ADOLESCENCE IN AMERICA

An Encyclopedia

The American Family

The six titles that make up **The American Family** offer a revitalizing new take on U.S. history, surveying current culture from the perspective of the family and incorporating insights from psychology, sociology, and medicine. Each two-volume, A-to-Z encyclopedia features its own advisory board, editorial slant, and apparatus, including illustrations, bibliography, and index.

Adolescence in America

EDITED BY Jacqueline V. Lerner, Boston College,
and Richard M. Lerner, Tufts University;
Jordan W. Finkelstein, Pennsylvania State University,
Advisory Editor

Boyhood in America

EDITED BY Priscilla Ferguson Clement, Pennsylvania State
University, Delaware County, and Jacqueline S. Reinier,
California State University, Sacramento

The Family in America

EDITED BY Joseph M. Hawes, University of Memphis,
and Elizabeth F. Shores, Little Rock, Arkansas

Girlhood in America

EDITED BY Miriam Forman-Brunell,
University of Missouri, Kansas City

Infancy in America

EDITED BY Alice Sterling Honig, Emerita, Syracuse University;
Hiram E. Fitzgerald, Michigan State University;
and Holly Brophy-Herb, Michigan State University

Parenthood in America

EDITED BY Lawrence Balter, New York University

ADOLESCENCE IN AMERICA

An Encyclopedia

Volume 2
N–Y

Jacqueline V. Lerner, EDITOR
Boston College

Richard M. Lerner, EDITOR
Tufts University

Jordan Finkelstein, ADVISORY EDITOR
Pennsylvania State University

FOREWORD BY **Mark L. Rosenberg**
Center for Child Well-Being
Atlanta, Georgia

A B C ☰ C L I O

Santa Barbara, California
Denver, Colorado
Oxford, England

Library of Congress Cataloging-in-Publication Data
Adolescence in America: an encyclopedia / Jacqueline V. Lerner and Richard M. Lerner, editors; Jordan Finkelstein, advisory editor.
        p. cm—(The American family)
Includes bibliographical references (p. 827) and index.
        ISBN 1-57607-205-3 (hardcover)—ISBN 1-57607-571-0 (e-book)
        1. Adolescence—United States—Encyclopedia. I. Lerner, Jacqueline
V. II. Lerner, Richard M. III. Finkelstein, Jordan. IV. American family
(Santa Barbara, Calif.)
    HQ796.A33244 2001
    305.235′0973′03–dc21
                                        2001002276

07 06 05 04 03 02 01   10 9 8 7 6 5 4 3 2 1 (cloth)

ABC-CLIO, Inc.
130 Cremona Drive, P.O. Box 1911
Santa Barbara, California 93116-1911

This book is also available on the World Wide Web as an e-book. Visit www.abc-clio.com for details.

This book is printed on acid-free paper ∞
Manufactured in the United States of America

ABOUT THE EDITORS

Jacqueline V. Lerner is professor of psychology and chair of the Counseling and Developmental Psychology program at Boston College.

Richard M. Lerner holds the Bergstrom Chair in Applied and Developmental Science in the Eliot-Pearson Department of Child Development, Tufts University.

Jordan Finkelstein is professor of behavioral health, human development, and pediatrics at Pennsylvania State University.

CONTENTS

A-to-Z List of Entries

N

Native American Adolescents

Today's Native American adolescents may choose to identify as American Indians, as Indians, as members of their tribe, or simply by their given name. They share many of the same concerns as other groups of teenagers: identity, daily living, teenage pregnancy, alcoholism and substance use, getting a good education, having a good career, having access to youth groups and activities, and having access to positive role models and mentors.

In the United States in 1996, there were reportedly 237,000 American Indians between ten and fourteen years of age (120,000 boys and 117,000 girls). Current population figures for 2000 indicate that 17.4 percent of American Indians (418,000) are between the ages of five and thirteen, 8.2 percent (196,000) are between fourteen and seventeen years of age, and 12.6 percent (238,000) are between the ages of eighteen and twenty-four; moreover, all three totals are declining (www.doi.gov/nrl/StatAbst/Aldemo.pdf). Indeed, American Indians are regarded as the "invisible minority" because of their small presence, in terms of both numbers and percentages.

Native American teenagers today struggle with many of the same identity issues that their parents and grandparents confronted in the past. For native teens even the simple question "Who am I?" is made more difficult by the fact that they feel they live in two worlds: one Indian and one European. They strive to maintain their native culture while trying to fit in with and adapt to the larger society (one that is not very friendly toward them)—a struggle commonly referred to as biculturalism. Several native youth have expressed their difficulty with identity issues by stating that they need role models to show them how to live their life on a day-to-day basis, and to do so successfully (Grand Rapids Youth Groups, 2000). Indeed, as C. Farris (1976, p. 387) notes in writing about the efforts of Indian children to survive in this dual world, "Indian children critically need to have meaningful contact with successful role models who are also Indians and can accurately interpret and teach their mutual tribal heritage."

Unlike generations before them, today's native teenagers live with their families and attend public, private, charter, or year-round Native American schools. In 1978, Congress passed the Indian Child Welfare Act in order to prevent the removal of native children from their families of origin. Prior to this year, native children could be removed from their families because of poverty or alcoholism and sent to live in boarding schools or non-Indian homes, often hundreds of miles away from their parents.

Of the current population of American Indians, estimated at 2 million, 65.6

Contemporary Native American teenagers struggle with many of the same identity issues that their parents and grandparents confronted in the past. (Miguel Gaudert/Corbis)

percent have a high school education or higher (www.doi.gov/nrl/TribalPop/pdf). The degrees earned by Native American graduates in the U.S. population break down as follows: 0.9 percent Associates, 0.5 percent Bachelor of Arts, 0.4 percent Master of Arts, 0.3 percent Doctorates, and 0.5 percent First Professional Degrees (www.doi.gov/nrl/StatAbst/Aleduc.pdf). Education continues to be a main concern among American Indian families because children are seen as the community's most valuable resource.

Government statistics show that 45 percent of first-time mothers in the Native American community are under age twenty, compared to an average of 24 percent in all other races. Moreover, the

infant mortality rate among Native Americans is 30 percent higher than the average rate for all other races, although it has dramatically decreased (by 61 percent) since 1972. The leading causes of infant deaths among Native Americans are sudden infant death syndrome (SIDS) and birth defects (www.doi.gov/nrl/StatAbst/Birth_inf_matern_mort.pdf).

Native American adolescents want the general public to know that they are not all alcoholics, substance users, high school dropouts, and aimless teens. They continue to fight many of the same stereotypes and myths that their parents and grandparents fought in past generations. For example, native youth complain that others do not understand their culture. Many of these youth feel left out and lack a sense of belonging because of differences in their cultural practices. Native adolescents uphold the principle of diversity; central to their culture is the belief that difference is to be valued, respected, and appreciated. Unfortunately, however, many native male teens have been teased by peers because they have let their hair grow long, honoring an age-old cultural practice. It is not uncommon to hear stories about male adolescents who have cut their hair because of such peer pressure—in an attempt to fit in, to belong.

Native teens also want the general public to know that they take pride in their heritage. They are grateful that they can practice their religious and cultural ceremonies without the fear that their ancestors experienced, thanks to passage of the American Indian Religious Freedom Act in 1978. They are trying to better their lives and to make a difference for native adolescents in the future. And they are emphatically fighting the stereotype that they are apathetic, aimless teens with no direction in life and no ambition to make something good of themselves. Indeed, many native youth are actively involved in youth groups, leadership councils, cultural activities that educate others about who they are, theater productions, community presentations, and community sobriety walks in conjunction with powwows. Above all, they are strong, positive role models for the generations to come. As such, they are living proof that "knowing one's heritage, place of origin, and identity, as well as passing that knowledge from one generation to the next, is a critical form of resistance to racial/cultural oppression and annihilation" (Kawamoto and Cheshire, 1999, p. 98).

Le Anne E. Silvey

See also Ethnic Identity; Identity; Racial Discrimination

References and further reading
Farris, C. 1976. "Indian Children: The Struggle for Survival." *Social Work* 21: 386–389.
Grand Rapids Youth Groups. 2000. Nishnabek Youth Leadership Council and People of Our Time. Personal communication (January 25).
Kawamoto, Walter T., and Tamara C. Cheshire. 1999. "Contemporary Issues in the Urban American Indian Family." Pp. 94–104 in *Family Ethnicity: Strength in Diversity*, 2nd ed. Edited by Harriette P. McAdoo. Thousand Oaks, CA: Sage.

Neglect

Neglect is the most prevalent form of maltreatment facing American children and adolescents today. According to *The Third National Incidence Study of Child Abuse and Neglect* (NIS-3), 879,000 children and adolescents are neglected each year (Sedlak and Broadhurst, 1996). Based on a conservative index established by the U.S. Department of Health and Human Services, this figure equates to 13.1 acts of neglect per 1,000 children and adolescents.

Each year 16.3 percent of all reports to Child Protective Services (CPS) agencies involve youth ages twelve and older (USDHHS, 1997). Yet the NIS-3 study indicates that only 18 percent of all neglect cases are eventually investigated by CPS agencies. This finding implies that adolescent neglect incidents are more likely to be underreported to CPS agencies than other forms of maltreatment or neglect incidents involving younger children. In addition, compared to other forms of maltreatment such as physical and sexual abuse, reports of neglect are less likely to be substantiated once investigated.

Adolescent neglect generally falls into three categories: physical, educational,

Adolescent neglect generally falls into three categories: physical, educational, and emotional. (Urban Archives, Philadelphia)

and emotional. *Physical neglect* is typically defined in terms of refusal to provide healthcare, delay in providing healthcare, abandonment, expulsion of an adolescent from the home, inadequate supervision, failure to meet food and clothing needs, and clear failure to protect an adolescent from hazards. *Educational neglect* is associated with acts of omission and commission that permit chronic acts of truancy, failure to enroll an adolescent in school, and inattention to individual academic needs. *Emotional neglect* includes such behaviors as failing to meet the nurturing or affection needs of an adolescent, exposing a minor to severe and chronic spousal abuse, allowing the use of alcohol or other controlled substances, encouraging an adolescent to engage in antisocial behaviors, refusal to provide psychological care, delaying the provision of mental healthcare, and other forms of inattention to an adolescent's developmental needs (Gelles, 1999). The NIS-3 study found that the highest rates of emotional neglect occur during late childhood and adolescence, between the ages of nine and seventeen. It is important to recognize that many adolescents experience more than one form of maltreatment and that the boundaries between the subcategories of neglect are often blurred.

Potential Contributors to Neglect

Adolescent neglect is often associated with risk factors such as stress, social isolation, and involvement with delinquent peers. According to the NIS-3 study, children and adolescents in families with an income under $15,000 per year were twenty-two times more likely to be victims of neglect than children in families with an income over $30,000. The rate of neglect was also significantly higher among children living with a single parent. Nevertheless, most children raised in low-income or single-parent families do not experience neglect, and within low-income communities, families who neglect their children are viewed as deviant (Black and Dubowitz, 1999).

Outcomes of Neglect

Neglected adolescents have been found to display deficits in cognitive and social-emotional functioning in conjunction with socially withdrawn behavior. For example, research by John Eckenrode and his colleagues (1993) indicates that neglected children and adolescents perform more poorly in school than nonmaltreated children and adolescents. And although some neglected youth show signs of passivity and withdrawal, research by Cathy Spatz Widom (1989) suggests that other neglected youth exhibit higher levels of violent behavior compared to abused children.

Protective Factors and Interventions
Studies indicate that a positive temperament, good intellectual capacity, and flexibility serve as protective factors for at-risk youth. Resilient youth are able to recognize and change undesirable emotions such as fear, anger, and sadness. Moreover, the use of external support systems by adolescents and their families promotes competent functioning in the presence of adversity.

Adolescents who have experienced neglect may need interventions centered on overcoming deficits in cognitive, academic, and social skills. Interventions that have been proven to be helpful include (1) special education programs to remedy deficits in cognitive stimulation and motivation to learn, (2) school- or community-based tutorial programs using professional teachers or volunteers to provide academic assistance and encourage relationships with nurturing adults (e.g., mentoring), and (3) enrichment classes for older children and adolescents designed to develop personal and life skills appropriate to their ages and developmental levels (Gaudin, 1999, p. 227). According to Diane DePanfilis (1999), the "integral ingredients" in all such interventions include helping alliances and partnerships with family members, empowerment of families to cultivate and use their strengths, and a flexible service model to better meet the needs of different families. Indeed, educators, counselors, and parents need to adopt a difference, rather than deficiency, perspective that allows them to be sensitive to the many cultural variations intrinsic to the process of rearing children. Adolescent neglect is most readily understood when each youth is examined within the context of the many systems in which she or he is embedded (Bronfenbrenner, 1979).

Lyscha A. Marcynyszyn
John Eckenrode

See also Accidents; Child-Rearing Styles; Coping; Foster Care: Risks and Protective Factors; Parent-Adolescent Relations; Parental Monitoring

References and further reading
Black, M. M., and Howard Dubowitz. 1999. "Child Neglect: Research Recommendations and Future Directions." Pp. 261–277 in *Neglected Children*. Edited by Howard Dubowitz. Thousand Oaks, CA: Sage Publications.
Bronfenbrenner, Urie. 1979. *The Ecology of Human Development*. Cambridge, MA: Harvard University Press.
DePanfilis, Diane. 1999. "Intervening with Families When Children Are Neglected." Pp. 211–236 in *Neglected Children*. Edited by Howard Dubowitz. Thousand Oaks, CA: Sage Publications.
Eckenrode, John, Molly Laird, and John Doris. 1993. "School Performance and Disciplinary Problems among Abused and Neglected Children." *Developmental Psychology* 29, no. 1: 53–62.
Gaudin, J. M. 1999. "Child Neglect: Short-Term and Long-Term Outcomes." Pp. 89–108 in *Neglected Children*. Edited by Howard Dubowitz. Thousand Oaks, CA: Sage Publications.
Gelles, R. J. 1999. "Policy Issues in Child Neglect." Pp. 278–298 in *Neglected Children*. Edited by Howard Dubowitz. Thousand Oaks, CA: Sage Publications.
Sedlak, Andrea J., and Diane D. Broadhurst. 1996. *The Third National Incidence Study of Child Abuse and Neglect*. Washington, DC: National Clearinghouse on Child Abuse and Neglect Information.
U.S. Department of Health and Human Services (USDHHS), Administration on Children, Youth, and Families. 1997. *Child Maltreatment 1997: Reports from the States to the National Child Abuse*

and *Neglect Data System.* Washington,
DC: U.S. Government Printing Office.
Widom, Cathy S. 1989. "Does Violence
Beget Violence? A Critical Examination
of the Literature." *Psychological
Bulletin* 106, no. 1: 3–28.

Nutrition

The teenage years comprise a period involving the most rapid growth and physiological maturation since infancy, requiring greatly increased amounts of calories and nutrients. However, the psychological, emotional, and social changes experienced at this time often lead to exploratory and experimental behaviors that, in turn, result in food choices placing teens at risk for poor or less than optimal health during adolescence as well as subsequent adulthood.

Specific Nutrient Requirements

As noted, the rapid growth and developmental changes of adolescence require significant increases in nutrients. Recommended dietary allowances (RDAs), which reflect current knowledge of nutrient needs, have been established for different gender and age groups. These allowances include a safety factor and are intended as guidelines for optimal nutrition. Energy, in the form of calories, is required to support rapid linear growth and increased lean body mass: Daily calorie recommendations range from 2,200 calories per day for girls between eleven and fourteen to 3,000 calories per day for boys between fifteen and eighteen. At the same time, there is wide variation in the caloric needs of both sexes, depending upon their rate of growth (which may not be apparent until a growth spurt is completed) and physical activity.

Protein recommendations, which are based on height and growth rates, range from 44 grams per day for girls between fifteen and eighteen to 59 grams per day for boys between fifteen and eighteen. Most teens consume considerably more than the RDA for protein; however, in cases where energy intake is inadequate (as when a teen is dieting, chronically ill, or unable to afford sufficient food), protein may be used for energy rather than for growth needs, thereby compromising linear growth and augmentation of lean body mass.

Mineral needs increase significantly during adolescence. For example, because almost half of an individual's skeletal mass is deposited during adolescence, calcium requirements are significantly higher than during childhood. The Recommended Dietary Allowance (RDA) for calcium is 1,300 milligrams for all adolescents. National surveys indicate, however, that average calcium intakes during adolescence are less than two-thirds of this amount. In addition, many teens drink large amounts of soft drinks (comprising up to 15 percent of their total caloric intake), and the increased amounts of phosphorus and caffeine in these beverages may interfere with metabolization of calcium in the body. This, in turn, may affect calcium skeletal deposition and final total bone mass—especially in girls who drink inadequate amounts of milk. Such girls are at greater risk for osteoporosis in later adulthood.

Both males and females need extra iron during adolescence to support increased blood volume and increased lean body mass (and, in females, to replenish menstrual losses). Iron recommendations are 12 and 15 milligrams per day for males and females, respectively. However, surveys indicate that 12 percent of boys and 14 percent of girls are iron deficient. The need for most other minerals, as well as for vitamins, also surges during adolescence. For example, larger amounts of B vitamins such as thiamine, niacin, and riboflavin are required for the increased energy processes, tissue syntheses, and cell growth characteristic of this period.

Physical Changes

Puberty is defined, in part, as the orderly growth and development that occur from childhood to adult maturity. Part of this development manifests as linear growth and body composition changes (Spear, 2000, p. 263). Although the pubertal process is sequential and predictable, there is wide variation among individuals in terms of initiation of puberty, rates of growth, and growth completion, with resulting differences in specific indicators such as menarche and growth spurts. Teens gain about 15 percent of their adult height and, as noted, almost half of their adult skeletal mass during adolescent growth. On average, girls attain their adult height at about four and one-half years after menarche (approximately seventeen years of age), and boys, at about twenty-one years of age. During this period, teens also gain about one-half of their ideal adult body weight and experience significant body shape and composition changes. Girls tend to gain weight slightly before they achieve gains in height, whereas boys tend to gain weight and height at the same time. As children, girls and boys have similar body proportions of fat and muscle (about 15 percent and 20 percent, respectively). During maturation, however, such proportions change to those of mature adulthood: Girls attain about 23 percent body fat and boys about 15 percent.

Psychosocial Changes

In addition to the significant physiological changes that occur with physical growth

Healthy growth during adolescence requires greatly increased amounts of calories and nutrients. (Wartenberg/Picture Press/Corbis)

and maturation, adolescents shift from the status of children to more independent adult roles. This transition involves a number of processes and experiences, including experimentation. Most teens test boundaries and try new behaviors—especially eating behaviors. They eat more meals and snacks away from home; family meal patterns and food behaviors may be at least partly replaced by social meals and snacks with peers at fast-food restaurants or shopping malls. Many teens skip meals, especially breakfast. And they often try new food styles such as vegetarianism or diets to lose or gain weight. Busy schedules—with time allocated to school, outside activities such as sports or the arts, and part-time jobs—influence when and where teens eat. Another factor is the amount of money they are able to spend. Fast food and other meals away from home often provide calories and protein but are usually low in nutrients such as vitamins, minerals, and fiber. In addition, fast food tends to be high in calories, fat, sodium, and simple carbohydrates such as sugar, relative to the other nutrients provided. In short, it has low nutrient density. Adolescents typically try new food choices and behaviors and then gradually return to the familiar food patterns of their childhood and families of origin.

Other Influences on
Adolescent Eating Behaviors

Although peers and outside activities affect adolescent eating behaviors, the family food milieu is, for many teens, the strongest influence on their eating habits. Teens raised in families with healthy attitudes toward food are used to making food choices and may thus feel free to experiment with new behaviors and then return to more healthy ones. Ellyn Satter (1987) describes a healthy food relationship as one in which the parent or caretaker provides a reasonably well balanced selection of foods on a regular schedule (i.e., meals and snacks) in a safe and pleasant environment; each family member is then responsible for deciding how much to eat or even whether to eat. Children raised in such a food environment are likely to respond to interior eating cues such as fullness or satiety as a signal to stop eating rather than to exterior cues such as a clean plate. Other components of a positive food environment include healthy attitudes toward body size and shape as well as a moderate approach to

exercise. Parents who obsess about thinness, dieting, or exercise encourage children and teens to adopt similar attitudes and behaviors, just as parents who require that children "learn to like" certain foods or that they "eat their vegetables before having dessert" often end up creating aversions for the very foods they hoped would be consumed. In contrast are those parents who model good food behaviors, present their families with reasonable food choices, and let family members make individual eating choices, thus encouraging their children to accept a wider variety of foods and to attend to internal cues as signals to eat or not to eat. Parents can also influence their family's eating habits through careful selection of the foods they purchase as well as through healthy food preparation methods. Indeed, since teens tend to prefer foods to which they have been regularly exposed, those who are accustomed to foods prepared with large amounts of fat or sugar will tend to prefer such foods themselves, whereas those whose parents have regularly offered lower-fat food choices and lots of fruits and vegetables will more often make these healthy choices in their own lives.

Yet another influence on adolescent eating behaviors is passive recreation. Research indicates that television viewing and computer use are associated with higher-than-normal weight levels among children and teens. Time spent in front of a television or computer screen involves very low energy use, and television viewers, in particular, often simultaneously consume high-calorie snacks. In addition, most food advertisements targeted at youth are for snack foods with high sugar and fat content; studies show that children frequently exposed to such advertising request more of the advertised foods than do children not so frequently exposed. Less is known about how food advertising affects teens, but given that food habits tend to persist over time, it seems logical to assume that early childhood choices for advertised foods could have long-term influences.

Surveys of food choices indicate that many American adolescents fail to select the kinds and amounts of foods most desirable for optimal health and growth. (Interestingly, teenage boys are more likely than teenage girls to meet their nutrient and energy recommendations by choosing appropriate kinds and amounts of foods.) The Food Guide Pyramid was created by the U.S. Department of Agriculture as a model to help individuals make healthy food choices. Its daily recommendations include six or more servings of grain products, two or more fruits, three or more vegetables, and two or more servings from milk and meat groups. (Fats and sweets are considered "extras" to be chosen in small amounts.) Teens who choose foods based upon this guide are likely to consume the recommended amounts of nutrients; conversely, those who neglect one or more food groups are likely to have inadequate intakes of specific nutrients. For example, teens who avoid the milk group almost always have low calcium intakes, and those who rarely choose foods in the fruit or vegetable groups tend to have low vitamin and fiber intakes. In fact, teen diets overall are characterized by low levels of selections from milk, vegetable, and whole-grain groups, with resulting low calcium, vitamin, and fiber intakes.

A related factor is dental health. Dental caries and gum disease have multiple causes including genetics, diet, and oral hygiene. Frequent exposure to sweet or sticky foods increases the risk for caries. Since as much as 80 percent of the average person's dental decay occurs during adolescence, this age range is a time to choose foods conducive to good dental health such as vegetables, fruits, and dairy products; to continue the use of fluoridated water; and to get regular oral hygiene and dental checkups.

Obesity and Eating Disorders

The incidence of overweight and obesity among adolescents (as well as adults and children) is increasing at a rapid rate in the United States and other countries. Based on the body mass index (BMI) definition of obesity, data from the National Health and Nutrition Examination Survey show that adolescent obesity increased from to 5.7 percent of adolescents in 1976–1980 to 12 percent of adolescents in 1988–1994, and, more recently, that 21.7 percent of males and 21.4 percent of females are classified as overweight. Obesity is a major concern because of its association with various health and psychosocial risks. Among adolescents it is associated with elevated blood lipid levels and abdominal obesity, which lead to elevated risk for cardiovascular disease in adults; glucose intolerance; noninsulin-dependent diabetes (NIDDM), which is increasing rapidly among children and adolescents (since 1982 its incidence has increased tenfold in Cincinnati) (Dietz, 1998); gallstones; elevated liver enzymes; hypertension; sleep apnea; and orthopedic complications. Possible psychosocial effects of adolescent obesity include negative self-image, low self-esteem, disturbed body image, and decreased socioeconomic status, educational level, and marriage rates (Dietz, 1998).

Other weight-related disorders include binge eating, unhealthy dieting practices such as inappropriate weight loss and poor food choices, and anorexic and bulimic behaviors such as laxative use, overexercising, and self-induced vomiting. These conditions may be causally related to such factors as individual inherited susceptibility, cultural pressures for thinness in women and a muscular physique among men, and adverse individual and family experiences such as a history of overweight or need for control. Surveys indicate that as many as 60 percent of girls consider themselves overweight and that 40 percent of girls and 15 percent of boys are dieting at any given time. Approximately 30 percent of clinically overweight teens and 2.5 percent of all college students have binge eating disorder, 10–20 percent of adolescents have exhibited anorexic or bulimic behaviors one or more times in their lives, 1–3 percent of adolescents are diagnosed with bulimia, and 1 percent of adolescents (primarily young women) are diagnosed with anorexia nervosa. Treatment of weight-related disorders is difficult, and long-term outcomes are poor. Dieting to lose weight rarely results in permanent appropriate weight stabilization (rebound and regain are more common), and bulimia and anorexia often lead to long-term deleterious physical effects or even death. Diagnosis and treatment of the latter two conditions, especially, should be made by an interdisciplinary team experienced in short- and long-term physiological and psychological treatment of eating disorders.

Athletics

Teens who participate in organized sports such as gymnastics or wrestling are sometimes pressured to "make weight" or to attain a specific body shape or composition. Such attempts are not recommended, however, because they can be extremely harmful—to the point of impeding normal growth and development. Carbohydrate loading, though occasionally recommended for endurance activities such as swimming or track, has been shown to have widely varying individual effects and may compromise performance. Similarly, numerous dietary supplements such as amino acids have been promoted as muscle building and endurance enhancing but usually enhance only the wallet of the seller. To avoid such outcomes, all participants in athletics (and their coaches) are advised to consult a registered dietitian with training and experience in sports nutrition for expert advice on performance nutrition.

Physical Activity

Activity level influences caloric use and thus body weight. Numerous factors account for the decreased physical activity of many teens today: Not only television and other sedentary work and play activities such as computer use and video games but also transportation and technological home and work improvements have resulted in lower physical output and caloric consumption. Moreover, fewer and fewer schools offer regular physical education from kindergarten through high school, and even fewer require it. The combined effect of these factors has been to divide adolescent population into two groups: one that has little or no exposure to school-affiliated physical activities and another that regularly participates in organized sports and is more active and physically fit.

Any individual's weight is a delicate balance between growth and maintenance, calorie intake and activity. Regular physical activity is an important part of good health and weight regulation. It is also a significant factor in preventing adult maladies such as cardiovascular disease and diabetes.

Food and Nutrition Advice
Teens are often faced with conflicting advice: They are encouraged, on the one hand, to eat more (or at least to eat better) and, on the other, to eat less and be slim.

Many groups and organizations offer recommendations on making good food choices in the interest of good health and disease prevention; these include the American Heart Association, the American Cancer Association, the American Public Health Association, and the American Dietetic Association. The U.S. government, too, has issued guidelines such as the Food Guide Pyramid and Dietary Guidelines for Americans as well as specific nutrient recommendations such as RDAs and dietary reference intakes (both of which can usually be found on food labels). In addition, numerous books offer food or nutrition advice; some provide reliable information, others do not. It is often difficult to decide which information is beneficial—let alone to follow it! The best advice for teens and others interested in good nutrition and health is to aim for moderation, balance, and, especially, variety in food choices. For most of us, the easiest model to use is probably the Food Guide Pyramid. Choosing foods that are low in fat (such as skimmed milk and lean meats) and high in fiber (vegetables, fruits, and whole-grain products) not only contributes to healthy weight control but also helps prevent chronic diseases such as cardiovascular disease, cancer, and diabetes. Daily physical activity

is also recommended. Indeed, good eating habits and exercise will help youth feel better, gain more energy, and stay on track to good health throughout the teen years and beyond.

Marcia Vandenbelt

See also Acne; Anemia; Body Build; Body Fat, Changes in; Diabetes; Eating Problems; Sports, Exercise, and Weight Control

References and further reading
Birch, Leann L., and Jennifer O. Fisher. 1998. "Development of Eating Behaviors among Children and Adolescents." *Pediatrics* 101 (suppl.): 539–549.
Clark, Nancy. 1996. *Nancy Clark's Sports Nutrition Guidebook.* Champaign, IL: Human Kinetics Publishers.
Dietz, William H. 1998. "Health Consequences of Obesity in Youth: Childhood Predictors of Adult Disease." *Pediatrics* 101 (suppl.): 518–525.
Haworth-Hoeppner, S. 2000. "The Critical Shape of Body Image: The Role of Culture and Family in the Production of Eating Disorders." *Journal of Marriage and the Family* 62: 212–227.
Hill, James O., and John C. Peters. 1998. "Environmental Contributions to the Obesity Epidemic." *Science* 280: 1371–1374.
Kelder, Steven H., Cheryl L. Perry, Knut-Inge Klepp, and Leslie L. Lytle. 1994. "Longitudinal Tracking of Adolescent Smoking, Physical Activity, and Food Choice Behaviors." *American Journal of Public Health*, 84, no. 7: 1121–1126.
Munoz, Kathryn A., Susan M. Krebs-Smith, Rachel Ballard-Barbash, and Linda E. Cleveland. 1997. "Food Intakes of U.S. Children and Adolescents Compared with Recommendations." *Pediatrics* 100, no. 3: 323–329.
Neumark-Sztainer, Dianne, and Jillian K. Moe. 2000. "Weight-Related Concerns and Disorders among Adolescents." Pp. 288–317 in *Nutrition throughout the Life Cycle.* Edited by Bonnie S. Worthington-Roberts and Sue Rodwell Williams. Boston: McGraw-Hill.
Satter, Ellyn. 1987. *How to Get Your Kid to Eat . . . But Not Too Much: From*

Birth to Adolescence. Palo Alto, CA: Bull Publishing.

Spear, Bonnie A. 2000. "Adolescent Nutrition: General." Pp. 262–287 in *Nutrition throughout the Life Cycle.* Edited by Bonnie S. Worthington-Roberts and Sue Rodwell Williams. Boston: McGraw-Hill.

Troiana, Richard P., and Katherine M. Flegal. 1998. "Overweight Children and Adolescents: Description, Epidemiology, and Demographics." *Pediatrics* 101 (suppl.): 497–504.

Walsh, Timothy B., and Michael J. Devlin. 1998. "Eating Disorders: Progress and Problems." *Science* 280: 1387–1390.

P

Parent-Adolescent Relations

Adolescence is a time when both changes in the individual and changes within their relationships are markedly evident. In particular, adolescents undergo many alterations in their relationship with their parents. Many parents experience apprehension and concern about their children beginning with the adolescent years. In fact, the teenage period has often been referred to as one of storm and stress, a time marked by conflict, rebellion, and acting-out. But is this really the case for most adolescents or is this a stereotype that has been perpetuated over the years? Although changes in adolescents are evident, contemporary research suggests that most adolescents and their parents continue to have a positive relationship during the adolescent period of development.

It is true that adolescents do undergo a variety of changes that may, to varying degrees, alter the parent-adolescent relationship. For example, the period of adolescence is marked by physiological, social, and psychological changes. Specifically, physiological alterations such as those involved in puberty, including hormonal changes, bodily growth and maturation, and sexual maturation and awareness, are all part of adolescence. Social transitions also take place, such as the transition from elementary to middle school or junior high school. These transitions are important ones for the adolescent in several ways. In many cases, the young person experiences changes in school structure, and, often, these changes require adjustment to a larger school, to different grading procedures, to more stringent teacher expectations, and to a less personal overall school environment. In addition, as a consequence of changes in school environments, adolescents may experience alterations in their friends and peer groups. They are also confronted with new temptations, which may include engaging in sexual activity or participating in deviant behavior or substance use. Finally, psychological changes result, for example, in the need for increased independence from parents that is yet another alteration from the childhood years to the teenage years. Adolescence is a period in the life span when changes begin that contribute to one's life course development. Taken together, these changes represent major adjustments and transitions from the earlier childhood period. Consequently, it would seem reasonable that some changes would occur in the parent-adolescent relationship as well during this period of development.

The adjustment of both adolescents and their parents to these changes is related, at least in part, to the nature and quality of their relationship prior to the onset of the adolescent years. For example, a child who was overprotected by her parents during her early years may find it especially difficult to adjust to the new expectations for independence and self-reliance during adolescence. On the other hand, a child who was reared permissively may be more likely to give in to new temptations such as engaging in delinquent or in sexual behavior. Because of the multiple changes and transitions that are associated with this period of the life span, social scientists have paid a considerable amount of attention to the influence of the family on adolescent development and to the nature of parent-adolescent relations during the adolescent years.

Research suggests that despite the pervasive influence of parents on youth behavior and development across the adolescent period, there is generally a decrease in the amount of time that adolescents spend with their parents. For instance, one study reported that the amount of time adolescents spent with their families decreased from 35 percent to 14 percent of waking hours as youth progressed through adolescence (Larson et al., 1996). At the same time, adolescents begin to spend more time with their peers. Often this change in where adolescents spend their time is a result of the pressure put on youth to achieve independence from parents during this period. Whatever the cause, these gains in autonomy can alter the parent-adolescent relationship and can heighten family conflict. In turn, some research has found that families with adolescents are more likely to be less cohesive and more chaotic than families with either younger or older children. This finding is not really surprising. As noted, adolescents are at a time where they are striving to gain independence and autonomy and thus spend less time with parents and

more time with peers. It would follow then that families with adolescent children would seem to be less cohesive than families with younger children where independence is not a focal concern, or with families with older children who have already undergone the transition. Moreover, adolescents strive to gain more influence over decision making as a result of their increasing independence, and since they typically spend less time with parents, one might anticipate a more chaotic environment due to these factors.

Additional research suggests that alterations in the parent-child relationship may be a function of puberty. For example, E. R. Anderson and colleagues have found that pubertal development is related to decreases in mothers' warmth and involvement with their children. Mothers were also reported to monitor their adolescents less effectively. This research lends support to what L. Steinberg has termed the *distancing hypothesis*. That is, as pubertal development proceeds, relationships within the family become increasingly disengaged as a result of pubertal maturation. On the other hand, the *acceleration hypothesis* suggests that disengagement in the parent-child relationship may result in accelerated physical maturation. In fact, Steinberg reported that greater distance between adolescents and their mothers was associated with faster pubertal development for girls in one study. Similar results were not reported for boys, however.

Adolescents, Mothers, and Fathers
Much of the research that has been done on adolescents and their parents focuses on adolescents and *mothers* in particular. This is due, at least in part, to the fact that mothers still spend the most time

with their children, despite the fact that increasing numbers of mothers are working outside the home. In fact, adolescents feel that their mothers know them better than their fathers do. Moreover, many families in the United States today are single-parent families, and the overwhelming majority of all single-parent homes are homes without a father. Thus, much of what we know about parents and adolescents specifically pertains to mothers and adolescents.

In contrast to the vast literature on mothers and children, there is a paucity of empirical research on fathers' contributions to their adolescents' development. However, literature is beginning to emerge that documents the importance of the role of the father in parent-child relations and in child adjustment. The greater attention to father-child relations may be due to increased interest in the role of the father in general, and to the recent assumption by many fathers of the more traditional caretaking roles that have been previously held by mothers. This shift may be primarily due to increases in women's employment and to changes in societal expectations regarding fathers' involvement with their children.

Research suggests that mothers and fathers engage in different types of interactions with their children. In the early years, for example, in contrast to mothers, who specialize in caretaking and nurturance, fathers specialize in play. M. E. Lamb reports that although mothers may actually spend more time in play activity, clearly fathers spend a greater proportion of their time with children engaged in play. During the adolescent years, differences between mothers and fathers are evident as well. For example, D. M. Almeida and N. L. Galambos report that fathers have been found to have less feeling for and show less understanding toward their adolescents than mothers. Fathers also, however, were reported to have less intense conflicts with their children as compared to mothers. This may be related to the fact that, in general, mothers are more involved with their children's day-to-day activities than fathers are. In fact, research has supported this idea. When fathers were more involved with their adolescents, they also reported having more conflict with them than less involved fathers.

Contemporary Research on the Family and Adolescent Adjustment

Self-esteem has been the focus of a considerable amount of adolescent research. Perhaps this focus is due, in part, to the key developmental issue concerning this period of the life span, the formation of one's identity. According to Erik Erikson, the most important task of the adolescent period is that of achieving an identity. The knowledge that the adolescent has gained thus far of who he is is challenged by the changes that begin during the early adolescent period: changes in physical, psychological, cognitive, and social dimensions. Thus, the adolescent is forced to evaluate himself in light of these changes, and is faced with the question, Who am I? This is basically a question that requires information (knowledge) about the self. In addition, if this development allows the youth to find a socially approved role in society, Erikson argues, then positive self-esteem will accrue.

Because of the multiple transitions associated with adolescence, self-esteem has been an important focus of research and has been given much attention by social scientists. The family, and the interactions that occur within the family, are considered of primary importance for the development of one's self-concept. For instance, adolescent self-esteem and well-being have been related to supportive, close family relationships. David Demo and his colleagues found that adolescents' perceptions of communication within the family and participation with parents were related to adolescent self-esteem. Parental control was reported to have an inverse relationship to adolescent self-esteem. Further, sons' self-esteem, more so than daughters', was related to dimensions of the parent-child relationship, including communication with parents and with youth participation in joint activities with them. Similarly, other research reported that adolescents' perceptions of parents' supportive behaviors were related to positive self-esteem in the mother-daughter dyad. Parental coercive behavior was negatively related to self-esteem in the father-daughter dyad.

In addition to self-esteem, parenting behavior is related to adolescents' academic achievement. Studies assessing parenting styles in relation to scholastic achievement report that children with authoritative parents have higher grades and have more positive attitudes toward school as compared to children with authoritarian or permissive parents. Authoritative parents also tend to be more involved in their children's education, for instance, through participating in activities and helping with homework. Researchers such as A. E. Gottfried and D. L. Stevenson and D. P. Baker have also confirmed that the more parents are involved in their children's education, the better they do in school.

Moreover, researchers have reported that other parental characteristics are related to adolescents' academic achieve-ment. For example, school achievement in adolescence has been positively related to parents' educational aspirations for their children. Similarly, positive parental beliefs and attributions about their adolescent's capabilities are positively related to adolescent academic achievement. High levels of parental control and high parental responsiveness were also related to positive achievement outcomes for adolescents. One study reported that the way adolescents themselves perceived the quality of parenting they received and how they assessed the degree of their parents' involvement in their lives mattered more for their achievement in school than the way the parents saw their own parenting (Paulson, 1994).

Although some research finds negative outcomes for the parent-adolescent relationship during this period, other research suggests that the *majority* of adolescents feel they get along well with their parents and in general report feeling positive about their relationships with their parents. And, although some research reports heightened conflict between parents and children, these disruptions are often temporary and not long-lasting. In addition, despite the fact that there is generally a decrease in the amount of time that adolescents spend with their parents, research indicates that youth still most often seek parental advice on matters regarding further education, career choice, and financial matters. In essence, then, past research indicates that, despite quantitative and qualitative changes in the parent-child relationship, parents still play an important role in the socialization of their adolescents, and most adolescents and parents maintain an overall positive relationship during this period.

Domini R. Castellino

See also Academic Achievement;
Allowance; Child-Rearing Styles; Family Composition: Realities and Myths;
Family Relations; Fathers and Adolescents; Identity; Mothers and Adolescents; Parenting Styles; Parental Monitoring; Sibling Relationships

References and further reading
Almeida, D. M., and N. L. Galambos.
1991. "Examining Father Iinvolvement
and the Quality of Father-Adolescent
Relations." *Journal of Research on
Adolescence* 1, no. 2: 155–172.
Anderson, E. R., E. M. Hetherington, and
W. G. Clinempeel. 1989.
"Transformations in Family Relations
at Puberty: Effects of Family Context."
Journal of Early Adolescence 9, no. 3:
310–334.
Demo, D. H., S. A. Small, and R. C. Savin-
Williams. 1987. "Family Relations and
the Self-Esteem of Adolescents and
Their Parents." *Journal of Marriage and
the Family* 49: 705–715.
Erikson, E. H. 1963. *Childhood and
Society*. New York: Norton.
Gottfried, A. E. 1991. "Maternal
Employment in the Family Setting:
Developmental and Environmental
Issues." Pp. 63–84 in *Employed Mothers
and their Children*. Edited by J. V.
Lerner and N. L. Galambos. New York:
Garland.
Lamb, M. E. 1997. *The Role of the Father
in Child Development*, 3rd ed. New
York: Wiley.
Larson, R. W., M. H. Richards, G. Moneta,
G. Holmbeck, et al. 1996. "Changes in
Adolescents' Daily Interactions with
Their Families from Ages 10 to 18:
Disengagement and Transformation."
Developmental Psychology 32, no. 4:
744–754.
Paulson, S. E. 1994. Relations of Parenting
Style and Parental Involvement with
Ninth-Grade Students' Achievement.
Journal of Early Adolescence 14:
250–267.
Steinberg, L. 1988. "Reciprocal Relation
between Parent-Child Distance and
Pubertal Maturation. *Developmental
Psychology* 24: 122–128.
Stevenson, D. L., and D. P. Baker. 1987.
The Family-School Relation and the
Child's School Performance. *Child
Development* 58: 1348–1357.

Parental Monitoring

Parental monitoring is the activity that allows parents to be knowledgeable about their adolescents' whereabouts, activities, and companions. Parents monitor their adolescents when they keep track of them from a distance. Parents who are effective monitors know about their adolescent's day and are aware of their adolescent's experiences.

Monitoring is not an isolated activity but part of the parent-adolescent relationship. Parents who are good monitors are interested in their adolescents and make an effort to establish open channels of communication with them. Because most of the information parents have about their adolescents comes from the adolescents themselves, adolescents must be willing to share their experiences with their parents and be honest about those experiences. Effective parental monitoring emerges from a trusting relationship between interested and involved parents and open and truthful adolescents.

Parental monitoring is more than just knowing where adolescents are, what they are doing, and whom they are with. Good monitors attempt to influence the behavior of their adolescents and try to shape their experiences. Good parental monitoring not only includes knowledge of adolescent behaviors but also includes attempts by parents to instill positive behaviors and discourage adolescent deviant behavior.

Researchers who study parent monitoring typically measure it by comparing the responses of adolescents and parents to questions about typical or specific experiences of the adolescent. Adolescents answer questions about themselves, their friends, and their recent activities, and these answers are compared to the same questions asked of parents about their

Parental monitoring involves actions that enable parents to be knowledgeable about their adolescents' whereabouts, activities, and companions. (Laura Dwight/Corbis)

adolescents. Questions include items that assess knowledge about an adolescent's activities in school and after school, television watching, and interactions with friends. One cannot be certain which individual more accurately portrays the reality of the adolescent's experiences, but researchers usually assume that the adolescent's report is accurate and examine the match between parent report and adolescent report.

What adolescents say they do and what parents think their adolescents do is frequently at odds, oftentimes to a significant degree, and especially in regard to illegal and unhealthy behavior. For example, in one study of ninth graders by Deborah Cohen and Janet Rice, 19 percent of parents indicated that they thought their adolescents had used alcohol or drugs, a percentage in striking contrast to the 55 percent of these same adolescents who reported that they had used these substances. Many parents believe that other adolescents use drugs and alcohol, but their own adolescents do not.

Although monitoring is a specific aspect of parenting, it is related to several other components of parenting. A study by Debra Mekos and colleagues found that parents who are good monitors are also likely to be warm and supportive and to have relationships with their adolescents that are low in conflict and negativity. Parental monitoring is positively related to using discipline effectively and reinforcing healthy adolescent behavior. Monitoring is also positively related to family cohesion and good parent-adolescent communication. All of these findings suggest that effective monitoring is built upon a healthy and positive parent-adolescent relationship.

In general, mothers are better monitors than fathers; they know more about the everyday whereabouts of their adolescents and their activities. This gender difference is not only true for mothers who are full-time homemakers but even for mothers who are employed full-time outside the home. Ann Crouter and Susan McHale found that fathers seem to calibrate the extent to which they monitor their adolescents based in part on the availability of mothers. Fathers monitor their adolescents more when mothers work than when they do not, but fathers typically monitor their adolescents less than mothers in either work situation.

Even though mothers know more about their adolescents than do fathers, parents of both genders know more about their same-sex adolescent than they do their opposite-sex adolescent. Several factors may play a part in this same-sex matching: fathers and sons, as well as mothers and daughters, may have more related interests and engage in more similar activities; parents may be more interested in the lives of same-sex adolescents; and same-sex adolescents may be more likely to confide in a parent of the same sex.

Debra Mekos and colleagues also found that in remarried families parents monitor their biological children more closely than they do their stepchildren. The low monitoring of stepchildren may be one reason stepchildren are more likely to engage in problem behavior than biological children. In general, stepparents seem to adopt a disengaged style of parenting with stepchildren, especially when the stepchildren are adolescents.

Between childhood and late adolescence there is a marked decrease in parent monitoring. What this means is that as adolescents get older they spend an increasing amount of time away from home and parents, and that parents are not well informed about where their adolescents are, what they are doing, and whom they are with. Many adolescents handle this increase in freedom and autonomy well, but for some adolescents a decrease in parent monitoring is associated with contact with deviant peers and participation in unhealthy and illegal activities.

Many studies have shown that effective parent monitoring of adolescents decreases adolescents' involvement in unhealthy and deviant behavior. Low parental monitoring is associated with adolescent academic problems; tobacco, alcohol, and marijuana use; and antisocial behavior. In addition, parents who are ineffective and inconsistent monitors are more likely to have sons who engage in sexual intercourse at an early age. The pathway from low parental monitoring to adolescent problem behavior is through association with deviant peers, which increases the risk of involvement in illegal and unhealthy behavior. Monitoring plays a pivotal role in the prevention of adolescent problem behavior. When parents are aware of where their adolescents are spending their time and with whom, the opportunity for engaging in deviant behavior is reduced.

Monitoring becomes an especially important aspect of parenting during adolescence, when adolescents spend more unsupervised time with peers after school and in the evenings. In general, studies with adolescents show that poor parental monitoring is more highly related to adolescent problem behavior than any other aspect of parenting. Overall, adolescents who do well in school, do not abuse alcohol or drugs, and do not engage in delinquency have parents who are good monitors and who are warm and supportive.

Raymond Montemayor

See also Child-Rearing Styles; Employment: Positive and Negative Consequences; Family Relations; Fathers and Adolescents; Maternal Employment: Historical Changes; Maternal Employment: Influences on Adolescents; Mothers and Adolescents; Parent-Adolescent Relations; Parenting Styles

References and further reading
Ary, D. V., T. E. Duncan, A. Biglan, C. W. Metzler, J. W. Noell, and K. Smolkowski. 1999. "Development of Adolescent Problem Behavior." *Journal of Abnormal Child Psychology* 27: 141–150.

Bahr, S. J., R. D. Hawks, and G. Wang. 1993. "Family and Religious Influences on Adolescent Substance Abuse." *Youth and Society* 24: 443–465.

Capaldi, D. M., L. Crosby, and M. Stoolmiller. 1996. "Predicting the Timing of First Sexual Intercourse for At-Risk Adolescent Males." *Child Development* 67: 344–359.

Cohen, Deborah A., and Janet C. Rice. 1995. "A Parent-Targeted Intervention for Adolescent Substance Use Prevention: Lessons Learned." *Evaluation Review* 19: 159–180.

Crouter, Ann C., and Susan M. McHale. 1993. "Temporal Rhythms in Family Life: Seasonal Variation in the Relation between Parental Work and Family Processes." *Developmental Psychology* 29: 198–205.

Crouter, Ann C., H. Helms-Erikson, K. Updegraff, and Susan M. McHale. 1999. "Conditions Underlying Parents' Knowledge about Children's Daily Lives in Middle Childhood: Between- and Within-Family Comparisons." *Child Development* 70: 246–259.

Forehand, R., K. S. Miller, R. Dutra, and M. W. Chance. 1997. "Role of Parenting in Adolescent Deviant Behavior: Replication across and within Two Ethnic Groups." *Journal of Consulting and Clinical Psychology* 65: 1036–1041.

Hetherington, E. M., and W. G. Clingempeel. 1992. "Coping with Marital Transitions." *Monographs of the Society for Research in Child Development* 57 (2–3, serial no. 227).

Jacobson, K. C., and L. J. Crockett. 2000. "Parental Monitoring and Adolescent Adjustment: An Ecological Perspective." *Journal of Research on Adolescence* 10: 65–97.

Mekos, Debra, E. M. Hetherington, and D. Reiss. 1996. "Sibling Differences in Problem Behavior and Parental Treatment in Nondivorced and Remarried Families." *Child Development* 67: 2148–2165.

Patterson, G. R., and M. Stouthamer-Loeber. 1984. "The Correlation of Family Management Practices and Delinquency." *Child Development* 55: 1299–1307.

Stoolmiller, M. 1994. "Antisocial Behavior, Delinquent Peer Association and Unsupervised Wandering for Boys: Growth and Change from Childhood to Early Adolescence." *Multivariate Behavioral Research* 29: 263–288.

Parenting Styles

The term *parenting style* refers to a cluster of parental attitudes and practices that tend to produce certain identifiable patterns in child and adolescent adjustment outcomes. Research has demonstrated that particular parenting styles may differentially impact an adolescent's psychosocial adjustment, achievement level, success in school, and involvement with drugs or alcohol. Many factors are likely to influence what type of parenting style a particular family adopts when their child reaches adolescence. For instance, research suggests that the cognitive, social, and emotional changes that developing adolescents experience are likely to influence which parenting styles their parents adopt. Individual characteristics of parents, and the parenting style adopted earlier in their child's development, may also influence which parenting style is most prominent in their child's teenage years.

It is generally accepted that there are two dimensions of parenting, demandingness and responsiveness, and these two dimensions are used to define four parenting styles (authoritative, authoritarian, permissive, and rejecting-neglectful; see table). Demandingness refers to the extent to which parents supervise and discipline their offspring and place age-appropriate demands on them.

		Demandingness	
		High	Low
Responsiveness	High	Authoritative	Permissive
	Low	Authoritarian	Rejecting-Neglectful

Parenting style refers to the set of behaviors and attitudes used by parents to raise their children. (Jennie Woodcock; Reflections Photolibrary/Corbis)

Responsiveness refers to the degree to which parents are accepting of their offspring and how attentive and sensitive parents are to their changing needs. The four styles of parenting are defined in terms of these two dimensions: Authoritative parents are both highly responsive and demanding; permissive parents are highly responsive but not demanding; authoritarian parents are highly demanding but not responsive; and rejecting-neglectful parents are neither demanding nor responsive.

History of Parenting Styles

Parenting styles have been extensively researched during the past sixty years. Over the course of that time there have been several major developments that have shaped the way in which we think about parenting styles today. Scholars in the 1960s and 1970s employed factor analytic techniques to identify parenting constructs that repeatedly emerged from parenting questionnaires and interviews. The first major development in this field was the emergence of two dimensions, warmth-hostility and permissiveness-restrictiveness, that seemed to account for most of the variation in parenting attitudes and practices. Building on research that spurred these dimensional constructs, a classification system that categorized parents as being authoritative, authoritarian, permissive, or rejecting-neglectful was employed to further describe the differences between parents. These four categories were defined by two-dimensional constructs that were different in name but quite similar in nature to the earlier dimensional ideology. The revised dimensions, termed demandingness and responsiveness, were quickly adopted into the literature and became very influential in further research endeavors. The four categories of parenting style and the two-dimensional constructs upon which they are based comprise the classic nomenclature in this field and are mentioned in some way by most studies on parenting styles.

Another key development in the field of parenting styles was the discovery of discrete parenting characteristics, other than those captured by the responsiveness and demandingness dimensions, that seemed to consistently cluster with particular categorical parenting styles. In an effort to represent these characteristics, the existing classification system was broadened to include four hybrid terms: authoritative-reciprocal, authoritarian-autocratic, indulgent-permissive, and indifferent-uninvolved. Since this last major development in the field, researchers on parenting styles have continued to come up with new terminology to more accurately and precisely classify parenting characteristics. Despite the evolving nature of this classification system, a basic understanding of the four most widely used parenting styles (authoritative, authoritarian, permissive, and rejecting-neglectful) is the key to understanding and interpreting this body of research.

In order to better understand the classic categories of parenting styles, one must clearly understand what researchers mean by responsiveness and demandingness. Responsiveness refers to how attuned parents are to the individual needs of their adolescents. A parent who is responsive is highly aware of his adolescent's development and is able to foster social and emotional development in his adolescent. Demandingness refers to the extent to which a parent places maturity demands on his adolescent, as well as the way in which a parent chooses to enforce those demands. A parent who is moderately demanding is able to teach his adolescent social responsibility and the value of delayed gratification. Additionally, a moderately demanding parent is likely to set reasonable goals and demands for his adolescent and follow up with consistent but nonpunitive discipline. The most successful parenting happens when demandingness and responsiveness are in balance with one another. As will be discussed, when there is either too much or too little of either responsiveness or demandingness, negative outcomes can ensue. A better understanding of how these are integrated into parenting styles requires taking a closer look at each parenting style and its associated outcomes in terms of adolescent psychosocial adjustment.

Authoritative, Permissive, Authoritarian, and Rejecting-Neglectful Parenting Styles

Research has shown that the most successful parents are those who adopt an authoritative parenting style. Authoritative parents are highly responsive as well as somewhat demanding. Parents who are authoritative work with their adolescent to establish clear and reasonable rules to live by, and they expect that their adolescent will be responsible and behave in an age-appropriate manner. Authoritative parents may make demands on their adolescent, but they also allow their adolescent to make demands upon them. In this sense, authoritative parents foster a partnership with their adolescent that is mutually respectful and reciprocal in nature. When an adolescent misbehaves, an authoritative parent will provide consistent but reasonable disciplinary action. At the same time, an authoritative parent provides a warm and supportive environment in which their adolescent is encouraged to make her own decisions, express her own opinions, and strive for autonomy. Authoritative parents typically raise adolescents who have a positive sense of themselves, are well socialized, are high achievers, do well in school, and are not likely to get involved with drugs, alcohol, or antisocial activities.

A permissive parenting style is highly responsive but not demanding. Permissive parents are warm and accepting but do not set appropriate rules or reprimand their adolescent, and in an effort to avoid confrontation, permissive parents will not hold their adolescent accountable for misconduct. Permissive parents may try too hard to be friends with their adolescent, and as a result these parents typically do not provide enough adult influence and guidance in the home environment. Permissive parenting generally produces adolescents who are comparable to adolescents of authoritative parents, except that adolescents of permissive parents tend to have difficulty in school and to be at increased risk for drug and alcohol use.

Authoritarian parents are highly demanding but not responsive. Authoritarian parents set extensive rules and guidelines for their adolescent and do not tolerate a cooperative or reciprocal relationship with their adolescent. Authoritarian parents frequently assert parental power by enforcing punitive discipline when their adolescent does not adhere to rules or live up to parental expectations. Adolescents raised by authoritarian parents tend to have psychological difficulties (depression or anxiety), difficulty in school, low self-esteem, and even though these adolescents typically exhibit good self-control, they are at risk for involvement with drugs, alcohol, and illegal activities.

The rejecting-neglectful parent is low on both responsiveness and demandingness. A rejecting-neglectful parent is uninvolved with his adolescent and does not provide either support or structure. The rejecting-neglectful parent may view parenting as a burden and therefore may limit both the quality and quantity of time he spends with his adolescent. As a result, adolescents raised by rejecting-neglectful parents tend to have a significant amount of internalizing difficulties, problems asserting themselves, a high frequency of drug and alcohol use, and may have lower cognitive skills and academic abilities than adolescents raised by authoritative parents.

Parenting Attitudes and Practices

Parental attitudes and parental practices are both important components of a parenting style. However, there are distinct differences between these three terms. Parenting attitudes represent the way in which parents think or believe they should raise their adolescent. Parenting style is the term used to describe a constellation of parenting attitudes. As such, parenting styles set the emotional tone of parent-adolescent interactions and provide the framework for the parent-adolescent relationship. Although parenting styles define the contextual features of a parent-adolescent relationship, the manner in which parents actually impose their belief systems (i.e., parenting practices) may actually comprise the nuts and bolts of parenting. Therefore, although parenting styles greatly influence which parenting practices are implemented, these two constructs are not interchangeable. Research has shown that parenting practices directly impact adolescent outcome, while parenting attitudes or styles have a more indirect role. It is not difficult to see how this relationship unfolds; a parent believes their adolescent should behave in a certain way, but simply having these beliefs (parenting attitudes or style) does not directly influence an adolescent. It is the manner in which a parent chooses to enforce these beliefs (parenting practices) that directly affects the adolescent.

It is especially important that parenting practices be fluid, reflecting the developmental changes of the adolescent as she progresses into young adulthood. Parents who are inflexible with their parenting practices are likely to be in conflict with their adolescent. This parent-adolescent conflict typically occurs when parenting practices that worked well during childhood are viewed by an adolescent or young adult as an infringement on her autonomy. The most successful parents are those who are in sync with the changing needs of their adolescent. Though it is difficult to generalize across all adolescents, parenting is most likely to be effective when parents allow the power structure in the family to shift as their adolescent matures. Thus, while a more parent-centered family structure is appropriate for young children, a more balanced structure between parents and their maturing adolescent is necessary. It has been found that parents who are able to balance the power structure and adopt fluid and responsive parenting practices, while at the same time maintaining stability in the home environment, have better relationships with their adoles-

cents, and their adolescents have higher self-esteem and are more satisfied with their lives.

The influence of different parenting styles has been relatively consistent across socioeconomic status, gender, age, and family composition. However, most of the research on parenting styles has been focused on European Americans, and research with other ethnic groups in the United States and abroad is relatively new. Developing a better understanding of cross-cultural differences in parenting styles will require further research.

Rachael B. Millstein
Grayson N. Holmbeck
Sean N. Fischer
Wendy E. Shapera

See also Child-Rearing Styles; Family Relations; Fathers and Adolescents; Mothers and Adolescents; Parent-Adolescent Relations; Parental Monitoring

References and further reading

Baumrind, Diana. 1973. "The Development of Instrumental Competence through Socialization." Pp. 3–46 in *Minnesota Symposia on Adolescent Psychology*, vol. 7. Edited by Anne D. Pick. Minneapolis: University of Minnesota Press.

———. 1991. "Parenting Styles and Adolescent Development." Pp. 746–758 in *Encyclopedia of Adolescence*, vol. 2. Edited by Richard M. Lerner, Anne C. Peterson, and Jeanne Brooks-Gunn. New York: Garland.

Darling, Nancy, and Laurence Steinberg. 1993. "Parenting Style as Context: An Integrative Model." *Psychological Bulletin* 113, no. 3: 487–496.

Holmbeck, Grayson, Roberta Paikoff, and Jeanne Brooks-Gunn. 1995. "Parenting Adolescents." Pp. 91–118 in *Handbook of Parenting*, vol. 1. Edited by Marcus H. Bornstein. Mahwah, NJ: Erlbaum.

Maccoby, Eleanor E., and John A. Martin. 1983. "Socialization in the Context of the Family: Parent-Adolescent Interactions." Pp. 1–101 in *Handbook of*

Adolescent Psychology, vol. 4. Edited by Paul H. Mussen. New York: Wiley.

Steinberg, Laurence. 1999. "Families." Pp.118–149 in *Adolescence,* 5th ed. Boston: McGraw-Hill.

Steinberg, Laurence, Nina Mounts, Susie Lamborn, and Sanford M. Dornbusch. 1991. "Authoritative Parenting and Adolescent Adjustment across Varied Ecological Niches." *Journal of Research on Adolescence* 1, no. 1: 19–36.

Peer Groups

As children make the transition into adolescence, they exhibit increased interest in their peers and a growing psychological and emotional dependence on them for support and guidance. One reason for this growing interest is that many young adolescents enter new middle school structures that necessitate interacting with larger numbers of peers on a daily basis. In contrast to the predictability of self-contained classroom environments in elementary school, the uncertainty and ambiguity of multiple classroom environments, new instructional styles, and more complex class schedules often result in students turning to each other for ways to cope, information, and social support. Interest in sexuality and dating also increases at this age, widening the focus of peer interactions from same-sex to opposite-sex peers. As a result, young adolescents quickly form groups based on factors such as mutual interest, values, activities, or ethnicity; group membership is a hallmark of adolescent society well into the high school years. Typically, adolescent peer groups are studied in two ways. Peer crowds reflect fairly large, reputation- and status-based collectives of peers who have common interests, values, or attitudes. Peer networks or cliques are characterized by smaller groups of self-selected friends who interact with each other on a frequent basis.

Peer crowds are largely defined by stereotypic characterizations of individuals based on interests, attitudes, behavioral repertoires, values, or even race and social class. Therefore, crowd membership is typically a function of how a student is perceived by her peers rather than what she is really like or the extent to which she actually interacts with the other students in the crowd. In fact, although a peer crowd is often thought of as a group to which an individual actually belongs, students do not necessarily think they belong to a crowd to which their peers assign them. Moreover, peer crowds can serve as reference groups for those who would like to be a part of the crowd but are not. In other words, students observe crowd behavior for information about acceptable behavior, popular styles, and what they should be like. In general, the importance of belonging to a crowd peaks during early adolescence and then decreases over the course of the high school years.

Although adolescents themselves seem to define and organize their own groups, adults can play a critical role in group formation. For instance, class size can determine the size of peer cliques, and ability grouping and tracking practices can determine their composition. The degree to which schools emphasize group activities, such as sports and music, or academics also can influence the types of crowds that are formed and their relative status in a school.

Peer crowds differ on a range of characteristics, including the social status associated with group membership, the ease with which the group accepts new members, and the degree to which the group is

Young adolescents form groups based on factors such as natural interest, values, activities, or ethnicity. (Skjold Photographs)

similar to or different from other groups. Most peer crowds are easily recognized by the defining norms or activities of the group. For instance, most schools have groups that students label as *nerds, jocks, druggies, populars,* and *loners.* Nerds, or brains, are students who earn high academic grades and are perceived as being smart. Jocks are students who like and participate in sports and physical activities. Druggies, in contrast, are typically known for using drugs and for antisocial forms of behavior. Populars are those students perceived as having many friends, going to lots of parties, being cool, and having fun. Loners are perceived as not belonging to any particular crowd and not being accepted by peers in general. Although these groups are typically found in all schools, other crowds based on ethnicity, social class, or specific activities are also common.

During the early adolescent years, peer crowds are often large and typically represent only two or three distinct sets of interests or levels of social status. For instance, middle school crowds might simply consist of those students who are popular and those who are not. It is relatively difficult to move in and out of these crowds, and many students remain associated with a crowd for two or more years. As adolescents progress through high school, crowds become more differentiated, with five or six groups representing the peer population. In contrast to young adolescent crowds, which are defined primarily on the basis of behavioral styles and activities, crowds of mid-adolescents are defined to a greater extent according to abstract and personality-based qualities. For instance, at this time crowds might have highly distinct characteristics, as represented by labels such as nerds, druggies, punkers, or populars. High school crowds also represent varying levels of the social status hierarchy, although students often are able to move from one crowd to another. By the end of high school, social status becomes less important in defining peer crowds. At this age, students can and do move from crowd to crowd with relative ease.

In contrast to peer crowds, peer networks or cliques are smaller and based on mutual relationships. Peer cliques can also be formed on the basis of common activities such as study groups, athletic teams, or music and arts activities. A young adolescent in sixth grade might be affiliated with a crowd comprised of roughly a half or a third of her class while at the same time belonging to a peer clique of seven or eight peers. Members of peer cliques based on friendships are likely to have similar behavioral styles, similar orientations toward aggression, for instance, or similar tendencies to be cooperative and prosocial, as well as similar personality styles. Adolescents belonging to the same friendship network also tend to be similar in terms of levels of emotional stress or psychological well-being.

Members of peer cliques interact with each other frequently, although not exclusively. Like peer crowds, networks can be characterized according to the visibility and importance of the group within a classroom, and they often differ in the social status accorded their members. The status and centrality of specific individuals in a particular network also help define these groups. Adolescents often belong to several peer networks and make new friends as a result. Because of the changing nature of adolescent friendships, network membership is more unstable than crowd membership.

Adolescent peer groups seem to play several important roles in the social and emotional development of young people. Peer crowds are believed to serve two primary functions, to facilitate the formation of identity and self-concept and to structure ongoing social interactions. With respect to identity formation, crowds are believed to provide adolescents with values, norms, and interaction styles that are sanctioned and commonly displayed. Behaviors and interaction styles that are characteristic of a crowd are modeled frequently, and so they can be easily learned and adopted by individuals. In this manner, crowds provide prototypical examples of various identities for those who wish to try out different lifestyles and can easily affirm an adolescent's sense of self. As adolescents enter high school and the number of crowds increases, identities associated with crowds are more easily recognizable and afford the opportunity to try on various social identities with relatively little risk.

Because crowds are associated with specific norms and patterns of behavior, they also tend to structure the nature of adolescents' social interactions. For instance, crowd affiliation can determine the quality of one's friendships. Members of popular crowds often have friendships that are fairly superficial and status based, whereas members of low-status crowds tend to form friendships marked by loyalty, stability, and commitment. Because it is often easier to move to one crowd with similar characteristics than to another crowd that has very different norms and values, crowd membership also tends to determine how many friends an individual might have and the ease with which friends can be made outside one's crowd.

A specific example of the power of crowd influence is reflected in relations between crowd membership and adolescents' attitudes toward academic achievement. Peer crowds differ in the degree to which they pressure members to become involved in academic activities, with jock and popular groups providing significantly more pressure for academic involvement than other groups. Ethnic group status also appears to be a factor, in that white and Asian American adolescents tend to value an education, whereas in African American samples valuing education is less prevalent. At a more general level, the degree to which adolescents are able to establish positive relationships with groups of peers is related to their adjustment to and ultimate success in school. Students who believe that their peers support and care about them tend to be more engaged in positive aspects of classroom life than students who do not perceive such support. In particular, perceived social and emotional support from peers has been associated positively with prosocial outcomes such as helping, sharing, and cooperating, and related negatively to antisocial forms of behavior. In contrast, young adolescents who do not perceive their relationships with peers as positive and supportive tend to be at risk for academic and behavioral problems.

Of additional interest with respect to academic achievement, however, is that being liked by teachers might offset any negative effects of peer rejection on adolescents' adjustment at school. For instance, young adolescents who have few friends but are not necessarily disliked by their peers are often highly motivated students if they are well liked by their teachers. These adolescents tend to remain academically and socially well adjusted over the course of the middle school years. Therefore, it appears that the absence of peer relationships does not inevitably influence motivation to achieve and academic performance if supportive relationships with teachers exist.

The function of peer networks is believed to be somewhat different from that of peer crowds. Peer networks typically provide members with the help, support, companionship, and mutual aid typical of close friendships. Peer networks also play a role in defining social boundaries and status hierarchies that help to maintain social control and enforce conformity to group norms and practices. Social control can be accomplished when adolescents provide each other with positive types of support such as instrumental help and emotional validation. In addition, however, social control can be maintained by peer interactions that are less helpful and often quite negative.

Adolescent gossip is a typical mechanism of social control that conveys approval or disapproval of behavior to group members. It is clear that adolescents are often highly motivated to conform to peer standards of behavior for fear of rejection or ridicule. Indeed, emotional distress has been linked consistently to peer rejection and lack of peer support during this stage of development. Interestingly, adolescents who believe that approval from peers makes them feel good about themselves suffer from the negative emotional effects of peer rejection, whereas adolescents who believe that feeling good about one's self leads to peer acceptance do not.

Perhaps one of the more interesting questions with respect to peer groups is how great the strength of their influence is when compared to that of parents and other adults. It often is assumed by researchers as well as the general public that adolescent peer groups provide alternative and competing influences to those of parents. Interestingly, however, this is not entirely the case. Although adolescents vary in the extent to which they succumb to peer pressure, adolescents typically follow parental advice when faced with conflicting advice from parents and peers, especially if decisions involve future plans such as choosing and attending a college. As adolescents get older, they tend to make important decisions on their own, independently of advice or pressures from peers or parents.

Exceptions to this pattern are found in adolescents who associate with delinquent gangs. In this case, peers have an enormous amount of influence on individual gang members. However, the strength of gang influence is in large part due to parents who have been ineffective in providing their children with social skills and emotional support. In the case of gang cultures that evolve among children from poor immigrant or ethnic-minority groups, economic hardships, cultural discontinuities, and lack of supportive programs in the schools serve to weaken further the role of parents in adolescents' lives. As a result, these adolescents who have become detached from family and school cultures tend to group together into gangs that offer them friendship, emotional support, a sense of security, and protection. Most adolescents, however, do not engage in gang activities and are able to negotiate the

world of peer groups successfully, especially if they have the support of patient and nurturing parents.

Kathryn R. Wentzel

See also Cliques; Dating; Ethnic Identity; Ethnocentrism; Identity; Proms; Social Development; Youth Gangs

References and further reading
Brown, Bradford B. 1989. "The Role of Peer Groups in Adolescents' Adjustment to Secondary School." Pp. 188–215 in *Peer Relationships in Child Development*. Edited by Thomas J. Berndt and Gary W. Ladd. New York: Wiley.
Brown, Bradford B., Margaret S. Mory, and David Kinney. 1994. "Casting Adolescent Crowds in a Relational Perspective: Caricature, Channel, and Context." Pp. 123–167 in *Personal Relationships during Adolescence*. Edited by Raymond Montemayor, Gerald R. Adams, and Thomas P. Gullotta. Newbury Park, CA: Sage.
Epstein, Joyce L. 1989. "The Selection of Friends: Changes across the Grades and in Different School Environments." Pp. 158–187 in *Peer Relationships in Child Development*. Edited by Thomas J. Berndt and Gary W. Ladd. New York: Wiley.
Furman, Wyndol. 1989. "The Development of Children's Social Networks." Pp. 151–172 in *Children's Social Networks and Social Supports*. Edited by Deborah Belle. New York: Wiley.
Kindermann, Thomas A., Tanya McCollam, and Ellsworth Gibson. 1996. "Peer Networks and Students' Classroom Engagement during Childhood and Adolescence." Pp. 279–312 in *Social Motivation: Understanding Children's School Adjustment*. Edited by Jaana Juvonen and Kathryn R. Wentzel. New York: Cambridge University Press.
Urberg, Kathryn A., Serdar M. Degirmencioglu, Jerry M. Tolson, and Kathy Halliday-Scher. 1995. "The Structure of Adolescent Peer Networks." *Developmental Psychology* 31: 540–547.

Peer Pressure

Peer pressure is the influence that peer groups exert, through implicit or explicit demands, on individual members to conform to a group's activities, beliefs, or norms. Although peer pressure can be in positive directions, the focus has primarily been on the negative impact that peer pressure can have on adolescent development. It is popularly believed that peer pressure is one of the key causes of deviant and antisocial adolescent behavior. This belief has influenced social policies and research concerning peer pressure in adolescence, generating policy and research biases toward discovering ways to keep adolescents from succumbing to the negative influence of peer pressure, neglecting positive effects that it might have. However, concerns over research design and methods of data collection have raised questions about the impact that peer pressure has. Studies that address these concerns demonstrate that although peer pressure plays a role in adolescent development, the importance of that role has been overstated. Additionally, other research shows that peer pressure is not experienced uniformly by all adolescents. Factors such as age, gender, group status, the nature of the peer group demands, and parenting style all play a role in determining susceptibility to peer pressure.

Peer pressure is popularly perceived as a major cause of deviant behavior among adolescents. This belief has its roots in neo-Freudian theories of adolescent detachment, according to which "healthy" adolescents "break free" of parents during puberty, a detachment that occurs with a concomitant attachment to peers. Belief in the rejection of parental influence and increase in peer influence is reinforced by the positive correlation consistently found between individual levels of antisocial behavior (e.g., smoking, substance use, delinquency, and the like) and antisocial behavior among peers. Thus, social programs aimed at preventing these antisocial behaviors typically target peer groups, attempting to inoculate adolescents against conformity pressures. The most famous example of such a program was First Lady Nancy Reagan's "Just Say No" American antidrug campaign, in which teens were advised to say "no" to peer demands. Programs such as this one operate under the assumption that peer groups exert a large influence over adolescent behavior and use this influence to enforce antisocial norms. Thus, many studies investigating peer pressure focus on how peers initiate and maintain negative pressure. Studies investigating positive aspects of peer pressure are seldom conducted, overlooking the role that peers can have on socially desirable outcomes, for example, school achievement. Given the negative emphasis society and social policy place on peer pressure, it is important to understand the impact it has on adolescent behavior.

Due to research designs, the importance of peer pressure in the lives of adolescents tends to be overstated. Peer pressure is not a reflection of how similar peer group members are, but of the degree to which the group influences the behaviors of individual members. Investigations that use a single time period to explore the relationship between an adolescent's behavior and that of her peer group are assessing similarity, not peer pressure. These studies confound peer selection with peer influence; not all similarities between peers are due to conformity demands. Adolescents tend to join peer groups that have similar inter-

Peer pressure is one of the key causes of deviant and antisocial adolescent behavior. (Shirley Zeiberg)

ests. For example, a teenager who is in the school band is not forced by peer pressure to learn to play an instrument. Instead, the teenager typically joins the band if she already knows how to play an instrument. Therefore, measuring the level of similarity among band members' musical ability needs to account for the fact that they may have originally been highly similar. In order to assess the degree to which an adolescent changes to conform to peer pressure, she needs to be studied over time, in a longitudinal research design. Although peer groups have an impact on adolescent behavior, studies using a longitudinal design find that the majority of similarities observed are due to initial selection.

A similar research problem arises in how information is gathered about adolescent and peer similarity. Many researchers have chosen to use a single adolescent informant. That is, one teenager provides information for both his behaviors and the behaviors of peers. Thus, a positive relationship between a teenager and peers could partially reflect the teenager projecting his behaviors onto peers. Studies that have collected information from both adolescents and peers support this idea. Peer pressure is still found to have an impact when it is measured with multiple informants; however, its impact is significantly lower than when assessed with a single informant.

Additionally, researchers investigating peer pressure have found various factors that influence the impact of peer pressure. One of the most reliable findings is the role of age. Conformity to peer pressure appears as an inverted U across time. That is, adolescent conformity to peer pressure increases as individuals enter adolescence, peaks during middle adolescence (approximately twelve to fifteen years old), and declines thereafter.

Gender has also proven a relatively consistent modifier of susceptibility to peer pressure. Although male and female adolescents generally display similar levels of susceptibility to peers, males are more likely to conform to peer demands to engage in antisocial activities than are females. Both genders are equally susceptible to peer pressure concerning musical preferences, but females are less susceptible to peer pressure involving illegal activities. Classic views of peer pressure as a negative phenomenon, therefore, are more applicable to the adolescent male experience.

The status a teenager has in a peer group also affects the nature of peer pressure. Low-status group members are usually subject to unilateral influences from the peer group; the peer group pressures the adolescent and she conforms. Higher status adolescents also experience peer pressure, but in a more subtle and bidirectional manner. Higher-status teens can influence and guide the peer group, yet their status and influence are bound by group expectations. Thus, although higher status members appear more influential, their behaviours are guided in less obvious ways by the demands of the group.

The degree to which adolescents conform to peer pressure also depends on what the peer group is demanding. Adolescents are more likely to be influenced by peer pressure involving neutral behaviors than peer pressure involving antisocial or deviant behaviors. Thus, although teenagers may readily conform to peer demands to attend a certain film, they are less likely to conform to similar pressures to take illegal drugs. On a related point, teenagers are also more susceptible to peer pressure in some areas of their life than others. Life decisions involving short-term and transient outcomes are highly subject to peer pressure, but peer pressure has a smaller impact on long-term decisions. For example, peer pressure plays a larger role in the color that a teenager dyes his hair but a smaller role in college selection.

The broader social context of the adolescent, especially her relationship with parents, also modifies the impact that peer pressure has on behavior. Permissive or authoritarian parents tend to increase the degree to which a teen is susceptible to peer pressure. Additionally, it has recently been shown that autocratic parenting influences adolescent susceptibility differently, depending on whether peer pressure is positive or negative. Teens with highly autocratic parents are more influenced by positive peer pressure and less influenced by pressure to engage in positive rather than negative behaviors than are teens with less autocratic parents.

Douglas W. Elliott

See also Cliques; Conflict and Stress; Dating; Decision Making; Ethnocentrism; Identity; Juvenile Crime; Moral Development; Substance Use and Abuse; Teasing; Youth Gangs

References and further reading

Berndt, Thomas J. 1979. "Developmental Changes in Conformity to Peers and Parents." *Developmental Psychology* 15: 608–616.

Berndt, Thomas J., and Keuho Keefe. 1995. "Friends' Influence on Adolescents' Adjustment to School." *Child Development* 66: 1312–1329.

———. 1996. "Transitions in Friendship and Friends' Influence." Pp. 57–84 in *Transitions through Adolescence: Interpersonal Domains and Context.* Edited by Julia A. Graber, Jeanne Brooks-Gunn, and Anne C. Petersen. Mahwah, NJ: Lawrence Erlbaum Associates.

Brown, B. Bradford, Donnie Rae Classen, and Sue Ann Eicher. 1986. "Perceptions of Peer Pressure, Peer Conformity Dispositions, and Self-Reported Behavior among Adolescents." *Developmental Psychology* 22: 521–530.

Bukowski, William M., Andrew F. Newcomb, and Willard M. Hartup. 1996. *The Company They Keep: Friendship in Childhood and Adolescence.* New York: Cambridge University Press.

Chassin, Laurie, Clark C. Presson, Steve J. Sherman, Daniel Montello, and John McGrew. 1986. "Changes in Peer and Parent Influence during Adolescence: Longitudinal versus Cross-Sectional Perspectives on Smoking Initiation." *Developmental Psychology* 22: 327–334.

Kandel, Denise B. 1978. "Homophily, Selection, and Socialization in Adolescent Friendships." *American Journal of Sociology* 84: 427–436.

Mounts, Nina S., and Laurence Steinberg. 1995. "An Ecological Analysis of Peer Influence on Adolescent Grade Point Average and Drug Use." *Developmental Psychology* 31: 915–922.

Youniss, James. 1980. *Parents and Peers in Social Development: A Sullivan-Piaget Perspective.* Chicago: University of Chicago Press.

Peer Status

What characteristics of the person and of his context enhance the quality of his peer status? How can adolescents be aided in building healthy and supportive friendships? Although there has not been a lot of theoretical attention paid to conceptualizing what individual and contextual variables may help answer these questions, research does indicate that there are three dimensions of peer relationships, or friendships, that affect the course of youth development: first, simply having friends; second, the kind of person one has as a friend; and third, the quality of the friendship. Variations in all three of these dimensions are related to differences in the adjustment of youth.

Clearly, unless one has a friend, the other influences of friendship on adolescent development cannot act. There is a diverse set of individual and contextual variables that shape the formation of friendships in adolescence.

Friendships are formed more readily by youth who are more age-mate oriented than family oriented in their attempts to establish new social relationships with peers. Also, the ability to take the perspective of other people whom one is meeting is important in establishing new friendships in adolescence. In addition, knowledge of what are appropriate and inappropriate strategies to use in making friends is important in establishing acceptance by peers. Knowing these strategies, along with the ability to take someone else's perspective, can be quite useful, since being able to fit one's style of behavior to that desired by peers is a key factor in positive peer relations and popularity.

Useful strategies in establishing friendships include managing conflicts in ways that avoid any disruption in the relationship (that is, that avoid "stopping talking" for a while) and using display behaviors to enhance one's attractiveness to others.

Friendships marked by stability, engagement, and lack of deviance in the friend are associated with positive self-esteem among adolescents. (Skjold Photographs)

For instance, and in light of the fact that physical attractiveness is linked to better peer relations in both boys and girls, each gender may use a set of behaviors that they believe is associated with greater physical attractiveness. For instance, in order to try to appear more attractive, girls have been found to display chin strokes, hair flips, head tilts, coy looks, and movements designed to make themselves appear physically smaller.

To the extent that these behaviors and characteristics are successful in forming a friendship, *and* if the adolescent can then become engaged in a friendship that is marked by the qualities of

1. stability (duration over time);

2. engagement (i.e., being involved in activities with a best or close friend); and
3. lack of deviance in the friend (that is, a friend who does not get into trouble, a friend who has behaviors and attitudes that are socially positive),

then it is likely that positive self-esteem will develop in the youth.

However, not all friendships are formed with youth who are engaged in positive behaviors and who avoid trouble and deviance. When friendships are formed with youth having negative characteristics, the implications for adolescent development are not favorable. For instance, when a youth's friends engage in antisocial behavior or in disruptive behavior, it is likely that the youth will follow the same course.

In addition, young people and their friends frequently have the same feelings of internal distress, and such personality characteristics can be associated with both adolescent and peer substance abuse. Involvement with deviant peers and feelings of depression increase the likelihood that the adolescent will use drugs. Similarly, changes in youths' grades and drug use are linked to these same changes in their friends.

Such associations may develop through a process involving both hostile and low-reciprocity relationships with a close friend, occurring in relation to feelings of depression and self-destructive behaviors in a youth. Indeed, such a process has been found to be related to high levels of alcohol use among adolescents.

In sum, a range of types of friendships exists in adolescence. As with peer relations in general, there are specific implications for youth behavior and development of the type of friendships they possess.

Richard M. Lerner

See also Cliques; Ethnocentrism; Loneliness; Social Development

References and further reading
Hartup, Willard. 1993a. "Adolescents and Their Friends." *New Directions for Child Development* 60: 3–22.
———. 1993b. "The Company They Keep: Friendships and Their Developmental Significance." *Child Development* 67: 1–13.
Kolaric, G. C., and Nancy L. Galambos. 1995. "Face-to-Face Interactions in Unacquainted Female-Male Adolescent Dyads: How Do Girls and Boys Behave?" *Journal of Early Adolescence* 15, no. 3: 363–382.
Laursen, Brett. 1993. "Conflict Management among Close Peers." *New Directions for Child Development* 60: 39–54.
Lerner, Richard M. In press. *Adolescence: Development, Diversity, Context, and Application.* Upper Saddle River, NJ: Prentice-Hall.
Rubin, Kenneth A. 1998. "Peer Interaction, Relationships, and Groups." Pp. 619–700 in *Handbook of Child Psychology*, vol. 3. 5th ed. *Social, Emotional, and Personality Development.* Edited by W. Damon and N. Eisenberg. New York: Wiley.
Windle, Michael. 1994. "A Study of Friendship Characteristics and Problem Behaviors among Middle Adolescents." *Child Development* 65: 1764–1777.

Peer Victimization in School

Peer victimization can be defined as the repeated bullying, insulting, terrorizing, or intimidating of youth that takes place in and around school in contexts where adult supervision is minimal. Although victimization is of concern to teachers, administrators, and parents of school-aged children at any age level, early adolescence may be a particularly critical developmental period for understanding the nature of chronic harassment, as well as its causes and consequences. Both the pubertal changes that signal the onset of adolescence and the transition to middle school bring about major shifts in the importance of the peer group to individual well-being. Given their heightened concern about finding their niche, fitting in, and peer approval in general, adolescents who are targets of peer victimization may be particularly vulnerable to adjustment difficulties. Academic problems may also be exacerbated among adolescent victims, since they must

Peer victimization is repeated bullying, insulting, terrorizing, or intimidating of youth. (Skjold Photographs)

learn to cope with the general decline in motivation that often accompanies the middle school transition and adjust to a school structure that provides more opportunities for avoidance (e.g., skipping classes).

Types of Peer Victimization

Peer victimization takes many forms. It can be either direct, entailing face-to-face confrontation, or it can be indirect, usually involving a third party. Direct victimization can be further distinguished as either physical (e.g., assault, damage to one's property) or verbal (e.g., name-calling, threats, racial slurs). Indirect victimization usually involves spreading nasty rumors, gossiping, or other kinds of behaviors that are designed to exclude or ostracize the victim from his or her peer group. The most common types of victimization reported by middle school students are being the target of nasty rumors, name-calling, and public ridicule. Overt physical victimization appears to decline from childhood to adolescence, whereas the psychological types, both direct and indirect, increase from elementary to secondary school.

How pervasive is peer-directed victimization in schools? Harassment begins as early as preschool, and its effects are evident at a relatively young age. For example, survey data reveal that children as young as age seven list feeling unsafe at school as one of their greatest worries. Other studies indicate that more than one-third of all aggressive acts against twelve- to fifteen-year-olds take place at school, with another 20 percent occurring on the way to school. Furthermore, anywhere from 40 percent to 80 percent of students report that they personally have been victimized at school, with the reported incidents ranging from verbal abuse and intimidation to property damage and serious assault (Hoover, Oliver, and Hazler, 1992). In some urban secondary schools most of the youth who carry weapons to school claim that they do so for self-defense. All of these findings suggest that psychological abuse, physical threat, and direct aggression have become accepted facts in American schools, and that the perpetrators of hostility are becoming more aggressive and the targets of their abuse are feeling more vulnerable.

Although the public tends to think of peer victimization as a dyadic interaction between a perpetrator (bully) and her victim, it may be more accurate to portray victimization as a group phenomenon involving multiple social roles. As many as six participant roles that children may assume during a victimization incident have been identified. In addition to bully and victim, these roles are bully's assistant, bully's reinforcer, victim's defender, and bystander. In studies among middle and high school students, a greater percentage of students report taking on roles that encourage and maintain peer abuse as opposed to roles that discourage it. For example, at least 35 to 40 percent of adolescents act as bullies, assistants, or reinforcers. If those in the bystander role are included, there are as many as 60 to 70 percent of students who do nothing to stop bullying. In contrast, only about 20 percent of students report that they take on defender roles (Salmivalli, 1999).

There are no clear gender differences in victimization. Girls and boys are about equally likely to be harassed by their peers, although they tend to be harassed in different ways. Boys are more often physically victimized, whereas girls are more typically indirectly or relationally victimized by being excluded from social groups. Verbal harassment, such as name-calling, occurs with about the same frequency among males and females.

As a special type of peer victimization, sexual harassment in school does have clear links to gender. Girls are more likely to report being the victim of unwanted sexual attention than boys. The most common types of sexual victimization reported in school are being the target of sexual comments, jokes, or gestures, and being touched, grabbed, or pinched in a sexual way. The least common types reported are voyeurism (i.e., being spied on as one gets undressed in the locker room) and forcible rape. Sexual harassment is likely to occur more often and be perceived as more severe in high school than in middle school, and among older than younger high school students. Because sexual harassment is unique and has its own developmental course, it is not included in the sections that follow on the causes and consequences of peer victimization.

Risk Factors for Peer Victimization
Although large percentages of students report some experiences with victimization, only about 10 to 15 percent of school children are *chronic* victims (Olweus, 1991). These are the youngsters who are repeatedly harassed by their peers. Chronic victimization can last from a few weeks to several years.

The reasons why some children become chronic victims are not well understood, but there are both individual and family factors that place a child at particular risk. Because victimization occurs when there is an imbalance of power between individuals, one characteristic that appears to directly contribute to victimization is physical weakness. Physically weak children are often increasingly victimized over time because they lack the ability

and confidence to ward off the attacks of their peers. Late pubertal development relative to one's peers has been linked to victimization for boys, because boys who mature later are typically smaller and physically weaker in middle school than their on-time and early-maturing male classmates.

A second risk factor for victimization is being different from others. Habitual teasing is especially likely for children who look different due to, for example, being fat, wearing glasses, being an ethnic minority, or having speech problems or an obvious physical disability. Youngsters who behave in a deviant way are also at increased risk. Hyperactivity and other kinds of annoying or disruptive behavior often invite peer harassment. Hence, the dimensions of difference that can cause victimization may be both within the potential victims' control (e.g., annoying behavior) and outside of their control (e.g., looking different).

The absence of good-quality friendship networks is a third risk factor for victimization. It has been shown that children who are vulnerable in other ways are less likely to be harassed by peers if they have even one close friend. A close friend provides not only emotional support but also someone who will stick up for the child if victimization does occur. Studies have shown that bullies prefer to attack friendless children because there is little risk of retaliation from others. On the other hand, the quality as well as the quantity of one's friendships can also be an important consideration. Chronic victims who do have more than one friend often have chums who themselves are weak, timid, and fearful. Nevertheless, victims often do have close relationships that can offer much in the way of support or protection against bullies.

A fourth risk factor can be traced to the chronic victim's family relationships. Children who display what is called *insecure attachment* to parents are often the targets of peer harassment. As infants and toddlers, insecurely attached children are easily upset by novelty, have difficulty separating from their parent, and are not easily comforted by their parent when they are upset. When these children reach school age, they tend to be anxious and reluctant to explore or try new things, and they cry easily. Such behaviors often invite harassment by classmates. Parenting styles also are related to victimization. Overprotectiveness or intrusiveness by mothers, particularly toward their sons, can interfere with the boy's development of physical play and risk taking, which are behaviors that are valued by the male peer group and that protect against victimization. In contrast, overcontrolling parents who use coercion and threat of love withdrawal to insure compliance are more likely to be a risk factor for girls. Parents who employ such tactics may foster self-doubts in their daughters about their ability to develop the kind of interpersonal relationships that are more expected of girls.

In summary, there are individual child factors and family factors that can be causes of victimization. It is important to remember, however, that the presence of these risk factors does not mean that victims are responsible for their plight. Peer-directed victimization would not take place if there were no bullies to initiate it and if there were better ways to supervise and monitor all children at school.

Consequences of Peer Victimization

The psychological and behavioral consequences of chronic victimization are overwhelmingly negative. Chronic victims tend to have low self-esteem, and they feel more lonely, anxious, unhappy, and insecure than their nonvictimized peers. Studies of victimization over time reveal that these psychological consequences can have long-term effects. For example, one large-scale study conducted in Norway showed that chronic victimization in ninth grade predicted depression, negative self-views, and suicide attempts ten years later when the former victims were young adults.

One reason why many victims suffer from low self-esteem and depression is that they blame themselves for what happens to them. That is, when youngsters are harassed by others, they often ask themselves, "Why me?" To the extent that their answer to this question focuses on their own perceived weaknesses (e.g., "I'm a wimp," "I'm the type of person who deserves to be picked on"), they will feel worse about themselves. Victims who attribute their plight to situational factors (e.g., "This school has a lot of tough kids") that do not single them out (e.g., "These kids pick on everybody") show better coping and adjustment.

There is increasing evidence that chronic victims are also at risk for school difficulties. Victims of all ages report that they like school less than do nonvictims. At the secondary level, victimization is associated with attendance problems, such as tardiness and unexcused absences. Such findings may indicate that victims use avoidance as a way of coping with chronic harassment by others. Less is known about how victimization directly affects actual school performance, as measured by grade-point average. What is clear, however, is that when victimization is accompanied by psychological problems, such as low self-esteem or depression, adolescents are at particular risk for diminished academic performance.

In addition to suffering from negative self-views and school difficulties, victims tend to be rejected by the general peer group, especially during early adolescence. In addition to showing dislike, studies on peer attitudes document that young adolescents express little concern that victimization might cause pain and suffering for the target of such behavior. In general, adolescents appear to be unsympathetic toward victims and to endorse the belief that these children bring their problems on themselves. This may partly explain why peers take on the role of participants in the victimization process and why victims have difficulty finding peers who will either protect them or come to their aid.

As a result of negative self-views and peer rejection, many victims become passive and withdrawn, and they yield to bullies' demands with little or no protest. Other victims, in contrast, become hostile and aggressive themselves. When picked on by others, they react with exaggerated displays of anger and hostility. But such youngsters are rarely successful in their attempts to defend themselves or gain acceptance from the peer group. The long-term consequences of being an aggressive victim can be just as devastating as those associated with being a passive victim. One such consequence is perhaps best illustrated by the series of school shootings that took place in America over a two-year period in the late 1990s. A common factor underlying almost all of these shootings was that the perpetrator had a history of being teased and taunted by fellow classmates, and that he felt picked on and persecuted.

In summary, research on the consequences of chronic peer harassment portrays a dismal picture of the school life of victimized youth. Victims feel bad about themselves, lonely, isolated, and depressed. They are also disliked by their peers, who are very unsympathetic to their plight. The behavioral consequences of victimization involve both turning inward, with submissiveness and withdrawal, and turning outward, with hostility and aggression. Chronic harassment can also lead to poor school performance.

School-Based Interventions for Victimization

The negative consequences of victimization highlight the need for intervention, and a few different approaches have been offered. One approach focuses on the victim, in order to teach social skills and strategies for dealing with harassment. These may include assertiveness training, where victims learn to defend themselves in nonaggressive ways; the learning of effective problem-solving tactics; and friendship development training, such as learning cooperation and sharing.

Many victims are reluctant to tell anyone about their experiences out of fear of further retaliation or being singled out as an easy mark. To address this problem, victim hot lines have been established as a second approach. A phone call to counselors at the victim's discretion is thought to both protect their privacy and encourage help seeking.

Yet a third kind of approach has been designed to change the school environment where peer harassment takes place. The goal is to target everybody in the school setting, including staff, teachers, and all students. This kind of approach is guided by the belief that victimization can be combated only if two things happen: First, teachers and administrators must take harassment seriously and know how to handle it. And second, the student body must become less tolerant of victimization and more empathetic toward victims. Schoolwide programs are multifaceted, in that they typically include a curriculum for staff development and empathy training for all students, as well as specific interventions for both victims and bullies.

Given the pervasiveness and seriousness of peer victimization in schools today, it seems that schoolwide programs will be the most effective strategy for both prevention and intervention. Only when the school community comes to accept the fact that the problem of victimization is everyone's responsibility will the climate be right for effective and lasting change.

Sandra Graham

See also Cliques; Conflict and Stress; Ethnocentrism; Identity; Shyness; Teasing

References and further reading
Graham, Sandra, and Jaana Juvonen. 1998. "A Social Cognitive Perspective on Peer Aggression and Victimization." *Annals of Child Development* 13: 21–66.
Hoover, J., R. Oliver, and R. Hazler. 1992. "Bullying: Perceptions of Adolescent Victims in Midwestern USA." *School Psychology International* 13: 5–16.
Juvonen, Jaana, and Sandra Graham, eds. 2000. *Peer Harassment in School: The Plight of the Vulnerable and Victimized.* New York: Guilford Press.
Lee, Valerie, Robert Croninger, Eleanor Linn, and Xianglei Chen. 1996. "The Culture of Sexual Harassment in Secondary Schools." *American Educational Research Journal* 33: 383–417.
Olweus, Dan. 1991. "Bully/Victim Problems among School Children: Basic Facts and Effects of a School-Based Intervention Program." Pp. 411–454 in *The Development and Treatment of Childhood Aggression.* Edited by Debra Pepler and Kenneth Rubin. Hillsdale, NJ: Erlbaum.
Rigby, Ken. 1996. *Bullying in Schools and What to Do about It.* Melbourne: Austrailian Council for Educational Research.
Salmivalli, Christina. 1999. "Participant Role Approach to School Bullying: Implications for Intervention." *Journal of Adolescence* 22: 453–459.
Verlinden, Stephanie, Michael Hersen, and Jay Thomas. 2000. "Risk Factors in School Shootings." *Clinical Psychology Review* 20: 3–56.

Personal Fable

The personal fable is a story adolescents tell themselves, about themselves. The personal fable emerges during adolescence when they begin to think differently about the world. While they are developing new cognitive abilities, adolescents become self-centered or egocentric. Aspects of egocentrism are extreme self-consciousness, a sense that one is always under critical scrutiny of others, and a feeling that one is different from everyone else. In the personal fable the adolescent portrays herself as special or unique. People at all stages of their lives have personal fables that help them to overcome difficult times. For adolescents, however, the fable dominates their thinking and understanding.

The period of adolescence is marked by dramatic changes in ways of thinking. Adolescents gain the ability to think abstractly and hypothetically. For instance, they can now think about what might happen given certain circumstances. Adolescents can reflect on their own and other people's thinking and can consider the point of view or perspective of others. However, with these new abilities come errors in judgment. These errors contribute to the personal fable.

Personal fables can lead to adolescents' feeling they are invulnerable or indestructible. (Shirley Zeiberg)

The personal fable may appear in many different forms. Adolescents may fail to distinguish between experiences and feelings that are unique to them and those that are common to humanity. They may underestimate how much other people can relate to their experiences. For example, a young man may have his heart broken and believe that no one has experienced the pain he feels. Alternatively, adolescents often believe that others share their own concerns and preoccupations. A young woman with a blemish on her face is likely to think that everyone else notices it, too, and cares about it as much as she does.

Another part of the personal fable is that adolescents have a feeling of invulnerability or indestructibility. They believe that "bad things happen to other people but not to me." Since they are special and unique, they are not vulnerable to the same dangers as other people. This belief may lead to risk-taking behavior. For instance, although adolescents know drunk driving is dangerous and may even know of someone who was involved in a drunk-driving accident, they do not think it could ever happen to them.

The personal fable can be adaptive for adolescents, since it protects them from being overwhelmed by fears and experiences that they did not have to deal with as children. As their thought processes mature, adolescents begin to realize the many threats in the world that were not of concern to them previously. The personal fable may also protect and help develop self-esteem at a time when adolescents are particularly vulnerable to criticism.

In general, personal fable behavior begins to diminish as young people begin to develop friendships in which intimacies are shared. Once young people begin to share their personal feelings and thoughts, they discover that they are less unique and special than they originally thought. In addition, the sense of loneliness in being special and apart from everyone else diminishes. As adolescents move into adulthood, self-esteem increases and the need to fit in diminishes, as does the need for the personal fable.

Susan Averna

See also Accidents; Ethnocentrism; Identity; Lore

References and further reading
Buis, Joyce, and Dennis Thompson. 1989.
"Imaginary Audience and Personal Fable: A Brief Review." *Adolescence* 24, no. 96: 774–781.

Elkind, David. 1978. "Understanding the Adolescent." *Adolescence* 13, no. 49: 127–134.

Lapsley, Daniel, Matt Milstead, Stephen Quintana, Daniel Flannery, and Raymond Buss. 1986. "Adolescent Egocentrism and Formal Operations: Tests of a Theoretical Assumption." *Developmental Psychology* 22, no. 6: 800–807.

Personality

Each person is different, not like anybody else, unique. This uniqueness is a very complex set of biological characteristics, ideas, memories, motivations, attitudes, and values. Theoretically, the number of characteristics that each person possesses is unlimited or at least very large. Moreover, these characteristics themselves are not equal; they define a very complicated system called a human being, and they define it in different ways. Some of these characteristics can be observed directly and established objectively (like eye color or height), some could be judged based on a person's action (like kindness or anxiety), some influence a person's behavior in life situations (for instance, sociability), and some do not (again, eye color or, for instance, blood type).

Personality is defined as one's characteristics that *define one's behavior in life situations.* These characteristics are called personality traits. They are "individual differences in the tendency to behave, think, and feel in certain consistent ways" (Caspi, 1998, p. 312). Some of these traits are biologically determined (as properties of one's nervous system) and related closely to one's temperament; some are mostly cognitive (like values and attitudes) and related to a person's self, a mental structure that encompasses a person's views and beliefs about him/herself and the world around them. Personality can be viewed as a kind of geometrical shape with multiple facets, with each facet representing a personality characteristic, and all the facets with unique joints between them should be taken into consideration if one wishes to explain or predict a person's behavior in any given moment. This shape is personality. There are numerous traits, so it would be hard or maybe impossible to describe a particular personality without some kind of generalization. In the early years of research on personality, scholars noted that those characteristics might be grouped, reducing their number and making descriptions, explanations, and comparisons much easier. Continuing to use a geometrical metaphor, if the shape is viewed from a distance, the edges between some facets would be blurred and several of them would be perceived as one, bigger facet. The number of facets we see will depend on the distance, or, more scientifically, the number of traits to take into consideration will depend on the level of analysis.

In sum, personality might be thought of as a hierarchy of traits, from broadest domains that correspond to the most general tendencies of a person's behavior, to smaller traits, as well as the values and ides that may influence his reaction to a particular situation.

On the top of the hierarchy are the *Big Five* factors, the broadest qualities each of which encompasses several more precise personality characteristics. Most researchers agree that these five factors are:

- *Extraversion,* or Positive Emotionality, defining to which extent a person actively engages in life on the whole and likes to seek new experiences; extraverts are usually

Personality is defined as the characteristics that define an adolescent's behaviors, emotions, and motivations. (Skjold Photographs)

active, assertive, enthusiastic, outgoing, humorous, and sociable;

- *Neuroticism,* or Negative Emotionality, defining to which extent a person sees the world as hostile, distressful, and threatening; people who possess this quality are basically anxious, self-pitying, concerned with adequacy, not self-reliant, worrying, and have fluctuating moods;

- *Agreeableness,* defining warm, giving, and sharing quality of a person's interpersonal nature; manifests itself in generousness, kindness, warmth, compassion, and trust;

- *Conscientiousness,* or Constraint, or the strength of one's self-controlling ability; conscientious people are organized, planful, reliable, and responsible;

- *Openness,* or Intellect, defining the complexity of one's intellectual life; as it is obvious, it is directly related to a person's intellectual level and expresses itself in creativity, curiosity, width of interests, the depth of understanding experiences, artistry, and fantasy.

The above schema is widely accepted by most scholars of personality and represents the two highest levels of the personality hierarchy. Yet the complexity of a human being cannot be represented in one, even one very well developed and very precise schema. In many instances one cannot predict their own behavior or the behavior of others. In fact, human personality is much more complex than any schema can represent, and, in addition, it is constantly changing. It is also interesting that the very nature of our understanding of personality is full of contradictions. Some of these are:

- between the holistic nature of personality and the need, already discussed, for some classification and generalization;
- between objectivity and subjectivity—there is *no* way of objectively measuring any personality traits;
- between stability and change;
- between the roles of heredity, environment, and the conscious will in development of one's personality.

The first contradiction is that there are a large number of traits, attitudes, and values that influence any act in any situation. These numerous traits were invented by psychologists to describe and measure personality with a certain degree of precision, but in reality all of these qualities are at work simultaneously.

The ability to generalize is useful if we want to compare two personalities, or if we want to measure change in one's personality over time. However, these scales and dimensions are approximations. For instance, we may want to describe someone as outgoing, agreeable, extravert, kind, generous, self-reliant, yet not planful enough, who likes to avoid responsibility, yet is always devoted to his friends. Based on these characteristics, a person can be judged. Yet, it would still be an approximation, and it would be impossible to predict this person's behavior in a given situation just based on that description. Thus, the first contradiction lies in the idea of personality as a scientific concept.

The second contradiction is evident when one attempts to measure all the qualities that are considered to be part of personality. How do we know that the person is kind, or sociable, or optimistic? How do we compare one person with another and claim that one of them has more of a certain quality than another?

How can we judge our own qualities? In other words, the question is how some degree of objectivity is reached while making judgements about personality characteristics.

One measurement strategy is to judge personality based on a person's actions. A kind person does more for the others. A sociable person has more friends. Yet, there are at least two problems with using this way of measuring. First, there is no way of recording ALL of a person's actions and behaviors, even during some short period of time. Second, one's actions and behaviors in any situation depend on the situation no less than they depend on one's personality characteristics, so to make a comparison between two people, for instance, we would need to compare their actions in absolutely identical situations, which is not realistic. In addition, there are some personality traits (like optimism) that do not display themselves directly into actions and define more global attitudes toward life. However, using actions to measure personality is common in questionnaires and interviews. Another way to capture one's personality is to rely on people's opinions, and, if opinions of several people concur, then that our measurement has at least some degree of objectivity.

The next contradiction is between continuity and change. As it can be inferred from the definition of personality traits, traits are consistent qualities. At the same time, human personality is an ever-changing system. The questions that arise out of the notion of a changing system have to do with whether change is possible; if it is possible, is it necessary; and last, what changes?

First of all, change is possible. Moreover, the scholars in the field of behavioral genetics, who deal with the prob-lems of heredity in temperament and personality characteristics, claim that change is genetically programmed; in other words, people are born with predispositions for more or less change. For instance, it is well known that twin studies have shown that all twins, even those who grow up in the same family, during the life course always grow apart or become less similar. At the same time, those studies have shown that different pairs of twins (even of one kind, monozygotic, or biologically most similar twins) display different degrees of change. Since in such studies all the other variables seem constant (all monozygotic, all growing together in a normal environment), the only logical explanation would be that the proneness to change is another genetic characteristic.

Most of the change happens in the first part of life, from birth until early adulthood. In other words, this change is part of usual maturation, which is, as we know, biologically inevitable. On the other hand, people change for the rest of their lives, though this change, happening beyond young adulthood, is less drastic and more environmentally than biologically influenced.

Trying to draw conclusions about whether change is necessary is more difficult. It implies that change should be evaluated as positive or negative for development.

Basically, researchers agree that stability is positive and that people whose personalities remain relatively stable from adolescence to adulthood are more intellectually, emotionally, and socially successful than those who exhibit higher degrees of change (Block, 1971). Some have hypothesized that stability, or consistency of personality characteristics, is related to the very important and definitely positive human trait—integrity, which means a person's stability and strength in the face of different life events.

To answer the question of what changes is difficult. Human personality is a complex construct that is hierarchically organized. There are global traits (domains), there are specific ones, and there are ideas and attitudes situated at the lowest levels of hierarchy. Keeping in mind that all change is relative to consistency, it is nevertheless possible to claim that there is at least one global rule of change that holds true for most human personalities. The more global the trait is, the slower it changes. The most stable across the life span are the five factors, or domains, which are mostly biologically determined and thus harder (yet not impossible) to change. The less stable are traits, values, and attitudes that are culturally and cognitively created and thus are possible to reshape when a new culture, new environment, or a new stream of events comes into play.

The last contradiction that arises when the topic of personality is looked at is the one between heredity, environment, and conscious will in shaping one's personality. This problem is probably the most important one, since some information in this field would promote one's understanding of the forces shaping his personality and his own role among these forces.

On one hand, the most basic personality traits are biologically determined, hence inherited, hence hard to change. Yet taken literally, this fact contradicts, the very idea of contemporary developmental psychology, which states that *nothing, or very little in human psyche, is predetermined and impossible to change; everything is the result of a very complex interplay of biology and envi-*

ronment. There are different opinions about this issue in the field.

First of all, the scholars of behavioral genetics claim that heredity is responsible for from 22 to 46 percent of variation in different personality characteristics, more so for Extraversion and Neuroticism and less for the rest of the factors (Agreeableness, Constraint, Openness). These numbers seem pervasive. But if one thinks about it not in terms of bare numbers but in terms of people and imagine that, for instance, if two people have the same inherited level of sociability, and then for one of them it remained as it was but for another one it increased four times (this could be true, since this is the difference between inherited 22 (25) percent and the 100 percent that we have as the result of different life influences), even without being acquainted with these two people we can say that they will be quite different.

So a great deal of flexibility and unpredictability exists here, and it is easier to understand if we think of the fact that "we do not inherit personality traits or even behavioral mechanisms as such. What is inherited are chemical templates that produce and regulate proteins involved in building the structure of the nervous system and the neurotransmitters, enzymes, and hormones that regulate them. . . ." (Zuckerman, 1991). These biological characteristics are *always somehow influenced by the environment,* so it is in a sense artificial to talk about biological characteristics as separate factors.

Another consideration that may evolve here is the idea that in *usual* studies researchers deal with *usual* environmental influences and do not deal with environments especially designed for a specific goal, for instance, in families where parents put all of their efforts to suppress aggression and develop sociability in their child. Since the effect of such an experiment would be impossible to measure (we could never know how this child would develop under normal circumstances), we cannot estimate it in terms of numbers and percentages, but we can suppose that the impact of such a special, goal-oriented environment might be impressive.

Another example of an environmental impact is what we call "a self-made person." This can be understood in the context of the previous example, with the only difference being that this is the person himself, and not his parents who created a special environment for developing special personality traits. The mechanism of this change is a little more complex than for any other change, since to create the environment the person needs to understand exactly what the difference between his ideal self and his real self is and how to eliminate this difference. To do this, he needs to understand exactly and correctly his real self, and to determine the means of change. It is very hard, but still possible, and though, as in the previous examples, the effects of the impact of an intentionally created environment would be impossible to measure, it is here that the complex, yet flexible and open to perfection nature of human personality is clearly seen.

Janna Jilnina

See also Autonomy; Conformity; Disorders, Psychological and Social; Emotions; Ethnocentrism; Gender Differences; Identity; Moral Development; Motivation, Intrinsic; Rebellion; Self; Self-Consciousness; Sex Roles; Shyness; Social Development; Temperament

References and further reading
Block, Jack. 1971. *Lives through Time.* Berkeley, CA: Bancroft Books.
Caspi, Avshalom. 1998. "Personality Development across the Life Course." In *Handbook of Child Psychology.* Edited by W. Damon and N. Eisenberg. New York: Wiley, pp. 311–388.
Caspi, Avshalom, Glen Elder, and Ellen Herbener. 1990. "Childhood Personality and the Prediction of Life-Course Patterns." In *Straight and Devious Pathways from Childhood to Adulthood.* Edited by Lee N. Robins and Michael Rutter. Cambridge: Cambridge University Press.
Zuckerman, Marvin. 1991. *Psychobiology of Personality.* Cambridge: Cambridge University Press.

Physical Abuse

There is no single definition of what constitutes child physical abuse. Arriving at a consensus definition is difficult because of diverse beliefs and values regarding parents' rights to discipline their children using physical means. Within the United States, some national leaders and child welfare experts believe that hitting a child in any way (e.g., spanking, slapping) should be considered abuse, whereas others believe that physical punishment is an appropriate method of discipline. Following the lead of Sweden, several European countries forbid all physical punishment. No state in the United States forbids parents from using physical punishment on their children.

Given that it is not unlawful for parents or guardians to use corporal punishment, when does physical discipline become abuse? Most states employ guidelines that define physical abuse as inflicting physical injury to a child causing abrasions, lacerations, and fractures. However, a determination of abuse involves taking into consideration such

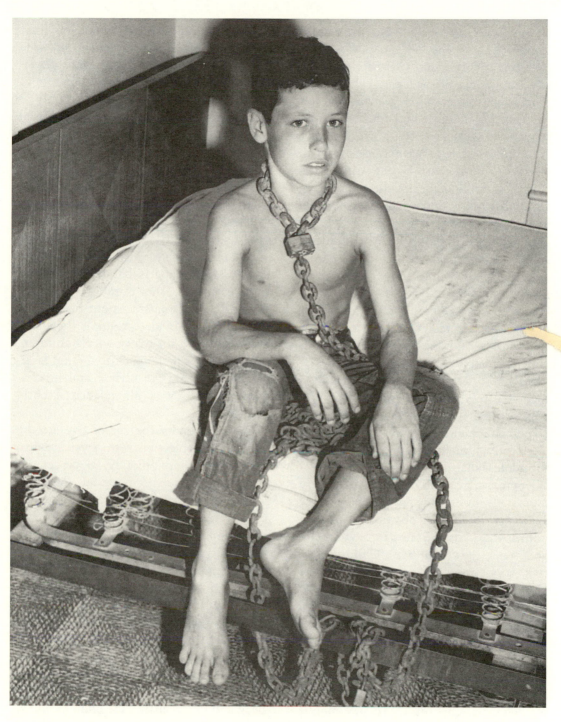

A child who has been the victim of physical abuse is at risk for juvenile delinquency, drug and alcohol abuse, and criminal activity. (Corbis/Bettmann)

factors as the age of the child, the extent of injury, and the circumstances surrounding the incident. Ultimately, federally mandated state agencies, called child protective services, are responsible for determining if abuse has occurred. Child protective services often work in conjunction with the police because physical abuse can be a criminal act. Child protective services can seek the removal of children from parents and placement in foster care through court action if children are determined to be at substantial risk of further harm.

Prevalence

Historically, parents in the United States have used physical methods to punish their children for perceived misbehavior. National surveys indicate that approximately 97 percent of Americans have received physical discipline at some point during their childhood. More than 50 percent of adults report that they were physically punished by their parents during adolescence.

Approximately 205,000 children were identified by child protective service agencies as being physically abused within the United States in 1998 (a rate of 2.9 per 1,000 children). Child protective service records showed that the physical abuse rate was 3.2 per 1,000 among 12-15 year-olds and 1.9 per 1,000 among 16-17 year-olds; these victimization rates are based on cases known to the authorities and are likely to significantly underestimate the number of adolescents who are physically abused. Physical abuse occurs in all socioeconomic groups, yet children from families who earn less than $15,000 are at least fifteen times more likely to experience physical abuse than children who are from families with incomes of more than $30,000.

A 1995 Gallup poll of parents on their use of physical punishment concluded that 49 children per 1,000 were physically abused; this estimate of the rate of abuse indicated that approximately 3 million children were physically abused that year. However, parents are not likely to be completely candid about their use of physical discipline in an interview, so these data are also likely to underestimate the prevalence of physical abuse.

There were 1,110 child fatalities in 1998 as the result of child maltreatment, which includes both neglect and physical abuse. Many experts believe this figure underestimates the number of deaths resulting from maltreatment because of the difficulty in determining the exact cause of death for many young children. Several states have instituted child fatality review teams to review and investigate the causes of all accidental child deaths.

Children under the age of five are the most vulnerable to severe physical harm and death (approximately 85 percent of child deaths due to physical abuse involved children under five) because they cannot flee from harm, verbalize what has happened, or defend themselves, and they have only minimal contact with adults beyond their families. Further, their bodies are the most vulnerable to physical injury. The most frequent cause of serious injury (brain damage) or death for children under the age of three is shaken baby syndrome. Shaken baby syndrome can occur when an adult grabs an infant by the shoulders and shakes the child; the child's head bobs back and forth causing the brain to hit the skull resulting in internal hemorrhaging.

Although many school-aged children are injured by their caregivers each year, school-aged children are less likely than younger children to suffer severe injuries due to physical abuse. The reduction in serious injury is attributed primarily to their greater physical development and access to teachers, principals, and counselors who are mandated to report any suspected abuse to child protective services. If a child discloses any form of child maltreatment to school officials, these professionals must immediately make a report to child protective services. Teachers and other professionals (e.g., counselors, doctors, nurses) who fail to report suspected abuse are subject to criminal prosecution.

Causes

No single factor has been identified as the cause of physical abuse. Research reveals that there are many factors that contribute to child abuse. These include parents who have a history of being physically abused as children, are of low socioeconomic status, are young and single, have less than a high school education, have poor impulse control, lack social supports, are under significant stress, and/or have a special needs child. Statistics indicate that 70 percent to 80 percent of parents who abuse their children were physically abused themselves. However, the majority (60–70 percent) of physically abused children do not harm their children when they become parents. Fifty to 80 percent of all physical abuse cases occur when parents are intoxicated or using illegal substances. A link has also been established between domestic violence and child abuse; many men who batter their spouses or partners also abuse the children in the home.

Effects

Children who experience physical abuse are frequently reluctant to disclose what has occurred. They are often threatened with further punishment, fearful of getting their parents into serious trouble, or frightened of the unknown consequences following disclosure. Some children, in order to maintain secrecy regarding their victimization, may hide their injuries by wearing extra clothing, creating fictitious stories about their injuries when questioned, or stay at home until the injuries are healed. Children who believe that a nonoffending parent will support them are far more likely to disclose their abuse than children who feel unsupported.

It is common for abused children to think that they deserved the physical abuse they received. Children are taught to love and respect parents; consequently, they may believe that parents are acting in their best interest even when physical injury occurs. This is especially true for younger children. Unless children become aware that there are legal limits to physical discipline, they may be subject to continuous abuse without considering seeking help to prevent further incidents.

The impact of physical abuse on physical development varies. Beyond immediate physical pain and temporary injury, research indicates that abused children have a greater likelihood of neurological impairment. Sensory and motor skills problems are associated with physical abuse. In cases of severe abuse, children may experience a lifetime of physical limitations.

The effects of physical abuse are not limited to bodily harm. There are also psychological consequences for children and adolescents who have been emotionally traumatized by the experience of physical abuse. The most significant consequence is that victims of abuse often view the world around them as a hostile, unpredictable place that threatens them with harm. Abused children and adolescents learn that in order to survive they must physically, psychologically, and emotionally protect themselves from others. They can become distrustful and suspicious of any adult.

Research shows that adolescents who have been physically abused are more likely than nonabused peers to act out in an aggressive manner or to withdraw from peers. They may have difficulty initiating and maintaining positive social relationships during adolescence, and this pattern may still be evident in adulthood. Adolescents with a history of physical abuse frequently show low levels of self-esteem and have a much greater probability of suffering from depression and anxiety disorders than nonabused adolescents; they also report thinking more often about committing suicide than other adolescents. Physical abuse has been linked to other problem behaviors in adolescence and adulthood. Having been physically abused increases the probability of participation in juvenile delinquency, drug and alcohol abuse, and criminal activity. More than 80 percent of adult criminals in prison for assault reported being physically abused as children.

Remediation and Treatment
Several factors can mitigate the harmful effects of physical abuse. Less severe abuse, shorter duration, and being older than five have all been linked to fewer negative consequences. Studies consistently show that the most powerful factor in minimizing or eliminating the harmful consequences of abuse is experiencing a trusting, supportive relationship with an adult, preferably the nonoffending parent. Such relationships serve to provide children with physical and psychological safety; they can reduce feelings of fear, betrayal, and self-blame that are often found in victims of physical abuse.

Psychotherapy is the recommended treatment for abused children. The specific type of therapy utilized (play, cognitive behavioral, group, and/or family therapy) depends on the age of the child, familial support, and circumstances surrounding the physical abuse. The primary issues include assisting children in expressing feelings, gaining a sense of control over traumatic memories, personal empowerment, enhancing self-esteem, building positive relationships, and developing alternatives to acting-out behaviors. Children and adolescents may need to participate in psychotherapy for varying lengths of time and at different stages of development to overcome the effects of physical abuse. Victims of abuse who have participated in psychotherapy report significant benefits to self-esteem and interpersonal relationships. In addition, they are able to resolve traumatic memories and reduce feelings of self-blame.

James Henry
Tom Luster

See also Aggression; Alcohol Use, Risk Factors in; Anxiety; Bullying; Coping; Counseling; Emotional Abuse; Foster Care: Risks and Protective Factors; Neglect; Parent-Adolescent Relations; Rights of Adolescents; Self-Injury; Sexual Abuse; Violence; Youth Gangs

References and further reading
Dote, Martha. 1999. "Emotionally and Behaviorally Disturbed Children in the Child Welfare System: Points of Preventative Intervention." *Children and Youth Services Review* 21, no. 1: 7–29.
Egeland, Byron. 1993. "A History of Abuse Is a Major Risk Factor for Abusing the Next Generation." Pp. 197–208 in *Current Controversies on Family*

Violence. Edited by Richard J. Gelles and Donileen R. Loseke. Newbury Park, CA: Sage.

English, Diana. 1998. "The Extent and Consequences of Child Maltreatment." *The Future of Children* 8, no. 1: 39–51.

National Clearinghouse on Child Abuse and Neglect Information. 1999. "Child Fatalities Fact Sheet." Washington, DC: U.S. Government Printing Office, pp. 1–3.

Straus, Murray A., and Glenda K. Kantor. 1994. "Corporal Punishment of Adolescents by Parents: A Risk Factor in the Epidemiology of Depression, Suicide, Alcohol Abuse, Child Abuse, and Wife Beating." *Adolescence* 29, no. 115: 543–560.

Urquiza, Anthony J., and Cynthia Winn. 1999. "Treatment for Abused and Neglected Children: Infancy to Age 18." National Clearinghouse on Child Abuse and Neglect Information. Washington, DC: U.S. Government Printing Office, pp. 1–16.

Political Development

Teenagers typically consider politics a boring topic with little relevance for their lives, probably because by politics they mean the business of elected officials. But politics is a much broader domain. It concerns rights and responsibilities and a commitment to the principles that bind us together as a society. Political participation is the way in which we stabilize our society and make our communities a good place to live. It is also the way in which we challenge our society and contribute to social change.

Political comes from the word *polis*, which means the public sphere of society. Aristotle referred to the polis as a network of friends working together for their common good. The common good or public sphere refers to those things that members of a community share, that no one individual or group owns but that belong to everyone—like public

schools, public parks, or public roads. They exist for the people, and the people have a stake in making them work well.

Political participation is the way people work together to make their communities good places to live. In this sense it is very similar to civic work or public service. When teenagers do volunteer work in their communities—whether cleaning up a river or helping children learn to read—they are doing civic work. Such work benefits the public, that is, all citizens, not just the individuals that the adolescent helps. When a river is polluted, everyone for whom it was a source of drinking water or of recreation loses out. Likewise, if a child doesn't learn to read, as an adult she will be poorly prepared to find work that can support a family or to make informed decisions that affect the entire community.

When politics is conceived in this broader way, teenagers are very engaged. In fact, the results of an annual nationwide study of college freshman found that 81 percent of the class of 2000 had done volunteer work and 45.4 percent had participated in an organized demonstration, but only 28.1 percent said that they were interested in keeping up with politics (Kellogg, 2001). This is a far cry from the self-absorbed and apathetic picture that is sometimes painted of youth. In fact, adolescents are real assets to their communities—with fresh ideas and the energy to make things happen.

Getting involved as a teenager seems to predict a lifetime of political participation and civic engagement. Adults who are active in the civic and political affairs of their communities were active in extracurricular activities at school and in other community and youth groups when they were teenagers (Verba, Schlozman, and Brady, 1995). Why this is so is

Political participation is the way people work together to make their communities good places to live. (Skjold Photographs)

not entirely clear. However, it is likely that by being a member of a group and helping to define and work toward common goals, one gets a sense of what it means to work for the common good. The feeling of group solidarity is a good one, and membership in the group becomes part of who one is. One identifies with the group, cares about the other members, and wants to help accomplish the goals of the group. This group identification is an essential part of political development because political goals are rarely accomplished by individuals. They result from group effort.

Getting involved in extracurricular activities or community groups is not the only factor that promotes political or civic participation. Families also play an important role, especially in the values they teach children. In a large study of adolescents in seven different countries, Flanagan et al. found that youth in each country were more likely to be involved in civic work if their parents had taught them that it was important to empathize with others' feelings and needs and not just their own. In fact, research by Wendy Rahn and John Transue shows that increasing materialist aspirations among youth over the past few decades have eroded their feelings of trust in others, and low levels of social trust are related to lower levels of political participation. Social trust does increase, however, as a result of participating in community activities. Thus, youth participation in community service should increase their trust in others.

The adolescent and young adult years are generally considered an ideal stage in life for reflecting on political issues. Adolescence is the period when questions of identity—who I am, where I am headed, what meaning my life has—come to the fore. Questions of values—what I stand for, what ideals I believe in, and where my society is headed—may also emerge. Erik Erikson held that an ideology was a psychological necessity for adolescents, offering them, among other things, a correspondence between the inner world of ideals and the social world and helping them frame a perspective for the future. Our political views reveal something about ourselves and our view of the world. And the political views that evolve during the adolescent years are concordant with the person the teen is becoming and with his personal aspirations, values, and beliefs (Flanagan and Tucker, 1999).

As they search for a direction in life, adolescents experiment with different ideas, roles, and lifestyles. Indeed, there is a certain freedom during this time to search because, compared to adults, adolescents are relatively free from responsibilities, especially for families. For these reasons, Karl Mannheim argued that it was during the late adolescent and early adult years that youth experienced a fresh contact with their society. They saw it from a new vantage point and could decide how their own ideals meshed with their social order and which aspects of that order were in need of change. As each new generation of youth comes of age, the particular political and historical events of the era are the context for their decisions about personal identity and political action. Politics is a world of con-

tested views, and in their choice of music or the clothes they wear, youth make political statements. They decide who they are and with which groups and cultural messages they are aligned. And by the culture they create as a generation, they shape the world around them. According to generational theorists, social change occurs because each new generation of youth, with their own set of experiences, ideals, and choices, replaces the generation before them. Although political views continue to evolve after the adolescent and young adult years, the way an individual grapples with social and political issues during this period and the values to which she commits are formative of her personality and behaviors thereafter.

Constance Flanagan

See also Autonomy; College; Conformity; Decision Making; Ethnic Identity; Ethnocentrism; Family Relations; Freedom; Gender Differences and Intellectual and Moral Development; Identity; Media; Moral Development; Parent-Adolescent Relations; Peer Pressure; Racial Discrimination; Religion, Spirituality, and Belief Systems; Rights of Adolescents; Self; Social Development; Transition to Young Adulthood; White and American: A Matter of Privilege?; Youth Culture; Youth Outlook

References and further reading
Erikson, Erik H. 1968. *Identity: Youth and Crisis.* New York: Norton.
Flanagan, Constance A., and Leslie S. Gallay. 1995. "Reframing the Meaning of 'Political' in Research with Adolescents." *Perspectives on Political Science* 24: 34–41.
Flanagan, Constance A., and Corrina Jenkins Tucker. 1999. "Adolescents' Explanations for Political Issues: Concordance with Their Views of Self and Society." *Developmental Psychology* 35, no. 5: 1198–1209.
Flanagan, Constance A., Jennifer Bowes, Britta Jonsson, Beno Csapo, and Elena Sheblanova. 1998. "Ties That Bind:

Correlates of Adolescents' Civic Commitments in Seven Countries." In *Political Development: Youth Growing Up in a Global Community. Journal of Social Issues* 54, no. 3: 457–475.

Kellogg, Alex. 2001. "Looking Inward, Freshmen Care Less about Politics and More about Money." *Chronicle of Higher Education* Jan. 26: A47–A49.

Mannheim, Karl. 1952. "The Problem of Generations." Pp. 276–322 in *Essays on the Sociology of Knowledge.* London: Routledge and Kegan Paul. (Original work published 1928).

Rahn,Wendy M., and John E. Transue. 1998. "Social Trust and Value Change: The Decline of Social Capital in American Youth, 1976–1995." *Political Psychology* 19: 545–565.

Verba, Sidney, Kay Lehman Schlozman, and Henry E. Brady. 1995. *Voice and Equality: Civic Voluntarism in American Politics.* Cambridge, MA: Harvard University Press.

Youniss, James, Jeffrey A. McLellan, and Miranda Yates. 1997. "What We Know about Engendering Civic Identity." *American Behavioral Scientist* 40: 620–631.

Poverty

Income and poverty levels and trends are important, because adolescents in low-income families may experience marked deprivation in such basic areas as nutrition, clothing, housing, and healthcare, and because differences in family income influence an adolescent's chances of achieving economic success during adulthood. Many adolescents throughout the past half-century have experienced the deprivations associated with low family incomes, and the proportion has increased over the past two decades. Using a poverty measure that is most appropriate for historical and international comparisons, about one-fourth of adolescents in the United States lived in relative poverty in 1998, a proportion substantially higher than for other rich Western countries

(U.S. Bureau of the Census, 1998). The proportion who ever experienced relative poverty at any time during childhood or adolescence is substantially higher. The primary factors determining both levels and trends in adolescent poverty have been the trends in fathers' and mothers' employment and income earned from their work. Poverty is higher among adolescents in the United States than in other rich countries primarily because government income transfer programs in other countries are much more generous than in the United States.

Adolescents in the United States have experienced two distinct eras of economic change during the past half-century, with corresponding changes in poverty and economic inequality. The post–World War II era of rising prosperity and improved opportunities was followed by declining economic circumstances and prospects. An understanding of the consequences of these changes for adolescents requires attention both to changes in average economic levels and to shifts in inequality in access to economic resources.

In a specific year, one-half of families have incomes below the median family income, and one-half have incomes above the median. During the twenty-six years from 1947 to 1973, median family income more than doubled. But twenty-five years later, in 1998, median family income was only 12 percent greater than in 1973, despite the enormous jump in mothers' labor force participation. In fact, because increased mothers' labor force participation requires additional work-related expenditures including transportation, clothing, and childcare (Ruggles, 1990; Citro and Michael, 1995), the average income actually available to families for nonwork-related expenditures increased less than indicated by change in the median income during the post–World War II era.

Economic deprivation is often measured by the official U.S. poverty rate, which was developed in the 1960s, based on income levels, or poverty thresholds, that were designed to measure the minimum income needs experienced by families as of the early 1960s. The official poverty rate for adolescents ages twelve to seventeen fell sharply during the 1960s from 24 percent in 1959 to 15 percent in 1969 (Hernandez, 1993, p. 260). Since then, official poverty has increased somewhat for adolescents, rising to 16 percent as of 1998.

For studies of long-term change, however, increasing numbers of scholars call into question the official poverty measure. One major limitation of the current official measure is that it fails to take into account changing social perceptions about what income levels are viewed as "normal" or "adequate." Given the enormous increase in real income between World War II and 1973, for example, it would be surprising if a corresponding change had not occurred in social perceptions regarding the amount of income needed to maintain a "normal" or "adequate" level of living.

That such judgments are relative has been noted for at least 200 years. Adam Smith emphasized in *Wealth of Nations* that poverty must be defined in comparison to contemporary standards of living. He defined economic hardship as the experience of being unable to consume commodities that "the custom of the country renders it indecent for creditable people, even of the lowest order, to be without" (cited in U.S. Congress, 1989, p. 10).

More recently, John Kenneth Galbraith also argued, "People are poverty-stricken when their income, even if adequate for survival, falls markedly behind that of the community. Then they cannot have what the larger community regards as the minimum necessary for decency; and they cannot wholly escape, therefore, the judgment of the larger community that they are indecent. They are degraded for, in a literal sense, they live outside the grades or categories which the community regards as respectable" (1958, pp. 323–324).

Based on these insights, and Lee Rainwater's comprehensive review of existing U.S. studies and his own original research, as well as additional literature, Hernandez developed a measure of income inequality that classifies family income levels in terms of "relative poverty," "near-poor frugality," "middle-class comfort," or "luxury," based on income thresholds set at 50, 75, and 150 percent of median family income in specific years and adjusted for family size (1993, pp. 241–242).

This measure shows that adolescents experienced a sharp drop in relative poverty after the Great Depression from 37 percent in 1939 to 30 percent in 1949, and then a continuing rapid decline to 23 percent in 1959. The 1960s and 1970s brought a much smaller decline of only 3 percentage points, but these gains were lost during the 1980s and 1990s. By 1998, nearly one in four adolescents, 24 percent, lived in relative poverty.

At the opposite extreme, adolescents in families with luxury-level incomes declined from 23 percent in 1939 to a nearly constant 20 to 21 percent during the 1940s and 1950s. The proportion living in luxury then increased to about 24 percent in 1979, and 27 percent in 1988 and 1998. As a result adolescents living in middle-class comfort or near-poor frugality increased from 38 percent in 1939 to 58 percent in 1969, but declined to 56 percent in 1979, and further to 49 percent in 1988 and 1998.

All told, income inequality for adolescents narrowed markedly after the Great Depression, but then expanded substantially beginning in the 1970s.

What accounts for these trends in relative poverty and income inequality? Further analysis indicates that change in available fathers' incomes can account for much of the post-depression decline and subsequent increase in childhood relative poverty, and that changes in mothers' incomes acted to speed the earlier decline in relative poverty and then slow the subsequent increase. Additional income from relatives other than parents in the home had little effect on poverty trends after 1949, and the total effect of cash welfare programs on these trends is no more than 2–3 percentage points, although the effects of taxes and the value of noncash government benefits would be important, if they were taken into account (see below). Finally, the rise of mother-only families, which often leads to lack of access to fathers' incomes in many of these families, has also contributed to the recent poverty increase, but the prime factor in determining both levels and trends in childhood poverty has been trends for fathers' and mothers' employment and income earned from their work (Hernandez, 1993, p. 371; 1997, p. 33).

For example, between 1964 and 1974, employed men became substantially less likely to have low earnings, that is, annual earnings below the official poverty level for a four-person family (U.S. Bureau of the Census, 1992b). Since 1974, but especially since 1979, substantial increases have occurred in men with low earnings, especially among men working full-time year-round, and of the ages when children are most likely to be in the home. Among year-round full-time workers, the proportion with low earnings for men ages thirty-five to fifty-four dropped from 13 to 5 percent between 1964 and 1974, but then climbed to 9 percent by 1990 (Hernandez, 1993).

The trends were similar for white, black, and Hispanic males with full-time, year-round work, but the proportions with low earnings were much higher for blacks and Hispanics than for whites. It is not surprising that trends in relative (and official) poverty rates have followed a similar pattern during the past quarter-century, and that black and Hispanic children are much more likely to live in poverty.

In 1998, for example, relative poverty rates of 44 to 45 percent for black and Hispanic adolescents were three times greater than the rate of 14 percent for non-Hispanic white adolescents. In fact, while about one-fourth of non-Hispanic white adolescents (26 percent) lived in relative poverty or near-poor frugality, more than three-fifths of black and Hispanic adolescents, 62 and 66 percent, respectively, lived in families with relatively poor or near-poor incomes. Hence, while most non-Hispanic white adolescents (74 percent) live in families with middle-class or luxury-level incomes, fewer than four-fifths of black (38 percent) or Hispanic (34 percent) adolescents live in families with middle-class or higher income levels.

Adolescents experience economic inequality not only among themselves but also compared to younger children. In 1959 and 1969, for example, adolescents were slightly (2 percentage points) less likely than young children ages zero to five to live in relative poverty, but this gap expanded to 5 percentage points in

1979, and to 7 percentage points in 1988 and 1998. Thus, the transition from early childhood to adolescence has involved a decline in relative poverty for children born during the past half-century.

Adolescents also experience economic inequality compared to adults. At least since the Great Depression, the economic situation has been less favorable for adolescents than for adults. The 8 percentage point gap in relative poverty separating children from adults shrank to only 3 percent in 1969, but then expanded to 7 percentage points in 1988, virtually the same as in 1939. Meanwhile, the 12 percentage point deficit in 1939 in the proportion of adolescents, compared to adults, living in families with luxury-level incomes expanded to 14 percentage points in 1949, and then fell to the nearly constant level of 10 percentage points between 1969 and 1988.

Among adults, poverty trends for parents with children under eighteen in the home have been most similar to those for children, since such parents and children share the same households, but other working-age adults have experienced quite different trends. Immediately after the Great Depression, relative poverty declined more slowly for adults without children than for parents, but by 1969 the gap had closed, and after 1979 children and their parents experienced substantial increase in relative poverty, while working-age adults without children experienced a slight decline.

At the opposite extreme, parents, like children, experienced declines in luxury living between 1939 and 1969, followed by substantial increases to 30 and 22 percent, respectively, as of 1988, while working-age adults without children at home experienced high rates of 38–42 percent during the Great Depression,

with increases, especially after 1969, to 45–50 percent.

Adolescents experienced less relative poverty than the elderly until the 1980s. But if the value of homes owned by the elderly is taken into account (since elderly homeowners have lower current housing costs than other groups), adolescents experienced less relative poverty than the elderly until the 1970s, when a sharp reversal occurred as social security pensions increased and other federal policies favorable to the elderly were enacted. Adolescents have been about as likely as the elderly to live in luxury since 1996.

Economic status measures presented here are based on before-tax income, that is, before the reduction in available income associated with paying taxes, and not including as income the value of health insurance and other noncash benefits provided by employers or governments. Because such taxes and benefits effectively decrease or increase the economic resources actually available to persons and families, they should be taken into account to accurately measure levels and changes in economic status. Empirical estimates for long-term historical change taking these factors into account do not exist, but an overall assessment of how broad conclusions would be altered based on available evidence is possible.

First, tax law changes between 1965 and 1989 tended to increase relative poverty and economic inequality, but the trend then reversed during the 1990s, because of the increasing value of the earned income tax credit for low-income working families. Second, increasing private health insurance, especially for middle-class and higher-income families between 1939 and the mid-1950s, tended to increase inequality and relative poverty, while the subsequent spread downward of private insurance, and growth of public insurance (Medicaid and Medicare) after 1965, tended to reduce relative poverty. But during the early 1980s, declining Medicaid coverage for the relatively poor and near-poor, and increased private coverage for the middle class, tended to increase relative poverty. Third, the effect of other cash and non-cash welfare programs changed little between 1939 and the mid-1960s, but then tended to reduce relative poverty by several additional percentage points as of 1979. From 1979 to 1991, the effect of these programs remained about constant (U.S. Bureau of the Census, 1992a, p. 98), while subsequent changes tended to reduce relative poverty during the early 1990s and increase relative poverty during the later 1990s.

Altogether, then, taking these three factors into account might yield the following. During the 1940s and 1950s, actual adolescent relative poverty probably declined less than the estimated 14 percentage points. During the 1960s and 1970s, actual adolescent relative poverty probably declined by more than the estimated 2–3 percentage points, although about 29 percent of relatively poor and near-poor persons remained without health insurance by 1980. Since the early 1980s, actual adolescent relative poverty probably has increased by more than the estimated 4 percentage points, since access to health insurance among low-income families has declined, while little change has occurred in the combined effect of changes in taxes and in the value of other cash and noncash benefits.

Another approach to measuring poverty is to estimate the proportion of persons who experience a low family income during one or more years over an extended period of years. By this accounting, the proportion of adolescents ever experiencing low family incomes before reaching adulthood is much higher than indicated here, because some children fall into poverty, while others rise out of poverty from one year to the next. Compared to other developed countries, poverty rates for U.S. children in general, and no doubt for adolescents in particular, are unusually high. Using a measure similar to the relative poverty measure described above, for example, U.S. children in the mid-1980s were substantially more likely to live in poverty than were children in Canada, Germany, Sweden, France, or the United Kingdom. At the extreme, U.S. children were about nine times as likely as Swedish children to be living in relative poverty (27 versus 3 percent), and U.S. children in single-parent families were about fourteen times as likely as corresponding Swedish children to be living in poverty (63 versus 4 percent) (Smeeding and Torrey, 1993, p. 874; 1995, p. 10).

What accounts for these international differences in poverty rates? Part of the explanation is the low levels of support provided by U.S. government transfers compared to Sweden. In the United States around 1980, for example, the average poor family with children received only about $2,400 per year in government transfers, compared to $6,400 in Sweden. An additional part of the explanation is the low proportion receiving any government transfers. Among the United States, Australia, Canada, Germany, Sweden, and the United Kingdom around 1980, only 73 percent of poor families with children in the United States received government transfers—27 percent received none—while in all the other countries 99–100 percent of poor families with children received government transfers

(Hobbs and Lippman, 1990, pp. 12, 36). These comparisons suggest that the high and increasing poverty rates experienced by U.S. children of all ages, including adolescents, are not inevitable, but result at least partly from explicit public policy decisions.

Donald J. Hernandez

See also Coping; Homeless Youth; Intervention Programs for Adolescents; Juvenile Crime; Maternal Employment: Historical Changes; Runaways; School Dropouts; Self-Esteem; Social Development; Welfare

References and further reading
Citro, Connie, and Robert Michael. 1995. *Measuring Poverty: A New Approach.* Washington, DC: National Academy Press.

Duncan, Greg J., and Willard L. Rodgers. 1988. "Longitudinal Aspects of Childhood Poverty." *Journal of Marriage and the Family* 50: 1007–1021.

Galbraith, John Kenneth. 1958. *The Affluent Society.* Boston: Houghton Mifflin.

Hernandez, Donald J. 1993. *America's Children: Resources from Family, Government, and the Economy.* New York: Russell Sage Foundation.

———. 1997. "Poverty Trends." Pp. 18–34 in *Consequences of Growing Up Poor.* Edited by Greg J. Duncan and Jeanne Brooks-Gunn. New York: Russell Sage Foundation.

Hobbs, Frank, and Laura Lippman. 1990. "Children's Well-Being: An International Comparison." U.S. Bureau of the Census, International Population reports, series P-95, no. 80. Washington, DC: U.S. Government Printing Office.

Rainwater, Lee. 1974. *What Money Buys: Inequality and the Social Meanings of Income.* New York: Basic Books.

Ruggles, Patricia. 1990. *Drawing the Line: Alternative Poverty Measures and Their Implications for Public Policy.* Washington, DC: Urban Institute Press.

Smeeding, Timothy M., and Barbara Boyle Torrey. 1993. "Poor Children in Rich Countries." *Science* 242: 873–877.

———. 1995. "Revisiting Poor Children in Rich Countries." Unpublished manuscript.

Smith, Adam. 1776. *Wealth of Nations* (London: Everyman's Library, cited in "Alternative Measures of Poverty." A Staff Study Prepared for the Joint Economic Committee (of the U.S. Congress), October 18, 1989, p. 10.

U.S. Bureau of the Census. 1992a. *Measuring the Effects of Benefits and Taxes on Income and Poverty: 1979 to 1991.* Current Population Reports, series P-60, no. 183. Washington, DC: U.S. Government Printing Office.

———. 1992b. *Workers with Low Earnings: 1964 to 1990.* Current Population Reports, series P-60, no. 178. Washington, D.C.: U.S. Government Printing Office.

———. 1998. "Poverty and the United States: 1997." Current Populations reports, series P-60, no. 178. Washington, DC: U.S. Government Printing Office.

U.S. Congress. 1989. "Alternative Measures of Poverty." A Staff Study Prepared for the Joint Economic Committee, October 18.

Pregnancy, Interventions to Prevent

Teen pregnancy is a significant social, economic, and political concern. Although rates of teen pregnancy have decreased in the United States in recent years, they are higher than any other industrialized nation. In 1997, the U.S. rate was 52.3 births per 1,000 women aged fifteen to nineteen. In the 1950s and 1960s, birthrates were almost double what they are today. Teen pregnancy increases the risk of negative outcomes for mothers and their children. Teen mothers are more likely to have poorer school and job outcomes, and their children are at risk for behavior and school problems.

There are many reasons why teens become pregnant. Although teen pregnancy occurs in all segments of society, it

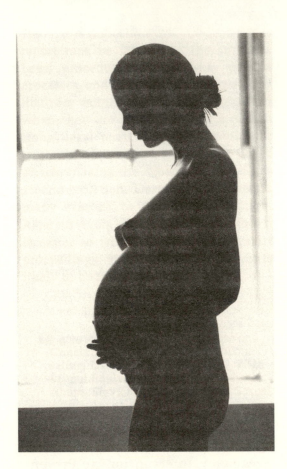

Teen pregnancy is most common among teenagers living in poverty. (Anna Palma/Corbis)

is more frequent among teens living in poverty. Pregnancy and parenthood may appear to be positive options for teens living in poor communities with few positive role models and no job opportunities. Some teens may be imitating the behavior of their peers, and others may be seeking emotional closeness by having a baby.

As a result of the widespread concern about teen pregnancy, many intervention programs have been established with the goal of reducing teen pregnancy. These interventions include pregnancy preven-

tion education, providing access to contraception, and community-based programs offering a broad variety of educational and job skills as alternatives to pregnancy. The programs use a variety of approaches, including hospital- or clinic-based, school-based, and home visitation services.

Pregnancy Prevention Education

Pregnancy prevention education or family life education is a common approach of intervention programs. Data from the 1995 National Survey of Family Growth indicates that 90 percent of women eighteen to nineteen years of age report that they have received formal instruction on safe sex. Many pregnancy prevention education programs provide information about sexuality, reproduction, decision making, and sexual relationship issues. In addition, these programs often promote abstinence as the major method of birth control. Many of the abstinence-based programs focus on attitudes about early sexual initiation and communication with parents and peers about abstinence-related values. Pregnancy prevention education programs by themselves have been successful in increasing teen's short-term knowledge about contraception and reproduction; however, long-term impact is less certain.

Programs that provide teens with factual information and skills to negotiate difficult peer relationships are more successful than programs that focus on knowledge about sexuality alone. One such program is Postponing Sexual Involvement. This program was developed in Atlanta, Georgia, and was designed to provide teens sixteen years of age and younger with skills to resist peer pressure. The main message of the program is to delay sexual intercourse. The program consists of ten sessions that are lead by a male and female senior high school student. The program targets low-income students. Results of the program showed that by the end of the eighth grade, boys who did not participate in the program were three times more likely to engage in sexual intercourse than boys who participated in the program. At the end of the eighth grade, females not participating in the program were fifteen times more likely to have engaged in sex than females who participated in the program. Similar programs have been developed in other areas of the country in schools and other community groups. Another program, Reducing the Risk, was a sex education program in health education classes in high schools in California. Teens who received this program were less likely to have started sex than other teens and less likely to report engaging in unprotected sex. In general, education programs that use small groups, teen counselors, and community-based components have been most successful preventing teen pregnancy. As a result, program developers have begun to incorporate an educational/informational component of teen pregnancy into larger, more comprehensive programs.

Contraceptive Services Approaches
Programs that provide family planning services can be an important method for preventing teen pregnancy. In recent years, new methods of birth control have also been available to teens. For example, some teens using depo provera injections have a lower incidence of pregnancy than those using the birth control pill. Contraceptive services approaches to teen pregnancy prevention also may be useful in promoting healthy, responsible behavior related to birth control. The most suc-

cessful of these programs have focused on contraceptive use by promoting problem-solving and decision-making skills and addressing difficulties in accessing birth control.

Research indicates that teens are more likely to use contraceptive services if services are teen-friendly and easy to obtain. A large number of teens receive contraception services through family planning clinics. For example, data from the 1995 National Survey of Family Growth indicates that almost 30 percent of fifteen- to nineteen-year-old females were seen by a healthcare provider for at least one family planning visit during the past year. Program results indicate that contraceptive service programs also need to engage teens just before their first sex. Recent figures from the 1995 National Survey of Family Growth show increases in the use of contraceptives at the time of first sex for both teen and adult women. Teens, however, are still more likely to delay birth control services until well after their first intercourse, and this delay can have serious consequences.

School-based clinics can be a way to provide primary healthcare to students who may otherwise have difficulty getting access to health services. Although school-based clinics often incorporate counseling and sex education into their programs, fewer than 20 percent actually provide contraception services on-site. In addition, their services can be limited to students and miss the highest risk teens, who may have dropped out of school. One well-known, successful school-based program in Baltimore, Maryland, provided middle and high school students with classroom instruction, group discussion, and individual consultation about sexuality and reproduction. A community clinic provided contraceptive services across the street from the high school. A social worker provided individual counseling, and a nurse provided education about reproduction and contraception. Presentations were made at homeroom classes, during lunch hours, and after school. A peer leader component was also used for small-group discussion. Results of this program indicated that pregnancy rates for teens participating in the program decreased 30 percent at a three-year follow-up period. Pregnancy rates for teens not enrolled in the program increased by 58 percent (Zabin et al., 1986, p. 18).

Family planning programs may be useful in answering questions related to increasing use of contraception. One clinic-based pregnancy prevention initiative in Philadelphia involved tailoring services to the need of teens. It incorporated additional hours for teens and it trained staff about the special needs of teens. The program also offered a media campaign and school- and community-based components. Results of this citywide program indicated that teens who received the teen-friendly services were more likely to continue using a birth control method than a group who received traditional contraceptive services. Other programs include a series of integrated psychological counseling visits and medical appointments.

*Community-Based Life
Options Programs*
In recent years community-based pregnancy prevention initiatives have become more common. Many hospital- or university-based prevention programs have developed community partnerships. Community-based programs are a promising approach to teen pregnancy prevention. They go beyond pregnancy preven-

tion to providing ways of increasing teens' life options. Successful programs provide comprehensive services, including recreational programs, education about birth control, physical and mental health services, mentoring, job skills training, and even admission to local colleges. When teens feel successful and confident in their academic or employment skills, they may feel less pressure to define success by becoming a parent. Increasing educational and employment incentives for teens may be an effective approach to preventing pregnancy among teens.

An example of a community partnership is the Adolescent Pregnancy Prevention Coalition of North Carolina, a group of community members and professionals who assist groups in the community to implement programs to reduce teen pregnancy. The statewide coalition has followed state teen pregnancy rates from 1978. Community media and outreach campaigns have also become more prevalent. Some community marketing campaigns have used public-service announcements, condom vending machines, and small-group workshops focusing on decision-making skills. Results of some of these programs have demonstrated that during the campaign there was a significant increase in a specific behavior such as condom use, but after the campaign ended, condom use returned to preprogram levels.

Many of the community programs stem from grassroots agencies. One grassroots initiative is Pain Talk. This program targets six communities across the country. Its goal is to increase teens' knowledge about sexuality and communication between teens and adults about sexuality issues. Individual communities identify a contact agency, which works with community members to address teen pregnancy in their community. Another program has even offered guaranteed admission to a local college.

Finally, some programs have used concrete monetary investments in teens, rather than job training per se. For example, teens are paid for each hour they spend in the program. They can work toward a savings account, and they receive bonuses after working a certain number of hours.

Programs to Reduce Repeat Pregnancy
Approximately 30 percent to 35 percent of all first-time teen mothers have a repeat pregnancy within two years after the first delivery (East and Felice, 1996, p. 36). A variety of programs aimed at reducing repeat pregnancy have been developed. Successful programs that reduce repeat pregnancy are comprehensive and focus on areas that extend beyond the prevention of a second pregnancy, including peer support and educational and occupational skills. Some programs also have used monetary incentives to reduce repeat pregnancies among teen mothers. Mothers can receive a specific amount of money per week if they do not become pregnant again. Another kind of program to prevent repeat pregnancy is a home visitation program in rural areas that provides counseling and comprehensive health services. Programs to reduce repeat teen pregnancy also need to intervene with other members of the teen's family and enlist their help and support, either through family counseling or home visitation. Programs have begun to include the father of the baby and the grandmother of the baby. Programs increasing positive family relationships and support may lead to better pregnancy prevention.

Federal and State Programs
In response to the high rates of teen pregnancy, the federal and state governments have developed various agencies to help reduce teen pregnancy. These agencies can be sources of important information for teens and their families. For example, Congress passed the Adolescent Family Life Act (AFL) in 1981. The main objective of the AFL was to decrease the negative consequences associated with teen pregnancy and parenting. As part of this legislation, the Adolescent Family Life Program was created as part of the Office of Population Affairs of the U.S. Public Health Service. The AFL Program has funded demonstration, care, and research projects related to teen pregnancy and parenting. In recent years other organizations have been created with the purpose of reducing the high rates of pregnancies and births among teens. For example, the National Campaign to Prevent Teen Pregnancy is a recent initiative whose goal is to reduce the teen pregnancy rate by one-third by the year 2005. Grants help communities develop innovative approaches to preventing teen pregnancy by promoting good health and preventing unhealthy behaviors in both boys and girls.

Numerous state initiatives have also been developed. For example, the California Department of Education implemented a grant program targeting high-risk youth to prevent teen pregnancy. Similarly, the state of Maryland formed the Governor's Council on Adolescent Pregnancy Prevention and funds pregnancy prevention programs throughout the state.

Effective Programs
Effective teen pregnancy prevention programs have certain components that parents and teens can look for. Effective

programs focus on sexual behaviors that lead to pregnancy, such as not using contraception or initiation of sexual intercourse. These programs have a clear message about using condoms or abstaining from sex. A second component is that effective programs are age appropriate and sensitive to the culture of the program participants. For example, programs need to be tailored differently for middle and high school students and for African American and Hispanic teens. Culturally based programs need to address the positive contributions of a cultural group with the belief that by strengthening cultural awareness, they will help teens to be less likely to engage in unprotected sex.

In addition, programs need to be of sufficient duration for teens to acquire the skills necessary for pregnancy prevention. Programs must be long enough to provide opportunities to complete comprehensive services. Programs that offer a variety of teaching methods including mentoring, role playing, and practicing communication skills that help teens resist peer pressures also may be more effective than programs offering only one style of teaching. Successful programs also provide practice with regard to peer communication and assertiveness training. Developing specific skills is essential to negotiating peer situations that involve sexuality.

In addition, programs with multiple approaches, which focus on issues that go beyond individual decisions about birth control, are also more successful. There are multiple predictors of adolescent pregnancy and childbearing. Poverty, school failure, family problems, and being the child of an adolescent parent increase the risk for adolescent pregnancy. Teen pregnancy prevention programs should recog-

nize the impact of family, neighborhood, and community influences on sexual behavior and address these issues.

Effective programs also recognize that some programs may need to be tailored to the individual needs of each teen. Some youth may require long-term, intensive intervention, whereas others may only require information and birth control. It is important to differentiate which components are effective for different teens and to determine the level of intensity that is required by each teen. Programs need to disseminate their findings so that successful programs can be replicated in other parts of the country.

Programs should also include males or other family members in their interventions. For many years programs on adolescent pregnancy focused only on females and virtually ignored males. In recent years programs have begun to focus on the partners of teen mothers. Young fathers have many of the same characteristics as young mothers, including low educational and occupational attainment. However, many fathers of the children born to teen mothers are not teens themselves. Programs need to include males and consider the role of males in teen pregnancy prevention. Programs also need to intervene with other members of the teen's family and enlist their support. Family instability often precedes adolescent pregnancy. Thus, programs to enhance family functioning should lead to lower rates of teen pregnancy. Recently, programs have begun to focus on the younger sisters of teen mothers. Adolescent mothers are strong role models for early parenthood to younger sisters. Therefore, programs need to target this high-risk group.

Different strategies are also needed for teens who have not yet experienced a first pregnancy and teens who have already given birth. For adolescent mothers, the return to school within a relatively short period of time may be more important in preventing a repeat pregnancy than birth control alone.

Obviously from this discussion, many programs are already targeted toward reducing births to teenagers. Given our nation's high teen pregnancy rates, we still need to continue to develop programs that offer incentives to delay pregnancy and make them accessible to all of our country's youth.

Katherine Nitz

See also Abstinence; Contraception; Dating; Decision Making; Family Relations; Health Promotion; High School Equivalency Degree; Menstrual Cycle; Peer Pressure; Programs for Adolescents; Risk Behaviors; Sex Education; Sexual Behavior; Sexually Transmitted Diseases; Single Parenthood and Low Achievement

References and further reading
Abma, J., A. Chandra, W. Mosher, L. Peterson, and L. Piccinino. 1997. "Fertility, Family Planning, and Women's Health: New Data from the 1995 National Survey of Family Growth." National Center for Health Statistics. *Vital Health Statistics* 23, no. 19.
Alan Guttmacher Institute. 1994. *Sex and America's Teenagers.* Washington, DC: Author.
California Senate Office Research. 1997. *Issue Brief: California Strategies to Address Teenage Pregnancy.* Sacramento, CA: Senate Printing Office.
Delgado, D. 1994. "The Annie E. Casey Foundation's Plain Talk Initiative." *PSAY Network* 2: 1–12.
East, P. L. 1996. "Do Adolescent Pregnancy and Childbearing Affect Younger Siblings?" *Family Planning Perspectives* 28: 148–153.
East, P. L., and M. E. Felice. 1996. *Adolescent Pregnancy and Parenting: Findings from a Racially Diverse Sample.* Mahwah, NJ: Erlbaum.
Howard, M., and J. McCabe. 1990. "Helping Teenagers Postpone Sexual Involvement." *Family Planning Perspectives* 22: 21–26.
Hughes, M. E., F. F. Furstenberg, and J. O. Teitler. 1995. "The Impact of an Increase in Family Planning Services on the Teenage Population of Philadelphia." *Family Planning Perspectives* 27: 60–65.
Kirby, D. 1997. *No Easy Answers: Research Findings on Programs to Reduce Teen Pregnancy.* Washington, DC: National Campaign to Prevent Teen Pregnancy.
Peterson, S., and C. Brindis. 1995. *Adolescent Pregnancy Prevention: Effective Strategies.* San Francisco: National Adolescent Health Information Center.
Zabin, L. S., M. B. Hirsch, E. A. Smith, R. Street, and J. Hardy. 1986. "Evaluation of a Pregnancy Prevention Program for Urban Teenagers." *Family Planning Perspectives* 14: 15–21.

Private Schools

In the United States most schools fall under one of two broad categories: private or public. Approximately 46 million students from kindergarten through grade 12 are enrolled in public schools in the United States, while 6 million students in the same grades are enrolled in private schools (National Center for Education Statistics, 1997, p. 87). The discussion of private schools here pertains to both religiously affiliated and nonsectarian (i.e., schools that are independent or have no religious affiliation) day schools whose goal is to place the majority of their students in two- or four-year colleges. This discussion does not include boarding schools or trade schools.

Private schools differ from public schools in three key areas: school attributes (e.g., school organization and climate), student/family attributes, and teacher/administrator attributes. There

Approximately 46 million students from kindergarten through grade 12 are enrolled in public schools in the United States, while 6 million students in the same grades are enrolled in private schools. (David H. Wells/Corbis)

is an ongoing debate regarding the merits of private schools versus public schools. Some of the differences that exist favor public schools, while others favor private schools.

Regarding school attributes, school organization encompasses many features. The defining organizational distinction of private school, however, lies in the sources of financial support. Public schools depend primarily on local school district, state, and federal funds to finance the operation of a school, which includes, but is not limited to, basic maintenance of building and grounds; teacher, staff, and administrator salaries and benefits; classroom and teacher supplies and materials; and whatever equip-

ment or supplies are necessary to maintain a variety of extracurricular activities. Private schools have virtually all of the same expenses but receive no public monies. Instead, private schools are usually funded by tuition, grants, charitable donations, and large-scale fund-raising campaigns. Tuition varies considerably by grade level and whether or not the school has a religious affiliation. Tuition ranges anywhere from $2,000 to $20,000 per year, with religiously affiliated schools tending toward lower tuition rates than nonsectarian schools.

Tuition represents one form of selectivity characteristic of private schools. Although many schools offer academic and financial scholarships, the majority of students attending a private school tend to come from families in higher income brackets who can afford to pay the tuition of one or more of their children over the course of several years. Another form of selectivity exercised by private schools is through an admissions process. Schools vary considerably in how selective they are and in the criteria they use for selection; however, there is almost always an application process. This process generally entails completing various application forms, taking an entrance examination, obtaining teacher recommendations from one's previous school, spending a day at the school, and engaging in student and parent interviews with principals, headmasters or headmistresses, and/or an admissions committee.

Another feature of school organization is size. Private schools and classes within private schools tend to be considerably smaller than public schools. For example, public schools tend to have up to three or four times as many students overall, and classes may contain nearly twice as many students. There is a good deal of recent research emphasizing the merits of smaller school and class sizes. For adolescents, who tend to desire closer contact with peers and need close, positive contact with adults, smaller schools tend to promote a sense of community between and among students and teachers. In addition, smaller schools and classes are thought to be easier to manage and to allow teachers more opportunities to provide students with individual attention as needed. To the extent that one values small school and class size, this distinguishing feature of private schools is a significant advantage.

Since private schools tend to have admissions policies and criteria that require students to demonstrate their academic potential and commitment, the curriculum or academic program in private schools also tends to be more rigorous. For example, the National Commission on Education and the Economy has proposed that all high school graduates be required to complete four years of English, three years each of social studies, science, and mathematics, and some foreign language study. Private schools tend to have similar requirements, so virtually all students in private schools will have completed this course work as required for graduation. In addition, a large proportion of private school students are more likely to have taken advanced mathematics and science courses. This is not to say that public schools do not provide rigorous classes or requirements, but rather that the proportion of students in a public school who opt for more rigorous programs and/or are able to manage them tends to be smaller.

With regard to academic programs, requirements, and performance in public school settings, it is important to emphasize that public schools vary considerably according to their location and the population served. For example, public schools located in wealthier, suburban areas where the majority of students and parents are oriented toward college and postgraduate professional education (e.g., advanced degrees in medicine, law, and business) tend to resemble private schools in their programs and requirements. These families tend to resemble families found in private schools, when we consider such characteristics as parents' educational level and family income level.

School climate refers to the degree to which the school environment promotes and is conducive to positive social, emotional, and educational experiences for students and teachers. Neither students nor teachers can work to the best of their ability when schools are unsafe or if teaching and learning are disrupted by persistent behavior problems. Private school students tend to experience far less exposure to crime and violence than do public school students, particularly public school students in urban settings also characterized by higher rates of crime and violence.

Alcohol and drug use among adolescents also contributes to the quality of a school's climate. Although alcohol and drug use is a rampant problem among adolescents regardless of socioeconomic, racial, or cultural backgrounds, there are significant differences in the degree to which such use affects school climate. For example, private schools tend to have fewer occurrences of alcohol consumption or drug use during the school day on school premises. Perhaps the most significant difference between private and public schools lies in their ability to control and create safe environments. Private schools are not obliged to retain students who pose persistent and serious behavior problems or threaten the potential safety and learning of others. As a result, private schools can more effectively maintain school climates conducive to teaching and learning.

Along with the differences in parent education and income levels discussed above, private schools tend to be less racially and ethnically diverse than public schools. As a result, minority students attending private schools may feel isolated or alienated at times. For this reason, it is especially important that private schools emphasize the richness of diverse cultures, which is a difficult undertaking when that richness does not appear to be immediately present. Although many private schools, especially those located near or within urban settings, are eager to build more diverse student and faculty populations, the recruitment of such students and faculty is difficult as long as the school remains largely homogeneous (i.e., middle- to upper-middle-class white families, teachers, and administrators).

To the extent that one sees racial and ethnic diversity as an asset and as affording an opportunity to teach students respect and tolerance for differences, the diversity of public schools serves as a potential advantage over private schools. However, it is often an advantage in potential only; the benefits of diversity are not always part of daily school experience, because such diversity can also pose great challenges and tension in a school. Part of what *may* make private schools easier to "manage," as mentioned earlier, is lack of diversity and the wide array of challenges and tensions this can also bring.

Private schools also tend to differ from public schools in terms of teacher/ administrator attributes. Teachers in private schools tend to earn lower salaries than do public school teachers, but are less likely to perceive students and their families as having problems that interfere with learning and are more likely to perceive themselves as effective in making a difference in the lives of their students. Teachers in private schools also tend to enjoy greater autonomy in the classroom. That is, they tend to have a certain amount of control over what and how they teach. Thus, it appears that teachers in private schools may be willing to accept lower salaries as a trade-off for enjoying smaller classes, fewer discipline problems, a stronger sense of community, and more influence over curriculum, teaching, and policy.

Private schools have historically been accessible to those who can afford them, that is, white, middle- to upper-middle-class students and their families. At the same time, these schools have many attributes that potentially promote a more positive and safe environment for students and teachers alike and that are in keeping with the academic and social recommendations made by educators, policymakers, and parents. In the last five to ten years private, religiously affiliated middle schools have been opening in inner-city areas around the country. These schools are private in the sense that they do not receive financial support from local school district, state, or federal educational offices. Some schools are still tuition based, but tuition is nominal and set according to what families can afford. Others have corporations and sponsors who financially support a class throughout its four years of middle school. Additional financial and material support comes largely from grants, charitable donations, and fund-raising efforts, both within and beyond the local community. Such schools are committed to providing early adolescents with the organizational and curricular benefits of private school in combination with the rich racial and ethnic diversity generally found in public school settings.

Imma De Stefanis

See also Academic Achievement; College; Gifted and Talented Youth; Homework; Middle Schools; School Engagement; School, Functions of; School Transitions; Schools, Single-Sex; Teachers; Tracking in American High Schools

References and further reading
Alexander, Karl L., and Aaron Pallas. 1983. "Private Schools and Public Policy: New Evidence on Cognitive Achievement in Public and Private Schools." *Sociology of Education* 56, no. 4: 170–182.
National Center for Education Statistics. 1997. *Public and Private Schools: How Do They Differ?* Washington, DC: U.S. Department of Education, Office of Educational Research and Improvement.

Programs for Adolescents

Youth today have more discretionary time than ever before in America. For instance, one research study found that approximately 40 percent of the waking hours of a sample of high school youth were spent in leisure time (Csikszentmihalyi and Larson, 1984). It is also important to note that most of that time is spent without companionship or supervision from adults. Often this discretionary time is not spent in constructive activities; rather, it is spent on watching television, talking on the phone with friends, and playing computer games. Yet unstructured time is an opportunity for youth to engage either in positive activities that enhance their development and foster their competency or in negative activities that increase their chances of yielding to social pressures to engage in drug use, sex, and antisocial activities. For example, FBI statistics indicate 47 percent of violent juvenile crime occurs on weekdays between the hours of 2 P.M. and 8 P.M. (Sickmund, Snyder, and Poe-Yamagata, 1997).

Creating structured activities through youth programs during the nonschool hours offers a strategy for promoting the positive development of youth. Programs for nonschool hours include not only after-school programs and activities but evening, weekend, and summer programs. By being engaged in constructive activities, youth have an opportunity to explore their world, develop skills, and

Youth programs allow adolescents to see themselves as a part of their community. (Kevin R. Morris/Corbis)

gain a sense of belonging with peers and adults. This entry will present some of the evidence for the importance of these programs, followed by an overview of the critical components of quality youth programs. A youth program is defined here as any structured activity offered during the nonschool hours. Youth programs include but are not limited to sports programs, after-school clubs, service clubs, faith-based organizations, 4-H Youth Development, Boys and Girls Clubs, Boy Scouts and Girl Scouts, YMCA, and programs run by other youth-serving organizations.

Importance of Youth Programs
Nonschool programs offer youth an opportunity to meet their developmental needs while decreasing the likelihood that youth will engage in risky behavior that threatens their life chances. These programs provide youth the chance to develop positive relationships connecting them to peers, other adults, and their communities. The development of these relationships in conjunction with the structured activities provided by a program increases the likelihood that youth will successfully navigate the challenges they face as they move toward adulthood. Participation in quality youth programs engages young people in reflective learning experiences. These experiences enhance youths' understanding of self and others. Moreover, youth are able to see themselves as a part of their community, become invested, and engage in activities that better the community.

In a recent synthesis of research findings, Peter Scales and Nancy Leffert examined the impact that involvement in youth programs had on young people. Their review of more than thirty research studies suggests that involvement in youth programs is linked to the following:

- Increased self-esteem, sense of personal control, and enhanced identity development
- Better-developed life skills, leadership skills, public speaking skills, and decision-making skills, and increased job dependability and responsibility
- Increased academic achievement
- Improved protection of students at risk of dropping out of school
- Improved likelihood of college attendance
- Increased involvement in constructive activities in young adulthood
- Increased safety
- Increased family communication
- Decreased psychological problems, such as loneliness, shyness, and hopelessness
- Decreased involvement in risky behaviors

This synthesis of numerous research studies provides strong scientific evidence of the positive influence that programs can have on youth development. Programs do more than occupy the idle time of youth; they provide them a playing field on which they can learn essential life lessons, develop practical life skills, and build strong positive relationships with adults and peers. Yet not all youth programs are the same in their effectiveness. The impact that participating in a youth program has on a young person is determined by the quality of that program.

Key Components of Quality Youth Programs

According to a recent study, engagement in youth programs was the most pervasive positive influence and common predictor of positive youth outcomes (Scales et al., 2000). The level of positive influence that a youth program has on a young person is dependent on the focus of the program, on the level of youths' participation, and on the adults leading it. Programs that focus on promotion of skills and competencies in addition to prevention are more likely to have a positive influence on youth. By becoming thoroughly engaged in programs, youth increase the number of core experiences and opportunities for positive development. Adult leaders who possess a strong sense of commitment to the youth and their engagement are going to foster the positive development of youth. For example, a coach who emphasizes the growth and development of each player and the team as a whole would create a very positive learning experience, one that would provide youth with opportunities to learn teamwork, problem solving, fine and gross motor skills, and sportsmanship. On the other hand, a coach who emphasizes winning at all costs can create a negative learning experience, one that would increase the likelihood of youth learning inappropriate behaviors that could negatively influence their life trajectory. Therefore, programs and the staff who conduct them must establish a clear focus that intentionally includes time for positive relationship building between the adults and youth.

Besides offering access to caring adults and responsible peers, high-quality youth programs provide skill-building activities that reinforce positive values and skills. Scholars in the youth development field have identified the following characteristics of quality youth programs (Carnegie Council on Adolescent Development, 1992; Quinn, 1995; Roth et al., 1998).

- Good youth programs provide youth an opportunity to have an ongoing one-on-one positive relationship with a caring adult. These interactions are organized around concrete productive purposes. In addition, the program offers frequent opportunities for youth to interact with other adults through intergenerational events and activities.
- Good youth programs provide youth with social support by connecting youth to a positive peer group.
- Good youth programs create a strong sense of belonging with clear rules and expectations, responsibilities, and, at the same time, flexibility. Flexibility means being able to adapt a program to meet the unique needs of the young people involved.
- Good youth programs focus on the specific needs and interests of young people. Therefore, a quality program engages youth as partners in the identification of the needs a program will meet, as well as in the planning, implementation, and evaluation of the program. Youth can be engaged in these processes through various methods (e.g., focus groups, concept mapping, and coleadership).
- Good youth programs offer young people the opportunity to hold meaningful leadership roles within the program and the parent organization. Moreover, youth are engaged in organized service activities within the community.
- Good youth programs provide an accessible safe haven for youth both physically and emotionally. They provide youth with a sense of a positive group experience.
- Good youth programs provide learning opportunities that are active and participatory. Therefore, programs use experiential learning opportunities and encourage young people to take positive risks. All attempts, successful or unsuccessful, are viewed as part of the learning process. Thus, learning how to take risks also involves learning how to "fail courageously." This approach empowers youth to consistently take new risks without fear of being rejected.
- Good youth programs focus on recruiting and retaining young people from diverse backgrounds (e.g., diverse in race, ethnicity, family income, family structure, and gender) by intentionally designing activities that address their needs.
- Good youth programs provide multiple opportunities for youth to engage in activities with their families and communities.
- Good youth programs encourage parental involvement by offering a variety of possibilities for participation (e.g., social events, parental workshops, volunteer opportunities).
- Good youth programs are designed and conducted based on explicit theories of adolescent development. The theory may be helpful

in the identification of the target population and in the types of activities to be implemented within the program.

- Good youth programs strive to assist youth in avoiding identified problem behaviors by providing them with other opportunities. These opportunities are designed to enhance skills (e.g., goal setting, decision making, problem solving, and accepting delayed gratification), civic responsibility, and prosocial behavior.

- Good youth programs offer skill-building activities that reinforce the values and skills linked with doing well in school and maintaining good physical health.

- Good youth programs are ongoing and occur on a frequent basis. They are at least a year in length and have built-in follow-up sessions.

- Good youth programs offer a variety of resources through collaboration with other youth-serving community organizations and schools.

- Good youth programs have clearly stated goals that are assessed on a regular basis. These goals are linked to outcomes for youth (e.g., development of decision-making skills, problem-solving skills, and conflict-resolution skills) that emphasize the benefits of program participation. The evaluation strategy being used allows for mid-course corrections in the program.

- Good youth programs have well-trained staff: The staff have appropriate educational backgrounds and are diverse, the program provides for frequent staff in-services, and the turnover rate for staff is low. Staff are visible advocates for youth.

- Good youth programs have a visible organizational structure and are well organized and managed.

- Good youth programs have established strategies for recognizing the accomplishments of their participants.

No one program can address all the needs of young people. However, the research is clear—youth who are engaged in programs are making a positive difference in their world now and are increasing their chances of being successful as adults. As with anything, however, too much of a good thing can be bad. Researchers have found that youth who are engaged in more than twenty hours of extracurricular activities a week are more likely to engage in risky behaviors compared to youth who engage in five to nineteen hours of extracurricular activities. Therefore, young people's participation in youth programs must be balanced with meeting other demands for their time (e.g., school and family).

Young people develop as the result of core experiences with diverse persons and systems, communities, and the institutions in those communities. Communities and institutions can be supportive influences in youths' lives through programs. Communities that offer a variety of programs and encourage youth participation are more likely to harness youths' energy toward the common good. Programs, through positive connections and activities, empower youth to develop their skills, build their capacity to be resourceful, and increase their self-confidence.

In order for programs to provide all youth with the developmental opportunities that they need, communities and citizens are going to have to intentionally commit themselves to expanding those programs. For example, some 29 percent of the adolescent population, approximately 5.5 million, are not being served by any existing youth programs. Most of these young people are in impoverished neighborhoods and are in dire need of a safe place to be challenged. Thus, barriers to participating in youth programs need to be addressed in order to provide equal access.

If we as citizens want our children and youth to do more than avoid risky behaviors, if we want them to be contributing, engaged members of society, then we must take the initiative to create places and opportunities that nurture their development. The core experiences that young people can gain from participating in youth programs during the nonschool hours can provide them with a clear sense of direction as to what they should be doing.

Daniel F. Perkins

Lynne M. Borden

See also Alcohol Use, Risk Factors in; Apprenticeships; Children of Alcoholics; Counseling; Delinquency, Mental Health, and Substance Abuse Problems; Drug Abuse Prevention; Eating Problems; Foster Care: Risks and Protective Factors; Gay, Lesbian, Bisexual, and Sexual-Minority Youth; High School Equivalency Degree; Intervention Programs for Adolescents; Juvenile Justice System; Schools, Full-Service; Services for Adolescents; Sex Education; Substance Use and Abuse; Suicide

References and further reading
Carnegie Council on Adolescent Development. 1992. *A Matter of Time: Risk and Opportunity in the Nonschool Hours.* New York: Carnegie Corporation.
Csikszentmihalyi, M., and Reed Larson. 1984. *Being Adolescent: Conflict and Growth in the Teenage Years.* New York: Basic Books.
Durlack, Joseph A. 1998. "Common Risk and Protective Factors in Successful Prevention Programs." *American Journal of Orthopsychiatry* 68: 512–520.
Larner, Mary B., Lorraine Zippiroli, and Richard E. Behrman. 1999. "When School Is Out: Analysis and Recommendations." *The Future of Children* 9: 4–20.
Quinn, Jane. 1995. "Positive Effects of Participation in Youth Organizations." Pp. 274–303 in *Psychosocial Disturbances in Young People: Challenges for Prevention.* Edited by M. Rutter. New York: Cambridge University Press.
Roth, Jodie, Jeanne Brooks-Gunn, Lawrence Murray, and William Foster. 1998. "Promoting Healthy Adolescents: Synthesis of Youth Development Program Evaluations." *Journal of Research on Adolescence* 8: 423–459.
Scales, Peter C., and Nancy Leffert. 1999. *Developmental Assets: A Synthesis of the Scientific Research on Adolescent Development.* Minneapolis: Search Institute.
Scales, Peter C., Peter L. Benson, Nancy Leffert, and Dale A. Blyth. 2000. "Contribution of Developmental Assets to the Prediction of Thriving among Adolescents." *Applied Developmental Science* 4: 27–46.
Sickmund, Mellisa, Howard Snyder, and Eileen Poe-Yamagata. 1997. *Juvenile Offenders and Victims: 1997 Update on Violence.* Washington, DC: U.S. Department of Justice, Office of Juvenile Justice and Delinquency Prevention.
Zill, Nicholas, Christine W. Nord, and Laura S. Loomis. 1995. *Adolescent Time Use: Risky Behavior and Outcomes: An Analysis of National Data.* Washington, DC: U.S. Department of Health and Human Services.

Proms

Discussions of dresses and tuxedos, limousines and flowers—is there a wedding on the horizon? Not necessarily. If it's springtime, it's prom time for most teenagers, and that means an American tradition is about to occur—a rite of passage for many teens that signals the prospect of romance and glamour. Throughout history, traditional cultures around the world have invented rituals that signify the passage from childhood into adulthood. These cultural rituals often involve tests or celebrations of physical endurance, intellect, and maturity, and serve as a way for society to guide young men and women through a period of developmental challenges. Modern American teenagers often refer to prom as a significant milestone in their development, as much more than an ordinary school dance. Upon close examination it is apparent that proms incorporate many of the components of other cultural rituals, both cognitive and physical. Cognitive aspects of prom can range from community efforts, such as planning the celebration, to the more personal aspects, such as self-esteem. Physical aspects of prom involve appearance, such as style of dress, but also more serious concerns about body image and sexuality.

Most often, a high school prom is an annual event that is recognized by teenagers as a culmination of social activity. The effort involved in organizing a prom is tremendous, and usually a committee is selected by the student body. This committee manages the organizational details, such as location (hotel or school cafeteria?), theme ("Enchantment under the Sea" or "Dream Date"?), music (band or disc jockey?), food (chicken or filet mignon?), and price of admission. Local stores tend to donate items or services in return for advertising, and the whole community may choose to take part in the event. Attention to prom extends past the immediate community into the larger teenage community, as the media hype topics such as "prom fashions" and "finding the perfect date." There are thousands of Web sites dedicated to proms, and numerous books, such as Sheryl Berk's *The Ultimate Prom Guide*, that provide suggestions and strategies for the occasion. However, for many teenagers, the prom can still be an anxiety-provoking experience.

The stresses of prom night begin well before the night of the prom. Problems are most often associated with girls, perhaps because they articulate their worries more frequently than boys, and society dictates that boys aren't supposed to care as much about prom as girls. Both parents and their teens invest time and money in prom night, which can put a strain on the family.

More subtle strain comes from worries such as, "What if no one asks me to the prom?," "What will I wear?," and "Who will pay for the tickets? Limo? Dinner?" These questions often plague girls and boys as the prom looms in the distant future. Once the prom arrives, new worries replace old worries, such as, "How do I look?," "I think I blinked in our picture," and "What does she think will happen when we're alone tonight, after the prom?" For those students who are either not asked to the prom or are rejected by prospective dates, the negative associations can leave painful, long-lasting imprints on the teenager's self-esteem. Books such as Sean Covey's *The 7 Habits of Highly Effective Teens* aim to help teens navigate through some of these issues, most of which are not limited to prom season.

Physical concerns associated with prom night vary, but the first and most common concern is about physical appearance. Clothes, hair, makeup, and accessories are important factors in the prom experience. Students sometimes spend up to a thousand dollars on a prom "look," and those students who cannot afford such lavish expenditures most definitely notice the contrast between the "haves" and "have nots." This serves as a blatant reminder of economic differences that are usually diluted because of related social differences. Physical appearance also includes weight and height, and many teens resort to dieting or purging to lose a few pounds before prom. The outcomes of these behaviors can have serious, sometimes dangerous, outcomes.

The implications of prom fashions also extend to issues of sexuality, particularly sexual intercourse. In addition to the social rite of passage, a large number of teenagers include an additional rite of passage from so-called "innocent" youth into the realm of sexually active individuals. At a time when sexual intercourse can result in life-threatening viral infections, many parents and educators worry about the physical well-being of their student population. Alcohol consumption and drug use are other concerns for adults, since drugs and alcohol often accompany the prom celebration, and intoxication can be lethal if a student decides to drink and then drive to or from the dance. Many communities create hot lines, staffed by parent volunteers, that a teen may call if he requires assistance of any kind. The no-questions-asked policy and promise of confidentiality make this an invaluable teen resource.

The American prom experience may have changed in some ways over the years. For example, it is not uncommon for boys and girls to go with same-sex partners to the dance, and an increasing number of students choose to go without a date ("stag"), rather than miss the big event. Yet, much of the tradition remains the same as it was fifty years ago. There are still dresses and tuxedos, corsages and boutonnieres, and dancing until students' feet are swollen. Prom is perceived by many teens as an American rite of passage, not a rite of exclusion. It is the embodiment of life's joys and anticipation about the future.

Lisa B. Fiore

See also Alcohol Use, Risk Factors in; Appearance, Cultural Factors in; Appearance Management; Conformity; Dating; Decision Making; Gay, Lesbian, Bisexual, and Sexual-Minority Youth; Peer Groups; Peer Pressure; Rites of Passage; School Transitions; Schools, Single-Sex; Sexual Behavior; Substance Use and Abuse; Transitions of Adolescence; Youth Culture

References and further reading
Berk, Sheryl. 1999. *The Ultimate Prom Guide.* New York: HarperCollins Juvenile Books.
Covey, Sean. 1998. *The 7 Habits of Highly Effective Teens: The Ultimate Success Guide.* New York: Simon and Schuster.

Prostitution

Prostitution is engaging in sexual relations in return for material goods. Prostitution is not a problem just in the United States; it is a profitable industry all over the world. Young children and adolescents are routinely sold or lured into sexual labor. In the United States, many teenage prostitutes are youth who have run away from homes where they have experienced physical, mental, and/or sexual abuse. Their parents may be abusing drugs or alcohol and may be neglectful. These young people often describe themselves as "latchkey" kids. Children run away to escape difficult home lives, but the problem of teenage prostitution cannot be blamed entirely on the family. Although these young people may be estranged from their families, they are often experiencing difficulty in school and with peers as well. They feel they have nowhere to go, no option but to run away to a "better life." Only the life is not always what they expect.

Adolescents often do not know of services that can help them to escape a dysfunctional home environment, or these services are inadequate to meet their needs. Once young people run away from home, they typically attempt to seek legitimate employment. Often they are thwarted in these attempts by legal restrictions on employment for young people or by an inability to find jobs that will support their needs for food, shelter, and other basic necessities. In many cases, they cannot find a job at all. Searching through dumpsters for food and begging is frequently the next step, but often these acts are not enough to support adolescent needs. As a consequence, young children and adolescents may turn to prostitution in order to make money to survive.

In the United States, many teenage prostitutes are youth who have run away from homes where they have experienced physical, mental, or sexual abuse. (Robert Holmes/Corbis)

Male and Female Teenage Prostitutes

Although most people think of prostitutes as female, estimates are that one-third of the teenage prostitutes currently on the street are male. It is often harder for male prostitutes to find someone to take them in, so they are very susceptible to beatings, theft, and other dangers of the street. There is little written about young male prostitutes, and what is written is often focused on the sexual orientation of these young men. Male prostitutes are not necessarily homosexual. They are often lured into prostitution by the same means used to lure young female prostitutes: the promise of money, food, protection, and shelter, as well as attention and friendship from their pimps (men who get clients for prostitutes) or madams (women who run houses of prostitution, and get clients for prostitutes).

Young prostitutes, both male and female, are in demand by customers. Young prostitutes are wanted because there is a mistaken belief that the younger prostitutes are "cleaner" (i.e., do not have sexually transmitted diseases), and thus the client will not catch anything from the young person. The exact number of young prostitutes on the street is difficult to measure precisely, as there are debates regarding what constitutes prostitution (e.g., whether to include those adolescents involved in child pornography). In addition, there is no consistency in defining what ages are considered, and the information on gender inclusion is often absent. One estimate puts the number of child prostitutes currently within the wide range of 300,000–600,000, while a slightly more optimistic count places the number at 100,000–300,000.

Pathways to Prostitution

Resistance to prostitution is often broken by forced sex. Many teenage runaways are raped during their first months on the street. The young person is then approached by a paying client, and he finds it difficult to resist offers of food, shelter, drugs, and attention. Often, for female prostitutes, men will offer the attention and companionship these young girls are desperately seeking, making the young girl feel loved. The first-time sexual experience as a teenage prostitute can be emotionally confusing. Prostitutes will describe their feelings of shame and guilt for having performed sexual acts in exchange for money, and yet they also feel relief over having earned often desperately needed money. For street children, prostitution becomes a survival strategy.

Most prostitutes work for a pimp or madam in return for promises of money and protection. Pimps can cast themselves in the role of boyfriend and protector, while at the same time exploiting the young man or woman for money. The young people then become the victims of violence at the hands of their pimps if they aren't "working hard enough."

Madams and pimps will isolate young prostitutes in order to keep them under control and create a sense of dependency, so that they feel they have no one else. This isolation is achieved by not allowing the young person to have outside friends, a boyfriend or girlfriend, other jobs, or to attend school. The pimp or madam will also try to ensure that the teenage prostitute does not make any attempts to contact her family. Threats of violence from their pimp or madam, the lure of money, and a perceived lack of options keep many young people in prostitution. Pimps and madams often take the lion share of teenage prostitutes' earnings, thus further keeping the young people under their control by making them financially dependent. They also keep a close eye on their prostitutes to make sure they will not escape.

Although pimps are often portrayed as adults, young prostitutes often work for pimps who are young people themselves. One example would be a girlfriend prostituting for her boyfriend. The boyfriend will convince the young woman that the sex will not mean anything emotionally but will help them financially. However, there does not have to be this form of a relationship for a young person to pimp for another young person.

Pimps or madams use teenage prostitutes to recruit other young people into the world of prostitution. They will lure other young people on the street into prostitution with the promise of lots of money and protection, while hiding the dangers of the work. They glamorize the freedom of life on the streets. Once new prostitutes have been lured in, competition between the prostitutes is fierce, and is in fact promoted by the pimps and madams. This fierce competition is another way to keep the young prostitutes isolated and loyal.

Dangers of Teenage Prostitution

Teenage prostitutes are subject to a variety of dangers. Many teenage prostitutes become addicted to drugs and become the victims of rape and/or other forms of violence. These young women and men live in constant fear of being beaten, raped, or even murdered. Since drug use is often associated with life on the streets and prostitution, these teenagers are also at risk for addiction, overdosing, and diseases associated with intravenous drug use (e.g., HIV/AIDS).

Although laws vary by state, the risk of jail time for prostitution is very real. Prostitutes often find their pimp or madam will abandon them when it comes time to pay for an attorney or to post bail money. Thoughts of self-destruction and suicide are very real risks for teenage prostitutes.

Clients will pay extra money not to use protection, and the teenage prostitute is often overcome by the lure of money, or uninhibited because of drugs and alcohol, and will thus engage in unsafe sex practices. Female prostitutes face the risk of getting pregnant, thus having to choose between abortion, adoption, or raising a child in an already difficult lifestyle. Unprotected sex with multiple partners also increases the chances of contracting HIV/AIDS and other sexually transmitted diseases (STDs), such as gonorrhea and chlamydia. Even oral sex, once thought to be safer than vaginal or anal intercourse, is now known to be quite dangerous for the transmission of HIV. Contracting an STD can also leave a woman unable to have a child and can cause sterility in men.

Prostitution also interferes with the successful completion of many of the important developmental tasks of adolescence. In adolescence, there is a conflict between needing to belong and creating an identity, which is difficult to resolve when under the control of another person such as a pimp or madam. Selling one's body for sex can also cause confusion about the role of sexuality in relationships and causes problems for establishing sexual identity. Intimacy is another developmental task of adolescence. Prostitution inhibits the forming of intimate relationships. Prostitutes distance themselves from the psychological dimension of the physical act of sex. Whether this is through denial, drug and alcohol use, or other methods, the result is the same—the failure to meet the developmental task of learning to form intimate relationships.

Finally, although most of this article has been focused on street prostitution, young people also end up involved in so-called high-class prostitution. This form of prostitution is presented as being cleaner and safer than street prostitution. However, young people involved in white-collar prostitution face all the same risks of violence, sexually transmitted diseases, and failure to develop psychologically as do teenagers in street prostitution.

Helpful Resources for Teenage Prostitutes

There is no one reason why a young person ends up in prostitution. Prostitution is the end result of a variety of problems faced by the young person in the family, school, and peer context. Lack of support for exploration of gender roles, lack of social services to recognize children at risk for running away, the failure to provide such youth with counseling and assistance, and problems with the welfare system all contribute to youth prostitution. Given the diversity of reasons youth engage in prostitution, there are several useful approaches to helping teenage prostitutes.

Although there have been no longitudinal studies of the long-term effects of childhood prostitution, there are organizations that report success stories of young women and men escaping the life of prostitution. Former prostitutes can go on to live productive, drug-free lives with the right assistance from a variety of organizations. This assistance is offered through agencies or community-based programs that offer resources for teenagers thinking about running away, currently on the streets, or involved in prostitution. These organizations and programs provide support and referrals, they help young people get off the streets, and they provide them with resources such as education, food, shelter, clothing, and counseling. They include the following:

- The National Runaway Switchboard, 1–800–621–4000, www.nrscrisisline.org
- Children of the Night, 1–800–551–1300, www.childrenofthenight.org
- Boys Town, 1–800–448–3000, www.boystown.org
- Covenant House, 1–800–999–9999, www.covenanthouse.org

Deborah L. Bobek

See also Counseling; Delinquency, Mental Health, and Substance Abuse Problems; High School Equivalency Degree; Homeless Youth; Juvenile Crime; Juvenile Justice System; Physical Abuse; Programs for Adolescents; Rape; Risk Behaviors; Runaways; Sexual Abuse; Sexual Behavior; Sexually Transmitted Diseases

References and further reading
Bell, Laurie. 1987. *Good Girls/Bad Girls: Feminists and Sex Trade Workers Talk Face to Face.* Toronto: The Women's Press.
Ennew, Judith, Kusum Gopal, Janet Heeran, and Heather Montgomery. 1996. *Children and Prostitution: How Can We Measure and Monitor the Commercial Sexual Exploitation of Children?* New York: UNICEF.
Hart, Jordana. 1998. "Young and on the Run after Fleeing Home, They Often Find a World of Rape, Prostitution and Drugs." *The Boston Globe,* February 2, A1.
Jesson, Jill. 1993. "Understanding Adolescent Female Prostitution: A Literature Review." *British Journal of Social Work* 23, no. 5: 517–530.
Schissel, Bernard, and Kari Fedec. 1999. "The Selling of Innocence: The Gestalt of Danger in the Loves of Youth Prostitutes." *Canadian Journal of Criminology* 41, no. 1: 33–56.
Strauss, David Levi. 1992. "A Threnody for Street Kids: The Youngest Homeless." *The Nation* 254: 752–755.
Weisberg, D. Kelly. 1985. *Children of the Night: A Study of Adolescent Prostitution.* Lexington, MA: Lexington Books.

Psychosomatic Disorders

The term *psychosomatic disorders* indicates that a physical disease is the consequence of the interaction between the mind (or *psyche*) and the body (or *soma*). Examples of psychosomatic disorders are asthma, neurodermatitis, ulcers, migraine headaches, and hypertension (high blood pressure). Psychosomatic disorders are studied, among others, by the field of behavioral medicine, which is concerned with the integration of behavioral and medical knowledge and techniques for the prevention, diagnosis, and rehabilitation of illness. Since adolescence is a time of rapid and often stressful change, psychosomatic disorders are common, and an understanding of the mechanics of these disorders is useful to anyone who deals with adolescents.

Psychosomatic disorders are also sometimes called *psychophysiological disorders*, and in the fourth edition of the *Diagnostic and Statistical Manual of Mental Disorders (DSM-IV)*, the term *psychosomatic* was replaced by the diagnostic category of "psychological factors affecting medical conditions." This last concept specifies that psychological factors can adversely affect the person's physical condition, and the influence of these factors is made evident by the temporal association between the psychological factors and the initiation, exacerbation, and aggravation of, or delayed recovery from, the general condition. Some general psychological factors that could affect physical conditions are mental disorders (e.g., depression), psychological symptoms (e.g., anxiety, depressive symptoms), personality traits or coping style (e.g., not recognizing or denying the need of a surgery), maladaptive health behaviors (e.g., overeating, unsafe sex, lack of exercise), and stress-related physiological responses (e.g., headache produced by tension or stress).

Psychosomatic disorders are distinguished from the concept of *somatization*, which refers to a tendency to experience and express physical symptoms in the absence of a known physical illness. For example, a sudden blindness without a demonstrated biological cause is an example of somatization. In these cases, nothing is physically wrong with the patient, although the physical problems are real in the patient's mind. The person usually does not recognize and may even deny that the psychological distress might be related to the illness. Somatization might be useful to the individual because, through it, he may attain certain psychological and/or social gains (e.g., extra attention or relief from responsibilities). A bad headache, for example, may exempt a student from taking an exam that she does not want to take. Constant stomachaches might result in frequent visits to the doctor's office, which would mean more attention from adults. In other words, somatization can be used as an unconscious strategy to cope with the demands and frustrations of life.

Psychosomatic disorders, on the other hand, do involve real, organic pathology. They are real physical illnesses that involve a clear disturbance of the body, in which anxiety is the main emotion involved in producing the symptoms. In other words, if the person is not able to process or handle emotions on a psychological level, the conflicting emotions may be transferred to the body.

The tendency to experience and communicate distress through the body rather than through a psychological mode exists in different societies, but it does not necessarily imply that the individual displaying it has a psychiatric disorder. After all, we all somatize at some point of our lives, because we all go through stressful times in life. It is not uncommon to experience dizziness, headaches, stomachaches, shortness of breath, palpitations, or other symptoms during these stressful periods.

In the case of psychosomatic illnesses, there can be changes in the perceptual, structural, or functional responses of the body. This happens because the brain, the organ of the mind, is connected to the organs of the body through nerves and hormones. Through these connections, the mind can contribute to the creation and course of illnesses that reside in the body, such as neurodermatitis, peptic ulcer, and asthma, among others. Changes in the organs of the body are more likely to occur when the mind is overwhelmed by certain emotions, and the changes are a way of dealing with these emotions (Dubovsky, 1997).

Emotions give rise to mental and physical changes in the body. When emotions are expressed openly (e.g., when anger is openly discussed or expressed with the person we are angry with), the mental and physical activities in which the individual engages help to end the physiological changes that occur in the body because of those emotions (Dubovsky, 1997). When we feel angry, for example, there is more blood flow to the muscles and our heart rate accelerates. These physical changes prepare the person for an action to deal with the emotion, such as yelling at the source of anger to relieve the anger. Normally, the physiological state created by the emotion returns to its usual functioning after the action is done and the emotion is relieved. In the case of anger, the muscles relax and the heart rate returns to its usual level of activity. If, instead, the feelings and emotions are repressed or relegated to the unconscious mind, the physiological changes will not be terminated through action, and the body may continue to respond to the emotion. Physiological changes such as rapid heartbeat, elevated blood pressure, muscle tension, headache, or an upset stomach will continue until the emotion is resolved (Dubovsky, 1997). Repressed anger and anxiety, for example, have been associated with a particular type of neurodermatitis in which the person loses hair very rapidly due to the altered emotional state (e.g., repressed anger). Rapid hair

loss, at the same time, produces great levels of anxiety because of the fear of becoming bald—establishing a pattern of anxiety, hair loss, anxiety—which may be quite difficult to treat.

The continuous physical stimulation of undischarged emotions is not necessarily dangerous for a body that is healthy. However, a body that is vulnerable and that is subjected to intense and prolonged somatic responses to stressful situations may be permanently changed. For example, a person who is continually angry and whose heart is vulnerable might experience rapid, uncontrollable cardiac rhythms. With time, the person's heart may adjust to the rapid beating, and "may reset itself to a pathological level of functioning that is independent of the emotional state that originally mobilized it" (Dubovsky, 1997, p. 47).

Obviously, certain experiences may give rise to emotions that are natural in human beings, such as anger, anxiety, grief, love, or sexual desire. Under certain circumstances, it may be difficult to express these feelings and emotions openly, or they may become too strong. Thus, they may become uncomfortable. For example, an adolescent who is becoming aware of his growing sexual thoughts and impulses might feel anxious due to these newly felt desires. Societal conventions do not allow a free expression or immediate satisfaction of these desires, which can make the adolescent feel even more anxious about his new emotions. He might feel shame, guilt, and, sometimes, fear in relation to these emotions. When anxiety and feelings of guilt, fear, or shame become too strong, the conscious mind might try to push these problematic responses into the unconscious mind, into the part of the mind that will keep them out of his awareness. In order for these problematic feelings to remain out of the person's awareness, the conscious mind needs continuous vigilance over them. When a person is having difficulty dealing with the emotions on a psychological level, the emotions can take the form of different psychological symptoms such as phobias or depression, which might not be as difficult for the person to deal with as the original ones were. However, these symptoms also reflect the same strong, hidden, and unconscious emotions. In some of these cases, it is also possible for the conflict to be transferred to the body.

We also know that certain personality types are more prone to physical damage than others. These are those who seem more incapable of dealing with their problems, and they tend to keep them from getting out (e.g., from leaving the unconscious mind). Again, when people cannot deal with their problems efficiently, the problems may turn into a body dysfunction. In this way, getting sick may be an unconscious way of dealing with guilt, of manipulating others, or of obtaining care and attention. People who have learned that it is wrong to express their feelings and emotions directly may communicate them indirectly through, for example, physical symptoms (Dubovsky, 1997). In the case of psychosomatic disorders, the idea of somatic involvement does not mean, as early theoreticians believed, that either the organs or the autonomic nervous system can actually express an unconscious idea. However, it does mean that there is an interaction between the body and the mind, through which the mind and psychological factors can affect physiological changes in the body.

Stress is a factor that is involved in the origin and course ("etiology") of psychosomatic disorders. It has been defined as a challenging event that requires physiological, cognitive, and behavioral adaptation (Oltmanns and Emery, 1998). Stress is known to play an essential role in the onset or exacerbation of most physical illnesses. It can be caused by many events in a person's life, such as the death of a spouse, a divorce, detention in jail or other institution, the death of a close family member, a major personal injury or illness, a major change in behavior or health of a family member, pregnancy, sexual difficulties, gaining a new family member (e.g., birth, adoption, oldster moving in, etc.), major change in the financial state, outstanding personal achievement, beginning or ceasing formal schooling, a major change in life conditions (e.g., remodeling a home), a change in residence, or a change to a new school.

Some people distinguish between external and internal stress. External stress refers more to observable events that happen or have happened to a person, such as pressures at work, difficult deadlines, troubles at home, or heavy traffic. Internal stress, on the other hand, refers to the different ways in which people can react physiologically to stress. Some people may perceive some challenges of life differently than others. For example, for some people a minor event might be perceived as something extremely stressful. Nowadays, however, most researchers argue that stress is the result of the interaction between the environment and the person, as well as how the person perceives the challenges of the environment.

As we all know, adolescence is a time of many physical, intellectual, emotional, and social changes that occur in a short period of time. There are changes in the anatomy and physiology of the body, changes in cognitive abilities, changes involved in the transition from childhood and dependence toward adulthood and independence, and even changes in or restructuring of relationships with family and friends. It is a time of transitions and adaptations.

According to Hendren (1990, p. 249), the typical adolescent stressors are pubertal growth and hormonal changes, heightened sexuality, change from dependence to independence, changed relationship between parents and adolescents, newly developed cognitive abilities, cultural and social expectations, gender role, peer pressure, parental psychopathology, school changes, family moves, parental marital discord and divorce, encounters with legal authorities, sexual mistreatment, and physical illness and hospitalization. Adolescence is thus a period that involves important transitions, increasing responsibilities, and changes in the roles the individual plays in society.

All of these changes require adaptations and thus bring with them a certain amount of stress, which adolescents have to learn to deal with. The young person's coping skills, the family's functioning, and the sociocultural environment influence reactions to these normal developmental changes (Hendren, 1990). Environmental stressors, such as divorce or school changes, may increase the risk of developing stress-related illnesses. Stress is known to produce anxiety, and anxiety may contribute to the worsening of the conditions of psychosomatic illnesses. Indeed, anxiety is an important component in the following illnesses: insomnia, asthma, tensional headache, dermatitis, digestive disorders, chronic pain, eating disorders, and cardiovascular disorders.

A high prevalence of psychosomatic symptoms has been documented among adolescents, with chronic headaches and stomachaches as some of the most common symptoms related to stress. Because of the high prevalence of these symptoms, it has been argued that some psychosomatic symptoms may even represent a normal and temporary adolescent reaction to changes in the body. However, it has also been argued that these symptoms are indeed specifically related to stressful life experiences and psychological distress. It is extremely important for families to learn to recognize symptoms of stress in adolescents, in order to seek professional help if needed. Although a certain amount of stress seems to be usual in adolescence, psychosomatic symptoms are potential markers of psychosocial and emotional distress, which need to be attended to, particularly because a significant proportion of these symptoms can persist into adulthood.

In our society, there is a general belief that stress is always bad, since it is the cause of many illnesses, and that it should be avoided. However, evidence now suggests that under the right conditions, stress can promote emotional strength rather than disorders. Thus, a certain amount of stress can be adaptive. Moreover, learning more adaptive ways of coping with stress can limit the recurrence or improve the course of many physical illnesses. One key to helping adolescents who are suffering from psychosomatic illness is not to try to remove all stress from their lives but to help them learn to maintain a balance between being challenged and being overloaded by stress.

Susanna M. Lara Roth

See also Chronic Illnesses in Adolescence; Counseling; Disorders, Psychological and Social; High School Equivalency Degree; Self; Self-Consciousness

References and further reading

American Psychiatric Association. 1994. *Diagnostic and Statistical Manual of Mental Disorders (DSM-IV)*, 4th ed. Washington, DC: American Psychiatric Association.

Dubovsky, Steven L. 1997. *Mind-Body Deceptions: The Psychosomatics of Everyday Life.* New York: Norton.

Hendren, Robert L. 1990. "Stress in Adolescence." Pp. 247–265 in *Childhood Stress.* Edited by L. E. Arnold. New York: Wiley.

Kaplan, Harold I., Benjamin J. Sadock, and Jack A. Grebb. 1994. *Kaplan and Sadock's Synopsis of Psychiatry: Behavioral Sciences, Clinical Psychiatry,* 7th ed. Baltimore: Williams and Wilkins.

Krishkowy, Barry, et al. 1995. "Symptom Clusters among Young Adolescents." *Adolescence* 30, no. 118: 351–362.

Oltmanns, Thomas F., and Robert E. Emery. 1998. *Abnormal Psychology,* 2nd ed. Upper Saddle River, NJ: Prentice-Hall.

Petrie, Keith J., and John A. Weinman, eds. 1997. *Perceptions of Health and Illness.* Amsterdam: Hardwood Academic Publishers.

Pitts, Marian, and Keith Phillips. 1998. *The Psychology of Health: An Introduction,* 2nd ed. London: Routledge.

Psychotherapy

There are many different theories and forms of psychotherapy and adolescents decide to become involved in psychotherapy for many different reasons. Most basically, however, psychotherapy (also commonly referred to as therapy or counseling) is a process through which a trained psychotherapist or counselor seeks to help a person learn and change in ways that contribute to psychological growth and well-being. The person who has sought psychotherapy is commonly referred to as a client.

The goals of psychotherapy should be decided upon by the client and therapist prior to the start of psychotherapy. Although the goals of therapy may change over time, it is important that the process begin with an agreed-upon goal. Many adolescents find psychotherapy helpful for coping with the many challenges and transitions that accompany the teenage years. Adolescents may find therapy helpful in learning how to deal better with everyday concerns or in resolving more serious conflicts. One of the most common reasons for seeking therapy is dissatisfaction with some aspect of one's life, such as family conflict, feelings of sadness, anxiety, suicidal thoughts, loneliness, dissatisfaction with school or occupational achievement, difficulties in making friends, issues concerning sexuality, and problem behaviors, such as lying or stealing. Adolescents sometimes enter therapy because they want assistance in coping with a difficult or traumatic life event, such as the death of a family member, an incident of physical or sexual abuse, or the aftermath of an accident or physical disaster. Therapy may also be sought for help in adjusting to changes, such as changing schools, parental divorce or remarriage, starting college, or the breakup with a romantic partner. In these circumstances, therapy may focus on enhancing coping skills to deal with the stresses of these transitions. Adolescents may also decide to enter psychotherapy because they are looking for guidance in future planning or because they want to learn more about themselves and ways that might enhance their success at school, at work, or in social relationships.

Therapy can be practiced in many forms. Therapists often meet individually with clients or with groups of clients. Group therapy is a therapeutic format in which a small number of individuals, often with common concerns,

Psychotherapy is a process through which a trained psychotherapist seeks to help a person learn and change in ways that contribute to psychological well-being. (Richard T. Nowitz/Corbis)

meet together with a therapist. Many adolescents find group therapy helpful because they can share feelings and learn from other teenagers, as well as the therapist. Family therapy occurs when all family members meet together with the therapist to change problematic family relationships. Oftentimes, family therapy is initiated because one family member is experiencing a specific problem. Family therapy can help adolescents and other family members learn to communicate and understand one another better. Individuals often participate simultaneously in several modalities of therapy, such as individual and group, or individual and family.

Trained psychotherapists generally have one of several graduate degrees and are licensed by the state in which they are practicing. Clinical social workers and mental health counselors are trained at the master's level; psychologists are trained at the doctoral level, receiving either a Ph.D. or Psy.D. degree; and psychiatrists are trained physicians with an M.D., and a residency in the specialization of psychiatry. Psychiatrists are licensed to prescribe medications, as well as to provide psychotherapy. Some adolescents who are prescribed medications to help with depression or anxiety may meet with a psychiatrist, as well as with a psychologist.

The process of psychotherapy usually relies upon a verbal interaction between a therapist and client. The nature of the verbal interaction and the extent to which the verbal interaction is supplemented by other activities will depend upon the theoretical orientation of the therapist. Psychodynamic therapists, for example, may focus on using the verbal interchange as a way to increase client understanding of the self and one's history. The psychodynamic therapist believes that this understanding or insight will enable the individual to change in desirable ways. A behavioral therapist is not interested in client understanding or insight, but instead focuses on change in specific behaviors. In behavior therapy, a verbal interchange may focus on identifying the conditions that maintain negative behaviors, so that the antecedents and consequences of those negative behaviors can be changed. The behavioral therapist and client might establish a contract, which the client agrees to follow and through which a system of rewards is expected to modify undesirable behavior. The cognitive therapist focuses on changing the way in which the client thinks, believing that human behavior and feelings are caused most directly by what we think. From a cognitive perspective, the causes of depression include negative thoughts about the self ("I am worthless"), about others ("No one likes me"), and about the future ("This situation is hopeless and will not change"). The cognitive therapist might supplement verbal dialogue, with role playing or doing therapeutic homework, such as practicing new skills learned in the therapy session. A family systems therapist may focus on how the family interacts as a whole, may focus on interactions among family subsystems (children vs. parents), and may be interested in how social systems beyond the family, such as the neighborhood, school, or workplace, impact the family.

Adolescents often enter therapy because an adult in their lives, such as parent or guardian, or a school official, has decided that they would benefit from it. Sometimes adolescents decide on their own that they would benefit from counseling and approach a parent, guardian, or school counselor for assistance in obtaining therapy. A therapist or counselor needs permission from a parent or guardian in order to provide therapy to persons under the age of eighteen. Therapists often provide progress reports to parents, so they will have a broad understanding of the goals and progress of therapy. The specifics of what the youth says during therapy, however, are confidential, and are thus not generally shared with others. There are limits to confidentiality, however. The therapist must report to appropriate authorities indications that the client is being physically or sexually abused, or indications that the client intends to cause harm to oneself or another person.

Maureen E. Kenny

See also Anxiety; Counseling; Depression; Disorders, Psychological and Social; High School Equivalency Degree; Intervention Programs for Adolescents; Programs for Adolescents; Self

References and further reading
Patterson, Lewis E., and Elizabeth Reynold Welfel. 2000. *The Counseling Process*, 5th ed. Belmont, CA: Wadsworth.
Prout, H. Thompson, and Douglas T. Brown. 1998. *Counseling and Psychotherapy with Children and Adolescents*, 3rd ed. New York: Wiley.

Puberty: Hormone Changes

Adolescence is the period of the life span that includes roughly the second decade of life. It is characterized by physical, hormonal, psychological, and emotional changes. *Puberty* is the term used to describe the physical and hormonal changes that occur during adolescence. It is a process that takes years to complete and consists of many different changes.

Puberty is characterized by more rapid physical changes than at any time since infancy. These changes are brought on by complicated interactions among genes, hormones, the brain, and the environment where the adolescent lives. This entry will focus on hormones and the role they play in the physical changes of puberty. Hormones as a group are one of the factors responsible for increases in height and weight and changes in body size and body proportions at puberty. Changes in hormones, along with physical growth, are thought to be related to changes in moods and behavior at puberty.

There are many hormones that contribute to the physical changes at puberty, but there are three main types of hormones that change at puberty: gonadotropins, gonadal hormones, and adrenal hormones.

The term *gonadotropins* refers to two hormones, luteinizing hormone (LH) and follicle stimulating hormone (FSH). Gonadotropins are produced by the pituitary gland at the base of the brain. They stimulate the production of two other hormones, estrogen and testosterone. In early puberty, the gonadotropins rise during sleep, but as puberty advances they are present during the day as well.

The second group of hormones that rise at puberty consists of the gonadal hormones, estrogen and testosterone. As gonadotropins rise, so do the gonadal hormones, estrogen and testosterone. Gonadal hormones are produced by the gonads. The term *gonads* refers to the testicles in boys and the ovaries in girls. During puberty, estrogen is produced mainly by the ovaries in girls and is several times higher in girls than in boys. Estrogen is responsible for growth and the development of secondary sexual characteristics, that is, breasts and other organs that humans need to reproduce. Testosterone is produced mainly by the testicles in boys and is several times higher in boys than in girls. Testosterone is responsible for the development of sperm and other organs involved in reproduction, like the penis and testicles. Estrogen and testosterone begin to rise at approximately age eight to nine in girls and ten to eleven in boys.

The adrenal hormones that change at puberty are dehydroepiandrosterone (DHEA), dehydroepiandrosterone sulphate (DHEAS), and androstenedione. Adrenal androgens are produced by the adrenal glands, which sit on top of the kidneys. The adrenal androgens begin to rise at approximately age seven to eight in girls and boys. Adrenal androgens contribute to the development of a prepubertal growth spurt and pubic and underarm hair in boys and girls.

Boys and girls can vary widely in the age at which they begin to have an increase in all three groups of hormones. Shortly after these hormones begin to rise, adolescents begin to show physical changes. Girls will begin to develop breasts. Boys will begin to develop a larger penis and testicles. Both boys and girls will develop pubic and underarm hair. Girls begin to show physical changes eighteen to twenty-four months before boys. At around ages twelve to thirteen in girls and fourteen to fifteen in boys, height will increase very rapidly. This rapid increase in height is referred to as the growth spurt. The growth spurt lasts about two years. Adolescents will continue to grow after the growth spurt, but at a slower rate. Growth hormone, along with other growth factors, contributes to the rapid rise in height at puberty. In early puberty, growth hormone is secreted mainly at night. For girls, menarche, the beginning of the menstrual period, is a late event of puberty that usually occurs after the growth spurt. Cyclical (monthly) changes in some of the hormones occur during the menstrual cycle.

Girls and boys vary in when they will exhibit the hormonal and physical growth changes of puberty, although the majority of boys and girls begin to show changes at about the same age. Those who experience changes in hormones and, in turn, physical changes earlier than their same-age friends are called early maturers and those who begin later are called late maturers. The timing of hormone changes can be affected by many factors, which include genetic influences, stress, socioeconomic status, nutrition, diet, exercise, and chronic illness. In some cases, both early and late maturers can have problems coping with their time of maturation. These problems include changes in moods (from sadness to anger to happiness, and so on), disobedience, and more serious problems, like aggression and delinquency. Much more research needs to be done on how the timing of the physical changes of puberty will affect adolescents' physical and mental health later on in life.

Elizabeth J. Susman

See also Acne; Aggression; Appearance, Cultural Factors in; Body Fat, Changes in; Body Hair; Delinquency, Trends in; Emotions; Gender Differences; High School Equivalency Degree; Menarche; Menstruation; Pregnancy, Interventions to Prevent; Sex Differences; Sexual Behavior; Sports, Exercise, and Weight Control; Transition to Young Adulthood

References and further reading
Bourgignon, J., and T. M. Plant, eds. 2000. *The Onset of Puberty in Perspective. Proceedings of the 5th International Conference on the Control of the Onset of Puberty.* Amsterdam: Elsevier.
Griffen, J. E., and S. R. Ojeda. 1996. *Textbook of Endocrine Physiology.* New York: Oxford University Press.
Herman-Giddens, M. E, E. J. Slora, R. C. Wasserman, C. J. Bourdony, M. V. Bhapkar, G. G. Koch, and C. Hasemeier. 1997. "Secondary Sexual Characteristics and Menses in Young Girls Seen in Office Practice: A Study from the Pediatric Research in Office Settings Network." *Pediatrics* 99: 505–512.

Puberty: Physical Changes

The physical changes of puberty occur some time after the hormonal changes have begun. This time interval is not accurately known, but it is assumed to be about six months to one year after the hormonal changes. There is a wide range of ages of both onset and completion of various physical sexual stages of development. These changes typically span the second decade of life, involving early adolescence (around ages ten to fourteen or fifteen), middle adolescence (ages fifteen to seventeen), and late adolescence (ages eighteen to twenty). Boys who do not experience testicular enlargement by thirteen and a half years, or who have no pubic hair development by age fifteen years, or who take more than five years to complete development are considered to have delayed pubertal development. Boys who show development prior to age nine years are considered to have precocious puberty. Girls who do not have breast development by age thirteen, who have no pubic hair by age fourteen, and fail to menstruate by age sixteen are considered to have delayed puberty. Appearance of these changes in girls younger than eight years has been considered abnormal. Some recent studies have reported that the onset of changes in girls was in fact more variable and that changes occurring earlier than eight years were not uncommon especially among black girls. This phenomenon has not been noted for boys.

Between about six and ten years of age, but before the onset of true puberty, all children experience hormonal changes called adrenarche. These hormones may cause some physical sexual change in a small proportion of children. The most common of these changes is the appearance of an adult type of armpit odor, but some children also experience the appearance of axillary or pubic hair. These changes are normal in the vast majority of children.

The primary physical sexual changes of true normal puberty are changes in development of the gonads (testes or ovaries). All other physical sexual changes are called secondary sexual characteristics—they are secondary to the hormones secreted by the gonads.

In general, although there is a wide range of time of onset and rate of progress, there is an orderly sequence of the physical changes of puberty. For boys, the earliest visible change is enlargement of the testes. Testicular size greater than 2.5 cm is considered to represent pubertal development. Average adult testis size

is approximately 5 cm. The scrotum also shows development early in puberty. It becomes thinner, and increases in blood supply can easily be seen in its walls. Pubic hair appears next, either on the scrotum or around the base of the penis, and gradually spreads laterally. The penis enlarges next, first in length and later in width. Deepening of the voice occurs by mid-puberty. Axillary and facial hair appear late in puberty. The adolescent growth spurt in boys is also a rather late event in puberty, as is the increase in maximum muscle strength. Mature sperm appear early in boys, at about twelve and a half years on average. A significant proportion of boys will experience some breast development during middle puberty, which is benign and usually regresses without treatment.

Breast development is usually the earliest indication of pubertal physical development among girls. Breast development may take place on one side only for a while. It is not uncommon for girls to complain about soreness of the nipple. This is caused by the thin-skinned nipple rubbing against clothing and will disappear as development proceeds and the skin of the nipple thickens. Pubic hair appears before or at the same time as breast development in a significant number of girls. A significant increase in body fat occurs in middle puberty, causing the more rounded body configuration seen in most young women. Peak growth spurt is a middle pubertal event. Axillary hair and the first menstrual period are late events in puberty. Most girls will grow an average of two more inches after they experience menarche.

There are very obvious changes in behavior during puberty, but there is little data to suggest that these changes are related to the changes in hormones that

The physical changes of puberty typically begin earlier for girls than for boys. (Shirley Zeiberg)

cause the physical changes of puberty. The bodily changes of adolescence involve, then, a period during which the person reaches an adult level of maturity. One aspect of that new level of maturity is that the person becomes capable of reproduction: of becoming pregnant, or being able to impregnate. But puberty is not synonymous with all maturation changes. Puberty is the process that is complete when the person is able to reproduce and it is only one event within the pubescent phase. For instance, puberty is not synonymous with menarche (the first menstrual cycle) in females or with the first ejaculation (the release of semen) in males. The initial menstrual cycles of females, for instance, typically are not accompanied by ovulation. Similarly, for males there is a gap between the first ejaculation, which usually occurs between eleven and sixteen years of age, and the capability to fertilize. Nevertheless, these most striking physical changes give a powerful message and play a significant role in the transformation to which we give the name of puberty.

Jordan W. Finkelstein

See also Acne; Appearance, Cultural Factors in; Appearance Management; Attractiveness, Physical; Body Build; Body Hair; Body Image; Gender Differences; High School Equivalency Degree; Menarche; Menstrual Cycle; Nutrition; Pregnancy, Interventions to Prevent; Self-Consciousness; Sex Differences; Sexual Behavior; Sports, Exercise, and Weight Control

References and further reading
Berkow, Robert B., ed. 1997. *The Merck Manual of Medical Information: Home Edition*. Whitehouse Station, NJ: Merck Research Laboratories, pp. 1254–1257.
Clayman, Charles B., ed. 1994. *The American Medical Association Family Medical Guide,* 3rd ed. New York: Random House.
Katchadourian, H. 1977. *The Biology of Adolescence*. San Francisco: Freeman.
Paikoff, Roberta, and Jeanne Brooks-Gunn. 1991. "Do Parent-Child Relationships Change during Puberty? *Psychological Bulletin* 110: 47–66.

Puberty: Psychological and Social Changes

Pubertal maturation is characterized by increased production of steroid hormones (estrogens in females and androgens in males). These hormones lead to the development of secondary sexual characteristics, such as the growth spurt, the development of breasts in girls, and the formation of masculine hair patterns in boys.

Gradual physical alterations heighten young people's awareness of their bodies and increase their self-consciousness. Their concept of self, now focused primarily on physical self, becomes more psychological. Gradually, young adolescents reach a higher level of self-understanding and come to see themselves as distinct from others and as carrying rather stable personality characteristics. This process of forming a coherent personal identity is at times characterized by crisis, which must be resolved if healthy development is to occur. Research has shown that adolescents' ability to successfully resolve their pubertal identity crisis can shape their emotional outlook and impact their self-esteem and life choices. Some children tend to experience prolonged identity confusion and might later exhibit temporary pathological symptoms. However, most of these children successfully overcome the negative symptoms through the course of their normal development.

The search for a new identity and the desire to establish interpersonal intimacy are important components of adolescents' psychological and social development during puberty. (Skjold Photographs)

While trying to reach a feeling of comfort with their new body image and identity, adolescents also develop a need for more autonomy and begin to seek more contacts and support outside the family. They turn increasingly to peers, and through peer relations they look for friendships that offer loyalty and intimacy. Loyalty among friends becomes a necessary component of mutual understanding that develops during puberty, while peer relations provide a way to satisfy a longing for more intimate relationships with the members of the opposite or the same sex.

The search for a new identity and the desire to establish interpersonal intimacy are important components of children's psychological and social development during the pubertal stage. However, what course one's pubertal psychological and social functioning will take depends to a great degree on the timing of physical maturation, that is, whether adolescents reach puberty early (before the rest of their peers), late (after their peers), or "on time" (when most of the rest of their peers reach puberty). In addition, the influence of puberty on psychological and social functioning depends on the context within which the maturation takes place. All girls and boys go through puberty, but society does not regard their early, on-time, or late maturation in the same way.

This differential treatment often increases children's vulnerability to health risks (such as eating disorders) and/or problem behaviors (such as drinking).

Sexual Differences and Pubertal Development

The timing of pubertal development is different for boys and girls. The onset of puberty falls between the ages of 8 to 13 years for girls, and between the ages of 9.5 and 13.5 years for boys. Puberty is considered to be early if the first physical changes occur around the age of eight in girls and nine in boys, and it is considered to be delayed if no physical signs of change appear prior to age thirteen in girls and fourteen in boys. Since puberty is the time when children are absorbed in social comparisons and do not want to be different from their peers, being an early- or late-maturing person has important implications for self-esteem and self-concept in young adolescents.

Early-maturing girls usually weigh more and are taller than most of their classmates. Poor body image and negative self-evaluations are common in these girls. Since being thin is a norm for female popularity among peers, the desire for popularity prompts the girls to try to control their physical transformation by dieting. During the course of this preoccupation with physical appearance, some of the girls have been found to develop eating problems.

Being an early maturer has more positive consequences for boys than for girls. During the process of their physical changes, boys experience not only a growth spurt but also a gain in muscle mass. These changes are favorable factors for gaining popularity among the peers of early-maturing boys. However, given the value placed on physical strength, sports, and macho behavior among boys, this norm can also put late-maturing boys at a disadvantage, since it prompts the boys to develop negative self-evaluations and lower self-esteem.

In addition to the impact of timing on young adolescents' psychological and social behavior, the context within which the onset and development of puberty occur is equally important. Many parents may be uncomfortable about discussing puberty issues with their children. Fathers, in particular, report feeling uneasy about raising the subject of pubertal maturation with their children, especially their daughters. If they are unable to overcome their uneasiness, such an omission leaves children isolated in their efforts to understand the reasons for pubertal changes in their body shape.

In their search for identity, for a self-definition that would be both personally satisfying and socially effective, children turn to social cues. The media are a prominent source of such cues. Through media such as television, teen magazines, and movies, young adolescents learn of and come to accept cultural preference for thinness in girls and muscularity in boys. The emphasis on specific body images puts pressure on girls to maintain a prepubertal figure and asks of boys to affirm themselves through engagement in sports.

The possible negative effects that pubertal physical changes and their timing can have on young adolescents' psychological and social adjustment can be illustrated among those adolescents whose involvement in athletic or professional training requires a particular body shape. An example of this requirement in boys would be participation in sports such as football, which promotes aggressiveness and the expectation of rigorous building up of muscle mass. If a child is a late maturer, meaning that he is not physically mature enough to be able to build up his muscles as well as are early or on-time maturers, the physical expectations imposed on the child may negatively affect his psychological development. As for girls, professions that call for vigorous physical exertion and/or particular thinness regardless of one's age may not only delay onset of menarche but also affect the girls' successful identity development. In one study conducted by psychologists Jeanne Brooks-Gunn and E. O. Reiter, ballerinas from two different settings were studied. One setting was a highly competitive and physically strenuous ballet school and the second setting was a regular school. Brooks-Gunn and Reiter found that the different pressures of the settings for having a thin body figure were related to body image. Late-maturing ballerinas had better body image than did on-time ballerinas. However, ballerinas had more problems with body image and eating than did girls in the regular school setting.

Pubertal changes can also alter young adolescents' interactions with their parents. Indications of increased conflicts have been found between mothers and their pubertal sons. Mothers and sons tend to interrupt each other during conversations more during the initial pubertal period. However, conflict decreases by the time sons reach the height of their pubertal maturation.

Timing of physical maturity has a certain value not only for adolescents themselves but also for adults who interact with them, specifically parents. At the beginning of puberty, children who are early maturers are taller than most other children in their age group. They are often expected to perform more demanding jobs or to show more socially adult

behavior. Furthermore, parents may give girls and boys who are physically more mature than their peers more freedom to go out. This treatment may make it more likely that these young adolescents will start dating earlier than expected.

Interactions between puberty, psychological and social functioning, and the context in which children are embedded may increase children's vulnerability to problem behaviors and health risks. Both male and female early maturers are more likely to engage in adult behaviors (such as smoking, drinking, and sexual activity) at an earlier age than are on-time and late maturers. However, it has been shown that these problem behaviors depend somewhat on the characteristics of the children's peers. Although early-maturing girls are generally likely to start drinking or dating at an earlier age, they are more likely to act that way if their friends are older. Early-maturing girls with older friends expect fewer sanctions from their peers and tend to break more norms than is the case with early-maturing girls who do not have older friends.

Societal preference for thinness can put young adolescents also at a health risk. Current ideals of slimness, as portrayed by the entertainment and fashion industries, inspire dieting at the time of puberty. Adolescents are affected by this societal value to such a degree that dieting and poor self-image increase as the body is developing. Thus, in some cases, adolescents can develop eating disorders, such as anorexia nervosa (avoidance or loathing of food, often accompanied with psychological problems) or bulimia (uncontrolled binge eating and purging behavior). While girls are prone to anorexia nervosa, boys seem to be more vulnerable to physical anorexia (a type of anorexia that can be found in runners, for example). In either case, eating problems in young adolescents are prevalent, and, as some clinical studies show, both boys and girls can exhibit eating problems as early as eight years old.

Eating problems in young adolescents are sometimes accompanied by depression. Early-maturing girls and late-maturing boys who are dissatisfied with their body image might find it hard to feel happy. This unhappiness is likely to increase depressive tendencies in the children. Depressed males and females are found to be dissatisfied with their body weight and shape even when their peers do not rate them as less attractive.

With all the psychological and social changes taking place during children's transition to adolescence, and with all the risks associated with it, what is it that parents and children can do to help each other combat the risks? First, it should be understood that although parent-child relationships undergo important changes during children's transition through adolescence, parents still continue to hold an important role in their children's lives during this period. Parents are involved in their children's lives by directly communicating their knowledge and values to them, and by indirectly providing emotional support for their teenagers' attempts to form friendships outside their home.

Adolescents turn to their parents for guidance when the actions that they are taking may have implications for their academic goals and future plans. Adolescents value their peers' input over their parents only when it comes to issues of popularity and status in different teenage cliques. However, acceptance of particular peer values does not necessarily imply that adolescents will suddenly refuse to rely on their parents' guidance alto-

gether. In their search for autonomy through expansion of peer relations and, at the same time, motivated by a desire to remain connected to their families, adolescents look for ways to establish peerlike relationships with their parents. The authority of adults in the parent-child relationship remains, but adolescents now seek to be respected and seen by their parents as their equals (which is exactly what they find in their peer relationships). At times when parents and their teenage children are able to meet halfway in this manner, mutuality of respect and communication between parents and their adolescent children tend to emerge.

Second, as noted earlier, pubertal maturation is a rather stressful developmental period during which one's success in resolving the identity crisis may shape one's emotional outlook, self-esteem, and acceptance of oneself and one's actions. Parents should help children understand that puberty is a developmental stage that everyone goes through, that they themselves went through, and that it does not last forever. In addition, for many girls the onset of menstruation is a cause for embarrassment and discomfort. Parents need to make an effort to explain to their pubertal daughters what the menstrual cycle is and what sorts of feelings the cycle usually brings up in females. Daughters should also be informed on how to conduct their menstrual hygiene.

Third, puberty is also a time when parents need to be aware that their own behavior can elicit much greater variations of both negative and positive behaviors from their pubertal children. For example, factors such as family stressors (e.g., marital conflict or parental divorce) tend to be consequential for girls' pubertal development, much more than for boys'. A high level of family conflict is associated with early menarche (the first menstrual period) in girls. This is the case even when biological factors such as girls' weight and nutrition are controlled for. Furthermore, some studies point out that many early-maturing girls tend to have absent biological fathers, and that the longer the period of father absence, the earlier is the onset of menarche in these girls. At the same time, however, stressful family context does not always necessarily result in early maturation.

Requirements of particular environmental/social contexts may delay pubertal maturation as well. For example, the delay may be either environmentally imposed or personally desired and attained, as is the case with delayed menarche in ballerinas (mentioned earlier in this article) or in girls who engage in excessive exercise and dieting. For this reason, parents of adolescents should pay more attention to their diet-conscious girls and late-maturing boys. Family meals should be modified in order to ensure that the adolescents get enough calories while eating more healthy foods. Parent-child discussions regarding the child's physical appearance should be structured in a way that meets the child's need for emotional understanding and affirmation.

Parents should also consider the possible effects that their own dieting or emphasis on muscular build and athletic involvement can have on the pubertal maturation of their children. For example, parents who actively foster weight control are likely to communicate to their pubertal children their own perceptions, beliefs, and attitudes regarding physical appearance and body shape. In addition, both parents and children need to be aware that in families with more than one child of pubertal or prepubertal age it is a common occurrence that siblings may behave similarly. Specifically, younger siblings are often found to imitate some of the behaviors of their older siblings. Thus, early-maturing girls and boys who engage in dieting, excessive exercise, drinking, or sexual activity may put their younger siblings (in particular, the younger siblings who are close in age to them) at a greater risk of developing similar problem behaviors themselves.

In the end, it is equally important to propose that adolescents should explore different ways in which to communicate to their older siblings and parents any concerns that they might have regarding their maturational state and identity dilemmas and insecurities, as well as possible social pressures. By helping parents understand better what their adolescents' concerns are, adolescents will enable parents to communicate with them more successfully and, thereby, know how to be supportive in a way that meets the developmental needs of their adolescent children.

Aida Bilalbegović

See also Appearance, Cultural Factors in; Attractiveness, Physical; Body Image; Conformity; Dating; Decision Making; Emotions; Ethnocentrism; Family Relations; Freedom; Gender Differences; Identity; Parental Monitoring; Peer Groups; Peer Pressure; Peer Status; Personality; Rites of Passage; Self; Self-Consciousness; Sex Differences

References and further reading
Aquilino, William S. 1997. "From Adolescent to Young Adult: A Prospective Study of Parent-Child Relations during the Transition to Adulthood." *Journal of Marriage and the Family* 59, no. 3: 670–686.
Brooks-Gunn, Jeanne, and E. O. Reiter. 1990. "The Role of Pubertal Process."

Pp. 16–53 in *At the Threshold: The Developing Adolescent*. Edited by S. Shirley Feldman and Glen R. Elliott. Cambridge, MA: Harvard University Press.

Graber, Julia A., Jeanne Brooks-Gunn, and Anne C. Petersen, eds. 1996. *Transitions through Adolescence: Interpersonal Domains and Context*. Mahwah, NJ: Erlbaum.

O'Koon, Jeffrey. 1997. "Attachment to Parents and Peers in Late Adolescence and Their Relationship with Self-Image." *Adolescence* 32, no. 126: 471–482.

Simmons, R. G., and D. A. Blyth. 1987. *Moving into Adolescence: The Impact of Pubertal Change and School Context*. New York: Aldine de Gruyter.

Puberty, Timing of

The term *timing of puberty* refers to the time at which pubertal maturation begins. Timing of puberty usually is referred to as "early," "on-time," or "late" with respect to a defined norm, such as the peer group, the grade in school, or available norms used by the healthcare profession. The adolescent's own perception of timing of puberty, or that of the parents, may be different from that defined by healthcare providers. Timing of puberty is known to have physical and psychological significance.

The issues around timing of puberty actually encompass both physical changes and psychosocial changes in adolescence, since one can influence the other. This entry will focus on two primary aspects of timing of puberty. First, it describes what is meant by early and late puberty in adolescent boys and girls, which is sometimes referred to as off-time pubertal development. Second, it discusses the potential physical and psychological significance of off-time puberty with respect to healthy adolescent development.

Off-time puberty usually refers to the early or late development of physical changes that occur during puberty. These changes primarily include breast or genital development and pubic hair development as well as the first menstrual period (menarche). Clinicians use charts and tables that describe the average time of the beginning of pubertal development to evaluate the progression of these physical characteristics. There is an average age of onset of puberty, but the normal age range for development of these characteristics is wide. For example, some charts say that menarche is on time if it occurs anywhere from age ten to age sixteen. Based on these ages, early timing would be younger than age ten and later timing would be over age sixteen. (Recent evidence on timing of puberty is discussed in the next paragraph.) For boys, testicular development usually is the first observable change in puberty, and normally testes begin to increase in size anywhere from age nine to age thirteen and beyond. Based on the developmental norms, if testicular development begins before nine or so, that may be called early timing, and if after thirteen, it may be called late. However, clinicians do not look at just one developmental change to determine early or late development. They look at everything that should change at puberty. If there is evidence of some change, like a growth spurt or new presence of body odor, this may indicate that breast or genital development will occur soon. As a clinician, one cannot pay attention just to one change; one has to look at all of the changes together to make a decision about the timing of puberty. Moreover, many of the old charts that describe age of onset of puberty were based on only information from Caucasian adolescents. Now there is more information on minority adolescent development norms as well.

There has been some recent research in 1997 showing that girls may be entering puberty earlier than before. Marcia Herman-Giddens and her group collected physical examination information on more than 17,000 girls in the United States aged three to twelve. They found that on average, girls are physically developing at a younger age than the norms that have been used. African American girls also develop earlier than Caucasian girls. This includes breast and pubic hair development and menarche. For example, about 48.3 percent of African American girls had begun physical development by age eight compared to about 14.7 percent of Caucasian girls (Herman-Giddens et al., 1997, p. 505). New guidelines reported by Paul Kaplowitz and colleagues suggest that early development needing a medical evaluation would be in an African American girl with either breast or pubic hair development before age six and in a Caucasian girl before age seven. (This information is not yet available for boys.) If a girl shows development at a young age, it may still be important to see a pediatric healthcare provider. The physician will look at all the signs of growth and development together, in order to determine that the early development is not worrisome. For example, early (or precocious) development can be caused by something going wrong in the body. In that case, the evaluation and any necessary follow-up or treatment for the problem would be important in order to prevent future health problems. One could then know if development was truly too early. Early puberty can also occur in overweight or obese girls. Sometimes a pediatric physician who specializes in growth and hormone problems of children and adolescents, that is, a pediatric endocrinol-

ogist, may do the evaluation. Pediatric endocrinologists also evaluate those who are developing late.

Importance of Off-Time Pubertal Development

Off-time pubertal development may be important from both a physical and a psychological viewpoint. Physically, we have already touched upon the importance of a pediatric healthcare provider evaluating early or late pubertal development. In this case, early or late puberty is important from a medical viewpoint. We also do not yet know what influence early or late pubertal timing has on brain development and, in turn, behavior and thinking. Some scientists are now beginning to evaluate the influence that puberty and its timing may have on brain development. At this point it is too early to speculate, but soon we will have more information on brain development and pubertal timing. Off-time puberty also may be important psychologically, and this aspect has been studied by a number of scientists. Some of these studies have looked at the relation of off-time puberty to moods or behavior problems. The definition of "off-time" has often varied. Sometimes it has been based on the same norms that the medical profession might use, such as the charts and tables mentioned above.

When it is based on the physical changes of puberty, those changes may be measured by an actual physical exam or by parent or adolescent report of development. Other times the scientists have defined timing with respect to the way the peer group (others in the study) has developed. Still other studies have actually asked adolescents a question like, "Compared to your friends, is your development at puberty earlier, later, or at about the same time?" For some studies, this last question may be more important, because how adolescents perceive their development may have more influence on certain moods or behaviors than what charts say about timing of development. An adolescent may be on time for development based on norms used by healthcare providers, but they may *feel* early or late compared to how other friends are developing, which in turn makes them feel out of place.

There is some inconsistency in the conclusion of studies about timing of puberty. One group of studies shows that girls and boys who are off time in their pubertal development, that is, early or late, have a more difficult time adjusting at adolescence. They may be under more stress and may have more mood and behavior problems. Being off time, they may not have the same social support from peers, since they are now different from their peer group.

A second group of studies supports the idea that early timing results in adjustment problems for girls. Early developers are assumed to be under stress more than on-time developers. They also may have missed the opportunity to complete normal psychological and social developmental tasks of middle childhood. That is, they missed time in childhood to develop and gain experience. These earlier maturers look more adult and therefore others expect adult behaviors. However, often an adolescent's thinking ability and emotional control is not fully developed. Because early maturers look older than they are, they may be tempted to hang out with older adolescents and participate in more risky behaviors.

Some of the studies show that early or late pubertal timing may be different for girls and boys. In general, early puberty seems more difficult for girls than for boys, whereas late puberty seems more difficult for boys. The early-maturing girls tend to engage in more adult behaviors, which they may not be ready for, and they may be less happy with their body changes. For boys, early maturation means an advantage in some things. Early-maturing boys may have an advantage in social development and in sports and leadership. On the other hand, late-maturing boys may be less accepted by peers and therefore have more social difficulties. In contrast, there is some evidence that late-maturing girls may have an advantage when it comes to academics.

Understanding differences in these studies can be somewhat confusing. There are no hard and fast rules about the psychological effects of off-time pubertal development. Adjusting to these changes can be very individual and may depend upon physiological differences, coping abilities, support, past experiences, and factors we don't even know about yet, like genetic background.

Lorah D. Dorn
George P. Chrousos

See also Body Image; Conformity; Gender Differences; Menarche; Nutrition; Self-Consciousness; Sex Differences

References and further reading
Dorn, Lorah D., Stacie F. Hitt, and Deborah Rotenstein. 1999. "Psychological and Cognitive Differences in Children with Premature vs. on-Time Adrenarche." *Archives of Pediatrics and Adolescent Medicine* 153: 137–145.
Graber, Julia A., Peter M. Lewinsohn, John R. Seeley, and Jeanne Brooks-Gunn. 1997. "Is Psychopathology Associated with the Timing of Pubertal Development?" *Journal of the American Academy of Child and Adolescent Psychiatry* 36: 1768–1776.
Hayward, Christopher, Joel D. Killen, Darrell M. Wilson, Lawrence D.

Hammer, Iris F. Litt, Helena C. Kraemer, Farish Haydel, Ann Varaday, and C. Barr Taylor. 1997. "Psychiatric Risk Associated with Early Puberty in Adolescent Girls." *Journal of the American Academy of Child and Adolescent Psychiatry* 36: 255–262.

Herman-Giddens, Marcia E., Eric J. Slora, Richard C. Wasserman, Carlos J. Bourdony, Manju V. Bhapkar, Gary G. Koch, and Cynthia Hasemeier. 1997. "Secondary Sexual Characteristics and Menses in Young Girls Seen in Office Practice: A Study from the Pediatric Research in Office Settings Network." *Pediatrics* 99: 505–512.

Kaplowitz, Paul B., Sharon E. Oberfield, and the Drug and Therapeutics and Executive Committee of the Lawson Wilkins Pediatric Endocrine Society. "Reexamination of the Age Limit for Defining When Puberty Is Precocious in Girls in the United States: Implications for Evaluation and Treatment." *Pediatrics* 104: 936–941.

Nottelmann, Editha D., Elizabeth J. Susman, Gale E. Inoff-Germain, Gordon B. Cutler Jr., D. Lynne Loriaux, and George P. Chrousos. 1987. "Developmental Processes in American Early Adolescents: Relationships between Adolescent Adjustment Problems and Chronological Age, Pubertal Stage, and Puberty-Related Serum Hormone Levels." *Journal of Pediatrics* 110: 473–480.

R

Racial Discrimination

Those who compile statistics for the U.S. Bureau of the Census predict that in the next few decades, the number of ethnic minorities in the United States will approach 50 percent (U.S. Bureau of the Census, 1994). Living in a multicultural society means that individuals from all cultures may come in contact with adults and peers from other ethnic groups who knowingly or unknowingly hold stereotypic prejudices. These prejudices may result in acts of racial discrimination. An act of racial discrimination is an action that denies equal treatment to persons based on their race. Experiences with racism and discrimination are often a common experience for members of ethnic minority groups. These encounters can lead to stress, anxiety, and increased health problems. Teaching youth strategies to deal with encounters with racial discrimination, strengthening their self-esteem, and providing information about diverse ethnic cultures all help to alleviate feelings of distress that could put them at risk for developmental problems.

- An Asian student feels pressured to do well by teachers, often being told he is a "model" minority. He does not agree that it is fair to burden all Asians with such high academic expectations.
- A white student gets into an argument because she is often told she has unfair advantages due to "white privilege." She does not feel the stereotype applies because she grew up in a poor rural neighborhood with few resources.
- A black teen walks into a store and is hassled by the store clerk. He leaves frustrated that he is unable to browse like all the other customers.
- A Hispanic teen is upset after being told to "go back to his country" because he is speaking Spanish. He was born and raised in the United States and does not feel he should be made to feel bad because he is proud of his cultural heritage and chooses to speak Spanish among his friends.

A recent research study of a multiethnic sample of adolescents showed that teenagers often experience scenarios like these and are highly distressed by them (Fisher, Wallace, and Fenton, 2000). Although many American youth report experiences of discrimination, they often experience them in different forms. For example, teenagers of African descent have long family histories of harsh oppression rooted in legally sanctioned slavery and segregation. Historical and contemporary

Teaching youth strategies to deal with racial discrimination and providing information about diverse ethnic cultures may help alleviate feelings of distress associated with such discrimination. (Skjold Photographs)

histories of teenagers of Hispanic, Native American, and East and South Asian heritage are marked by military conquest, displacement, and economic exploitation. Some youth of European descent share family histories of discriminatory immigration laws and experiences with oppression in their homelands.

Old prejudices and historical forms of ethnic and racial discrimination are giving way to new, more subtle forms of ethnic stereotypes (Essed, 1991). The work of bodies like the Federal Glass Ceiling Commission and U.S. Sentencing Commission, as well as several recent studies, indicate that discrimination in jobs, housing, education, juvenile justice, and social serv-ices continues to be a risk factor for minority youth. The effects of these experiences with discrimination can be great. For adolescents belonging to visible minorities in particular, negative self-evaluations may emerge from continuous experiences with discriminatory exclusion from opportunities and racially prejudiced attitudes (Spencer, 1999; Steele, 1997).

Research with African American, Mexican American, and Chinese American families suggests that parents who socialize their children to be proud of their racial/ethnic heritage help them to develop coping styles to deal with discriminatory practices and negative ethnic stereotypes (Thornton, et al., 1990).

The term that has come to be applied to this helpful kind of socializing is *social construction*. Social construction involves helping people restructure their experience with racism. A young person is apt to see a racial incident as his own fault; instead, parents should help their child place the blame for the problem on the perpetrator. It is also important to teach youth how to assert themselves during racist encounters. This is a difficult task, as most people prefer to ignore or avoid threatening encounters. However, addressing the racist incident directly and in an appropriate manner can be empowering. Teenagers socialized to be aware of and respond proactively to racism have been found to have a greater sense of personal efficacy and self-esteem (Phinney and Chavira, 1995).

For many ethnic minority members, values within their communities may come into conflict with the values of mainstream society. This conflict may add to the stress experienced due to hostile and discriminatory experiences. There are strengths in the ability to understand and work within mainstream culture. Therefore, it is important for parents to strengthen their children's identification with both "American" culture and their family's cultural heritage.

Teaching tolerance and diversity is an effective tool in decreasing stereotypic views and prejudicial attitudes. Therefore, it is also important to help broaden an adolescent's knowledge of various cultures. Participating in social events, reading, and studying diverse cultures are just a few of the methods helpful to gaining cross-cultural appreciation.

Scyatta A. Wallace
Celia B. Fisher

See also African American Adolescents, Identity in; African American Male Adolescents; Asian American Adolescents: Comparisons and Contrasts; Asian American Adolescents: Issues Influencing Identity; Chicana/o Adolescents; Ethnic Identity; Latina/o Adolescents; Native American Adolescents; Peer Groups; Political Development

References and further reading
Essed, P. 1991. *Understanding Everyday Racism: An Interdisciplinary Theory.* Newbury Park, CA: Sage.
Federal Glass Ceiling Commission. 1995. *Good for Business: Making Full Use of the Nation's Human Capital. The Environmental Scan.* Washington DC: U.S. Government Printing Office.
Fisher, C. B. S. A. Wallace, and R. E. Fenton. 2000. "Discrimination Distress during Adolescence." *Journal of Youth and Adolescence* 29: 679–695.
Phinney, J. S., and V. Chavira. 1995. "Parental Ethnic Socialization and Adolescent Coping with Problems Related to Ethnicity." *Journal of Research on Adolescence* 5: 31–53.
Ridley, C. 1995. *Overcoming Unintentional Racism in Counseling and Therapy.* Thousand Oaks, CA: Sage.
Spencer, M. B. 1999. "Social and Cultural Influences on School Adjustment: The Application of an Identity Focused Cultural Ecological Perspective." *Educational Psychologist* 34: 43–57.
Steele, C. M. 1997. "A Threat in the Air: How Stereotypes Shape Intellectual Identity and Performance." *American Psychologist* 52: 613–629.
Thornton, M. C., L. M. Chatters, R. J. Taylor, and W. R. Allen. 1990. "Sociodemographic and Environmental Correlates of Racial Socialization by African American Parents." *Child Development* 61: 401–409.
U.S. Sentencing Commission. 1995. *Special Report to the Congress: Cocaine and Federal Sentencing Policy.* Washington, DC: U.S. Sentencing Commission.

Rape

Rape, or forced sexual intercourse, can happen in different situations, including dating situations, incest, rape in marriage,

While both men and women are victims of rape, women tend to be at a much greater risk. (Richard T. Nowitz/Corbis)

and rape by a stranger. Rape is a very common crime and has intense physical, mental, and emotional consequences for the victims and their loved ones. While both men and women are victims of rape, women tend to be at a much greater risk. A recent national survey found that 700,000 women were victims of rape, attempted rape, or sexual assault in 1997 (National Crime Center and Crime Victims Research and Treatment Center, 1997). Statistics often underestimate the prevalence of rape because many incidents go unreported. Unfortunately, the topic of rape is very relevant to teenagers because they represent a high-risk group. According to the Justice Department, one in two rape victims is under age eighteen; one in six is under age twelve (U.S.

Department of Justice, 1992). Although there is a common misperception that rape is most often perpetrated by a stranger, in fact, the most common form of rape is date or acquaintance rape.

Because teens are at high risk, they need information about self-protection and defense and about the best ways to cope with the aftermath of rape. Although there are no guarantees against rape, there are steps a person can take to reduce her/his risk. Drinking or taking drugs increases the chances of being raped considerably; abstaining from drugs and alcohol or drinking only in moderation is a simple preventive skill. Another preventive skill is learning to trust one's own instincts. Women are often taught to be "nice" no matter what;

this makes it difficult for many women to trust their instincts and get away when they feel uncomfortable in a social setting. Lastly, there are many self-defense programs available that teach people how to fight off attackers. Many people find these programs very helpful and empowering. Although there are ways to reduce one's vulnerability to rape, rape is *never* the victim's fault, *ever.*

Self-defense and rape prevention strategies can reduce risk, but they are not a guarantee against rape. If a person has experienced rape, the first step she should take once she is safe is to visit an emergency room as soon as possible. Visiting a doctor after being raped, however, can be very difficult for many reasons. Victims often experience shame and this makes reporting rape difficult. In addition, the examination process can feel like a second violation of privacy. Victims are often unaware that they have the right to assert their needs in the hospital setting and insist on a doctor they feel safe with or to refuse any exam that makes them feel uncomfortable. This information could be given to teenagers at home or in school settings.

Attending to the physical injuries of rape is only the first step in the process of recovery. Rape leads to profound and far-reaching psychological trauma. Some rape victims may develop symptoms of post-traumatic stress disorder. This is a term used to describe a set of symptoms associated with trauma. Symptoms include flashbacks (in which a person may have vivid and intrusive memories of the event that seem frighteningly real), nightmares, intrusive thoughts, disassociation, memory loss, and hyper-vigilance. The aftermath of trauma may also include a spectrum of troubling, negative emotions including anger,

depression, despair, anxiety, shame, or fear. Often, the pain of rape is intensified by feelings of guilt or shame about what has happened. The survivor may blame herself for being in the wrong place at the wrong time, for wearing clothes that were "too provocative," or for being involved with drinking, drug use, or other reckless behaviors. One of the more devastating consequences of rape is the feeling of isolation and secrecy. Victims of rape often feel that they cannot talk about what happened to them. Survivors may fear that no one will understand, or that they will be blamed, or they may not want to burden other people with their pain. Keeping all the pain and confusion about rape to oneself leads to profound feelings of isolation. Professional psychological counseling is recommended to aid survivors in breaking the isolation and addressing the emotional damage of rape.

There are multiple methods of therapy for survivors of rape. Individual counseling usually focuses on re-creating safety and a sense of control in the victim's life. Some survivors find groups a powerful healing tool. Support groups can help with feelings of isolation, guilt, shame, and depression. As survivors share their stories with others, they often find that offering support to other group members helps them feel more accepting of themselves and less alone. Groups also help survivors feel empowered to take action on their own behalf and on behalf of other survivors.

In addition to psychological healing, there are also legal aspects of rape. Some women decide to press charges, while others do not. In 1996, less than one in every three rapes was reported to law enforcement officials (U.S. Department of Justice, Bureau of Justice Statistics,

1997). It is important that the decision to report rape be left up to the survivor. Legal procedures can be very painful processes, and the law often makes it difficult for women to win their cases, even when they are equipped with a professional legal team. Too often a victim's truthfulness and lifestyle comes under attack, making the experience feel like a second violation. Despite this, there are many reasons to pursue legal action. Rape survivors should be informed that it is easier to win their case if they start proceedings sooner because there is likely to be more evidence available.

Lauren Rogers-Sirin

See also Abortion; Adoption: Issues and Concerns; Aggression; Coping; Counseling; Dating; Decision Making; High School Equivalency Degree; Physical Abuse; Services for Adolescents; Sexual Abuse; Sexually Transmitted Diseases; Violence

References and further reading
Herman, Judith. 1992. *Trauma and Recovery: The Aftermath of Violence— From Domestic Abuse to Political Terror.* New York: Basic Books.
Koss, Mary P., Lisa A. Goodman, Angela Browne, Louise F. Fitzgerald, Gwendolyn Puryear Keita, and Nancy Felipe Russo. 1994. *No Safe Haven: Male Violence against Women at Home, at Work, and in the Community.* Washington, DC: American Psychological Society.
Levy, Barrie, ed. 1991. *Dating Violence: Young Women in Danger.* Seattle: Seal Press.
National Crime Center and Crime Victims Research and Treatment Center. 1997. *Rape in America: A Report to the Nation.*
Pierce-Baker, Charlotte. 1998. *Surviving the Silence: Black Women's Stories of Rape.* New York: Norton.
Pirog-Good, Maureen, and Jan E. Stets, eds. 1989. *Violence in Dating Relationships: Emerging Social Issues.* New York: Praeger.
U.S. Department of Justice. 1992. *Child Rape Victims.* Washington, DC: Bureau of Justice Statistics.
———. 1997. *The Sourcebook of Criminal Justice Statistics, 1997.* Washington, DC: Bureau of Justice Statistics.
Wiehe, Vernon, and Anne Richards. 1995. *Intimate Betrayal: Understanding and Responding to the Trauma of Acquaintance Rape.* Thousand Oaks, CA: Sage Publications.

Rebellion

Development during adolescence involves extensive physical and psychological changes that provide youths with new perspectives of themselves and the world around them. Because of these new perspectives, many adolescents feel compelled to seek out and push the limits of discipline. However, the rebellious behavior of adolescents can be interpreted not as a disrespectful rejection of parental or social values, but as a drive to independently examine the world on their own terms.

Prior to adolescence, children are less able to manage the complexities of daily life and rely on their parents and other authority figures for structure and guidance. As children move through adolescence they develop independent thinking (or *cognitive*) skills. They are increasingly able to balance multiple concepts, solve complex problems, and think abstractly. They begin to recognize and use their own skills and perspectives to guide themselves. These burgeoning abilities to look at and deal with the world are an important step in the development of autonomy. Growth in autonomy is a normal part of development, as adolescents gradually learn to think and behave independently. The development of autonomy is not always a smooth process and often involves mild conflicts with authority figures, as adolescents learn to manage themselves within the "real world."

Adolescent development of autonomy can be a mixed blessing for parents. Not having to constantly manage their adolescent child's life can be a positive and almost liberating thing for parents. However, although their adolescent children may have increased capacities for independence, they still have a great deal of development ahead of them and so still require parental guidance and structure. When parents continue to enforce rules and regulations, their adolescent children may begin objecting to what they see as burdensome restrictions.

Along with their cognitive skills, adolescents are developing their sense of self, an identity of their own. This is no easy task! Even though they are now beginning to recognize themselves as individuals, they do not yet have the independent experience and knowledge to help shape their own identities. Nevertheless, adolescents may rebel against their parents in order to experiment with new ideas and values. Parents should not despair; most adolescents continue to respect and adopt their parents' values, even while they sometimes act in defiance of them.

It is not uncommon for adolescents to feel constrained and frustrated by their parents' efforts to maintain rules and regulations. This can lead to conflicts between parents who want to keep their children safe and adolescents who want to experience the world on their own terms. The passion with which adolescents pursue freedom to explore and discover can translate into emotional and sometimes impassioned defiance of parental restrictions.

Conflicts and disagreements with parents may actually serve to teach adolescents valuable skills of independent thinking and social problem solving. We may think of the family as the "minor league" of social interaction. It is place where social skills are developed and practiced within a supportive and accepting context. Imagine if adolescents had to learn how to argue a point to an adult in the outside world without any practice! Although parents usually do have a better perspective on a situation than their adolescent children, it is important that adolescents feel as though they have a voice in the family that is listened to and valued.

Adolescents are generally more prone to getting themselves into trouble because they face more new situations and challenges than older, more experienced adults do. They have less practice, fewer skills, and less confidence than adults and so are more likely to make mistakes. These mistakes can range from excessive driving speed to not wearing a condom during sex. The mistake itself is not usually an angry rejection of adult authority but the result of an uniformed step over an unfamiliar line. It is counterproductive to assume that adolescents are troublemakers, since most try to perform well and behave within acceptable standards.

Communication between parents and their adolescents is a crucial ingredient to ensuring that adolescents are informed and supported throughout their journey toward adulthood. Adolescents may sometimes feel as though they do not need help or support and may object to parental interference in their affairs. However, adolescents actually do need to have support and structure in their lives even as they may rebel against it. It is very important that parents remain a consistently loving and supportive resource for their adolescents.

As difficult and frustrating as it may be, parents should understand that adolescents do still require rules and restrictions. Simply removing boundaries can leave adolescents exposed to potentially dangerous personal and social complexities that they may not be ready to handle on their own. With gradual and careful widening of parental restraints, the mistakes that adolescents will inevitably make will remain learning opportunities rather than inescapable pitfalls.

George T. Ladd

See also Conflict and Stress; Conformity; Emotions; Ethnocentrism; Family Relations; Freedom; Identity; Juvenile Crime; Parent-Adolescent Relations; Peer Groups; Peer Pressure; Transitions of Adolescence; Youth Outlook

References and further reading
Dacey, John S., and Alex J. Packer. 1992. *The Nurturing Parent.* New York: Fireside.
Kett, Joseph F. 1977. *Rites of Passage: Adolescence in America, 1790 to the Present.* New York: Basic Books.
Larson, Reed W., Maryse H. Richards, Giovanni Moneta, Grayson Holmbeck, and Elena Duckett. 1996. "Changes in Adolescents' Daily Interactions with Their Families from Ages 10 to 18: Disengagement and Transformation." *Developmental Psychology,* 32, no. 4: 744–754.
Paikoff, Roberta, and Jeanne Brooks-Gunn. 1991. "Do Parent-Child Relationships Change during Puberty?" *Psychological Bulletin* 110: 47–66.
Turner, Rebecca A., Charles E. Irwin, Jeanne M. Tschann, and Susan G. Millstein. 1993. "Autonomy, Relatedness, and the Initiation of Health Risk Behaviors in Early Adolescence." *Health Psychology* 12, no. 3: 200–208.
Youniss, James, and Jacqueline Smollar. 1985. *Adolescent Relations with Mothers, Fathers, and Friends.* Chicago: University of Chicago Press.

Religion, Spirituality, and Belief Systems

Background

Many modern ideas about religious development during adolescence can be traced to the early-twentieth-century work of G. Stanley Hall, considered to be the founder of developmental psychology. Adolescence, according to Hall, is *the* critical period for religious development. He viewed religious "conversion" as central to the experience of adolescence, the culmination of physical, cognitive, and spiritual development that takes place during adolescence. Conversion was not only the giving of one's life to Christ but a transformation of the adolescent's understanding of the world, involving moving from a belief system that is internally motivated to one that is externally motivated, actively seeking new ideas instead of passively accepting them, and rationally deciding how to direct the life course instead of unquestioningly following adult authority.

The place of religion in the study of human development, however, shifted soon after Hall. Religion is no longer central to the study of contemporary adolescent development, and as such, is seldom an item of investigation. Nevertheless, although organized religion is not necessarily a part of every American adolescent's experience, youths are still charged with forming a set of beliefs about themselves, the world around them, and whatever higher powers they may or may not believe in. Hall's broader definition of the

Spirituality is defined as a personal relationship with things above and beyond the self, while religion comprises the organizational aspects of a "search for the sacred." (Skjold Photographs)

conversion of the adolescent's entire belief system, a spiritual coming-of-age similar to the physical, cognitive, and social coming-of-age already well documented in adolescence, remains a useful paradigm for understanding religious development during adolescence.

Definitions

Recent summaries of the literature have noted the need for an integrative theory and a consensus on definitions and concepts. In their absence, *spirituality* is defined as a personal relationship with things above and beyond the self. Spirituality requires a personal search or quest and cannot be imparted by labels, such as Muslim or Jewish, or by institutions, such as Evangelicalism or Islam. *Religion* comprises the organizational aspects of a "search for the sacred"; it is possible to use such labels as Protestant, Wiccan, or Catholic to name a religious belief system. According to these conventions, someone can be spiritual (feeling a strong connection to the supernatural) but not religious, religious (following doctrines and practices of a belief system social context) but not spiritual, both religious and spiritual, or neither religious nor spiritual. To echo Hall's integrative perspective, the term *belief system* is defined as a person's individual relationship with the supernatural and overarching principles of existence, without the assumption that a belief system is necessarily either religious or spiritual.

Given this background and set of definitions, the purpose of this article is to provide basic data on the social context of religion in America; describe the contributions of cognitive, social construction, and motivational perspectives on religious development and applications toward resiliency and coping; organize existing research in a new way, according to the developmental paths it examines; and suggest directions for future research.

Demographics and Contextual Considerations

Popular sources agree that the religious landscape of America is changing, but no consensus exists as to how. Although Evangelical Christian sources decry the decline of family values and the plight of today's young people, these claims are not supported by survey data. Nationwide, Christian church attendance has remained roughly the same across the past few decades, with membership in more established, liturgically focused denominations (e.g., Episcopal and Catholic) decreasing, and membership in new, evangelical denominations (e.g., Assembly of God, Church of Christ) increasing. Church attendance of adolescents has declined only slightly over the years, and their religious interest has not changed.

Concerns with adolescents "falling away" from religion are borne out by longitudinal data, which confirm that over the life course the transition to adolescence predicts a drop in church attendance. Other studies find conversion to a religious identity from a nonreligious background to be relatively rare, while apostasy, or falling away from religion, is far more common; however, most youth continue in the religious identity in which they were raised. Although these findings can be synthesized into a larger contextual picture of belief system development, most research only includes Protestant and Catholic participants, complicating access to the unique perspectives of other traditions.

A further challenge is understanding the multiple contexts within which youth experience spirituality and religion. The interaction between the interpersonal and intrapersonal contexts of belief systems would be particularly salient, for example, to a hypothetical Christian adolescent who attended a parochial school until eighth grade and then went to a public high school. Surrounded by people who do not necessarily share her beliefs and an institution that is not supportive of religious behavior, the youth's expression of religion would have to change if it were to fit a new secular context. She would have to decide whether religion meant deeply held spiritual beliefs or daily corporate prayer in class and constant interaction with those at least nominally of the same faith.

Rite-of-passage rituals are also important to understand in context. Cultural literature has praised religion as a source of resiliency in the face of adolescent anomie. For example, ceremonies such as bar mitzvah or confirmation are intended to provide a meaningful religious transition to adulthood. However, they are traditionally celebrated at age thirteen, yet in the context of American society, adolescents do not receive adult privileges until age sixteen and are not considered adults until they are eighteen or twenty-one. Many adolescents find that the only meaningful change in status they experience through these rite-of-passage rituals is limited to religious institutions. This example illustrates that adolescent belief system development can only be adequately understood if experiences at the individual, family, church/organizational, and cultural levels are considered in combination.

Cognitive Stage Theories

Several modern theories, such as those proposed by David Elkind and James Fowler, frame religious development in terms of cognitive stages. Fowler's first stage, primal faith, begins with a child's relationship to caregivers. As children become increasingly capable of concrete operational thought, they can perceive God as separate from their parents, as well as imagine and comprehend symbols and images of the sacred. Formal operational thought marks the breakthrough into Elkind's abstract, undifferentiated religious reasoning stage and Fowler's synthetic-conventional faith stage. The adolescent's belief system is synthesized from childhood religious teaching, personal experiences, and a more adultlike understanding of the way the world works. The development of relativistic reasoning in late adolescence or young adulthood allows for a broader interpretation of beliefs beyond social contexts. Relativistic reasoning is possibly the developmental precursor to Lawrence Kohlberg's postconventional stage of moral development, as well as C. Daniel Batson's "quest" approach to religion.

Although cognitive stage theories might prove capable of predicting an individual's understanding of religion, separate from a social context it cannot predict the beliefs that a person will actually have. In addition, these theories have been criticized on the grounds that the majority of people do not reach the highest stages. One of the more dangerous extensions of the cognitive viewpoint has been explored in studies that show a negative correlation between "cognitive complexity" and religious orthodoxy and fundamentalism. Closely related is the construct of "quest" religion, in which doubting and questioning are the essence of mature faith. The danger lies in the logical conclusion that fervently held religious beliefs are a sign of a weak conflicted mind. However, according to recent findings, religious adolescents are more involved in community service, more flexible and open-minded, less susceptible to internalized racism, and have greater ego strength than nonreligious adolescents. Finally, stage theories of religious development make the precarious assumption that everyone goes through roughly the same experiences in the same order. An alternative perspective, the social construction viewpoint, holds that context has profound effects on belief system development

The Social Construction Viewpoint

The theory of the social construction of religion focuses on how well observable social factors predict adolescent religious commitment and participation. Using large samples and modern statistical techniques, investigators have shown that family religiosity, group identity of the adolescent's religious organization, religious education, devotional behavior at home, and a generally supportive family environment predict adolescent church attendance and mature beliefs. Because this research has been conducted with populations that are homogenous with respect to religious background, the generalizability of these findings is limited.

Joseph Erickson's data (1992) are particularly interesting because they can be interpreted to show that religious participation does not necessarily follow directly from religious belief and commitment. His model tested various predictive factors for adolescent religious belief and commitment, which, in turn, would directly predict adolescent religious worship behavior. The model more or less worked, with devotional behavior at home and parents' religiosity emerging as the strongest predictors of adolescent religiosity; peer influence and church attendance were also significant. The genius of Erickson's study, however, lies in the difference between the expected and the observed models. Belief and commitment were strongly correlated with worship behavior, but other factors directly predicted worship behavior and did not have as strong of a correlation with belief and commitment. Motivation for religious participation might have been the invisible mediator that caused the striking difference between the observed and expected models. According to Erickson's findings, it makes sense to study religion both in terms of the observable aspects of what adolescents are doing and the unobservable aspects of why they are doing it.

Motivational Theories

Motivational theories of religious commitment, first proposed by Gordon Allport (1950) and developed by Richard Gorsuch (1988), address the question of why people are involved in religion. Since the seminal work of Allport, motivations are usually classified as *intrinsic*, in which a person's "master motive" is religion and the religion is an integral part of the individual's identity, or *extrin-sic*, in which a person is involved in religion as a means to an end. Empirical studies report that people of intrinsic orientation consistently fare best when evaluated for positive views of human nature, internal locus of control, prosocial behavior, lack of depression, psychological health, lower levels of prejudice, and lower levels of homophobia. Based on these findings, it would be logical to investigate religious motivation development with regard to resiliency, but, to date, this has not been done.

Resiliency and Coping Applications

Research on religion as a source of resiliency in adolescence has focused on specific cultural contexts, such as Angela Brega and Lerita Coleman's recent study on the resilience of African American youth against internalized racism. Combining social construction and motivational perspectives, these researchers found that participants who attended church and were internally motivated to attend church scored lower on internalized racism.

This study suggests the possibility of investigating religion in and of itself as a potential source of resiliency and as a predictor of positive coping behavior in adolescence. Clinical case histories relate situations in which a client's religion had to be affirmed and used to make progress in therapy, and a client had to reconsider religious values as a necessary part of the belief system in order to work through negative experiences with religion. These cases indicate that religion can be a source of resiliency as well as a source of risk during adolescence, depending on the individual and the social context. Future investigations should not assume that every adolescent goes through identical experiences with religion, but consider the possibility of individualized paths to belief system development.

The Path of Continuity

Various trajectories of belief system development have been investigated. One line of research has been concerned with the continuity of religious identity or how well children who are raised in a particular faith tradition internalize the spiritual values and participate in the religion as adults. Family religiosity, religious education, and a supportive family environment have been found to predict religious identity continuity during adolescence. Such youths also have higher levels of ego strength, hope, will, purpose, fidelity, love, and care than nonreligious adolescents, which suggests that they also have a greater degree of resiliency. Brega and Coleman demonstrate the importance of motivation for continuing religious participation, especially intrinsic religious motivation, which is so clearly correlated with positive outcomes in adulthood. Investigating religious motivation could reveal differences in belief systems and resiliency of adolescents who are internally motivated to participate in religion versus adolescents who participate for social reasons (e.g., compelled by parents) or who are spiritual but do not participate in religion.

Further research should also focus on the continuity of nonreligious identity. If adolescents do not experience religion in the home, receive education about religion, participate in devotional behavior at home, or internalize what they learn about religion, they are not likely to be religious adults. Research that examines similarities between adolescents who simply grew up in a nonreligious home and others who report having been "raised Jewish" or "raised Catholic" but are otherwise not religious is needed. This could reveal important differences in how the experience of religion in multiple contexts affects the belief system of adolescents.

The Path of Apostasy

Apostasy, giving up a religious identity, has been a concern of organized religions for many years. Representing one school of thought on apostasy, the influential Puritan sermons of Cotton Mather at the beginning of the eighteenth century viewed adolescents as doomed to fall away from salvation without immediate and heavy-handed adult intervention. Taking the opposite and more empirically valid perspective, G. Stanley Hall 200 years later viewed apostasy as unlikely as long as ministers and rabbis working with youth provided the education and empathetic guidance necessary to help adolescents find God on their own terms. Investigators report that the correlates of apostasy are a poor relationship with parents, an intellectual approach to life, and perception of religious adults as hypocritical. Research should explore these "bad example" findings further, because they could have direct implications for the practices of religious leaders and parents. Research on apostasy should also distinguish among adolescents who were once religious but actively rejected it, those who came from a home that was only culturally or nominally religious and saw no point in continuing this into adulthood, and those who are simply experimenting with new adult choices without forsaking their beliefs.

Future research also needs to investigate motivational differences in apostasy, given the correlation between resiliency and motivational variables. The research of Kenneth Pargament and his colleagues has recently found religion-positive patterns of coping with life stressors more adaptive and prevalent than religion-negative patterns of coping. They also identified a pattern of coping that involved doubting, questioning, and even blaming God, as well as reassessing long-held beliefs. This underscores the need for research that investigates not whether but for whom religious and spiritual methods of coping are adaptive.

The Path of Conversion

Conversion is the path of an adolescent who was not raised religious but experiences a spiritual awakening on the way to young adulthood. Converts are the most celebrated stories of Christian youth ministers, yet they do not occur in large enough numbers to constitute a meaningful longitudinal research sample. Further complicating research is the social construction of conversion itself, which might lead converts under the microscope of retrospective research to embellish the details of how horrible things were before they found God. Brian Zinnbauer and Pargament found no significant differences between sudden and gradual types of conversion. As fascinating as these stories are to religion researchers, dramatic and sudden religious conversion (as exemplified in the biblical story of Saul on the road to Damascus) does not emerge as a common phenomenon in the life course.

Pehr Granqvist's 1998 study is part of a new trend of framing the question of religious development in terms of attachment style. The predictions were that the relationship of young adults to God would either correspond with their attachment to their parents or compensate for its absence, and therefore be different from their attachment to parents. Participant religiosity and spirituality turned out to be correlated with secure attachment and religious parents, supporting the findings about the resiliency of adolescents with continuous religious identity. Participant religious changes also turned out to be correlated with insecure attachment and nonreligious parents, which supports a separate path of conversion to the same destination of religious identity. The last two studies indicate that traumatic life events or a general need to connect with something greater than the self predict conversion. Future research needs to investigate the distinction between conversion to a spiritual belief and conversion to a religious identity.

Conclusions

Belief system development is the product of the interaction between the adolescent and the environment. Prior research has made it clear that features of self-development and identity exploration in adolescence, among them extreme thinking, unique patterns of judgment, and the desire to revise childhood attachments into more adult relationships, characterize belief system development during adolescence. Additionally, the direct interplay between individual belief systems and the cultural context must be acknowledged, although the unique developmental path of the individual necessarily mediates this relationship. With this caveat, more finely differentiated predictions can be made within and across developmental paths about what affects and is affected by belief system development. Without it, one could conclude that religious involvement and the importance of religion globally affect certain outcome variables, which might be true for some adolescents but not for others.

G. Stanley Hall is often thought to have believed that conversion is a universal feature of adolescence; critics have ignored his broad and integrative view of the concept of conversion as comprising all the changes an adolescent's belief system undergoes during the transition to adulthood. This integrative view accommodates findings that not every adolescent follows the same path toward belief system development, and that some do not develop a belief system that includes the supernatural. It is the task of future empirical work to validate a working model of differential developmental paths of belief system development and to discern which trajectories lead to resiliency and mental health. Certainly, adolescents' relationships with the higher powers of the universe are as diverse as adolescents themselves, and researchers must direct their energies toward learning from that diversity.

Geoffrey L. Ream

See also Cognitive Development; Cults; Decision Making; Gender Differences and Intellectual and Moral Development; Identity; Moral Development; Self; Youth Culture

References and further reading
Allport, Gordon W. 1950. *The Individual and His Religion: A Psychological Interpretation.* New York: Macmillan.
Batson, C. Daniel, Patricia Schoenrade, and W. Larry Ventis. 1993. *Religion and the Individual: A Social-Psychological Perspective.* New York: Oxford University Press.
Bireley, Marlene, and Judy Genshaft, eds. 1997. *Understanding the Gifted Adolescent: Educational, Developmental, and Multicultural Issues.* New York: Teachers College Press.
Bjarnson, Thoroddur. 1998. "Parents, Religion, and Perceived Social Coherence: A Durkheimian Framework of Adolescent Anomie." *Journal for the Scientific Study of Religion* 37, no. 4: 742–754.
Brega, Angela G., and Lerita M. Coleman. 1999. "Effects of Religiosity and Racial Socialization on Subjective Stigmatization in African-American Adolescents." *Journal of Adolescence* 22: 223–242.
Donelson, Elaine. 1999. "Psychology of Religion and Adolescents in the United States: Past to Present." *Journal of Adolescence* 22: 187–204.
Elkind, David. 1971. "The Development of Religious Understanding in Children and Adolescents." Pp. 655–685 in *Research on Religious Development.* Edited by M. P. Strommen.
Erickson, Joseph A. 1992. "Adolescent Religious Development and Commitment: A Structural Equation Model of the Role of the Family, Peer Group, and Educational Influences." *Journal for the Scientific Study of Religion* 31, no. 2: 131–152.
Fowler, James W. 1981. *Stages of Faith: The Psychology of Human Development and the Quest for Meaning.* San Francisco: Harper and Row.
Gorsuch, Richard L. 1988. "Psychology of Religion." *Annual Review of Psychology* 39: 201–221.
Granqvist, Pehr. 1998. "Religiousness and Perceived Childhood Attachment: On the Question of Compensation or Correspondence." *Journal for the Scientific Study of Religion* 37, no. 2: 350–367.
Hall, G. Stanley. 1904. *Adolescence: Its Psychology and Its Relations to Physiology, Anthropology, Sociology, Sex, Crime, Religion, and Education.* New York: D. Appleton.
Hood, Ralph W., Jr., Bernard Spilka, Bruce Hunsberger, and Richard Gorsuch. 1996. *The Psychology of Religion: An Empirical Approach.* New York: Guilford Press.
Kohlberg, Lawrence. 1981. *The Philosophy of Moral Development: Moral Stages and the Idea of Justice.* San Francisco: Harper and Row.
Lerner, Richard M. 1998. "Adolescent Development: Challenges and Opportunities for Research, Programs,

and Policies." *Annual Reviews of Psychology* 49: 413–446.

Lovinger, Sophie L., Lisa Miller, and Robert J. Lovinger. 1999. "Some Clinical Applications of Religious Development in Adolescence." *Journal of Adolescence* 22: 269–277.

Markstrom, Carol A. 1999. "Religious Involvement and Adolescent Psychosocial Development." *Journal of Adolescence* 22: 205–221.

Ozorak, Elizabeth Weiss. 1989. "Social and Cognitive Influences on the Development of Religious Beliefs and Commitment in Adolescence." *Journal for the Scientific Study of Religion* 24, no. 4: 448–463.

Pargament, Kenneth I., Bruce W. Smith, Harold G. Koenig, and Lisa Perez. 1998. "Patterns of Positive and Negative Religious Coping with Major Life Stressors." *Journal for the Scientific Study of Religion* 37, no. 4: 710–724.

Silverman, Wendy K., and Thomas M. Ollendick, eds. 1999. *Developmental Issues in the Clinical Treatment of Children.* Boston: Allyn and Bacon.

Streib, Heinz. 1999. "Off-Road Religion? A Narrative Approach to Fundamentalist and Occult Orientations of Adolescents." *Journal of Adolescence* 22: 255–267.

Wulff, David M. 1991. *Psychology of Religion: Classic and Contemporary Views.* New York: Wiley.

Youniss, James, Jeffrey A. McLellan, and Miranda Yates. 1999. "Religion, Community Service, and Identity in American Youth." *Journal of Adolescence* 22: 243–253.

Zinnbauer, Brian J., and Kenneth I. Pargament. 1998. "Spiritual Conversion: A Study of Religious Change among College Students." *Journal for the Scientific Study of Religion* 37, no. 1: 161–180.

Responsibility for Developmental Tasks

Adolescents reach a point in their lives when it is not possible to proceed in the same way they did as children. It is the responsibility of each adolescent to achieve the developmental tasks of adolescence, with support and guidance from parents, teachers, mentors, and the community. The nature of these developmental tasks depends on our culture's definition of normal development at different points throughout the life span. According to Robert Havinghurst, adolescents must conquer eight developmental tasks: achieving emotional independence from parents and other adults, achieving new and more mature relations with peers of both sexes, achieving a masculine or feminine gender role, accepting one's physique and using the body effectively, preparing for an economic career, preparing for marriage and family life, and developing an ideology, which involves acquiring a set of values and an ethical system as a guide to behavior. Most essentially, adolescents must develop autonomy, identity, social roles, gender roles, and morals and values to achieve a sense of self that will promote the transition from the childhood they must leave behind to the adulthood they must enter.

Autonomy

Autonomy signifies being independent and responsible for one's actions. Some parents label the increased independence that typifies adolescence as rebellious. However, in many instances this new independence represents the adolescent's pursuit of autonomy, rather than a reflection of the adolescent's feeling toward parents. Adolescents' quest for autonomy and a sense of responsibility can create confusion and concern for many parents. Therefore, it is important for parents to assess the appropriate times to relinquish control in the areas in which the adolescent can make reasonable and responsible decisions. Moreover, it is important

The responsibility of achieving the developmental tasks of adolescence can occur with support and guidance from parents, teachers, mentors, and the community. (Skjold Photographs)

for parents to give guidance when the adolescent's knowledge and skills are more limited and for the adolescent to receive and accept the guidance. This combination will gradually lead to the development of mature decision making and will support the adolescent's struggle to master the developmental task of achieving emotional independence from parents and other adults.

Identity

Due to Erik Erikson's theory of psychosocial stages of development, identity is a key concept in adolescent development. Identity versus identity confusion is Erikson's fifth developmental stage, which

individuals experience during adolescence. Throughout this stage, adolescents are struggling to find out who they are, what they are about, and what their purpose in life is. Before adolescence, children identified with their parents. Adolescents attempt to move beyond the identity organizations they once had by integrating elements of their earlier identity into a new whole, one that includes their own interests, values, and choices. This is a time for adolescents to explore different roles, form knowledge systems, identify goals, and develop self-regulatory skills. Adolescents who are able to cope with the conflicting identities emerge with a new sense of self that is satisfying and acceptable. However, adolescents who do not successfully resolve this identity confusion may withdraw, thereby isolating themselves from their family and peers, or may immerse themselves in their peer world, which can result in the loss of identity in the crowd. Moreover, if the process of making self-defining choices is not attempted in adolescence, the transition to adulthood will be problematic.

Social Roles

Peer relations are an essential component of adolescent development. Peer relations are considered necessary for normal social development. When adolescents interact with peers, they participate in new activities that allow them to explore different norms and values. Thus, adolescents have the opportunity to reconstruct their identity with peers by relinquishing some of the norms and values that were previously developed.

It is extremely important for most adolescents to be popular. Research in the field has discovered that popular adolescents listen carefully, maintain open lines of communication with peers, are generally happy, and are self-confident but not conceited. Friendships within adolescence involve sharing intimate conversations, sharing private information, listening, and comforting; however, it is the decision of each individual what and how much information is shared with others. It is the adolescent's responsibility to achieve the developmental task of developing new and more mature relations with peers of both sexes, to facilitate the attainment of emotional independence from parents and other adults.

Gender Roles

Gender refers to the sociocultural dimension of being either male or female. A gender role is a set of expectations that specifies how an individual should think, act, and feel as a male or female. Society has expectations pertaining to the ways girls and boys should behave and creates social pressures, which tend to force individuals to conform to these expectations. Moreover, during adolescence many physical and social changes are occurring in females and males that cause them to come to terms with new definitions of their gender roles. It is important to understand that there are many influences contributing to the way adolescents perceive their gender role, including parents, teachers, peers, and the media. Through these influences, several gender role stereotypes have been formed based on what is believed or expected of males or females. However, these differences have often been exaggerated. In the process of developing one's sense of gender identity, it is important to accept one's physical characteristics and to use one's body effectively with the purpose of achieving a gender role that feels comfortable.

Morals and Values

Moral development involves rules and values about what people should do in their interactions with others. Most adolescents indicate that experiencing success in school and at work, providing better opportunities for their children, and maintaining strong relationships with family and friends are most important. These would be considered examples of morals and values. Adolescent morals and values begin to develop at an early age, usually shaped by attitudes and beliefs that have been communicated by parents. Most adolescents actually internalize and apply these morals and values that have been established by their parents. However, adolescents also begin to discover the ways in which their views differ from their families by experimenting with different perspectives to search for their own identity. Through this process, adolescents will be able to develop a sense of who they are and develop effective strategies for their school, work, families, and friendships. Moreover, this process will contribute to the fulfillment of the final adolescent developmental tasks of preparing for an economic career, preparing for marriage and family life, and developing an ideology.

Deborah M. Trosten-Martinez

See also Autonomy; Decision Making; Developmental Challenges; Transition to Young Adulthood

References and further reading
Brandtstädter, Jochen, and Richard M. Lerner. 1999. "Introduction: Development, Action, and Intentionality." Pp. ix–xx in *Action and Self-Development: Theory and Research Through the Life Span.* Edited by Jochen Brandtstädter and Richard M. Lerner. Thousand Oaks, CA: Sage.
Cobb, Nancy J. 1998. *Adolescence: Continuity, Change, and Diversity,* 3rd ed. Menlo Park, CA: Mayfield Publishing.
Erikson, Erik H. 1963. *Childhood and Society,* 2nd ed. New York: Norton.
Havinghurst, Robert J. 1972. *Developmental Tasks and Education.* New York: David McKay.
Head, John. 1997. *Working with Adolescents: Constructing Identity.* New York: Falmer Press.
Pugh, Mary Jo V., and Daniel Hart. 1999. "Identity Development and Peer Group Participation." Pp. 55–70 in *New Directions for Child and Adolescent Development: The Role of Peer Groups in Adolescent Social Identity: Exploring the Importance of Stability and Change,* no. 84. Edited by Jeffrey A. McLellan and Mary Jo V. Pugh. San Francisco: Jossey-Bass.
Santrock, John W. 1996. *Adolescence: An Introduction,* 6th ed. Dubuque, IA: Brown and Benchmark.

Rights of Adolescents

Why should today's teenagers be entitled to rights? Indeed, what is the real meaning of rights applied to persons who have not reached the age of majority? In this chapter we discuss the concept of children's rights and the implications this has for children as citizens. It is important to point out that in the language of rights, children are defined as persons under age eighteen. As child development researchers, we highlight our approach to working with children, one that requires a fundamental readjustment in the nature of the adult-child relationship. In redefining the status of the child in civil society, we show how this idea has become universal in scope and revolutionary in content.

A decade ago the General Assembly of the United Nations voted to establish a body of international law that would define, and hold governments responsible for, the rights of children (Van Bueren, 1995). This document, known as the Convention on the Rights of the Child (CRC), consists of forty-one articles that define a series of human rights as they relate specifically to the lives of children. Accompanying this delineation of rights is a series of articles that define the obligations states have to implement those rights. Although no sanctions are mentioned if a nation fails to support these rights, there is a strong moral authority that accompanies acceptance of the CRC. Looking back on the ten years since the CRC was introduced, it is both heartening and surprising that nearly all the countries in the world have ratified the CRC. In record time it has become the most widely endorsed treaty ever introduced by the UN. Only two countries have not fully ratified it: the United States and Somalia (UNICEF, 1995).

The articles of the CRC are divided into four broad categories: the right to survive, to be protected and feel secure, to have one's life chances promoted, and to participate in decisions and activities that have a direct bearing on one's own well-being. Many of these are considered positive as opposed to negative rights in the sense that they represent children's entitlement to opportunities and resources within in their own society, rather than the protection of individual liberties or the freedom from domination and oppression. The CRC is one of the few human right documents to balance positive and negative entitlements.

To take the CRC seriously, one must understand and accept the fact that it reflects a major revision in the history of childhood (Bardy, 1994). In the evolution of international treaties it completes the process that had its origins in the Declaration on Human Rights. By recognizing the developmental capabilities of children, the document brings the circumstances of children into the same human rights framework as women, racial and ethnic minorities, and indigenous peoples. Children are elevated to the status of full-fledged citizens. It is ironic that as the world's oldest democracy, the United States has not joined the global community in ratifying the CRC. America's children, looked upon as the most modernized and independent in the world, still do not have a government that recognizes them as citizens (Wilcox and Neimark, 1991). As one colleague responded, "the problem is that children have too many rights." Our response to this cynical comment is: were the rights of ethnic minorities or women the issue, would not that idea seem objectionable? Are children a sufficiently different lot of humanity?

In our work with street children in Brazil and South Africa, and profoundly deprived infants in Romanian orphanages, it became painfully obvious that simply being a signatory to the CRC does little to protect children or promote their well-being (Carlson and Earls, 1997; Earls and Carlson, 1999). The existence of a law does not guarantee its acceptance. Yet the presence of a law does change things. It becomes a standard against which injustices and insecurity can be measured. It is this legal and ethical standard that has compelled us to treat children with a higher level of respect and dignity.

It is worth emphasizing that the child rights movement had its origins in the context of international human rights, not at a local or grassroots level. This means that implementation is subject to the acceptance of the child rights agenda within local milieus that differ in history, educational and economic development, and tradition. In the United States, the sources of resistance to adopting the CRC relate to a host of issues such as parental versus children's rights in instances of custody, adoption, medical care, and the treatment of serious juvenile offenders as adults. Children have little impact on school policy and are deemed incompetent in decisions regarding their own medical treatment and participation in research. At the same time the conditions for child survivorship and the protection of children from exploitation and abuse are relatively well developed in the United States. This amounts to an inconsistency in the recognition and support for a universally established child rights agenda.

Our work has been focused mainly on participatory rights, which are of particular importance during the teen years. Specifically, these rights are indexed in Articles 12 to 15 of the CRC (see sidebar) and refer to the child's right to voice opinions, to form groups, and to deliberate in matters that bear on their own best interests. We first began to understand the importance of this matter while working with street children in Brazil. There we learned that a national organization of street boys and girls had successfully lobbied for a "Bill of Rights" for children in the new Constitution of Brazil of 1989 (Rizzini et al., 1994). Despite their deprivation, these adolescents viewed themselves as citizens and from this vantage maintained a sense of personal dignity that was obvious in our discourse with them.

We returned to the United States with this lesson and began working with small groups of adolescents as research collaborators. The effort began by introducing them to the CRC as a framework for gaining the perspective of youth and for bringing attention to those particular rights that they viewed as important to their well-being. We introduced them to research methods in social science and had daily intensive dialogue sessions over an eight-week period in the summer.

Favorable results using this approach were obtained in two very different settings. In Chicago, the work has been conducted within the context of a large study examining the impact of neighborhood organization on children's behavioral and social adjustment. The aim was to gain a wider perspective on the measures used in the survey and to develop new insights into ways that children interpreted the local worlds we were investigating from the perspectives of adult academics. The teens involved in this project decided to focus their attention on the issue of standard of living as defined in Article 27 of the CRC. They viewed this standard as a function of the

---

U.N. Convention on the Rights of the Child (CRC): Selected Articles

Participatory Rights
Article 12: The Child's Opinion
The child's right to express an opinion, and to have that opinion taken into account, in any matter or procedure affecting the child.

Article 13: Freedom of Expression
The child's right to obtain and make known information, and to express his or her views, unless this would violate the rights of others.

Article 14: Freedom of Thought, Conscience and Religion
The child's right to freedom of thought, conscience and religion, subject to appropriate parental guidance and national law.

Article 15: Freedom of Association
The right of children to meet with others and join or set up associations, unless the fact of doing so violates the rights of others.

Standard of Living
Article 27: Standard of Living
The right of children to benefit from an adequate standard of living, the primary responsibility of parents to provide this, and the State's duty to ensure that this responsibility is first fulfillable and then fulfilled.

---

level of adult commitment toward children in their communities (parents, teachers, and police officers). They designed a questionnaire to scientifically measure the quality of relationships with these authority figures and went on to administer it to a sample of their peers. The insights and findings derived from their work have informed subsequent stages in the larger study (see newsletters at http://phdcn.harvard.edu, click on Young Citizens Program).

The second venue was an ethnically diverse high school in Cambridge, Massachusetts. Again using participatory rights as a starting point and extensive dialogue sessions as a way of sharing perspectives to gain a consensus, a representative group of students decided to produce a video to explore the theme of internal or self-segregation at their school. The range of opinions that surfaced in their own discourse and the complexity of this issue led them to create a research questionnaire that is being used to survey their entire student body and the school's faculty. The purpose of this study is to broaden the discussion of this important issue as it relates to academic success, emotional well-being, and quality of the school environment.

These exercises represent a new orientation to young people and to our research. Once the rights approach is understood and adopted, it becomes non-negotiable. It is no more possible to retreat from the posture that children are rights holders than it is to deny citizenship to ethnic minorities and women. The child rights movement is mobilized, the history of childhood has been revised, and the future of children's well-being should be more promising as a result.

Felton Earls
Maya Carlson

See also Political Development; Rights of Adolescents in Research; Transition to Young Adulthood

References and further reading
Bardy, Margitta. 1994. "The Manuscript of the 100-Year Project: Toward a Revision." Pp. 299–317 in *Social Theory, Practice and Politics.* Edited by Jan Qvortttup, Margitta Bardy, and Hans Winterberger. Aldeshot, UK: Avebury Press.
Carlson, Maya, and Felton Earls. 1997. "Psychological and Neuroendocrinological Sequelae of Early Social Deprivation in Institutionalized Children in Romania." *Annals of the New York Academy of Science* 807: 419–428.
Earls, Felton, and Maya Carlson. 1999. "Children at the Margins of Society: Research and Practice." *Homeless and Working Youth around the World: Exploring Developmental Issues.* Edited by Marcela Raffaelli and Reed Larson. San Francisco: Jossey-Bass.
Rizzini, Irene, Irma Rizzini, Monica Munoz-Vargas, and Lidia Galeano. 1994. "Brazil: A New Concept of Childhood." Pp. 55–99 in *Urban Children in Distress: Global Predicaments and Innovative Strategies.* Edited by Cristina Szanton Blanc. Langhorne, PA: Gordon and Breach Science Publishers.
UNICEF. 1995. *State of the World's Children.* New York: Oxford University Press.
Van Bueren, Geraldine. 1995. *The International Law on the Rights of the Child.* Dordrecht, Germany: Martinus Nijhoff.
Wilcox, Brian, and Hans Neimark. 1991. "The Rights of the Child: Progress towards Human Dignity. *American Psychologist* 46: 49–55.

Rights of Adolescents in Research

Research on adolescent development is important, because it provides knowledge about factors that contribute to psychological adjustment or place teenagers at risk for problem behaviors. Such knowledge helps parents, practitioners, and policymakers determine the best ways to promote healthy psychological development. To provide knowledge about such adolescent problems as delinquency, school failure, drug abuse, and other health-compromising behaviors, scientists may ask teenagers to answer survey questions, observe their behaviors, give them specific tasks to complete, or collect blood or other physical samples to determine if there is a biological basis for some problems. All such research poses both potential risks and benefits for those who participate. For example, in addition to contributing to society's understanding of and strategies for ameliorating problems of youth, these methodologies can increase distress by focusing teenagers' attention on emotionally charged issues, introduce them to forms of risk taking of which they may have been ignorant, or inflict knowledge about a medical condition for which they or their families may not be prepared. Consequently, the Office for Protection from Research Risks has developed federal guidelines to insure that scientists protect the rights and welfare of individuals who participate in their research.

Formal ethical standards for the protection of research participants did not exist before World War II. Public outcry, in response to the Nazi medical research atrocities conducted on concentration camp prisoners during World War II, led to the establishment in 1946 of the first international set of regulations for biomedical research, called the Nuremberg Code. This code laid the foundation for current federal guidelines (e.g., Department of Health and Human Services [DHHS], 1991) and regulations put forth by professional organizations that have as their members individuals who conduct research with minors (e.g., Society for Research in Child Development [SRCD], 1993; American Psychological Association [APA], 1992).

Current regulations for the ethical conduct of research are based upon three principles. The first, *beneficence*, requires that when designing a research study, investigators make every effort to maximize the benefits and minimize the risks of the research to participants. The second principle, *justice*, requires investigators to ensure that the benefits of research are available to persons from diverse backgrounds. The third principle, *respect*, draws attention to the scientist's duty to protect the autonomy and privacy rights of participants. This last principle requires that individuals understand their rights in research, are capable of protecting themselves if their rights are violated, and volunteer without coercion or pressure to conform.

A hallmark of the principle of respect is the researcher's obligation to obtain *informed consent* from all research participants and their guardians. Informed consent means that before an individual agrees to participate in a study, the investigator must explain the purpose of the research, what participants will be asked to do, the potential risks and benefits of participating in the study, how participant privacy will be protected, and participants' right to refuse to participate or to withdraw from the study at any time.

Children and young adolescents are thought to be incapable of giving informed consent for three reasons. One is that their intellectual skills are not fully developed and, therefore, they cannot fully understand the information needed to make an informed decision. This assumption, however, has been a source of debate when adolescents aged fourteen years and older are involved. Another assumption is that even if they possess mature intellectual skills, teenagers lack experiences that are necessary to understand the true nature of their participation. Finally, actual and perceived power differences between teenagers and adults may make adolescents particularly vulnerable to coercion. For example, teenagers may perceive themselves as powerless to refuse a researcher's request to participate in a study or fail to question an unethical action by a researcher because they are taught not to question those in authority.

To ensure that teenagers' best interests are protected and that they are not vulnerable to rights violations, federal and professional guidelines require that in most situations scientists obtain the informed consent of a legal guardian before an adolescent can participate in research. Federal guidelines also recognize, however, that there are times when guardian permission may not be in the youths' best interest (e.g., when child abuse or neglect is being studied) or parental permission cannot be obtained (e.g., when problems confronted by teenage runaways are the focus of study). Under these circumstances, guardian permission may be waived if the investigator appoints an independent advocate to protect the teenagers' rights. Guardian permission may also be waived when adolescents agree to participate in research about their reasons for and reactions to medical and mental health treatment (e.g., venereal diseases and abortions) that they are allowed by state law to obtain without parental permission.

Out of respect for teenagers as developing persons, federal regulations and professional codes also require that in addition to guardian consent, adolescents must provide their informed *assent* before they can participate in research. Researchers must provide teenagers with information about the study at a level that they can understand. In addition, when a minor refuses to participate, this decision must be respected even if the legal guardian has given permission.

When teenagers are asked to participate in a research study, it is important that both they and their parents know their rights in research. These rights include the following:

1. *The right to be fully informed about the research.* Potential research participants and their parents should be given all information that might influence their decision to participate. Such information includes who the researchers are and which institutions they are affiliated with, why the project is being conducted, what the teenager will be asked to do, how long the study will take, when and where it will occur, and the risks and benefits of participation.

2. *The right to participate or not in the research.* Research participation is always voluntary. Participation in research cannot be required (e.g., for course credit), and teenagers should not be pressured by investigators, teachers, or others to participate.

3. *The right to ask questions.* At any point in the research, adolescents and their parents should feel free to ask questions, and the researcher must answer these questions as honestly as possible.

4. *The right to withdraw from the study or not complete all aspects of the research.* Once a study begins, teenagers can always tell the investigator that they do not wish to continue. In addition, the investigator should make it clear to teenage participants that they do not have to answer specific questions or engage in specific behaviors that make them uncomfortable. There should be no penalties for not fully completing a study.

5. *The right to privacy and confidentiality.* Under most circumstances anything a teenager does or says when participating in a research study should remain confidential. Researchers cannot share the names of individuals who participate in a study, nor can they tell others what the teenager did or said. To protect confidentiality, investigators usually give participants a code number and keep the information they collect on individuals in secure files; when they publish the results of the study they only report how groups of individuals responded, not how an individual teenager responded. However, researchers are ethically obligated to disclose information if they learn that a teenager is being abused or is in danger of harming himself or someone else.

6. *The right to be protected from harm.* Teenagers should not experience any physical, social, or mental discomfort when participating in a research project. If something unforeseen does happen during the study, the researcher must address the problem as soon as possible.

7. *The right to know the results of the study.* When the study is completed, the researcher should share her findings with participants. This information can be distributed to teenagers and their parents in a written summary. It often takes many months for an investigator to analyze and interpret research findings, and during that time, teenage participants may have moved, changed classes, or graduated from the school at which a study was conducted. Consequently, investiga-tors often ask that teenagers and parents who would like a summary of the results provide their addresses when consenting to the research.

8. *The right to understand and use these rights.* These rights should be explained to teenagers and parents in an easily understandable way. If English is not a parent's first language, then the investigator should have available consent forms in a language the parent can understand. Finally, teenagers should be allowed to exercise these rights without any penalties.

Parents can play a key role in insuring that teenagers make an informed decision to participate in research. To help a teenager understand and exercise his or her research rights, the following steps are recommended:

- Ensure that the teenager understands what will be expected of him or her for participation in the research. After explaining the purpose and procedure, ask the teenager to tell you in his or her own words what he or she will be doing.
- Encourage the teenager to ask questions throughout the study and to expect answers from the investigator.
- Discuss with the teenager his or her desire to participate or not in the study before you make your decision. This will allow the individual to make a decision without feeling pressured by your choice.
- Be sensitive to the fact that the teen may feel pressure from peers or teachers to participate. Encourage him or her to make an independent decision about whether he

or she would like to be in the study, rather than give in to pressure to be part of a group.

- Tell the teenager that the researcher does not have authority over him or her. Emphasize that even if he or she agrees to participate, he or she does not have to complete any part of the study and can withdraw from the study at any time.
- Explain to the teenager that answers will not be shared with other people, including yourself. Because of this, the individual can feel comfortable answering questions honestly.
- Encourage the teenager to tell the researcher if some aspect of the study bothers or upsets him or her. Explain that it is the researcher's responsibility to help alleviate any anxiety or discomfort.

In today's complicated world, research on teenage development is an essential tool for helping parents, teachers, practitioners, and policymakers solve the practical problems of adolescence. Adolescent research is a partnership among investigators, teenage participants, and parents, in which partners respect and learn from each other.

Jean-Marie Bruzzese
Celia B. Fisher

See also Rights of Adolescents

References and further reading
American Psychological Association. 1992. "Ethical Principles of Psychologists and Code of Conduct." *American Psychologist* 47: 1597–1611.
Belter, Ronald W., and Thomas Grisso. 1984. "Children's Recognition of Rights Violations in Counseling." *Professional Psychology and Practice* 15: 899–910.
Bersoff, Donald N. 1983. "Children as Participants in Psychoeducational Assessment." Pp. 149–178 in *Children's Competence to Consent*. Edited by Gary B. Melton, Gerald P. Koocher, and Michael J. Saks. New York: Plenum Press.
Department of Health and Human Services. 1991. "Protection of Human Subjects." *Code of Federal Regulations*. Title 45 Public Welfare, Part 46. Washington, DC: DHHS.
Fisher, Celia B. 1993. "Integrating Science and Ethics in Research with High Risk Children and Youth." *Social Policy Report. Society for Research in Child Development* 7, no. 4: 1–27.
Fisher, Celia B., Michi Hatashita-Wong, and Lori Isman Greene. 1999. "Ethical and Legal Issues in Clinical Child Psychology." Pp. 470–486 in *Developmental Issues in the Clinical Treatment of Children and Adolescents*. Edited by Wendy K. Silverman and Thomas H. Ollendick. Boston: Allyn and Bacon.
Fisher, Celia B., Kimberly Hoagwood, and Peter Jensen. 1996. "Casebook on Ethics: Issues in Research with Children and Adolescents with Mental Disorders." Pp. 135–238 in *Ethical Issues in Research with Children and Adolescents with Mental Disorders*. Edited by Kimberly Hoagwood, Peter Jensen, and Celia B. Fisher. Mahwah, NJ: Erlbaum.
Freedman, Benjamin. 1975. "A Moral Theory of Informed Consent." *Hastings Center Report* 5, no 4: 32–39.
Gaylin, Willard, and Ruth Macklin. 1982. *Who Speaks for the Child: The Problems of Proxy Consent*. New York: Plenum Press.
Grisso, Thomas, and Linda Vierling. 1978. "Minors' Consent to Treatment: A Developmental Perspective." *Professional Psychology* 9: 412–427.
Holder, Angela R. 1981. "Can Teenagers Participate in Research without Parental Consent?" *Irb: Review of Human Subjects Research* 3: 5–7.
Keith-Spiegel, Patricia. 1983. "Children and Consent to Participate in Research." Pp. 179–211 in *Children's Competence to Consent*. Edited by Gary B. Melton, Gerald P. Koocher, and Michael J. Saks. New York: Plenum Press.

Koocher, Gerald P., and Patricia C. Keith-Spiegel. 1990. *Children, Ethics, and the Law.* Lincoln: University of Nebraska Press.

Rau, Jean-Marie B. 1997. *The Ability of Minors to Define and Recognize Their Rights in Research.* Dissertation #97-30, 105. Fordham University, NY.

Rogers, Audrey Smith, Lawrence D'Angelo, and Donna Futterman. 1994. "Guidelines for Adolescent Participation in Research: Current Realities and Possible Resolutions." *Irb: Review of Human Subjects Research* 16: 1–6.

Society for Research in Child Development. 1993. "Ethical Standards for Research with Children." Pp. 337–339 in *Directory of Members.* Ann Arbor, MI: SRCD.

Thompson, Ross A. 1990. "Vulnerability in Research: A Developmental Perspective on Research Risk." *Child Development* 61: 1–16.

———. 1992. "Developmental Changes in Research Risks and Benefits: A Changing Calculus of Consensus." Pp. 31–64 in *Social Research on Children and Adolescents.* Edited by Barbara Stanley and Joan E. Sieber. Newbury Park, CA: Sage.

Weithorn, Lois A. 1983. "Children's Capacities to Decide about Participation in Research." *Irb: Review of Human Subjects Research* 5: 1–5.

Weithorn, Lois A., and Susan B. Campbell. 1982. "The Competency of Children and Adolescents to Make Informed Consent Treatment Decisions." *Child Development* 53: 1589–1598.

Risk Behaviors

Far too many youth across America are dying—from violence, drug and alcohol use and abuse, unsafe sex, poor nutrition, and persistent and pervasive poverty. And among those who are not dying, their life chances are being squandered. They experience school failure, under-achievement, and dropout; crime; teen-age pregnancy and parenting; lack of job preparedness; and challenges to their health such as lack of immunizations, inadequate screening for disabilities, poor prenatal care, and insufficient infant and childhood medical services. They often experience feelings of despair and hopelessness as they watch their parents struggle with poverty and see themselves as having little opportunity to do better—to have a life marked by societal respect, achievement, and opportunity.

There are numerous indications of the severity and breadth of the problems facing the youth, families, and communities of this nation. For instance, the quality of life that the United States offers its children and youth is poor in comparison to that provided by other modern industrialized countries. Indeed, as reported by the Children's Defense Fund, although America leads other such nations in productivity related to military and defense expenditures, health technology, and the number of individuals who attain substantial personal wealth, it falls far behind other nations in indicators of child health and welfare. In fact, the poverty rate for children in the United States is *highest* among the major eighteen industrialized countries. Although the total number of American children living in poverty decreased by 1 percentage point between 1985 and 1996, one out of every five of this nation's youth remains poor.

Risk behaviors in late childhood and adolescence fall into four major categories:

1. Drug and alcohol use and abuse
2. Unsafe sex, teenage pregnancy, and teenage parenting
3. School underachievement, school failure, and dropout
4. Delinquency, crime, and violence

Participation in any one of these behaviors could diminish a youth's life chances—or, indeed, possibly eliminate the young person's chances of even having a life. Unfortunately, such risks to the life chances of American children and adolescents are occurring at historically unprecedented levels.

There are approximately 39.4 million American youth between the ages of ten and nineteen years. Researcher Joy G. Dryfoos has estimated that about 50 percent of these adolescents engage in *two or more* of the above-noted categories of risk behaviors. She further estimates that 10 percent of the nation's youth engage in *all* of the four categories of risk behaviors. Dryfoos's work suggests that risk behaviors are highly interrelated among adolescents.

Drug and Alcohol Use and Abuse
Adolescents drink alcohol and use a wide variety of illegal/illicit drugs and other unhealthy substances (e.g., inhalants such as glues, aerosols, butane, and solvents). They also extensively use cigarettes and other tobacco products. Recent national trends in the use of all these substances have shown some declines. For instance, according to the University of Michigan's *Monitoring the Future Study*, which has been tracking this behavior among high school students since the 1970s, smoking rates among eighth, tenth, and twelfth graders, involving youth between thirteen and eighteen years of age, decreased slightly between 1997 and 1998. Similarly, youth in these grades showed some decline in using illicit drugs during the 12-month period prior to the survey. Nevertheless, the use of such substances is still widespread.

The magnitude of this problem is well illustrated by the following examples:

- The proportion of students who indicated that they smoked at all during the thirty days prior to a national study had decreased by 1.9 percent over the previous two years among eighth graders (to 19.1 percent), by 2.8 percent among tenth graders (to 27.6 percent), and by 1.4 percent among twelfth graders (to 35.1 percent). However, in a nationally representative sample of students in grades 9 to 12, the study found that 70.2 percent of all students had tried cigarette smoking, 36.4 percent had smoked on one or more days in the thirty days prior to the survey, and 9.5 percent of students had used smokeless tobacco on one or more days prior to the survey.

- An estimated 3 million underage smokers purchase 947 million packs of cigarettes and 26 million cans of smokeless tobacco each year.

- According to a national survey of students in grades 9 to 12, 79.1 percent reported having initiated alcohol use. In addition, 50.8 percent reported having had at least one drink on one or more days in the thirty days prior to the survey, and 33 percent of high school seniors reported being drunk at least once in that thirty-day period.

- Marijuana continues to be the most widely used illicit drug, with 22 percent of all eighth graders in 1998 saying that they had used marijuana and 49 percent of all twelfth graders reporting that they had done so.

- According to a nationwide survey conducted by the Centers for Disease Control and Prevention, 8.2 percent of students had used some form of cocaine, 3.3 percent had used cocaine on one or more days in the thirty days prior to the survey, 17 percent had used other illegal drugs (e.g., LSD or heroin), and 16 percent had used inhalants.

Unsafe Sex, Teenage Pregnancy, and Teenage Parenting
Adolescents have always engaged in sex. Indeed, historical records indicate that sexually transmitted diseases (STDs) and pregnancy have always been problems among this age group. What is different today, however, is the extent of adolescents' involvement in sex and the increasingly younger ages at which this involvement occurs.

Consider the following examples:

- More teenagers today are initiating sexual intercourse before age thirteen than in the past. For example, 10.8 percent of ninth graders report having had sexual intercourse before age thirteen compared to 4.7 percent of twelfth graders. And among girls younger than fifteen, the incidence of pregnancy rose 4.1 percent between 1980 and 1988—a rate higher than for any other adolescent age group.

- In 1997, 61.9 percent of high school seniors reported having had sexual intercourse and 21 percent of high school seniors reported having had four or more sexual partners. Seven percent of ninth graders reported similar activities. Among sexually active female adolescents overall, 27 percent of those fifteen to seventeen years old, and 16 percent of those eighteen to nineteen years old, said that they use no method of contracep-

tion. The proportions of Latino, African American, and European American adolescent females not using contraception are 35 percent, 23 percent, and 19 percent, respectively.

- Each year, 1 million adolescents nationwide become pregnant; about half have babies. This amounts to about one baby born every minute.

- In 1991, 38 percent of the pregnancies experienced by fifteen- to nineteen-year-olds ended in abortion.

- Among the married adolescents who give birth, 46 percent go on welfare within four years, compared to 73 percent of unmarried adolescents.

- Youth between fifteen and nineteen years of age account for 25 percent of STD cases each year. Moreover, 6.4 percent of adolescent runaways, who number between 750,000 and 1 million each year in America, register positive on serum tests for the AIDS virus. These runaway youth often engage in unsafe sex, prostitution, and intravenous drug use.

- Among all young women ages fifteen through nineteen, 15 percent of births occurred out of wedlock in 1960, compared to 76 percent in 1996.

- By age nineteen, 15 percent of African American males have fathered a child; the corresponding rates for Latinos and European Americans are 11 percent and 7 percent, respectively.

- Thirty-nine percent of the fathers of children born to fifteen-year-old mothers, and 47 percent of the fathers of children born to sixteen-year-old mothers, are older than twenty years of age.

- About 20 percent of adolescent girls in grades 8 through 11 are subjected to sexual harassment, and 75 percent of girls under the age of fourteen who have had sexual relations are victims of rape. In short, sex is often forced on adolescent girls.
- About $25 billion in federal money is spent annually to provide social, health, and welfare services to families begun by teenagers.

School Underachievement, School Failure, and Dropout

About 25 percent of the approximately 48 million children and adolescents enrolled in America's 82,000 public elementary and secondary schools are at risk for school failure. Indeed, each year about 700,000 youth drop out of school, and about 25 percent of all eighteen- and nineteen-year-olds have not graduated from high school. The costs to society—and to the youth themselves—are enormous.

Remaining in school is the single most important action that adolescents can take to improve their future economic prospects. For example, in 1992, a high school graduate earned almost $6,000 per year more than a high school dropout. In the same year, college graduates earned an average income of $32,629, compared to only $18,737 earned by high school graduates. Completion of a professional degree added $40,000 to the average annual income of college graduates.

Despite these advantages, however, youth continue to drop out of school. Moreover, even among those who remain in school, many do not achieve at the levels expected of them.

There are numerous indicators of the seriousness of the problems of underachievement, school failure, and dropout among today's youth. Some examples follow:

- Although U.S. eighth graders scored above the international average in both mathematics and science, they were outperformed in science by students in nine other countries and in mathematics by students in twenty other countries. U.S. twelfth graders scored below the international average in both mathematics and science assessments.
- About 4.5 million ten- to fourteen-year-olds are one or more years behind in their modal grade level.
- In 1996, about five out of every hundred young adults enrolled in high school dropped out. In 1997, 9.5 percent of Hispanics were dropouts, compared with 3.6 percent of European American students and 5 percent of African American students.
- Over the last decade, between 300,000 and 500,000 tenth-, eleventh-, and twelfth-grade students dropped out.
- At any point in time, about 18 percent of dropouts eighteen to twenty-four years old, and 30 percent of dropouts twenty-four to twenty-nine years old, are under the supervision of the criminal justice system. Among African Americans, the corresponding percentages are about 50 and 75 percent.
- In 1997, youth living in families with incomes in the lowest 20 percent of all family incomes were nearly seven times as likely as

their peers from families in the top 20 percent of the income distribution to drop out of high school.

- Each added year of secondary education reduces the probability of public welfare dependency in adulthood by 35 percent.

Delinquency, Crime, and Violence
Of all the problems confronting contemporary youth, no set of issues has attracted as much public concern and public fear as youth delinquency and violent crimes. People point not only to the increased number of youth gangs in urban centers as well as rural communities but also to their territorial battles, drug trafficking, shootings, and random street violence. Also observable today is the increasingly younger ages of the gang members themselves.

The magnitude of such problems as delinquency, crime, and violence among youth is daunting. To illustrate:

- In 1996, 79 out of every 1,000 students (ages twelve to eighteen) were implicated in thefts at school. Theft accounted for about 62 percent of all crime against students at school that year.
- Although the Violent Crime Index arrest rate among juveniles dropped 23 percent between 1994 and 1997, the 1997 rate was still about 30 percent greater than the average rate in the years between 1980 and 1988.
- Nationwide, juveniles commit about one in four of all violent crimes. In 1997, according to victims' reports, 70,000 serious violent crimes involved one or more juvenile offenders between the ages of twelve and seventeen.

- In 1997, about 2,100 murder victims were younger than eighteen years of age—a level 27 percent below that of the peak year of 1993, when 2,900 juveniles were murdered. During the same year, the number of juveniles murdered in the United States exceeded, by more than 300, that in a typical year during the 1980s. About 6 juveniles are murdered daily.
- In 1997, 84 percent of murdered juveniles aged thirteen or older were killed with a firearm. No other age group in that year exhibited a higher proportion of firearm homicides.
- The National Center for Health Statistics lists homicide as the third leading cause of death for children aged five to fourteen and the second leading cause of death for youth aged fifteen to twenty-four.
- At any point in time, about 20 percent of all African American youth are involved with the criminal justice system.
- In 1997, 26 percent of juvenile arrests were arrests of females. Between 1993 and 1997, arrests of juvenile females increased more (or decreased less) than male arrests in most offense categories.
- Even with the large increase in female rates, the 1997 Violent Crime Index arrest rate for juvenile males was five times the arrest rate for juvenile females.
- African Americans experience rates of rape, aggravated assault, and armed robbery that are approximately 25 percent higher than those for European Americans, rates of motor vehicle theft that

are about 70 percent higher, rates of robbery victimization that are about 150 percent higher, and rates of homicide that are between 600 and 700 percent higher.

- In a nationally representative sample of ten- to sixteen-year-olds, 25 percent experienced an assault or abuse in the previous year. Approximately 20 percent of the documented child abuse and neglect cases in 1992 involved young adolescents between the ages of ten and thirteen years.

- The suicide rate among adolescents aged fifteen to nineteen has nearly doubled from 5.9 per 100,000 in 1970 to 9.7 per 100,000 in 1996. And among youth aged fifteen to twenty-four, the suicide rate has increased from 12.9 per 100,000 in 1992 to 14.9 per 100,000 in 1994.

- In 1993, the cost of providing emergency transportation, medical care, hospital stays, rehabilitation, and related treatment for American firearm victims aged ten through nineteen was $407 million.

- An estimate of the current value of preventing a single youth from leaving school and turning to drugs and crime as a way of life is $1.7–$2.3 million.

All told, about 50 percent of America's youth are at risk for engaging in unhealthy, unproductive, even life-threatening behaviors—a crisis the country needs to address promptly and thoroughly.

Richard M. Lerner
Daniel F. Perkins

See also Accidents; Aggression; Alcohol Use, Risk Factors in; Bumps in the Road to Adulthood; Eating Problems; Juvenile Crime; Peer Pressure; Rebellion; Self-Injury; Sexual Behavior Problems; Sexually Transmitted Diseases; Substance Use and Abuse; Teenage Parenting: Consequences; Youth Gangs

References and further reading
Carnegie Council on Adolescent Development. 1995. *Great Transitions: Preparing Adolescents for a New Century.* New York: Carnegie Corporation.
Children's Defense Fund. 1996. *The State of America's Children.* Washington, DC: Children's Defense Fund.
Dryfoos, Joy G. 1990. *Adolescents at Risk: Prevalence and Prevention.* New York: Oxford University Press.
Johnston, Lloyd D., Jerald G. Bachman, and Patrick M. O'Malley. 1999. *The Monitoring of the Future Study.* Washington, DC: U.S. Department of Health and Human Services.
Lerner, Richard M. 1995. *America's Youth in Crisis: Challenges and Options for Programs and Policies.* Thousand Oaks, CA: Sage.
Lerner, Richard M., and Nancy L. Galambos. 1998. "Adolescent Development: Challenges and Opportunities for Research, Programs, and Policies." Pp. 413–446 in *Annual Review of Psychology,* Vol. 49. Edited by J. T. Spence. Palo Alto, CA: Annual Reviews.
National Center of Education Statistics. 1997. *Digest of Education Statistics, 1997.* Washington, DC: National Center of Education Statistics.
U.S. Department of Health and Human Services. 1996, 1998. *Trends in the Well-Being of America's Children and Youth.* Washington, DC: Child Trends.

Risk Perception

Speculation about adolescents' competence in recognizing and assessing risk has existed since the time of Aristotle. Adolescents are frequently portrayed as believing they are invulnerable to harm, a portrayal that implies a compromised ability to judge risks. Yet at the same time, others view adolescents as being able to make informed and competent decisions, and having capabilities equivalent to those of adults. Perceptions of adolescents as incompetent to judge risks provide the basis for many legal limitations on adolescents' rights, while selected policies that allow adolescents to take part in research or to undergo certain types of medical treatments without parental permission reflect a belief in adolescents' competence to judge risks. Resolving these contradictory views of adolescents' capabilities to judge risks thus has important and far-reaching implications.

Most research on risk perception has focused on adults rather than adolescents. What we have learned from these studies is that risk assessment is inherently subjective, and prone to significant bias. Even experts demonstrate biases under certain conditions. Some of the most pervasive biases occur when people are asked to estimate their own risk status. Adults overestimate the probability that good things will happen to them, and underestimate their own vulnerability to many negative events. They also view their personal risk status as more favorable than the risk status of others. For example, people view themselves as better than average drivers, more likely to live past eighty years of age than others, less likely to die as a result of various factors, and less likely to be harmed by the products they use.

Given the bias in adults' perceptions of risk, it should not surprise us to find that adolescents demonstrate bias as well. Like adults, adolescents are inaccurate in their assessments of risk, overestimating some risks while underestimating others. They, too, view their personal risks as being less than those of their peers. Adolescents also rely on cognitive shortcuts

when assessing risks, a practice that makes them susceptible to bias. However, studies do not show adolescents to be unable to judge risks. Even young adolescents appear to have the ability to consider risks and benefits associated with the consequences of engaging in risky behaviors and events like medical procedures. There is also little evidence to support the notion that adolescents, by virtue of their developmental status, are less likely than adults to perceive themselves as vulnerable to harm. Only three studies have directly compared adolescents' risk judgments with those of adults—an important comparison because it allows us to identify whether adolescents' risk judgments are quantitatively different from those of legal adults. Findings from these studies show that adolescents actually appear to be less likely than adults to see themselves as invulnerable, and only a small minority of adolescents evidenced such perceptions. When asked to judge how risky various situations are, adolescents also judge risks as higher than do adults, and younger adolescents perceive risks as higher than older adolescents.

Does this mean that adolescents are better able to judge risks than adults? Not necessarily. For one thing, they are less accurate than adults. Most people think that risks are higher than they actually are, but adults' judgments are closer to reality. There are also other things that we do not know about how adolescents assess risks that are relevant to their abilities in this regard. For example, do risk assessments that take place in research settings bear resemblance to those that occur spontaneously in adolescents? What effects does emotion have on adolescents' risk judgments?

There are, of course, many other factors that influence perceptions of risk. One of the most important is experience. People who engage in risky behaviors see the risks as lower than do people who do not engage in the behaviors. This probably occurs because most individuals who take risks do not suffer negative consequences, and thus do not perceive their behavior as dangerous. Judgments of lower risk among people with behavioral experience suggest that some of the age-linked variation in risk judgments may be attributable to experiential differences, since older people generally have more experience. Perceptions of control are also important. When people believe that risks are controllable, they tend to downplay them.

Perceptions of risk are viewed as important because of the role they are thought to play in people's behavior. Conventional wisdom holds that people avoid things they think are harmful, but longitudinal studies of adolescents have not been conducted to confirm this. If we think of risk judgments as reflecting generalized feelings of vulnerability or anxiety, it would make sense that these feelings would inhibit individuals from engaging in behaviors. But it is also possible, and likely, that other factors motivate adolescents to engage in risky behaviors, and that risk judgments play only a small role.

The actual risks posed by many of the behaviors we want to protect adolescents from are serious but small. Few adults would suggest providing adolescents with information about the actual statistical risk. On the other hand, continuing to emphasize the likelihood of negative outcomes could be counterproductive if young people already feel a sense of vulnerability; it could also backfire as adolescents become aware of the reality that most experiences with risky behaviors do not lead to negative outcomes. Given these considerations, perhaps a more appropriate goal for educating youth about health risks is to find ways to make small probabilities real to adolescents, without raising anxiety to unproductive levels. Efforts to decrease public and scientific perceptions of "the invulnerable adolescent" may also be warranted. Such perceptions can perpetuate negative views about young people that can have far-reaching implications for adolescent-related programs, policies, and legal statutes.

Susan Millstein

See also Accidents; Cognitive Development; Conduct Problems; Conformity; Decision Making; Delinquency, Mental Health, and Substance Abuse Problems; Ethnocentrism; Peer Pressure; Personal Fable; Thinking; Youth Culture

References and further reading
Cohn, Lawrence, Susan Macfarlane, Claudia Yanez, and Walter Imai. 1995. "Risk-Perception: Differences between Adolescents and Adults." *Health Psychology* 14, no. 3: 217–222.
Gochman, David, and Jean-Francois Saucier. 1982. "Perceived Vulnerability in Children and Adolescents." *Health Education Quarterly* 9, nos. 2 and 3: 46–58, 142–154.
Halpern-Felsher, Bonnie L., Susan G. Millstein, Jonathan M. Ellen, Nancy E. Adler, Jeanne Tschann, and Michael C. Biehl. In press. "The Role of Behavioral Experience in Judging Risks." *Health Psychology* 20: 120–126.
Jacobs-Quadrel, Marilyn, Baruch Fischhoff, and Wendy Davis. 1993. "Adolescent (In)vulnerability." *American Psychologist* 48, no. 2: 102–116.
Millstein, Susan G. 1993. "Perceptual, Attributional, and Affective Processes in Perceptions of Vulnerability throughout the Life Span." Pp. 55–65 in *Adolescent Risk Taking.* Edited by Nancy Bell and Robert Bell. Newbury Park, CA: Sage Publications.
Urberg, Kathryn, and Rochelle Robbins. 1984. "Perceived Vulnerability in

Adolescents to the Health Consequences of Cigarette Smoking." *Preventive Medicine* 13: 367–376.

Rites of Passage

In its traditional sense, a rite of passage can most easily be thought of as walking across a one-way bridge: It represents a journey from one way of being, through a transformational period of change and growth, into a new way of being. This process can be described as one way because people who cross are usually not allowed or encouraged to return. These rites of passage, also called coming-of-age ceremonies or initiations, usually occur at puberty and serve at least three important purposes: (1) marking and facilitating the transition of children into adulthood, (2) transmitting and maintaining cultural values, traditions, and beliefs from one generation to the next, and (3) influencing the development of adolescents' selves within a given cultural context. Rites of passage are an example of structured cultural practices that vary from one culture to another. Despite this variation, rites of passage have been identified in many cultures around the world and tend to be ceremonial, ritualized, and festive occasions.

The most successful and significant rites of passage tend to be found in highly religious, seasonally based, stable, and preindustrial societies, where significant importance is given to individual development and the individual's role within the larger society. Researchers generally agree that most rites of passage have some characteristics in common, including a generalized three-phase structure: (1) rites of separation, (2) rites of transition, and (3) rites of incorporation. The first phase involves the physical or sym-

bolic separation from an individual's old habits, responsibilities, support group, and identity. The separation process may involve fear, uncertainty, crisis, and a feeling of instability.

The rite-of-transition phase represents a time of change and development within a new support group. During this phase, participants are taught about the knowledge, history, and religion of the culture as well as their new responsibilities as adults. In addition, the transitional phase may involve learning humility, respect for elders, and gaining an appreciation for the growth and change that they are going to experience. It is not uncommon for the transitional stage to include one or more forms of physical mutilation, ranging from cutting of the hair to tattooing, circumcision (for boys), excision (for girls), ritual scarring, piercing or cutting of the ears, or other ritualized practices. These physical rites serve to mark the participant in a permanent manner, in such a way that they are now the same as other adults. The final stage of incorporation represents a return to the community, physically and symbolically, of a transformed individual who is now widely accepted and respected as an adult. The incorporation phase brings celebration, new habits, roles, responsibilities, support groups, and peers, as well as a growing sense of stability and comfort in the role of adulthood.

In addition to a three-phase structure, successful rites of passage are (1) recognized and valued by the culture as a critically important part of becoming an adult, (2) usually public in nature so that the entire community participates or is at least aware of the events, and (3) usually finish with some sort of significant closure, such that the participant and the community feel certain that the

Rites of passage represent culturally specific transitions from youth to adulthood. (Ted Spiegel/Corbis)

participant has been fully transformed into an adult.

The following is a generic example of a rite of passage compiled from several different tribes in Australia. Boys are expected to live with their mothers and the other children until the rite of separation. This expectation clearly separates the men from the boys. At a certain time, chosen by the elders, boys are violently separated from their mothers by the men of the tribe. Following the separation, boys are often secluded and may be painted white or black, thus symbolizing their death as boys. Often, the participants are considered to be dead by the

tribe for the remainder of the rite of passage. During this time, the boys endure a period of physical and mental weakening in seclusion. This experience will deepen the sense of permanent separation from childhood and may also be intended to inspire humility, spiritual awakening, and respect for elders. Following this, the boys are symbolically resurrected and begin the rites of transition, during which they are taught the laws of the tribe, adult rituals, dances, ceremonies, myths, and other secret knowledge. Before the boys are returned to the community (rites of incorporation) they complete a traditional religious ceremony, which often involves some form of physical mutilation, such as circumcision or ritual scarring, that will identify them to all others as a full adult member.

Traditional rites of passage such as these are not widely used in the westernized world. Culturally specific rites of passage, such as the Jewish bar mitzvah or the Christian confirmation, are still in use, but even these traditional ceremonies no longer have the ability to serve as effective rites of passage for all, or even the majority, of adolescents in any given country. As cultures become increasingly large and diverse in beliefs, traditions, and values, it also becomes increasingly difficult to have a single effective rite of passage from adolescence into adulthood. Other reasons for this difficulty include industrialization and formalized education, both of which may postpone the achievement of social adulthood until the early twenties. Some researchers have argued that graduation from high school represents a rite of passage for adolescents in the United States. While graduation is important and valued, high school graduates do not experience separation, training in being an adult, or a return to society as a fully accepted adult member. Indeed, high school graduation is not even an attainable goal for all members of society. Although eighteen–year-olds are considered legally adult, they continue to experience numerous restrictions on what they are allowed to do, and many adults do not view an eighteen-year-old as an adult.

Other researchers have found that adolescents in cultures lacking traditional rites of passage will develop their own. Examples include smoking, sexual experimentation, gang initiation ceremonies, and the use of drugs or alcohol. Although these experiences may demonstrate a desire to be seen as an adult or to belong to a specific group, they do not provide for a successful, culturally sanctioned rite of passage, which helps the individual achieve adulthood in the eyes of the larger community.

The lack of universal rites of passage within westernized cultures has been identified as a potential cause of cultural problems ranging from teen violence to the breakdown of marriage. Although it may be true that westernized cultures often lack widely accepted rites of passage, it is more likely that the long-term and broad-ranging effects of the industrial revolution and formalized education (which helped to make rites of passage obsolete) are largely responsible for the ongoing cultural changes we are experiencing. Westernized cultures have, moreover, developed alternative mediums for the formation of adults, such as an extended period of education, internships, and job training. Current attempts to develop culturally sanctioned rites of passage within smaller communities do exist, and it will be some time before we know whether they have been effective.

The reasons for the existence of rites of passage are not well understood. Researchers have attempted to identify patterns and theoretical associations between different cultures that have rites of passage. Unfortunately, such attempts have been largely unsuccessful at pinpointing precise biological, ecological, financial, or geographic reasons for their existence. What is clear, however, is that rites of passage provide a culturally supported medium for the education and training of children and their transition into adulthood, thus maintaining social structure, customs, and values within a given culture over many generations.

Benjamin D. Locke

See also College; Dating; Employment: Positive and Negative Consequences; Identity; Menarche; Puberty: Hormone Changes; Puberty: Physical Changes; Religion, Spirituality, and Belief Systems; Self; Sexual Behavior; Transition to Young Adulthood; Transitions of Adolescence; Why Is There an Adolescence?; Youth Gangs

References and further reading
Alves, Julio. 1993. "Transgressions and Transformations: Initiation Rites among Urban Portuguese Boys." *American Anthropologist* 95, no. 4: 894–928.
Dunham, Richard M., Jeannie S. Kidwell, and Stephen M. Wilson. 1986. "Rites of Passage at Adolescence: A Ritual Process Paradigm." *Journal of Adolescent Research* 1, no. 2: 139–154.
Gennep, Arnold Van. 1960. *The Rites of Passage.* Translated by Monika B. Vizedom and Gabrielle L. Caffee. Chicago: University of Chicago Press. (Original work published in 1908.)
Kett, Joseph F. 1977. *Rites of Passage: Adolescence in America, 1790 to the Present.* New York: Basic Books.
MacDonald, Kevin. 1991. "Rites of Passage." Pp. 944–945 in *Encyclopedia of Adolescence*, Vol 2. Edited by Richard M. Lerner, Anne C. Petersen, and Jeanne Brooks-Gunn. New York: Garland.

Shweder, Richard A., Jacqueline Goodnow, Giyoo Hatano, Robert A. LeVine, Hazel Markus, and Peggy Miller. 1998. "The Cultural Psychology of Development: One Mind, Many Mentalities." Chap. 15 in *Handbook of Child Psychology.* Vol. 1, *Theoretical Models of Human Development.* New York: Wiley.

Zeagans, Susan, and Leonard Zeagans. 1979. "Bar Mitzvah: A Rite for a Transitional Age." *The Psychoanalytic Review* 66, no. 1: 117–132.

Runaways

The National Statistical Survey on Runaway Youth, completed by the National Opinion Research Corporation, is the most comprehensive study ever completed on runaway behavior. The results revealed that 5.7 percent of households with teenagers had at least one runaway incident the year of the study. Extrapolations to the general population of the United States suggest over 1 million runaway episodes per year. According to some figures, 71 percent of runaways are between the ages of ten and seventeen years (National Opinion Research Corporation, 1976, p. 14; Adams, 1997). Based on an analysis of a variety of studies, the estimate is that one in three adolescents consider running away at some time, that one in five actually run away, and that girls are more likely to run away than boys (Adams, 1997).

About half of teens who run away do not run far and stay with friends, relatives, or neighbors. The majority of runaways are gone for brief periods of time, most commonly overnight. For those who stay away longer, more than 80 percent return or reconnect with the family in one month.

There are clear patterns in adolescents' psychological and social circumstances that predict running away. Adolescents with a psychological profile that includes a combination of low self-esteem, signs of depression, a sense of loss of control, impulsiveness, and a history of poor interpersonal relationships are likely to run away. Often the home environment is filled with conflict, weak involvement by parents, poor communication, and perhaps physical or sexual abuse. Often parents are ineffective in supervising their children. Parents of runaway adolescent boys seem to be unable to control their sons, whereas parents of runaway adolescent girls are overcontrolling and punitive with their daughters.

The list of potential negative consequences are staggering. The risks include alcohol and substance abuse, coercive sexual behavior, physical injury, sexually transmitted diseases, confrontation with the law, unwanted pregnancy, general health and nutrition problems, and loss of educational training opportunities, among many other problems.

The two greatest threats to the runaway adolescent are abusing drugs and contracting a sexually transmitted disease (Adams, 1997). Runaways are very likely to sell drugs to support their habit, and the potential for addiction is extremely high. To get along, many runaways become sex workers. Prostitution in North America is filled with young teenage boys and girls, doing "tricks" for drugs or money. The threat of contracting HIV is large and looming for these street kids.

For the unfortunate number of young runaway women who become pregnant, their future is often dismal. Early pregnancy can often have negative health consequences for the mother, and it also places the fetus and baby at risk for numerous medical problems. Looking further into these young women's lives,

If adolescents who run away from home live on the streets they may have a life filled with insecurity, fear, depression, alienation, and risks to survival. (Steve Raymer/Corbis)

the young children of a runaway adolescent woman are at great risk of becoming socially maladjusted, prone to temper tantrums and impulsivity, and having a variety of forms of learning disabilities.

There are a variety of things that parents and families can do to avoid serious runaway behavior. The formula is simple. Talk to teenagers, listen to their problems and issues, and don't make light of what they consider serious. Provide guidance without telling them what they have to do. Simple indirect suggestions, encouragement to face their teenage issues, and reassurance that the teen can deal with problems are the tools of good parenting. Allow teenagers to express views that are different from the parents; recognize that the adolescent

and parent can differ on some points and still love and respect each other.

Promote positive peer relationships and healthy teen activities. Get teenagers involved in groups where the adolescent has a chance of making friends. Don't devalue or degrade your teenager's friends. Encourage involvement in school activities, sports, support groups, volunteer activities, and the like.

If a teenager runs away from home, she is likely to return. Often she returns angry, afraid, depressed, and uncertain about the family's response to coming back home. The most frequent reaction, unfortunately, is for families to express anger and frustration as the youth returns. The teenager needs instead to be welcomed, recognized, and told she is loved and needed. Most often families fail to talk about the issues that precipitated the runaway episode. Instead, families often settle into either a form of cold war where people don't speak to each other or a series of small confrontations that keep the emotions hot and frustrating. Neither withdrawal nor rejection will help the runaway readjust. Instead, a series of open and frank discussions should be held about the issues that the teenager sees in her life and family. The goal should be to identify the issues and work together to find an acceptable compromise. This means, of course, that both the adolescent and the family need to make changes.

Often it is best for all concerned to enter into family therapy. A family therapist uses a systemic approach to healing and recovery. When the whole family participates, including siblings, the underlying family issues are likely to be exposed and addressed in a therapeutic discourse. Considerable success has been observed using systemic or multisystemic approaches to healing and recovery among adolescent populations.

It seems that there are two major forms of runaways (see pp. 418–419 in Gullotta, Adams, and Markstrom for a full discussion). One form involves runaways who have a home where they have a chance to return. These families want the runaway back home, safe and sound, loved and involved with the family. The other form includes throwaways, children and teenagers who are told to go and not to return. Often this form of runaway behavior is an action taken out of necessity, as a way to survive. The former form of runaway behavior is likely to be resolved over time by making readjustments in the dynamics of the family. The latter form is more complex, and those teenagers who recover often do so outside of the family. Throwaways are left to the streets and/or social services that will embrace them. To this date, they remain a major challenge to the social and mental health agencies in cities around the world. When life on the street gives a young person more than he could have at home, we all know the circumstances at home are destructive. Children of the streets live a life of insecurity, fear, depression, alienation, and bare survival.

The problems of runaways are extremely hard to address. Most of these teenagers are angry, hurt, and often rejected by family and society. Runaway shelters provide a temporary fix. In some states, the social and legal system allow a formal declaration of independence and assistance is provided. The use of residential foster homes has brought mixed results. Communities continue to struggle with finding a satisfactory solution to this social problem.

Gerald R. Adams

See also Family Relations; Homeless Youth; Parent-Adolescent Relations; Programs for Adolescents; Rebellion; School Dropouts

References and further reading
Adams, G. R. 1997. "Runaway Youth." Pp. 826–828 in *Primary Pediatric Care*, 3rd ed. Edited by R. A. Hoekelman et al. St. Louis: Mosby.
Adams, G. R., and G. Munro. 1979. "Portrait of North American Runaways: A Critical Review." *Journal of Youth and Adolescence* 8: 359–371.
Gullotta, T. P., G. R. Adams, and C. Markstrom. 2000. *The Adolescent Experience*. New York: Academic Press.
National Opinion Research Corporation. 1976. *National Statistical Survey on Runaway Youth*. Princeton, NJ: NORC.
Young, R. L., et al. 1983. "Runaways: A Review of Negative Consequences." *Family Relations* 32: 275–289.

S

Sadness

Sadness is an emotion that people of all ages and cultures experience once in a while. Sadness involves emotional discomfort, lethargy, and lack of pleasure or interest in enjoyable activities. Negative events can cause a person to feel sad (e.g., death, the loss of a friend, or something hoped for that does not happen). In other cases, the reasons for sadness may be less obvious. During adolescence, teens often experience frequent and intense periods of sadness, which may include feelings of hopelessness and loneliness, and negative feelings about one's self. These feelings are often an emotional reaction to the many changes that teens experience physically, psychologically, and socially. When, however, sad feelings persist for more than two weeks and involve other symptoms, this may be a sign of an illness known as depression.

Approximately 10–15 percent of teens experience brief, occasional depressive symptoms. However, 3 percent of teens experience a more chronic mood disorder known as dysthymia, and 5 percent develop major depressive disorder. Symptoms of depression include changes in energy level and sleep patterns and changes in weight that are not caused by dieting. Other symptoms are excessive crying, lowered self-esteem, feelings of guilt or self-blame, constant stomachaches or headaches, and loss of interest in friends. Depressed adolescents are often extremely self-critical and perceive all events negatively. Adolescents with depression may perceive their selves as worthless and their future as hopeless. This negative pattern of thinking can place depressed teens at risk for committing suicide. Suicide is currently the third leading cause of death among teenagers (Centers for Disease Control, 2000).

Abrupt changes in mood are common during adolescence and can involve intense feelings of sadness that occur suddenly. These feelings can cause adolescents to withdraw from social activities and desire to be left alone. During puberty, endocrine glands such as the pituitary, thyroid, and adrenal glands secrete hormones into the body. Once activated, these glands cause the body's metabolism to increase and rapid growth to occur. Increased spurts of growth coupled with changing levels of hormones can intensify an adolescent's emotional experiences. For example, girls between the ages of twelve and eighteen years produce 60 percent higher levels of the hormone prolactin than boys do, which is released in tears when individuals cry. Crying is a normal process that relaxes muscles, lowers blood pressure, and releases emotional tension. Girls report crying four times more often than boys do during adolescence.

As in all periods of life, sadness is an emotion experienced by many adolescents. (Skjold Photographs)

The pituitary glands activate the development of secondary sex characteristics such as female breasts and male facial hair, which can be noticeable to others and make teens feel self-conscious about their bodies. Teens may also feel frustrated and not understand the source of heightened sexual impulses that can emerge as the pituitary gland releases hormones. For girls, puberty involves the beginning of menstruation, which is often accompanied by increased body fat and weight gain. Adolescent girls often report lower body satisfaction and negative feelings about their selves as their bodies become different from current images of thinness idealized in the media. Regardless of the actual weight gained, girls who see their body image negatively are more likely to experience depressed feelings. Girls who get their period at a younger age than peers may feel unable to talk to their friends who have not yet experienced this marker of maturity. These girls may be less prepared and experience greater self-consciousness as they deal with these changes separate from peers.

During adolescence, teens often try to define their personal values and show who they are as individuals distinct from their parents. As teens seek independence from their families, they also have a strong need to identify with peers and belong to a social group. Friends often help each other by sharing similar personal experiences, providing emotional support, and accepting each other socially. Being accepted into a social group, however, can involve conforming (going along) with behaviors that an adolescent feels uncomfortable with. Peers may pressure adolescents to participate in delinquent acts, experiment with drugs and alcohol, or engage in sexual acts that they are not ready for. Adolescents who don't conform to their friends' standards may be ridiculed, ostracized, or rejected.

Adolescents who do not share the values of their peers may face social rejection as they reveal an identity that is different from the majority of teens. Adolescents who feel that they don't belong to a social group may feel helpless and lonely. Minority groups such as gay and lesbian adolescents are at especially high risk for experiencing social isolation and sadness. Gay and lesbian adolescents may feel separate from their peers and receive little or no social support from friends or family when they reveal their sexual orientation. Similarly, other minority groups face prejudice from others, experience discrimination, and are exposed to negative stereotypes of their group depicted in the media. Some teens may even face life-threatening aggression from others who see them as different. The experience of not being accepted by peers for who one is as a person can contribute to sad, depressed feelings.

Everyone gets the blues now and then, but generally these feelings pass. When sad feelings don't seem to go away, they may be symptoms of clinical depression. Depression can affect an adolescent's ability to concentrate in school, remember things, or make decisions. Often depressive symptoms can keep an adolescent feeling despair, helplessness, and hopelessness about the future. Suicide may seem like the only solution that will solve one's problems.

Rates of teen suicide have risen dramatically in the past decade, with 9.5 per 100,000 adolescents aged fifteen to nineteen committing suicide in 1999 (Centers for Disease Control, 2000). The rate of suicide is six times higher during adolescence than childhood. Boys are four times more likely to commit suicide, but adolescent girls are twice as likely to attempt suicide. Many adolescents use alcohol or drugs to ease sadness and to forget about their problems. Unfortunately, alcohol and drug use often leads to more serious problems, such as motor vehicle accidents, school failure, involvement in crime, unwanted pregnancy, and health problems. For thousands of teens, early substance abuse can lead to alcohol dependency, which serves to further complicate and increase problems.

As common as occasional sadness may be, individuals who work with teens need to be aware that sadness can lead to more serious problems.

Angela Howell

See also Coping; Counseling; Depression; Emotional Abuse; Emotions; Fears; Loneliness; Peer Victimization in School; Personality; Youth Outlook

References and further reading
Arbetter, Sandra. 1995. "Am I Normal? Those Teen Years." *Current Health* 2, no. 21: 6–7.
Centers for Disease Control and Prevention. 2000. "Profile of the Nation's Health." In *CDC Factbook 2000/2001*. Washington, DC: Department of Health and Human Services.
Frey, William H. 1985. Crying: *The Mystery of Tears*. New York: Harper and Row.
Garrison, Carol Z., et al. 1997. "Incidence of Major Depressive Disorder and Dysthymia in Young Adolescents." *Journal of the Academy of Child and Adolescent Psychiatry* 36: 458–465.
Gullota, Thomas P., Gerald R. Adams, and Carol A. Markstrom. 2000. *The Adolescent Experience*, 4th ed. San Diego: Academic Press.
Gullota, Thomas P., Gerald R. Adams, and Richard Montemayor, eds. 1995. *Substance Misuse in Adolescence*. Thousand Oaks, CA: Sage.
Kist, Jay. 1997. "Dealing with Depression." *Current Health* 23, no. 5: 25–28.
Peterson, Anne C., Nancy Leffert, and Barbara Graham. 1995. "Adolescent Development and the Emergence of Sexuality." *Suicide and Life-Threatening Behaviors* 25: 4–17.
Powers, Mick J. 1999. "Sadness and Its Disorders." Pp. 497–519 in *Handbook of Cognition and Emotion*. Edited by Tim Dalgleish and Mick J. Power. Chichester, UK: Wiley.
Rierdan, Jill, and Elissa Koff. 1997. "Weight, Weight-Related Aspects of Body Image, and Depression in Early Adolescent Girls." *Adolescence* 32, no. 127: 615–625.
Rutter, Michael. 1991. "Age Changes in Depressive Disorders: Some Developmental Considerations." Pp. 273–300 in *The Development of Emotion Regulation and Dysregulation*. Edited by Judy Garber and Kenneth Dodge. Cambridge: Cambridge University Press.
Smucker, Mervin R., Edward W. Craighead, Linda Wilcoxen, and Barbara J. Green. 1986. "Normative and Reliability Data for the Children's Depression Inventory." *Journal of Abnormal Child Psychology* 14, no. 1: 25–39.

School Dropouts

A student who withdraws from school before completing the graduation requirements as defined by the school is commonly identified as a school dropout. The exact definition of a dropout varies widely across states and school districts, and even among schools within the same district. For example, some schools may not include students who drop out over the summer, while others do include them in the dropout total. On average, 6 percent of students in the United States drop out of school each year (U.S. Department of Education, 2000). In October 1999, some 3.8 million sixteen- to twenty-four-year-olds were not enrolled in a high school program and had not completed high school (U.S. Department of Education, 2001). Major factors that contribute to a student's dropping out of school are poverty, location of residence and school, the student's behavior in school, and the student's academic performance. School dropouts are more likely to develop mental and physical problems and to require social services during their lifetimes. Thus, dropping out of school is a complicated social problem, which has multiple causes and a number of negative consequences for the individual and for society in general.

The U.S. Student Dropout Rate

There are three different methods of calculating the dropout rate. The *event dropout rate* indicates the proportion of students who drop out in a single year without completing school. In October 1997, 5 percent of students who were in high school the previous October dropped out of high school sometime during the year (U.S. Department of Education, 2000). The *status dropout rate* indicates the proportion of all individuals in the population who have not completed their respective school and were not enrolled at a given point in time. In 1993, the national status dropout rate for sixteen- to twenty-four-year-olds was 11 percent. The status dropout rate is much higher than the event dropout rate, since it reflects the number of students in a given age range who have dropped out of school over a number of years, rather than the rate for a single year. The third dropout calculation method is the *cohort dropout rate,* which reflects the percentage of dropouts in a single age group or specific grade level over a given period of time. The cohort rate for sophomores in 1990 and 1992 was 5.6 percent (U.S. Department of Education, 2001).

Nationwide, all dropout rates have declined during the last few decades. The event dropout rate for ages fifteen through twenty-four in grades 10 through 12 has fallen from 6.1 percent in 1972 to 4.5 percent in 1993. Similarly, the status dropout rate for sixteen- to twenty-four-year-olds declined from 14.6 percent in 1972 to 11 percent in 1992 and 1993. The cohort dropout rate for students who were sophomores in 1980 and dropped out between grades 10 and 12 was 11.4 percent, while the cohort rate for a comparable group of 1990 sophomores was 6.2 percent. All the indicators of the dropout rate declined over the last two decades, but they still mean that a large segment of the population is not completing high school. For example, in October 1997, some 3.6 million teenagers were not enrolled in a high school program and had not completed high school (U.S. Department of Education, 2001).

Gender and Racial Differences in Dropout Rates

Although the dropout rates are about the same for males and females, the rates are not the same for students from different ethnic groups or different income levels. In general, rates are higher for minority students and students from disadvantaged backgrounds. For example, Latino teenagers in the United States have higher status dropout rates than either whites or blacks. In 1997, 25.3 percent of Latino young adults were status dropouts, compared to 13.4 percent of blacks and 7.6 percent of whites. Hispanic students were also more likely than white and black students to leave school before completing a high school program: in 1997, 9.5 percent of Hispanics were event dropouts, compared with 3.6 percent of white and 5 percent of black students.

Event dropout rates were not significantly different between white and black students, but rates for American Indians and Alaska Natives are quite high, while those for Asian American students are quite low (U.S. Department of Education, 2001).

Family Characteristics That Contribute to School Dropout

Parents play a critical role in keeping teenagers in school. Family characteristics that influence dropping out of school include such factors as a stressful home environment, low socioeconomic status, minority membership, siblings who did not graduate from high school, single-parent households, poor education of parents, and primary language other than English. In 1997, teenagers living in families with incomes in the lowest 20 percent of all family incomes were nearly seven times as likely as their peers from families in the top 20 percent of the income distribution to drop out of high school (U.S. Department of Education, 2001). Students whose parents did not complete high school had a substantially higher dropout rate than did those whose parents had graduated. Similarly, students whose parents or siblings were dropouts are themselves more likely to drop out than their peers who come from families without any dropouts. In addition, those who marry and have children before graduating from high school are more likely to drop out of school than their peers who stay single and have no children while at school. Finally, the national data indicate that the dropout rate is greater in cities than in other suburban and rural locations, and is highest in the West and South of the United States.

Although risk factors associated with socioeconomic status, family structure, and ethnicity are correlated with dropping out, this does not mean that these factors create school dropouts. Risk factors have an impact on whether a student drops out of school, but most dropouts come from backgrounds that are not usually thought of in connection with risk of school failure. Similarly, the majority of students with any particular risk factor do not drop out. In other words, each individual student creates her school experience in a unique way, and students may drop out or stay in school for different reasons. Thus, most dropouts cannot simply be predicted from their family background. For example, an analysis of the dropouts from the 1980 sophomore class yielded rather surprising results: Sixty-six percent were white, 86 percent spoke English at home, 68 percent came from two-parent families, and 71 percent had never repeated a grade (U.S. Department of Education, 1989).

Individual Characteristics That Contribute to School Dropouts

School dropouts are more likely to fall into the general pattern of academic underachievement and social and emotional problems. They generally perform below their grade level and have problems in school, both with their peers and with the school personnel. Many researchers have found that students with poor grades, who have repeated a grade, who are below average for their grade, or who are frequently absent are more likely to become dropouts than other students. More specifically, truancy, tardiness, suspension, and other disciplinary infractions along with a poor attendance record during the first few months of tenth grade are important indicators of a possible dropout.

Researchers studying why students leave their school before graduating found a number of personality characteristics that are common among dropouts. First, many school dropouts indicate that they are not interested in school and do not believe that the school personnel are there for them when they need them. Dropouts point out that they did not feel as though they belonged to their school and say they were not identified with any part of the school environment. They also expressed that they did not share their decision to drop out with any of the school personnel because they did not believe that anybody in school would have helped them. In some cases, even though students wanted to contact somebody in school, they did not know whom to contact. It was also found that school dropouts are more likely to be transfer students who have experienced more than one school system. Finally, many school dropouts described problems in their family such as divorce, death, separation, and child abuse.

Consequences of Dropping Out of School

After leaving school, dropouts show even higher rates of high-risk behaviors, such as premature sexual activity, early pregnancy, delinquency, crime, violence, alcohol and drug abuse, and suicide. They also experience more isolation from their families and friends. School dropouts have more difficulty getting jobs than do graduates. For example, the unemployment rate for high school dropouts was about 25 percent by the early 1990s, while unemployment for high school graduates stayed around 14 percent. High school dropouts are three times more likely to slip into poverty than their peers who have finished high school (Brown, 1998).

The issue of school dropouts must be considered as a social and economical problem in addition to a personal problem. In addition to individual efforts, dropout prevention requires the efforts of fellow students, parents, teachers, administrators, community-based organizations, and business, as well as governmental agencies. This is particularly critical to respond to multiple contextual and personal contributors of school dropout as well as the diverse individual needs of students at risk for school dropout.

Selcuk Sirin

See also Academic Achievement; Decision Making; Family-School Involvement; High School Equivalency Degree; School Engagement; School, Functions of

References and further reading
Brown, Duane. 1998. *Dropping Out or Hanging In: What You Should Know before Dropping Out of School.* NTC Publishing Group.
Dorn, Sherman. 1996. *Creating the Dropout: An Institutional and Social History of School Failure.* Westport, CT: Praeger.
Dryfoos, Joy G. 1999. *Safe Passage: Making It through Adolescence in a Risky Society.* New York: Oxford University Press.
Fine, Michelle. 1991. *Framing Dropouts: Notes on the Politics of an Urban High School.* Albany: State University of New York Press.
U.S. Department of Education, National Center for Education Statistics. 1989. "Dropout Rates in the United States: 1988." ED 313–947. Washington, DC: U.S. Department of Education.
———. 2000. "Dropout Rates in the United States: 1998." NCES 2000–022. Washington, DC: U.S. Department of Education.
———. http://nces.ed.gov/ The dropout rates reported in this entry were the most recent data available as of January 2000. One can get the latest dropout rates as well as other related statistics from this home page.
———. 2001. "Dropout Rates in the United States: 1999." NCES 2001–022.

Washington, DC: U.S. Department of Education.

West, Linda L., ed. 1991. *Effective Strategies for Dropout Prevention of At-Risk Youth.* Gaithersburg, MA: Aspen.

School Engagement

Any discussion of school engagement involves two ideas. The first is the idea that certain behaviors indicate whether a student is engaged in school. These behaviors include attending school, coming to school prepared, completing school assignments, and participating in class. Other behaviors associated with school engagement are initiating dialogues in the classroom, seeking help when needed, and participating in activities such as sports and clubs.

The other idea behind school engagement is school identification. The degree of school identification depends on whether students feel as though they belong in school and whether they value what school has to offer in the way of an education. Although both school engagement behaviors and school identification are important in determining whether a student stays in school and achieves, in some instances it is the school behavior that is most important, and in other cases it is the school identification that is key.

Many students become engaged in school early on. Due to the positive experiences they have in school and the support they receive from parents and friends, they come to view school as a valuable place to be, a place that can offer them opportunities in the future if they do well in school. Research indicates that students who are engaged in school are more likely to be academically successful than their peers who are not engaged in school. It also indicates that self-esteem (whether one views who one is in a positive or negative manner) and future education expectations (how optimistic and realistic one is about one's future) influence school engagement as well as academic performance.

Although many students are engaged in school early on, as some students progress through school, they begin to disengage from school. For example, as students make the transition between elementary school and middle school, and between middle school and high school, many of them experience frustration and a drop in their self-esteem, which causes them to disengage from school. One reason for this change is that each time students make a transition, they have to become familiar with a new environment. Sometimes those environments are not designed to be developmentally appropriate for students. Let's take the example of middle school. Students in middle school are generally between the ages of eleven and thirteen. Students at this age tend to worry about friendships and romantic relationships with peers, relationships with adults, and gender expectations (e.g., Is it okay for a girl to play sports? Is it okay for a boy to be in a cooking class?), and they are concerned about becoming competent in the areas that are important to them (e.g., sports, academic subjects, music, etc.). Unfortunately, many middle schools are not designed to support students in these areas. Students are often moved from class to class with multiple teachers throughout the day. As a result, teachers don't have enough time to provide students with the one-on-one attention they may desire.

For a variety of reasons, including a lack of money and choosing other priorities, many schools no longer offer activi-

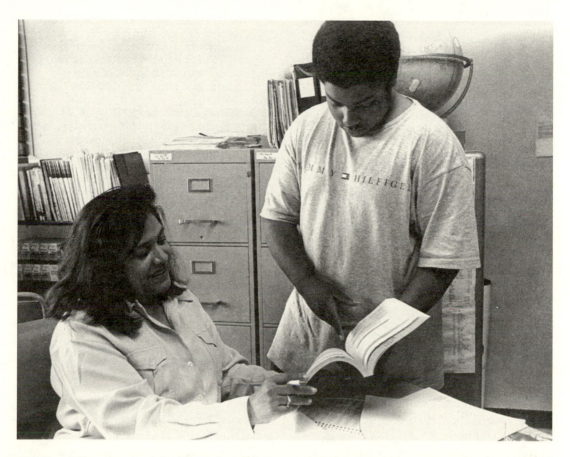

Students who are engaged in school are likely to be more academically successful than youth who are not engaged in school. (Shirley Zeiberg)

ties such as art, music, and sports. Students then have fewer opportunities to express themselves and to learn about who they are and what they want to become. As for gender expectations, because students and adults have less and less time to meet and talk, many students struggle with relationships with members of the opposite sex. Girls are often pressured to dress a certain way and behave in ways that get the attention of boys. Boys can be pressured to hide their feelings and emotions and instead to act brave or strong all the time. Feeling a desire to be liked, yet at the same time struggling to create an identity for themselves, students can often find themselves feeling alone and alienated from their peers.

Although transitions can be challenging for many students, for others school can become a place where they feel alienated and alone for another reason. Students of color (including African American, Asian American, Latino/a, and Native American students) often feel that school is not a place where they are welcomed. They may be treated poorly by European American students who do not understand or respect their language or cultural practices. In addition, in many schools, teachers do not teach about a variety of cultural groups and practices, instead choosing to focus on the history and accomplishments of European Americans. This, too, can make students of color feel that they do not belong and that school does not have anything of value to offer them and their futures. As a result they may disengage from school and have low academic performance.

There are many programs in schools that are designed to help students stay engaged. Many schools offer school tutoring and mentoring programs. In these programs students can receive help with academic work, as well as connect with an adult and build a trusting relationship that might provide them support when things get difficult. Community agencies also offer programs after school and on the weekends to build student self-esteem and confidence. Many of these programs also help students think about their futures and begin making plans. With that kind of help, often students begin to see school as valuable again (or for the first time), become engaged, and start to do better in school.

Lisa R. Jackson

See also Academic Achievement; Academic Self-Evaluation; Cognitive Development; College; Family-School Involvement; Learning Styles and Accommodations; Motivation, Intrinsic; School Dropouts; School, Functions of; Teachers

References and further reading
Davidson, Ann Locke. 1996. *Making and Molding Identity in Schools: Student Narratives on Race, Gender, and Academic Engagement.* New York: State University of New York Press.
Fine, Michelle. 1986. "Why Urban Adolescents Drop Into and Out of Public High School." *Teachers College Record* 87: 393–409.
Finn, Jeremy. 1993. *School Engagement and Students at Risk.* Washington, DC: U.S. Department of Education, National Center for Education Statistics.
Israelashvili, Moshe. 1997. "School Adjustment, School Membership and Adolescents' Future Expectations." *Journal of Adolescence* 20: 525–535.
Mickelson, Roslyn Arlin. 1990. "The Attitude-Achievement Paradox among Black Adolescents." *Sociology of Education* 63: 44–61.
Skinner, Ellen, James Welborn, and James Connell. 1990. "What It Takes to Do Well in School and Whether I've Got It: A Process Model of Perceived Self-Control and Children's Engagement and Achievement in School." *Journal of Educational Psychology* 82, no. 1: 22–32.

School, Functions of

Schools perform many functions. Schools have been viewed as training institutions, as agents of cultural transmission designed to perpetuate and improve a given way of life, and as a means to inculcate both knowledge and values. In addition, schools have been regarded traditionally as fulfilling a *maintenance-actualization* role, that is, as representing a way in which the adolescent can be happy and yet challenged. In other words, schools are a place to develop optimal personal and interpersonal attributes, and in that way the ability to contribute to society.

Schools also provide a context for social interactions and relationship development. They can facilitate the adolescent's emancipation from parents through giving youth an opportunity to earn their own social status. Students may earn status concurrently with school attendance

Schools can be viewed as training institutions, as agents of cultural transmission, and as a means to gain knowledge and values. (Skjold Photographs)

by demonstrating a mastery of the curriculum, by attaining high class standing, and by nonacademic interactions with the peer group in school activities such as organized athletics or clubs. Students may also prepare to earn social status in the future through the training and education attained in school. In addition, the school serves a custodial role in society, in that a system of compulsory education, such as that found in the United States, highly structures the time and activity of students.

However, the structure provided by schools is not necessarily beneficial for all youth. For example, Native American youth do not perform as well in academics as do their European American peers. A study comparing Native American and European American youth found that the Native Americans tended to perceive that the structure of the school created barriers to their success; this perception was associated with lessened school performance.

Teachers are obviously a critical part of the school context, and their behaviors, attitudes, and expectations—apart from their skills as instructors per se—can influence youth behavior and development. For instance, in a longitudinal study of sixth- to eighth-grade students, Kathryn Wentzel found that perceptions by the adolescents that their teachers cared about them were associated with enhanced motivation to achieve positive social as well as academic outcomes. Teachers who cared were described as having attributes akin to those associated with authoritative parents. That is, they showed democratic interaction styles, developed expectations for their students that were based on the individual characteristics of the adolescents, and provided constructive feedback.

Schools exist in relation to the other key contexts of adolescent development—the family, peers, and the community. All of these contexts strengthen or detract from the ability of schools to function as society intends.

Support from the family context can enhance school performance. For instance, for African American, European American, and Latino students, such social support is associated with students' grades, scores on a standardized achievement test, and teacher ratings. In addition, students' self-esteem is enhanced by the support they receive. Similarly, middle school girls who have the ability and motivation to do well in mathematics show positive attitudes toward the subject when their mothers are also positive about it.

In turn, among the offspring of African American teenage mothers, family support is among the key factors reducing the likelihood of dropping out of high school. The decrease in the chances of discontinuing school is related to high maternal educational aspirations for the child in early life, number of years the father was present, being prepared for school, and not repeating an elementary school grade.

The culture transmitted through socialization by the family, as well as by peers, influences school performance. Positive family climate and peer group norms supporting positive behaviors for youth have been found to be associated with school achievement. Social support from parents has also been found to be related to youth feeling open to, excited by, and involved in school-related activities; furthermore, a family climate that challenged the young person to succeed was related to an adolescent focusing on important goals. Youth who lived in families where both support and challenge were present had the best school experiences.

Other research has found that mathematics scores of Asian American students are higher than those of European American students, but lower than those of Chinese and Japanese students. Factors associated with the achievement of Asian and Asian American students include having parents and peers who hold high standards, believe that one succeeds through effort, have positive attitudes about achievement, study diligently, and are less apt to distract youth from studying. Moreover, the psychological adjustment of Asian American and European American students is not different, suggesting that the higher performances and family and peer influences on the former group do not interfere with positive psychological functioning.

Parents and peers can have negative as well as positive effects on school performance. Low parental academic achievement and ineffective child-rearing practices are linked to antisocial behavior and to decreases in engagement with course work among adolescent boys. In turn, African American students' awareness of the discrimination toward people of their race that exists in America was found by Ronald Taylor and his colleagues to be associated with their perceptions that academic achievement was not important. However, when ethnic identity was high, students showed both school engagement and school achievement.

Taylor's study also found that in addition to family and peer influences, the neighborhood or community context of the school has an influence on the academic performance of youth. For instance, African American youth attending neighborhood schools report feeling "stuck" in a setting where they perceive that they have little access to community culture and to the wider society. On the other hand, when African American youth from the same neighborhood attend a citywide school, they perceive that they possess such access.

In addition, African American males are more likely to graduate from high school if they live in neighborhoods having a high percentage of residents working in white-collar occupations, or in middle-class neighborhoods more generally. However, the same does not hold true for females. Other research also has found that African American males from higher-income neighborhoods are more likely to stay in school.

Similarly, other research supports the link between the type of occupations present in a community and a high school dropout rate. A higher percentage of service occupations in a community was associated with increased dropout rates; in turn, a higher percentage of managerial/professional occupations was associated both with a lowered dropout rate and a greater likelihood that high school graduates would continue their education.

In sum, differences in the families and peer groups of youth are related to differential outcomes of school experiences. In addition, individual differences (diversity) among adolescents in their psychological and behavioral characteristics may moderate the potential influences of the school on youth development.

Richard M. Lerner
Jacqueline V. Lerner

See also Academic Achievement; Career Development; Cognitive Development; College; Gifted and Talented Youth; Higher Education; Learning Disabilities; School Engagement; Schools, Full-Service; Vocational Development

References and further reading
Chen, Chaunsheng, and Harold W. Stevenson. 1995. "Motivation and Mathematics Achievement: A Comparative Study of Asian American, Caucasian American, and East Asian High School Students." *Child Development* 66: 1215–1234.
Dryfoos, Joy G. 1994. "Full Service Schools: A Revolution in Health and Social Services for Children, Youth, and Families." San Francisco: Jossey-Bass.
———. 1995. "Full Service Schools: Revolution or Fad?" *Journal of Research on Adolescence* 5, no. 2: 147–172.
Ensminger, Margaret E., Rebecca P. Lamkin, and Nora Jacobson. 1996. "School Leaving: A Longitudinal Perspective Including Neighborhood Effects." *Child Development* 67: 2400–2416.
Lerner, Richard M. 1994. "Schools and Adolescents." *Visions 2010: Families and Adolescents* 2, no. 1: 14–15, 42–43. Minneapolis: National Council on Family Relations.
———. In press. "Adolescence: Development, Diversity, Context, and Application." Upper Saddle River, NJ: Prentice-Hall.
Rathunde, Kevin. 1996. "Family Context and Talented Adolescents' Optimal Experience in School-Related Activities." *Journal of Research on Adolescence* 6, no. 4: 605–628.
Taylor, Ronald D., Robin Casten, Susanne M. Flickinger, Debra Roberts, and Cecil D. Fulmore. 1994. "Explaining the School Performance of African-American Adolescents." *Journal of Research on Adolescence* 4: 21–44.
Wentzel, Kathryn R. 1997. "Student Motivation in Middle School: The Role of Perceived Pedagogical Caring." *Journal of Educational Psychology* 89, no. 3: 411–419.
Wood, Peter B., and W. Charles Clay. 1996. "Perceived Structural Barriers and Academic Performance among American Indian High School Students." *Youth and Society* 28, no. 1: 40–61.

School Transitions

A transition refers to a passage from one state, stage, or place to another. The term *school transition* refers to a change in school settings in particular. Normative school transitions are changes that most students in a community experience at particular points in time. For example, adolescents may experience as many as three school transitions: (1) from elementary to middle or junior high school, (2) from junior high school to senior high school, and (3) from senior high school to college, military service, or work. The change from elementary school to middle or junior high school has received the most attention from educators, psychologists, and policymakers. The change from high school to whichever path a student chooses to pursue (e.g., college, military service, or work) is also an important one, but for different reasons. The transition to high school, on the other hand, has received far less attention. Students generally enter high school from a kindergarten through eighth grade (K–8) school or from a middle or junior high school. There is some evidence to suggest that students who enter high school from a middle or junior high school appear to have more difficulty making the transition in comparison to those who come from a K–8 school.

The terms *elementary school, middle school,* and *junior high school* are used very freely, but the schools themselves may look quite different from place to place. The term *elementary school* may refer to a school that consists of kindergarten through fifth-grade classes, kindergarten through sixth-grade classes, or kindergarten through eighth-grade classes. The terms *middle school* and *junior high school* are often used interchangeably; they can refer to schools that offer fifth through eighth grade, sixth through eighth, or seventh and eighth grade only. The term *middle school* will be used here, but encompasses any one of these three types of school settings.

The change from elementary school to middle school can be difficult for many students who are also trying to manage several other changes (physical/biological, social, emotional, cognitive) associated with puberty and early adolescence. For example, the typical eleven- or twelve-year-old begins to experience any combination of the following: bodily changes, increased self-awareness and self-consciousness, increased importance of peer relationships, attraction to the opposite sex, dating-type behavior, more critical and complex thinking skills, and an increased need for a trusting and supportive adult figure. Handling several changes at once requires a great deal of energy and effort, and for some adolescents this experience can be overwhelming.

Psychologists have done research that indicates that during the transition to middle school many students experience declines in motivation, in positive attitudes toward school, and in self-assurance or confidence in their abilities. Declines in these areas, in turn, tend to result in a drop in grades. Although some students recover after the first year following a transition, many others have trouble bouncing back. Evidence from the research of both psychologists and educators suggests that the typical middle school environment does not fit with the needs and capabilities of most young adolescents. Early adolescent development is characterized by increases in desire for autonomy, peer orientation, self-focus, self-consciousness, importance of identity issues, concern over heterosexual relationships, capacity for abstract cognitive activity, and desire for opportunities to demonstrate higher-order thinking skills and problem-solving skills. The clash between the characteristics of the middle school setting and the characteristics of the early adolescent constitute what is referred to as a developmental mismatch.

School size, departmentalization, and instructional style have been identified as three problematic characteristics of middle schools. Very often students go from smaller, neighborhood elementary schools to larger middle schools drawing students from several different elementary schools. At a time when adolescents are becoming capable of and require greater intimacy and closeness with peers and adult role models, the sudden change from a smaller, neighborhood school to a larger middle school can foster alienation, isolation, anonymity, and difficulties in communication and intimacy. Some schools have emphasized the role of homerooms and/or an advisory system in order to offset the isolating effects of a large school, as well as to foster the development of relationships with peers and teachers.

Departmentalization poses a second problem. Whereas students in elementary school tend to spend the better part of their day with the same teacher and the same group of students, departmentalization forces students to change from classroom to classroom, and from teacher to teacher, thereby imposing a series of disruptions throughout the day and providing fewer opportunities for students to develop closer relationships with others. When students are able to move more as groups, rather than as individuals, this interference with the young adolescent's growing ability and need for closer communication and contact can be lessened.

The instructional style of the typical middle school causes problems by conflicting with three characteristics of the developing adolescent: increased need for autonomy, higher cognitive ability, and more self-consciousness.

Researchers have discovered that most middle school teachers, instead of allowing more autonomy, tend to exert more control over student behavior, maintain stricter rules and discipline, and allow less student input in decision making than do most elementary school teachers. This approach often prevents the development of positive student-teacher relationships, which also prevents the development of relationships with much-needed supportive adult role models. Student reactions to seemingly unfair and punitive control over the environment can range from acting-out to losing interest altogether. Wherever possible it is important that the structure and process of general classroom and school management respond to and foster adolescents' growing capacity for autonomy, responsibility, and critical thinking.

As for cognitive ability, adolescents generally become more capable of logical and abstract thinking; they can formulate and test hypotheses or ideas mentally, use more effective strategies for studying and remembering class material, and plan, monitor, and evaluate the steps they take in solving a problem. Upon entrance to middle school many students encounter increased work demands and stricter grading policies, but not necessarily a demand for higher-order thinking and problem-solving skills. Rather, they tend to find less cognitively challenging work than they experienced in the last year or so of elementary school.

Lastly, middle school classes tend to involve occasions of public comparison regarding achievement, where achievement is based on a competitive, rather than a collaborative, model of task completion and academic success. Researchers have shown that such experiences for the early adolescent can result in still sharper increases in self-consciousness as well as a decrease in motivation in all but the highest-performing students.

While the transition from elementary school to middle school is characterized by the degree to which schools match, or fail to match, developing adolescents' needs and capabilities, the transition from high school to a self-chosen path, on the other hand, is the first change that concretely represents movement toward adulthood and taking responsibility for oneself. Adolescents generally pursue one of four paths: a four-year college, military service, a community college, or full-time employment. Although different paths may involve different questions or concerns pertaining to the future, there are certain experiences common to all groups to varying degrees: termination of relationships with friends, a general sense of loss, confusion and anxiety (despite the openly expressed attitude of "I can't wait to get out"), and concern over the possibility that peers who provided a source of support all along may no longer be able to do so due to differing pursuits.

For students going on to a four-year college or university, the pertinent issues include the following: learning to take care of oneself; dealing with "loss" of family, friends, boyfriends, girlfriends, and the like; fears regarding academic pressure and success; financial worries; making new friends; and the general process of separation, or what is called individuation. One can support these students in many ways, for example, by encouraging them to talk about their hopes, anxieties,

and sadness; by recognizing the importance of saying good-bye to friends, some of whom they may have known nearly all of their lives; by exploring with them the different ways of saying good-bye; by clarifying that the sadness and difficulty associated with leaving is not to be equated with childishness; and by discussing the impact of extracurricular activities, a social life, and possible part-time employment on academic demands and success during college.

Students who choose military service encounter many of the same issues encountered by students pursuing a four-year college; however, the nature and purpose of military service introduces additional concerns and questions. Military service carries very real possibilities of war, heroism, and death, for oneself and others. Students may need to explore how their personal ideals and values intersect with the requirements of military service. For females, there is the additional reality of entering into a male-dominated field and how to manage possible experiences of feeling unwelcome. The need for saying good-bye and for talking about fears, hopes, and anxieties can be more difficult for this group of students, depending upon their perception of the life-risking purposes and potentials accompanying military service.

Students who attend community colleges tend to fall into one of two groups: those who intend to transfer to a four-year college and those who are seeking solely an Associate degree. Although some students attend community colleges for financial reasons, the greater proportion of students attend community colleges because their high school grades together with their SAT scores have prevented acceptance to a four-year college. For these students, the emphasis is less on saying good-bye and more on dealing with possible feelings of being left behind. Students may feel some tension or ambiguity around living at home while also trying to gain the adult independence that many of their peers will gain by virtue of distance from their parents. A counselor can play a key role in helping students to articulate their struggles, recognize the importance of academic performance if the goal is to transfer to a four-year college, and consider the impact of commuting, a social life, and a possible part-time job on academic success.

Students making the transition from high school to full-time employment potentially struggle at two levels: They may not receive the same kind of structured support as college- and military-bound students, whose pursuits more strongly depend on and are mediated by ongoing contact with school staff and counselors, and they tend to be in the minority relative to their college and military-bound peers and thus may find it especially difficult identifying peers they feel understand and support them in their experiences of transition. For this group the choice or need to pursue full-time employment entails more than the personal loss of high school friendships and familiar support systems. Work-bound students lose a way of life that permits continued exploration of educational and career possibilities, social contact with and support from peers, and the attainment of skills and experiences that bring further career and economic advancement.

Although high school graduates are more likely to find employment than those who drop out of school, they have fewer work opportunities than were available to this population several decades ago. When they are able to find work, jobs attained by high school graduates tend to be low-paying, unskilled positions with little or no possibility for long-term training or vocational counseling. These students may also struggle with the tension between assuming adult roles and responsibilities yet remaining financially dependent. In the United States, more adolescents are employed during high school than in any other developed country; most work in order to earn personal spending money. However, work-bound high school graduates, particularly low-income students, very often work to meet living expenses as well, whether family-related or personal. That is, the financial demands of food, rent, bills, transportation, and so on can be quite overwhelming and stressful.

Regardless of the nature and direction of change involved in the transitions high school seniors make, it is critical that school staff and/or counselors provide students with information regarding all possible career and educational avenues; help students to process the impending transition, particularly with regard to termination and separation; wherever possible invite past graduates to come talk to students about various issues, questions, concerns, and hopes; and create opportunities for peer and adult support.

Imma De Stefanis

See also Academic Achievement; Academic Self-Evaluation; College; Family-School Involvement; Higher Education; Homework; Learning Styles and Accommodations; Middle Schools; Peer Groups; Private Schools; School Engagement; School, Functions of; Schools, Full-Service; Schools, Single-Sex; Teachers; Tracking in American High Schools

References and further reading
Eccles, Jacquelynne, Carol Midgley, Allan Wigfield, and Christy M. Buchanan.

1993. "Development during Adolescence: The Impact of Stage Environment Fit on Young Adolescents' Experiences in Schools and in Families." *American Psychologist* 48, no. 2: 90–101.

Goodnough, Gary E., and Vivian Ripley. 1997. "Structured Groups for High School Seniors Making the Transition to College and to Military Service." *The School Counselor* 44: 230–234.

McCormick, John F. 1995. "'But, Nobody Told Me about . . .': A Program for Enhancing Decision Making by College-Bound Students." *The School Counselor* 42: 246–248.

Wigfield, Carol, and Jacquelynne Eccles. 1994. "Children's Competence Beliefs, Achievement Values, and General Self-Esteem: Change across Elementary School and Middle School." *Journal of Early Adolescence* 14, no. 2: 107–138.

Schools, Full-Service

Among contemporary youth, risk behaviors—such as drug use, unsafe sex, delinquency, and school failure—occur together. A key tactic has been taken to prevent the occurrence of these interrelated risks: the creation of "full-service" schools. Most youth experts agree that schools by themselves are unable to deal adequately with the multiple problems facing many of their adolescent students.

Full-service schools are involved in community-wide, multiagency, collaborative efforts that work to prevent adolescent risk. (Shirley Zeiberg)

The problem is that schools are not part of community-wide, multiagency, collaborative (partnership) efforts that work to prevent and ameliorate adolescent risk. The leading spokesperson for the creation of full-service schools that are involved with the community in this manner is Joy G. Dryfoos.

The call for the creation of full-service schools constitutes an appeal to reorganize and reform the structure and function of these schools. Research, although still in its initial stages, suggests that such revisions have positive influences on youth. For instance, when middle schools undertook reforms that included building school-community partnerships; enabling teachers of different subject areas (e.g., math, science, social studies, and language arts) to work together on interdisciplinary teams; and bringing community volunteers into the school to help the students discuss connections between social studies and art, students' awareness of art increased, they developed attitudes and preferences of particular styles of art, *and* their movement from concrete to abstract thinking was enhanced. Thus, changing a school's organization, in the direction of the reforms described by Dryfoos, can be beneficial to youth.

Richard M. Lerner

See also Academic Achievement; Cognitive Development; Health Promotion; Learning Disabilities; Learning Styles and Accommodations; Mentoring and Youth Development; School, Functions of; Teachers

References and further reading
Dryfoos, Joy G. 1994. *Full-Service Schools: A Revolution in Health and Social Services for Children, Youth, and Families.* San Francisco: Jossey-Bass.
———. 1995. "Full-Service Schools: Revolution or Fad?" *Journal of Research on Adolescence* 5, no. 2: 147–172.
Epstein, Joyce L., and Susan L. Dauber. 1995. "Effects on Students of an Interdisciplinary Program Linking Social Studies, Arts, and Family Volunteers in the Middle Grades." *Journal of Early Adolescence* 15, no. 1: 114–144.
Lerner, Richard M. In press. *Adolescence: Development, Diversity, Context, and Application.* Upper Saddle River, NJ: Prentice-Hall.

Schools, Single-Sex

Most experts on adolescent development agree that the junior and senior high school years provide teenagers with many challenges and opportunities in preparation for future life in wider society, or in the "real world." The debate over single-sex (SS) schools versus coeducational (CE) schools is a long-standing one with some new wrinkles, but little resolution. Increasing interest in SS schools in the public sector stems largely from the positive effects it is said to have on the education and socialization of young people, particulary females, as documented by nearly thirty years of research. Although SS schools have traditionally been private (i.e., tuition-based) schools, most of which have been religiously affiliated (usually Roman Catholic or Orthodox Jewish), it is this movement into the public sector that raises the question again: What are the benefits of single-sex education?

Public education in the United States remained all-male until about the mid–nineteenth century when early women's rights advocates fought their traditional training in household management, arguing that to be thoroughly taught meant being taught with men in the same classes. By 1900, all but 2 percent of the nation's public schools were coeducational, and gender equity had seemingly been achieved. Today, advocates of SS education argue that CE settings do not assure gender equity, and may even perpetuate gender-based stereotypical attitudes and behaviors. Equity in an educational context generally refers to the concepts of equal treatment and equal opportunity for all students, regardless of sex.

Supporters of SS education believe that even though males and females may occupy the same classroom space, they do not mature at the same rate physically, cognitively, socially, or emotionally, and so their educational needs and experiences differ as well. Although research studies have supported the general benefits of a SS education for both males and females, the overwhelming majority of studies have focused on the advantages for females in particular.

The central argument in support of SS schools in general is based on a belief in male-female differences in the rate and style of development in several areas. An SS environment can be more sensitive to varying emotional, cognitive, and social needs. Very often CE schools are portrayed as dominated by a culture of "rating" and social maneuvering to which SS schools are immune. The main tension between advocates of CE schools and SS schools revolves around this issue: CE advocates believe that the CE environment mirrors a gender-stratified society, while advocates of SS education maintain that social and sexual pressures can detract from social, emotional, and academic development. Research has shown that males and females who attend SS schools tend to have higher academic achievement and educational aspirations, as well as fewer stereotypical attitudes about gender and course subject or career (Lee and Bryk, 1986; Riordan, 1990).

Regarding the benefits of SS education for boys, the research is sparse. Advocates of SS schools believe there are several social and emotional benefits to the developing male adolescent: Since males mature at a slower rate than girls, all-male schools can better accommodate their social/emotional needs and development; SS schools yield improved behavior and a healthy sense of structure and discipline among male adolescents, who otherwise tend toward restlessness and unruliness; and the greater number of male faculty provides more role models than is possible in CE schools, where the majority of teachers tend to be female. This last argument has been pivotal in the recent initiatives to open public SS schools in low-income areas serving minority males, for whom a positive role model may be lacking. Additional goals here include lowering high school dropout rates and delinquent/criminal behavior.

In terms of academic gains, boys in SS schools tend to take more math and science and to have higher general academic achievement than their counterparts in CE schools. Those who oppose SS schools for boys primarily claim that, without the presence of girls, boys' schools run the risk of fostering sexist attitudes and behaviors toward females.

The central argument in favor of girls' schools is related to the issue of gender equity. In 1992, the American Association of University Women released a report summarizing the findings of 1, 331 studies of girls in schools and demonstrated that there is ample evidence to show that in CE environments males tend to dominate over females. This report showed a pattern of unequal support and attention when both sexes are in the same classroom, at all levels, from preschool to college. For example, males are permitted to call out answers, are called upon more often, are asked higher-level questions, are assisted more often by the teacher in arriving at the "right" answer, and are more often given specific and affirming feedback. An SS school can be one antidote for gender inequities, which also lead to other difficulties, including lowered self-esteem, learned helplessness, lowered expectations about one's own ability to succeed, lowered motivation, and a lowered sense of control over one's life.

Nearly thirty years of research shows that girls who attend SS schools show improved motivation and performance, do more homework, take more math and science classes, hold less stereotypical sex role attitudes, have a stronger self-concept, more often pursue leadership positions and athletic activities, hold higher educational and career aspirations, and benefit from a greater number of female role models in positions of authority (e.g., administrators) than are found in CE schools (Lee and Bryk, 1986; Riordan, 1990; Sadker, Sadker, and Klein, 1991).

Although the arguments favoring SS schools for girls can appear more compelling and numerous than those for boys, it is important to remember that the research on all-girls' schools far exceeds the work on all-boys' schools. More research is needed in the areas of male SS schools, public SS schools for both males and females, and the possibility that individual student differences (e.g., in needs, preferences, styles, temperament, and so on) may be just as important in assessing the best fit between students and school type.

Imma De Stefanis

See also Academic Achievement; Academic Self-Evaluation; Dating; Family-School Involvement; Gender Differences; Middle Schools; Peer Groups; Private Schools; School Engagement; School, Functions of; Services for Adolescents; Sports and Adolescents

References and further reading
American Association of University Women. 1992. *How Schools Shortchange Girls: The AAUW Report.* Washington, DC: American Association of University Women Educational Foundation.
Carelli, Anne O. 1988. *Sex Equity in Education.* Springfield, MA: Charles C. Thomas.
Lasser, Carol. 1987. *Educating Men and Women Together: Coeducation in a Changing World.* Urbana: University of Illinois Press.
Lee, Valerie E., and Anthony S. Bryk. 1986. "Effects of Single-Sex Secondary Schools on Student Achievement and Attitudes." *Journal of Educational Psychology* 78, no. 5: 331–339.
Riordan, Cornelius. 1990. *Girls and Boys in School: Together or Separate?* New York: Teachers College Press.
Sadker, Myra P., David M. Sadker, and Susan Klein. 1991. "The Issue of Gender in Elementary and Secondary Education." *Review of Research in Education* 17: 269–334.

Self

Although there is little agreement about how to define the term *self,* both in everyday conversation and in social and behavioral science research, the self is presumed to be complex and to include both the subjective experiences and objective characteristics that distinguish a person as a unique individual apart from others. Across academic disciplines, scholars and researchers not only define self differently but also highlight different dimensions of the self-system; however, the contributions of each discipline provide valuable insights into the broader picture of how self is central to the human experience. How we both experience and understand our own selves is influenced by our capacity for cognition and self-consciousness, the current

Physical, social, and cognitive aspects of a young person's sense of self develop during adolescence. (Shirley Zeiberg)

ment that it is possible to distinguish at least two parts of the self that need to be accounted for in any discussion of self. The first is called the *subject*, the *I*, or the *knower*—the awareness that an individual has of herself as a separate being in everyday life. The second part is given names that are counterparts to each of these, being called the *object*, the *me*, or the *known*—the capacity of an individual to consciously think about herself and the characteristics that distinguish her from others.

For some psychologists and cognitive scientists, the most interesting part of the self is the subjective self-consciousness, self-awareness, and self-understanding that the mind creates as the individual lives his life. From this perspective, everything the individual thinks and does is always interpreted with regard to how it has meaning for his own self, and the primary focus of all self activity is in the brain.

For social psychologists and sociologists, the self is presumed to come primarily from the social world and is structured in the form of a self-concept that includes all the labels, characteristics, and descriptions that the individual applies to herself. The conceptions the individual has of herself are multiple and occur at a number of different levels. For example, while some of the individual's self-conceptions are known to others as part of the public self, other things the individual thinks and feels about herself may only be known to herself and therefore reside in the private self. One part of the private self might be the ideal self or the person she wishes she could really be. However, when there is a big gap between the person the individual wishes she were and the person she believes herself to be, then problems of self-esteem or self-

beliefs of our culture about how persons fit into the larger world, and internalization of the everyday interactions we have in the social world. Adolescence as a stage of development has special implications for changes in self-experience and self-understanding, because both the adolescents' physical selves and social selves are changing dramatically at the same time as new cognitive abilities to reflect about the self in the social world are increasing.

Dimensions of Self

Although the self is one of the central dimensions of humans studied by cultural anthropologists, sociologists, psychologists, and philosophers, there is little agreement about what the self really is. There is, however, some general agree-

worth may emerge. While self-esteem refers to a general sense of personal worth or value, self-efficacy is the part of the self-concept that specifically reflects an individual's belief about her competence or ability to meet social expectation and demands.

A different psychological orientation to the study of self focuses on the structure and strength of the individual's character, motivations, and other dimensions of personality. For psychologists who take this approach, the ego is presumed to be the most central part of the self, as it is what allows each individual to navigate the social demands of life, constantly balancing what is socially expected and what is personally desirable. Although much of this ego is presumed to be at a conscious level, self or ego psychology also assumes that at least some portions of the ego work at a subconscious level. An additional element of self that emerges from the ego as it negotiates the individual's interactions in the world is identity or the way the individual chooses to identify himself as a member of the social world.

Across both psychology and sociology, an increasing number of researchers are beginning to examine the personal narratives, or *self-stories*, that people tell about themselves and their lives. These scholars believe that when people think about themselves across time, they think of themselves as the main character of a story and connect events in their experiences in such a way as to make sense of their own experience in life. From this perspective, our personal stories or narratives are tools for organizing how to think about who we are, how we became the persons that we are, and why we are making choices about the person we are still to become. Since different stories can be constructed out of the same experiences (e.g., how parents' divorce either ruined life or provided opportunity for growth), this means that individuals are able to reinterpret self-experience by changing the stories they choose to tell (e.g., changing the events to include, or the interpretation of, the motivations behind actions).

Humanistic psychologists have a special interest in both the subjective experience, or *phenomonology*, of self, and the degree to which human self-control and free will are possible. From this perspective, all persons have a unique potential, and if they can have their basic needs met and make appropriate choices that allow for growth, they can self-actualize or reach the highest potential that is possible for them. As with the narrative perspective, the idea is that, since choice resides within the individual, self is not something that just develops or is fully determined by the social world; rather, it can be discovered, chosen, and actively created by the individual.

Influences on Self-Experience and Self-Understanding

Regardless of the definition of self used or the dimension of self examined, there are key influences on how the self of any person develops and key forces that limit the type of self that any one person can have. These influences and forces include the nature of cognitive functioning, the beliefs and norms of the broader culture the individual resides in, and interactions of the individual in the social world.

Without the functioning of the brain, no self-conscious thought can exist. For example, few people imagine that a rock has a sense of self or a self-concept. Even an ant, which is part of the animal kingdom, is not presumed to have the mental capacity to have a sense of self; as we move up the animal chain, however, to species with more complex mental abilities like chimpanzees and dolphins, the questions about the nature of self these animals can have are much less clear. Similarly, when humans are first born, their mental capacities are limited and so, therefore, are their abilities to recognize that they are separate persons with their own individual characteristics and identity. As cognitive abilities increase, so does the potential for persons to construct complex self-concepts and personal stories. The importance of the mind in shaping the experience of the self is also reflected in the incomplete or confusing sense of self for persons who are diagnosed with cognitive disorders such as autism or schizophrenia.

How the brain makes sense of the self experience in the world is, however, also shaped and constrained by the worldview or the cultural beliefs about the self and the world that the person is raised in. For example, while most Western cultures, including the United States, place a high priority on individuality and the rights of each person as a separate human being, many Eastern cultures put a much higher emphasis on the individual as an interdependent member of a broader collective. Similarly, not all cultures share beliefs about the degree to which human action is controlled by the self versus other forces including spirits and God. In either case, because people mentally internalize the usually unquestioned beliefs of the culture they are raised in, both the everyday experience of self-consciousness and the more reflective self-understanding of persons in each culture will be different as they filter their experience of reality through a different cognitive lens.

Although both the mind and culture may set the limits and potentials for the development of the self, the self of any one individual must develop through actual interactions with the social world. From birth, as parents and other caregivers begin to interact with newborns, an awareness of the distinction between self and others begins to develop in the mind. As children learn to use language, they recognize that they have their own names and that certain labels and words are applied to them and describe who they are presumed to be. Soon, children also are able to describe themselves in terms of the language of the culture, using the appropriate labels to describe their physical characteristics (e.g., tall), the social roles they have to perform (e.g., sister, student), and even the personality characteristics that are typically ascribed to them by others (e.g., shy, funny). Over time, as they compare themselves to others, reflect on their relative successes and failures in adjustment, and see the pattern of how others respond to them through what is called the looking-glass self, a more stable sense of self begins to form.

Adolescence and Self
Both the changes of puberty and the social transitions into more mature social roles (e.g., getting a license, starting high school) change the everyday subjective experience of adolescents and force them to more consciously reflect on who they are and how they fit into the social world. How these changes are experienced by the self are, however, complicated by new cognitive abilities, which allow the adolescent to think about themselves in more complicated ways. For example, as they move through adolescence, individuals are able to think

more abstractly, to imagine the future more completely, and to see ideas from multiple perspectives. Although these cognitive changes increase the capacity for self-understanding and self-aware-ness, they also have some negative con-sequences for self as well.

Because adolescents do not yet have the perspective on self that will come with experience, these cognitive develop-ments, along with the other changes that come after puberty, can lead to a height-ened sensitivity to self-experience and a preoccupation with what others think about them. *Adolescent egocentrism* is the term for this adolescent self-focus, and it includes two different dimensions of experience, the *imaginary audience* and the *personal fable*. The imaginary audience refers to the heightened self-consciousness, with the belief that every-one is watching, that emerges out of the interaction between these cognitive, physical, and social changes. The per-sonal fable refers to the false sense of invincibility and self-importance that comes with this personal preoccupation. These two elements are of special con-cern, because they mean that, as adoles-cents turn to new reference groups (e.g., peers) to define who they are as persons, they are more likely to be influenced by peer conformity or to take risks in social situations (e.g., drug use, drinking and driving) without acknowledging the real-ity of the negative consequences that can follow. These factors also contribute to the concerns with body image and other mental health problems that increase across the adolescent years.

All these changes in the experience of the adolescent also provide a new drive to make sense of how the self fits into the world as a soon-to-be adult. With new social expectations for choices (e.g., whether to get a part-time job, what elec-tives to take in school) and a new orien-tation toward the future, adolescents are confronted with the challenge of choos-ing an identity, a coherent sense of self that defines who one is and wants to be in the future. Although some adolescents may experience this challenge to define one's self as a crisis and may explore a range of possible selves they could be, most adolescents are able to successfully achieve a sense of identity that provides continuity, stability, and unity to their sense of self in the world.

Phame Camarena

See also Autonomy; Conformity; Ethno-centrism; Identity; Peer Groups; Peer Pressure; Personality; Self-Conscious-ness; Self-Esteem; Temperament

References and further reading
Baumeister, Roy F. 1986. *Identity: Cultural Change and the Struggle for Self.* New York: Oxford University Press.
Brinthaupt, Thomas, and Richard Lipka, eds. 1992. *The Self: Definitional and Methodological Issues.* Albany: State University of New York Press.
Brown, Jonathon W. 1998. *The Self.* Boston: McGraw-Hill.
Damon, William, and Daniel Hart. 1988. *Self Understanding in Childhood and Adolescence.* Cambridge: Cambridge University Press.
Kihlstrom, John F., and Stanley B. Klein. 1997. "Self-Knowledge and Self-Awareness." Pp. 5–17 in *The Self across Psychology: Self-Recognition, Self-Awareness, and the Self-Concept.* Edited by Joan Gay Snodgrass and Robert L. Thommpson. New York: New York Academy of Sciences.
Lester, Marilyn. 1984. "Self: Sociological Portraits." Pp. 19–68 in *The Existential Self in Society.* Edited by Joseph A. Kotarba and Andrea Fontana. Chicago: University of Chicago Press.
Levin, Jerome D. 1992. *Theories of the Self.* Washington, DC: Hemisphere Publishing.
Scheibe, Karl E. 1995. *Self Studies.* Westport, CT: Praeger.

Turner, John C., and Rina S. Onorato. 1999. "Social Identity, Personality, and the Self-Concept: A Self-Categorization Perspective." Pp. 11–46 in *The Psychology of the Social Self*. Edited by Tom R. Tyler, Roderick M. Kramer, and Oliver P. John. Mahwah, NJ: Lawrence Elbaum Associates.

Self-Consciousness

Self-consciousness involves thinking and feeling critically about oneself and may also involve a sense that one is being scrutinized by others. Self-consciousness is related to identity development, which is one of the major developmental tasks of adolescence and young adulthood. Feelings of self-consciousness are common in adolescents, and yet many adolescents do not realize that their peers have similar feelings. Self-consciousness often keeps teenagers trapped with their own feelings of insecurity, fearing that if they share these feelings they will be met with ridicule from others. Understanding that these feelings are normal and common is an important step in helping teenagers feel somewhat more comfortable with themselves.

Self-consciousness is not specific to adolescents; many if not most people have feelings of self-consciousness at one time or another. However, adolescence seems to be a period of heightened self-consciousness. There have been some interesting theories suggested to explain this phenomenon. Some psychologists suggest that adolescents are in a period of egocentrism. Egocentrism is defined as self-absorption. This self-absorption leads to a view of the world that tends to be self-focused and to exclude other people's point of view. Adolescent self-absorption can make teens highly critical of others, in that they do not necessarily consider the perspective of another when making a judgment. Instead, teens make judgments based solely on their own point of view and assume that others share their point of view.

There are two components of adolescent egocentrism. The first component, which refers most directly to self-consciousness, is called the imaginary audience. The imaginary audience is the adolescent's perception that he or she is the focus of the attention of others. The imaginary audience is used to explain the adolescent perception that everybody is looking at them, for better or worse. In other words, adolescents often feel as though people are staring at them, noticing every blemish and shortcoming. For example, in a room full of people many teenagers are certain that everyone else has noticed their bad hair day or the pimple on their forehead. The imaginary audience also suggests that teenagers often feel as if they are "on stage." This helps to explain why teens often seem to wonder, both to themselves and out loud, why everybody is staring at them, even when in fact nobody is paying any attention to them at all.

The second component of adolescent egocentrism is known as the personal fable. The personal fable suggests that at the same time that teenagers are certain that everyone is watching them, they also believe themselves to be unique and unlike anyone else. Teens often believe that nobody else can possibly understand their experience, because it is completely unique. This personal fable has a number of practical implications. Feeling that one is unique and that one's experience is unlike that of anyone else can create a sense of isolation and distance. Teens may find it hard to believe that parents and other adults can understand them or empathize with them, since they see themselves and their experience as so dif-

Self-consciousness involves thinking and feeling critically about oneself. (Skjold Photographs)

ing and thus hamper judgment and decision making. It is not uncommon for adolescents to engage in risky behavior and report that they did so because they did not believe that anything bad could happen to them. For example, teenagers who drink and drive rarely believe that they will hurt themselves or others. Similarly, despite book knowledge to the contrary, teens engaging in unprotected sex do not believe that they will become pregnant, make someone pregnant, or contract AIDS or other sexually transmitted diseases. Feelings of invulnerability and invincibility are certainly interesting given the elevated level of self-consciousness among adolescents. On one hand, teens are highly critical of themselves and others, always sure that they are being watched. On the other hand, they seem to have difficulty accepting the very real risks to their safety that do exist.

Deborah N. Margolis

See also Anxiety; Body Image; Conformity; Ethnocentrism; Fears; Identity; Self; Self-Esteem; Shyness

References and further reading
Elkind, David. 1998. *All Grown Up and No Place to Go,* revised ed. Cambridge, MA: Perseus.
Kastner, Laura, and Jennifer Wyatt. 1997. *The Seven Year Stretch.* New York: Houghton Mifflin.
Ryan, R., and R. Kuczkowski. 1994. "The Imaginary Audience, Self-Consciousness, and Public Individuation in Adolescence." *Journal of Personality* 62: 219–238.
Rycek, K. E., S. L. Stuhr, J. McDermott, J. Benker, and M. D. Swartz. 1998. "Adolescent Egocentrism and Cognitive Functioning during Late Adolescence." *Adolescence* 33: 746–750.

ferent and distinct. For example, a teenager experiencing family problems may believe that she must keep these problems to herself because no one else could possibly have similar problems or feelings. This, in fact, may be related to and help explain the isolation that many teens feel in their own self-consciousness.

Beyond feelings of uniqueness, the personal fable may create a sense of invulnerability and invincibility for the adolescent. Invulnerability and invincibility refer to feelings of being immune to or safe from problems that plague others. Feelings of invulnerability and invincibility can seriously distort adolescent think-

Self-Esteem

Self-esteem refers to an individual's self-evaluation. Self-acceptance, respect for

Adolescents with high self-esteem are often motivated to succeed. (Laura Dwight)

quency. Since the developmental stressors of adolescence pose risks to self-esteem and emotional well-being, an understanding of the development of self-esteem, especially during adolescence, is crucial to anyone who works with young people.

Obviously self-esteem is important, and scholars have paid a good deal of attention to how it develops. Some psychological theorists suggest that support, caring, and nurturance from parents and other caretakers during infancy and childhood contribute to a view of oneself as worthy of care. This does not mean that self-esteem is determined only by experiences early in life. Ongoing experiences at school and in the neighborhood and community also affect self-esteem. Adolescents who feel that they are liked by their close friends, classmates, teachers, and parents are also likely to feel good about themselves. Whether or not they are successful in areas they judge to be important also affects their self-esteem. For example, if athletics and academic achievement are important to a person, doing well in those areas will be important to maintaining positive self-esteem.

Self-esteem may fluctuate at different ages. For example, between the ages of eleven and thirteen, some adolescents experience a drop in self-esteem. The increased freedom experienced by teens after age thirteen is believed to contribute to a gradual increase in self-esteem during the high school and college years. Not all teens, however, experience loss of self-esteem in early adolescence. In fact, across the transitions to middle school and to college, some teens experience gains in self-esteem, while others report little change.

Social, biological, and cognitive factors have been used to explain the changes in

one's own worth as a person, and liking oneself are all aspects of self-esteem. Self-esteem can be simply assessed by answering the question, "How much do I like the kind of person I am?" Research indicates that self-esteem is important to mental health and achievement. Adolescents with high self-esteem are often motivated to succeed and do well in school. They typically have positive ways of solving life's problems and effective ways of coping, which reduce the harmful effects of stress. Low self-esteem, on the other hand, has been associated with a variety of emotional and behavioral disorders, including anxiety, depression, eating disorders, and delin-

self-esteem that sometimes occur during early adolescence. Socially, early adolescents are often making the transition from the security of an elementary school classroom, where they are well known by teachers and close friends, to the more impersonal and larger environment of the middle school, where they have to deal with many teachers who expect them to complete more difficult work with less teacher support. More competition among classmates, stricter grading, and decreased teacher attention can threaten self-esteem. Biologically, some early adolescents are entering puberty and may be stressed by coping simultaneously with changes at school. Teenagers who are physically mature may experience high social and academic expectations by adults and peers who assume these teens are older than they really are. Teenagers may also become more focused on their physical appearance and attractiveness to members of the opposite sex, which can also contribute to negative self-evaluation. Early puberty and a preoccupation with physical appearance make some early adolescent girls especially vulnerable to a decline in self-esteem.

Cognitively, thinking processes move from being more concrete to more abstract during the adolescent years. Whereas a child is likely to describe the self in physical terms (e.g., tall, brown-eyed) or simple feelings (e.g., happy), adolescents are more likely to describe the self using abstract concepts, such as wishes, motivations, and complex emotions. Since these abstract characteristics are more difficult to assess in direct ways, some adolescents develop unrealistic self-concepts and self-evaluations. Abstract reasoning skills also enable the adolescent to become more introspective or inward looking. They often become more self-conscious and concerned about what others think. When they imagine that peers and important adults are thinking about them negatively, self-esteem can suffer. Adolescents also describe themselves in a greater number of social roles. The self may interact differently with mother, father, close friend, teacher, coach, classmate, and romantic partner, and adolescents may evaluate themselves differently in each of these relationships. This can be confusing to the younger adolescent, who is not able to figure out who is the "real me." The more advanced cognitive skills of older adolescents enable them to realize that it is common to behave and interact differently with different people and enable them to develop views of the ideal self or the self that one would like to be. Although these ideals can contribute to negative self-evaluations, they can also be a source of motivation and incentive to work hard.

Although teenagers do not have control over many factors that impact self-esteem (such as family conflict, societal prejudices, and job opportunities available for young people), there are a number of strategies that adolescents can employ to maintain or enhance self-esteem. Adolescents should become actively involved in activities that match their interests and skills. Teens can learn how to identify caring adults in their schools, neighborhoods, and communities who can provide support, guidance, and assistance as needed. The support of these adults may be enlisted in developing and carrying out plans for improvements in the schools, neighborhoods, and communities. Recognizing that one has done something positive to enhance one's community or improve one's future often provides a boost to self-esteem. Because the opinions of others often impact self-esteem, teens should critically evaluate the sources and accuracy of information that are being incorporated into the evaluation of self. Sometimes one discovers that negative self-evaluations are based upon inaccurate views of the self. It is important that teens and the adults who care about them recognize that there are many strategies that can help teens cope with the challenges of adolescence in ways that contribute to enhanced self-esteem.

Maureen E. Kenny

See also Academic Achievement; Academic Self-Evaluation; Attractiveness, Physical; Developmental Assets; Ethnocentrism; Identity; Mentoring and Youth Development; Self

References and further reading
Hart, Daniel. 1988. "The Adolescent Self-Concept in Social Context." Pp. 71–90 in *Self, Ego, and Identity.* Edited by Daniel Lapsley and F. Clark Power. New York: Springer-Verlag.
Harter, Susan. 1999. *The Construction of the Self: A Developmental Perspective.* New York: Guilford Press.
Markus, Hazel, and Paula Nurius. 1986. "Possible Selves." *American Psychologist* 41: 954–969.

Self-Injury

Self-injury can be defined as deliberate attempts to harm or damage oneself without suicidal intent. A number of terms have been used to describe the habit of self-injury, including self-mutilation, self-abuse, and deliberate self-harm, and it can include such behaviors as cutting, burning, scratching, hair pulling, interfering with the healing of wounds, head banging, swallowing sharp objects, and bone breaking. Self-injurious behaviors occur on a broad continuum, and it is important to understand the behaviors in the individual's context. For example, tattoos and body piercings by U.S. teens, while altering the skin or damaging it, are not considered self-injurious because of the acceptance of these behaviors in Western culture. Although self-injury can occur in a variety of populations and across the life span, self-injury has become an increasingly serious problem for adolescents, who use self-injury as a means of coping with extreme psychological distress.

The reasons why adolescents engage in self-injurious behaviors are complex, and researchers have only begun to identify the characteristics of those who self-injure and the causes of their behavior. Often superficial to moderate self-injury occurs in the context of psychiatric conditions or disorders. More severe and stereotypic (i.e., repetitive and rhythmic) self-injury is associated with developmental disorders (e.g., mental retardation) and psychotic disorders. Superficial or moderate self-injurious behaviors typically begin in early adolescence, involve methods with a low level of lethality, and can occur once or may continue over many years with repetitive episodes. Self-injury can begin as experimentation, but may become a habitual way of coping with stress. Skin cutting is the most prevalent type of self-injurious behavior, but most individuals engage in multiple methods. The damage is rarely life threatening, and the wounds are often made on hidden parts of the body. However, self-injury can be dangerous, resulting in permanent scarring or infections; it can even lead to death by accidentally cutting a vein. Often adolescents who self-injure feel a sense of shame or social stigma, which may result in hiding these behaviors and wounds from others. For this reason, research on determining the rate of self-injury among teenagers has been difficult. Researchers have estimated that approximately 2 million Americans engage in superficial or moderate self-injury each year (Favazza and Conterio, 1988). Although most evidence suggests that more girls than boys engage in self-injurious behaviors, boys are still at risk

Self-injury usually occurs in a trance-like state called dissociation. Adolescents who self-injure often cannot resist the impulses to commit these acts, and they seek out the physical pain as a calming effect to counter the distress they are feeling. Self-injury, however, may have several intentions, including to release tension, to return to reality, to establish control, to gain a sense of security and uniqueness, to influence others, to counter negative perceptions of the self, to vent anger, or to enhance or repress sexual feelings. Self-injury is sometimes viewed as an attempt at self-help that provides fast, but temporary, relief from overwhelming psychological distress. Self-injury can also be a means of being in control, of channeling anger, of keeping in touch with reality, and of avoiding a severe depression. Biological factors have been implicated in perpetuating self-injury. For example, hormones (e.g., endorphins) are released when the body is injured that fight anxiety and depression.

Adolescents who self-injure often feel powerless, have difficulty trusting others with emotions, feel isolated or alienated, feel afraid, and have low self-esteem. Self-injury is also associated with a number of clinical symptoms and disorders, including depression, drug and alcohol abuse, negative body image, frequent problems with eating and eating disorders, and obsessive-compulsive disorder.

Self-injury has been viewed as a method of relieving the adolescent of emotional pain brought on by overwhelming psychological distress, such as depression, anxiety, or extreme anger.

In addition, self-injury in adolescents has also been associated with disrupted family situations, such as family conflict and parental alcoholism and depression. Self-injury may also occur in adolescents who experience a loss or disruption of an important interpersonal relationship. Self-injurious behaviors can occur as a generalized reaction to stress in relationships, as a means to reduce the adolescents' own feelings of frustration, anger, or anxiety, while at the same time communicating their feelings to others. Adolescents engaging in self-injurious behaviors often have difficulty verbally expressing their feelings and gain a sense of relief from overwhelming feelings after committing these acts. Some adolescents may also be exbihitionistic about their self-injurious behaviors in order to gain the attention of important people in their lives.

Histories of trauma have also been associated with self-injurious behaviors in adolescents. For example, childhood physical and sexual abuse, as well as parental neglect and parental separation, are strongly associated with adolescent self-injury. Other evidence suggests a relationship between self-injury and body alienation, which may be related to chronic childhood illnesses. Adolescents who have had childhood illnesses, such as diabetes, asthma, epilepsy, and cardiac illnesses, and ongoing or invasive medical treatments, have been found to be more likely to self-injure than those who have not had childhood illnesses or major surgical procedures.

Often, self-injurious behaviors are mistaken for suicidal gestures. It is true that some adolescents who self-injure also become suicidal. The two phenomena are, however, distinct in important ways, such as intent, method, lethality, and number of acts. Still, both behaviors are self-directed, result in concrete physical harm, are often the result of frustrated psychological needs, and reflect lifelong coping patterns. Both are of grave concern to friends, parents, teachers, counselors, and other mental health professionals.

Most adolescents seek treatment for other problems, such as depression, and not for self-injurious behaviors. However, not everyone who engages in self-injurious behaviors has a severe psychological problem. Some warning signs to be aware of include increased depression, feeling overwhelmed with relationship or sexual issues, having been abused, or hurting oneself to manage one's emotions. Individuals who self-injure may seek treatment from community mental health centers, local clinics, hospitals, and other specialized treatment programs.

Laura A. Gallagher

See also Depression; Physical Abuse; Risk Behaviors; Self-Consciousness; Suicide

References and further reading
Favazza, Armando R. 1996. *Bodies under Siege: Self-Mutilation and Body Modification in Culture and Pyschiatry,* 2nd ed. Baltimore: Johns Hopkins University Press.
———. 1989. "Why Patients Mutilate Themselves." *Hospital and Community Psychiatry* 40, no. 2: 137–145.
Favazza, Armando R., and Karen Conterio. 1988. "The Plight of Chronic Self-Mutilators." *Community Mental Health Journal* 24, no. 1: 22–30.
Levenkron, Steven. 1998. *Cutting: Understanding and Overcoming Self-Mutilation.* New York: Norton.
Strong, Marilee. 1998. *A Bright Red Scream: Self-Mutilation and the Language of Pain.* New York: Viking.
Suyemoto, Karen L., and Marian L. McDonald. 1995. "Self-Cutting in Female Adolescents" *Psychotherapy* 32, no. 1: 162–171.
Walsh, Barent W., and Paul M. Rosen. 1988. *Self-Mutilation: Theory, Research, and Practice.* New York: Guilford Press.
Winchel, Ronald M., and Michael Stanley. 1991. "Self-Injurious Behavior: A Review of the Behavior and Biology of Self-Mutilation." *American Journal of Psychiatry* 148, no. 3: 306–317.

Services for Adolescents

This entry summarizes state-of-the-art knowledge about services for adolescent behavioral, emotional, and mental health problems discussed in other chapters. Adolescence is a time of high morbidity and mortality related to problems including violent behavior, substance use, unwed pregnancy, depression, suicide, anxiety, school failure, and peer difficulties. Each of these problems is associated with a youth's community and family environment and mental health. However, existing interventions are scarce and fragmented. Treatment, when provided, usually attempts to intervene only with the individual, often focuses on attitudes rather than the actual problem, and ignores the environment. Nevertheless, on the positive side, there is increasing recognition of the need for effective action. Recently, prompted by the dramatically increasing rates of adolescent problems, governmental and public health sectors have jointly called for mobilization and coordination of comprehensive efforts to develop new interventions.

The Services Needs of Adolescents
Adolescence is a very unusual period physiologically and historically. Except for the infancy/toddler age, it is charac-

Youth services provide sources of support and guidance for young people. (Urban Archives, Philadelphia)

terized by the steepest growth curve in a human's life. Unlike a baby, the adolescent is conscious of these changes and must confront them to establish a sense of identity. Also, today, for the first time in history, adolescents are more at risk for permanent injury and death from problems that are not primarily biomedical. The initiation of risky behavior is occurring at progressively younger ages, and the proportion of adolescents who come from disadvantaged groups (who are at higher risk for behavior problems) is increasing. Adolescence is a time to develop the skills and knowledge that will lead to a productive, satisfying, healthy adulthood. Yet many adolescent

risk behaviors threaten future development. These include unwed pregnancy, unprotected sexual activity, violent behavior, and substance use. Further, risk behaviors seldom occur alone. Adolescents engaging in one risk behavior are likely to engage in many such behaviors and have other associated mental health problems. Many of these behaviors increase in frequency and intensity during adolescence, and many mild risk behaviors (such as experimentation with tobacco use or occasional alcohol use) serve as gateways for more risky involvement in later adolescence or adulthood.

Need for services may be conceptualized in terms of diagnoses, symptoms, or functioning. Many adolescents have clusters of symptoms severe enough to be distressing or disabling. Research has estimated that between one-quarter and one-fifth of adolescents need services because they have mental health problems that meet diagnostic criteria. The rates for need of services by those who have distressing or disabling symptoms yet who do not meet diagnostic criteria would be much higher.

Where Adolescents Can Find Services
Adolescents are minors, and they are often reluctant or unable to seek services on their own. For example, youths may not be able to obtain services without a guardian's permission, may not have the money or insurance to pay for services, may not have transportation to get to services, or may not believe that services can help them. Youths tend to be directed to services by their parents, teachers, physicians, social workers, juvenile justice authorities, and other adults. Large proportions of these "gateway" individuals come from four types of public-service sectors: primary health, child welfare, juvenile justice, and education. Providers from these sectors or informal sectors (e.g., clergy, family, friends, or self-help groups) often have the first contact with the youth and identify the problem. Even when they cannot offer direct services for behavioral or emotional problems, their actions in referral, consultation, and liaison help youth access services.

The primary health and education sectors would appear to be universal sources of gateway services. In fact, few youths actually receive services in specialty mental health settings (e.g., mental health clinics, community mental health centers, or psychiatric outpatient departments); most receive such care through the education or primary health gateway sectors. Unfortunately, the financial capacity of the educational system to provide services is limited. Primary health providers, such as family doctors and city health clinics, are the second most likely gateway providers to be consulted; however, youths frequently do not discuss their emotional or behavioral problems with their healthcare providers.

In order to provide services, these gateway providers must recognize that a youth needs services. Yet research shows large discrepancies between need for services and provider identification of need. The clustering of several mental health problems, functional impairments, and risk factors all influence identification of need for services. Gateway providers, including teachers, may be more likely to recognize behavior that disrupts classes or disturbs others, and fail to pay attention to problems such as depression or anxiety. However, even when a provider knows a youth needs services, services and treatments specifically designed for adolescents are often unavailable.

Risk Factors
Services for problems need to focus on factors that cause or maintain those problems, or factors that might protect a youth from such problems. A number of risk factors might predispose youths to need services. These risk factors include biological or genetic contributions, the youth's environment (both social and physical), individual personality factors, and behavioral factors (or lifestyles). In addition, a number of protective factors can also fall into any of the above categories. For instance, a supportive family

environment and other external support systems may protect highly stressed youth.

We know that risks and protectors work together in complex ways. The ecological and bio-psycho-social perspectives focus on interactions among multiple systems as they determine physical and mental health and social functioning. Research within the field of developmental psychopathology has examined the complex interplay between personal and environmental risk and protective factors in determining behavioral and mental health outcomes. The difficulty lies in distinguishing the relative influence of biological, psychological, social, communal, and economic factors so that services can efficiently target the most important factors.

Individual Risk Factors. Individual differences may be present from birth. For example, physiology contributes to many behavior and mental health problems. Many youths with such problems also have problems with attention, memory, and social-cognitive processing. These problems may have their roots in hormonal or neurotransmitter problems, or may be related to environmental contaminants such as lead poisoning. Several studies show an association between genetics and other mental health problems, specifically depression, suicidal tendencies, and substance abuse.

Peer Risk Factors. Peers provide the motivation, rationalization, attitudes, opportunities, and reinforcement for many adolescent behavior problems, including violence, unprotected sex, and substance use. In fact, peers may even punish prosocial behaviors.

Family Risk Factors. Many behavior or mental health problems may have roots in early childhood through physical abuse, as well as observation of similar behaviors in families and in the community. Intervention studies support this association by showing that when parents adopt more positive, consistent, and less physical styles of discipline, their children's antisocial behavior declines.

School Risk Factors. Youths who have mental health or behavioral problems often also have school problems. This suggests that school environment and student attitudes toward education are important risk factors. When school is valued and considered a viable option, misbehavior is reduced. Alternatively, some assert that school problems and other behavioral or mental health problems are both symptoms of deeper root problems.

Community Risk Factors. Aspects of the community or neighborhood may make a youth more likely to need services. Community problems include the presence of gangs, underemployment, economic deprivation, the availability and use of illicit drugs, and access to lethal weapons. In the United States, many risk factors are associated with minority status and low socioeconomic status. For example, minority communities have high rates of violent behavior, unprotected sex, substance use, suicide, and the like. Nevertheless, much of the racial variation in such behaviors may be due to community differences. Increased levels of such problems are also associated with community mobility, social disorganization, breakdowns of formal and informal social controls, and tolerant attitudes toward such behaviors.

Prevention Programs
Although we know about the types of risk factors, we do not understand why, given similar risk factors, some youths never develop problems, some engage in sporadic experimentation with problem behaviors and then desist, and some develop serious problems. Obviously there must be some protectors at work. Prevention programs help youths resist the development of serious problems by mitigating risks and enhancing potential protectors.

The literature on prevention programs remains woefully underdeveloped. It consists largely of calls for action. Knowledge about prevention is fragmented, with little good outcome research. Prevention focuses on reducing access to means for problem behaviors such as substance use or violence, controlling media, enhancing prosocial skills, intervening with peers and families, reducing risk factors, and intervening at multisystemic community levels.

Prevention by Reducing Access to Risks.
Some preventive interventions to reduce substance abuse have focused on carding teens who try to purchase cigarettes, enforcing age minimums for alcohol purchase, and prosecuting illicit drug dealers and users. Similarly, some preventive interventions for violence have focused on firearm reduction by enforcing current laws and reducing the availability of firearms.

Prevention through the Mass Media.
Volunteer groups and legislators have called on the media to deglamorize unprotected sex, substance use, and violence. For example, legislators have demanded more accurate portrayal of violence and its consequences by the entertainment industry.

Prevention through Developing Life Skills. Life skills training teaches communication approaches, conflict resolution, anger management, and social skills. Such programs assume that many behavior problems are learned, and so they can be changed and prevented. Thus, these programs usually target youths from dysfunctional families or communities with high rates of problems. They may address factors indirectly associated with a problem, such as low academic achievement or drug use for gang prevention, and may include a combination of life skills training, mentoring, self-esteem development, peer tutoring, and education. These programs may begin as early as preschool in order to prevent later behavioral problems.

Clearly, many youths lack such skills as problem solving, communication, and anger control. However, we know that these skills can be learned, particularly if the training is implemented at an early age. Therefore, preschool or elementary school social skills training would be an appropriate preventive intervention. Effective prevention would also involve changing youths' future outlook through goal setting and/or job training. Many youths involved in problem behavior have no future goals, and cannot visualize themselves respectably and gainfully employed. Therefore, changing the individual youth's perception of her future, and preparation for that future, would be helpful. Note that it is financially easier to influence the perception of one's future than it is to influence actual opportunities. However, it is also possible to better prepare youths to take advantage of existing opportunities.

School-based life skill programs have one distinct advantage: Because school attendance is mandatory, the programs can involve virtually all youths in a community. Unfortunately, data suggest that such interventions have limited behavioral success within the school setting, and no studies show that reducing problem behavior in primary school generalizes to later behavior in the community. It is especially difficult to transfer prosocial behaviors to youths' everyday environments if those environments are disadvantaged or nonsupportive.

Prevention through Peers. Peer counseling and peer mediation are used to decrease violence, delinquency, and antisocial behaviors, as well as to increase the likelihood of using protection during sexual behavior, and so on. The rationale behind such peer programs is that adolescents may listen to the advice of their peers more than to that of adults. Unfortunately, no conclusive data show that peer programs are effective. In fact, some have concluded that peer counseling may even have negative effects on delinquency and associated risk factors, such as academic failure, rebelliousness, and lack of commitment to school. However, youth-led programs that document personal experiences or provide activities to fill idle time (such as basketball tournaments, game room activities, and dancing) give some evidence of effectiveness.

Prevention through the Family. Attempts to alter high-risk family systems are another common approach to the prevention of behavioral and mental health problems in adolescence. Such programs generally target at-risk families with younger children. Parent training programs teach child and family management skills, and address both family conflict and early antisocial behavior. Marital and family therapy approaches focus on changing the dysfunctional patterns of family interactions, and addressing risk factors such as poor family management, family conflict, and early antisocial behavior. Studies of these interventions have demonstrated a significant reduction in children's antisocial behavior and possible long-term preventive effects on delinquency. However, such programs are least successful with the most high risk families (e.g., those with multiple problems, including high conflict, unemployment, poverty, illness, and low stability).

Prevention through Community Intervention. The personal interventions of skills training, goal setting, influencing perception, and efforts to develop self-esteem are all likely to fail unless intervention includes consideration of youths' environments. Youths' environments include families, school, peers, and neighborhoods. The acceptability and modeling of problem behaviors must be reduced at all levels. This is not easy, as issues of censorship, the profit-making motive of the media, societal welfare, and individual freedom must be balanced.

Community interventions are based on the presumption that resource inequity, high tolerance of problem behaviors, and a sense of powerlessness and lack of control compound youths' problems. Community prevention, therefore, focuses on decreasing cultural acceptance of the problem behaviors (such as violence, unwed pregnancy, or substance use), decreasing racial and gender discrimination, and supporting more positive role models. Community interventions include resource enhancement such as mobilizing community members and coordinating better financing for mental health, drug abuse, and social service programs. They also include services such as providing role models, family interventions, neighborhood projects, education, and job training. Often they include criminal justice involvement through improving police images and increasing police-resident interaction. The youths' environment must have increased positive opportunities for activities that will reduce the likelihood of engaging in problem behavior and decrease the opportunities for problem behavior to flourish. Many adolescent problem behaviors occur during idle moments when groups of youths are unsupervised. Programs trying to increase constructive idle time include midnight basketball leagues and other clubs, sports activities, or choir activities sponsored by churches and community centers.

Neighborhood environments can be enhanced through positive adult role models and desirable future opportunities. Many gender- and ethnic-specific mentor and role-model programs have already been instituted. These programs must also provide the educational, financial, and social support youths need to emulate the models. In many areas where risk behaviors are highest, the most common employment opportunities are through an underground illicit economy that allows the growth of gangs, unprotected sex, substance use, and violent behaviors. Real possibilities for gainful employment and for adequate, effective, and appropriate education would be effective services. Unfortunately, although community approaches with an evaluation component have produced evidence of attitudinal changes, they have been unable to document changes in behavior.

Services Available to Adolescents Who Already Have Serious Problems
Because we have addressed programs targeting at-risk youths and communities in the prevention section, the following discussion concentrates on adolescents who already have serious behavioral or mental health problems. Treatment approaches have the same major problems as prevention approaches. In addition, in many areas, services for teens, such as drug abuse treatment, are unavailable. Even when services for a problem are available, communities are often not involved, and services are both uncoordinated and underfunded.

Therapeutic Approaches. Treatments for youths are based on three different psychological perspectives: (1) psychosocial, (2) humanistic/nondirective, and (3) behavioral. (Note that we are excluding a discussion of psychopharmacological treatment in this chapter, as that is a separate medical issue.) Under each of those three categories, a whole range of specific approaches can be listed. For example, the psychosocial approach includes psychodynamic, psychoanalytic, and interpersonal approaches. The behavioral approach includes social learning and cognitive behavioral approaches. All three psychological perspectives share the concept that problems are due to a shortcoming within the individual, and treatment can be either short or long term. Additionally, a number of short-term treatments, largely deriving from the behavioral perspective, focus primarily on solving problems. These include task-centered or solution-focused therapies, psychoeducation, and bibliotherapy.

All three psychological perspectives assume that, if interventions target the deficiency in an individual, effective and healthy behavior will follow. Some reviewers of evaluated interventions conclude that no approach is clearly superior. Others argue that the results of repeated evaluation studies tend to support the effectiveness of behavioral approaches.

Unfortunately, many therapeutic interventions are crippled by the problematic nature of the families of disturbed youths. For instance, youths may be coping with an incarcerated parent, a drug-using parent, and/or an unstable and violence-filled home. Further, youths may lack adequate food and shelter, supervision, and schooling. Youths themselves may have addiction problems that limit their ability to take advantage of other therapies. Also, many problem behaviors revolve around alcohol and drugs, which both make users more apt to engage in problem behaviors by lowering their inhibitions and create a need to continue to engage in other problem behaviors to obtain alcohol and drugs.

Residential or Inpatient Treatments. Residential or inpatient treatments provide youths with individual intervention while removing them from society. Unfortunately, services are not always available and are expensive, and positive results may not transfer to youths' homes upon release. Further, many programs are designed to address a single issue, and are thus unprepared to cope with a youth who is, for example, both a substance abuser and suicidal. Also, youths with extreme behavioral problems may tax the resources of residential placements and put other residents at risk. Therefore, many programs are unwilling to accept youths with violent antisocial behavior problems. Many such youths are shuffled from one program to another and finally end up in jails.

Criminal Justice Treatment. Traditionally, youths engaging in delinquent, vio-

lent, or substance abuse behaviors were removed from society and placed in juvenile detention centers or jails. Mainstream criminology views clinical services as ineffective and prefers punishment. However, the criminal justice approach alone has never been proven effective. Crowded and poorly supervised residential, inpatient, or juvenile detention facilities expose healthier youths to more disturbed youths. Sometimes the justice system also provides psychological treatment, and that approach has produced a substantial reduction in recidivism. Such services include more intensive treatment of higher risk cases, services targeted at reducing the offenders' need to commit criminal behavior, and services tailored to the abilities and learning style of the offenders. For youths whose major service option appears to be jail, diversion programs are popular. Examples of diversion programs include wilderness experiences and boot camps. Wilderness camping programs attempt to remove youths from their normal surroundings and challenge them to cooperate for survival. Unfortunately, neither program consistently shows long-term positive effects.

Systems Approaches

A number of therapeutic approaches take a more systemic approach by looking at youths' environments. This addresses what we know about the many interacting causes and protectors of risk behaviors. Originally systems theory approaches focused on the family system. But it has become clear that individuals interact with multiple systems, including their families, their peers, their communities, and their schools. Therefore, a spate of systems-based interventions, ranging from family therapy to group therapy, has incorporated the theoretical approaches of the individual therapies. They deal with the youth's problem as it interacts with the family, the school, peers, neighborhoods, communities, and so on.

Recently, some treatment approaches for adolescents have broadened their approach to attempt to deal with multiple and interactive causalities. For example, multisystemic treatments (MST) combine cognitive intrapersonal strategies with family, peer, and school interventions. The approach involves collaborative work with the school, parents, teachers, and peers. Research shows behavioral improvements lasting up to one year, and reduced recidivism at a four-year follow-up.

Clearly, adolescent behavioral and mental health problems are manifestations of complex economic, environmental, political, cultural, educational, and behavioral factors. Services must echo that complexity through the coordination of services (including public health, healthcare, mental health, criminal justice, social service, education, and the media) and foci of responses. Further, prevention programs must be developmentally and culturally appropriate and comprehensive, they must target risk groups, and they must include assessment.

Literature, research, and experience quite clearly point to the necessity of increasing multifaceted interventions targeting multiple risk factors. Improvement of access to care would be easier to achieve if there were coordination of care across services and service sectors. Then multifaceted and multilevel services could take into account adolescents' internal factors, developmental stages, social networks, and cultural backgrounds.

Arlene Rubin Stiffman

See also Counseling; High School Equivalency Degree; Intervention Programs for Adolescents; Programs for Adolescents

References and further reading
Bandura, Albert. 1986. *Social Foundations of Thought and Action: A Social Cognitive Theory.* Englewood Cliffs, NJ: Prentice-Hall.
Bronfenbrenner, Urie. 1980. "Ecology of Childhood." *School Psychology Review* 9, no. 4: 294–297.
Burns, Barbara, Carl A. Taube, and John E. Taube. 1990. *Use of Mental Health Sector Services by Adolescents: 1975, 1980, 1986.* Paper prepared under contract for the Carnegie Council on Adolescent Development and the Carnegie Corporation of New York, for the Office of Technology Assessment, U.S. Congress, Washington, DC. Springfield, VA: National Technical Information Service (NTIS No. PB 91–154 344/AS).
DiClemente, Ralph J., William Hansen, and Lynn Ponton, eds. 1996. *Handbook of Adolescent Health Risk Behavior.* New York: Plenum Publishing.
Henggeler, Scott W., Sonja K. Schoenwald, Charles M. Borduin, Melisa D. Rowland, and Phillippe B. Cunningham. 1998. *Multisystemic Treatment of Antisocial Behavior in Children and Adolescents.* New York: Guilford Press.
Hurrelmann, Klaus, and Stephen F. Hamilton, eds. 1996. *Social Problems and Social Contexts in Adolescence: Perspectives across Boundaries.* New York: Aldine de Gruyter.
Jessor, Richard, and Shirley L. Jessor. 1977. *Problem Behavior and Psycho-Social Development: A Longitudinal Study of Youth.* New York: Academic Press.
McWhirter, J. Jeffries, Benedict T. McWhirter, Anna M. McWhirter, and Ellen Hawley McWhirter. 1993. *At-Risk Youth: A Comprehensive Response.* Pacific Grove, CA: Brooks-Cole.
Rolf, Jon E., Ann S. Masten, Dante Cicchetti, Keith H. Nuechterlein, and Sheldon Weintraub, eds. 1990. *Risk and Protective Factors in the Development of Psychopathology.* Cambridge, UK: Cambridge University Press.
U.S. Department of Health and Human Services. 1990. *Healthy People 2000:*

National Health Promotion and Disease Prevention Objectives. Washington, DC: U.S. Government Printing Office.

Sex Differences

Adolescence is the stage during which sex differences become much more marked, and it is crucial that those who work with adolescents understand the nature of those differences and be prepared to help young people understand them. At the same time, they need to be aware of the controversies that remain over whether those differences are caused by nature or nurture.

There are many ways in which females and males are different. Some of these differences can be seen before birth, while others develop later in life. Some differences are biological, while others are influenced by society and experience. This section will address sex differences in physical development and growth, as well as differences in ability. The emphasis of this section is on *sex differences,* or those differences between males and females that are thought to be influenced primarily by biology and genetics (i.e., nature). *Gender differences,* on the other hand, are differences between males and females that are primarily shaped by society, culture, and the environment (i.e., nurture).

The distinction between sex differences and gender differences is not always clear. Even experts in these areas of research do not always agree on where to draw the line between nature and nurture. How much are differences between people due to the fact that they are genetically female or male, and how much are they due to the way society raises girls and boys? For example, it is often found that males perform better than females on tasks that involve mentally moving and turning objects in their minds (spatial tasks), a finding that will be discussed later. Some experts interpret this difference as biological in nature, which would explain why males tend to be drawn toward working with tools and physical sports more than women are. However, other experts believe that this difference is due to the opportunities and experiences that males have through childhood and adolescence, such as playing sports or working with tools, which increase their ability for spatial tasks. In reality, it is likely that nature and nurture both contribute to the development of sex differences, with some differences being influenced more by nature than nurture and vice versa.

Basic Differences

The most basic sex difference between females and males is their genetic makeup. At conception, genes from the mother and father are combined. It takes a pair of chromosomes to create a human being, and each parent contributes one chromosome to the pair. The mother always contributes an X chromosome, and the father always contributes a Y chromosome. Two X chromosomes (XX) create a female offspring, while one X and one Y chromosome (XY) create a male.

One of the most obvious differences between females and males is the appearance and function of their sexual organs. Although this difference is obvious in children and adults, it is impossible to tell the difference between females and males by looking at the genitals of fetuses. In fact, all fetuses look more like females than males until the sex organs develop. The fetus needs to receive certain hormones at important stages of

*During adolescence sex differences in various behaviors may become much more prominent.
(Wartenberg/Picture Press/Corbis)*

development in order to become male. If these hormones are not present, it will not develop male genitals, and will appear externally female, even though it is genetically male. The reverse can also occur, in which the baby is genetically female, though it appears externally male. This is known as having *undifferentiated* or *ambiguous* genitalia.

Differences in Physical Development
Females and males differ in how they grow and develop *physically*. Girls and boys have different biologically determined schedules for development, and this difference is most pronounced at adolescence. Sex differences in growth and development are first seen before birth, when the skeletal development of female fetuses can be as much as three weeks ahead of that of male fetuses at the same stage of pregnancy. Female development is more advanced than that of males at birth, and this difference continues through puberty. At puberty, females' skeletal structures are up to two years more advanced than males. This female "advantage" is also seen during puberty. Females begin and end puberty, on average, earlier than males. They tend to develop the first signs of puberty earlier, and reach their maximum height earlier, as well.

Growth spurts are characteristic of adolescence, and a common way of measuring physical growth. Females have their growth spurts about six months earlier than males, on average. Girls experience their growth spurts around the ages of four and a half, six and a half, eight and a half, and ten years. Boys are close behind at just over four and a half years, and at seven, nine, and ten and a half years. Although females grow faster, males are generally larger. From birth to three years old, boys are about two pounds heavier and one to two inches taller than girls are. Using height spurts as a sign of puberty, females tend to reach puberty (ten and a half years) and end puberty (fourteen years) earlier than males, who begin puberty around twelve and a half years and tend to end around eighteen years.

Puberty is also characterized by sexual development, both primary and secondary. *Primary sex characteristics* are those that are directly related to sexual functioning and reproduction. This includes, in both sexes, the ability to reproduce. In females the development of primary sex characteristics at puberty involves beginning of ovulation and menstruation (menarche). In males it means the ability to produce sperm. There are also *secondary sex characteristics* that develop during puberty. Before puberty, girls and boys look physically similar. Except for the genitals, and gender-stereotyped clothing and hair, it can be difficult to tell a girl from a boy. After puberty it is usually easy to tell women from men physically. Both sexes develop more body hair than they had before puberty, but males develop more of it, and in different places. Females develop breasts and their hips widen. Males' shoulders broaden, and their voices deepen significantly.

Differences in physical size other than height also become evident at puberty. Males begin to develop more muscle mass and become leaner, losing fat. Males also become larger overall than females. On the other hand, females gain fat at puberty but are, as a group, smaller than males once they reach adulthood. These differences may have evolutionary roots. For example, if males are designed to hunt and fight, they need to have more muscle mass and less fat. In contrast, one major role of females throughout evolution and across most species is to bear offspring. Pregnancy requires a lot of energy and nourishment, and some people think that the increase in female body fat at puberty is the body's way of preparing itself for childbearing. In modern culture, females generally do not reproduce when their bodies are first ready to. However, the female body does not know that, and will prepare itself for that basic task, regardless of cultural body ideas for women.

Differences in Ability

There are also sex differences in ability, but this area of research is much more controversial and speculative than differences in development. Sometimes the controversy arises regarding whether there are actual sex differences in certain abilities. When actual sex differences are found, debate centers around whether the differences are caused by sex (i.e., they are natural or genetic), or whether they are influenced by society (i.e., being raised as a girl or boy). Although experts do not always agree on the causes of these differences (again the debate on nature versus nurture), there are distinct sex differences in some types of ability.

First, there are sex differences in *physical ability*. Generally, females are better at activities that require agility, such as dancing and gymnastics, and fine motor skills, such as manipulating small objects with their fingers. Males tend to be better at activities that require power and force, such as weight lifting. These differences are due, in large part, to biology. After adolescence, males have much more muscle mass than females, which helps them excel at activities requiring power. In childhood, these sex differences are not as great as they become at puberty, but even then males still slightly outperform females on tests such as grip strength, jumping, running, and throwing distance and velocity. It is easy to assume that these differences are purely biological. Sex differences in very young children may indicate that there are biological roots to these differences, since sex differences in children are less influenced by society. At infancy, male infants are more active than female infants, suggesting a biological predisposition for activity. However, society helps shape the activities females and males will participate in, and subsequently become good at.

Second, sex differences are found in abilities that are more *mental* than physical. One of these abilities is called spatial ability. Spatial ability is measured with puzzles that require a person to rotate a shape or object in the mind. Males have been found to perform better than females on these tasks in certain situations. Some experts would argue that the reason that males perform better is because they have more experience than females with games that promote spatial ability (throwing, building, and the like). Others would say that the differences are due to differences in the brain. *Lateralization* refers to which side of the brain is dominant. The left side of the brain is thought to deal primarily with verbal tasks, while the right side is thought to deal with mathematical and spatial tasks. However, there is little evidence of sex differences in brain lateralization

between females and males. Differences in lateralization between adult males and females could be due to environment and socialization.

Although males, as a group, outperform females, as a group, in spatial orientation tasks, females tend to be better than males at *orientation toward others.* This term refers to how people acknowledge and interact with other people. Psychologists have studied this behavior by measuring length of eye contact with others, responses to people in distress, recognizing faces, and the amount of attention people pay to pictures of faces. Females outperform males on all of these behaviors. By childhood, some of these differences may be due to learning, but differences are seen in infancy.

In sum, while sex differences in several areas are evident, it is clear that real differences between males and females are the result of both biology and socialization. Researchers continue to make progress in answering questions about both the biological and environmental differences between the sexes.

Matthew Jans

See also Body Build; Gay, Lesbian, Bisexual, and Sexual-Minority Youth; Gender Differences; Gender Differences and Intellectual and Moral Development; Puberty: Hormone Changes; Puberty: Physical Changes; Puberty, Timing of; Services for Adolescents

References and further reading
Bancroft, John, and June Machover Reinisch, eds. 1990. *Adolescence and Puberty.* New York: Oxford University Press.
Geary, David C. 1998. *Male, Female: The Evolution of Human Sex Differences.* Washington, DC: American Psychological Association.
Hoyenga, Katharine B. 1993. *Gender-Related Differences: Origins and Outcomes.* Boston: Allyn and Bacon.

Jacklin, Carol Nagy. 1992. *The Psychology of Gender.* New York: New York University Press.

Reinisch, June Machover, Leonard A. Rosenblum, and Stephanie A. Sanders, eds. 1987. *Masculinity/Femininity: Basic Perspectives.* New York: Oxford University Press.

Sex Education

During the adolescent years, sexual development speeds up, and sexuality become a central focus for adolescents. Adolescents grapple with the physical, behavioral, and physiological aspects of their sexuality. It is not unusual for the adolescent to experience a certain amount of confusion and anxiety as a result of this increase in sexual drive and development. Specialists in child development agree that educating the young adolescent about sexual issues is a proactive way of reducing not only anxiety about sex but also behaviors that may result in disease or unwanted pregnancy. Although it may seem reasonable for adolescents to obtain information from their parents, they usually do not do so. Adolescents consistently identify their peers as their primary source of sex education, with parents and schools as lesser sources. Most adolescents get much of their information regarding sex from their peers, who are often misinformed about this topic. Research that has focused on the sex education occurring in the home has found it to be lacking. However, in some studies there have been positive outcomes when parents do talk to their adolescents about sex. For example, adolescents are less likely to engage in certain sexual behaviors, and if they do have sex they are more likely to use effective contraception and have fewer sexual partners if their parents talk to them about sexual issues.

Parents usually agree that some sex education should be done in the schools, but a significant minority is strongly opposed to it. In a large opinion study, most parents reported that they thought public high schools should include sex education in their instructional program (Gallup, 1987). Unfortunately, schools rarely have teachers who have had specific training regarding human sexuality. Healthcare providers are another possible source of sex education, but many have had little training in this area. During a health checkup, most providers spend only a few minutes talking with teenagers about any topic. In many other Western and some Asian countries, sex education is a regular part of the curriculum and is taught in every grade according to the developmental stages of the child. Information collected from these countries suggests that there are no unwanted effects of using this curriculum (e.g., no increase in promiscuity) and also suggests that there are fewer problems related to adolescent sexuality (e.g., a lower rate of unwanted pregnancy among adolescents) (Zabin and Hayward, 1993). Below several potential problems and possible solutions in regard to sex education are discussed.

Teaching Adolescents about Sexuality
Peers provide the most information about sex to teens. Teens are more comfortable talking about private issues with their friends. Unfortunately, peers are often uninformed or misinformed about the issues and facts, and base their statements on their own personal experience or that of a few friends. If there were a standard curriculum for sex education, this problem could be eliminated,

because all adolescents would be exposed to similar, accurate information. There are several reasons why parents are not typically a source of sex education for their children. First, it is likely that they have had no formal exposure to sexuality issues. In addition, most parents do not feel comfortable talking to their kids about sexual issues. The main exception is that most mothers tell their daughters about menstruation.

Schools are the source of some sexual information. Most girls get to see a film on menstruation, often shown after most girls have already reached menarche. Boys are almost never allowed to see this film, especially at the same time and in the same room as girls. Some schools show boys a film about sexual development, but never in the same room and at the same time as girls. The practice of separating the sexes during instruction that applies to both of them sends a rather peculiar but common message in regard to sexuality. This message suggests that sex is something so private and mysterious that one sex should not know anything about the other sex.

In the past, the teacher designated to be the instructor in sexual matters in schools did not have particular training or expertise in this area. Many times the person was the athletic coach, often by default. Today, all schools are required to provide students with information regarding AIDS. Children are informed about how AIDS is contracted and how it is not contracted, but little information is provided on explicit sexual practices. Most states have developed a standard curriculum to address this subject and have provided training for teachers who teach this topic. However, many states do not allow teachers to talk about any ways to prevent AIDS except by avoiding having sexual relations. Some school systems have developed a curriculum that they require every child to complete. If parents do not want their adolescent exposed to the curriculum in the school setting, they may administer the curriculum at home or have another responsible and appropriate person (healthcare provider, religious leader, or the like) supervise the curriculum at a location other than the school. All students must pass a standard test based on the curriculum, regardless of where it was taught. Schools in other developed countries have successfully instituted courses in human sexuality, integrating it into the curriculum in appropriate places.

Perhaps the media represent the largest source of information about sex in the United States. Sexually intimate behavior, often quite sexually explicit, is displayed by the media with increasing frequency. Films run in public theaters have been rated to exclude younger teens from certain movies. Although there have been attempts to do this for television, it is not known how much parents actually control what their adolescents watch, or how many younger adolescents still watch material considered inappropriate. Specifically pornographic films, videos, and magazines are also available. Part of the problem relates to the use of sexually suggestive advertisements whose message often is use this product and you will be sexually rewarded. So the teenager is often faced with mixed messages, hearing on one hand the message based on Judeo-Christian belief, which says that sexuality is a personal and private issue of intimacy between one man and one woman, and on the other hand the message of the media and businesses that advertise using the media, which suggests that sex is all right anytime, anyplace, with anyone. Another part of the problem relates to the apparent absence of consequences for sexual behaviors displayed on-screen. Multiple sexual partners, no use of contraception or methods to prevent sexually transmitted disease, yet no ill effects, and the emotional side effects of sexual behaviors are rarely shown. This may give the message to adolescents that there are no unwanted consequences of sexual behaviors.

Sex Education Curriculum—The Problem of What to Teach

The question of the content of sex education programs creates anxiety in parents. There is little agreement among parents and teachers about the appropriate content of sex education curriculum. Anatomy (body parts), physiology (how the body works), changes associated with puberty, pregnancy, childbirth and infant care, sexually transmitted diseases, and family planning can be thought of as relatively scientific topics, but some parents feel that even mentioning some of these topics is a violation of their and their child's right to decide on what is appropriate information to give to adolescents. Some parents also are concerned that if their children get information, they may become very curious about the information and want to act on it—they may become sexually active. Some parents feel that if their child is not sexually active, providing them with information about sex may make them think that there is something wrong with them because they may think that everyone else is sexually active except them.

Many sex educators have felt that they should only provide scientific information and avoid discussing the ethical and moral issues involved in human sexuality. Many parents feel that the ethical and moral issues are of major importance and that only they as parents can know what these issues are for their families. It seems fairly clear, however, that almost everyone agrees about the basic ethical and moral issues of the Judeo-Christian philosophy. It is difficult to imagine that parents, teachers, or healthcare providers would advocate premarital intercourse, teenage unplanned pregnancy, promiscuity, and the like, or that they would not consider abstinence advisable for all adolescents. These and other commonly agreed upon points should be covered in any sexuality curriculum. Issues related to gender identity, gender roles, gender preferences, and abortion are extraordinarily complex issues compared with the topics mentioned previously. Inclusion of these issues in sexuality curricula will depend on the availability of experts in these areas.

When to Teach Children about Sexual Issues

Sexuality education should ideally begin at home during infancy and childhood. Parents have many opportunities to provide important and appropriate information to their children in the preschool years. If they did so, it would serve to appropriately prepare a child to experience a school-based curriculum regarding sexuality. To a great extent the practice of using a curriculum designed for each developmental age group will best suit most people. It would be inappropriate to discuss contraception with children in kindergarten, but an appropriate presentation of pregnancy would be important, since the mothers of many of this group will be pregnant.

A different presentation of pregnancy would be most appropriate for high school juniors and seniors, since many of them will become parents within a few years. The concept that sexuality education should begin at puberty does not recognize the importance of child development in sexuality education. It also fails to recognize that all children are sexually curious and engage in sexual behaviors throughout development (e.g., genital fondling is common during the toddler and early childhood years, and masturbation typically begins in early adolescence), and therefore all children need information and guidance concerning this important aspect of life at all stages of life. Sexuality begins in the developing fetus and continues throughout all stages of life. Sexuality education should parallel these changes. Too often sex education is introduced after the adolescent is already sexually active.

The essential point is that all children will become sexually educated. There is an abundance of information from informal sources such as peers and the media, and there is no way to shelter an adolescent from information and misinformation. All sources that adolescents elicit information from (parents, peers, clergy, teachers, and medical professionals) need to provide accurate and responsible information. Adolescents should have a means to discuss their sexual attitudes and behaviors in an open and honest way.

Jordan W. Finkelstein

See also Abortion; Abstinence; Contraception; Pregnancy, Interventions to Prevent; Sex Differences; Sexual Behavior; Sexuality, Emotional Aspects of; Sexually Transmitted Diseases

References and further reading
Bourgeois, Paulette, and Martin Wolfish. 1994a. *Changes in You and Me: A Book about Puberty, Mostly for Boys.* Kansas City: Andrews and McMeel.
———. 1994b. *Changes in You and Me: A Book about Puberty, Mostly for Girls.* Kansas City: Andrews and McMeel.
Faulkenberry, Ray, M. Vincent, A. James, and W. Johnson. 1987. "Coital Behaviors, Attitudes, and Knowledge of Students Who Experience Early Coitus." *Adolescence* 22: 321–332.
Gallup, Gordon, Jr. 1987. *The Gallup Poll: Public Opinion 1986.* Washington, DC: Scholarly Resources.
Irvine, Janice M. 1994. *Sexuality Education across Cultures.* San Francisco: Jossey-Bass.
Koch, Patricia. 1991. "Sex Education." In *Encyclopedia of Adolescence.* Edited by Richard Lerner, Anne Petersen, and Jeanne Brooks-Gunn. New York: Garland.
Measor, Lynda, with Coralie Tiffin. 2000. *Young People's Views on Sex Education: Education, Attitudes, and Behavior.* London and New York: Routledge/Falmer.
Zabin, L., and S. Hayward. 1993. *Adolescent Sexual Behavior and Childbearing.* Newbury Park, CA: Sage.

Sex Roles

Sex roles are the prevailing societally defined male and female roles, or gender roles. All societies define expected role behaviors for males and females. In the United States, the traditional male sex role is an instrumental one, and the traditional female sex role is an expressive one. These roles are reversed in some other cultures, because they are not entirely biologically determined. Sex roles are learned in the same manner as other social behaviors and roles, through direct training, by parents, for example, or through peer pressure, observational learning (e.g., watching models such as parents or the way males and females behave in the media), and other socialization techniques. Because sex roles influence the view of the self, impact on vocational decision making, shape views of marriage and parenting, are related to general psychological adjustment, and have an influence in a number of other ways, many consider sex roles to be at the center of the personality. During adolescence there is a heightened awareness of sex roles and of the importance of behaving in accord with them. Hence, understanding sex roles is an important component to understanding adolescent behavior and personality development.

Defining and Measuring Sex Roles
The traditional instrumental masculine sex role involves traits such as independence, aggressiveness, assertiveness, being a doer, and being successful as a manipulator of the environment. The traditional feminine sex role in the United States involves being nurturing, gentle, sociable, and nonaggressive. Those who view themselves as possessing the traditional masculine traits to a relatively high degree and the traditional feminine traits to a relatively low degree are called masculine. Those with the reverse self-perspective are called feminine. Some individuals view themselves as possessing both traditional masculine and traditional feminine sex role characteristics to a relatively high degree. These people are called androgynous. Some view themselves as neither very masculine nor very feminine. These individuals are called undifferentiated.

Several instruments have been developed to measure sex roles. In general, each instrument assesses the degree to which individuals ascribe traditional masculine and feminine characteristics to the self. For example, after reading a sex role descriptor such as "sensitivity to others" or "willing to take risks," the individual indicates the degree to which the characteristic accurately describes her by selecting from alternatives ranging from "Never or Almost Never True of Me" to "Always or Almost Always True of Me." A masculinity and a femininity score are obtained for each person by summing their scores on the items composing the masculinity and femininity scales. These scores are then compared to the median score (the score that divides all the subjects' scores on each scale in half). Individuals whose scores are below the median are considered to be low on the scale; those with scores above the median are considered "high" on the scale. People then can be classified into one of the four sex role groups.

A word of caution about these scales is in order. Most were developed in the 1970s, and because there have been important changes in sex-typed behavior since then, they may not be as accurate an indicator of sex roles as they once were. For example, the number of women in the workforce and the number of women entering and completing college today reflects changes in the traditionally masculine traits of being the primary wage earner and being more oriented toward achievement.

Sex Role Development
Sex roles change in several ways. First, they evolve and change within their cultural context. That is, there are changes in the traditional sex roles as the culture changes and evolves. What may be considered traditionally feminine at one point in history may become much less sex-typed later on. Second, individuals' sex roles change as they grow and develop.

The traditional sex roles have a historical basis in biological sex differences. At one time they probably were an adaptive means of insuring survival. Many argue, however, that the historical necessity for capitalizing on biological sex differences—for example, the males' greater strength as related to hunting successfully—has long since passed. They view the traditional sex roles as overly restrictive on both males and females, limiting their ability to develop as a person and engage in a variety of rewarding behaviors, and call for a blending of the traditional sex roles—androgyny.

In order for sex role stereotypes to change, broad changes must occur within the culture. A significant shift in the percentage of women, and especially of mothers, who are in the workforce is an example of a cultural change that has given impetus to altering the traditional sex roles in the United States. Being a wage earner outside the home no longer is as exclusively a part of the masculine sex role as once was the case. Because gender is no longer strongly related to whether or not one works outside the house, working is no longer a strongly masculine trait. Similar changes, in sports opportunities, for example, and going to college, have resulted in other traits, such as being athletic and achieving, becoming less sex-typed.

In some other ways, however, the traditional sex role stereotypes remain. Women still are the primary child caretakers (although changes are occurring), and many women still plan on leaving the workforce for some period of time to remain home with children. And, women continue to remain the primary person who runs the household. These are some ways in which traditionally sex-typed behaviors, and therefore sex roles, have not changed.

Sex roles not only change with shifts in cultural values, they also change during the person's development. Evidence shows that the proportion of androgynous males increases with age and the proportion of androgynous females decreases with age, with more females taking on a more traditional feminine sex role. In other words, we do not learn a sex role and then never change. Changes of this kind reflect other cultural pressures. For example, in current society it is more acceptable for female adolescents to behave in what once were considered masculine ways (e.g., being an achieving, striving person) than it is for males to behave in a more feminine manner. This has resulted in changes in current sex role stereotypes.

Societal definitions of sex roles change as the culture evolves and changes. Individuals' sex roles change with their development and particular circumstances. These changes occur because sex roles are not biologically determined but are learned, just as other social behaviors are. Because they are learned, they can and do change.

Sex Roles and Psychological Adjustment

Those who argue that traditional sex roles are limiting often suggest that an androgynous sex role is preferable to either the stereotypical masculine or feminine sex role. In other words, the view is that an androgynous sex role is associated with better psychological adjustment during the adolescent years. The evidence supporting this view is very clear. Adolescents who are androgynous, who view themselves as being comfortable when behaving in either traditionally masculine or traditionally feminine ways, show advantages in a number of realms. They are less likely to be depressed, have better self-esteem and identity development, feel healthier, cope better in a variety of situations, practice better health behaviors, and generally are more psychologically well adjusted than adolescents who are more traditionally sex-typed.

It is also clear that being traditionally sex-typed is better than being undifferentiated (viewing the self as not possessing either traditionally defined masculine or feminine characteristics to a relatively high degree). Undifferentiated adolescents generally score the lowest on measures of psychological adjustment, perhaps because they feel relatively incompetent or uncomfortable in a wide variety of situations. These findings underscore the importance of sex roles within the larger context of our social institutions and sex role stereotypes. Being sex-typed as masculine or feminine, then, may be personally limiting and not as beneficial as being androgynous, but it is better than being undifferentiated.

Adolescent Development and Sex Roles
Adolescence is a time of important personality and identity development, especially in regard to learning how to navigate a number of interpersonal social roles. In many ways, learning how to behave as a male or female, that is, learning culturally defined sex-typed behaviors, is important to traversing the transition into adulthood. This task entails resolving conflicts between personal ideals and prevailing social standards, learning to adjust to feeling different, and learning to accept having goals that may differ from existing societal norms. As these norms change, such adaptations will become easier and we will see further changes in sex role norms.

Jerome B. Dusek

See also Gay, Lesbian, Bisexual, and Sexual-Minority Youth; Gender Differences;

Gender Differences and Intellectual and Moral Development; Maternal Employment: Historical Changes; Media; Sex Differences; Sexual Behavior

Reference and further reading
Brovermann, I. K., S. R. Vogel, D. M. Broverman, F. E. Clarkson, and P. S. Rosenkrantz. 1994. "Sex-Role Stereotypes: A Current Appraisal." Pp. 191–210 in *Caring Voices and Women's Moral Frames: Gilligan's View.* Edited by B. Puka. New York: Garland.
Dusek, Jerome B. 1996. *Adolescent Development and Behavior.* Upper Saddle River, NJ: Prentice-Hall.
Endo, K., and T. Hashimoto. 1998. "The Effect of Sex-Role Identity on Self-Actualization in Adolescence." *Japanese Journal of Educational Psychology* 46: 86–94.
Karniol, R., R. Gabay, Y. Ochion, and Y. Harari. 1998. "Is Gender or Gender-Role Orientation a Better Predictor of Empathy in Adolescence?" *Sex Roles* 39: 45–59.
Norlander, T., A. Erixon, and T. Archer. 2000. "Psychological Androgyny and Creativity: Dynamics of Gender-Role and Personality Trait." *Social Behavior and Personality* 28: 423–435.

Sexual Abuse

Although legal definitions vary from state to state, sexual abuse involves the initiation of inappropriate sexual activities with a child or adolescent by an adult or someone who is considerably older than the victim (Finkelhor, 1994). Sexual abuse can involve physical contact, such as the abuser touching sexual portions of the child's body, having intercourse, or causing a child to touch the abuser in a sexual manner. However, there is also noncontact sexual abuse, such as exhibitionism, voyeurism, or having a child pose for pornographic pictures.

Prevalence
It is difficult to know precisely how many children and adolescents have been

sexually abused because most cases of sexual abuse are never reported to authorities. Based on surveys of adults who have been asked to recall any experiences of sexual abuse while growing up, it has been estimated that at least 20 percent of females and 5 percent to 10 percent of males in the United States have experienced some type of sexual abuse (Finkelhor, 1994, p. 31). Various surveys suggest that females are two to four times as likely as males to be sexually abused. For both males and females, the perpetrator of the abuse is likely to be male and someone who is known to the victim. Sexual abuse is less likely than physical abuse or neglect to be perpetrated by a parent or parent figure, but the perpetrator is viewed by the victim as an authority figure in about half of the cases.

Sexual abuse can occur at any time from infancy through adolescence. In one national survey of adults, 34 percent of the female and 39 percent of the male victims reported that the sexual abuse occurred during adolescence (i.e., from ages twelve through eighteen) (Finkelhor et al., 1990, p. 21).

Consequences

What are the consequences of sexual abuse for those who have been abused? The consequences of sexual abuse vary from individual to individual, with some adolescents coping well with the experience (i.e., appearing to be very similar to adolescents who have never been abused) and other adolescents having serious negative consequences. Typically, studies of the consequences of abuse compare victims of abuse with peers who have never been abused to determine if the two groups, on average, differ on some outcome. Not surprisingly, these studies show that more problems are found in the group that experienced sexual abuse than in the comparison group.

Some of the differences involve how the victims feel. On average, adolescents who have been abused are more likely than their peers to feel fearful, anxious, angry, or depressed. Some victims even have suicidal thoughts because of the psychological pain they are experiencing. Other adolescents report that memories of the abuse intrude on their thoughts during the day or at night in the form of nightmares.

How adolescents feel as a result of the sexual abuse may affect how they behave. Some victims of abuse become more socially withdrawn and are generally less trusting of others. Other adolescents who have been victimized may find it more difficult to concentrate on schoolwork, and their school performance may suffer. Victims of sexual abuse are more likely than their peers to engage in binge drinking and to use drugs; substance abuse may be one way that adolescents try to cope with the experience of sexual abuse, but it is a coping response that has its own negative consequences.

Sexual abuse can also affect sexual behaviors. Children who have been victims of sexual abuse tend to show an early interest in sex that is evident in their play or through excessive masturbation. Adolescents who have been sexually abused may have sexual intercourse at an earlier age or have more sexual partners than their peers during the adolescent years. In contrast, some adolescents or adults may fear having normal sexual contact or may find it to be less pleasurable than others when they are having consensual intimate experiences.

Adolescents who have experienced sexual abuse may act out in various ways. Sexual abuse is associated with an increased risk of conduct problems, aggressive behavior, and delinquency. However, it is important to point out that no one is likely to show all of the symptoms that have been linked to sexual abuse, and as noted earlier, many adolescents who have been abused show none of these symptoms.

Mitigating Factors

Why do some victims of sexual abuse fare better than others? It seems likely that the consequences of sexual abuse depend on the adolescents' experience prior to the abuse, to the nature of the abuse they experienced, and to what occurs after the abuse ends. Children who have had very positive relationships with their parents and other adults prior to the abuse experience and who have experienced success in areas that are important to them (e.g., school, sports, peers relationships) are more likely than children from less fortunate circumstances to have the personal resources to cope effectively with the abuse. The long-term consequences are likely to be less severe if the abuse represents a painful event in an otherwise happy childhood.

The nature of the abuse is also likely to vary from individual to individual. More negative consequences are found when the sexual abuse is severe (usually defined as involving penetration) or involves the use of force. The duration and frequency of the abuse may also be important factors. Adolescents who have experienced physical abuse as well as sexual abuse are at higher risk for having problems than adolescents who have experienced only one type of abuse. The relationship that the adolescent had with the perpetrator is another important factor; victims who feel betrayed by someone with whom they have had a close relationship, such as a father, are likely to be negatively impacted by the abuse, the betrayal, and the loss of a close relationship. Although one would expect the experience of sexual abuse and how it is processed to be markedly different for very young children and adolescents, the effect of experiencing sexual abuse at different ages is not well understood at this time.

For those victims who disclose the abuse, what happens after disclosure in their family and in the legal system can also influence the long-term impact of sexual abuse. Victims fare better when their mothers believe them, are supportive, and take steps to protect them following disclosure. Those who disclose also tend to have fewer problems if the case is settled quickly either in court or through a plea bargain, if the victims are not forced to testify repeatedly, and if they feel supported by Protective Service workers, prosecutors, and other officials dealing with their case. The outcome of the case, the acquittal or conviction of the alleged perpetrator, seems to have little effect on how victims fare.

The victim's experiences after the sexual abuse has ended are also important. Victims of abuse have fewer problems if they have supportive relationships with their mothers and fathers. They are less likely to engage in problem behaviors, like binge drinking, if their parents monitor whom they are with and what they are doing when away from home. In general, victims of sexual abuse show an abatement of symptoms if they experience supportive environments once the abuse ends. In contrast, adolescents or adults who are victimized again (e.g., another incident of sexual abuse, rape, or domestic violence) exhibit more long-term problems than their peers. Although sexual abuse can result in long-term difficulties, one of the most important findings to come out of the research is that much can be done by families, case workers, and the judicial system to support the victims and reduce the negative consequences of sexual abuse.

Tom Luster

James Henry

See also Aggression; Coping; Counseling; Emotional Abuse; Physical Abuse; Rape; Sexual Behavior Problems

References and further reading
Briere, John N., and Diana M. Elliott. 1994. "Immediate and Long-Term Impacts of Child Sexual Abuse." *The Future of Children* 4, no. 2: 54–69.
Finkelhor, David. 1994. "Current Information on the Scope and Nature of Child Sexual Abuse." *The Future of Children* 4, no. 2: 31–53.
Finkelhor, David, Gerald Hotaling, I. A. Lewis, and Christine Smith. 1990. "Sexual Abuse in a National Survey of Adult Men and Women: Prevalence, Characteristics, and Risk Factors." *Child Abuse and Neglect* 14: 19–28.
Henry, James. 1997. "System Intervention Trauma to Child Sexual Abuse Victims Following Disclosure." *Journal of Interpersonal Violence* 12: 499–512.
Kendall-Tackett, Kathleen A., Linda M. Williams, and David Finkelhor. 1993. "Impact of Sexual Abuse on Children: A Review and Synthesis of Recent Empirical Studies." *Psychological Bulletin* 113: 164–180.
Luster, Tom, and Stephen A. Small. 1997a. "Sexual Abuse History and Number of Sex Partners among Female Adolescents." *Family Planning Perspectives* 29: 204–211.
———. 1997b. "Sexual Abuse History and Problems in Adolescence: Exploring the Effects of Moderating Variables." *Journal of Marriage and the Family* 59: 131–142.
Trickett, Penelope K., and Frank W. Putnam. 1998. "Developmental Consequences of Child Sexual Abuse." Pp. 39–56 in *Violence against Children in the Family and the Community.* Edited by Penelope K. Trickett and Cynthia J. Schellenbach. Washington, DC: American Psychological Association.

Sexual Behavior

Although one of the most prominent features of adolescence is development into sexual maturity, what is understood about this development is limited and not organized by any particular theory. In fact, much of the research on adolescent sexual behavior is atheoretical and is a piecemeal collection of promising variables and different methods of assessing outcome, varying from self-report of coitus to pregnancy rates. The main theories that do exist on adolescent sexual development are typically a blend of cognitive and self-control models that focus on the individual.

Unfortunately, the need for developmental research on sexual behavior has grown as the result of a focus on two health consequences of sexual activity: pregnancy and infection with sexually transmitted diseases (STDs), including the human immunodeficiency virus (HIV). In the United States, pregnancy among adolescents has been a growing concern of educators, governmental agencies, and service providers since the 1970s and has been the focus of much research, largely because of the generally poor outcomes for teenage mothers and their children. Compared to other adolescents, teenage mothers are less likely to complete their education, which may result in inadequate economic opportunities, are more likely to become dependent on public assistance, experience more economic instability (since pregnancy typically occurs outside of marriage), and

Healthy sexuality requires a focus on positive and negative emotional aspects of sexuality, such as the qualities of respect and responsibility in relationships with a potential partner. (Jennie Woodcock; Reflections Photolibrary/Corbis)

commonly experience prenatal complications and a lack of adequate prenatal care.

Although the research on the antecedents and consequences of teen pregnancy has been expanding over the last twenty-five years, there remains the need to increase the knowledge base because of two key limitations of the research to date. The first limitation is that teen pregnancy and early motherhood have been examined extensively among majority groups in the United States, but have only recently been the focus of attention among different ethnic minorities. This has resulted in a dearth of information on the nature of the process for minority teens. The second limitation of previous research on teen pregnancies and adoles-

cent sexual behavior is that the research has typically examined adolescents aged fifteen to nineteen, which is usually after the onset of sexual activity has occurred.

Although the HIV infection rate is not currently of epidemic proportions among adolescents, numerous authors have suggested that given the increasing prevalence of HIV among heterosexual individuals in their twenties, and the long latency of the virus, it is possible that a number of these individuals were infected as adolescents. Estimates for other STDs are also high, suggesting high rates of unprotected intercourse. Younger adolescents may not consider themselves at risk for STDs and may have less information about HIV than older adolescents, who have taken sexuality education classes. Furthermore, the cognitive skills required for consistent condom use (the most effective barrier against disease transmission) may not have fully evolved among younger adolescents.

Developmental literature suggests several possible trajectories for adolescents' sexual development. For instance, there may be a normative pattern in which the onset of sexual behavior occurs later in adolescence or in early adulthood. Many believe that this sequence is optimal because the older adolescents have more cognitive, educational, and economic resources that protect them from the undesired consequences of sexual activity. Another possibility is a more risk-filled developmental trajectory in which the adolescent engages in sexual activity at an early age. Younger adolescents are less cognitively mature, suggesting poor decision-making skills, are biologically ill prepared for pregnancy, and are less likely to attain their educational goals; also, their maturity levels do not make it likely they will be able to provide good parenting for children. Early onset of sexual activity has also been correlated with a greater number of lifetime sexual partners, which increases the probability of exposure to sexually transmitted diseases such as HIV/AIDS. Recent research has also shown that younger adolescents are less likely to use contraception.

The number of factors that have been examined with regard to the early onset of sexual activity is extensive. Individual factors such as self-esteem, locus of control, level of knowledge on sexual information, attitudes toward sexuality, pubertal status, and cognitive skills have been examined. Peer factors, such as actual peer activity and perceptions about peer activity, have also been exam-

ined. The influence of familial factors, such as parent-child communication, parental monitoring, parental support, maternal age, and other demographic factors, have also been researched. Less frequently, contextual factors such as acculturation have been explored.

Estimates for the onset of sexual intercourse among adolescents vary according to race, ethnicity, location, and historical period of the data. Although the onset of sexual intercourse is an important marker in determining risk of negative consequences for adolescents, some researchers have suggested that heterosexual sexual development occurs in a sequence of behaviors. This sequence involves increases in intimacy, as couples move from kissing to fondling and petting before reaching intercourse. However, some authors have not found the same sequence of behaviors before intercourse for black adolescents. On the other hand, a later study by Judith S. Brook and colleagues did find a similar sequence for African American and Puerto Rican adolescents. The applicability of this sequence is not clear for younger adolescents, as their reports state that intercourse is an unpredictable and a spontaneous event. Also, it is often a demanding task to survey younger adolescents about these behaviors because of the sensitive nature of these topics and the difficulty of obtaining parental permission for interviews on these topics.

Age and pubertal status are two factors that have been the subject of much investigation regarding the onset of sexual activity. Udry and colleagues explained in their study on adolescent female sexuality that social scientists have often assumed that "puberty supplies the hormones that create the motivation for sexual behavior" (1986, p. 217). In a later study, Udry noted that certain social control variables might interact with the biological to predict the onset of sexual activity. Daniel J. Flannery and colleagues (1993) recommended separating age and physical maturation because the two are distinct social phenomena that interact with one another and are frequently entangled in the studies on adolescent development. Yet the relationship between age and pubertal status may be related more importantly to the subsequent effects on other psychosocial factors. In other words, pubertal development at younger ages may influence how the adolescent is perceived by family and peers.

There have also been studies to examine whether early pubertal development is associated with the early initiation of sexual activity. Brent C. Miller and Kristin A. Moore reported on the basis of their 1990 review on the research of the 1980s that substantial evidence showed that early pubertal development is associated with early initiation of sexual activity. Although the importance of early pubertal maturation on sexual activity is clear, social factors must be considered in relation to hormonal effects. Although there is much individual variability in timing, part of early pubertal development is the corresponding development of secondary sexual characteristics, which may attract the attention of parents and peers in the adolescent's environment. Yet, as noted by Roberta Paikoff and Jeanne Brooks-Gunn, the meaning of pubertal events and familial relationships may vary by ethnicity, which may affect how these variables are related.

Parental monitoring (in other words, parents supervising their children and being knowledgeable of their whereabouts) has been examined as a parenting practice important in relation to delinquent behavior, drug use, and early sexual behavior. The influence of parental monitoring on early sexual behavior, in particular, may be important by virtue of the fact that if parents decrease and control their child's association with peers of the opposite sex, they may reduce the possibility of sexual activity. Jeanne Brooks-Gunn and Frank Furstenberg (1989) note that with greater parental supervision, the onset of intercourse occurs later. Some researchers have speculated that parents who use greater monitoring have more access to their child's activities while parents who use low monitoring permit their child to associate with deviant peers.

Although clearly the consequences of adolescents' sexual activity can be devastating or even life threatening, what is sadly missing from the study of adolescent sexual development is a focus on the development of healthy sexuality. In one of the few discussions of healthy sexuality for adolescents, Jeanne Brooks-Gunn and Roberta Paikoff suggested in their 1993 essay that as adolescents mature, the most optimal outcome is to develop a sense of what they call sexual well-being. They defined sexual well-being as having positive feelings about one's body, accepting feelings of sexual arousal and desire in sexual behaviors, and if engaging in intercourse, practicing safe sex. Developmental research, interventions designed to prevent pregnancies and STDs, and society as a whole may benefit by shifting the focus of adolescent sexuality from purely the prevention of risk to the promotion of a positive sense of sexual well-being.

Cami K. McBride
Roberta L. Paikoff

See also Contraception; Dating; Gay, Lesbian, Bisexual, and Sexual-Minority Youth; Love; Sexual Behavior Problems; Sexuality, Emotional Aspects of; Sexually Transmitted Diseases

References and further reading
Brook, Judith S., Elinor B. Balka, Thomas Abernathy, and Beatrix A. Hamburg. 1994. "Sequence of Sexual Behavior and Its Relationship to Other Problem Behaviors in African American and Puerto Rican Adolescents." *Journal of Genetic Psychology* 155: 107–114.

Brooks-Gunn, Jeanne, and Frank F. Furstenberg. 1989. "Adolescent Sexual Behavior." *American Psychologist* 44: 249–257.

Brooks-Gunn, Jeanne, and Roberta L. Paikoff. 1993. "'Sex Is a Gamble, Kissing Is a Game': Adolescent Sexuality and Health Promotion." In *Promoting the Health of Adolescents: New Directions for the Twenty-First Century.* Edited by Susan G. Millstein, Anne C. Petersen, and Elena O. Nightingale. New York: Oxford University Press.

Brown, Larry K., Ralph J. DiClemente, and Nancy I. Beausoleil. 1992. "Comparison of Human Immunodeficiency Virus Related Knowledge, Attitudes, Intentions, and Behaviors among Sexually Active and Abstinent Young Adolescents." *Journal of Adolescent Health* 13: 140–145.

Flannery, Daniel J., David C. Rowe, and Bill L. Gulley. 1993. "Impact of Pubertal Status, Timing, and Age on Adolescent Sexual Experience and Delinquency." *Journal of Adolescent Research* 8: 21–40.

Ford, Kathleen, and Anne Norris. 1993. "Urban Hispanic Adolescents and Young Adults: Relationship of Acculturation to Sexual Behavior." *Journal of Sex Research* 30: 316–323.

Hayes, Cheryl D. 1987. *Risking the Future: Adolescent Sexuality, Pregnancy, and Childbearing.* Washington, DC: National Academy Press.

Hovell, Melbourne F., et al. 1994. "A Behavioral-Ecological Model of Adolescent Sexual Development: A Template for AIDS Prevention." *Journal of Sex Research* 31: 267–281.

Katchadourian, Herant. 1991. "Sexuality." In *At the Threshold: The Developing Adolescent.* Edited by Shirley S. Feldman and Glen R. Elliott. Cambridge, MA: Harvard University Press.

Miller, Brent C., and Kristin A. Moore. 1990. "Adolescent Sexual Behavior, Pregnancy, and Parenting: Research through the 1980s." *Journal of Marriage and the Family* 52: 1025–1044.

Miller, Kim A., Rex Forehand, and Beth A. Kotchick. 1999. "Adolescent Sexual Behavior in Two Ethnic Minority Samples: The Role of Family Variables." *Journal of Marriage and the Family* 61, no. 1: 85–98.

Murphy, Debra A., Mary Jane Rotheram-Borus, and Helen M. Reid. 1998. "Adolescent Gender Differences in HIV-Related Sexual Risk Acts, Social-Cognitive Factors and Behavioral Skills." *Journal of Adolescence* 21, no. 2: 197–208.

Paikoff, Roberta L., and Jeanne Brooks-Gunn. 1991. "Do Parent-Child Relationships Change during Puberty?" *Psychological Bulletin* 110: 47–66.

Paikoff, Roberta L., Sheila H. Parfenoff, Stephanie A. Williams, and Anthony McCormick. 1997. "Parenting, Parent-Child Relationships, and Sexual Possibility Situations among Urban African American Preadolescents: Preliminary Findings and Implications for HIV Prevention." *Journal of Family Psychology* 11, no. 1: 11–22.

Parfenoff, Sheila H., and Roberta L. Paikoff. 1997. "Developmental and Biological Perspectives on Minority Adolescent Health." Pp. 5–27 in *Health-Promoting and Health-Compromising Behaviors among Minority Adolescents.* Edited by Dawn K. Wilson, James R. Rodrigue, and Wendell C. Taylor. Washington, DC: American Psychological Association.

Romer, Daniel, Maureen Black, Izabel Ricardon, Susan Feigelman, Linda Kaljee, Jennifer Galbraith, Rodney Nesbit, Robert C. Hornik, and Bonita Stanton. 1994. "Social Influences on the Sexual Behavior of Youth at Risk for HIV Exposure." *American Journal of Public Health* 84: 977–985.

Udry, J. Richard. 1988. "Biological Predispositions and Social Control in Adolescent Sexual Behavior." *American Sociological Review* 53: 709–722.

Udry, J. Richard, Luther M. Talbert, and Naomi M. Morris. 1986. "Biosocial Foundations for Adolescent Female Sexuality." *Demography* 23: 217–227.

Sexual Behavior Problems

Depending on their values, people may differ on the definition of what constitutes a sexual problem. Most researchers who study adolescent sexuality would agree on at least one fact—that a greater number of adolescents have sexual intercourse before reaching adulthood now than at any previous time in this country's history. Moreover, whatever values they may hold, most people would agree that when adolescents are forced to have sex they do not want, have unwanted pregnancies, bear children they are neither emotionally nor financially capable of supporting, or contract sexually transmitted diseases, their sexuality is associated with problems and full of risk for their future healthy development.

Unfortunately, as statistics from the U.S. Department of Health and Human Services (1996) bear out, there are numerous illustrations of the presence of such sexual problems and risks among contemporary adolescents:

- Each year, 1 million adolescents become pregnant and about half have babies. Indeed, about every minute, an American adolescent has a baby.
- Of adolescents who give birth, 46 percent go on welfare within four years; of *unmarried* adolescents who give birth, 73 percent go on welfare within four years.
- By age eighteen years, 25 percent of American females have been pregnant at least once.

- Over the last three decades the age of first intercourse has declined. Higher proportions of adolescent girls and boys reported being sexually experienced at each age between the ages of fifteen and twenty in 1988 than in the early 1970s. In 1988, 27 percent of girls and 33 percent of boys had intercourse by their fifteenth birthday.
- Pregnancy rates for girls younger than fifteen years of age rose 4.1 percent between 1980 and 1988, a rate higher than for any other teenage age group.
- In 1993, the proportion of all births to teenagers that were to unmarried teenagers was 71.8 percent. This rate represents an increase of 399 percent since 1963.
- By the end of adolescence about 80 percent of males and about 70 percent of females have become sexually active. These rates represent significant increases across the last fifteen years.
- Among sexually active female adolescents, 27 percent of fifteen- to seventeen-year-olds, and 16 percent of eighteen- to nineteen-year-olds, use no method of contraception. Among Latino, African American, and European American adolescents, the percentage of females not using contraception is 35 percent, 23 percent, and 19 percent, respectively.
- Among sexually active male adolescents in 1991, 21 percent report using no contraception at their last intercourse; an additional 56 percent of males used a condom and 23 percent relied on their female partner to use contraception.

- By age 20, 74 percent of males and 57 percent of females who became sexually active by age fourteen or younger have had six or more sexual partners.
- In 1991, thirty-eight of the pregnancies among fifteen- to nineteen-year-olds ended in abortion.
- By age nineteen, 15 percent of African American males have fathered a child; the corresponding rates for Latinos and European Americans is 11 percent and 7 percent, respectively. Moreover, 74 percent of European American youth, 76 percent of Latino youth, and 95 percent of African American youth are unmarried at the birth of their first child. In addition, teenage fathers are often absentee fathers. Among fourteen- to twenty-one-year-old fathers, about 40 percent were absentees.
- However, 39 percent of the fathers of children born to fifteen-year-old females, and 47 percent of the fathers of children born to sixteen-year-old females, are older than twenty years of age. Between 30 percent and 40 percent of adolescent mothers have been impregnated by males who have not yet reached their twentieth birthday.
- Women who become mothers as teenagers are more likely to find themselves living in poverty later in their lives than women who delay childbearing. Although 28 percent of women who gave birth as teenagers were poor in their twenties and thirties, only 7 percent of women who gave birth after adolescence were living in poverty in their twenties and thirties.
- About $25 billion in federal money is spent annually to provide social, health, and welfare services to families begun by teenagers.
- In 1992, the federal government spent nearly $34 billion on Aid to Families with Dependent Children, Medicaid, and food stamps for families begun by adolescents.

The breadth and variation of these problems pertinent to contemporary adolescent sexual behavior are staggering. The magnitude and diversity of the manifestation of these problems is challenging the educational, healthcare, and social service systems of America.

Richard M. Lerner

See also Rape; Sexual Abuse; Sexual Behavior; Sexually Transmitted Diseases

References and further reading
Carnegie Corporation of New York. 1995. *Great Transitions: Preparing Adolescents for a New Century.* New York: Carnegie Corporation of New York.
Lerner, Richard M. 1995. *America's Youth in Crisis: Challenges and Options for Programs and Policies.* Thousand Oaks, CA: Sage Publications.
———. In press. *Adolescence: Development, Diversity, Context, and Application.* Upper Saddle River, NJ: Prentice-Hall.
U.S. Department of Health and Human Services. 1996. *Trends in the Well Being of America's Children and Youth; 1996.* Washington DC: U.S. Department of Health and Human Services.

Sexuality, Emotional Aspects of

Healthy sexuality requires awareness about sexuality in many ways, to include accurate knowledge, recognition of one's own and others' feelings and intentions, personal decision making, and common sense about behaviors that are appropriate for the individual adolescent. Some of these themes have been addressed elsewhere in these volumes. Tied to all of them is the importance of dealing with what is considered by many to be a taboo topic in relation to sexuality—emotions.

"Sexuality itself and sexual feelings and desire are veiled in silence," said Leena Ruusuvaara (1997, p. 411). Sex education classes, parents, books, public policymakers, even peers, show little concern about promoting the idea of good communications, pleasure, and egalitarian sexual relations among teenagers.

The focus from adults is on abstinence in the hope that adolescents will not engage in risky sexual behaviors; one careless, unthinking act can result in a life-threatening disease. Therefore, the primary foci of discussions regarding sex include abstinence because premarital sex is "bad," contraception use if one does have sexual intercourse, and the use of condoms for safer sex, given the potential for various sexually transmitted diseases (STDs), and especially to protect against AIDS. Indeed, there is some reluctance to discuss even these topics, for fear that it will encourage adolescents to engage in sexual behavior. Research supports the opposite. The more knowledgeable one is, the less likely one is to engage in sexual behavior until an appropriate age, meaning when one makes decisions responsibly, with safety, respect for self and others, and care. The same should apply to understanding the emotional implications of engaging in sexual behaviors.

Technical information is essential but not sufficient. Many adolescents choose to be sexually active, even if that only means kissing or having oral sex. Healthy sexuality requires a focus on positive and negative emotional aspects of sexuality, such as the qualities of respect and responsibility in relationships with a potential partner. One of the primary problems for adolescents is the continued use of double standards that deny both genders the right to enjoy their sexuality. This must be understood and challenged. The double standard refers to the social assumption that a male "should" demand sex (oral, anal, or vaginal) and a female "should" expect this demand and then "should" place limits on his advances. This places emotional pressures on both genders to engage in a sexual dance. If the adolescent male doesn't try, there is something wrong with his manliness and her attractiveness. Males need to develop the personal strength to recognize and disregard these social pressures as well as to honor female adolescents as whole individuals, not as sex objects to be used to prove one's manhood and to provide self-pleasure. Female adolescents need to understand that they have the right to determine their own expressions of sexuality. They need to place less value on male sexual advances as standards for their self-worth.

Many females who choose to be sexual with a partner do so with the understanding that there is affection, love, perhaps commitment, implied in this behavior. But most adolescent relationships are very short. While some males, too, engage in sex only when they feel affection for their partner, many more males than females do so for the sexual experience per se. This can result in devastating negative emotions. As described by Thomas Lickona (1994), discovering that one has been "used" can result in the loss of self-respect and self-esteem. It can shake one's sense of trust in self and others. It can trigger rage over betrayal by a partner who may have used the popular phrase, "If you love me, you'll . . ." and then broke off the relationship within days or weeks. With intercourse may come fear about pregnancy or AIDS or guilt that one has dishonored family and/or violated one's religious values. Shattered trust may make it very difficult to establish later commitments to what could be genuine quality relationships. In some instances, it can trigger depression and thoughts of suicide. Male adolescents may feel guilt for their manipulativeness and the destruction they may cause to young women.

Sexual pleasure can be experienced through touching, kissing, and petting, negotiated jointly with respect for both partners. Focusing on oral, anal, or vaginal sex as "sex" is very limiting and stifles the emergence of a healthy interest in sexuality. With a more encompassing view of one's sexuality, sexual pleasure could be acknowledged more easily as healthy, natural, and appropriate as a topic for discussion within the family, with peers, and in the classroom.

The emotions associated with sexuality thus are many—some positive, some negative. In order to address these emotions in a healthy way it is important to do several things. One is to accept one's individual self as a sexual being. Adolescents are not encouraged to think this way. However, all humans are sexual, and we are so from the very beginning of our development. We may express it in different ways throughout our lives, but it is an integral part of who we are. Some people are very passionate, and others feel little interest in their own sexuality. For example, while many individuals may thoroughly enjoy masturbating frequently, others do so with embarrassment and guilt, and still others may feel no interest in engaging in this behavior. At some times in our lives and with certain people we may feel more sexual than at other times or with other people. For example, while the sight of one person may trigger strong feelings of lust, another person may be perceived as a great friend with whom one has a comfortable, platonic relationship. A very wide range of possibilities is normal. When one accepts one's self as a sexual being, one can more comfortably develop one's own perspective on how one feels at any given time. That openness to sexual self-awareness allows one a greater opportunity to think about choices. It contributes to feeling comfortable about one's sexuality and can increase one's sense of confidence in making personal decisions about what behaviors feel good and right and what behaviors feel wrong for the individual adolescent.

Another thing that is important is to become comfortable with one's changing body, and for adolescents this is particularly the case regarding pubertal development. Subsequent to puberty, one needs to accept one's body image as well. The mainstream culture of the United States has made it very clear that being thin and beautiful is a necessity for female popularity and acceptance by one's peers. And the need for a male to be macho, a muscle man, captain of some sports team parallels these expectations. It is essential for all adolescents to cut through this nonsense. These stereotypes leave the vast majority of adolescents feeling low self-esteem with body shame, because 95 percent or more of adolescents cannot fit these images. If one cannot feel comfortable with one's own body, it is extremely hard to enjoy sharing any aspect of it with another person. The media, such as television and magazines, should not be convincing people that the appearance of less than 5 percent of the population should dictate what is to be valued and desired by all. Adolescents need to feel proud of their own bodies, enjoy them, and keep them healthy. This self-comfort would allow both males and females greater pleasure in discovering each other's sexual being at an appropriate time.

Yet another helpful factor is development of self-efficacy, including personal power to exercise control over sexual situations. One needs to be able to anticipate how it would feel to engage in particular sexual behaviors in the future. Then one should assess the extent to which one has the capability to affect what will or will not be done. Adolescents, in particular, must include in this formula how to handle peer pressure, and the potential for lack of acceptance, or even rejection. They must ask themselves whether they will be able to mobilize their energy and persevere even in the face of all the pressures that may be placed on them by those dictating social norms for their age group. If they anticipate feeling regret or guilt or anger, then they may choose to avoid the behaviors. Emotionally, this can provide a positive sense of self-worth. It may afford them the confidence to communicate with a potential sexual partner and negotiate cooperation about how far to go or it may make it possible for a couple to practice safer sex because they have planned for it together.

Accepting one's nature as a sexual being, being comfortable with one's own body and its sexual pleasures, and developing a sense of self-efficacy regarding sexual choices all are major contributors to enjoying healthy sexuality. This understanding of one's own sexual self and respect for others and their right to make their own choices should enhance the chances of being able to discuss sexual feelings and behaviors with others without embarrassment or fear of offending the other. It should increase as well the likelihood that young people will prepare for those risky behaviors if they choose to proceed to oral, anal, or vaginal sex together.

Sally Archer

See also Dating; Dating Infidelity; Love; Sexual Behavior

References and further reading
Bakker, A. B., B. P. Buunk, and A. S. R. Manstead. 1997. "The Moderating Role of Self-Efficacy Beliefs in the Relationship between Anticipated Feelings of Regret and Condom Use." *Journal of Applied Social Psychology* 17, no. 2: 2001–2014.
Bandura, A. 1986. *Social Foundations of Thought and Action: A Social Cognitive Theory.* Englewood Cliffs, NJ: Prentice-Hall.
Coleman, J., and D. Roker, eds. 1998. *Teenage Sexuality: Health, Risk and Education.* Canada: Harwood Academic Publishers.
Lickona, Thomas 1994. "The Neglected Heart." *American Educator* (Summer): 34–39.
Ruusuvaara, Leena. 1997. "Adolescent Sexuality: An Educational and Counseling Challenge." Pp. 411–413 in *Adolescent Gynecology and Endocrinology: Basic and Clinical Aspects.* Edited by G. Creatsas, G. Mastorakos, and G. Chrousos. New York: Annals of the New York Academy of Science, Vol. 816.

Sexually Transmitted Diseases

Sexually transmitted diseases (STDs) are a group of infections that are spread by intimate sexual contact; teenagers are much more likely than adults to get STDs, and the consequences of STDs are more serious in teens than in older adults. Nearly thirty different types of infections can be spread through sexual contact. An estimated 15.3 million STD incidences occurred in 1996 in the United States. A majority of people with STDs do not feel sick and are not aware of their own infections. Whether there are symptoms or not, STDs can lead to serious health consequences and are infectious. Many STDs, such as chlamydia, gonorrhea, and trichomoniasis, can be cured, if treated appropriately. Viral STDs, such as genital herpes, genital warts, and HIV infections, are among the STDs that cannot be cured, although treatment is available and some form of treatment is necessary. A person infected by one type of STD is more likely to catch another type of STD.

Some prefer the term STI (infection) to STD (disease), for the reason that most sexually transmitted infections often do not have the kind of symptoms associated with disease. Again, sexually transmitted diseases are very serious, whether accompanied by any symptoms or not. A "silent" STD can become symptomatic at any time and is as contagious as a symptomatic STD. In addition, a silent STD in a mother can be transmitted to her baby during pregnancy or delivery. Thus, the term STD is commonly used for all types of sexually transmitted infections, regardless of whether there are any symptoms.

Most infectious agents that cause STDs are spread by body fluid exchange, such as semen, blood, vaginal or penile discharge, drainage or blood from blisters, sores, or cuts on mucosal membranes or skin. Some STDs can be transmitted from a mother to her baby, during pregnancy, in the birth canal, or by breast milk. Blood transfusion or sharing needles with an infected person can be a source of STD transmission. Those activities that can cause the spread of STDs are called STD risk factors, and those who engage in activities that are associated with STD risk factors are said to be at risk for STDs. STDs are a group of infections; not all STDs are transmitted exactly the same way.

Many teens do not know that STD screening is often not part of annual checkups or sports physical examinations. The fact that a person cannot tell whether his or her partner is infected by the way that he or she looks puts many teens at risk for STDs. It is important to make sure both partners are STD free before initiating sexual intercourse.

The most important fact to remember about STD symptoms is, as emphasized before, that a great majority of STDs are asymptomatic until a complication sets in. Another important fact is that many teens with STD symptoms end up ignoring the symptoms because they tend to believe, "It cannot happen to me." Also, STD symptoms are often missed or misinterpreted by the person who has the infection because the symptoms are mild, nonspecific, or transient (in that they may disappear spontaneously, without treatment). Even a physician may not recognize STD symptoms, if the patient does not reveal his or her STD risk. Another complicating factor is that, as with all types of infections (including the common cold, chicken pox, and the like), STDs have an incubation period, a time between exposure to the infection and the appearance of a symptom or a positive test result. Many STDs have a long incubation period (weeks to months). Thus, a symptom of an STD may appear long after the exposure, and after the incident (or incidents) that caused it has been forgotten.

A list of STDs that are common in adolescents, along with typical symptoms, appears below. Some STDs (e.g., syphilis, HIV/AIDS, herpes) can affect other organs of the body, as well as sexual/genital organs. The same syndrome (group of symptoms) or medical condition may stem from different types of STDs, and one STD can cause more than one syndrome or medical condition. Common syndromes and medical conditions that may originate from STDs are urethritis syndrome, cervicitis, cystitis (bladder infection–like symptoms), PID (pelvic inflammatory disease), TOA (tubo-ovarian abscess), ectopic pregnancy, infertility, epididymitis, Reiter's syndrome, DGI (disseminated gonococcal infection), GUD (genital ulcer diseases), chronic pelvic pains, cervical dysplasia (ASCUS), and AIDS. Cancers associated with STDs include hepatoma (cancer of the liver), cervical cancer in women, penile cancer in men, and Kaposi's sarcoma. This list is not comprehensive. (For detailed descriptions and more information, please see the works listed at the end of this entry.)

A doctor can diagnose certain types of STDs by taking a history and making a simple physical examination. For most STDs, however, specimen collection for a special test is necessary. For some infections, a swab specimen is necessary, which involves a pelvic examination and/or a specimen collection with a thin swab. For others, a blood specimen is needed for the diagnostic test. Some, including chlamydia and gonorrhea, can be tested now by use of a urine specimen and new DNA amplification, such as ligase chain reaction (LCR) or polymerase chain reaction (PCR). This is convenient for the patient and the doctors, but availability of these new tests is limited at the time of this writing. A doctor will order a special test for each type of STD suspected or will carry out a set of screening tests for certain types of STDs that are common in the region.

A correct diagnosis must be made before treatment can begin. Some types of treatments are available for all STDs, but as mentioned before, not all STDs can be cured. A special medication taken by mouth only once will cure some STDs such as chlamydia, gonorrhea, and trichomoniasis. If the treatment is longer, it is important to take all of the medication as instructed by the doctor. Sex partners must be treated, whether they have symptoms or not. Although there is no cure for viral STDs, treatments are available to reduce the severity of the symptoms, prevent symptoms and later complications from showing up, or reduce the risk of spreading the infection. Management of a person with an STD is not complete until all her sexual partners are appropriately assessed and treated.

The only sure way not to get STDs is to abstain from any sexual exposures or limit sexual exposure to an infection-free partner. Both partners should be tested for STDs, including HIV, before initiating sexual intercourse. Female condoms or male condoms used correctly and with spermicidal gels or foam are effective in preventing STD transmission, but abstinence is the only 100 percent effective prevention measure. At the time of this writing, FDA-approved vaccines are available for hepatitis B and hepatitis A. New vaccines are being tested for a number of STDs and may be approved for use in the near future. Hepatitis B vaccine is recommended to all teenagers who have not been vaccinated previously, before they initiate sexual intercourse. Hepatitis A vaccine is recommended to individuals with special risk factors.

Nearly thirty different types of infections can be transmitted by intimate sexual contact. Following is a selective overview of some of these infections; please see consult works listed at the end of the entry for comprehensive information.

Chlamydia or chlamydial infection, caused by *Chlamydia trachomatis,* is the most common curable STD in teenagers and young adults in the United States. A variety of serious health problems result from untreated chlamydial infection, including PID (pelvic inflammatory disease). Chlamydial infection is the most common cause of preventable infertility in the United States. In males, chlamydia can cause epididymitis, a painful swelling of the scrotal sac. Although frequently asymptomatic in women and men, chlamydial infection can cause urethritis, cervicitis, or cystitis-like symptoms. Chlamydia is the most common cause of burning on urination among sexually active teenagers, a condition often misdiagnosed as a urinary tract infection (UTI), if a history of sexual intercourse is not revealed. The patient often misses vaginal or penile discharge associated with chlamydial infections. Diagnosis of chlamydia infection is made with a tissue culture or a variety of DNA tests of a swab specimen, or by a urine DNA amplification test. Uncomplicated chlamydial infection of the lower genital tract can be treated with a single dose of medication taken by mouth, or a seven-day treatment with an oral medication may be necessary.

Gonorrhea or gonococcal infection ("drips," "clap"), caused by *Neisseria gonorrhoeae,* is the second most common bacterial infection among teenagers. Gonorrhea is the most common cause of purulent (puslike) discharge from the genitals. Within a few days of exposure to an infected person, a thick yellow or greenish discharge appears. The discharge may disappear in a few days without any treatment. Complications of untreated gonococcal infections include PID, epididymitis, arthritis, and disseminated gonococcal infections (DGI or blood poisoning). A laboratory test for gonorrhea can be done with a swab specimen or by a urine test. DGI is diagnosed with a blood culture or a microscopic examination of the fluid from the associated skin rashes. Uncomplicated gonococcal infection can be treated by a single dose of medication given by injection or taken by mouth.

Trichomoniasis or trichomonas vaginitis, caused by a parasite called *Trichomonas vaginalis,* is one of the most common causes of vaginitis in women of all ages. Trichomoniasis can cause vaginal discharge and itching, and is often confused with vaginal yeast infections. A microscopic examination of a vaginal swab specimen can confirm the diagnosis. A culture is also available. In males, diagnosis of trichomoniasis is often difficult. This infection is curable with special antibiotics taken by mouth.

Genital herpes, caused by herpes simplex virus (HSV, type II mostly), is by far the most common incurable STD in the United States and the most common cause of genital ulcer disease. It starts with a painful blister, often spreading to many blisters and painful ulcers in the genital area and accompanied by painful swelling in groins. One of the unique features of this infection is the unpredictable recurrence of the blisters and ulcers. Each blister is full of virus particles that are highly contagious. Breakage of the mucosal surface due to genital herpes can become an entry point of other types of germs, increasing risk of contracting other STDs and HIV. HSV can cause serious problems, including the death of a newborn exposed to the infection during birth. A culture of fluids from a blister or ulcer or a blood test will provide the diagnosis. Although HSV cannot be completely cured, treatment with antiviral agents helps heal the ulcers, and used appropriately may control the recurrence of genital ulcers.

Genital warts, or condyloma accuminata, caused by human papillomavirus (HPV), are common in adolescents and young adults, and the most common cause of abnormal Pap smears in adolescent girls. Certain types of HPV have been linked to cancer of the uterine cervix, anus, and penis. However, most HPV infections are asymptomatic or unrecognized. Warts in external genitals are recognized by typical bumps of various sizes and colors in the vagina, vulva, penis, perineal area (the area between the anus and genitals), and anus. An HPV infection of the uterine cervix is often identified by an abnormal Pap test (dysplasia). Type-specific viral DNA tests are available but are not widely used at this time. Symptoms are managed with topical application of medications, biopsy, or surgical removal of precancerous lesions. Once a person has been infected, the HPV cannot be eradicated. The HPV particles can be swallowed by a newborn during delivery, causing warts in the throat of the baby, called pharyngeal papilloma. Pharyngeal papilloma may be life threatening, and treatment of pharyngeal papilloma is very difficult.

Pubic lice, or "crabs," are often transmitted by intimate genital contact and cause itching in the pubic area. Diagnosis is made by presence of the lice or their eggs attached to public hair. Application of a specific shampoo or lotion will eradicate pubic lice. All bedding materials and underwear must be washed in hot water at the same time.

Hepatitis B is caused by Hepatitis B virus (HBV). Sexual transmission accounts for 30 to 60 percent of all HBV infections occurring annually in the United States. Hepatitis is an infection of the liver. The symptoms of hepatitis B vary from no symptoms to flulike symptoms to jaundice. HBV is a cause of chronic hepatitis and may lead to cancer of the liver and death. Diagnosis of HBV infection is made by a blood test. There are at least five different types of viral hepatitis (A to E). Accurate type-specific diagnosis is important for the management of sexual contacts and prevention of further spread. No specific treatment is available at this time. Hepatitis B is a vaccine-preventable STD. If they have not been vaccinated as infants, teenagers are recommended to receive HBV vaccination before exposure occurs. Passive immunization with hepatitis B immune globulin (HBIG) within fourteen days of exposure can prevent infection in the majority of exposed persons. Thus, it is very important to consult a physician as soon as possible if exposed to an infected person.

Syphilis is an ancient STD, caused by a bacteria called *T. pallidum*. A painless ulcer in the genital area associated with swollen lymph nodes in the groin area is typical for this disease. The ulcers may not appear at all or may disappear without any treatment while the bacteria are being spread to other organs, resulting in a flulike disease. Other symptoms of syphilis include rashes on palms, soles, and other parts of the body. If not treated, syphilis can progress through different phases and result in damage to the heart and brain. Syphilis is diagnosed with examination of swabs from the genital ulcer or a blood test. If it is diagnosed early, treatment is very effective.

More information on STDs is readily available. A good place to start on the Internet is http://www.ASHASTD.org. There are also two hot lines, the National STD Hotline, 1-800-227-8922, and, specifically for HPV, the HPV Hotline, 1-877-HPV-5868, Monday to Friday 2–7 P.M., EST. Other resources, aside from those listed below, are local STD clinics, the public health department, and private doctors.

M. Kim Oh
Jeanne S. Merchant

See also Abstinence; Contraception; Gonorrhea; High School Equivalency Degree; HIV/AIDS; Sex Education; Sexual Behavior

References and further reading
American Social Health Association and Centers for Disease Control and Prevention hot line information Web site: http://www.ashastd.org
Cates, Willard, Jr. 1999. "Estimates of the Incidence and Prevalence of Sexually Transmitted Diseases in the United States." *American Social Health Association Panel: Sexually Transmitted Disease* (Suppl.): S2–S7.
Centers for Disease Control and Prevention. 2000. *Sexually Transmitted Disease Surveillance, 1999.* Atlanta, GA: U.S. Department of Health and Human Services, Public Health Services, Centers for Disease Control and Prevention. CDC's Web site for this report and other information, including diagnostic slides in color, is at http://www.cdc.gov/nchstp/dstd/dstdp.html
Eng, T. R., and W. T. Butler, eds. 1997. *The Hidden Epidemic: Confronting Sexually Transmitted Diseases.* Washington, DC: National Academy Press, Institute of Medicine.
Holmes, K. K., et al. 1999. *Sexually Transmitted Diseases,* 3rd ed. New York: McGraw-Hill.
"1998 Guidelines for Treatment of Sexually Transmitted Diseases." 1998. *Morbidity and Mortality Weekly Report* 47, no. RR-1: 1–116.

Shyness

Generally speaking, shyness may be defined as the experience of discomfort or inhibited behavior in social situations. The tendency to be very self-conscious is particularly characteristic of the shy person. However, shyness is a highly complex phenomenon that varies widely in its intensity and effects. Shyness may include physiological symptoms (e.g., pounding heart), cognitive symptoms (e.g., self-consciousness), and behavioral symptoms (e.g., awkward body language). Both genetic and environmental factors contribute to shyness. Adapting to all the changes of adolescence (e.g., adjusting to a changing body, beginning to date) can trigger the development of shyness or increase shyness in the already shy teen. Many adolescents experience a period of shyness when they develop what is called the *imaginary audience*—the belief of adolescents that other people are watching them and focusing on their appearance and behavior. Although being shy may present challenges (e.g., greater risk for loneliness), it is important that those who have contact with shy adolescents be aware that shyness also has positive consequences, such as greater empathy. Paradoxically, helping young people accept as well as understand their own shyness can also help them to deal with its challenges.

In considering the causes of lasting shyness, researchers have found strong evidence that genetic inheritance contributes to shyness. Shy children often have at least one shy parent, or they may have other shy family members. Shyness is considered to be the personality trait with the strongest genetic component.

Biological factors, which are influenced by genetic predispositions, contribute to shyness. During infancy, physiological differences are evident between shy and sociable babies. A subset of infants show extreme nervous system reactivity to common stimuli such as moving mobiles. These infants are described as highly reactive, and physiological studies indicate that they have an easily excitable sympathetic nervous system. Infants and older children who show this high reactivity display a pattern of inhibited behavior when they encounter unfamiliar people, objects, or situations. Interestingly, highly reactive infants show higher-than-average heart rates, and their higher heart rates are evident even before birth.

A number of other interesting biological factors are linked to shyness, including blue eye color, blond hair, pale skin, and allergies (especially hay fever). Women who are exposed to short day length during pregnancy (especially during the midpoint of pregnancy) are more likely to have shy children. These biological links are likely the result of complex physiological processes. For example, the hormone melatonin is thought to be responsible for the link between shyness and day length during pregnancy. It is suggested that during the winter months when there are fewer hours of daylight, the body produces higher levels of melatonin. This melatonin passes through the placenta to the developing fetal brain, where it may act to create the more highly reactive temperament characteristic of the shy.

Not all shyness is evident during infancy, and so it is important to make the distinction between what is referred to as early- and later-developing shyness.

Many adolescents experience a period of shyness when they develop what is called the imaginary audience, the belief of adolescents that other people are watching them and focusing on their appearance and behavior. (Skjold Photographs)

The early-emerging shyness, which typically appears during the first year of life, is referred to as fearful shyness. Wariness and emotionality, temperamental characteristics that both show a strong genetic component, influence the development of this fearful shyness. In contrast, a later-developing, self-conscious type of shyness first appears around age four or five, and coincides with the child's development of a cognitive sense of self. This self-conscious shyness increases in intensity around age eight as children engage in more social comparison, and it reaches a peak between the ages of fourteen and seventeen, as adolescents deal with the imaginary audience and identity issues. For some, early-developing shyness may continue into a lifelong pattern of shyness. However, others appear to grow out of their shyness. Similarly, whereas self-conscious shyness typically decreases over time, for some, this later-emerging shyness continues through their adult years.

Social factors such as poor relationships with parents have been linked to the development of shyness. Relationships with parents may also influence the course and intensity of shyness. Whereas many shy individuals report that they had poor relationships with peers but positive relationships with parents during childhood, men who exhibit social phobia are more likely to report that they had negative childhood relationships with both peers and parents, especially with their mothers. Conversely, parenting that is sensitive to the child's temperamental characteristics and social needs may lessen the impact of shyness.

Other negative experiences outside of the family, such as feelings of incompetence in comparison to peers or experiences of peer rejection during childhood and adolescence, may play key roles in the development of shyness. Interestingly, it is suggested that the expansion of technology in our society may both help and hurt shyness. Whereas the Internet and e-mail may provide a comfortable mode of communication for some shy individuals, a competing concern is that as people need to engage in fewer face-to-face interactions due to technological advances, the development of social skills may be impaired. Poor social skills may result in more shyness.

Cultural factors influence both the prevalence of shyness and attitudes about shyness. For example, the extent to which individual boldness and independence are valued and encouraged varies by culture. Within the United States, shyness is typically highest among Asian Americans and lowest among Jewish Americans. Similarly, in studies that have looked at shyness cross-culturally, lower reports of shyness are reported in Israel, whereas higher levels of shyness are found in Taiwan and Japan.

Shyness is generally viewed as an undesirable personality characteristic in the United States, especially for males. Because of their likelihood of higher reactivity, shy children may find themselves to be the targets of teasing and bullying. Shy individuals also are more vulnerable to experiencing loneliness. Lack of a social support network may contribute to greater health problems for shy individuals in adulthood. Family and work roles also may be affected by shyness. For example, some research has found that shy men marry and have children later, whereas shy women have been found to be less likely to work outside of the home.

It also is important to recognize the positive characteristics that may be found among shy individuals. Shy individuals have been described as more sensitive and empathic, and as good listeners. Modesty also may be viewed as a positive characteristic of the shy individual. Shy people are usually not perceived as negatively by others as they think they are. Furthermore, not all shy individuals view their shyness negatively. Many well-known and accomplished individuals in all fields of endeavor consider themselves to be shy, and many do not view their shyness as a weakness. We all have a unique constellation of temperamental characteristics that make us who we are. The diversity of personality styles—shy, bold, or in between—adds to the richness of our world.

There is help and hope for shy individuals who feel that their shyness is negatively impacting their lives. Recognizing which social environments are a good fit for a person's temperament can help. For some people, the thought of trying to meet other people at a noisy party is unpleasant. Recognition by these individuals that they may feel more comfortable gradually getting to know people through a common activity (e.g., a club) is an important aspect of self-knowledge. Some strategies that may be helpful to teenagers who want to overcome their shyness include identifying situations most likely to provoke shyness, building self-esteem through recognizing and developing areas of interest and talent, and practicing social skills (e.g., making eye contact, asking for others' opinions, and practicing starting conversations).

Pamela A. Sarigiani

See also Anxiety; Loneliness; Personality; Self-Consciousness; Social Development; Temperament

References and further reading
Carducci, Bernado, and Philip Zimbardo. 1995. "Are You Shy?" *Psychology Today* 28: 34–40.
Gortmaker, Steven L., Jerome Kagan, Avshalom Caspi, and Phil A. Silva. 1997. "Daylength during Pregnancy and Shyness in Children: Results from Northern and Southern Hemispheres." *Developmental Psychobiology* 31: 107–114.
Henderson, Lynne, and Philip Zimbardo. 1998. "Shyness." Pp. 497–509 in *Encyclopedia of Mental Health*, Vol. 3. Edited by Howard S. Friedman. San Diego: Academic Press.
Schmidt, Louis A., and Jay Schulkin, eds. 1999. *Extreme Fear, Shyness, and Social Phobia: Origins, Biological Mechanisms, and Clinical Outcomes.* New York: Oxford University Press.
Simon, Gary. 1999. *How I Overcame Shyness: 100 Celebrities Share Their Secrets.* New York: Simon and Schuster.
Zimbardo, Philip, and Shirley Radl. 1981/1999. *The Shy Child: A Parent's Guide to Preventing and Overcoming Shyness from Infancy to Adulthood,* 2nd ed. Cambridge, MA: Malor Books.

Sibling Conflict

Disagreements are an inevitable part of daily interaction in family relationships. Thus, it comes as no surprise that conflict constitutes a normal part of the sibling experience, even as children enter adolescence. Nevertheless, parents are often concerned by conflict between their adolescent siblings.

What Is Conflict?

Social conflict is the discord that transpires when two or more people disagree with one another. Conflicts between siblings may be marked by oppositional behaviors such as disagreeing, arguing, objecting, and may at times include physical aggression. Not all conflict, however, includes aggressive behavior, and many researchers recognize that conflict and aggression are not interchangeable terms. Whereas conflict involves mutual opposition and disagreement, aggression is behavior intended to cause harm to another individual.

Research shows that there are two distinct forms of sibling conflict. Destructive conflict is characterized by strong negative feelings and coercion. This form of conflict may include physical aggression and typically leads to unsatisfactory resolutions. Constructive conflict, in contrast, is less emotionally intense and more likely to be resolved by means of negotiation and compromise, which facilitates resolutions that are mutually acceptable.

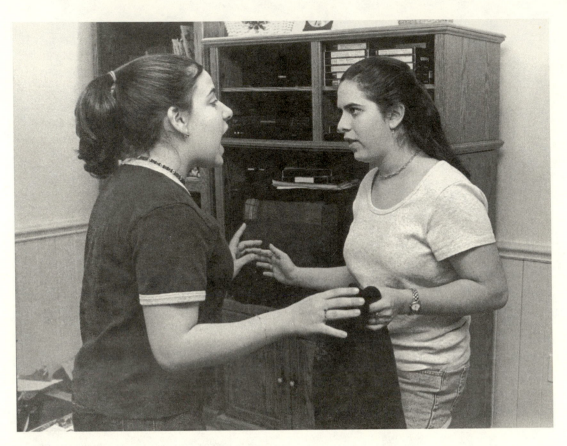

Sibling conflicts, although stressful, can enhance problem-solving skills among youths.
(Shirley Zeiberg)

What Constitutes Average Sibling Conflict?

Although conflict can be a defining feature of siblinghood early in life, some research indicates that sibling relationships actually become less emotionally intense as children move into adolescence. There is a slight decrease in warmth, disclosure, and even conflict between siblings. The lessening of tensions may be related to decreased sibling contact, as adolescents begin to spend more time outside the family. Nevertheless, siblings, especially those who continue to spend a great deal of time together, may still engage in frequent conflict. This is especially true for siblings who have a particular history of conflict.

Contrary to popular belief, opposite-sex siblings engage in more conflict than same-sex pairs. Similarly, siblings who are closer in age engage in more conflict than sibling pairs with wider age gaps. In addition, the presence of several personality characteristics are important predictors of sibling conflict. For example, adolescents who have more traditional sex role attitudes, who are highly active, less conscientious, and less agreeable, generally engage in more frequent conflict. In addition, siblings' personality characteristics may either mesh or clash. That is, not only the children's own personality traits per se influence conflict, but also their characteristics relative to one another.

Other family relationships can also influence sibling conflict. Children whose parents frequently quarrel with each other are more likely to engage in frequent sibling conflict. Likewise, children whose parents use more punitive or inconsistent discipline strategies, or favor one sibling over another, are more likely to engage in sibling conflict.

What Do Siblings Fight About?

Although it is often difficult for siblings themselves to know what their conflicts are actually about, it appears that conflict between siblings reflects the strains of group living. Thus, the most common themes of sibling conflict are personal property disputes, typically resulting from one sibling's unauthorized use of the other's belongings or space. Birth order differences do exist, in that older siblings are more likely to refer to privacy issues and the younger siblings' immature behavior as reasons for sibling conflict. Quarrels over duties, chores, and privileges or rivalry regarding special treatment by parents are less frequent themes. Interestingly, fighting or competing for parental love or attention is one of the least commonly reported themes of sibling conflict.

Who Starts Sibling Conflicts and How Do They End?

When asked who starts sibling conflict, adolescents, as opposed to younger children, are likely to assign equal responsibility to both participants. Adolescents tend to resolve sibling conflicts by using passive techniques such as withdrawal or ignoring their siblings, rather than using more active or constructive techniques such as negotiation or compromise. Another frequently used conflict resolution tactic is parental intervention, which includes parents voluntarily stepping in to end the conflict as well as children seeking the help of a parent.

Is Physical Aggression a Problem?

Destructive conflict among adolescent siblings may involve physical aggression such as kicking, biting, hitting, and slapping. In fact, this form of conflict between siblings is the most frequent source of physical harm for youngsters and the most common type of family violence, excluding homicide. Interestingly, girls are as likely as boys to report physical aggression as part of their sibling conflict. There is a growing concern among researchers that aggression between siblings as a means of settling conflict may generalize to situations outside the family. In cases where sibling conflict does become intensely physically violent, families may want to seek counseling or other types of professional intervention.

Can Sibling Conflict Be Beneficial?

Constructive sibling conflict can actually serve a number of important functions. First, siblings' ability to disagree openly may create a context where adolescents can assert themselves. Differences are articulated, and individual boundaries and family rules about sharing space are often clarified as part of sibling conflict. Thus, sibling conflict may provide a vehicle for improving relations by highlighting and resolving differences. Second, conflict may reflect age-appropriate issues of self-definition and foster a sense of uniqueness, ultimately helping adolescents develop an identity, one of the main tasks of adolescence. In addition, constructive sibling conflicts are believed to enhance problem-solving skills that may be generalized outside the family to other relationships and contexts.

Can Siblings Who Frequently Fight Still Love Each Other?

Although conflict may be seen as negative by parents, not all conflict is necessarily detrimental to the sibling relationship. In fact, adolescents report that the majority of sibling conflicts are neither positive nor negative, nor do they have negative long-term effects on the relationship. In addition, conflict is unrelated to emotional closeness, ratings of the siblings' importance, or relationship satisfaction. That is, siblings can experience intense bonds of warmth and affection as well as equally strong displays of conflict in the same sibling relationship. In the face of adversity, siblings who frequently fight may grow closer—adolescents rely on their siblings for advice about life plans and personal problems and turn to their siblings for support when experiencing problems with other children at school, during family illness, or after serious accidents. Furthermore, having a close sibling relationship can act as a protective factor for children who are experiencing the stress of parental disharmony and conflict.

Beth Manke
Deborah Corbitt-Shindler

See also Bullying; Conflict and Stress; Conflict Resolution; Family Relations; Sibling Differences; Sibling Relationships; Storm and Stress; Teasing

References and further reading
Brody, Gene H., and Zolinda Stoneman. 1996. "Sibling Relationships." Pp. 189–212 in *Sibling Relationships: Their Causes and Consequences.* Edited by Gene H. Brody. Norwood, NJ: Ablex Publishing.
McGuire, Shirley, Beth Manke, Afsoon Eftekhari, and Judy Dunn. 2000. "Children's Perceptions of Sibling Conflict during Middle Childhood: Issues and Sibling (Dis)similarity." *Social Development* 9: 173–190.
Prochaska, Janice M., and James O. Prochaska. 1985. "Children's Views of the Causes and 'Cures' of Sibling Rivalry." *Child Welfare* 114: 427–433.
Raffaelli, Marcela. 1992. "Sibling Conflict in Early Adolescence." *Journal of Marriage and the Family* 54: 652–663.
———. 1997. "Young Adolescent's Conflicts with Siblings and Friends." *Journal of Youth and Adolescence* 26: 539–557.
Reid, William J., and Timothy Donovan. 1990. "Treating Sibling Violence." *Family Therapy* 152: 49–59.
Vandell, Deborah L., and Mark D. Bailey. 1992. "Conflicts between Siblings." Pp. 242–269 in *Conflict in Child and Adolescent Development (Cambridge Studies in Social and Emotional Development).* Edited by Carolyn U. Shantz and William H. Hartup. New York: Cambridge University Press.

Sibling Differences

Most research that includes information about more than one child within a family tells the same story: Siblings differ markedly from one another. That is, sibling differences greatly exceed similarities for most characteristics. What little resemblance there is among siblings is due to hereditary similarity, not to the experience of growing up in the same family. Sibling differences, on the other hand, emerge for reasons of nurture (environment) as well as nature (genetics).

Adolescent Siblings Are More Different than Similar

The most common method for indexing sibling resemblance is to calculate the correlation between sibling pairs for various traits and behaviors. The extent to which the sibling correlation is less than 1.0 denotes sibling differences. Collectively, previous research suggests that siblings growing up in the same family are not very similar. For example, sibling correlations for height and weight rarely exceed .50, meaning that when we combine all of the genetic and environmental influences, siblings are only about 50 percent similar. The average sibling correlation for IQ is similar to that for height and weight, whereas siblings resemble each other even less for personality (.20), psychopathology (.20), and common diseases (.10) (Dunn and Plomin, 1990, p. 42). In short, we can see that sibling differences are as great, if not greater, than their similarities. One exception to this pattern of overwhelming sibling differences pertains to delinquency. Sibling correlations for delinquency are often as high as .70, suggesting siblings are very similar in their delinquent and antisocial behavior, perhaps because siblings are often "partners in crime." Why are adolescent siblings so different from each other for most traits and behaviors, despite the fact that most siblings grow up in the same home and are raised by the same parents? At the heart of this question is the debate over the origins of individual differences—over the relative influence of nature and nurture.

Genetic Influences—Nature

Biological siblings (those who share the same mother and father) are first-degree relatives and thus share half (50 percent) of their genes. Thus, if genetic factors (heredity) account for *all* of the variance of a trait, and thus are entirely responsible for sibling differences, we would expect the correlation for first-degree relatives to be .50. For no behavior, however, does heredity account for all of the variance—its influence is generally more limited, whereas environmental factors are key. Looking across all traits and behaviors, it appears that genetic differences account for 30 to 50 percent of the differences between siblings. Genetic differences account for a greater proportion of sibling differences in height and weight (80 percent), as the heritability of these traits is greater (Dunn and Plomin, 1990, p. 65).

Environmental Influences—Nurture

If heredity is responsible for 30 to 50 percent of sibling differences, what accounts for the remaining 50 to 70 percent of sibling differences? A simple answer is the environment. Environmental influences responsible for sibling differences are commonly referred to as nonshared environmental factors, as they are not shared by siblings and thus work to make siblings different, not similar. Much of the current research designed to pinpoint specific nonshared environmental factors responsible for sibling differences has focused on parental differential treatment, or the ways in which parents treat two children in the same family differently. At any one point in time, parents usually behave very differently to two children in the same family. This is not surprising, given that siblings (except for twins) are different ages and thus are often at different developmental stages. Interestingly, witnessing differential behavior to other children in the family may be more important for well-being than any similar experiences of direct interaction with parents. That is, children who are treated less warmly and/or more harshly than their siblings (or at least believe they are) experience more depression, lower self-esteem, lower academic achievement, and have more difficulties in their interactions with siblings and friends.

Although less studied, other salient sources of nonshared environmental influence might include adolescents' interactions with peers, romantic partners, and teachers. For example, having different experiences (e.g., more conflict, less disclosure, and the like) with one's friends, as compared to a sibling, may be particularly important for sibling differences in adolescent well-being. These extrafamilial sources of nonshared environment might become especially important as adolescents begin to spend more time outside of the family, unsupervised by parents.

Another source of nonshared environmental influence might include siblings' intentional efforts to differentiate themselves from each other. Not only is family discourse commonly replete with comparisons and evaluative judgments about the different family members, but children themselves begin to compare themselves to other siblings in the family at an early age. This process of social comparison may lead some adolescents to choose different activities, clothing, and behavior in an attempt to develop a unique identity, separate from that of their siblings. Finally, we should consider less systematic sources of nonshared environmental influence, such as chance or uncontrollable life events. It may be that the source of sibling differences lies to some degree in different experiences of accidents, chance meetings, and natural disasters.

Beth Manke
Deborah Corbitt-Shindler

See also Family Relations; Gender Differences; Sibling Relationships; Temperament

References and further reading
Dunn, Judy, and Robert Plomin. 1990. *Separate Lives: Why Siblings Are So Different.* New York: Basic Books.
Hetherington, Mavis, David Reiss, and Robert Plomin. 1994. *Separate Social Worlds of Siblings: The Impact of Nonshared Environment on Development.* Hillsdale, NJ: Erlbaum.

Sibling Relationships

Siblings are defined as people who share at least one parent. Siblings are either biologically related or legally related. The sibling relationship is usually an individual's longest relationship, typically lasting from birth or childhood to late adulthood or death. Sibling relationships can range from very close and intimate to distant and hostile. The sibling relationship is influenced not only by each sibling but also by outside forces such as parents and friends. Overall, the sibling relationship is a very important relationship throughout a person's life.

There are several different types of siblings. In fact, twenty-six different types of siblings have been counted. The most common types of siblings are full siblings, half siblings, stepsiblings, and adopted siblings. Full siblings are siblings who share the same two biological parents. Half siblings share only one biological parent. For example, half siblings may have the same biological mother, but have different biological fathers. Stepsiblings have different biological parents. However, they are related through the marriage of one of their biological parents. For example, a child's mother may marry a man who has children of his own. The woman's children and the

Siblings are defined as people who share at least one parent and are either biologically or legally related. (Kevin Fleming/Corbis)

man's children are not biologically related, but they are related through their parents' marriage. Lastly, there are adoptive siblings. Adoptive siblings are not related by shared biological parents but because a parent has adopted the child or children into his or her family. That is, the parent has legally made the child a part of the family. Often, adoptive siblings do not have any biological connections to other family members. Recently, between 14 percent and 20 percent of American families included half siblings or stepsiblings. The number of half siblings and stepsiblings has grown in recent years due to the rising number of divorces and remarriages.

Historically, there have of course always been siblings. However, over the last hundred years changes in the family have occurred. At the turn of the century, families were larger, and the ranges between children's ages were greater than they are today. Currently, it is much more common for couples to plan for children, to space their children, and to have fewer children than in past years.

Sibling relationships are unique. One unique feature of the sibling relationship is that it is not voluntary. That is, individuals do not choose who they want for a sibling as they can with friends. Moreover, the status of the relationship never changes. That is, brothers are always brothers and sisters are always sisters. Siblings cannot be disowned or separated from as can friends or spouses. The permanent status of siblings allows for a continued bond throughout life.

Sibling relationships are also important because it is one of the longest relationships people will have. Sibling relationships often begin in infancy or early childhood and last until late adulthood or death. The sibling relationship often lasts longer than relationships with parents, spouses, offspring, relatives, and friends. The long period of time that the sibling relationship exists can be an important aspect of the relationship. That is, siblings typically grow up in the same household, neighborhood, and community, and they typically share relatives and kin. Siblings often maintain contact as adults and into old age.

As already mentioned, full sibling and some half sibling and adoptive sibling relationships start when the second child is born, or when the parent begins to talk about the unborn child to the soon-to-be-older sibling. In fact, it appears that parents who prepare their children about the expected child are helping the older sibling adjust to the new child. In turn, older siblings are more accepting and helpful when they are prepared for a new sibling. All sibling relationships, though, may begin at any time in life.

Because sibling relationships last throughout different stages of life, there are some changes in the way siblings relate. For many siblings, the first few years of the sibling relationship often begin with the older sibling helping take care of the younger sibling and the younger sibling imitating the older sibling. However, as the younger child begins to develop language and thinking skills, the sibling relationship is viewed by both siblings as more equal. That is, by middle childhood most siblings equally share the power in the relationship; one sibling does not dominate the relationship. Although there are differences between siblings, such as intelligence, power, status, age, and achievements, feelings of being equal appear to last throughout life.

Sibling relationships are also typically characterized by helping behaviors. In early childhood, older siblings often help parents with caring for younger ones. Although the extent of help varies, many children help their parents with tasks related to a younger brother or sister. As the siblings grow older, siblings are more likely to help each other in other ways, such as in chores, sharing possessions, homework, dating, and family problems. Most siblings continue to help and support each other throughout their lifetimes.

Siblings also appear to influence one another's behaviors and attitudes. Children as young as six months old may imitate their siblings' behaviors. This kind of imitation actually helps younger children learn about the world and their role in it. During adolescence, older siblings seem to influence their younger siblings' sexual and problem behavior. For example, one sibling's aggressive behavior may influence the other sibling to be aggressive as well. Siblings also impact each other's positive behaviors, such as helping behaviors and doing well in school.

Sibling relationships are far from being all alike. Some siblings are close and affectionate, whereas others are distant and aggressive. One reason that siblings may be close or not so close is their personality characteristics. That is, if siblings have similar personalities, they are likely to share a close relationship. On the other hand, siblings who have very different personalities are less likely to share a close relationship. For example, if one sibling is outgoing and the other sibling is shy, the siblings are less likely to be close. This is not always the case, though. In some cases, siblings who have different personalities complement each other, such that an outgoing sibling helps a shy brother or sister to be more sociable.

The sibling relationship also appears to be influenced by siblings' ages and posi-tions within the family. Same-sex siblings are more likely to be close than are brother-sister relationships. Moreover, sisters are more likely to confide in each other than are brothers. In addition, siblings who are close in age (less than three years apart in age) are more likely to experience conflict than siblings who are far apart in age (four or more years age difference). Very widely spaced siblings (six or more years age difference) typically get along together very well.

Sibling relationships also vary by the age of the siblings. For example, during adolescence siblings are less likely to be involved with each other, and the intensity of the relationship lessens. The sibling relationship changes during adolescence partly because teenagers are spending more time with friends, and friends are considered more important than are siblings. Moreover, conflict and negative feelings between siblings increase during early adolescence (ages eleven to thirteen) but lessen as siblings reach the end of adolescence (ages seventeen to nineteen). Although there are changes in the sibling relationship during adolescence, many teenagers continue to feel that a sibling is an important person in their lives. Even if there has been a cooling off, by adulthood the intimacy between siblings is once again established, though on adult terms.

The sibling relationship is not only influenced by each sibling but also by the family. For example, sometimes the sibling relationship is influenced by the amount of stress the mother experiences. When mothers deal with a lot of stress throughout the day, siblings are more likely to describe their relationship as less close and less intimate. Moreover, how each sibling relates to the parent influences how the siblings relate to each other. That is, if siblings have a warm relationship with a parent, then they are likely to also have a warm relationship with their sibling. In addition, the closeness of the siblings' family impacts the closeness of the sibling bond. Lastly, how the siblings' parents relate to each other is often reflected in how siblings relate to each other. That is, the characteristics of the mother-father relationship are often similar to the characteristics of the sibling relationship.

Another influence on sibling relationships is whether the parent treats each child the same or favors a particular child. If parents treat their children differently, then siblings are more likely to be jealous or envious of each other. In addition, even if the parent treats each child the same, but one sibling thinks the parent treats the other sibling better than the parent treats him, then the sibling relationship will more likely be characterized by jealousy and conflict. Overall, the sibling relationship is important throughout development, including in adolescence.

Leanne J. Jacobson
Patricia L. East

See also Family Composition: Realities and Myths; Family Relations; Mental Retardation, Siblings with; Sibling Conflict; Sibling Differences; Twins

References and further reading
Brody, Gene H., ed. 1996. *Sibling Relationships: Their Causes and Consequences*. Norwood, NJ: Ablex Publishing.
Cicirelli, Victor G. 1995. *Sibling Relationships across the Lifespan*. New York: Plenum Press.
Dunn, Judy, and Shirley McGuire. 1992. "Sibling and Peer Relationships in Childhood." *Journal of Child Psychology and Psychiatry* 33, no. 1: 67–105.

Single Parenthood and Low Achievement

Family structure has for a long time been considered a predictor of school performance among children and adolescents. In particular, children and adolescents raised in single-parent households consistently score lower on measures of educational achievement. And as single-parent families continue to represent a growing percentage of households, whether due to higher rates of divorce or children being raised by parents who choose not to marry, policymakers are increasingly interested in outcome measures that demonstrate what, if any, consequence results from this demographic shift.

Historically, deviations from the typical two-parent family structure have been viewed as impediments to children's and adolescents' academic achievement, the result of presumed added stress and less social and/or financial support characteristic of this type of family composition. Against this backdrop, it is unsurprising that those reared without resident biological fathers are seven times more likely to be school dropouts, runaway teens, pregnant as teenagers, welfare recipients, delinquent adolescents, and, subsequently, criminals (Lykken, 1997). Thus, the lower achievement test scores of those raised by single parents are often ascribed to some inherent pathology within the one-parent household structure. Recent analyses of achievement test scores, however, contradict this supposition and suggest that these differences are not necessarily due to any intrinsic negative attribute associated with the single-parent household structure, per se. Below we explain the reasoning for this new insight.

Charlotte Paterson and her colleagues looked at income level and household composition, among other variables, as predictors of elementary school-aged children's school performance. Results showed that although the variables measured accounted for 25 percent of the variance in academic achievement, coming from a singe-parent household was the least significant predictor of scores.

In his study of the effect of single parenthood on school readiness in six- and seven-year-olds, Henry Ricciuti showed that school readiness and achievement for this age group were unrelated to, and therefore unhindered by, single parenthood, which was associated with lower income and lower maternal educational attainment. Findings from a number of other studies report the same outcome for adolescents. For example, Elizabeth Peters and Natalie Mullis showed that performance of fifteen- to sixteen-year-olds on the Armed Forces Qualification Test (AFQT) was not affected by growing up in a female-headed household; and controlling income eliminated any negative effects on years of schooling completed by age twenty-four to twenty-five (Ricciuti, 1999). In their study of one-year prospective effects of family, peer, and neighborhood influence on academic achievement among African American adolescents, Nancy Gonzales and her colleagues reported that family status variables, which included income, parent education level, and the number of parental figures present in the home, did not significantly predict school performance. In fact, they pointed out that this finding "contributes to the growing list of studies that refute the 'father absence' explanation of underachievement that once prevailed in the field" (p. 380). More noteworthy are their findings that neighborhood risk interacted with maternal restrictive control and moderated a positive effect of peer support to significantly

affect school performance—highlighting the need for more ecological models when examining this issue.

This trend of commensurate academic performance among adolescents of one- and two-parent households, when other background variables are controlled, is actually not new. Data from the 1988 National Education Longitudinal Study, conducted by the National Center for Educational Statistics of the U.S. Department of Education, showed that early adolescents from two-parent households scored higher on standardized achievement tests compared with those from nontraditional family types, including mother-only and father-only compositions. Although these data seem to favor the two-parent household, when the effects of background variables were adjusted, the differences in scores of adolescents being raised in mother-only and mother-father family structures were reduced to one-tenth of a standard deviation (Zill, 1996).

Similarly, in two large-scale meta-analyses of the literature on educational achievement and single-parent family structure, Mavis Hetherington and her colleagues and S. A. Salzman looked at a wide range of outcome measures: IQ scores, aptitude tests, overall achievement scores, quantitative-verbal IQ differences, and school grades. Although the majority of studies reviewed in both analyses favored two-parent households, differences in overall general achievement were small, and in the case of IQ scores, differences were not considered meaningful (Milne, 1996).

Thus, the evidence reviewed supports the idea that rather than being caused by some inherent pathological problem associated with the single-parent household, differences in school achievement may be attributable to the circumstances associated with the deficient economic and educational resources available to this group. Furthermore, there is a clear indication that we must look beyond family structure and include external, community-related variables as factors in models that attempt to predict school performance in adolescents.

The National Assessment of Educational Progress has reported on the average differences in American students' verbal and math test scores since the late 1960s. Recent analyses of differences in achievement as a function of such factors as race, family structure, parental educational attainment, and family income level have documented the illusory role of family structure (e.g., Bronfenbrenner et al., 1996). These findings indicate that although children and adolescents of single-parent households score 16.67 percent lower on verbal test scores (with similar differences found on tests of mathematical reasoning), such deficits were not the result of family structure, per se. In fact, these differences are almost entirely due to variations in income and parental education that happens to be collinear with single parenthood. Thus, when parental educational attainment and income are controlled for, the deficit in scores of adolescents being raised by single mothers is completely eliminated on tests of verbal and mathematical ability.

Taken together, these new findings refute previous notions about the pathological role of single parenthood in children's and adolescents' school performance. Instead, they are congruent with observations over the past twenty years that the largest gains in test scores have been made by the most disadvantaged groups, the consequence of increases in educational spending that have been disproportionately targeted to programs serving disadvantaged families, such as Title 1 and Head Start (Bronfenbrenner et al., 1996).

In sum, recent research on family structure demonstrates that controlling for differences in economic and other situational factors (particularly maternal educational attainment) reduces the gap in test scores associated with single parenthood. In those situations where single-parent families possess equivalent incomes to those of two-parent families, the children's and adolescents' test scores are very similar. In light of this evidence it seems that rather than focusing on family composition, future policy should instead concentrate on assisting single-parent households in the procurement of fiscal support, which may serve to alleviate the intergenerational cycle of disproportionate resources leading to poor achievement.

Paul B. Papierno
Stephen J. Ceci

See also Academic Achievement; High School Equivalency Degree; Pregnancy, Interventions to Prevent; Programs for Adolescents; School Engagement; Sex Education; Teenage Parenting: Consequences; Welfare

References and further reading
Bronfenbrenner, Urie, Peter McClelland, Elaine Wethington, Phyllis Moen, and Stephen J. Ceci. 1996. *State of Americans.* New York: Free Press.
Coleman, J., and T. Hoffer. 1987. *Public and Private High Schools: The Impact of Communities.* New York: Wiley.
Gonzalez, Nancy A., Ana Mari Cauce, Ruth J. Friedman, and Craig A. Mason. 1996. "Family, Peer, and Neighborhood Influences on Academic Achievement among African-American Adolescents:

One Year Prospective Effect." *American Journal of Community Psychology* 24, no. 3: 365–387.

Hetherington, E. Mavis, David L. Featherman, and Karen A. Camara. 1981. *Intellectual Functioning and Achievement of Children in One-Parent Households.* Washington DC: National Institute of Education.

Lykken, David T. 1997. "Factory of Crime." *Psychological Inquiry* 8: 261–270.

Milne, Ann M. 1996. Family Structure and the Achievement of Children." Pp. 32–65 in *Education and the American Family: A Research Synthesis.* Edited by W. J. Weston. New York: New York University Press.

Paterson, Charlotte J., Janis B. Kupersmidt, and Nancy A. Vaden. 1990. "Income Level, Gender, Ethnicity, and Household Composition as Predictors of Children's School-Based Competence." *Child Development* 61: 485–494.

Peters, Elizabeth H., and Natalie C. Mullis. 1997. "The Role of Family Income and Sources of Income in Adolescent Achievement." Pp. 340–381 in *Consequences of Growing Up Poor.* Edited by Greg J. Duncan and Jeanne Brooks-Gunn. New York: Sage.

Ricciuti, Henry R. 1999. "Single Parenthood and School Readiness in White, Black, and Hispanic 6- and 7-Year-Olds." *Journal of Family Psychology* 13: 450–465.

Salzman, S. A. 1987. "Meta-Analysis of Studies Investigating the Effects of Father Absence on Children's Cognitive Performance." Paper presented at the annual meeting of the American Educational Research Association, Washington, DC (April).

Steinberg, Laurence. 1989. "Communities of Families and Education." In *Education and the American Family: A Research Synthesis.* Edited by W. J. Weston. New York: New York University Press.

Zill, Norman. 1996. "Family Change and Student Achievement: What We Have Learned, What It Means for Schools." Pp. 139–174 in *Family-School Links: How Do They Affect Educational Outcomes?* Edited by Alan Booth and Judith F. Dunn. Mahwah, NJ: Erlbaum.

Social Development

Social development refers to the changes in both social interactions and expectations that one experiences across the life span. Understanding the processes involved in social development will aid adolescents in successfully negotiating their social world. Social and cultural forces as well as specific life experiences affect our relationships with others and how we think of ourselves. In each stage of development, we must uphold certain social roles and values. Some of these roles are possessed since birth (e.g., being a son), while others are taken on as one ages (e.g., being a teenager). Many roles are thrust upon us by circumstance or societal expectations (e.g., being a woman), while others are chosen by the individual (e.g., being a lawyer). Thus, roles may change throughout the life span as we progress through infancy, childhood, adolescence, and adulthood.

Humans are social creatures, and we are interested in understanding how other people interact with and achieve success in the environment. Throughout life those around us serve as models for our own behavior as we observe and learn from their actions. Those individuals who tend to be most influential as models are those who are effective in their environment, those who have nurtured or protected us, and those individuals we perceive as similar to ourselves. We attempt to mimic behavior that we believe will help us reach the goals that are important to us and "people like us." Through observation, modeling, and even direct instruction we are *socialized* to conform to the standards of our communities, but our social environment is complex and changes constantly. When describing how we develop socially, we must account for

Social development, often involving peers, is a significant feature of adolescence. (Laura Dwight)

the contribution of differences in culture, historical period, gender, group membership, and status to social development. Social pressures interact with personal traits, including physical health, self-esteem, perceived attractiveness, and intelligence, to affect our development. For example, a person considered attractive in his cultural context will have a different set of life experiences than one not considered attractive. In this way judgments about ourselves and others both shape and are shaped by our social activities and interactions.

As we are socialized into the world, we develop a self-concept, which will impact our future social interaction and development. This notion of self-identity involves knowledge of both our social roles and our personal values and morality. Throughout life self-concept is a powerful contributor to social and personal development. Our views of ourselves affect the impressions that other people will come to have of us as well as our success in both our professional and personal lives. For example, even in young children school achievement has been shown to rely on both academic ability and individual inferences about learning ability. Those children who believe certain tasks are beyond their ability often find that to be true, simply because their own self-doubts prevent success. Aspects of our self-concepts are carried with us throughout development, although the self-concept may change somewhat over time.

Although there are many socializing forces in the environment, it is important to recognize that we play an active role in our interactions with the environment to guide and direct social development. Decisions we make and the attitude and approaches we take when interacting with others will alter the course of our own socialization, as well as influencing the social development of others in the community.

During childhood, social development begins with the family. Children must rely on adults not only to provide food and shelter, but also to provide social and emotional support. Bonds with parents or other caretakers form the first meaningful relationships an individual will have. Parents interpret society and culture for their children, and begin to convey their values and attitudes to their children from the day that they are born. Newborns do not have some of the skills we tend to associate with adult social interaction, such as language, but they are still active participants in the social world. Children tend to be naturally social, showing almost immediate interest in faces and amazing sensitivity to emotions. Newborns are likely to look at faces for longer amounts of time than other objects of equal complexity, and may even be observed to mimic the facial expressions they see. Infants can soon distinguish people based on age, gender, and familiarity, and they are sensitive to the moods of their mothers. As early as two months of age, children even coordinate their attention and actions with those of others in their social world.

By eighteen months they exhibit a trait known as *social referencing:* They base decisions about their behavior on the facial expressions and conveyed attitudes of the adults around them. For example,

children of this age will show interest in a new toy if their mothers smile and encourage them. However, they will avoid the same item if their mothers appear afraid of it. Through observation and modeling, children learn to interpret motives, emotions, and actions and become familiar with norms, roles, and relationships in society. In this way children learn to do the social problem-solving tasks they will encounter every day for the rest of their lives. They learn how to participate in and respond to social situations, and ultimately they learn about the expectations they must meet as members of society.

It has been said that one cannot know herself without first having a sense of the other people in the world. Through experience with the world, infants develop an awareness of themselves as separate from the environment and learn that they can control their own behavior as well as certain aspects of the external world. This realization leads young children to compare themselves to others and to begin to assign labels to members of their social world. Young children tend to describe and categorize others in terms of their external characteristics such as gender, age, appearance, or observable behavior. As children grow, they begin to recognize internal traits such as personality and attitude as stable aspects of individuals.

One of the earliest categories that children use for classification is gender. This trend is not surprising, given that even before children are themselves able to distinguish reliably between the genders, parents and other adults treat them differently based on gender, beginning the process of sex role socialization. Female infants are referred to as "pretty," "good," and "sweet," while terms such as "handsome," "tough," and "active" are applied to males. These differences have even been seen in research settings where the same baby posed as both a male and a female. In fact, most differences in temperament and achievement between the genders are actually very small. Although there may be a small difference in the average performance between the genders on some measures, the variation within either gender is almost always far greater than the variability between the genders, leading to much overlap in ability. For example, males may be able to lift heavier objects on average than females, but the strongest female is much stronger than the weakest male, even within the same age and health range.

However that may be, children internalize the gender-related behaviors and concepts that are modeled for them both directly and indirectly, and they become part of their self-concepts. Thus, by about age five most children display some gender role stereotypes and by age six or seven they have come to think of gender roles as permanent. Although gender-role identity is a fundamental aspect of self-concept, it is not necessarily a rigid personality trait. Many individuals reevaluate at least some aspect of their gender roles and gender concepts at some point in their lives.

Parenting styles and individual temperament interact to shape early social development. Parenting styles have tended to be defined in terms of both how demanding the parents are and how responsive they are to their children's needs and desires. Parents may show appropriate levels of both (characterized as ("authoritative"), may be demanding without being responsive ("authoritarian"), may be responsive but not demanding ("indulgent"), or may be neither ("neglecting"). Variability in parenting styles across individuals and cultures tends to reflect the socialization goals of the family, and there is not a direct correspondence between parenting styles and future social development. Children in authoritarian households can attain the same levels and kinds of social success as those in indulgent households, depending on the cultural context and individual attitudes.

Studies do show that with humans and other primates inadequate or inappropriate early social contact can often have lifelong effects on physical and mental health as well as the ability to form later relationships. Orphans raised in institutions may show abnormal levels of emotional and physical disorders and high death rates, even when adequate food and medical care are provided. Similar outcomes may result from hostile family environments, but individuals may also show resilience and thrive even in the face of a negative environment. These resilient children tend to share certain traits, which are believed to insulate them from many of the harmful effects of improper social contact. These traits include social competence (feeling effective and successful in their social world), self-confidence, independence, and a drive to achieve. In addition, most of these individuals have at least a few positive social relationships that provide a sense of security and create a social support system.

Peer relationships in early childhood tend to be based on physical proximity. Our first friends are those people available to play with, and friendships can be made or broken very rapidly, while the family tends to provide the main source of social support. In adolescence, peers begin to compete with the family as a major socializing influence. Friendships become more long-lasting, and are marked by loyalty and intimacy as friends "stick together" and "can tell each other anything." This kind of friendship takes a long time to form, and such friends are difficult to replace.

During adolescence an individual begins to form an adult identity and to push for independence from his or her parents. This move toward independence can strain family relationships, but there is much variability in the actions and reactions of individuals and their parents. While individuals separate from their parents, relationships with their peers tend to intensify, moving toward greater mutual dependence. In this way adolescents come to rely on their friends for advice and social support. Gender roles also begin to be more clearly differentiated during this time, and romantic relationships may be initiated. While their relationships change, adolescents also begin to address future personal and career goals in anticipation of the transition to adulthood. At this point, people may begin to recognize the active role they play in shaping their own social world. Decisions can be made about school, career, family, and friends that will have lasting consequences, and society comes to expect the individual to take responsibility for his actions at this stage as well. As cognitive abilities expand, adolescents begin to think more explicitly about their social roles and values. They may come to realize there may be discrepancies between the idealized view of themselves and reality, coming to terms with their own inconsistencies. During this period, individuals show marked concern about how others regard them, but they also show a tendency to filter out cultural and social information that is inconsistent with their self-image. Moral views become particularly important

parts of the self-concept, as the individual begins to consider the ramifications of her actions and to make decisions about the kind of person she would like to be.

The transition from childhood to adulthood is marked by rites of passage in some cultures, and is often believed to be associated with a time of emotional upheaval. The conception of adolescence as a time of mood swings and unpredictable behavior is not necessarily accurate, however. Many non-Western cultures do not hold this preconception and do not see such patterns of behavior. Even in the United States antisocial behavior during adolescence is the exception and not the norm. Adolescence is also typically associated with the onset of puberty, but this conception of development is too simplistic. Puberty refers to the physical changes that occur as one enters reproductive adulthood, but adolescence is a social construct, describing the transition to social adulthood. In most cases both adolescence and puberty begin in the preteen or early teen years. However, adolescence may be observed to begin earlier or later than puberty and often has a different overall time course.

Typically, adolescence begins later for boys than for girls, as females tend to mature both physically and socially earlier than males. In the United States adolescence has no clearly defined beginning or end. Children who are given increased independence at an early age may share characteristics of adolescents before puberty, while others may remain "children" beyond the onset of puberty. In recent years, some have suggested that the duration of adolescence may be lengthening as individuals delay the "adult" roles associated with marriage and family in order to further their educational and professional goals. In some cases, however, individuals may pass almost directly from childhood to adulthood due to the demands of the situation. These factors can vary culturally, but in any context, situations such as loss of a parent or teen pregnancy can significantly alter the duration of this phase.

In adulthood social relationships and personal accomplishments are both emphasized. Commitments move beyond oneself and one's partner to include the family, work, society, and the future. Throughout adulthood, social intimacy is a key factor of psychological well-being: Those people with strong personal relationships tend to be happier. As with the earlier stages, adulthood is marked by transitional periods that are associated with major life reorganizations. Early and middle adulthood may be characterized by a focus on family, as marital relationships and having children take center stage. Career satisfaction and achievement may also contribute significantly to both social roles and self-concept at this time. Throughout adulthood, goals for career and family are set and periodically reevaluated.

In general, women seem much more conflicted between expectations for career and family than men. This trend may be due to relatively recent social changes to women's roles, as having a career has become socially acceptable and even expected for many women. For adults, gender role behavior varies with the situation, but it appears that gender roles may tend to become more traditional as individuals encounter major life stages. Thus, a couple who are dating may have more balanced or untraditional gender roles, while married couples tend to display a shift toward more traditional gender roles, with the male serving as the breadwinner and the female overseeing the home. This shift becomes even more apparent with the birth of children. However, as with all aspects of social development, there is wide individual variation.

Late in adulthood, social interactions shift somewhat to friends again, as children gain independence and individuals retire from their jobs. With growing life expectancies, the postretirement years mark the beginning of new roles and social obligations to friends, family, and the community at large, rather than an end to one's "usefulness." However, older adults are often faced with negative stereotypes of declines in intellectual and physical ability. These declines are not necessary (or normal) aspects of the aging process, but at each stage negative stereotypes can lead to self-fulfilling prophecies, as individuals tend to live up (or down) to expectations held by society and by themselves.

Individuals tend to have internal social clocks by which they judge the age-appropriateness of different activities. There are expectations about the roles that must be fulfilled at various stages of life, and events that are not in accord with these clocks tend to be more stressful for the individual than those that occur on schedule. Although societal pressures do still dictate when certain events appear to be appropriate, age clocks may be less rigid now than they were in the past, as people are more apt to postpone having children until later in life, go back to school after already establishing a career, and marry, divorce, and remarry throughout the life span.

Our social environment is complex and affects development throughout life. Societal expectations and self-concept both change as one matures. Adolescence often marks a time when social factors first *consciously* enter into decision processes about how to act within situations, and most adolescents are strongly influenced by social pressures introduced by their families, their peers, and the greater community. Having a realistic understanding of the factors involved in social development will help adolescents to negotiate their environments confidently and to understand how their actions affect the social world experienced by themselves and others around them.

Maya Misra

See also Cliques; Conformity; Dating; Peer Groups; Peer Victimization in School; Puberty: Psychological and Social Changes; Youth Culture

References and further reading
Anthony, E. James, and Bertram J. Cohler, eds. 1987. *The Invulnerable Child.* New York: Guilford Press.
Baltes, Paul B., and Orville G. Brim Jr., eds. 1979. *Life-Span Development and Behavior,* Vol. 2. New York: Academic Press.
Baumrind, Diana. 1975. *Early Socialization and the Discipline Controversy.* Morristown, NJ: General Learning Press.
Cichetti, Dante, and Marjorie Beeghly, eds. 1990. *The Self in Transition: Infancy to Adulthood.* Chicago: University of Chicago Press.
Damon, William. 1983. *Social and Personality Development: From Infancy through Adolescence.* New York: Norton.
Damon, William, and Daniel Hart. 1988. *Self-Understanding in Childhood and Adolescence.* New York: Cambridge University Press.
Elder, Glen H., Jr., John Modell, and Ross D. Parke, eds. 1993. *Children in Time and Place: Developmental and Historical Insights.* New York: Cambridge University Press.
Erikson, Erik H. 1963. *Childhood and Society,* 2nd ed. New York: Norton.
Hetherington, E. Mavis, Richard M. Lerner, and Marion Perlmutter, eds. 1988. *Child Development in Life-Span Perspective.* Hillsdale, NJ: Erlbaum.
Levinson, Daniel J. 1978. *The Seasons of a Man's Life.* New York: Knopf.
———. 1996. *The Seasons of a Woman's Life.* New York: Random House.

Spina Bifida

Adolescents born with spina bifida, a serious and widespread congenital birth defect, face challenges their able-bodied peers do not. They are likely to experience pubertal development before their peers, have difficulty walking, and may find social interactions difficult. They also are more likely than able-bodied peers to remain dependent on their families and must be encouraged to accept increasing responsibility in an age-appropriate and ability-appropriate manner. Although most adolescents with spina bifida are within the normal range of intellectual functioning, their unique learning difficulties are often inadequately addressed and may result in discrimination in the workplace as adults. Given these challenges, it is not surprising that these adolescents are at increased risk for attentional problems, anxiety, withdrawal, and depression. A healthy parent-child relationship and opportunities for meaningful and rewarding social interactions, however, can improve the self-image and self-confidence of adolescents with spina bifida and protect them from many of these emotional and behavioral problems.

Major medical advances have greatly increased the survival and functioning of those born with spina bifida, but much work remains to fully understand their development over the life span. As children with spina bifida become adolescents, it becomes increasingly important to focus not only on medical needs but also on psychosocial factors that can improve their quality of life through childhood, adolescence, and into adulthood.

Developing with Spina Bifida

Spina bifida is the second most common congenital birth defect in the world. It occurs during the first twenty-eight days of a pregnancy when the bones of the spinal column that surround the developing spinal cord do not close completely. The degree of impairment in spina bifida depends on the location and extent of the spinal lesion, shunt status (i.e., how effectively the shunt that removes excess fluid from the brain is working), and the severity of orthopedic deformities in the legs, feet, and spinal column. Most children require some mechanical aids (e.g., wheelchairs, crutches, or braces) to move around, and the majority incur bladder and bowel control difficulties.

Prior to the early 1950s, babies born with spina bifida rarely survived. Major advances in neurosurgery and urology, however, have increased the chances of survival, and today the majority of infants born with this birth defect will live into adulthood. As the life span of children born with spina bifida has increased, more attention has been given to the developing adolescent and the transition into adulthood.

Children with spina bifida tend to begin puberty earlier than their able-bodied peers, often starting as early as seven years of age. This precocious puberty results in fewer available years for bone growth and thus shorter and heavier stature overall. In addition, it may result in earlier breast development and menarche for girls. Even though they mature early, adolescents with spina bifida perceive themselves to be uninformed about the sexual implications of spina bifida. The effect of spina

bifida on sexual function depends on the lesion level and the degree of completeness of the lesion. In males with spina bifida, erection, intercourse, ejaculation, fertility, and sensation of orgasm can all be affected to varying degrees. In females, fertility, menstruation, and intercourse are rarely affected, but sensation of orgasm may be affected by the disability.

Parental Relationships

Adolescents with spina bifida often remain psychologically dependent on their parents much longer than their nondisabled peers do. As a result, a major goal for the family during this period is to help the adolescent function more independently. The process of transferring responsibility from the parent to the child should take place in a progressive manner with age-appropriate and ability-appropriate jobs. Parents who treat their children in an age-appropriate manner, do not inhibit their activities, and encourage achievement have a positive influence on their adolescents' self-image, as well as future employment, community mobility, and social activity.

Dependency on the family is evident in the passive approach many adolescents with spina bifida take toward healthcare. Most adolescents with spina bifida are aware of the functional implications of their disability (e.g., symptoms associated with shunt malfunction, the name and purpose of medications, and programs necessary in managing their disability) but are unaware of diagnostic information (e.g., lesion level, hydrocephalus, diagnosis). To become more active in healthcare and make informed decisions, adolescents with spina bifida must be educated about their disability, the associated health risks, and implications for functioning. Earlier exposure to terminology related to diagnosis and neurological status, as well as more direct decision making by the adolescent about treatment, where appropriate, might improve knowledge and encourage more responsibility.

Current research suggests that adolescents with spina bifida may be at increased risk for emotional and behavioral adjustment problems, particularly attentional problems and internalizing symptoms such as anxiety, withdrawal, and depression. The normal challenges of identity formation are complicated for the adolescent with spina bifida because they must integrate the permanence of the disability into the developing self-concept. Adolescents with spina bifida often feel less competent than do able-bodied peers in academic, athletic, and social interactions. On the positive side, they feel equally supported by friends and parents and more supported by teachers.

The key is for parents to provide support and at the same time encourage their adolescent's physical and emotional independence. Given the protective effect of having a healthy parent-child relationship, a physical disability does not necessarily result in psychosocial problems. Rather, the social expectations of significant others as well as opportunities for meaningful and rewarding social interactions are primary determinants of positive self-image.

Peer Interactions

Social isolation is a major problem for young adults with spina bifida. Peer relationships are generally characterized by extremely limited out-of-school contacts, minimal participation in organized social activities, and a tendency toward sedentary activities. Most adolescents with spina bifida have never dated and have only minimal social interactions with the opposite sex. Activities that involve age-appropriate tasks that other students will both benefit from and appreciate are most helpful in increasing self-confidence and social interaction in adolescents with spina bifida.

A study by Jan Lord and colleagues suggests that mere physical proximity to able-bodied peers does not necessarily promote increased social interaction and confidence. The study found that, even though adolescents in mainstream classes had the most normal scores for academic and social skills, those whose program combined general and special education classes reported the least loneliness. Class placement, therefore, should be carefully considered on an individual basis, since it appears that for some adolescents part-time placement in special education classrooms might have social advantages that decrease loneliness.

Academic and Vocational Functioning

Adolescents with spina bifida, although below the population average, are within the normal range of intelligence and can usually function academically in general education classrooms. They usually perform within the normal range on verbal tasks, but have unique learning disabilities that involve visual-motor integration difficulty and fine-motor coordination problems. These problems typically result in lower arithmetic achievement relative to nondisabled adolescents, while performance in areas such as reading and spelling keeps pace with age peers. Expanded education for teachers regarding spina bifida is necessary to address these specific limitations.

Adolescents with spina bifida are protected under the Individuals with Disabilities Education Act (PL 101-476), which requires that goals and objectives related to employment and postsecondary education, independent living, and community participation be included in Individual Educational Programs (IEPs) at no later than sixteen years of age. In a survey of needs by Suzanne Kennedy and colleagues, parents and young people with spina bifida felt that these needs were not being adequately addressed. They strongly suggested that vocational counselors become more understanding and realistic and that employers receive updated information regarding disabilities. To compete for employment, young people with spina bifida need to learn self-advocacy and self-marketing skills and to be aware of their employment rights, based on the Rehabilitation Act and the Americans with Disabilities Act.

Venette C. Westhoven
Grayson N. Holmbeck
Michelle Abdala
Sandra Alcala

See also Developmental Challenges; Learning Disabilities; Learning Styles and Accommodations

References and further reading
Ammerman, Robert T., Vincent R. Kane, Gregory T. Slomka, Donald H. Reigel, Michael D. Franzen, and Kenneth D. Gadow. 1998. "Psychiatric Symptomatology and Family Functioning in Children and Adolescents with Spina Bifida." *Journal of Clinical Psychology in Medical Settings* 5: 449–465.
Appleton, P. L., P. E. Minchom, N. C. Ellis, C. E. Elliott, V. Boll, and P. Jones. 1994. "The Self-Concept of Young People with Spina Bifida: A Population-Based Study." *Developmental Medicine and Child Neurology* 36: 198–215.
Erickson, David. 1992. "Knowledge of Disability in Adolescents with Spina Bifida." *Canadian Journal of Rehabilitation* 5: 171–175.
Erickson, David, and Laurel Erickson. 1992. "Knowledge of Sexuality in Adolescents with Spina Bifida." *Canadian Journal of Human Sexuality* 14: 195–199.
Kennedy, Suzanne E., Sherri D. Garcia Martin, John M. Kelley, Brian Walton, Claudia K. Vlcek, Ruth S. Hassanein, and Grace E. Holmes. 1998. "Identification of Medical and Nonmedical Needs of Adolescents and Young Adults with Spina Bifida and Their Families: A Preliminary Study." *Children's Health Care* 27: 47–61.
Lord, Jan, Nicole Varzos, Bruce Behrman, John Wicks, and Dagmar Wicks. 1990. "Implications of Mainstream Classrooms for Adolescents with Spina Bifida." *Developmental Medicine and Child Neurology* 32: 20–29.
Wills, Karen E., Grayson N. Holmbeck, Katherine Dillon, and David G. McLone. 1990. "Intelligence and Achievement in Children with Myelomeningocele." *Journal of Pediatric Psychology* 15:161–176.
Wolman, Clara, and Deborah E. Basco. 1994. "Factors Influencing Self-Esteem and Self-Consciousness in Adolescents with Spina Bifida." *Society of Adolescent Medicine* 15: 543–548.

Completion of this article was supported in part by Social and Behavioral Sciences Research Grant No. 12-FY93–0621, 12-FY 97–0270, and 12-FY99–0280 from the March of Dimes Birth Defects Foundation.

Sports and Adolescents

Adolescents and athletics are a natural mix. Although adolescents may struggle with many other aspects of their lives, sports are uniquely equipped to help the adolescent adapt to the physical, psychological, and social changes they are experiencing. In light of this, athletics becomes a valuable setting in which to understand adolescents. While much of the world (the family and school, for example) is struggling to adapt to the changes of adolescence, athletics by its very nature embraces those changes and the different ways in which they evolve. There are athletic opportunities for early-, on-time, and late-maturing adolescents, for adolescents who are tall or not as tall, thin but fast or heavy but strong, and interested in team sports or interested in individual sports.

The power of sports to provide a meaningful and positive environment for adolescents cannot be overstated. However, there is also the potential for sports to create negative experiences for young people. Coaches are expected to instill a range of important values and skills in the young participants, but agreement on what those values and skills are is up for debate. We want our young athletes to be team oriented and loyal, but not if it involves cheating or poor sportsmanship. We want them to be competitive but fair, to be satisfied with putting forth their best efforts but also to win. Because of the complicated nature of these values, coaches must be prepared to help young athletes come to an understanding of what it means to be a good athlete. Thus, the purpose of the present essay is threefold. First, it examines the relationship between athletics and the fundamental changes of adolescence. Second, it identifies how young people can benefit or suffer from sport experiences. Finally, it provides parents and coaches with some ideas about how to help young people deal with the challenges of being an athlete.

Biological Change and Athletic Participation

In sports, the biological changes of adolescence, specifically puberty, need to be appreciated in two distinct ways. First, it is important to explore how an adolescent's pubertal changes affect her athletic experiences. In turn, it is also important to attempt to understand how athletics affect puberty.

When adolescents are good at an activity that is important to them, such as sports, they are likely to develop positive feelings about themselves. (Skjold Photographs)

Effects of Puberty on Athletic Experiences

Although it is true that nearly all adolescents go through puberty, *how* they go through it varies considerably. Specifically, variations arise in terms of the tempo—how rapidly an individual completes puberty—and the timing—at what age an individual begins puberty compared to his peers. Pubertal tempo and timing may affect the type of sport an adolescent chooses to participate in, her level of success in that sport, and/or her willingness to participate at all. We know that boys and girls who mature early may fare differently from those who mature later. Boys who mature early are likely to be successful in a variety of team sports, such as football, baseball, swimming, track and field, and cycling. In turn, those boys who mature later are found to be more successful in such sports as hockey, distance running, and gymnastics. For girls, the picture becomes more complicated. We know most about girls who participate in individual sports such as figure skating and gymnastics. In these sports, later maturation is more likely to lead to success. For female swimmers, success does not appear to be a function of maturational timing. However, while boys are likely to participate in athletics regardless of their pubertal experiences, early maturation in girls appears to have an inhibitory effect on their sport participation. This may result from their general lack of comfort with the physical changes associated with puberty, for which neither they nor those around them may be prepared. In fact, for girls, athletic contexts may demand a certain level of comfort with one's physical self in order to be able to participate.

*Effects of Physical Activity
and Athletics on Puberty*
The effect of physical activity on puberty is more difficult to understand. There is some evidence to suggest that girls who train intensely in sports are likely to experience delayed menarche (first menstrual period). But it is not clear whether physical activity is the cause of this delayed menarche or whether girls who participate in sports are simply predisposed to a later age of menarche anyway. In addition, we know very little about the impact of intense training on boys' development. It can be said that intense athletic activity appears to have no effect on growth in height, skeletal maturation,

or the timing of the growth spurt. It does affect weight in both boys and girls, as would be expected, by increasing the level of lean mass (muscle) and decreasing the level of adipose tissue (fat).

*Psychological Changes and
Athletic Participation*
In addition to the fundamental biological changes associated with adolescence, critical changes are occurring psychologically as well. Of particular importance in athletics are changes in the thought processes of young people. In the realm of sports, motivation becomes a key issue to understand, since it affects both an adolescent's willingness to get involved and stay involved in a sport as well as the success he experiences in that sport. Two approaches to understanding motivation are worth noting. Joan Duda has focused extensively on the idea of achievement motivation and the importance of being task oriented, while Maureen Weiss has focused on issues of competence motivation and the importance of gaining mastery.

*Types of Motivation:
Intrinsic and Extrinsic*
What is motivation? For the purposes of this discussion, there are two types of motivational style. *Extrinsic motivation* involves relying on some type of tangible reward. Thus, a child who is extrinsically motivated would seek to be involved in sport in the hopes of winning trophies, money, ribbons, or some other form of reward. In addition, an individual who participates in sports to *avoid* feeling guilty for not having participated would be extrinsically motivated. In contrast, *intrinsic motivation* is generated internally by the individual, meaning they participate "for the fun of it," or because they

like how they feel about themselves when they take part in sports. Thus, intrinsically motivated children, although they may be excited about winning a trophy or ribbon, are not driven solely by the need to be rewarded by such objects.

Achievement Motivation and Sports
The study of sport-related achievement motivation focuses on attributions and goal orientations. Specifically, it asks to what children and adolescents attribute their successes and failures, and whether they are oriented toward mastering tasks (in other words, task oriented) or toward surpassing others (in other words, ego oriented). At the same time, the relationship between how children think about their successes and failures (attributional style) and how task oriented they are is impacted by changes in the thought patterns that occur during childhood and adolescence. Thus, a discussion of these factors is merited in order to appreciate the complexity of how motivation develops as well as what is required of adults in their attempts to enhance rather than impede the development of motivation.

Ability, Effort, and Task Difficulty. Is success a matter of luck while failure is a matter of personal ability? Is failure based on a lack of effort or lack of ability? Are sporting experiences something over which the child feels he or she has some control with respect to the outcome? As children grow up, they come to understand that their ability, their effort, and the difficulty of a task are independent factors affecting athletic performance. They also learn to more accurately evaluate their own performance and ability in comparison to that of their peers. Thus, young children tend to believe that if they can just try hard enough, they can

be best at a sport. However, adolescents are more sophisticated thinkers and can realize that "ability is capacity," meaning there are some tasks that are simply too difficult for them regardless of how much effort they put forth. They may never be as good as some of their more athletically competent peers.

Attributions. So if adolescents can tell they may always be mediocre, why do those adolescents stay involved in sports? The answer is attributional style. It is generally understood that young people try to find ways to be successful and show high ability. How positively young people perceive their competence is affected by how much success they experience athletically, but that is not the only factor. A young person who thinks his success results from personal qualities like ability and effort is more likely to feel competent, particularly if he or she believes the causes of the success are personal and consistent (like ability). In contrast, a young person who believes her success is the result of situational factors (such as luck or ease of task) is less likely to develop positive feelings of competence. Positive feelings can also result from failure experiences. A child who believes he failed due to lack of effort is more likely to think the outcome could be different the next time "if I just try harder." Thus, it is possible for both success and failure to have either a positive or a negative effect on a child's feelings of athletic competence and therefore on her motivation to achieve. It simply depends on how the child interprets each event.

Task Orientation versus Ego Orientation. However, the picture is more complicated if one is interested in understanding why adolescents not only get into sports but *stay* involved. The issue of personal competence (task mastery) becomes important at this point. Adolescents who concentrate on mastering a task are likely to put forth more effort, have more accurate and positive perceptions of their ability, and set more appropriate goals for achievement. In contrast, adolescents who compare themselves to others may exhibit one of two distinct patterns: If they also believe they have high ability, they are more likely to engage in behaviors that are both challenging and calculated to strengthen their sense of competence; if they believe they have low ability, they are more likely to choose activities that are too easy or too difficult for their ability level and so have no effect on their sense of competence.

Practically speaking, a teenager whose main focus is on self-improvement is more likely to continue participating in sports throughout adolescence. On the other hand, a teenager who is primarily concerned with outdoing his peers may not experience problems initially, but it is almost inevitable that an unsurpassable opponent will be encountered at some point. By age twelve or thirteen, young adolescents understand that there is an upper limit to their ability regardless of the amount of effort they put forth, a limit that makes some opponents unbeatable. Under such circumstances, additional effort is useful only when an individual seeks to achieve a skill level that reflects *her* greatest potential, irrespective of others' performances. Thus, teenagers who are most interested in doing their best are less bothered when they realize they are not as skilled as others and will maintain participation in sports, whereas those most interested in beating others are more likely, given the right circumstances, to drop out of sports.

Competence Motivation and Sports
While understanding achievement motivation provides those in the field with insights into why young people may choose to stay in or to drop out of sports, competence motivation becomes valuable for those interested in understanding how sports contributes to the self-esteem of young athletes. In general, the basic premise of this approach is that how a child judges his level of competence affects how well the child performs athletically, which affects the child's self-esteem. There are many factors that contribute to the process of developing and building competence and self-esteem.

Multiple Domains of Competence. First, there are several performance areas or domains in which adolescents can show competence. One important domain is physical competence, which includes athletic skill. When athletic competence is combined with the adolescent's personal interest in sport, we gain insight into how self-esteem begins to develop. For example, a child may view sports as important and want to perform well athletically. However, if the child is unable to perform as well as desired, this will affect both the way the child evaluates her competence as well as her continuing interest in sports. Generally then, this means that when children are good at something that is also important to them like sports, they are likely to develop positive feelings about themselves. In contrast, a lack of success is likely to lead to anxiety and negative feelings.

Optimal Challenges. For those adults interested in helping young people improve athletically, it is important to present them with the *optimal challenge*. An optimal challenge is one that is neither too difficult nor too easy for them to master: one that is tailored to their individual ability. Most often the optimal challenge requires the young person to work hard and may or may not result in a successful outcome. It is an optimal challenge if the young person is able to realize that with effort, he will eventually be able to achieve success. A simple task will not help him feel more competent, and a difficult one will often result in frustration; neither will positively impact self-esteem. An optimal challenge then, maximizes the potential for young people to perceive themselves in a positive way.

Significant Others. Competence and self-esteem develop over the course of many experiences and much time. Each is affected by several forces, one of the most important being significant others, or individuals important to the youth. Significant others can be parents, coaches, teachers, relatives, and even peers. The positive role significant others can play centers around showing approval for an adolescent's attempts to get good at something, a kind of approval that makes it more likely that he or she will keep trying even when struggling. By giving such approval, adults show young people that the process of developing better skills is more important than winning. In addition, adults are promoting the adolescent's sense of competence and control.

Intrinsic and Extrinsic Motivation. Adults are also pivotal in determining whether children learn to simply like to play sports or whether they need to be rewarded for playing. This is important because children in each of these categories tend to think about their successes and failures differently from one another.

Here is how the process works. When adults give praise to a child's effort and persistence at a task (i.e., the process), the child is more likely to simply enjoy the sport, to play "for the fun of it." On the other hand, when adults only praise children when they are successful (i.e., the product), children are more likely to play in order to get a reward. Thus, it becomes critical to reward children not only for their successes but also for their genuine attempts to be successful even when they are not.

This approach to understanding children and adolescents in sports is useful for at least two reasons. First, the concept of optimal challenges requires adults to think about young people as individuals; the typical "one-size-fits-all" approaches to coaching and teaching are not generally recommended, nor are they particularly successful. In addition, it requires those who work with young people to appreciate their normal growth and development and to realize that our strategies for helping them improve must become more sophisticated over time. Second, the concept of significant others encourages us to recognize that, although adults, in particular, parents, are of great importance to young athletes, peers take on great importance during adolescence. Thus, adolescents begin to look to age-mates for information regarding performance standards, for standards for evaluating their personal achievements, and for feedback regarding their competence.

Ultimately, regardless of which approach one uses, the key point is to facilitate in children and adolescents a degree of personal interest in sports, so that they will want to do well for their own satisfaction, not for outside rewards. These young people are more likely to initiate sport participation and maintain their participation into adulthood. In addition, they are more likely to feel good about themselves and to have a greater sense of control over their lives. Finally, they are more likely to see value in achieving their own greatest potential irrespective of their performance levels relative to others.

Social Changes and Athletic Experiences

Parents are keenly aware of the social changes that emerge during adolescence. Peers take on greater importance at this time; indeed, some feel that peers take on even greater importance than do parents. However, the adolescent social experience can be quite different for boys compared to girls. Thus, this section will explore the different experiences of boys and girls athletically and the extent to which parents and peers are influential in those experiences.

Relationship between Parental Involvement and Sport Participation. Parents can be influential with their young athletes in several ways. Parenting style—be it more democratic or more authoritarian—is the primary means by which this influence occurs. Specifically, parental pressure and parental support are important factors in how young people come to perceive their sport experiences. In terms of parental pressure, we know that in general young people tend to enjoy sports more if they perceive less pressure to perform from their parents. We also know that parental pressure is often associated with more negative self-worth, greater fears of failure, more physical complaints of illness or injury, feelings of inadequacy, guilt and anxiety, and unhappiness with sport involvement and participation. In contrast, parental support seems to be important for young athletes' getting involved in sports initially as well as in staying involved. In addition, support appears to be related to greater enjoyment of sports, higher self-esteem, more positive evaluations of performance outcomes, and the amount of importance the adolescent attributes to the sport.

Differences between Mothers and Fathers. These issues cannot be examined without considering differences between mothers and fathers in the way they affect young people's performances. In general, mothers' and fathers' involvement tends to take on different forms and have different impacts on young athletes. Mothers tend to be less invested in their child's performance per se, focusing more on the child's enjoyment, thereby adjusting their level of support and expectations to match the child's enjoyment of the sport. Fathers, in contrast, tend to be more interested in their child's ability and effort, increasing their involvement when they believe their child's effort or ability is low. This is an important issue. If fathers (or parents generally) become overinvolved in their child's performance, the child may begin to enjoy the sport less as she perceives greater parental pressure to perform. This, then, may lead to less effort on the part of the child, setting up a destructive cycle of self-defeating behaviors. Note that this is not a criticism of fathers, since society has generally placed athletics in men's domain, and therefore they are more likely to feel pressure from society for their children to perform well athletically.

There may also be parenting issues that arise differently based on the sex of child. Some have suggested that when children are first getting involved in sport, the influence of the same-sex parent is most important. However, others suggest that fathers are most influential in the introduction to and the continued sports participation of both boys and girls. In addition, athletic girls tend to get encouragement from both parents, whereas boys tend to get more encouragement from fathers. Thus, for girls to be athletic may require both parents' interest and encouragement, which may be the result of sports often being considered a male domain. How to show support and encouragement will be discussed in the last section of this entry.

Relationship between Peer Influence and Sports Participation. Consistently, adolescents identify sports participation as an important factor determining the popularity of their peers. However, this appears to be true for boys and girls in different ways. Specifically, boys can gain popularity simply by becoming involved in sports. Girls, on the other hand, may have to overcome a variety of obstacles in order for sports to have a positive effect on their peer popularity. It's useful to spell out these differences experienced by adolescent male and female athletes.

Sports Participation and Gender Roles of Adolescents. First, it is useful to recognize that sports are an integral part of the socialization experiences of boys throughout childhood and especially adolescence. It is during adolescence that boys become highly interested in demonstrating their masculinity to others, as is the case for girls and femininity. For boys, sports participation is not only encouraged, it is often expected. While girls' involvement generally requires support from mothers, fathers, and peers, boys' involvement in sport may simply be the result of a father's influence and

encouragement. For girls, sports participation may be viewed as contrary to what society expects from them. Adolescent girls may feel the need to either choose a more "feminine" sport, such as gymnastics or figure skating, or not participate at all.

Gender-Related Differences in Sport Experiences. Differences between boys and girls are also evident in the ways in which each experiences and values sport involvement. Boys' popularity has been consistently linked to their sports participation. They are also more likely to spend their free time playing sports. Girls' experiences tend to be more restricted. Girls are expected to play "feminine" sports by their peers. They are often more reluctant to play sports, believing they will not perform well. In fact, girls who are most likely to play sports are those who perceive themselves to be competent in all aspects of their lives—at school, with their peers, and in sports. Boys, on the other hand, play sports regardless of their level of competence in other aspects of their lives. Boys tend to focus on winning and like to keep score. Girls, in contrast, like to play cooperative games and to not keep score. Finally, boys value winning in sport, and, in fact, their continued interest and enjoyment in sports is likely to be contingent on winning, while girls focus on personal goals rather than the overall outcome of their participation.

Effects of Sports Participation on Adolescent Development

It can be seen that for adults working with young athletes, understanding how development affects and is affected by sports participation is valuable. It is also useful to recognize the variety of ways in which sports participation can both benefit adolescents as they develop and hinder their development.

Benefits of Participation. Sports participation in any form (i.e., formal or informal, team or individual, aerobic or anaerobic exercise) can have a variety of positive impacts on the adolescent's overall sense of self.

Maintaining an Active Self. Involvement in sport provides adolescents with a way to assess their physical capacities. It allows them to establish behavioral patterns and values that make physical activity a priority in their daily lives. It may also allow the adolescent to develop physical skills that he can use not only during adolescence but throughout life to promote health and well-being.

Exploring One's Identity. A key component of adolescence is developing a sense of identity; sport participation can be instrumental in this process. Young athletes can hone their decision-making and problem-solving skills. This is important, since many of the situations in which adolescents have to make decisions are too simple, as they are in school, where problems and answers are often controlled and evaluated by adults, or too complicated, as they are in friendships, where adolescents are often confronted with difficult choices and life-altering or even life-threatening options (e.g., sex, alcohol, drugs). Sports, in contrast, provide a setting where neither the questions nor the answers are too complex or too simple, and the outcomes can be unpredictable. Finally, sports participation teaches adolescents to use feedback and criticism to improve themselves, without taking the criticisms personally.

Developing Prosocial Skills. Sports can promote many positive social skills that will prove useful in adolescent as well as later in adult contexts. The value of teamwork is undisputed. Recognizing the need for and learning to work with others in order to accomplish a common goal will prove to be invaluable to the adolescent. Working hard not just for one's own benefit but for others is an important part of teamwork as well. In addition, learning to value others because of their assets and in spite of their deficits—that is, sportsmanship—can be a useful skill developed in sport contexts. Finally, understanding and appreciating loyalty to one's teammates, to a coach, or to a team can be a useful skill as well.

Positive Interpersonal Experiences. Sports participation can provide adolescents with a variety of opportunities to develop positive relationships with other adolescents and with adults. Team membership gives young people opportunities to establish a healthy peer network with others who share their goals and ideals about sports and life. In addition, it limits both the amount of time and the number of opportunities they have to get involved in antisocial activities. Sports participation also provides the potential for positive interactions with parents, with opportunities to connect over a common interest. Finally, young athletes have an additional caring adult in their lives—the coach—who can serve as a role model, give guidance and insights about life obstacles, and broaden the number of adults who are connected to the child in a caring manner.

Potential for Negative Effects of Sports Participation. Clearly, sports can have many positive effects on young participants; however, the potential for negative experiences cannot be overlooked. Negative influences can be exerted in a variety of forms, most often by those who have good intentions but who lack insight into key aspects of child development. Some of the ways in which adults can create negative effects for young athletes include the following:

- Adults may promote winning as the most important or the only goal
- Adults may define success in terms of winning
- Adults may fail to recognize individual best performances regardless of wins and losses
- Adults may allow teammates to berate one another, believing that peer pressure is an effective motivator (e.g., they may allow name-calling, yelling at, or blaming a team member for a bad play or a loss)
- Adults may berate young athletes, believing that is an effective motivator
- Adults may focus so strongly on winning that only certain members of a team get playing time
- Adults may require sports to take on a higher priority than other activities, like school
- Adults may allow adolescents to use sport to act out aggressive or violent tendencies
- Adults may not appreciate developmental and individual differences in athletic ability

The next, and last, section is designed to help parents and other adults advocate for their young athletes in order to minimize such negative influences and maximize the positive experiences they are likely to come across in sports.

Advocating for the Young Athlete

The interested parent needs to juggle several concerns. On the one hand, parents do not want their children to experience undue or unnecessary hardship physically or emotionally. On the other hand, parents need to allow their children to learn how to negotiate difficult situations where they may feel that the children are being unfairly treated. Parents must work hard to determine the best way to promote their children's development without being too involved or too protective, which limits their learning opportunities. The following is a brief list of how parents can help children gain positive experiences from sport involvement.

Stay Involved with Your Child's Activities. The best way for parents to help their children in sports is to talk to them about their experiences. Parents need to be proactive when it comes to communicating with their children. It is not a good strategy to assume your child will come to you if she is having a problem. Children may perceive that their parents want them to perform well athletically and may not want to talk about problems they are having. Parents need to ask their children about their sport experiences, to ask them whether they are having fun and whether they feel good about themselves in terms of sports, about their successes *and* their failures (or perceived failures), and to talk to them about their goals.

Monitor Practices and Competitions. Parents also need to get involved in both practices and competitions. Parents need to observe practices to see how the coach works with the athletes. Is the coach supportive? Does the coach favor some players over others? Does the coach model athletic skills to enhance learning? Does the coach help all the team members to set personal goals for success? How do team members interact, and to what extent does the coach promote positive interactions among teammates? If answers to these questions are consistently negative, parents may need to talk to the coach or perhaps seek a new team for their child. If, however, the picture is less clear, parents may decide that regular discussions with the child will be enough to counteract the negative messages from the coach, team members, or even other parents.

Help Child Maintain Proper Perspective on Self and Sports Generally. Parents need to emphasize to their children that sports are one of many aspects of life, not the only thing in life. Young people need to know that their athletic ability is not a measure of their worth, particularly in the eyes of their parents. They need to know that how they perform in sports is less important than their willingness to try, to set realistic goals and work toward them, and to work hard no matter what. Finally, children need to know that being a good athlete is valuable, but not at the expense of other life domains such as academics.

Set High Standards for Achievement not Based on Winning. When adults set high performance standards, young people are likely to believe they can achieve such standards and work to do so. If parents focus narrowly on winning, adolescents may easily become discouraged, since winning is only partially related to how hard one tries. A child who believes that

winning is everything is more likely to quit if he perceives that winning is impossible.

Use Athletics to Accent Life, Not Dominate It. For a variety of reasons, parents may find themselves and their children dominated by their children's involvement in sport. Running children to practices; driving long distances to games, meets, or matches; selling candy; buying tickets and uniforms and equipment—these are only a few of the multitude of ways in which families become enmeshed in their children's athletic experiences. It is important to set limits to involvement in a sport. Sports should be a way for children to expand their lives in a fun and meaningful way, not limit their opportunities. Sport should be an activity that helps bond a child to school, or that fills some (but not all) of a child's idle time, not time already committed to other activities.

Conclusion
The power of sports to affect our young people in many positive and meaningful ways is clear. That power must be accompanied by a sense of responsibility on the part of the adults involved—responsibility to nurture not only athletic prowess but psychological and emotional stability as well as respect and appreciation for others. Adults are pivotal in promoting the "right stuff" to young athletes, to help them set priorities in life and in sports, to establish goals and work to meet them, to seek to reach their own greatest potential and help others do the same. We must recognize that adolescent athletes are young people first, who are trying to navigate the complex experience of growing up. Involvement in sports should augment

the process of growing up; build on adolescents' emerging physical, cognitive,
and emotional capabilities; recognize
their limitations; and allow them to
learn about the sport, the coach, and the
other young athletes.

Lauren P. Jacobson

See also Body Build; Female Athlete
   Triad; Nutrition; Sports, Exercise, and
   Weight Control; Steroids

References and further reading
Sanders, Christopher, Tiffany Field,
   Miguel Diego, and Michele Kaplan.
   2000. "Moderate Involvement in Sports
   Is Related to Lower Depression Levels
   among Adolescents." *Adolescence* 35:
   793–797.
Viira, Roomet, and Lennert Raudsepp.
   2000. "Achievement Goal Orientation,
   Beliefs about Sports Success and Sport
   Emotions as Related to Moderate and
   Vigorous Physical Activity of
   Adolescents." *Psychology and Health*
   15: 625–633.

Sports, Exercise, and Weight Control

Exercise, sports, and weight control are
essential components of normal growth
and maturation, both physically and mentally. Health is an all-encompassing concept that not only includes physical and
mental well-being but also has an impact
upon social interaction and spirituality.
Health further involves the enhanced ability to engage in life, to successfully navigate challenges that inevitably arise in the
course of living, and to deal with stress.
Two of the most effective ways to achieve
health are through exercise and sport and
through nutrition. Exercise involves many
physical activities, including sports, that
improve both motor skills and general
cardiovascular and respiratory endurance.

Exercise prevents future negative health
outcomes such as cardiovascular disease
and hypertension. Good nutrition, in
combination with exercise, prevents similar negative outcomes. Moreover, short-
term benefits of both healthy eating and
exercise behavior include high energy levels, which allow one to actively engage *in*
life, weight control, improved mood,
improved ability to cope with stress, and
enhanced happiness with one's physical
appearance and identity.

Physical activity falls along a continuum of intensity and duration, and its
relationship to fitness depends on the
appropriate level of intensity and duration. Sports are a subset of physical activity. They involve more structured and
competitive physical activities that focus
on fine-tuning skill to succeed. Therefore,
physical activity can have two broad outcomes: skill enhancement and health
improvement. Skill enhancement encompasses hand-eye coordination, agility, and
so forth. The health outcomes of physical
activity refer to biological changes. These
are longer-term effects such as improved
cardiovascular functioning, increased
muscle endurance, and changes in fat distribution. Both components allow the
individual to function better in everyday
activities. Of more long-term importance
is the goal of improving long-term physical health, which may not be of immediate concern to the teenager but should be
a familial goal.

The aforementioned benefits of physical activity are more or less universally
accepted and serve as the foundation of
the goals of many school-based physical
fitness curricula. In sum, physical activity improves motor skill and endurance,
builds strength, and improves health.
Furthermore, sport as a social activity
promotes the societal values of fairness,

Given the health benefits of physical exercise, it is important for teenagers to be active. (Skjold Photographs)

being a good sport, and honest winning and gracious losing. Physical activity and sport also teach values that can be generalized to everyday life goals. Sport and exercise teach perseverance, determination, and tenacity, which spill over into all facets of the individual's life. Of particular importance, especially for teenagers, is that the aforementioned benefits of physical activity and exercise also serve to enhance self-esteem and self-confidence. By improving strength, or skill, by persevering to achieve a personal goal, one feels more confident and better about one's self. Finally, making activity a lifestyle from youth means that physical activity will be valued as an adult. Given these undeniable benefits of physical activity, the only question that

remains is why young people are entirely too inactive. A study conducted in 1990 of children aged eleven to sixteen showed that in a three-day period almost 90 percent of the girls did not raise their heart rate above 139 beats per minute for a continuous twenty-minute interval. Boys were more active, yet 75 percent of them did not raise their heart rate above 139 beats per minute in the specified period. These data indicate that youth in general are very sedentary and and that girls tend to be even less active than boys (Biddle and Mutrie, 1991, p. 22).

So, why are teens vying for the position of the most inactive population next to those who are disabled? Many issues are involved in inactivity, but some research provides insight into why teens *engage* in physical activity. Knowing the factors that promote an active lifestyle may illuminate the factors that may contribute to inertia. The Canada Fitness Survey indicates that teenagers are active for the following reasons: fun, to feel better, weight control, flexibility, challenge, and companionship (Biddle and Mutrie, 1991, p. 251). Documentation also shows that young people prefer activities that establish and enhance their sense of self. Activities that serve this function are challenging but within the participant's skill level. Csikszentmihalyi theorizes, based on his research, that for an optimal experience the individual must have the skill to meet the challenge. If the individual does not have the appropriate skill to adequately meet the challenge, then her anxiety will be high and the experience will be evaluated negatively. As an individual's skill improves, the individual needs to be faced with more advanced challenges, otherwise she will become bored. Finally, the activity must be intrinsically rewarding. This means that the individual engages in an activity because she wants to, and not for rewards or recognition from other people. Simply engaging in the activity and being able to meet the challenges is rewarding in and of itself.

These conclusions about the psychology of optimal experience are directly related to the reasons young people give when they explain why they participate in sports and other physical activities. The overarching conclusions derived from interviews with youth is that they engage in activities that are fun, that enhance their skills, and that are optimally challenging, in that they can be mastered, which gives them a feeling of personal accomplishment. Additionally, youth engage in activities that are chosen

autonomously, which means that no one forces the youth to participate; rather, he decides on his own. Furthermore, these activities have valued outcomes, produce a good mood and a good feeling about oneself, and are supported without qualification by family and friends (Whitehead and Corbin, 1997, p. 186). Obviously, for anyone who is trying to find an activity or sport that she will not quit, or for any family member trying to promote physical activity to a young person, these are important components to take into consideration.

The aforementioned characteristics of physical activities define the psychological components and benefits of sport and exercise. What are the physiological aspects of sport and exercise? There are two main classes of physical activity: aerobic and anaerobic. Aerobic activities require an increase in heart rate for a sustained period of time; twenty minutes or more is recommended for health benefits. Aerobic activity improves the health of your heart and enhances respiratory endurance and muscular stamina. In contrast, anaerobic activity involves a short, explosive burst of energy followed by rest. Anaerobic activity increases muscle strength and power. The difference between the two activities can be illustrated by comparing someone who runs long distances with a sprinter who runs only 100 meters at 100 percent speed or lifts weights. Aerobic activity increases metabolism; it burns fat in order to fuel the body during the sustained activity. Though anaerobic activity does not burn fat, it does increase muscle mass. The more muscle the body has compared to fat, the higher the metabolism and the more calories it burns when at rest. Given the health benefits of physical activity, it is important for teenagers to be active so that they can be healthy both now and in the future.

For the teen who is active, as well as for the sedentary individual, nutrition and weight control are important aspects of health. Nutrition concerns for teenagers tend to center around the transition to college, incorporating healthy eating into a busy schedule, and body image and physical performance. Often, teenagers do not seek dietary advice, which makes them highly susceptible to dietary fads. Teens who engage in fad diets restrict necessary nutrients for proper growth and maturation, such as iron and calcium. The School Service Research Review (see at www.ificinfo. health.org/insight/teentrnd.htm) published results indicating that teens do not eat enough fruit and vegetables. Furthermore, most teens' diets are deficient in iron, calcium, vitamin A, and beta-carotene (International Food Information Council [IFIC]). Teenagers who adopt vegetarian diets should seek professional advice to ensure that their diet consists of all of the necessary nutrients. The proper diet, in conjunction with exercise, helps maintain a proper weight.

Overweight in the teenage years is associated with negative health outcomes in late adulthood regardless of overweight in adulthood. The *New England Journal of Medicine* published results from the Harvard Growth Study that implicated adolescent obesity in a myriad of deleterious health outcomes. The study found that overweight teenage boys were two times more likely to die by seventy years of age and five times more likely to be diagnosed with colon cancer. Overweight teenage girls were 60 percent more likely to develop arthritis and two times more likely to develop heart disease by seventy years of age (IFIC).

A healthy nutritious diet is essential for proper growth and development. Moreover, it is particularly important for families to be aware of the diet and exercise behaviors of the teenagers in their households, because too much or too little can both have deleterious immediate and future outcomes. There has been a dramatic increase in overweight adolescents since 1963, and this increase is associated with a prevalence of inactivity. From 1963 to 1980, the prevalence of overweight increased 6 percent in twelve-year-old boys and increased 5 percent in girls of the same age. An interesting gender relationship emerged in which the prevalence of obesity decreased with age in boys, whereas it continued to increase up to 20 percent in girls aged fourteen to sixteen (Page and Fox, 1997, p. 230). In part, the growing incidence of obesity is due to the popularity of sedentary pastimes such as video games, computer activities, and television. A study found that in a group of twelve- to seventeen-year-olds the occurrence of obesity rose by 2 percent for each additional hour of television viewed daily (Page and Fox, 1997, p. 231). Therefore, initiatives to promote exercise and healthy eating are critical. Simultaneously, there is an opposing stream of influence that promotes attainment of the unrealistic emaciated body type, and exercise and dietary restraint are the most common means used to pursue that unattainable image. Given these influences, it is essential to get across the message that healthy exercise and eating habits, as opposed to exercise fads and extreme diets, are the key to attaining a healthy body, and that a healthy body is the only realistic goal.

Adolescence is a developmental period when teenagers both acquire and integrate attitudes and habits that will prevail throughout their lifetime. Therefore, the eating and exercise habits that the teenager forms are likely to last into adulthood. This means that it is important to adopt healthy behaviors at an early stage in life. Presently, teenagers engage in sedentary leisure-time activities and their diets are high in fat and simple carbohydrates (e.g., sugar). Food is essential to living and living well. Food affects mental functioning, emotions, energy levels, and strength, as well as general health; without question, food is a critical issue, not just for teenagers, but for everyone. The nature of our society requires that we all have to eat on the run, and this typically means fast food and/or eating out of the home. Prepared foods are typically high in fat, sodium, and cholesterol, as are the foods that you receive in any restaurant. Furthermore, American society values large portions, which means that people are consuming more calories than they are expending in activity. For those who are in the habit of consuming large portions of high-fat foods, it is important to exercise some restraint. A healthy diet consists of fruits, vegetables, and lean meats, and it means avoiding the fried foods, rich creamy dressings, and high-fat sweets. Ultimately, both eating healthily and eating junk food are a matter of habit. One learns to prefer one type of food through experience, which means that with time one will no longer crave the McDonald's diet plan.

A healthy diet is critical, but self-denial is not part of a healthy diet. Food is enjoyable and is central to social occasions, so food should not be a source of anxiety or frustration. When one denies oneself indulgences, food comes to have a power over one; one should not be afraid of eating fat or overwhelmed with concern about calories. Indulgences are okay. The problem arises if one indulges every day, three meals a day. The focus should not be on dieting. Dieting connotes restraint, eating less, and eliminating certain categories of food from your diet. Rather, the focus should be on eating healthily by eating a variety of foods and exercising. This combination results in a stable body weight and increases the metabolism. When one eats fewer calories than the body needs to function, the metabolism slows down to conserve energy, because the body thinks it is starving. The consequence is that one does not lose weight. The message is eat, but eat well and exercise. Furthermore, food restriction and elimination of any food group ultimately results in nutrient deficiency. Your body needs a certain amount of unsaturated fats, carbohydrates, and proteins to function normally. Therefore, it is not healthy to adopt a fad diet that eliminates or dramatically restricts consumption of any food group. For the growing teenager it is particularly important to eat diverse types of foods and healthy quantities in order to promote normal growth and development. Ultimately, by adopting a well-rounded, healthy diet and exercising one can maintain a stable weight.

Of course it is easy to preach the benefits of adopting a healthy diet and regular exercise regime, but a number of factors play a role in the decision to make behavior changes in accordance with a healthy lifestyle and the desire to control one's weight. There are four critical questions that one must explore before the decision to make a behavior change can be put into practice: "Who am I?," "Who do I think I am? / Who do I want to be?," "How much do I care?," and "What do I intend to do?" (Page and Fox, 1997, p.

235). The first question, "Who am I?," relates to the physical attributes and health status of the individual. The answer is grounded in biological and physiological factors, such as sex, developmental stage, weight, body size, and so forth. The evaluation of these factors determines what type of behaviors will be adopted, if any. For example, different exercises, such as weight training, are preferable at different developmental stages. Also, sex influences diet and exercise; premenopausal women need to maintain a constant source of iron due to iron lost each month during the menstrual cycle. The second question, "Who do I think I am? / Who do I want to be?," deals with the psychological components of self-esteem, body image, and self-perceptions. Decisions to make behavior changes revolve around the disparity between how one perceives himself now and how he ideally wants to be. This is often termed the disparity between the real and ideal self. If the individual perceives a discrepancy between where he is now and where he would ideally like to be, then he will make behavior changes to attain the ideal self. The third question, "How much do I care?," refers to the importance of weight control to the individual. Resolution of this question takes into account degree of self-acceptance, preoccupation with weight, and self-satisfaction. An individual who is dissatisfied with her weight and is preoccupied with weight loss will adopt new and enduring behaviors. The final question, "What do I intend to do?," involves behavioral strategies to control weight (Page and Fox, 1997, p. 235).

Teenagers who manage their weight do so for a variety of reasons based upon their answers to these questions. Not all weight management efforts are healthy, and weight control efforts should be evaluated according to the following criteria: The weight control efforts should be warranted, the methods should be healthy, not maladaptive, and the efforts should be effective, not futile. Individuals who are trying to lose weight even though they are at a normal weight, who use laxatives, purging, and so forth, and who are trying to reach a weight that cannot be maintained exhibit maladaptive weight control efforts. There is a prevalence of maladaptive dietary restraint and excessive exercise in our society due to societal and peer pressures to attain an idealized body image. The teenage population is particularly vulnerable to these pressures, because during adolescence self-concept becomes increasingly based on interpersonal interaction. Evaluations of the self, self-esteem, and personal satisfaction with physical attractiveness are based upon the perceptions and affirmation of others. Adolescence, in consequence, is marked by an increase in self-consciousness and self-image instability, coupled with a decline in self-esteem. In the female population, in particular, this is expressed in body dissatisfaction and a negative body image.

Society portrays the people who embody the ideal physique as successful, healthy, and affluent. Consequently, people are compelled to achieve a similar appearance in order to attain a similar level of regard and esteem. Susceptible individuals, and that includes approximately 90 percent of the entire female population of North America, are dissatisfied with their bodies, and consequently they are susceptible to the desire to change their bodies to conform to unattainable images presented by the media (Davies and Furham, 1986, p. 143).

What females and males are learning is that the body is "infinitely malleable" and that great rewards await them when they attain the desired shape (Brownell, 1991, p. 3). The lesson being taught is a spurious one, but ardently embraced nonetheless. The consequence is a misperception that normality means being underweight, which has tragically produced a plethora of young ladies and men working with frustrating and futile diligence toward this elusive "norm."

Advertising exacerbates the futile effort with assertions that claim if one finds the optimal combination of diet, exercise, and pills one can achieve the perfect body; it is simply a matter of finding what works for you. When you discover the magical combination and your actual body metamorphs into the perfect frame, you will be rewarded with success, health, and so forth. The idea that one can mold one's body into any image is ludicrous, and young people need to be made aware of this reality. Body size and shape are not determined solely by environmental factors. So, instead of trying to achieve a body one is not biologically destined to attain, one should focus on exercise for strength, health, and effective living rather than as a way to lose weight; the goal of losing weight breeds increasing frustration and anxiety if the individual is unable to bridge the gap between actuality and ideality. Ultimately, body image and body dissatisfaction are intertwined with normative misperceptions, low self-esteem, and negative self-concept. Accordingly, healthy exercise and eating behaviors combat, if not prevent, disordered behaviors. When youth engage in physical activities that make them feel better about themselves, it gives them a sense of mastery and self-efficacy. Therefore, exercise, sport, and good nutrition are strong foundations that are resistant to social pressures.

Sara Johnston

See also Appearance, Cultural Factors in; Body Build; Body Fat, Changes in; Body Image; Eating Problems; High School Equivalency Degree; Nutrition; Sports and Adolescents; Steroids

References and further reading
Biddle, Stuart, and Nanette Mutrie. 1991. *Psychology of Physical Activity and Exercise.* London: Springer-Verlag.
Brownell, R. D. 1991. "Dieting and the Search for the Perfect Body: Where Physiology and Culture Collide." *Behavioral Therapy* 22: 1–12.
Csikszentmihalyi, Mihaly. 1975. *Beyond Boredom and Anxiety.* San Francisco: Jossey-Bass.
———. 1997. *Finding Flow: The Psychology of Engagement with Everyday Life.* New York: Basic Books.
Davies, E., and A. Furham. 1986. "Body Satisfaction in Adolescent Girls." *British Journal of Medical Psychology* 59: 279–287.
Fox, Kenneth R., ed. 1997. *The Physical Self: From Motivation to Well-Being.* Champaign, IL: Human Kinetics.
International Food Information Council Foundation (IFIC) http://ificinfo.health.org/insight/teentrnd.htm
The Nemours Foundation. Kids Health www.kidshealth.org/teen/index.html
Page, Angela, and Kenneth R. Fox. 1997. "Adolescent Weight Management and the Physical Self." Pp. 229–256 in *The Physical Self: From Motivation to Well-Being.* Edited by Kenneth R. Fox. Champaign, IL: Human Kinetics
Whitehead, James R., and Charles B. Corbin. 1997. "Self-Esteem in Children and Youth: The Role of Sport and Physical Education." Pp. 175–203 in *The Physical Self: From Motivation to Well-Being.* Edited by Kenneth R. Fox. Champaign, IL: Human Kinetics.

Standardized Tests

A standardized test is a task or set of tasks, given under uniform conditions and scored according to uniform criteria, used to compare the performance of an individual to that of a larger group. Standardized tests are one set of tools used by schools to learn about students. More than 1 million standardized tests per school day are used in American schools alone. Adolescents are likely to encounter various types of standardized tests during their middle and high school years.

Standardized tests differ from typical classroom tests in that they are designed to provide a common measure of the performance of many students. To obtain this common measure, or *standard,* the test is first administered to a very large sample of students across the country. The average scores of this large sample then become the *norm,* or standard, upon which other students will be measured. When students take a standardized test their scores reflect their relative standing compared with the norming sample. There are many different ways of reporting this relative standing. One common method used is the percentile rank. A percentile rank of 80, for example, means that a student's score is equal to or higher than the scores of 80 percent of the students in the norming sample.

Standardized tests are designed to assess some aspect of a person's knowledge, skill, or personality. Standardized tests can differ from one another in a variety of ways, including the method of administration (e.g., individual versus group) and the response format (e.g., multiple choice, true-false, essay). Some common uses of standardized tests are to evaluate school programs, to report on students' progress, to diagnose strengths and weaknesses, to select students for special programs and groups, and to certify student achievement.

Standardized tests are often grouped into two categories, based on what they are attempting to measure. Standardized *achievement* tests measure knowledge about subjects such as reading, spelling, or mathematics. These tests are heavily dependent on formal learning acquired in school or at home and are often used to evaluate an individual's progress in the specified area. The emphasis of achievement tests is on what the individual can do at that particular time. Examples of achievement tests that may be administered to adolescents include the Iowa Test of Basic Skills (ITBS), the Metropolitan Achievement Tests (MAT), and the California Achievement Test (CAT). In many states, a passing score on an achievement test has become a requirement for promotion to the next grade or for graduation from high school.

Standardized *aptitude* tests attempt to measure students' abilities to learn in school or how well they are likely to do in future schoolwork. Unlike achievement tests, which measure knowledge of subjects taught in school, aptitude tests measure a broad range of abilities or skills that are considered important for success in school. The types of skills measured by aptitude tests include verbal ability and abstract reasoning.

High school students who are thinking about going on to college may take both aptitude and achievement tests as they begin the application process. The Preliminary Scholastic Assessment Test/National Merit Scholarship Qualifying Test (PSAT/NMSQT) is often a student's first step in this process. This aptitude test is often taken in the junior year, although it may be taken earlier. It measures critical reading, verbal reasoning, math problem solving, and writing skills. The PSAT/NMSQT is given for a number of reasons, some of which include providing practice for the Scholastic Assessment Test (SAT) and identifying students who may be eligible for scholarships. The SAT I Reasoning Test is an example of an aptitude test that is used to predict how well a student is likely to do in college. The SAT I is a three-hour test that is often taken during the senior year of high school. The SAT I measures verbal and mathematical reasoning abilities, which have been developing throughout students' lives. The SAT II (Subject Tests) and Advanced Placement (AP) exams are examples of achievement tests that may be used by colleges for admission, course placement, and advising students about course selection.

There are many factors that may impact students' scores on standardized tests. One important factor to consider is the type of preparation different students bring to the test situation. Although one cannot study for standardized tests by memorizing specific facts, it is possible to feel more comfortable with tests like the PSAT and SAT I, and to develop test-taking strategies. For example, there are long-term strategies that are helpful, such as taking solid academic courses, reading widely, and writing frequently. There are also more specific strategies: Students can learn the format and timing of the tests, become familiar with the kinds of questions asked, know the directions for each question type, and take complete practice tests. Information about these and other helpful short-term test-taking strategies is available in writing or on the Internet by contacting the College Board.

Other factors, in addition to the amount of preparation, may impact a student's performance on a standardized test. Nervousness, hunger, and fatigue are examples of internal conditions that may affect test results. Research on the relationship between test anxiety and test performance suggests that a slight amount of anxiety may be beneficial, whereas a large amount may be detrimental. External factors such as a noisy, poorly lit, or uncomfortable testing environment can also influence test scores. Although it is not always possible to control all of these factors, there are some simple steps that can be taken in order to minimize the influence of such variables. For instance, being well rested and eating a healthy breakfast are useful prior to taking any kind of test.

Standardized college admissions tests, like the SAT, provide an efficient means of comparing a diverse group of students. Issues related to fairness and cultural bias make such comparisons and predictions extremely difficult and important to examine. Test score differences between various groups that have been reported in the literature are difficult to interpret. Many more studies are required before we understand all the factors that contribute to these differences. Because of both the importance of standardized tests and the potential for bias, a code of conduct, which states the obligations of professionals who develop or use educational tests, provides guidelines that aim to advance the quality of testing practices. The Code of Fair Testing Practices in Education presents standards for developing and selecting tests, interpreting scores, striving for fairness, and informing test takers. Ethnic and cultural diversity must be considered at each step in the testing process.

It is important to remember that when students apply to schools, standardized test results are just one source of information that colleges use. No single test can account for the entire spectrum of abilities related to intellectual behavior. In determining who will succeed in college, additional factors such as high school grades, letters of recommendation, and participation in extracurricular activities provide valuable information. Even the best standardized tests are unable to measure a student's creativity, motivation, and special talents. A standardized test is only capable of sampling the individual's repertoire of skills at that particular time. Test scores can vary from day to day, depending on such things as whether students guess, receive clear directions, follow the directions carefully, take the test seriously, and are comfortable taking the test. Within the context of their recognized limitations, standardized tests remain useful tools for learning about students.

Alyssa Goldberg O'Rourke

See also Academic Achievement; Academic Self-Evaluation; Cheating, Academic; Cognitive Development; College; Higher Education; Intelligence Tests; Learning Disabilities; Learning Styles and Accommodations

References and further reading
Anastasi, Anne. 1988. *Psychological Testing*, 6th ed. New York: Macmillan.
College Board Online. 2000. www.collegeboard.com
Joint Committee on Testing Practices. 1988. *Code of Fair Testing Practices in Education*. Washington, DC: Joint Committee on Testing Practices.
Kaufman, Alan S. 1990. *Assessing Adolescent and Adult Intelligence*. Boston: Allyn and Bacon.
Lyman, Howard B. 1986. *Test Scores and What They Mean*, 4th ed. Englewood Cliffs, NJ: Prentice-Hall.
Miller-Jones, D. 1989. "Culture and Testing." *American Psychologist* 44, no. 2: 360–366.
Neisser, U., et al. 1996. "Intelligence: Knowns and Unknowns." *American Psychologist* 51, no. 2: 77–101.
Sattler, Jerome M. 1992. *Assessment of Children*, 3rd ed. San Diego: Jerome M. Sattler.

Steroids

Those who work with adolescents will think first of those steroids used to enhance appearance or athletic performance; given the side effects these produce, their use is a serious problem, but for these steroids as well as the rest, there are also legitimate medical uses. The term *steroid* refers to a group of hormones that are produced by the adrenal glands or the gonads (testes or ovaries). The adrenals are located at the top part of the kidneys, which are near the small of the back. They produce three classes of steroids:

1. Glucocorticoids such as hydrocortisone, which helps our body deal with stress
2. Mineralocorticoids, which help our body regulate salt and water balance
3. Sex steroids, which promote sexual development and the maintenance of our reproductive system

The amount of any steroid the body makes by itself is called the physiological or natural amount. Sometimes it is necessary to give steroids as treatment for a medical problem. The amount of steroid that is needed to treat a disease is called a pharmacological or extra amount. When most people think about someone taking steroids they usually think about athletes or bodybuilders who are taking one of the sex steroids (testosterone or a steroid like testosterone) to bulk themselves up, that is, to increase their muscle mass or strength. The use of so-called *anabolic* steroids for those purposes is banned by all official sports organizations.

However, some teenage boys do take anabolic steroids in order to improve their physical appearance. The doses used for these purposes are many times higher than the natural amount produced by the body. Therefore, those who use them may be at high risk for some of the side effects of anabolic steroid use. These side effects include severe liver damage, which may be permanent and could result in premature death or in the development of liver cancer. They also include the so-called roid rage, in which people become violent and aggressive and may injure or kill someone or be injured or killed themselves, as well as significant increase in acne, high blood pressure, mood swings, and stoppage of growth earlier than normal, resulting in short stature. Other effects in teenage boys include shrinkage and decreased function of the testes and breast growth. Teenage girls taking anabolic steroids may experience excessive hair growth on the face, arms, legs, and chest, enlargement of the clitoris, and deepening of the voice, all of which would be permanent. Breasts may shrink and periods may become irregular or stop altogether.

There is substantial controversy about whether anabolic steroids actually accomplish what the user wants them to do. There is no question that when anabolic steroids are used in higher than natural amounts and are combined with an exercise program, they can significantly increase muscle mass. The increase in strength may, however, be due to the increased exercise program alone. In any case, the risks of the side effects are significant, and anabolic steroids should not be used to enhance appearance or performance.

There are other medical indications for the use of all three classes of steroids. Glucocorticoids are used to treat many diseases because they act to reduce harmful processes that sometimes occur in a teen's body. There are certain diseases in which the immune system does not work properly, even perceiving a part of the body as foreign. It will then begin to try to protect the rest of the body by ridding the body of that part. An example of this kind of malfunction of the immune system is a disease called lupus. Giving pharmacological doses of glucocorticoids can turn off the immune system and stop the disease from progressing. Glucocorticoids are also used to help organ transplants survive; the recipient's body usually reacts to other people's organs as foreign, and glucocorticoids help prevent that. They are also used in treating other diseases, such as severe asthma, bad allergic reactions, and some severe skin diseases. Glucocorticoids in high doses also may have significant side effects, such as rapid weight gain, edema (swelling of hands and feet), development of diabetes, and problems in salt retention. Nevertheless, they can be very helpful and even lifesaving in treating some diseases. They are also used in natural amounts for people whose adrenal glands no longer work.

Mineralocorticoids help maintain the correct amount of water and salt in our body. They are mainly used in natural amounts for people whose adrenal glands no longer work.

Both the adrenal glands and gonads produce sex steroids. As described above, they should never be used in pharmacological amounts to enhance appearance or performance. In legitimate medicine, they are used for the most part in natural amounts for people whose gonads do not work. They are also used as the main ingredients in birth control pills or in older women who have experienced menopause (are no longer menstruating).

Jordan W. Finkelstein

See also Body Build; Body Image; Sports and Adolescents; Sports, Exercise, and Weight Control; Substance Use and Abuse

References and further reading
Berkow, Robert B., ed. 1997. *The Merck Manual of Medical Information: Home Edition.* Whitehouse Station, NJ: Merck Research Laboratories.
Clayman, Charles C., ed. 1994. *The American Medical Association Family Medical Guide,* 3rd ed. New York: Random House.

Storm and Stress

The term *storm and stress* is used to describe a set of beliefs based on the notion that adolescence is an extremely difficult developmental time period for children, perhaps more difficult than other developmental periods. Those who endorse such a perspective believe that increases in the following are markers of adolescent storm and stress: a child's desire for independence and autonomy, mood disruptions, risk-taking behavior, and conflict with parents. Other factors such as school difficulties and dependence on peer relationships are also believed to increase during adolescence. From this perspective, adolescents are believed to exhibit rebellious behavior and resistance to adult authority. These behaviors are thought to lead to increased parent-child conflict, accompanied by extreme mood swings. Advocates of this position posit that rapid physical and psychological growth during this stage of life could be responsible. The degree to which adolescence is a stormy and stressful developmental period is still debated in the research literature.

This overview of storm and stress beliefs is divided into several sections. First, early perspectives of adolescent development will be reviewed. Second, current perspectives of adolescence will be discussed. Third, it is suggested that overdiagnosis and underdiagnosis of adolescents' problems are a possible outcome of storm and stress beliefs. Finally, the common behavioral components of storm and stress will be discussed. The following sections provide insight into the common storm and stress notions and their effect on both parenting and on the diagnosis of adolescent problems.

Early Perspectives on Storm and Stress
G. Stanley Hall, in 1904, was one of the first scholars to discuss storm and stress issues in relation to adolescent development. His theories followed Lamarck's evolutionary ideas, which stressed that evolution occurs as a result of accumulated life experiences. Based on this notion, Hall believed that adolescent development is indicative of "some ancient period of storm and stress" (Hall, 1904, p. 13), and that there may have been a period in human evolution that was extremely difficult, so much so that the memory of that period has shaped later generations. This memory is therefore experienced in the development of each individual as storm and stress during adolescence. According to the theory, the storm and stress memory is especially apparent in the adolescent's inclination toward risk-taking behavior, conflict with parents and authority figures, and erratic mood swings. Hall believed that storm and stress is a biologically based tendency, but that environment

and culture shape the experience and expression of it for individual adolescents. The clash between the more technologically advanced and complacent life offered by urbanization and the adolescent's desire for exploration and adventure, as well as difficulties at school and in the family, can exacerbate storm and stress in adolescence.

Psychoanalytic theorists have also played a role in perpetuating storm and stress beliefs. Anna Freud and Peter Blos believed that the storm and stress of adolescence is a recapitulation of earlier childhood experiences, especially oedipal conflicts. According to this perspective, such conflicts lead to emotional instability when the adolescent ego tries to suppress depressed moods as the adolescent renders the oedipal parent impotent. Emerging id drives may be acted out in delinquent, antisocial behavior. Freud went further than Blos, claiming that the adolescent experience of storm and stress is universal and a part of each child's development into adulthood. From this perspective, lacking this experience is a possible indication of psychopathology.

"Storm and stress" refers to the belief that adolescence is an extremely difficult period for youth. (Skjold Photographs)

Current Perspectives on Storm and Stress

Contemporary studies support the continued existence of storm and stress beliefs in the general population. For example, in one study, college students and parents of young adolescents perceived adolescence as a more difficult period than the elementary school period. Problems experienced by adolescents (symptoms of internalizing disorders, parent-child conflict, identity crises, and risk-taking behavior) are believed to be less likely in early childhood.

Despite these beliefs, adolescence does not appear to be a difficult stage for all teenagers. People usually hold storm and stress beliefs for adolescents as a group (a kind of belief referred to as *category based*) but not for each individual child (a kind of belief referred to as *target based*). Category-based beliefs reflect societal stereotypes, whereas target-based beliefs are held for the individual adolescent regardless of other adolescents' actions and behavior. Although people appear to be susceptible to storm and stress beliefs, they may still view particular adolescents whom they know and are close to very differently from the way they view adolescents as a group or subculture.

The media may be partially responsible for the storm and stress view of adolescence. Category-based beliefs could be influenced by stereotypes that television and newspapers perpetuate. Rarely is a story of an upstanding, well-adjusted teenager depicted in the news. The media typically present negative images of adolescents.

The view that adolescents are less social, more unfriendly, more moody, and more disobedient than younger children could lead some to perceive all difficulties experienced by adolescents as acts of rebellion. Parents, in particular, may fear the potential onset of such rebellion and, as a result, clamp down on their own children as they make the transition into adolescence. By constraining the development of autonomy, some parents may hope to avoid future conflicts with their adolescents. However, young adolescents may resent such controlling parental authority and act out to assert independence. Storm and stress beliefs may create a self-fulfilling prophecy; adolescents may rebel when parents increase restrictions to prevent anticipated rebellion.

Diagnosing the Difficult Adolescent
Knowledge of developmental norms, not stereotypes, serves as a basis for making sound diagnostic judgments, assessing the need for treatment, and selecting the appropriate treatment. In terms of diagnosis, both overdiagnosis and underdiagnosis can result from lack of knowledge of developmental norms. A clinician who lacks knowledge that a behavior or attitude is typical of the adolescent age period (e.g., interest in sexuality) is much more likely to overdiagnose and to inappropriately refer such an adolescent for treatment. With regard to underdiagnosis, it is a common belief that adolescents have stormy and stressful relations with their parents and that detachment from parents is the norm. On the other hand, research has not supported this notion—it appears that only a minority of adolescents have such relationships with their parents. It is interesting to speculate about the clinical implications of such erroneous storm and stress beliefs. Some have warned that adolescents who are experiencing severe identity crises or extreme levels of conflict with their parents are not experiencing normal adolescent growing pains. A clinician who overlooks this possibility will underdiagnose the psychopathology owing to storm and stress beliefs.

Common Components of
Storm and Stress
The following sections highlight three components that are most often discussed in research on storm and stress: parent-adolescent conflict, mood disturbance, and risk-taking behavior. A review of such research will aid in evaluating the myth versus reality of storm and stress beliefs.

Parent-Adolescent Conflict. Conflict with parents has been shown to increase as a child enters early adolescence. Accordingly, the time that parents and children spend together decreases. Adolescent children tend to desire more independence from their parents, while some parents may be reluctant to grant independence to their children. This tug-of-war over decision making and autonomy could lead to increases in conflict between parent and child. Though increases in conflict do appear common, many parents and children report that they share core values and have a mutual attachment to each other. Typically conflict does not dissolve the parent-child relationship; it transforms it. Conflict is usually over daily decision-making issues such as dating and curfew rather than over major moral issues. On the other hand, adolescents may see these arguments over mundane issues as representative of a global parental restriction of freedom and independence.

Mood Disruptions. Adolescents appear to experience mood swings more often than younger childhood or adults. Adolescents may feel lonely, ignored, depressed, anxious, or awkward on a more regular basis than do children. Some researchers have found that this increase in negative affect is due primarily to cognitive and environmental factors rather than biological factors resulting from puberty. Adolescents' negative perceptions of arguments with their parents may be one source of mood disruptions. Teenagers who interpret stressful events as threats to their well-being may feel tense and unsatisfied with their daily life. The more negative life events adolescents experience, the more likely they are to experience mood disruptions. Thus, this evidence provides partial support for the storm and stress notion that adolescents show a greater tendency to exhibit emotional disruption and mood swings.

Risk-Taking Behavior. Risk-taking behavior (i.e., behavior that carries the potential for harm to oneself or harm to others) peaks during late adolescence (at eighteen to twenty years old), rather than early or middle adolescence. Though increases in risk behavior are evident in adolescence, not all adolescents engage in risk-taking behavior. However, rates of substance abuse, sexual activity, and automobile accidents tend to be much higher for late adolescents than adults. Crime rates rise among teenagers until the age of eighteen. After that, the rates drop steeply. Substance abuse rates peak around age twenty. Automobile accidents and fatalities occur most frequently in late adolescence. Young adults under the age of twenty-five contract the majority of sexually transmitted diseases (STDs). Adolescents typically view risk-taking behavior as exciting and pleasurable, yet the consequences can be quite devastating. From one perspective, such findings provide some support for a storm and stress viewpoint. On the other hand, the fact that not all children engage in these behaviors, and that those who do are more apt to do so in late adolescence, suggests that storm and stress theory is not generally applicable to all adolescents.

Christine M. Wienke
Grayson N. Holmbeck

See also Aggression; Anxiety; Conflict and Stress; Conflict Resolution; Rebellion; Violence

References and further reading
Arnett, Jeffrey J. 1999. "Adolescent Storm and Stress, Reconsidered." *American Psychologist* 54: 317–326.
Blos, Peter. 1904. *The Adolescent Passage.* New York: International Universities Press.
Buchanan, Christy M., and Grayson N. Holmbeck. 1998. "Measuring Beliefs about Adolescence Personality and Behavior." *Journal of Youth and Adolescence* 27: 607–627.
Freud, Anna. 1958. "Adolescence." *Psychoanalytical Studies of Children* 13: 231–258.
Hall, G. Stanley. 1904. *Adolescence: Its Psychology and Its Relations to Physiology, Anthropology, Sociology, Sex, Crime, Religion, and Education.* Englewood Cliffs, NJ: Prentice-Hall.
Holmbeck, Grayson N. 1994. "Adolescence." Pp. 17–28 in

Encyclopedia of Human Behavior, Vol. 1. Edited by V. S. Ramachandran. San Diego: Academic Press.

Holmbeck, Grayson N., and John P. Hill. 1988. "Storm and Stress Beliefs about Adolescence: Prevalence, Self-Reported Antecedents, and Effects of an Undergraduate Course." *Journal of Youth and Adolescence* 17: 285–305.

Larson, Reed, and Maryse H. Richards. 1994. *Divergent Realities: The Emotional Lives of Mothers, Fathers, and Adolescents*. New York: Basic Books.

Substance Use and Abuse

Drug abuse is recognized as a pattern of drug use that interferes with normal social and emotional functioning as thoughts and behaviors revolve around obtaining and using drugs.

Most adolescents in today's world are faced with complicated personal and social environments. As if life weren't complicated enough, the drugs that are available to adolescents typically serve only to interfere with the very independence and maturity that adolescents cherish. When drug use interferes with normal social and emotional functioning, a serious problem of abuse may be developing. Drug abuse–related behaviors can take over a person's life, as thoughts and actions increasingly revolve around obtaining and using drugs. For instance, although an adolescent's substance abuse may be interfering with responsibilities at school, work, or within the family, drug use continues along with the problematic behaviors that are related to it. Drugs can be powerful distorters of an adolescent's decision making abilities, thus playing into the cycle of abuse.

The problem of drug use and abuse has clearly been on America's social conscience the last few decades, and yet the challenges of adolescent drug use persist. The 1999 National Household Survey on Drug Abuse (NHSDA) found that even though underage alcohol use is illegal, 10.4 million youths aged twelve to twenty were consuming alcohol in 1999. The majority (6.8 million) of these underage drinkers were engaging in dangerous binge drinking, and an alarmingly large group (2.1 million) of youths could be classified as heavy drinkers. In spite of the pronounced dangers of smoking tobacco, 16 out of every 100 adolescents still smoke cigarettes. These youths were found to be seven times more likely to use illegal drugs than those who didn't smoke. According to the NHSDA (2000), more than 10 out of every 100 adolescents between the ages of twelve and seventeen were using illegal drugs in 1999. The future will likely be difficult for those adolescents who are presently using drugs, since adults who began using drugs at a young age were found to be more likely to be dependent on drugs than adults who didn't start using drugs until later in life. It is obvious to most that it is not a big step from casual drug use to dangerous abuse, and yet drug abuse remains a major pitfall for adolescents.

In this discussion of drug abuse, the term *drug* may be applied to any substance that has a physical or psychological effect on an individual. Whether in the form of beer, a marijuana joint, a syringe of heroine, or a tobacco cigarette, any drug can be dangerous and destructive to someone who uses it inappropriately. Inappropriate drug use does not just occur among under-age adolescents using illegal drugs. Mature adults, over the age of twenty-one, suffer and die throughout the United States as a result of the abuse of legal drugs like nicotine (in tobacco products) and alcohol.

Drug abuse, legal or illegal, is a serious problem for people of any age. Thousands of Americans are killed each year as a result of drug abuse. Billions of dollars are spent each year in dealing with the health-, law-, and work-related problems that drug abuse causes. Families are weakened and communities burdened by the prevalence of drug abuse and the pain and destruction that can result. Ironically, while overall drug use in America has been decreasing, adolescent drug use has continued to exist at high levels in spite of extensive nationwide efforts to curtail it. Parents, educators, community workers, and state and federal programs have all labored to help America's youths understand the real dangers that the abuse of drugs can create. Although increased prevention and treatment efforts have made a difference, adolescent drug use continues to present a major challenge to keeping young people safe and healthy.

How do we determine where to draw the line between drug use, abuse, and dependency? The use of drugs is simply a matter of gaining access to a drug and trying it at least once. Some adolescents mistakenly perceive a drug as a tool for dealing with themselves or the outside world and begin to rely on it while ignoring its dangers. They may use drugs to make themselves feel happier or more confident about themselves. Drug use may serve as a pleasant or numbing distracter from stress that can accompany personal and social situations. Some adolescents who feel socially isolated or rejected may turn to drugs as a way to deal with their pain or depression. Others may feel pressured to use drugs because they want to be a part of a group or activity. Drug use may serve to break the boredom adolescents who have little involvement in engaging activities might feel or may appeal to those who want to feel more mature. Adolescents who are struggling with emotional difficulties such as depression, low self-esteem, or anxiety are especially likely to turn to drugs as a means of dealing with their problems. Ironically, inappropriate use of drugs simply acts as a temporary shield and ultimately exposes adolescents to an even greater level of emotional hardship and vulnerability.

Abuse and Dependency

Although drug dependency is traditionally thought of as a more serious condition than substance abuse, the primary difference is actually a matter of episodic versus chronic use. Substance abuse is episodic; only certain aspects of an individual's life are involved or affected by the use of drugs, leaving other aspects of life seemingly untouched. For instance, an adolescent may consume excessive alcohol at weekend parties but not during the school week. Drug dependency is a chronic condition, as drug use is involved in and persistently interferes with many more aspects of an individual's life. It is not uncommon for drug abusers to become dependent on drugs as their episodic behaviors escalate toward more pervasive and chronic ones.

Reinforcement

The escalation from experimentation and social use to abuse and dependency is usually driven by a powerful force involved with the use and effects of drugs: reinforcement. Reinforcement can be defined as any condition that promotes or decreases the occurrence of a particular behavior. There are two primary forms of reinforcement, positive and negative. Positive reinforcement occurs when the pleasant effects of a drug influence the individual to continue using the drug in order to reexperience the positive condition of feeling good. For instance, the condition of euphoria associated with the use of a particular drug may reinforce the continued use of that drug by the user. Negative reinforcement involves the increase or decrease of a behavior due to the removal or avoidance of an unpleasant stimulus. If an individual is experiencing stress or anxiety (unpleasant stimuli), a drug may serve to numb that person, thus temporarily removing the unpleasant feeling.

Tolerance and Withdrawal

Adding to the psychological and physical challenges that drug abuse can present the individual is the development of tolerance to a drug. Tolerance is the body's tendency to become less sensitive to a drug as it is administered over time. This change occurs as a result of the body's physiological responses, which are designed to counteract the effects of a drug. In order to maintain an optimal internal balance, the body releases chemicals that have the opposite effect of the administered drug. Over the course of continued drug use, the body's counteracting response becomes more powerful, thus elevating the amount of drug required to create an effect. This condition forces the drug user to administer larger and larger doses of a drug in order to achieve the desired level of effectiveness. As a drug user's body progressively builds a tolerance to a drug over time, unpleasant withdrawal effects can be experienced if drug use is stopped. Withdrawal involves the occurrence of effects that are usually the opposite of those produced by the use of a particular drug. For instance, alcohol use produces euphoric,

calming effects, and yet the withdrawal effects of alcohol use include nervousness and agitation. When drug use is discontinued, the body's compensation response is left unmatched by the effects of the drug. The unpleasant effects of this withdrawal condition often compel a drug user to resume drug use in order to avoid these withdrawal effects.

There are four types of drugs that are commonly abused, including narcotics, depressants, stimulants, and psychedelics.

Narcotics

Narcotics include drugs such as opium, morphine, codeine, and heroin. Narcotic drugs are derived from the opium poppy plant or are synthetically manufactured to produce physiological effects similar to those produced by the opium poppy in its natural form. Generally, narcotic drugs produce the effects of analgesia (relief of pain), euphoria (strong feelings of well-being), and drowsiness. When used inappropriately, narcotics are very dangerous. Tolerance to narcotic drugs develops very quickly, requiring the consumption of greater quantities in order to achieve a satisfying level of potency. An individual abusing narcotics is usually compelled to continue consuming the drug in order to avoid severely unpleasant withdrawal symptoms such as tremors, sweating, nausea, cramping, and diarrhea. In effect, a narcotic abuser can rapidly become a slave to the drug, constantly chasing the pleasurable effects and avoiding the negative withdrawal symptoms.

Depressants

Depressants drugs act to depress (slow) physical and psychological functioning. They can reduce anxiety or tension at low doses, while higher doses can induce drowsiness or sleep. The two major types of depressants include alcohol and sedative-hypnotics. Sedative-hypnotic drugs are sometimes used as sedatives or anesthetics; they include several varieties such as barbiturates, sedatives, and tranquilizers. Although some specific effects on the body and mind differ, depressant drugs all serve to calm physical and mental processes. Certain types of inhalants used by adolescents to achieve effects similar to the depressant drugs include model glue, paint thinner, and gasoline. The use of inhalants is particularly risky because neurological damage and asphyxiation (suffocation) are potential outcomes of abuse.

Alcohol (ethyl alcohol) is one of the most commonly used drugs in America and can be found within beer, wine, and distilled spirits. Since it is relatively easy to obtain it is the most widely abused drug among adolescents. When taken in low doses, alcohol produces a mild form of euphoria and tends to reduce anxiety. Thinking, perception, language, and coordination are all impaired to varying degrees depending on dosage level. Alcohol use dulls inhibitions, allowing individuals to behave in ways that they may not otherwise feel comfortable with. At higher doses, alcohol acts to sedate the user, and with increased dosage can induce drowsiness and sleep. Alcohol also depresses respiration (breathing) and at high doses can lead to death, as respiration becomes too shallow to sustain life. With continued use, alcohol produces both tolerance and the development of physical dependence. Since alcohol produces both positive and negative reinforcement, its influence over the individual can be powerful. Unlike the withdrawal effects of narcotic use, the effects of alcohol withdrawal are potentially life threatening. Full-blown alcohol withdrawal (among those dependent on alcohol) can last a week and will move through a series of stages that become progressively more unpleasant, culminating in delirium tremors, which can be lethal.

Stimulants

Stimulants are drugs that produce increased activity or alertness within the brain and nervous system. There are four main types of stimulants that are commonly abused: amphetamine, caffeine, cocaine, and nicotine. Amphetamine is a single name used to describe three similar drugs: amphetamine, dextroamphetamine, and methamphetamine. Methamphetamine, more commonly referred to as "speed," is the most abused of the three amphetamine drugs. Amphetamine drugs are typically taken as sleep and appetite suppressants and have the overall effect of physically and emotionally energizing the user. Cocaine is a drug derived from the coca plant. It produces similar effects to amphetamine drugs such as alertness and the production of a euphoric emotional state. At moderate doses, cocaine can cause negative experiences such as nervousness, paranoia, and anxiety. However, at high doses, the drug can cause sleeplessness, nausea, tremors, and psychotic mental states. Continued high levels of the drug can cause seizures, stroke, respiratory arrest, and death. Although tolerance develops to some of the drug's effects such as emotional euphoria, continued use can actually sensitize an individual to the convulsive effects of the drug. Cocaine withdrawal is relatively mild, and so negative reinforcement (by the discomforts of withdrawal) does not play a large role in dependence. However, the psychological dependence on cocaine, driven by positive reinforcement, is extremely powerful. Cocaine abusers can spend a great deal of money, time, and effort in obtaining the drug to the detriment of other aspects of their lives. The recent popularity of "crack" cocaine (a nugget form of the drug) is driven by its very low cost; it can sometimes be obtained for as little as a few dollars.

Caffeine and nicotine are legal stimulant drugs that are widely used in many different forms. Caffeine is a colorless, bitter chemical derived from various types of plants and is an ingredient within soft drinks and coffee. Caffeine can also be found in pill form, usually as nonprescription diet pills. Nicotine is derived from the leaves of the tobacco plant and is found within cigarettes, cigars, chewing tobacco, and nicotine gum or patches. The effects of caffeine and nicotine are milder but similar to those of amphetamine and cocaine. Although both caffeine and nicotine are relatively mild drugs in their legal forms, abuse and dependency are not uncommon when the drugs are used excessively. The easy availability of nicotine products and social attraction to their use, contribute to widespread dependency across all age groups. Although the withdrawal effects of nicotine are unpleasant, smoking or chewing tobacco in order to experience the effects of nicotine have been shown to increase the risks of developing various types of cancer (lung, mouth, throat) and chronic emphysema.

All four types of stimulants involve a rapid development of tolerance and so compel users to increase dosages in order to achieve desired levels of effect. Abuse of the stimulant drugs cocaine and amphetamine can give rise to serious paranoia, delusions, and hallucinations. These powerful and irrational side effects can lead to violent behaviors. The withdrawal effects of stimulants include sluggishness, sleepiness, and depression. Although these are rarely lethal, they do tend to compel people to continue using the stimulant drug in order to avoid them. In some cases, the depression that severe stimulant withdrawal involves can increase the risk of suicide.

Psychedelics

Psychedelic drugs (also called hallucinogens) cause serious alterations in the ways people perceive and process sensory experience. The drug-induced changes caused by psychedelics can create exaggerated emotional reactions and irrational interpretations of the surrounding environment. Just as each individual is unique, each individual's experience while taking a psychedelic drug will be different. This adds to the unpredictability and potential for panic or distress that can accompany a psychedelic drug experience. Some psychedelic drugs are found within certain plants, while others are synthetically manufactured. Mescaline is a psychedelic chemical compound drawn from the peyote cactus. Its effects are very powerful, sometimes lasting as long as five to ten hours. Marijuana (and its derivative, hashish) is another natural psychedelic derived from the marijuana or hemp plant. The active psychedelic ingredient in marijuana is called delta–9-tetrahydrocannabinol or THC. When marijuana is taken at low doses it acts as a mild sedative, while at higher doses the drug can produce psychedelic effects. LSD ("acid") and PCP ("angle dust") are both synthetic psychedelic drugs produced within a laboratory. As with other drugs, people who consistently use marijuana develop tolerance to it in addition to withdrawal symptoms such as restlessness, irritability, and nausea. Tolerance also develops with the use of other psychedelics, but there may be no withdrawal symptoms. A particular danger involved with the long-term use of PCP is the potential for neurological deficits in language, memory, and vision.

Anabolic Steroid

Steroids are included in this discussion of substance abuse as they can have powerful effects on the individual and can be dangerous when they are abused. Anabolic steroids are a synthetic form of the male hormone testosterone, which plays a role in muscle growth and development. When used inappropriately by adolescents, steroids can cause problems with the cardiovascular and reproductive systems of males and females, while also increasing the risk of certain cancers. In spite of these dangers, adolescents are sometimes so driven to improve themselves physically and athletically that they put themselves at great risk. Certain features of the adolescent's emotional and physical development may play into the attraction to steroid use. Moving through a period of awkward or underdeveloped body structure is a normal part of adolescent development. Yet the sensitivity of adolescents to the expectations and perceptions of others can create feelings of dissatisfaction with themselves physically. In addition, adolescents can be susceptible to pressure from peers and authority figures who may be pushing for greater athletic performance. These factors, combined with an adolescent's typically lower self-esteem, can create a strong motivation to improve themselves physically by inappropriate means such as steroids. Adolescents can actually become psychologically dependent on steroids as they become invested in looking more muscular or performing at higher levels athletically. To the detriment of their internal emotional development, adolescents who use steroids come to focus much of their self-worth on external appearance and performance.

Prevention

No single strategy for preventing adolescent drug abuse has been shown to be effective on its own. Effective prevention must involve several strategies combined and applied consistently over time. The most important aspect of this overall strategy is to provide children and adolescents with a supportive and nurturing environment from which they may develop a strong sense of belonging and identity. Positive social and emotional development requires investment from others so that adolescents can begin to invest in themselves. A second aspect to drug abuse prevention involves educating children and adolescents about the realities of drugs along with teaching them realistic strategies for dealing with the feelings and situations that can lead to drug use. The third important aspect involves providing adolescents with opportunities to get involved in a variety of scholastic and extracurricular activities. Adolescents who have alternatives available to them usually choose positive pathways in life, provided they have mentors to assist them.

For more information about drug abuse and prevention, the National Clearinghouse for Alcohol and Drug Information can be reached at 1-800-729-6686 for assistance in English or Spanish, or at TDD 1-800-487-4889 for hearing-impaired callers. PREVLine, an electronic communication system, is accessible through the Internet at www.health.org, and provides online forums and direct access to educational materials. "Preventing Drug Use among Children and Adolescents" provides 14 prevention principles based on 20 years of research to help schools and community groups develop more effective drug prevention programs. Call for a free copy at 1-800-729-6686.

Treatment
There are many types of drug treatment available to adolescents and their families. The first step in seeking out treatment should always involve seeking out local school or community support services. Support groups for adolescents with alcohol or drug troubles exist throughout the United States such as *Alanon* or *Alateen* (1-800-356-9996). Other regional and national support groups exist to provide information and referral should they be needed. For information about drug abuse treatment and referral call the National Drug Information and Treatment Referral Hotline, 1-800-662-HELP. This hot line provides drug-related information to people seeking a local treatment program, and directs those affected by the substance abuse of a friend or family member to support groups or services. Valuable resources can also be found on the Internet including, the National Institute on Drug Abuse (www.nida.nih.gov) and the National Institute on Alcohol Abuse and Alcoholism (www.niaaa.nih.gov). Adolescent drug abuse is a serious matter and requires the involvement of experienced support persons or professionals in order to properly address the problem. Do not hesitate to seek out help.

George T. Ladd

See also Alcohol Use, Risk Factors in; Alcohol Use, Trends in; Children of Alcoholics; Cigarette Smoking; Drug Abuse Prevention; Inhalants; Intervention Programs for Adolescents; Peer Pressure; Risk Behaviors; Steroids

References and further reading
American Psychiatric Association. *Diagnostic and Statistical Manual of Mental Disorders*, 4th ed. Washington, DC: American Psychiatric Association.
Cadogan, Donald A. 1999. "Drug Use Harm." *American Psychologist* 54: 841–842.
Carlson, Neil R. 1998. *Physiology of Behavior.* Boston: Allyn and Bacon.
Department of Health and Human Services, Substance Abuse and Mental Health Services Administration. 2000. *1999 National Household Survey on Drug Abuse.* Rockville, MD. DHHS.
MacCoun, R. 1998. "Toward a Psychology of Harm Reduction." *American Psychologist* 53: 1199–1208.
Winger, G., F. G. Hofmann, and J. F. Woods. 1992. *A Handbook on Drug and Alcohol Abuse: The Biomedical Aspects.* New York: Oxford University Press.

Suicide
Definition
Suicidal behavior can be defined as thoughts, verbalizations, or actions that have the intention of causing one's own death. Suicidal behavior is generally considered as extending along a continuum from ideation to actual completion. Suicidal ideation is characterized by thoughts or verbalizations about causing one's own death. A suicidal threat is the verbalization of an imminent suicidal action. A suicide attempt is a self-destructive action that realistically could lead to death (e.g., ingestion of a potentially fatal dose of drugs). A suicide completion is an action that ultimately leads to death. Other behaviors, such as risk taking, recklessness, or self-destructive actions without suicidal intent, although potentially life threatening (e.g., driving fast, abusing drugs, engaging in unsafe sex), are generally not considered suicidal by tradi-

tional definitions. Actions that are self-inflicted and result in injury without the intention of causing death (e.g., superficial wrist cutting, burning) have been termed self-injury, self-mutilation, or parasuicide, and are discussed in another entry in this volume.

Many teens at some point have thought about or contemplated suicide, but most teens decide that life is worth living. Other teens who are in crisis, however, view their problems and pain as inescapable. Teenagers who attempt and complete suicide often have intense and overwhelming feelings of despair, hopelessness, and helplessness. Other feelings include feeling unable to stop the pain or sadness, not being able to see a way out of the crisis, and worthlessness. Often, these youth become socially isolated and withdraw from their family and friends, have difficulty with sleeping and eating, have sudden changes in their personality, lose interest in activities they once found pleasurable, begin or increase their use of drugs or alcohol, have physical complaints, have difficulty concentrating, and have problems with their schoolwork. Many of these signs are quite similar to the symptoms of depression. Other warning signs include evidence of preparing for death, such as making out a will and final arrangements, giving away treasured or prized possessions, or having a preoccupation with death. Teens who are planning to commit suicide will often make direct or indirect statements about their suicidal intentions (e.g., "I won't be a problem for you any longer").

Suicide is the third leading cause of death among youth ages 15 to 24. (Philip James Corwin/Corbis)

Prevalence
Among teenagers in the United States, suicide is the third leading cause of death, following unintentional injuries and homicide. Since the middle of the last century, the rates of completed suicide have increased among youth between the ages of ten and nineteen, but the rates have declined since 1994. Although suicide attempts and completions are uncommon before puberty, the rates increase dramatically through middle adolescence. The Centers for Disease Control reported that, in 1997, 303 youth between the ages of ten and fourteen committed suicide in the United States. Of youth ages fifteen to nineteen, 1,802 committed suicide.

The incidence of suicide attempts by teenagers is more difficult to determine because of the number of attempts that go unreported and the number of attempts that may have been classified as accidental. According to a study by Lewinsohn and colleagues (1996), 2 percent of adolescents in a community sample had attempted suicide during the past year. However, 7 percent of the adolescents had attempted suicide in their lifetime. About one-half of all youth who attempt suicide will eventually make further attempts, and it has been estimated that approximately one-quarter to one-third of adolescent suicide victims have made at least one previous suicide attempt. Furthermore, occasional suicidal ideation is surprisingly common in the general adolescent population. These rates, however, become significantly lower for moderate to extreme suicidal intent.

Differences between adolescent boys and girls have been documented for the rates of suicide completions, attempts, and ideation. In general, boys are about four times more likely to commit suicide than girls. Suicide rates have increased among fifteen- to nineteen-year-old males since the 1960s, but have remained relatively stable for females in that age group and for the ten- to fourteen-year-old-age group. Teenage girls, however, are much more likely to report suicidal ideation and attempt suicide than teenage boys.

Furthermore, rates of suicidal ideation, attempts, and completions vary across ethnic groups in the United States. The risk of suicide among young people is greatest for young white males. The rates of completed suicide are generally higher in Native American youth and lower in African American youth. However, the rates of suicide have increased dramati-cally for African American males in the past two decades. The rates of suicide have also increased for Hispanic youth in recent years.

Moreover, much discussion and debate has arisen regarding the relation between sexual orientation and suicide. Although it has been suggested that gay, lesbian, and bisexual youth are at greater risk than heterosexual youth for completed suicide, research has not been conclusive. Because of a lack of societal acceptance of homosexuality, struggling with issues of sexuality may place youth at a greater risk for depression and other psychological problems, including suicidal behavior.

The most common method of completed youth suicide is by use of a firearm. Other common means of completed suicide are suffocation (e.g., hanging) and poisoning (e.g., intentional overdose). The most common methods for those adolescents who attempt suicide are intentional overdose and wrist cutting. Gender differences have also been found in the methods used for suicide, with girls primarily using ingestion and cutting, while boys primarily using guns and hanging. Suicide attempts made by older adolescents and males tend to have more serious intent and lethality.

The vast majority of suicide attempts are deliberate and planned. A high proportion of youth report suicidal ideation prior to attempting suicide. Youth who attempt suicide without previous apparent suicidal ideation usually commit the act impulsively, and are more likely to be under the influence of drugs or alcohol. The majority of depressed youth report suicidal ideation at some point, but not all youth who express suicidal ideation actually attempt it. The suicide attempts of youth with depression almost never occur when they are symptom free.

Risk Factors

Suicidal behavior in adolescents is a complex phenomenon. Although there is no typical suicidal adolescent, a number of variables have been identified by researchers as potential risk factors. Some of these factors include reduced family influence, economic stress, peer pressure, alcohol and substance use and abuse, sexual pressure, fear of AIDS, media, and gang influences. Although suicide has many causes, there is no particular formula to determine who will commit suicide. However, many factors have been documented in current research and have been crucial in identifying teenagers who may be at risk.

One of the strongest known risk factors for suicide attempts and completions is a past history of suicide attempt. In addition, suicide attempts almost always occur in the context of significant psychopathology or a psychiatric disorder (e.g., major depression, alcohol and drug abuse/dependence, disruptive behavior disorders, and, to a lesser extent, anxiety disorders). The majority of adolescents who commit suicide have a psychological disorder. Youth who have more than one psychiatric disorder have an increased risk of attempting suicide. However, having a psychiatric disorder does not mean that an adolescent will attempt suicide. It is important to note that most youth with a psychiatric disorder do not attempt suicide. Major depression, with feelings of low self-esteem, helplessness, hopelessness, loneliness, and a sense of guilt, is the most common psychiatric disorder of those youth who attempt or complete suicide. Although suicide with-out depression is rare, it is not necessary to be depressed to commit suicide.

Other psychiatric disorders that are associated with suicidal behavior are related to poor impulse control and low self-esteem. For example, disruptive behavior disorders (e.g., conduct disorder), and associated chronic difficulty with authority, is another common disorder that is associated with suicide. The risk for suicide is even greater if the young person is using drugs or alcohol. Drugs and alcohol cause disinhibition and can impair judgment and impulse control. Similar to differences in rates and methods of completion, differences between adolescent boys and girls also exist in regard to the risk factors for suicide. Among girls, the most significant risk factor for completed suicide is the presence of major depression. Another major risk factor for girls is a previous suicide attempt. For boys, a previous suicide attempt is the most important predictor, followed by depression, disruptive behavior disorders, and substance abuse.

A number of factors in a teenager's social environment have been linked to completed suicides, including stressful life events and interpersonal difficulties. Suicide in youth often occurs after the teenager has experienced some sort of recent disappointment, loss, or rejection. For example, interpersonal losses and disciplinary problems increase suicide risk. The following stressful life events may be predictive of future adolescent suicide attempts: many arguments or fights, the attempt of a relative or friend to commit suicide, problems of a relative or friend with alcohol or drugs, a disruption in the adolescent's living situation, the death of a relative or friend, an arrest or legal trouble, and a breakup of an intimate relationship. Interpersonal loss has been found to increase the risk of suicide, especially for boys. Since the reasons for completing suicide are complex and multidetermined, these stressful life events are rarely a sufficient cause for suicide. These events can, however, be precipitating factors for teens.

Other risk factors for suicidal behavior include a family history of depression or substance abuse, ineffective coping skills, functional impairment due to an illness or injury, or having been born to a teenage mother. The presence or the availability of the means to kill oneself has been associated with increased suicide risk. For example, having a firearm in the home has been found to greatly increase the risk of youth suicide. In addition, suicide completers have been found to have experienced more physical abuse, more exposure to family violence, residential instability, and parental unemployment, and more parent-child conflict. The occurrence of these stressful life events and circumstances should serve as warning signs for clinicians or parents of suicidal adolescents. It is important to note, however, that these events most often occur without suicide as a consequence.

Treatment and Interventions

Depression and suicidal feelings are treatable mental disorders. Unfortunately, very few youth who have committed suicide have been in treatment at the time of their death. Adolescents who express that they want to kill themselves should always be taken seriously, and they should seek an evaluation from a mental health professional. Although people often feel uncomfortable talking about death and suicidal feelings, addressing the depression and suicidal thoughts can be helpful and provide some relief. Asking questions regarding suicidal thoughts does not prompt suicidal behavior; rather, it can provide reassurance that someone cares, offers support, and is listening.

Often, inpatient hospitalization is the necessary form of intervention if the adolescent is in imminent danger of self-harm. The most important aspect of treatment for the youth in crisis is to provide a safe environment. If someone is in imminent danger of harming herself, do not leave her alone. When someone is actively suicidal, it is also important to limit her access to dangerous weapons, such as firearms, lethal doses of medications, or knives. Emergency steps may need to be taken, such as calling 911 or taking the person to a crisis center or emergency room. Other resources to contact in an emergency include community mental health agencies, a private therapist or counselor, school counselor, psychologist, or family doctor.

Laura A. Gallagher

See also Coping; Counseling; Depression; Intervention Programs for Adolescents; Psychotherapy; Self-Injury; Substance Use and Abuse; Youth Outlook

References and further reading
Berman, Alan L., and D. A. Jobes. 1991. *Adolescent Suicide: Assessment and Intervention.* Washington, DC: American Psychological Association.
Centers for Disease Control and Prevention. 1998. "Youth Risk Behavior Surveillance—United States, 1997." *CDC Surveillance Summaries, August, 14, 1998. Morbidity and Mortality Weekly Report* 4, no. SS-3.
———. 1999. *Suicide Deaths and Rates Per 100,000.* Available at: http://www.cdc.gov/ncipc/data/us9794/suic.htm
Gould, Madelyn S., et al. 1998. "Psychopathology Associated with Suicidal Ideation and Attempts among Children and Adolescents." *Journal of*

the *American Academy of Child and Adolescent Psychiatry* 37: 915–923.

Gould, Madelyn S., Prudence Fisher, Michael Parides, Michael Flory, and David Shaffer. 1996. "Psychosocial Risk Factors of Child and Adolescent Completed Suicide." *Archives of General Psychiatry* 53: 1155–1162.

Hoyert, Donna L., Kenneth D. Kochanek, and Sherry L. Murphy. 1999. "Deaths: Final Data for 1997." *National Vital Statistics Reports* 47, no 19. Hyattsville,

MD: National Center for Health Statistics.

Lewinsohn, Peter M., Paul Rohde, and John R. Seeley. 1996. "Adolescent Suicidal Ideation and Attempts: Prevalence, Risk Factors, and Clinical Implications." *Clinical Psychology: Science and Practice* 3: 25–46.

Shaffer, David, and Leslie Craft. 1999. "Methods of Adolescent Suicide Prevention." *Journal of Clinical Psychiatry* 60: 70–74.

T

Teachers

Teachers are rarely mentioned by adolescents as having a significant or important influence in their lives. Adolescents often describe teachers as providing aid and advice, but only as secondary sources relative to parents and peers. Moreover, studies of teacher characteristics and teacher-student relationships have not often been done with adolescents in middle and high school. However, teachers can have a profound effect on the academic and social lives of students. Recent studies have linked specific characteristics of teachers to adolescents' educational aspirations, values, and self-concept. In middle school, students' perceptions that teachers care about them have been related to positive aspects of student motivation such as pursuit of social and academic goals, mastery orientations toward learning, and academic interest. When perceived support from parents, peers, and teachers is considered together, perceived support from teachers has the most direct link to how much students like school and to how well they perform academically.

The most widely documented influence of teachers on school adjustment concerns the degree to which adolescents perceive teachers as being supportive and caring. Several authors have suggested that feelings of belongingness and of being cared for can foster the adoption and internalization of goals and values of caregivers. With respect to schooling, this explanation translates into the notion that students will be motivated to engage in classroom activities if they believe that teachers care about them. Middle school students characterize caring and supportive teachers as those who demonstrate democratic and egalitarian communication styles designed to elicit student participation and input, who develop expectations for student behavior and performance in light of individual differences and abilities, who model a caring attitude and interest in their instruction and interpersonal dealings with students, and who provide constructive rather than harsh and critical feedback.

Students' perceptions that teachers are indeed supportive and caring predict positive motivational orientations toward school over the course of the middle school years. Specific qualities of middle school teachers, which include communicating high expectations, clear and consistent rule setting, positive and constructive feedback, fairness, and modeling of interest in learning on the part of teachers, relate positively to students' pursuit of socially valued goals, interest in schoolwork, and positive beliefs about personal control. Negative feedback from teachers appears to be a powerful and consistent predictor of students' social behavior and academic performance: Students

Teachers can have a profound effect on the academic and social lives of students. (Skjold Photographs)

who perceive teachers as being harsh and critical display antisocial and uncooperative classroom behavior and earn low grades relative to their peers. These findings underscore the potentially pervasive influence of teachers' negative and highly critical feedback on adolescents' overall adjustment and success at school.

Young adolescents' relationships with and perceptions of teachers appear to change dramatically with the transition from elementary to middle school. During this time, students often report heightened levels of mistrust of teachers, perceptions that teachers no longer care about them, and a decrease in opportunities to establish meaningful relationships with teachers. These reported declines in the nurturant qualities of teacher-student relationships after the transition to middle school also correspond to declines in academic motivation and achievement.

As students proceed through middle school, they also report that teachers become more focused on students earning high grades, on competition between students, and on maintaining adult control, with a decrease in personal interest in students. Students who report these changes also tend to report less intrinsic motivation to achieve than students who do not. When asked about their own perceptions of their teaching, however, teachers do not perceive their practice in the same way as students. Teachers report that they do not emphasize competition and grading as much as do students, nor do they think they convey a lack of caring to their students.

As adolescents change in their perceptions of their teachers as they progress through middle school, they also change in the degree to which they think teachers have authority over their decisions and behavior. In general, almost all adolescents believe that teachers have authority over issues such as stealing and fighting; somewhat less authority over issues such as misbehaving in class, breaking school rules, and smoking or substance abuse; and least authority over issues involving peer interactions, friendships, and personal appearance. Interestingly, when beliefs about teachers are compared to beliefs about the authority of their parents and friends to dictate their school behavior, adolescents believe that teachers have more authority with respect to moral issues such as stealing and fighting and conventional rules involving school and classroom conduct. They also believe that teachers have as much authority as parents with respect to smoking or substance abuse. Peers are seen as having legitimate authority only in personal matters such as friendships or personal appearance. These beliefs, however, tend to change as children get older, with younger adolescents in middle school believing teachers have legitimate authority in all areas of school conduct and older adolescents in high school believing that teachers have little authority over most aspects of their lives at school.

Little is known about teachers' opinions and beliefs about their adolescent students. In a recent interview study, however, middle school teachers spoke of a variety of important things that they did in the classroom, ranging from instruction to promoting students' social and emotional development (Wentzel, 2000). For instance, 47 percent of the teachers mentioned promoting social-emotional development as an important part of their job, 40 percent mentioned instruction and establishing positive teacher-student relationships, and 33 percent mentioned classroom management and the teaching of learning skills. In addition, a good day for teachers was typically described as one in which students are motivated and on task, whereas bad days were most often described as those in which classroom management issues and problems with instruction were prevalent. Most teachers also had images of ideal and nightmare students, with ideal students being described most often as motivated and self-regulated, and nightmare students as having motivational and behavioral problems. Finally, most teachers attributed their students' success to home and instructional factors. These findings document the complex nature of the day-to-day lives of middle school teachers, as well as their recognition that their students need support and guidance in areas that reflect social as well as academic concerns.

It is likely that teachers might be more crucial to some adolescents' adjustment to school than to others. Some students who are at risk for academic problems due to unstable or problematic home life attribute their success to teachers who have served as mentors and often surrogate parents in their lives. Teachers also might be able to offset the negative impact of low levels of acceptance and rejection from peers. For instance, research shows that some middle school students who are rejected by their peers but liked by teachers tend to do well academically over time. However, teachers can also exacerbate the negative impact of peer rejection on students, in that young adolescents who are disliked by their teachers as well as by their peers are at higher risk for academic failure and other school-related problems than their peers who have more positive relations with their teachers and peers.

What do we know about teachers' instructional practices and adolescents' adjustment to school? The most common finding is that teachers tend to have different expectations for and interactions with students depending on curricular tracks. For instance, some researchers have documented that teachers of students who are not in college-bound programs tend to establish classrooms with more structure and present subject matter in less interesting ways than teachers of college-bound students. Students in college tracks also tend to receive more praise and recognition and less criticism than other students.

The long-term implications of these differential practices seem to be twofold. Regardless of the quality of instruction, students who perceive that their teachers are interested in the subject matter and are trying to make it interesting for them are themselves more interested in the subject matter, do better academically, and are more motivated to behave in socially appropriate ways than students who believe their teachers are not interested in what they do. Therefore, college-bound students are likely to benefit from their classes more than other students, in part simply because teachers make them more interesting and motivating. In addition, less structured classrooms tend to promote more friendly and open interactions among students, and so college-track students may well benefit from more frequent opportunities to make new friends with a wider and more diverse set of peers than their noncollege-bound classmates.

Kathryn R. Wentzel

See also Academic Achievement; Academic Self-Evaluation; Apprenticeships;

Homework; Mentoring and Youth Development; School, Functions of

References and further reading

Csikszentmihalyi, Mihaly, and Reed Larson. 1984. *Being Adolescent.* New York: Basic Books.

Eccles, Jacqueline, Carol Midgley, and Terry Adler. 1984. "Grade-Related Changes in the School Environment." Pp. 283–331 in *Advances in Motivation and Achievement.* Edited by M. L. Maehr. Greenwich, CT: JAI.

Epstein, Joyce, and Nancy Karweit. 1983. *Friends in School.* New York: Academic Press.

Harter, Susan. 1996. "Teacher and Classmate Influences on Scholastic Motivation, Self-Esteem, and Level of Voice in Adolescents." Pp. 11–42 in *Social Motivation: Understanding Children's School Adjustment.* Edited by Jaana Juvonen and Kathryn Wentzel. New York: Cambridge University Press.

Juvonen, Jaana. 1996. "Self-Presentation Tactics Promoting Teacher and Peer Approval: The Function of Excuses and Other Clever Explanations." Pp. 43–65 in *Social Motivation: Understanding Children's School Adjustment.* Edited by Jaana Juvonen and Kathryn Wentzel. New York: Cambridge University Press.

Smetana, Judith, and Bruce Bitz. 1996. "Adolescents' Conceptions of Teachers' Authority and Their Relations to Rule Violations in School." *Child Development* 67: 1153–1172.

Wentzel, Kathryn R. 1997. "Student Motivation in Middle School: The Role of Perceived Pedagogical Caring." *Journal of Educational Psychology* 89: 411–419.

———. 1998. "Social Support and Adjustment in Middle School: The Role of Parents, Teachers, and Peers." *Journal of Educational Psychology* 90: 202–209.

———. 1999. "Social-Motivational Processes and Interpersonal Relationships: Implications for Understanding Students' Academic Success." *Journal of Educational Psychology* 91: 76–97.

———. 2000. *Middle School Teachers' Educational Goals and Perceptions of Their Students.* Unpublished manuscript, University of Maryland, College Park.

Teasing

Teasing involves making fun of another person. Teasing may involve poking fun at someone with whom one is friendly, but it can also be much more like bullying and may be a form of harassment. Teenagers who engage in teasing may feel that they are "only fooling" and thus may not understand that the behavior is hurtful. Teens may not recognize that the person being teased views the situation much differently. An adolescent who is being teased may also be reluctant to admit that the behavior is bothersome for fear that this admission will simply escalate the teasing or bring about other forms of ridicule from peers.

Although there may be many instances of good-natured fun when friends exchange harmless jokes about one another, this type of playful verbal exchange is qualitatively different from one-sided teasing, directed at an individual, that is hurtful in nature. A common adolescent situation is teasing that involves comments or consequences that are not harmless. Despite the old adage that we are taught when we are young, "Sticks and stones may break my bones but names will never hurt me," we actually know that words can be at least as hurtful as physical aggression. This is especially true when the harmful words, or teasing, are ongoing.

Often, teasing involves a power inequity. Power inequities occur in any life situation in which some people have more of something desirable. For example, there is often a power inequity that results from a difference in wealth. People with financial resources often have more power to influence others than do poor people. If you apply this model to adolescent social situations, there are

Teasing can take many forms and often focuses on issues of difference. (Shirley Zeiberg)

individuals with more social power. Social power may mean having more friends or at least having the attention of others. Someone with more social power may feel at liberty to pick on someone with less social power. In addition, someone with more social power may be able to influence others to pick on someone with less social power. In this way, groups of adolescents who are considered "in" or "cool" determine how others will be treated. Sometimes teens tease others with the hope of gaining social power. For example, teens who want to feel accepted by others may join in teasing (or initiate the teasing of) someone less popular. However, it is important to note that not all popular teens engage in teasing others. In fact, many popular teens are friendly and kind. Thus, popularity should not be an excuse for the mistreatment of others.

Teasing can take many forms and often focuses on issues of difference. Teasing may involve comments or jokes about a person's physical appearance. Young people who are overweight are at particularly high risk for teasing by peers. Sadly, this form of discrimination is also prevalent in adult society. Family situation or structure, as well as ethnic or racial background, may also be a source of teasing. Since teens spend the majority of their waking hours in school settings, school achievement can be another focus of teasing. At times, less competent students may be teased. However, this is highly dependent on the school culture and whether or not academic achievement is valued. In some settings, it is the more competent, higher-achieving students who may become the subject of ridicule by their less academically oriented peers. In many high schools, athletes are held in the highest regard, and so physical/athletic ability can be an additional source of teasing. Teens (especially males) who are not athletically oriented may find that they are teased by peers. Conversely, teenage girls who are athletic but may not be interested in stereotypically female activities may be subject to teasing by peers.

One of the most common forms of adolescent teasing involves issues of sexual orientation. When young people want to insult one another they often use slurs that are related to being gay. Since adolescence is a time during which there is often much confusion and self-consciousness about sexual identity, this type of teasing can be particularly hurtful. Some statistics suggest that gay teens are at even higher risk for suicide than straight teens and often feel that they have no one to turn to for help. Therefore, teasing about sexual orientation may have deadly consequences.

Though teenagers have the intellectual ability to understand that their behavior could have an impact on someone else, their emotional development during this period may limit their understanding. From a social/emotional standpoint adolescents are often thought to be experiencing a period of egocentrism, which means that they see situations only from their own point of view and may not spontaneously take the perspective of another when looking at a situation. As a result, a teen who make a comment that she thinks is funny and actually gets a laugh from others may not give one moment's thought to the impact that the comment has on the person being teased. Even when the behavior is pointed out, the most common teenage response is, "I was only fooling around." This answer focuses only on the intention, thoughts, and actions of the teaser and completely ignores the feelings of the teen being teased.

Teasing is sometimes related to bullying. Bullying is defined as physical or verbal aggression against another person. Bullying is a means of exercising power and domination. A bully may be an individual who has difficulty making friends in more socially acceptable ways and resorts instead to trying to control others through aggression and intimidation. Intimidation can be very powerful, in that victims are made to feel fearful as a result of implicit or explicit threats. Adolescents who already feel self-conscious may be reluctant to report incidents of bullying.

Teasing and bullying can make teenagers feel miserable. Unfortunately, adults often underestimate the impact of such behavior. Teenagers who feel teased or bullied should find an adult in whom they can confide. If teens do not feel able to confide in any adult whom they already know, they can seek professional help from a counselor or therapist trained to help teens. Adults often suggest that teens suffering from teasing or bullying need to express their displeasure to the aggressor. However, it is crucial for adults to understand that expressing displeasure may not make the behavior stop, especially if it is intentional on the part of the teaser. In fact, knowing that they have evoked a response may provide just the reinforcement needed to encourage a continuation of the behavior. Similarly, adults often suggest that teens ignore inappropriate comments made by others. Although this may work at times, this, too, can produce the opposite result, in that the teaser may simply escalate the attack in order to provoke the victim. Since most teasing involves a focus on those who are somehow deemed to be different, educating young children, teens, and adults about the importance of mutual respect and acceptance of differences is an important step toward curbing teasing behavior.

Deborah N. Margolis

See also Bullying; Conduct Problems; Conflict Resolution; Peer Pressure; Peer Victimization in School; Self-Consciousness; Self-Esteem; Sibling Conflict

References and further reading
Marano, Hara Estroff. 1998. *Why Doesn't Anybody Like Me?* New York: William Morrow.
Stein, Nan. 1996. *Bullyproof*. Wellesley, MA: Wellesley Center for Research on Women.

Teenage Parenting: Childbearing

Becoming sexually active is a normal part of human development for adolescents making the transition into adulthood. In earlier historical periods, adolescents expected to marry and begin childbearing at a relatively early age. In contemporary American society, however, adolescents typically do not expect to marry at an early age, and many adult women delay childbearing until near the end of their reproductive years. Our society offers adolescents no clear norms for the acceptable age and acceptable relationship for initiation of sexual activity. In this context of uncertainty, many adolescents initiate sexual activity. Some become pregnant and bear children.

Declines in Adolescent Pregnancy and Birthrates

The birthrate for adolescents has declined in the United States. The 1998 adolescent birthrate was 51 per 1,000 adolescent females (fifteen to nineteen years of age). Declines have occurred for all ethnic groups, although ethnic differences remain. Hispanic adolescents have the highest birthrate; African Americans and American Indians are higher than Caucasians and Asian Americans. Similarly, disparities remain in adolescent birthrates in the geographic regions of the United States, but declines have occurred in all geographic areas. Mississippi has the highest rate of births to adolescents, and Vermont, the lowest. Ethnic differences must be interpreted cautiously, however, because ethnicity is confounded with socioeconomic status in major studies. Socioeconomic status may contribute to ethnic differences in adolescent pregnancy and birthrates.

Pregnancy and birthrates differ by age within the adolescent years. Older adolescents have higher pregnancy and birthrates than younger adolescents. The birthrate for fifteen- to seventeen-year-olds is 34 per 1,000 for the United States. In contrast, the birthrate for eighteen- to nineteen-year-olds is 86 per 1,000. Young adolescents who become pregnant have different developmental needs from older pregnant adolescents who are making the transition into adulthood. Young pregnant adolescents also are more likely than older adolescents to have medical complications.

The abortion ratio, the ratio of abortions to pregnancies, is relatively low in the United States compared to other developed countries. In most developed countries, the abortion ratio is very high—more than 50 percent for fifteen- to seventeen-year-olds. The majority of younger pregnant adolescents in developed countries choose abortion, and they are more likely than older adolescents (eighteen- to nineteen-year-olds) to have abortions. The abortion ratio in the United States, in contrast, is 36 percent for fifteen- to seventeen-year-olds and 34 percent for eighteen- to nineteen-year-olds.

Adolescent childbearing occurs at a higher rate in the United States than in other developed countries. Even with the exclusion of ethnic groups with higher adolescent birthrates within the United States, the U.S. rate for Caucasian adolescents remains higher than that in other industrialized nations. The pregnancy rate, calculated by combining birthrates and abortion rates, is also higher in the United States than in most developed countries. Recent statistics show that the United States is one of five countries (including Belarus, Bulgaria, Romania, and the Russian Federation) with pregnancy rates of 70 or more per 1,000 adolescent females per year. There has been a general decline in adolescent pregnancy rates and birthrates over the past twenty-five years in industrialized countries, although great disparities in adolescent pregnancy and birthrates exist currently among these countries. Among developed countries, adolescent pregnancy rates range from a low of 12 per 1,000 in the Netherlands to a high of 100 per 1,000 in the Russian Federation. Japan and most Western European nations have adolescent pregnancy rates lower than 40 per 1,000.

Developmental Tasks of Adolescence
Despite these declines in adolescent birthrates in the United States and in other developed countries, adolescent childbearing still presents a substantial problem when it occurs. In the current social context, adolescent childbearing can interfere with the successful completion of the normal developmental tasks of adolescence, such as education, movement toward economic self-sufficiency, and the renegotiation of family relations and establishment of new social relations.

Education. The completion of formal schooling and successful entry into the job market may be compromised by early pregnancies, childbearing, and child rearing. The overall declines in early childbearing may be linked to the increased importance of education and the desire of young people to attain higher levels of education. For many young women, education is a more central and more immediate goal than motherhood.

Adolescents need to be motivated to prevent pregnancy. In addition to information about contraception and access to contraceptives, they need strong reasons to delay childbearing. As the Children's Defense Fund puts it, the "best contraceptive is a real future." Without other competing life goals, such as education, adolescents may see childbearing and motherhood as their major goals.

Educational attainment has increased for adolescents who have children as it has for adolescents in general. Adolescent child bearers today have higher educational attainment than adolescent child bearers in the past. Adolescent mothers who have the worst educational outcomes are those who drop out of school before their first birth. Another critical factor related to lower educational attainment for adolescent mothers is having a second birth.

Economic Self-Sufficiency. The increase in the years of formal schooling means an extended period of economic and social dependency for adolescents in general. A complex question is whether adolescent childbearing causes economic disadvantage and dependency, at a time in the life span when individuals should be moving toward economic self-sufficiency. An alternative possibility is that poverty leads to adolescent childbearing. For low-income women, early childbearing may present no more adverse consequences than those associated with poverty. Studies show that outcomes are negative for low-income young women, even when they delay childbearing. For example, a comparison of adolescent mothers with their sisters who delayed childbearing until twenty years of age or later revealed few differences in educational attainment and in later economic outcomes. Thus, with socioeconomic status held constant, differences between adolescent child bearers and those who delay childbearing are greatly diminished or nonexistent. Reducing adolescent childbearing will not eliminate the effects of poverty. Preventing early childbearing may widen the pathways out of poverty, however, or at least not exacerbate the effects of poverty.

Social/Family Relationships. The formation of satisfying, mature close personal relationships may be jeopardized by early births and the demands of child rearing. Although not all outcomes are negative, adolescent childbearing changes the entire family system, creating new roles, such as grandparent, and new social and economic demands for all family members. In addition to renegotiating existing family and social relationships, adolescent child bearers also must master the parenting role with their own children.

Adolescent child bearers in contemporary society are unlikely to be married, in contrast to the 1950s, when the relatively high rate of births to adolescents was masked by the correspondingly high rate of early, stable marriages and relative economic prosperity. Despite the high value generally placed on marriage as the context for childbearing and child rearing, negative effects of marriage, such as interference with continued education, increased likelihood of subsequent pregnancies, inadequate economic resources of young husbands, divorce, and instability for the adolescent mother and child, may occur. A study of birth records for a midwestern state indicated that few African American adolescent mothers were married. Hispanic adolescent mothers were more likely to be married, and, for those who were married, educational attainment was lower than for their counterparts who were not married. Another study found that African American adolescent mothers were more likely to live with their parents, to stay in school, and to remain unmarried than were Caucasian and Hispanic adolescent mothers, who tended to leave the family of origin, drop out of school, and marry if they could.

Adolescent childbearing occurs in a social context in which adult women increasingly have babies out of wedlock. Adolescents account for a small percentage of unwed births in the United States. The decline in marriage rates and increase in out-of-wedlock births are not uniquely adolescent problems. Marriage may be a more appropriate choice for older than for younger adolescents. Only a small percentage of adolescents become pregnant or bear children at ages earlier than fifteen years. It should be noted, however, that there has been a decline in the age at which it is possible for a young adolescent to begin having children. The average age at which girls reach menarche is twelve and a half years. The changing biological timetable for sexual maturation has moved in the opposite direction from the preferred social timetable for childbearing and child rearing. Childbearing and child rearing now occur toward the end of the reproductive years, especially for affluent women. An enormous investment of societal resources has made it possible for older women to bear children safely. These medical resources are available to affluent women but not to women generally. The social norm that has evolved favors a late beginning for childbearing, carefully controlled childbearing, and few children.

The majority of adolescent child bearers report that they did not want to or plan to become pregnant. Adolescents need help making the decision to avoid pregnancy and taking active steps to prevent pregnancy. Parents, however, may be uncomfortable discussing sexuality and contraception with their children. Parents may be ambivalent about encouraging their adolescents to use contraceptives, thinking they might hasten the adolescents' sexual initiation. Because of adults' discomfort and uncertainty, adolescents may not have sufficient adult guidance and may turn to peers for information and advice. Adolescents may get less attention and guidance from adults at one of the times they need it most. Coercion or unwanted sexual behavior may occur in adolescents' relationships. Childhood sexual abuse, however, is not associated with increased likelihood of adolescent preg-

nancy, when other variables such as age at first intercourse and contraceptive use at first intercourse are considered. In addition, concern about HIV and AIDS may affect contraceptive use.

Romantic relationships surrounding adolescent childbearing may be short-lived. Some perspectives on adolescent child bearers' relationships, especially ethnographic work, incorporate a negative picture of the relationships that lead to adolescent childbearing. In this view of adolescent childbearing, young men father children to prove their virility and adolescent females want to get pregnant. This line of research provides examples of adolescent mothers' participation in a "baby club," in which they compete to have the most attractive, best-dressed children. According to this perspective, the adolescent mothers' interest is not sustained as the children become older and are no longer "cute." When their interest wanes, some researchers assert, adolescent mothers relinquish care of their children to their grandparents.

Becoming a grandmother can be especially difficult for a relatively young grandmother. Grandmothers may not always be able to provide the emotional and financial support adolescent mothers need. High levels of support may be needed and readily accepted by younger adolescents. The same high levels of support may not be needed by older adolescents and may be perceived as inappropriate interference or control.

Most fathers of children born to adolescent mothers are not themselves adolescents but are young adult males. Power differentials may exist in the relationships between adolescent females and young adult males. For adolescent males who become fathers, studies find few differences in cognitive functioning, socioemotional characteristics, or sexual knowledge, attitudes, and behaviors, in comparisons with adolescent males who are not fathers. Further, adolescent fathers typically do not live with the mother and baby and may have difficulty maintaining meaningful involvement in the rearing of the child. The involvement of fathers may not always be welcome by the adolescent mother and her family or by programs set up to assist adolescent mothers. Continued involvement of the father, however, is related to the adolescent mother's psychological and economic well-being.

The majority of adolescent mothers keep their babies rather than release them for adoption. There is great concern for the educational and developmental outcomes for the children of adolescent mothers. Adolescent childbearing often occurs in a social milieu of poverty and low educational attainment. Thus, the children of adolescent mothers may have a less than optimal rearing environment. These children, however, do not fare worse than other children reared in poverty. In addition, despite the stereotype of a repeated cycle of adolescent child bearers, generation after generation, the majority of daughters of adolescent mothers do not themselves become adolescent child bearers.

Diverse Outcomes for Adolescent Parents

Longitudinal research shows substantial variability in outcomes for adolescent mothers and their children. Although some adolescent mothers and their children fare relatively well, the prevention of early pregnancy remains an important goal. Because the United States has higher adolescent birthrates than other developed nations, it is instructive to examine policies and practices in those countries. Other developed countries that have lower rates of adolescent childbearing than the United States have more generous health and welfare benefits for their citizens and more widely available sex education and contraceptive services for adolescents.

Diane Scott-Jones

See also Abortion; Abstinence; Child-Rearing Styles; Contraception; Decision Making; Parenting Styles; Programs for Adolescents

References and further reading
Anderson, E. 1999. *Code of the Street: Decency, Violence, and the Moral Life of the Inner City.* New York: Norton.
Bachrach, C. A., C. C. Clogg, and D. R. Entwisle, eds. 1993. *Pathways to Childbearing and Childbirth Outcomes of Adolescent and Older Mothers* [Special issue]. *Journal of Research on Adolescence* 3, no. 4.
Caldwell, C. H., and T. C. Antonucci. 1997. "Childbearing during Adolescence: Mental Health Risks and Opportunities." Pp. 220–245 in *Health Risks and Developmental Transitions during Adolescence.* Edited by J. Schulenberg, J. L. Maggs, and K. Hurrelmann. New York: Cambridge University Press.
Coles, R. 1997. *The Youngest Parents.* New York: Norton.
Furstenberg, F. F., J. Brooks-Gunn, and S. P. Morgan. 1987. *Adolescent Mothers in Later Life.* New York: Cambridge University Press.
Rosenheim, M. K., and M. F. Testa, eds. 1992. *Early Parenthood and Coming of Age in the 1990s.* New Brunswick, NJ: Rutgers University Press.
Scott-Jones, D. 1993. "Adolescent Childbearing: Whose Problem? What Can We Do?" *Phi Delta Kappan* 75: 1–12.
Singh, S., and J. E. Darroch. 2000. "Adolescent Pregnancy and Childbearing: Levels and Trends in Developed Countries." *Family Planning Perspectives* 32: 14–23.

Teenage Parenting: Consequences

Adolescent sexual behavior, pregnancy and childbearing (particularly among unmarried adolescents) have been a societal, economic, and political concern for centuries. Today, teenage pregnancy is viewed as a major problem placing burden on all involved: teenagers, their children, and taxpayers. Currently, over 1 million teenage women under the age of twenty become pregnant every year in the United States, with one female teenager becoming pregnant every thirty-one seconds.

The percentage of American teenagers who are sexually active has increased in recent years, while the age of first intercourse has decreased. Currently, approximately 56 percent of females and 73 percent of males have had sexual intercourse before their eighteenth birthday, with the average age of first intercourse being seventeen years for females and sixteen years for males. The rates for unintended teenage pregnancy and nonmarital births have increased in part because of earlier puberty, later age of marriage, greater numbers of teenagers having sex, and lack of contraceptive use. Among the 1 million teenage pregnancies each year in America, just under one-half are to females aged seventeen and younger, with approximately half of the teenage pregnancies resulting in live births, 35 percent ending in induced abortion, and 14 percent resulting in a miscarriage or stillbirth.

Historical Trends in the United States

The birthrate among U.S. teens has fluctuated over the decades. Historically, after World War II, during the 1950s and 1960s, teen birthrates in the United States reached their highest levels. During the 1970s, a decline in birthrates occurred as a result of the legalization of abortion and the development of different contraceptive methods. Birthrates among teenagers declined from 66.2 percent in 1972 to 46.7 percent in 1982, with the legalization of abortion occurring in 1973. From 1986 until 1991, overall birthrates rose steadily. Among 15–19 year old females, the birthrate rose from 50 (in 1986) to 62 (in 1991) per 1,000 females. Between 1991 and 1996, the birthrates declined 12 percent, however, the rate in 1996 (54.7 per 1,000) was still higher than in 1980. Currently, the United States has the highest rate of teenage pregnancies and births compared to other westernized countries. This has been a consistent pattern; for example, in 1988 and 1992, the United States had 53 and 61 births per 1,000 teen pregnancies (born to females ages 15 to 19 years old), as compared with Japan, which had 4 births per 1,000 teen pregnancies for both years, while in the Netherlands, there were 6 and 8 births, respectively.

Consequences for Teenage Mothers

A pregnant female can choose from the following options regarding her pregnancy: she can carry the child to term and choose to become a parent, have an abortion, or have the baby and give the baby up for adoption. The great majority of today's teenagers are choosing either to raise their child or to have an abortion (see entry on abortion for further information).

Teenage females who choose to give birth and raise their child face a multitude of consequences, both medically and psychologically. Medically, females who are younger than 17 years of age while pregnant have a higher incidence of medical complications than do adult women. Approximately one-third of pregnant teenagers receive inadequate prenatal care. Teenage mothers tend to have more obstetric problems (e.g., either inadequate or excessive weight gain,

Adolescent childbearing may interfere with the successful completion of developmental tasks of adolescence. (Shirley Zeiberg)

pregnancy-induced hypertension, ane-mia), which arise from various intercon-nected factors, including poverty, lack of prenatal care, and poor nutrition.

In addition to the medical complica-tions a teen mother may face, her future educational and occupational prospects are likely to decline as well. Adolescent mothers are less likely to complete school or to do so on time, be employed, or make high wages, and are more likely to live in persistent poverty, become wel-fare dependent, have larger families, and become single parents. Interestingly, it should be noted that many of these con-sequences are not a direct result of the pregnancy, but may have been character-istics of the mother or her social environ-ment prior to the birth. For example, a

majority of the teenagers were living in poverty at the time of birth, or they had a history of poor academic performance prior to birth and had either already dropped out or were at high risk of drop-ping out of high school. However, recent research findings suggest that with age, many women who were teenage mothers fare better than previously hoped. In long-term follow-up studies of teenage mothers, most had completed high school (approximately 70 percent by the time the mothers are 35 to 39 years old), moved off public assistance, and many had secure and stable employment.

Consequences for Teenage Fathers
Although most of the research on conse-quences of teenage pregnancy and child-

bearing has focused on the teenage mother, virtually little research has been conducted on the teenage fathers. Research has found that many fathers of children born to teenage women tend to be two to three years older than the women, with many being older than twenty years of age. It is hard to get an accurate estimate of the number of teenage fathers as well as the consequences they may experience for a number of reasons. Teenage fathers tend not to live with their children, and may not know or deny that they are fathers, leading to an underreporting of teenage fatherhood.

Consequences for Children of Teenage Mothers

Children born to adolescent mothers run the risk of many health and psychological problems. Infants of teen mothers (particularly mothers under sixteen years of age) are more likely to be born prematurely and with a low birth weight (two times the rate of infants born to adults), which is a big contributor to infant mortality, morbidity, and future health problems. Within the first twenty-eight days of life, infants of teen mothers are three times more likely to die than infants born to older mothers. These threats to the infants' health typically are not the result of the mother's actual age, but are results of factors associated with the mother being young, such as inadequate prenatal care, poor nutrition, or substance use.

Future consequences of teenage pregnancy on the children include an increased risk for future developmental delays, academic difficulties (e.g., school failure or withdrawal), behavior problems, substance use, and unplanned pregnancy as a teenager. Many of the same factors associated with teenage preg-nancy and childbirth also influence the children, often supporting intergenerational transmission of risk factors for teenage pregnancy such as poverty or low academic attainment.

Consequences for Taxpayers

Teen pregnancy has huge economic and social costs as well. Young unmarried women seventeen years or younger are more likely to go on public assistance and to spend more years on welfare once enrolled. It is estimated that taxpayers pay nearly $7 billion per year for the costs of births to adolescents, which includes Aid to Families with Dependent Children, Medicaid, and food stamps. These costs do not include additional support to families and children provided by social services, protective services, and education for the young mother.

What Can Be Done?

There have been many prevention and intervention programs developed to address the issue of teenage pregnancy in the United States, most programs focusing on the adolescent female. These programs primarily fall into five categories, those which: (1) teach about sex and/or HIV, (2) improve access to contraception, (3) are sexual education programs focusing on parent-child communication, (4) involve multiple components, and (5) focus on youth development. Everyone, from parents and adolescents to government and social agencies, must be involved in these prevention programs in order to make them a success, with the ultimate goal of curbing teenage pregnancy and helping America's teens remain healthy and successful.

Christine M. Lee
Jennifer L. Maggs

See also Abortion; Abstinence; Decision Making; High School Equivalency Degree; School Dropouts; Single Parenthood and Low Achievement; Welfare

References and further reading
Alan Guttmacher Institute. 1994. *Sex and America's Teenagers.* New York: Alan Guttmacher Institute.
American Academy of Pediatrics. 1999. "Adolescent Pregnancy—Current Trends and Issues: 1998." *Pediatrics* 103, no. 2: 516–520.
Centers for Disease Control. 1997. "State-Specific Pregnancy Rates among Adolescents—United States, 1990–1996." *MMWR* 46: 837–842.
Emilio, J. D., and E. B. Freedman. 1997. *Intimate Matters: A History of Sexuality in America.* Chicago: University of Chicago Press.
Kirby, D. 1997. *No Easy Answers: Research Findings on Programs to Reduce Teen Pregnancy.* Washington, DC: National Campaign to Prevent Teen Pregnancy.
Moore, K. A., and N. Snyder. 1994. *Facts at a Glance.* Annual newsletter on teen pregnancy. Washington, DC: Child Trends.
Moore, K. A., B. W. Sugland, C. Blumenthal, D. Glei, and N. Snyder. 1995. *Adolescent Pregnancy Prevention Programs: Interventions and Evaluations.* Washington, DC: Child Trends.
Stevens-Simons, C., and E. R. McAnarney. 1996. "Adolescent Pregnancy." In *Handbook of Adolescent Health Risk Behavior.* Edited by R. J. DiClimente, W. B. Hansen, and L. E. Ponton. New York: Plenum Press.
Stevens-Simons, C., and M. White. 1991. "Adolescent Pregnancy." *Pediatric Annals* 20: 322–331.

Television

With the exception of the Internet, television is the newest medium of all of our media. Newspapers, magazines, and radios were all vehicles for transporting information that existed before the television was invented. Its introduction into mainstream society forever revolutionized the way people could see the world and the events occurring around them.

There is not one person in particular who is credited with inventing television. Rather, there were many discoveries from many people in many places all over the world that led to the creation of television as we know it today. Similarly, it is somewhat unclear when the first display of television occurred. Many individuals and many companies made the claim that they were the first to produce a successful demonstration of television. For example, the *New York Times* reported on April 7, 1927, that American Telephone and Telegraph (AT&T) had successfully transmitted a speech by the secretary of commerce, Herbert Hoover, from Washington, D.C., to the Bell Laboratories in New York. Apparently, the newspaper had ignored the accomplishments of a scientist in England named John Logie Baird, who had given some successful demonstrations of his own some time before the AT&T demonstration. However, the *New York Times* cannot be blamed for poor reporting. It was fairly common practice at that time for each company in each country to boldly proclaim that they had given the first successful demonstration of television in history.

Television did not reach the American public until 1939. At that time, however, very few Americans actually owned a television set. Because of the fact that television broadcasting had not been perfected, and also because of the high prices of television sets at the time, the American public was not very interested in television. In an attempt to combat these problems, the government allowed for commercial television programming to begin in July 1941. However, with the onset of World War II, television for commercial purposes took a backseat to television for

High levels of media use are associated with some problems in adolescent behavior and development, but for the vast majority of youth the media has no long-term detrimental effects. (Michael Pole/Corbis)

military purposes. Many laboratories were working on ways to use television to guide missiles and spy on distant locations. After the war, television sales were still unimpressive at best. In 1947, there were only 60,000 television sets in the country (Boddy in Smith, 1998).

By the 1950s, America was ready for television. Sales skyrocketed, with more than 3 million television sets sold in the first six months of 1950 alone (Boddy in Smith, 1998)! By the end of the decade, nine out of ten homes had a television set (Baughman, 1997). The reason for this astronomical boost in sales can be attributed to both the good state of the economy as well as a decrease in the cost of television sets. However, perhaps even a more significant reason for the increase in television sales was the migration of much of the population away from the cities and into the suburbs. Television now provided people in the suburbs with entertainment in the comfort of their own homes. This was a mixed blessing of sorts for the television industry. On one hand, television sales were booming. Advertisers were eager to sponsor programs and the networks were eager to sell them airtime. On the other hand, television stations had to be very careful in determining what shows were appropriate for a family-based audience. This is, of course, a problem that still exists with television today.

Determining what was acceptable material for television programs was just one of the many problems that arose as television gained popularity. Many critics felt that the time that people would spend watching television would take away from time that could be spent doing more productive or educational things. Similarly, many people in radio and the movies feared that the time that people had spent listening to the radio or going to the movies would now be spent watching television. Unfortunately for them, this was exactly the case. The older media had to adapt to find new, receptive audiences. As a result, radio stations played more music in an attempt to attract the teenage audience. In addition, radios were installed in cars. Moviemakers had the even greater dilemma of convincing people who were now residing in suburbs to leave the comfort of their homes and travel to the cities to watch movies. In order to do so,

moviemakers produced films with spectacular scenes, such as Moses parting the Red Sea in the film *The Ten Commandments*. In addition, drive-in theaters began to pop up throughout the suburbs. If people were not going to go to the movies, the moviemakers were going to try to bring the movies to them.

As television grew increasingly more popular, researchers began to wonder what kind of effects television was having on society. In many cases the results are quite shocking. One famous study examined how the murder rate changed over the first ten years of television in three different countries: the United States, Canada, and South Africa. The results of the study showed that murder rates increased in all three countries after the first decade of television's inception in that country. It should be noted that these results do not mean that television was a direct cause in any given murder. There are other factors that could have influenced the results of the study as well. For example, it is possible that gun sales increased as well. However, one can state that the introduction of television was *correlated* with an increase in murder rates in the three countries.

Researchers also became interested in how violence on television effected children viewers. A revealing study not only demonstrated that the amount of violence children saw on television was highly correlated with how aggressive they were in adolescence, but that the reverse was also true (i.e., one could assess how much television violence these adolescents had seen by assessing how aggressive the adolescents were).

As was previously mentioned, many researchers were curious as to how time spent watching television replaced time that people used to spend doing other things. One study in Canada examined children from three communities that differed in how many television stations they received. The first community, which the researchers called Notel, had no television reception; the second community, Unitel, received one television station; the third community, Multitel, received several television stations. A particularly important finding from this study is that second- and third-grade children from Notel scored better on reading tests than children in Unitel, who in turn scored better on the tests than children in Multitel. In addition, once television did arrive in Notel, the children of that community no longer scored higher on the reading tests. These findings suggest that television viewing can have a negative effect on reading skills (though they do not suggest exactly how).

Many studies have specifically targeted how television effects the adolescent audience. Researchers find this age group to be particularly important to study because adolescents go through the process of discovering who they are as an individual. Given that television is a highly accessible and influential medium, it follows that adolescents could incorporate messages suggested in television into their personal identity. This is the very goal of many advertisers. If an advertiser can make a television viewer identify with the actors in an ad, then they hope that the viewer will use the same detergent as the actor or wear the same pants. While these are two harmless examples of how television might influence a viewer, consider the following studies. The first examined the effects of alcohol use in television shows and in ads on adolescents. Although the amount of alcohol consumption on TV has decreased since the 1980s, a large percentage of the public

believes that alcohol advertising is a major contributor to underage drinking. The study confirmed the public's concern by finding that many adolescents believe that people of influence and status, like those depicted in television shows and ads, drink alcohol and that drinking is a symbol of adulthood. It should be noted, however, that other studies have found such factors as parents' and peers' attitudes toward drinking to be more important predictors of future drinking than exposure to alcohol advertising.

A second study examined the role of television in adolescent women's dissatisfaction with their bodies and their drive for thinness. The study found that the amount of television watched did not effect body dissatisfaction, but watching certain programs did. Soap operas and movies, specifically, predicted body dissatisfaction, and women who watched music videos had a higher drive for thinness than those who did not.

Although these studies warn us of the negative effects of television, there is no doubt that television has had a positive impact on society, too. Television allows us all to see places we might never visit, to keep up with events all over the nation and the world, and even gives us glimpses into the depths of space. Its images are often so powerful that people remember them forever. Neil Armstrong's walk on the moon, the explosion of the *Challenger*, the tearing down of the Berlin Wall; these are all events that captured the attention of a nation and the world.

There have been attempts to make television more educational as well. Thus far, much of the effort to make television more educational has come in children's television. While the Notel study mentioned previously showed that television can have a negative impact on reading skills, television programs implemented for educational purposes can benefit children. *Sesame Street, Mister Rogers' Neighborhood,* and *Blue's Clues* are all among the more popular educational programs. These three programs are a reflection of how much progress has been made in trying to get more educational television programming on the air. *Sesame Street* has now been on the air for over thirty years, and continues to be popular. Along with *Sesame Street, Mister Rogers' Neighborhood* appears on public broadcasting. Appearing on public broadcasting allows for the programs to receive federal funding as well as contributions from grants and individual donors. Because public broadcasting receives this financial support, shows like *Sesame Street* can be presented without the influence of any commercial agencies. This is an important point to realize because one of the many dilemmas that has emerged in the past few decades is how commercial-based networks can be regulated to provide more educational programming to their audience. Success in this task had been minimal until recently. However, things have changed. Nickelodeon, which is not federally funded, has taken it upon itself to provide more educational programming. The network has implemented many previously unimaginable techniques for improving the quality of its educational programming. For example, *Blue's Clues* repeats the same exact episode for one entire week. While many networks would consider this lack of variety to be the kiss of death for any show, Nickelodeon has stood behind its show, claiming that research shows that children need repetition, practice, and reinforcement to best absorb the material they are learning on television. The success of *Blue's Clues* and Nickelodeon's efforts could inspire other networks to consider taking more chances with educational programming.

Another promising educational direction that television can now take is through its inevitable convergence with the Internet. With the technological advances that have been made in recent years, it is anticipated that people will soon be able to watch television and surf the Web on the same screen. It would seem that this convergence would allow for the development of some innovative new programming that can combine the resources of the Internet with those of television. Exactly how this will be done and the precise effects it will have on society remain to be seen.

Jason Sidman

See also Appearance, Cultural Factors in; Media; Television, Effects of; Violence; Youth Culture

References and further reading

Baughman, James L. 1997. *The Republic of Mass Culture: Journalism, Filmmaking, and Broadcasting.* Baltimore: Johns Hopkins University Press.
Centerwall, Brandon S. 1989. "Exposure to Television as a Risk Factor for Violence." *American Journal of Epidemiology* 129, no. 4: 643–652.
Fisher, David E. 1996. *Tube: The Invention of Television.* Washington, DC: Counterpoint.
Smith, Anthony, ed. 1998. *Television: An International History.* Oxford; New York: Oxford University Press.

Television, Effects of

Although the influence of media on youth behavior and development continues to be a topic attracting social and political debate, the data indicate that most forms of media have no major, enduring effects on the vast majority of youth. Put another way, current research indicates that only some youth, under specific circumstances, are influenced by exposure to the media.

A more specific finding is that levels of television viewing have only a small influence on adolescents' leisure reading, completion of homework assignments, school achievement, and physical and social activities. However, high levels of viewing can have some dramatic effects on these activities.

For example, extensive television viewing is associated with lowered school achievement, obesity, and decreased involvement in academic and extracurricular activities. First, although results from about two dozen studies of the association between television watching and school achievement indicate that there is virtually no overall relation between these two domains of youth behavior, A. C. Huston and J. C. Wright (1998) have found that lowered achievement does occur when adolescents spend thirty or more hours a week watching television—that is, when their amount of television viewing approaches the time devoted to many full-time jobs! Second, a longitudinal study of youth by W. H. Dietz and S. L. Gortmaker (1985) has found that early-life television viewing is linked to obesity in adolescence. And, third, M. Myrtek and colleagues (1996) have found that between sixth and eighth grades, high levels of television viewing are related to lower participation in organized school and community groups, decreased reading, diminished activities outside the home, completion of less homework, and reduced interest in hobbies.

High levels of TV viewing are associated with other problematic behaviors as well. For instance, researchers have found that adolescents' engagement in passive leisure activities such as television viewing is greater than their participation in active leisure activities such as playing a sport. The boredom generated by television viewing is associated with drug use and delinquency. Watching rock music videos is related to permissive sexual attitudes and behaviors, especially among girls with problematic family relationships. And television viewing in general is associated with socially and politically authoritarian attitudes, especially among youth from higher socio-economic backgrounds.

In sum, media are a major part of the life of most youth. Although high levels of media use are associated with problems in adolescent behavior and development, for the vast majority of youth the media have no pervasive or long-term detrimental effects. It will be important, however, to revisit this conclusion as more research is conducted about the possible influences of new and emerging media (e.g., interactive television) on youth development.

Richard M. Lerner

See also Appearance, Cultural Factors in; Attractiveness, Physical; Body Image; Computers; Television; Violence

References and further reading
Dietz, W. H., and S. L. Gortmaker. 1985. "Do We Fatten Our Children at the Television Set? Obesity and Television Viewing in Children and Adolescents." *Pediatrics* 75: 807–812.
Huston, A. C., and J. C. Wright. 1998. "Mass Media and Child Development." In *Handbook of Child Psychology*. Vol. 3, *Child Psychology in Practice*. Edited by I. E. Sigel and K. Renninger. New York: Wiley.
Lerner, Richard M. In press. *Adolescence: Development, Diversity, Context, and Application*. Upper Saddle River, NJ: Prentice-Hall.
Myrtek, M., C. Scharff, G. Brugner, and W. Muller. 1996. "Physiological, Behavioral and Psychological Effects Associated

with Television Viewing in Schoolboys: An Exploratory Study." *Journal of Early Adolescence* 16, no. 3: 301–323.

Temperament

Temperament serves as a source of individuality in children, and continues to play a role in adolescence. The characteristic ways that children approach and engage their world are often referred to as temperament. By understanding how temperaments, or predispositional qualities, function, we may know more about how adolescents will react to emotional events, handle stressors, or adapt to a new situation. Adolescence is characterized by rapid socioemotional growth in many areas, including cognitive development, physical maturation, expansion of interpersonal relationships, and emotional growth. Within developmental psychology, the role of temperament as a main contributor to social and emotional development has advanced our understanding of adolescence.

Temperament reflects differences in an individual's behavioral style or tendencies. Although there is no single definition of temperament, there is general agreement on a number of central criteria that define it. Temperament qualities emerge early in life, are relatively stable across time, vary among individuals, and have a hereditary basis. One perspective considers temperament as relatively stable, primarily biologically based, individual differences in *reactivity* and *regulation*. Reactivity refers to physiological arousal (e.g., increased heart rate) and displays of emotionality. Levels of reactivity correspond to responses of the autonomic and central nervous systems and responses of the endocrine system. Reactivity is typically measured with respect to

the intensity of a reaction and/or the time to recover from a challenging or stressful event. Self-regulation refers to internal processes that work to inhibit or promote physiological reactivity. Self-regulatory processes may include attention, self-soothing behaviors, and approach or avoidance behaviors.

Temperament is reflected in the ways children experience, react, and cope with issues of adolescence. For example, due to the underlying temperamental characteristics associated with a highly reactive temperament, anxious adolescents may be predisposed to experience extreme feelings of fear or anxiety, together with the accompanying bodily responses of increases in heart rate or blood pressure, in response to a stressful event. A stressful event may be defined as having to speak in front of a class or trying to approach an unfamiliar group of peers to make friends. However, there is not always a perfect relationship between *psychological experiences* (how tense an adolescent may feel or how fearful he perceives a situation to be) and *physiological reactivity* (increases in heart rate or blood pressure) for all adolescents, as differences exist among individuals, even within a group of anxious adolescents.

Temperament is often described in terms of types or profiles, with respect to different constellations of behaviors. The behavioral qualities that are often mapped onto temperament are emotion, attention, and activity. One major distinction between types contrasts *easy* and *difficult* temperaments. The former refers to such behaviors as ease of adaptability and positive approach, whereas the latter refers to such characteristics as negative emotionality and being socially demanding. For adolescents these broad categories may be expressed with a range of behaviors. For example, positive moods and ease in approaching and meeting new people may characterize an easy temperament, whereas a difficult temperament may be expressed as rigidity in adapting to the demands of a situation, or negative moods. It should be recognized that some researchers have criticized the construct of difficult temperament. Although the term may classify a certain profile of behaviors and adjustment style, it may neglect the parent's own point of view of his or her child, namely that a parent may not experience the child as "difficult." Furthermore, the construct has not always accounted for the fact that the behaviors may be more appropriate in a certain context (e.g., interacting with a stranger).

The term *goodness of fit* reflects the idea that development occurs in part as a result of interactions between an individual and her social environment. Thus, optimal development occurs when there is an appropriate fit between an adolescent's characteristics (e.g., temperamental predisposition) and her environment and its demands (e.g., caretaking style). For adolescents, their behavior is often an expression of their underlying temperament. Thus, when others respond positively to this behavior and provide appropriate feedback, they may promote positive interactions and thus healthy development and adaptation. In contrast, if these behavioral expressions do not match well with the environment, or they do not meet behavioral expectations, the resulting interaction may be negative and developmentally maladaptive.

As an illustration, adolescents who are extremely inhibited may have difficulty asserting themselves appropriately in intense social situations. They may develop peer relationship problems due

Temperament refers to a person's behavioral style, and is reflected in how young people approach their world, their intensity of reactions, and their mood. (Skjold Photographs)

to difficulties interacting in social situations, or they may develop academic difficulties if they are too inhibited to seek necessary assistance in a busy classroom. Furthermore, an adolescent with an active, social, and excitable temperament may fit better and have less conflict with a social and highly charged family, rather than with a less demonstrative family. That varying temperament types thrive differently, depending upon the environment, demands, or expectations with which they are matched, may even be seen within a single family. Due to the individual differences in temperamental dispositions, two siblings raised in the same household, by the same parents, may have very different reactions to the same parenting style. Therefore, caregivers (e.g., parents, teachers) need to be sensitive and appropriately responsive to children's temperament, as their reactions serve to shape children's subsequent development.

Furthermore, evidence for the importance of this fit between temperament and environment begins at an early age. For example, excessive input from the family environment was associated with lower cognitive development for difficult infants. In contrast, for easy infants more social input was associated with higher cognitive development. In addition, *high active* toddlers had better outcomes when their families were lower in stimulation intensity, whereas that was opposite the case for *low active* toddlers.

Finally, although temperament is often thought to be a precursor to personality, and as adolescents develop there is often more reference to their personality than to their temperament, they remain distinct concepts. Temperament should be understood to be qualitatively different from personality, as temperament emphasizes the dynamics and energy of responsiveness. Temperament encompasses constitutionally based individual differences in reactions and behavior, and functions at both the biological and behavioral level. Personality, on the other hand, refers to the relatively permanent traits, dispositions, or characteristics within an individual, and the concept implies a relative degree of consistency in how an individual deals with these traits and social experiences. The more that is known about possible outcomes associated with the interaction of temperamental traits and environment, the better the

understanding of adjustment problems for adolescents.

Christine M. Low

See also Anxiety; Coping; Developmental Assets; Identity; Personality; Self; Shyness

References and further reading
Buss, Arnold H., and Robert Plomin. 1975. *A Temperament Theory of Personality Development.* New York: Wiley.
Derryberry, Douglas, and Mary K. Rothbart. 1985. "Emotion, Attention, and Temperament." Pp. 132–166 in *Emotion, Cognition, and Behavior.* Edited by Carroll E. Izard, Jerome Kagan, and Robert Zajonc. New York: Cambridge University Press.
Goldsmith, H. Hill, Arnold Buss, Robert Plomin, Mary Rothbart, Alexander Thomas, Stella Chess, Robert Hind, and Robert McCall. 1987. "Roundtable: What Is Temperament? Four Approaches." *Child Development* 58: 505–529.
Kohnstamm, Gedolph A., John E. Bates, and Mary K. Rothbart, eds. 1995. *Temperament in Childhood.* UK: Wiley.
Thomas, Alexander, and Stella Chess. 1977. *Temperament and Development.* New York: Brunner/Mazel.

Thinking

Adolescence is a transition period between childhood and adulthood in a number of different ways. One very important way has to do with thinking. Thinking comes to play a more significant role in the lives of most teens than it did when these teens were children. Teens are capable of more complex kinds of thinking than are children. For example, they can readily engage in what is called *counterfactual* thinking, or imagining a course of events counter to reality, such as, "If I hadn't gone along with the other kids, this wouldn't have happened."

Teens are also likely to spend more of their free time engaged in thinking than do children. Some of this may be the brooding that comes with the task of constructing a personal identity: "Why did she look at me like that?" "How should I act with that group?" But much of this thinking serves a critical purpose, since teens differ from children in another way: They have more freedom to make decisions than do children. Some of these decisions, such as choice of clothing or music, may not be consequential in the long run, but many decisions that teens are faced with—decisions about the choice of friends, about alcohol, drugs, or sex—could have life-or-death consequences, for others as well as themselves.

Teens not only have greater freedom than do children in deciding what they will do. They also have greater opportunity to decide what they will believe. This new potential raises some basic questions: How do such decisions get made, and what kinds of thinking underlie them? Does more thinking, or certain kinds of thinking, lead to better decisions? Is thinking worth the effort it entails, or do the choices people make and the beliefs they hold turn out to be just as good without it? Is it important to know *why* one holds beliefs, to be able to support those beliefs with good, thoughtful arguments? Or is it enough just to be clear about *what* one believes? To put it a different way, are unexamined beliefs worth having?

It turns out that adult society holds conflicting views about teens' ability to think for themselves. Developmental psychologist David Moshman describes two U.S. Supreme Court decisions made about the same time. One sided with high school students who had been denied permission by their school to form a Bible study group, ruling that a school allowing extracurricular groups to meet

on its premises must extend this privilege to any such group. In another ruling, however, the Court upheld a high school principal's right to censor articles written by students for the school newspaper if the principal regards the article as "unsuitable for immature audiences." A similar ambivalence regarding the thinking of adolescents appears with respect to other important issues, such as whether teens who commit serious crimes should be tried as adults. Do teenagers have the privileges and responsibilities that follow from the ability to think as well as adults in deciding what to do or believe? Or do teens need special protection because of their "immature" thinking skills? The research evidence on this issue shows no striking differences between the thinking abilities of older adolescents and those of adults. It is important to keep in mind, however, that we can interpret this finding as a cup half full or half empty. Are teens as accomplished thinkers as adults, or do adults think as poorly as teens?

It is not only adults who show varied understandings of the thinking that teens may engage in. Teens themselves show this variation. Researchers who have studied the understandings that children, teens, and adults have about their own and others' thinking and knowing have found that these understandings change in predictable ways. At an early age, children hold the view that thoughts and assertions mirror an external reality. "It is impossible that I could hold a view that is incorrect." With time, children connect thoughts and assertions to the human minds that generate them, enabling them to comprehend the idea of a false belief. But knowing, at this point, remains a simple black-and-white affair: "If you and I disagree about something, it must be the case that one of us is right and one is wrong, and it is simply a matter of finding out which is which."

Next, and often during the adolescent years, comes the most striking and dramatic change in beliefs about knowing and thinking. In a word, now everyone is right. Knowledge becomes simply opinions, freely chosen by their holders, like pieces of clothing. As a result, they are not open to challenge. And from this belief comes the most treacherous step down a slippery slope: Because all have a right to their opinion, all opinions must be equally right. Tolerance for others' opinions, in other words, is confused with the inability to discriminate among them.

Only at the next, and most advanced, level of understanding do we see a coordination of the objective and subjective components of knowing. At this level, a person is able to acknowledge that knowing is necessarily uncertain, without abandoning the idea that knowledge claims can be evaluated with regard to their worthiness. Two people can both have legitimate positions on an issue—can both "be right"—but one can be more right than the other, to the extent that his position is better supported by argument and evidence. Although many teens have achieved this understanding, others will go through their entire adult lives as absolutists, who believe that all questions have simple right-or-wrong answers, or as multiplists, who believe that "anything goes."

These different ways of thinking about thinking have important consequences, for example, in the way teens approach their schoolwork. In the words of David Olson and Janet Astington, who have studied how teens understand texts, "The author must come to be seen (or imagined) as holding those beliefs for some reasons." Assertions in textbooks need to be understood as reasoned expressions of someone's beliefs, rather than as disembodied facts. One study (Paxton, 1997) showed that simply inserting expressions that make an author visible in the text (e.g., "I think" or "from my perspective") enhances high school students' evaluations of their textbooks.

Different ways of thinking about thinking also play an important role in teens' thinking outside of school. These implications have to do with their intellectual values, with whether they believe that thinking is worthwhile, that it will have productive consequences. Beliefs about an activity shape one's valuing of that activity, which in turn shapes one's disposition to engage in that activity (and hence likelihood of doing so). Someone may value drinking alcohol because she believes it enhances one's image among peers. This belief/value constellation greatly increases the likelihood that one will engage in the behavior. The same is true in the case of intellectual behavior, or thinking. If facts can be ascertained with certainty and are readily available to anyone who seeks them, as the absolutist understands, or if any claim is as valid as any other, as the multiplist understands, there is no point in expending the mental effort that the evaluation of claims entails. It is only at the evaluativist level of understanding, then, that thinking and reason are recognized to be an essential support for beliefs and action choices. Thinking is the only effective route that allows us to make choices between conflicting claims. Understanding this leads one to value thinking and to be willing to expend the effort that it entails.

Although valuing thinking is thus critical, it is not the whole story. Believing thinking is worthwhile does not by itself tell us how to do it well. Thinking develops into good thinking, and good thinking into better thinking, when it is exercised, frequently and vigorously. The analogy of developing an athletic skill is a useful one. It is also important, research has shown, that thinking be exercised in social contexts, that it be shared among peers. This has a number of benefits. One important benefit is simply making ideas explicit and clear, because of the need to communicate them to others. Another benefit of thinking as a social activity is the opportunity it affords to be exposed to other points of view. It is crucial to become aware that there *are* other reasonable views than one's own, as well as to learn what these view are. Examining and comparing alternative views on an issue, and the arguments that support each, offers valuable experience in the skills of coordinating theories and evidence. The same kinds of experience are relevant when the alternatives are action choices rather than assertions. Good personal decision making requires a thoughtful identification of *all* the choice options and the positive and negative consequences associated with each.

Many times, the same action choice can have different reasons supporting it. Two teenagers may decide to abstain from sexual activity for entirely different reasons. The implication is that one cannot assume to know the thinking that underlies an action based simply on the action itself. But this does not make thinking any less important to good decision making. Rather, it means that we must focus on the thinking that underlies a belief or action, rather than the belief or action itself.

Educational programs designed to teach decision-making skills to adolescents report some success. Still, it is not easy to become a careful, thoughtful decision

maker. A recent newspaper story (*New York Times* Science Times section, March 7, 2000), for example, reports about a study of the "Baby Think It Over" doll, designed to help young teens understand what parenting an infant is really like. The seven-pound doll bursts out in loud cries at intervals ranging from fifteen minutes to four hours, twenty-four hours a day. Three days of experience with the doll, the researchers found, did not alter the decisions that sixth- to eighth-grade girls from a neighborhood with a high teen pregnancy rate had made to become mothers by the age of twenty. In fact, the maternal intentions of 3 of the 109 girls became stronger as a result of the experience. And even those who found taking care of the surrogate baby harder than they expected expressed an unrealistic belief: Each of them believed her own child would be less trouble to care for. These girls appeared ready to take an action that would irrevocably change their lives in major ways, with little indication that careful, informed, and realistic thinking supported this decision.

Beliefs may be more reversible than actions, but it is not easy to change beliefs, even when much evidence exists to show that these beliefs are wrong. A good deal of psychological research shows that people cling to their beliefs in the face of disconfirming evidence. These findings point to the importance of helping teenagers to become as thoughtful about their own thinking as they can be. They need to know why they believe what they do, which they only do if they have examined the arguments and evidence supporting each of the positions on an issue and weighed them against each other. And they need to be ready to revise their thinking—and, as a result, their beliefs and actions—but only when the evidence warrants it. To change one's mind too readily, as a result of each new piece of input that comes along, is as detrimental as being too resistant to changing one's views.

In the end, the most important goal is to be in control of one's thinking. Adolescents want and need to feel that they are in control of themselves and their lives. Being watchful over and in control of one's thinking may be the most important component of the self-management that teens aspire to.

Deanna Kuhn
Wadiya Udell

See also Academic Self-Evaluation; Cognitive Development; Coping; Ethnocentrism; Gender Differences and Intellectual and Moral Development; Intelligence; Learning Styles and Accommodations; Memory; Self

References and further reading
Baron, Jonathan, and Rex V. Brown, eds. 1991. *Teaching Decision Making to Adolescents.* Mahwah, NJ: Erlbaum.
Kuhn, Deanna, and Michael Weinstock. In press. "What Is Epistemological Thinking and Why Does It Matter?" In *Epistemology: The Psychology of Beliefs about Knowledge and Knowing.* Edited by Barbara Hofer and Paul Pintrich. Mahwah, NJ: Erlbaum.
Kuhn, Deanna, Victoria Shaw, and Mark Felton. 1997. "Effects of Dyadic Interaction on Argumentive Reasoning." *Cognition and Instruction* 15: 287–315.
Moshman, David. 1993. "Adolescent Reasoning and Adolescent Rights." *Human Development* 36: 27–40.
Olson, David, and Janet Astington. 1993. "Thinking about Thinking: Learning How to Take Statements and Hold Beliefs." *Educational Psychologist* 28: 7–23.
Paxton, Robert. 1997. "'Someone with Like a Life Wrote It': The Effects of a Visible Author on High School History Students." *Journal of Educational Psychology* 89: 235–250.

Tracking in American High Schools

Tracking is a form of ability grouping that is found in most American public high schools. Ability grouping starts in elementary schools, often in the form of within-class grouping (e.g., high and low groups in reading or math within a single class). Tracking in high school is somewhat more structured, taking the form of between-class groupings that refer to the nature of the courses (e.g., honors, advanced, regular, remedial, or vocational). The importance of high school tracking is that the sequences of courses determine not only the content and quality of the learning experience but also the eligibility of the student for enrollment in four-year colleges and universities, with consequent implications for later career paths. The current tracking systems in high schools clearly do much to injure the life chances of those in the lower-track courses.

The meaning of high school enrollment has changed dramatically during the twentieth century. In the early years of that century, about 15 percent of the relevant age group attended high school, whereas at the end of the century over 80 percent graduated from high school (computed using U.S. Bureau of the Census data). Whereas enrollment in high schools was earlier limited primarily to middle- and upper-class students, today members of all social groups assume that secondary school enrollment should be required and available. The power of this movement toward mass education is best exemplified by the extent to which dropping out of high school is now viewed as a major national problem, at a time when dropping out is increasingly rare.

The United States was a world leader in the development of mass public secondary education, expressing a meritocratic ideology that equality in educational opportunities for different groups would lead to similar educational outcomes for those groups. The remaining individual differences in academic achievement would therefore reflect differences in merit. Differential rewards for differences in education would thus be appropriate and nondiscriminatory.

Sadly, the contemporary high schools of the United States provide little comfort for those who see the public school system as providing equality of educational opportunity. Racial, ethnic, and class differences in academic achievement are viewed by most observers as a major problem, and differences in the level of individual educational performance are often explained as a product of educational inequality of opportunity. The failure of tracking in American high schools is often described in terms of the perpetuation of inequality.

The educational system is linked to the system of social stratification in all modern societies. In earlier agricultural societies, parents passed on their wealth to their offspring through the inheritance of land and livestock. Today, the primary way in which most parents aid their children economically is by investing in their education. Thus, education is in part a mechanism for inheritance.

Although schooling is not the only factor leading to occupational attainment, it is the most important factor that parents feel they can directly influence on behalf of their children. This parental concern for education is not limited to the higher social classes. Lower-status parents' concern about education is typically equal to or greater than the concern of higher-status parents.

On the other hand, education is also viewed as crucial for social mobility. Access to education is viewed as providing an opportunity for those from less affluent backgrounds to improve their status, primarily because education is used as a rational means of selecting people to occupy higher occupational positions. Education serves, therefore, as a mechanism for both inheritance and mobility.

Indeed, credentialism in deciding who will enter higher positions in the occupational structure has dramatically increased the educational requirements for the better jobs in contemporary society. In personnel selection, having the appropriate level of education is often more important than having the appropriate level of skills. Since the payoff for higher education has markedly increased when compared with the payoff for graduation from high school, the distinction between curricula that are college preparatory and those that do not prepare for higher education has become even more important.

The nature of tracking in American high schools changed from 1965 to 1975. Prior to that period, students were assigned to a curricular grouping that determined most of the courses they would take during their high school years (e.g., college preparatory, general, vocational). After that period, students could enroll in courses that were discrepant from each other in the level of ability associated with each class. Theoretically, a student might enroll in the highest level of math class, by taking a calculus course, for example, while simultaneously taking a low-level English course. Most high schools now state that they do not track their students, since each student does not have an overall assignment to a particular level of courses. But the reality, despite numerous discrepancies, is that de facto tracking persists today in American high schools, and that many of the results of such tracking are similar to those found in the earlier period of overall curricular tracks.

The persistence of tracking is a reflection of an American stress on individual differences in ability. There are important national differences in the emphasis on ability or on effort. Asian schools, believing that almost all students can perform at a high level, emphasize student effort more than individual differences in ability. Teachers in Asian schools report that clarity of presentation is the primary characteristic of a good teacher.

In the United States, the relative emphasis on ability is much greater than in Asian countries. American teachers report that the essence of good teaching is understanding the individual differences among students. In the United States, variability in student performance is viewed as an obvious product of differences in ability.

Not surprisingly, students in Asian schools not only average better math performance than do American students, but Asian students also exhibit less variability in their math scores. Grading in the two countries is also influenced by the ideological emphasis on ability or effort. American teachers emphasize ability in their grading, sometimes awarding separate grades for effort. In Japan, teachers grade more often on improvements in demonstrated ability that indicate an increase in effort.

Almost all American public high schools track. Whether schools assign students into overall tracks or into ability levels on a course-by-course basis, what is taught and learned differs dramatically by track. Teachers take into account the ability levels of the students in each class, and the content of instruction varies accordingly. Not only do higher-level courses cover more material

than do lower-level courses, but the qualifications of teachers also vary. The best and most experienced teachers tend to be assigned to the higher-level courses and to be given greater resources, whereas beginning teachers are typically given lower-level courses to teach.

In addition, teachers of lower-track courses set lower academic standards for their students compared with teachers of higher-track courses. Well-intentioned teachers often feel they cannot expect much from students of low ability and, in a form of "racism without racists," demand and expect little from their students. The higher the track, the more learning occurs. Higher-track students gain at the expense of lower-track students. When teachers teach both lower-track and higher-track courses, they put more attention, concern, and effort into their teaching of college-track students. So those most in need of exceptional teaching are least likely to get it.

Educators generally assume that teaching classes that are relatively homogeneous in terms of ability will enable students to progress at a rate commensurate with their capacities. Prior school achievement is the strongest determinant of track placement. But critics of the tracking system argue that it serves as a mechanism for perpetuating ethnic and class divisions. Schools typically overestimate their ability to assess ability. Particularly among those in the middle level of ability, misassignment to a lower track is common. Not only is the possibility of improvement in performance reduced, but there are negative long-term consequences of such misassignment.

Even among students who expect to graduate from a four-year college and whose math skills are above the national average, many are assigned to lower-track math and science courses that make it almost impossible to enter a four-year college. Such misassignment is more likely when the student is from a disadvantaged minority or from a family with lower parental education. From this perspective, students are, in part, selected in terms of their social origins. In general, the noncollege tracks are predominantly filled with low-socioeconomic-status and disadvantaged minority students. An interesting exception to these tendencies is that assignment practices favor black students over nonblack students who are equal in school performance. A possible explanation is that most black students performed poorly in elementary school, largely as a result of poverty, segregation, and discrimination. The relatively few blacks who performed very well may be favored in order to redress the imbalance in assignments.

There is considerable overlap between measures of social origin, measures of ability, and track assignment. Students from advantaged families are more likely to have the cultural and social capital that leads to better school performance. Among those advantaged students whose performance is only average, parents are likely to engage in active management to make sure that their children are placed in a higher track. Parents are well advised in urging placement in the highest track that is potentially feasible for their child. There are also curricular differences at the level of entire schools. At the school level, when the school population is mainly composed of minority or low-status students, the proportion of lower-track courses is usually larger and the higher-track courses are less rigorous.

Some have reported that minority students in Roman Catholic schools perform better academically than minority students in public schools. One partial reason for this difference may be the structure of tracking within Catholic schools. Controlling for background characteristics, more students are in the college-preparatory track in Catholic schools than in the public schools, and more rigorous academic course work is required of students who are in the noncollege track in Catholic schools. Paradoxically, this improved result may be a function of the lack of financial resources in the Catholic schools. They are too poor to create a variegated curriculum that, for example, includes vocational courses, so they help their students by emphasizing the main college-prep curriculum.

Although there is considerable movement across track lines as students move through their high school years, the barrier between taking college-prep courses and other courses tends to be relatively less permeable. About 80 percent of all students end their high school years in the same general grouping, college-prep or noncollege-prep, as when they began their first year in high school (Dornbusch, Glasgow, and Lin, 1996). Being in the college-prep track leads to better academic achievements and greater occupational opportunities, even after controlling for prior school achievement and background characteristics. For above-average students (in the fiftieth to eightieth percentile on earlier standardized math scores), misassignment to lower-track math and science courses leads to a permanent loss of academic potential. Despite their high ability, they work less hard and learn less; seldom are they reassigned to the college-prep track.

It is clear that it is the lower-track students who pay the price for the current tracking system. Under that system, they learn less, develop attitudes that are less proschool, associate with more students who are antischool, and have lower educational expectations. Those students who are in the higher track either perform slightly better academically or, at least, do not suffer from being tracked. Since those in the higher track are typically of middle- or upper-class origin, powerful forces are at work to support the current system. Attempts at de-tracking schools have sometimes been successful, but, more typically, higher-status parents successfully support the status quo. Their children are perceived as advantaged by the current system, and they usually have much more political clout than do the parents of lower-track students.

Since the immediate overthrow of the tracking system is not a likely alternative in most high schools, some argue that the best feasible reform is to stress short-term remediation of specific deficiencies in skills. The advantage of such an approach is that each student can return to the mainstream class as quickly as possible, thus avoiding the disadvantages of long-term assignment to a lower track. Indeed, short-term remediation is likely to be more effective if instituted in the early grades, so that work habits and expectations are not diminished. Certainly, the persistence of the current tracking system, which leads to the loss of so much talent, is the source of a national tragedy.

Sanford M. Dornbusch

See also Academic Achievement; Academic Self-Evaluation; Cognitive Development; College; Intelligence; Intelligence Tests; Learning Disabilities; Learning Styles and Accommodations; Standardized Tests

References and further reading
Dornbusch, Sanford M., Kristan L. Glasgow, and I-Chun Lin. 1996. "The Social Structure of Schooling." Pp. 401–429 in *Annual Review of Psychology*, Vol. 47. Palo Alto, CA: Annual Reviews.
Lucas, Samuel R. 1999. *Tracking Inequality: Stratification and Mobility in American High Schools.* New York: Teachers College Press.
Oakes, Jeannie. 1985. *Keeping Track: How Schools Structure Inequality.* New Haven, CT: Yale University Press.

Transition to Young Adulthood

As the end of the adolescent period draws near, a new stage of development—young adulthood—presents its own challenges. The challenges for the person involve making choices about aspirations, careers, and relationships that serve both the needs of the individual and the needs of society. We must also keep in mind that the cultural setting of the adolescent influences these choices.

The transition from late adolescence to young adulthood may be especially problematic for contemporary young people. That is, the challenges of the young adult transition may be especially acute because, in modern society, there is an increasing delay between the attainment of physical maturity and the assumption of adult responsibilities. This gap creates a change in the period of dependency of youth on adults. Moreover, modern society is marked by a diversity of developmental paths (e.g., involving different career possibilities, some of which—such as software designer, e-commerce specialist, or manufacturer of digital television equipment—did not exist in earlier historical periods), and this diversity makes the achievement of adult independence more complicated. Different adult responsibilities (completion of career training, establishing an intimate adult relationship, establishing one's own home, paying off one's educational loans) are increasingly segmented and separated across chronological periods.

Complicating this transition still further is a relative lack of funding, public support, or public policies and programs facilitating the transition to adulthood for the half of the adolescent population that moves directly from secondary school to full-time work, that is, the half that does not go on to college from high school. College gives youth a slower transition to adulthood; it provides a "safe haven to experiment with a variety of adult behaviors, values, and life styles; the developmental opportunities provided by this privilege are not well explored, but that half of the population not attending college may be missing more than continued academic achievement" (Sherrod, Haggerty, and Featherman, 1993, p. 219).

The presence of a safe haven may be quite useful for adolescents making the transition to young adulthood. If there were problems of personal adjustment and/or of social relationships in high school, the transition to adulthood might provide an opportunity to get back on track.

For example, in a study of students randomly selected from three public schools in the Boston, Massachusetts, area, Susan Gore and colleagues found that relations with parents improved across the transition to adulthood, and these enhanced relations were associated with lower depressed mood and less delinquency among the youth. In addition, and also suggestive of using the transition to adulthood to get back on a healthy developmental track, among high school graduates prior mental health and behavior problems were not substantially related to posttransition mental and behavioral functioning, suggesting that graduation from high school may have given youth the chance to break away from the troubles of their past.

However, not all explorations of possible life tracks during the transition to young adulthood might be beneficial to youth. One problematic path is having babies out of wedlock. Not only are poor women more likely to have such births but also out-of-wedlock childbearing during late adolescence is associated with poverty after the transition to parenthood.

On the other hand, the presence of developmental problems, even chronic ones, need not preclude the achievement of a successful transition to young adulthood. A large national study by Steven Gortmaker and colleagues provides a dramatic illustration of this point. Of the youth who participated in the study, 1.9 percent were identified as having a chronic physical health condition between the ages of fourteen and twenty-one years. These conditions involved such disorders as asthma, anomalies of the spine, diabetes mellitus, rheumatoid arthritis, epilepsy, cerebral palsy, scoliosis, congenital heart anomalies, eye, lower limb, or foot anomalies, muscular dystrophy, and sickle-cell anemia. Although youth who had very severe chronic health conditions had substantial limitations in their transitions to adulthood, such severely debilitating conditions were rare. The great majority of chronically physically challenged youth made successful transitions to adulthood.

Getting back on track during the transition to young adulthood may be influenced by events in earlier developmental periods, that is, by the *antecedents* of the transition. In turn, the degree to which the person functions well during the transition to young adulthood has consequences for behavior and development in later life.

In regard to the antecedents of behavior during the transition to young adulthood, in a twenty-year follow-up of the children of African American teenage mothers, Jeanne Brooks-Gunn and colleagues studied the factors related to success in completing high school and in pursuing education beyond high school. Among the participants in the study, 37 percent had dropped out of high school, 46 percent had completed high school, and 17 percent had gone on to postsecondary education. Completion of high school was associated with the number of years the father was present in the life of the girl, high maternal educational aspirations in the child's first year of life, being prepared for school, and not repeating a grade in elementary school. In turn, continuing education beyond high school was related to few years on welfare, high cognitive ability in preschool, attending a preschool, and no grade failures in elementary school.

Research has found that failure to complete high school is associated with psychological dysfunction in young adulthood. In addition, unemployment during the transition to adulthood is related to a greater tendency to pursue gender-typical adult roles. For instance, young women who are unemployed during the transition have a higher probability than do other women of staying at home with children.

In addition to behaviors associated with high school completion and employment during the transition, behaviors associated with interpersonal relationships during this period can have later-life influences. For example, Allan Horowitz and Helen White found that cohabitation dur-

ing the transition to young adulthood may be linked to some later-life problems. In their longitudinal study of unmarried young adults who were assessed when they were eighteen, twenty-one, or twenty-four years of age and then retested seven years later, when they were twenty-five, twenty-eight, or thirty-one years old, respectively, cohabitation during the first assessment period was not related to depression at the time of the second assessment. However, men who had cohabited during the first assessment reported more alcohol problems than did men who were single or married at the time; similarly, women who had cohabited reported more alcohol problems than did women who were married during the first assessment.

On a more positive note, having children or being married during the transition to adulthood is associated with having family-related goals. The presence of these goals is related to both additional transitions in the family (e.g., having additional children) and feelings of well-being.

As is true for other aspects of youth development, the family appears to have a major influence on the nature of the transition to young adulthood and, as well, on behavior later in adult life. For example, a more prestigious vocational background of grandparents is related to higher educational levels among parents, which, in turn, is associated with both greater high school academic success and the attainment of gender-atypical careers.

Educational attainment and healthy ego development in young adulthood are related to mothers and fathers behaving in ways that both promote autonomy in their adolescents and maintain their relatedness to the family. Youth who come from relatively small, intact, middle-class families, where parents maintain the expectation for success of their children, attain more education and higher prestige jobs in young adulthood than do peers from other types of families. In addition, parents who encourage their children to pursue education beyond high school, and who encourage both the autonomy of their young adult children and their continuing relationship with them, are more likely to have youth who complete high school and who have better educational attainment and higher occupational prestige in young adulthood.

Researchers have also found that individuals who, as adolescents, had parents who granted autonomy to them are more psychologically healthy as young adults, for example, in regard to feelings of control and adjustment. Moreover, in such families, relationships between young adults and their parents tend to become more positive over time. Indeed, as young adults makes transitions to marriage, to full-time employment, and even to cohabitation (but not to parenthood), relationships with parents become closer, more supportive, and less conflicted.

On the other hand, family conflict or poor parenting practices during the late adolescent period are often related to both problematic parent-child relations and to negative behavioral or emotional outcomes in young adulthood. Feelings of well-being among young adults are lower in families that are characterized by marital conflict.

Young adults do not generally receive help from parents involved in low-quality marriages; in addition, divorce lowers help between fathers and young adults, although not between mothers and young adults. Similarly, low maternal communication and problem-solving ability and high maternal depression in adolescence are linked to delinquency during the transition to young adulthood. High levels of maternal problem-solving skills and the absence of maternal depression are linked to lower rates of delinquency during this transition.

Clearly, the transition to young adulthood is not easy. This transition challenges the young person to keep the course of his development on a healthy path, or, if it is off course, the period represents an opportunity to find a healthy path. The person leaving the period of adolescence and entering young adulthood must find a way to exit the world of adolescence—a world defined in large measure by the culture of high school—and enter the realm of adults—a context defined in the main by commitment to work and career.

Richard M. Lerner
Jacqueline V. Lerner

See also Autonomy; Career Development; College; Decision Making; Ethnocentrism; Mentoring and Youth Development; Rites of Passage; Vocational Development

References and further reading
Aquilino, William S. 1997. "From Adolescence to Young Adult: A Prospective Study of Parent-Child Relations during the Transition to Adulthood." *Journal of Marriage and Family* 59: 670–686.
Best, Karin M., Stuart T. Hauser, and Joseph P. Allen. 1997. "Predicting Young Adult Competencies: Adolescent Parent and Individual Influences." *Journal of Adolescent Research* 12, no. 1: 90–112.
Brooks-Gunn, Jeanne, Guang Guo, and Francis F. Furstenberg. 1993. "Who Drops Out of and Continues beyond High School? A 20-Year Follow-Up of Black Urban Youth." *Journal of Research on Adolescence* 3, no. 3: 271–294.

Gore, Susan, Robert H. Aseltine, and Mary Ellen Colten. 1993. "Gender, Social-Relational Involvement, and Depression." *Journal of Research on Adolescence* 3, no. 2: 101–125.

Gortmaker, Steven L., Charles A. Salter, D. K. Walker, and William R. Dietz. 1990. "The Impact of Television Viewing on Mental Aptitude and Achievement: A Longitudinal Study." *Public Opinion Quarterly* 54: 594–604.

Hammer, Torild. 1996. "Consequences of Unemployment in the Transition from Youth to Adulthood in Life Course Perspective." *Youth & Society* 27, no. 4: 450–468.

Horowitz, Allan V., and Helen R. White. 1998. "The Relationship of Cohabitation and Mental Health: A Study of Young Adult Cohort." *Journal of Marriage and the Family* 60: 505–514.

Klein, Karla, Rex Forehand, Lisa Armistead, and Patricia Long. 1997. "Delinquency during the Transition to Early Adulthood: Family and Parenting Predictors from Early Adolescence." *Adolescence* 32: 203–219.

Lerner, Richard M. In press. *Adolescence: Development, Diversity, Context, and Application.* Upper Saddle River, NJ: Prentice-Hall.

Nummenmaa, Anna R., and Tapio Nummenmaa. 1997. "Intergenerational Roots of Finnish Women's Sex-Atypical Careers." *International Journal of Behavioral Development* 21, no. 1: 1–14.

Sherrod, Lonnie R., Robert J. Haggerty, and David L. Featherman. 1993. "Late Adolescence and the Transition to Adulthood." *Journal of Research on Adolescence* 3: 217–226.

Sullivan, Mercer L. 1993. "Culture and Class as Determinants of Out-of-Wedlock Childbearing and Poverty during Late Adolescence. *Journal of Research on Adolescence* 3, no. 3: 295–316.

Transitions of Adolescence

Often, a transition refers to movement from one stage or state to another and where movement also involves change or growth. Adolescents experience transitions in a number of areas: physically/biologically, cognitively, socially, and emotionally. Although changes in all of these areas are *normative*, or are expected to occur around particular ages, it is also true that not everyone changes in exactly the same way or at the same rate.

The beginning of adolescence is marked by puberty, the biological changes that lead to physical growth and sexual maturation. On the average, girls tend to reach puberty about two years earlier than boys. Physical growth includes overall increase in height and weight; however, different parts of the body grow at different rates. For example, hands, feet, and legs usually show sooner and faster growth (also known as "growth spurts"), followed by growth of the torso. Physical growth is triggered by a growth hormone released by the pituitary gland, located at the base of the brain.

Sexual maturation is controlled by sex hormones; although estrogen is usually thought of as a female hormone and androgens as male hormones, everyone possesses both, but in different amounts. In females, the ovaries produce estrogen, which triggers *menarche* (the first menstrual period); growth of pubic and underarm hair; development of breasts; and the maturation of female reproductive organs. In males, the testes release testosterone, which triggers *spermarche* (the first production of sperm); growth of pubic, body, and facial hair; muscle growth; and maturation of male reproductive organs. For both males and females these changes carry, as well, an increase in sex drive.

Not everyone physically matures at the same rate. When adolescents mature much earlier or much later than their peers it can cause some distress or self-consciousness. Some studies have shown that the effects of early and late maturation can differ for males and for females. For example, early-maturing girls are often found to have less positive body images and feel more self-consciousness than later-maturing girls. On the other hand, it is late-maturing boys who experience less positive body images and increased self-consciousness.

Adolescents also experience cognitive transitions. Cognitive processes have to do with how we come to know and think about things. For example, adolescents begin to think more in terms of possibilities. This can include all the possible ways of solving a problem in the present or all the possible avenues one can pursue in terms of college and/or career in the future. In general, adolescents become more capable of logical and abstract thinking; can formulate and test hypotheses or ideas mentally; use more effective strategies for studying and remembering class material; and can plan, monitor, and evaluate the steps they take in solving a problem. Adolescents become more capable of questioning and evaluating the nature and quality of relationships, political and social issues, religious beliefs, cultural values, and so on. So not only do adolescents begin to think about different things, they also begin to think about things differently.

In school this may become evident as adolescents begin to show increased capability for grasping more complex mathematical and scientific concepts, understanding the underlying meaning of a poem or short story, thinking more critically about what they read and hear, and engaging in intellectual discussions. At home, cognitive growth may be evident in the questioning of parental rules and practices or in the experience of "argument for argument's sake." The adolescent's need to question and discuss, in combination with the increased need for freedom and independence, can lead to parent-adolescent conflict and tension, but can also lead to increased mutual awareness and understanding—parents can come to appreciate their son or daughter's increasing maturity and independence, and adolescents can come to appreciate their parents' values and reasons for certain practices. Typical parent-adolescent discussions about rules and independence often center on such issues as curfew, attendance at particular social events, whom one can date, and the like. Although mutual understanding does not necessarily lead to agreement, in the best of moments it can lead to healthy compromise and mutual acceptance.

Cognitive transitions not only include how adolescents think about and approach the world around them but also how they think about themselves. Adolescents grow in their capacity for introspection. That is, they can think about their own thoughts and feelings in ways they could not do as children. The ability to reflect on one's own thoughts and feelings, in combination with the physical and biological changes described above, can lead adolescents to see themselves as the focus of other people's attention and interest. Psychologists refer to this tendency as *imaginary audience*, when the adolescent feels that everyone is looking at him or her. This, in turn, can lead adolescents to become quite self-conscious, making them more sensitive to critical remarks from teachers and parents, especially when criticism occurs in front of others. Even remarks intended as helpful recommendations on the part of adults can be interpreted by adolescents as negative criticism.

The idea that others are focused on them can also lead many adolescents to develop an opinion of themselves as so special and unique that others could never understand what they are thinking, feeling, and going through. Psychologists refer to this belief as the *personal fable.* The personal fable also includes the feeling that one is invincible, or that certain things "will never happen to me," which can lead to increased risk taking. This belief is reflected, for example, in such behavior as unprotected sex or reckless driving.

There are several aspects of social and emotional transitions as well that become important for adolescents. The amount of time and attention directed toward family decreases, while the amount of time and attention directed toward peers increases. Peers include one's immediate circle of close friends, the larger group of age-mates, and relationships with members of the opposite sex. Regardless of type, peer relations can affect, to varying degrees, one's self-esteem and one's sense of belonging.

During adolescence, friendships begin to deepen and take on a quality of intimacy. When people enjoy psychological intimacy they are able to share their innermost thoughts, feelings, and dreams with each another. For the adolescent this intimacy can include feeling comfortable just being oneself without worrying too much about what the other person will think; working out problems regarding teachers, parents, or other peers; and dealing with stressful events or circumstances. By their very nature, relationships possessing an intimate quality tend to be far fewer in number than the relationships one has with the wider peer group.

The larger peer group consists of those whom one encounters at school or in social gatherings. Although the larger peer group may include intimate friendships, it is neither likely nor possible that all members of the peer group are intimate friends. The peer group, however, does take on increased importance for adolescents, such that it matters what others think and say about them. The experiences of peer pressure and conformity are largely tied to this sensitivity to peer perception and evaluation. This does not mean that parents or significant adults have no influence on an adolescent's thinking or decisions. Rather, adults and peers influence different aspects of life. For example, parents and adults tend to impact basic values, educational plans, and career goals, whereas peers tend to have a greater impact on short-term choices such as dress, music, and friends. The persistent concern, among adults, centers around short-term choice that can lead to long-term consequences (e.g., drinking and driving, unprotected sex that results in pregnancy or sexually transmitted disease, arrest for possession of drugs).

Regarding relationships with the opposite sex, sexual interest is largely initiated by hormonal changes, but the actual beginning of dating is regulated by the social and cultural expectations and norms of both one's peer group and one's family background. When dating first begins it can have more to do with social strategizing (e.g., whom to date, who will know or see them together, how to handle the good-night kiss) than with romance or companionship.

As adolescents become more experienced in dating, their social skills improve, and they become increasingly more comfortable with themselves and the date situation. As they become more mature, adolescents begin to date people they want to be with more than people they want to be seen with; however, different people date for different reasons, including fun, status, companionship, sexual experimentation, and intimacy. Experiences of disappointment or hurt often stem from two people dating for different reasons: for example, one person may date in the hope of achieving intimacy and the other for the purpose of sexual experimentation.

Along with the social and emotional transitions described so far, the adolescent begins to ponder such questions as, "Who am I?" and "Who do I want to be?" These are quite significant questions regarding one's identity. Identity does not simply consist of the adjectives one might use in describing oneself. Rather, there are several aspects of identity that an adolescent may need to explore and integrate—academic, social, sexual, political, religious. Exploration and integration take place over time and result in the young person's increasing ability to make commitments to ideologies (or the values and beliefs that guide one's actions), occupation, and relationships.

Regarding this process there are a few important points to bear in mind: (1) Choices and commitments should be self-chosen. For example, one should go to medical school because one wants to help people get well and not simply because one's mother is a doctor. (2) What one aspires to in the future should have some basis in a current reality. For example, if one is five feet tall a future in professional basketball is not a likely possibility, and one may need to be satisfied with recreational basketball and pursuing a career in some other area of interest. (3) Adolescence marks neither the beginning nor the end of the identity development process. Rather, we bring with us the lessons, values, and experiences gained during childhood and continue to adjust our desires and expectations well into adulthood. (4) Identity requires a balance between being connected with others and being one's own person. For example, one may weigh the advice of parents and friends, yet ultimately make a decision on the basis of one's own reflection and judgment.

For some adolescents the period of exploration can be cut short when adult roles and responsibilities are taken on before the end of adolescence, for example, by starting a family or entering the full-time workforce before or immediately following graduation from high school. The college experience often opens a new world of possibilities, thus leading a person to rethink choices made only a semester or a year earlier.

In the United States adolescents are confronted with several points at which they are granted partial adult status by society. For example, at thirteen an adolescent may be responsible for the care and well-being of younger siblings; at sixteen he begins to drive and may get a job after school; at around eighteen he/she graduates from high school and can vote and enlist in military service; at twenty-one he/she reaches legal drinking age in most states and may marry or be tried as an adult for a crime at any point during the adolescent years, depending upon the state in which he/she resides.

In the United States social transitions are marked at various points during adolescence; however, there is no formal way in which U.S. society recognizes the adolescent's growing maturity, competence, and autonomy across the several areas of transition. Adolescents move from one situation and set of expectations to another much more often than do either children or adults. The many transitions of adolescence can be facilitated and/or complicated by such factors as the degree to which various settings confer similar levels of privileges and responsibilities upon the adolescent; an adolescent's temperament (e.g., introverted versus extroverted); level of parental support and expectation; the degree to which school offers a sufficiently challenging academic program and opportunities for exploration of interests; the extent to which the values of family and peers resemble one another; and the presence or absence of intimate friendships.

Imma De Stefanis

See also Autonomy; Dating; Menstruation; Middle Schools; Puberty: Hormone Changes; Puberty: Physical Changes; Puberty: Psychological and Social Changes; Rites of Passage; School Transitions

References and further reading

Brooks-Gunn, Jeanne. 1988. "Antecedents and Consequences of Variations in Girls' Maturational Timing." *Journal of Adolescent Health Care* 9: 365–373.

Elkind, David. 1985. "Egocentrism Redux." *Developmental Review* 5: 218–226.

Elkind, David, and Robert Bowen. 1979. "Imaginary Audience Behavior in Children and Adolescents." *Developmental Review* 15: 33–44.

Lerner, Richard M. 1985. "Adolescent Maturational Changes and Psychosocial Development: A Dynamic Interactional Perspective." *Journal of Youth and Adolescence* 14: 355–372.

Petersen, Anne. 1985. "Pubertal Development as a Cause of Disturbance: Myths, Realities, and Unanswered Questions." *Genetic,*

Social, and General Psychology Monographs 111: 205–232.

Sebald, Hans. 1985. "Adolescents' Shifting Orientation toward Parents and Peers: A Curvilinear Trend over Recent Decades." *Journal of Marriage and the Family* 48: 5–13.

Twins

Twins are two individuals born at the same time from the same mother. Twins can be either identical (monozygotic) or fraternal (dizygotic). Identical twins result when a zygote (fertilized egg) splits in two within days after conception. These twins are genetically identical. That is, they share 100 percent of their genes. Fraternal twins result when the mother releases two ova (eggs) that are fertilized by two separate sperm. These twins are about 50 percent genetically similar. Genetically, fraternal twins are the equivalent of brothers and sisters; they just happen to be born at the same time. Therefore, although identical twins are always the same sex and appear to be physically identical, fraternal twins may or may not be the same sex, and they typically do not resemble each other more than do any other sibling pair.

Fraternal twins are more common than identical twins. The frequency of fraternal twin births ranges from 4 to 16 per 1,000 births, depending upon a variety of factors. One such factor is ethnicity. For example, fraternal twins are much more prevalent among African Americans (16 per 1,000 births) than among Caucasians (8 per 1,000 births) (Berk, 1997). Fraternal twins are also more likely to be born to older mothers, mothers who have taken fertility drugs, and mothers who themselves are fraternal twins (since this type of twinning runs in families). Because there has

Twins are two individuals born at the same time from the same mother and can be either identical or fraternal. (Shirley Zeiberg)

been an increase in the number of women using fertility drugs and the number of women who are postponing childbearing until they are older, the prevalence of fraternal twinning is on the rise.

In contrast, the prevalence of identical twinning across time and ethnicity has been relatively stable. The prevalence rate of identical twins is about 4 per 1,000 births. Factors such as ethnicity and age do not appear to influence this type of twinning. Moreover, identical twins do not run in families; identical twins appear to occur randomly. However, research using animals suggests that factors such as late fertilization of the ovum and temperature changes may increase the probability of animals having identical twins. It is unclear whether these factors similarly affect humans.

Research Using Twins

A great deal of research has been conducted using twins to determine whether traits and behaviors are influenced by genes or the environment. Researchers compare characteristics of identical twins and fraternal twins. Although both types of twins are believed to share similar environments, identical twins share more of their genes (100 percent) than do fraternal twins (50 percent). Therefore, if the concordance rate (similarity) for a trait is higher for identical twins than for fraternal twins, that trait is believed to be genetically influenced. For example, identical twins have been shown to be much more similar to one another in personality traits such as shyness, extraversion, and activity level than fraternal twins are. Therefore, researchers believe that these traits are influenced at least partially by heredity. Twin studies also have shown that other personality characteristics such as optimism (how positively a person views the world), drinking behaviors and alcoholism, psychopathology (e.g., schizophrenia, manic-depression), and IQ are all influenced partially by genes. It is important to realize that these traits are also influenced by the environment. On average, genetic influences explain about 50 percent of the variation of these traits (Santrock, 1992). Environmental factors such as socioeconomic status, family relationships, and peer relations may also play an important role in the manifestation of these traits.

Developmental Issues of
Twins during Adolescence

Adolescents are faced with many important developmental tasks. One such task is to develop a stable sense of identity. Not surprisingly, identity formation may be much more difficult for twins, especially identical twins. Some twins may fail to develop a separate sense of identity (leading to adult twins who dress alike, live together, do not marry, and so on). In contrast, other twins may desperately struggle with the issue of identity and attempt to be as different from one another as possible.

Another important developmental task during adolescence is the development of autonomy or independence. This task can be thought of as emotionally pulling away from parents and becoming an independent person. Most adolescents achieve a sense of autonomy during adolescence and begin to function more independently. However, this task may be more difficult for twins, mainly because in order to function as independent people, they not only need to achieve autonomy from their parents, but they also need to become autonomous from each other.

During adolescence, individuals begin to spend less time with their families and more time with their peers. Peer relationships become more important as adolescents learn to interact with larger groups of friends and the opposite sex. Some twins may opt to forego the experience of becoming involved with a large peer network simply because they are likely to receive a great deal of emotional and psychological support from their "lifelong best friend," their twin. It also may be difficult for identical twins to feel as though they are a unique and significant part of a peer group if their peers cannot tell them apart. Therefore, as with the struggle with identity formation, some twins may consciously seek out different peer groups, and others may not seek out peer groups at all.

Another developmental task that occurs during late adolescence and early adulthood is the development of intimacy or the ability to form close, intimate relationships with others. Unlike the difficulties that may be associated with the other primary developmental tasks of adolescence for twins, this task may be relatively easy for twins, since they have experienced the most intimate relationship with another from birth. In short, the achievement of developmental tasks during adolescence may be more or less difficult for twins, depending on the nature of the task as well as on the nature of the *individual* twin.

Christine McCauley Ohannessian

See also Family Relations; Sibling Conflict; Sibling Differences; Sibling Relationships

References and further reading
Berk, Laura E. 1997. *Child Development,* 4th ed. Boston: Allyn and Bacon.
Clegg, Averil, and Anne Woollett. 1983. *Twins: From Conception to Five Years.* New York: Van Nostrand Reinhold.
Freiberg, K. L. 1998. *Annual Editions: Human Development.* Guilford, CT: Dushkin/McGraw-Hill.
Juel-Nielsen, Niels. 1980. *Individual and Environment: Monozygotic Twins Reared Apart.* New York: International Universities Press.
Santrock, John W. 1992. *Life-Span Development,* 4th ed. Dubuque, IA: W. C. Brown Publishers.

V

Violence and Aggression

Violence and aggression among adolescents is not a new phenomenon in the United States. The quantity and severity of aggressive behavior in adolescence, however, has undergone change within the past ten to fifteen years. In 1991, a report released by the Federal Bureau of Investigation confirmed statistically that violent crimes by youth ages ten to seventeen had ballooned during the 1980s and is still surging upward in the 1990s (Curcio and First, 1993, p. 242). To understand fully the impact of violence on the lives of adolescents, it is essential to understand the many interrelated factors that contribute to violent behavior.

The American Psychological Association cites three main aspects of adolescent lives that contribute to violent behavior: (1) developmental factors, (2) social factors, and (3) individual factors.

Developmental Factors

From a developmental perspective, factors contributing to violent behavior include inherited and biological factors and learned patterns of behavior. These factors can contribute to a pattern of aggressive responses, conflict, and difficult interpersonal relationships.

One developmental influence on adolescent violence is child-rearing practices in early childhood. Parental indifference, permissiveness toward aggression, and lack of clear behavior limits are likely to set the stage for the development of aggressive behavior in adolescence. Negativism, overly controlling parenting methods, lack of warmth, and harsh, physical punishment contribute to patterns of aggressive and violent behavior and can lead to long-term aggressive behavior.

Research on aggression indicates that boys exhibit higher levels of aggression than girls. One possible explanation for these gender differences is that aggressive acts are aimed at damaging the goals that are valued by each gender group. Boys tend to exhibit overt forms of aggression such as hitting, pushing, or threatening to fight. These behaviors match goals that are important to boys within the peer group, such as power and control. Girls, however, are more likely to focus on relationship issues among their peers. Aggressive behavior in girls is evident in behaviors such as excluding a peer from a group, withdrawal of friendship, or spreading rumors. Both forms of aggression are predictors of long-term social problems.

Additionally, aggressive children know fewer solutions to social problems. Research on bullying indicates that children characterized as bullies have an aggressive pattern of behavior based on a need for power and dominance over others. A poor self-concept is evident in bullies,

Adolescents engage in violence for reasons relating to their personality, family, peer group, and community. (Skjold Photographs)

who tend to have feelings of being unloved, unimportant, and inferior. The best way to deal with these feelings is by placing them onto others and gaining power and control over them.

Social Factors

Social influences on violent behavior are defined by the attitudes that currently exist in the larger society. Complex events or combinations of events in the environment (in conjunction with individual variables) set the stage for displays of aggression.

On a larger scale, poverty and socioeconomic inequality contribute to aggres-

sive behavior. Poverty and its life circumstances deeply affect the way in which people live. In fact, although levels of violence are high in each of the ethnic minority groups, it is clear that one's socioeconomic status is a greater predictor of violence than racial or ethnic status. Also, rates of unemployment are higher among ethnic minority groups, resulting in greater levels of poverty. These factors can damage one's self-esteem and lead to family disruptions. Additionally, limited income prohibits access to some basic life necessities, adding to the stress. For these reasons, residence in urban areas is also a contributing factor to violence. If the area is characterized by low socioeconomic status, discrimination, poor housing, high population density, and high unemployment, the feelings that accompany these conditions (e.g., hopelessness, anger) increase the risk of exposure to violence.

Another sociocultural influence on violence is cultural differences. Cultural membership is not a cause of violence, but rather increasingly diverse cultures come together in social, economic, and cultural contexts that afford easier access and privilege to some, while excluding others. An adolescent's violent and aggressive behavior should be viewed in the context of the interaction between the parents' culture and the community and of the adolescent's assimilation into mainstream American society. This view offers the realization that for some adolescents and their families, access to society's benefits is not a reality. Further, because families in the United States today are more culturally and structurally diverse than families of previous generations, an understanding of aggression and violence also requires an understanding of the diverse nature of American society as a system of advantage based on race and ethnicity.

Individual Factors

The influence of individual experiences on aggression and violence are also significant. One example of an individual experience is relatively easy access to firearms and other weapons that are more likely to be owned by deviant youth. The use and abuse of alcohol and other drugs also plays a major role in interpersonal violence. Involvement in antisocial groups such as gangs increases the likelihood that a teen will be involved in conflict and violence. Gangs meet some important developmental needs for adolescents (needs for connection, belonging, self-definition), but increase the risk of involvement in violent behavior.

The strongest predictor of a child's involvement in violence is a history of previous violence. To make a reasonable transition to adulthood, adolescents need to feel a sense of safety and security, as well as a sense of hope about their futures. For these reasons, adolescents who are victims of violence and conflict or who live with the chronic pressure of violence require interventions to decrease their risk of future victimization and of future involvement in violence.

Judith E. Robinson

See also Aggression; Delinquency, Mental Health, and Substance Abuse Problems; Emotional Abuse; Juvenile Crime; Juvenile Justice System; Physical Abuse; Risk Behaviors; Sexual Abuse; Youth Gangs

References and further reading
American Psychological Association Commission on Violence and Youth. 1993. *Violence and Youth: Psychology's Response.* Washington, DC: Public Interest Directorate.
Arllen, Nancy L., Robert A. Gable, and Jo M. Hendrickson. 1994. "Toward an Understanding of the Origins of Aggression." *Preventing School Failure* 38, no. 3: 18–23.
Centers for Disease Control. 1991. "Homicide among Young Black Males: United States, 1978–1987." *Journal of the American Medical Association* 265: 183–184.
Crick, Nicki R. 1996. "The Role of Overt Aggression, Relational Aggression, and Prosocial Behavior in the Prediction of Children's Future Social Adjustment." *Child Development* 67: 2317–2327.
Crick, Nicki R., and Jennifer K. Grotpeter. 1995. "Relational Aggression, Gender, and Social-Psychological Adjustment." *Child Development* 66: 710–722.
Curcio, Joan L., and Patricia F. First. 1993. *Violence in the Schools: How to Proactively Prevent and Defuse It.* Newbury Park, CA: Corwin Press.
Gable, Robert A., Lyndal M. Bullock, and Dana L. Harader. 1995. "Schools in Transition: The Challenge of Students with Aggressive and Violent Behavior." *Preventing School Failure* 39: 29–34.
Olweus, Dan. 1993. *Bullying at School: What We Know and What We Can Do.* Cambridge, MA: Blackwell.
Slee, Phillip T. 1993. "Bullying: A Preliminary Investigation of Its Nature and the Effects of Social Cognition." *Early Child Development and Care* 87: 47–57.
Soriano, Marcel, Fernando L. Soriano, and Evelia Jimenez. 1994. "School Violence among Culturally Diverse Populations: Sociocultural and Institutional Considerations." *School Psychology Review* 2: 216–235.
Spivek, Howard, Alice J. Hausman, and Deborah Prothrow-Stith. 1989. "Practitioners' Forum: Public Health and the Primary Prevention of Adolescent Violence: The Violence Prevention Project." *Violence and Victims* 4: 203–212.

Vocational Development

One of the main tasks that teenagers face is to prepare themselves for the world of work. This preparation includes learning about themselves and about occupations. Researchers and educators refer to these tasks as vocational development. Vocational development during childhood and adolescence has far-reaching implications for an individual's future income, socioeconomic status, social relationships, and prestige in the community. Moreover, there is considerable evidence to suggest that, to a large extent, individuals define themselves through their occupation. This process of self-definition is often described as vocational identity development.

Not every adolescent experiences vocational development in the same way or at the same time. Variations are the result of gender and individual differences in interests, values, abilities, and opportunities. Looking at sex differences, it is readily apparent that the job aspirations of boys and girls are often quite different. This can be traced to the sex role stereotyping of occupations, which is a process whereby society determines which occupations are appropriate for males and females. This process has profound effects on the distribution of males and females within occupational groupings. For example, in the United States females dominate in nursing, while males dominate in auto mechanics. Sex role stereotyping of occupations may reduce the occupational options available to males and females, in spite of significant efforts that have been made in the media and in schools to reduce its detrimental impact. Although efforts to reduce sex role stereotyping have been directed mainly toward encouraging girls and young women to explore and enter male-dominated occupations, efforts have also been made to get boys to enter female-dominated fields.

As children and adolescents observe the world around them they learn about various features of different occupations. As a consequence of this and other forms of learning, which occur both within and outside of the family, they develop vocational interests. At first these may be fairly undifferentiated, with boys often choosing either stereotypic male occupations or the occupations of their fathers, and girls choosing stereotypic female occupations or the occupations of their mothers. With increasing maturity and more extensive exposure to the world of occupations, interests become more differentiated and are thought to reflect the individual's personality.

The most prominent instrument to assess vocational interests is Holland's Self-Directed Search (SDS). It provides a means for individuals to explore their interests and their competencies and to match them against occupations that are known to favor individuals with similar characteristics. The SDS partitions the world of work and the individual's personality into six dimensions: realistic, investigative, artistic, social, enterprising, and conventional. Upon completing the SDS, an individual can identify where she best fits within the world of work. Examples of realistic occupations include auto mechanic and farmer; investigative occupations include biologist and physicist; artistic occupations include musician and journalist; social occupations include clinical psychologist and high school teacher; enterprising occupations include salesperson and small business owner; and conventional occupations include bank teller and accounting clerk.

Occupational choices are also dependent on the values that individuals hold. For example, having a great deal of money is most important for some people, while others place priority on helping others. Moreover, as adolescents progress through their education and as they acquire firsthand experience in the world of work through part-time jobs, they realize that they are able to excel in some areas but not in others. Thus, individuals who do well in mathematics are more likely to choose engineering as their occupation than those who do not, and those who like socializing choose occupations that enable them to have more interactions with people.

Our discussion thus far has emphasized that vocational development involves multiple processes that ultimately lead to an occupational career. The formal beginning of such a career is an initial occupational choice. The majority of young adults, a generation ago, would have viewed such an initial occupational choice as a long-term commitment. In today's fast-paced occupational world that is shaped by rapid technological advances, however, initial occupational choices are often temporary and superseded by other choices down the road. It is thus increasingly important for teenagers to understand and appreciate the complex processes of vocational development and to master the skills involved in making good occupational choices.

In an ideal world, adolescents can choose the occupation that best reflects their abilities, interests, and values. Unfortunately, however, the opportunities for making such a choice are unevenly distributed in the United States and even more so in the rest of the world. Therefore, as adolescents begin to develop occupational preferences, it is important that they become aware of the opportunities as well as the limitations created by their own behavior, by their family and their community, and, more generally, by society. They often face the challenge of trying to realize their occupational preferences in a context that may not be supportive of their intentions. Therefore, in predicting a particular adolescent's vocational path, one must consider the complex interactions between the developing person and the contexts within which he is attempting to build an occupational future.

Vocational development represents both peril and opportunity. Teenagers who invest time and effort in exploring the world of occupations and work, on the one hand, and their own competencies, interests, and values, on the other, are most likely to end up choosing a career path that allows them to prosper both psychologically and materially. Teenagers who do not attend to these important issues tend to flounder in school and to experience uncertainty and confusion regarding their vocational identity. Vocational identity, in turn, plays a central role in teenagers' developing sense of identity in many other life domains, including relationships with others, religion, and politics. Because work is such a central part of the human experience, it is important that parents, educators, and other professionals facilitate adolescents' transition from adolescence to adulthood and from school to work by serving as positive role models and as facilitators of adolescents' vocational development.

Fred W. Vondracek
Erik J. Porfeli

See also Apprenticeships; Career Development; Employment: Positive and Negative Consequences; Mentoring and

Youth Development; Work in Adolescence

References and further reading
Holland, John L. 1994. *Self-Directed Search: Assessment Booklet.* Odessa, FL: Psychological Assessment Resources.
———. 1997. *Making Vocational Choices: A Theory of Vocational Personalities and Work Environments,* 3rd ed. Odessa, FL: Psychological Assessment Resources.
Sharf, Richard S. 1997. *Applying Career Development Theory to Counseling,* 2nd ed. Pacific Grove, CA: Brooks/Cole.
Vondracek, Fred W., Richard M. Lerner, and John E. Schulenberg. 1986. *Career Development: A Life-Span Developmental Approach.* Hillsdale, NJ: Erlbaum.

Volunteerism

Throughout the world Americans are known for being generous with both their time and resources. The generosity of Americans is not limited to adults; young people each year give of their time and resources. Like the adolescents of our earlier agrarian society who worked for the benefit of the family, youth today who are involved in service activities are assuming meaningful roles and responding to real needs of society, as well as to their own need to be needed. Service and volunteering provide opportunities for adolescents to contribute to society in meaningful and valued ways. Engaging in community service empowers teens to become contributors, problem solvers, and partners with adults in improving their communities and the larger society.

The last fifteen years have seen an explosion of volunteering or community service among youth both individually or in groups as a part of school or outside of school. Approximately 13.3 million teenagers ages twelve to seventeen are involved in some form of volunteerism (Independent Sector, 1996). The importance of volunteerism as a value of American culture is demonstrated in the fact that many high schools across the country are requiring a certain number of hours devoted to community service as a part of their curriculum and even as a requirement for graduation. Scholars have affirmed the benefits of volunteerism or community service, but only recently has research been conducted to provide strong evidence for those benefits. A few of the rationales for youth's engagement in community service include the meaningful role it provides for adolescents, the civic leadership and responsibility it instills, and the opportunity for age desegregation through partnerships between adults and young people.

Volunteerism, Community Service, and Service Learning

Volunteerism can be defined as people performing some service or good work of their own free will and without pay (with, for example, charitable institutions or community agencies). For example, many individuals have volunteered while growing up through 4-H, scouting, church youth groups, or other organizations. Community service is a specific type of volunteering done in the community without any formal attachment to any specific outcomes of learning. Learning may take place within the individual while participating in community service, but the focus of community service programs is on the task and not the learning. In addition, community service has been used as a punishment technique for delinquent behavior of youth and adults, but that is *not* what community service means in this entry. In fact,

Approximately 13.3 million teenagers ages twelve to seventeen are involved in some form of volunteerism and many high schools are requiring it for graduation. (Shirley Zeiberg)

throughout this entry the words volunteerism and community service are used interchangeably.

Community service and service learning are often confused and the lines separating the two blurred. Service learning is developed as part of an educational learning experience that is predominantly school based. The service is integrated into the students' academic curriculum, with structured time provided for students to think, talk, or write about what they did and saw during the actual service activity. Thus, their learning is extended beyond the classroom and into the community. The focus of service learning programs is on learning within the individual. The focus of this entry is on youth volunteering in the community outside of the parameters of school, thus on community service and not on traditional service learning opportunities.

Youth Volunteering
America's youth continue the long-held tradition of being generous with their time and talents. In fact, more than half of America's teenagers report volunteering in 1995 (Independent Sector, 1996). Fifty-nine percent of teenagers ages twelve to seventeen donated an estimated 3.5 hours per week and 2.4 billion hours per year in total (Independent Sector, 1996). Most youth report engaging in their community service through religious institutions, informal contacts and

efforts, youth development agencies, or educational organizations like schools. Youth volunteering represents a large dollar value, when one considers that their volunteer time is worth approximately $7 billion.

Youth volunteers are more likely to participate when directly asked to be involved. For example, when asked to volunteer, 93 percent of teens participated, whereas only 24 percent of the teens volunteered without being asked (Independent Sector, 1996). Additionally, youth who had volunteer experiences as children, usually through faith organizations, were more likely to be engaged in community service.

Community Service
Community service provides youth with a vehicle that facilitates their ability to be contributing members of a community; volunteering and community service have been found to have other positive influences on youth as well. Social scientists have found that community service has a positive impact on the psychological, social, and intellectual development of teenagers who participate in service. Community service has been linked with enhancement of self-esteem, growth in moral and ego development, increased use of critical thinking skills, and a greater mastery of skills and content directly related to the experiences of participants. Indeed, community service enables young people to gain a heightened sense of personal and social responsibility, more positive attitudes toward adults and others, and more active exploration of potential careers. Moreover, teens gain a sense of empowerment in community service when they have the power to define the problem they wish to solve and decide on a plan of action. As noted by Peter Scales and Nancy Leffert in their comprehensive review of research, community service and volunteering has been associated either directly or indirectly with all of the following benefits:

- Decreased school failure, suspension, and dropout; increased reading grades; increased performance; increased grades; increased school attendance; increased commitment to class work; increased effort for good grades
- Decreased behavior problems at school
- Reduced teenage pregnancy
- High levels of parents talking with young adolescents about school
- Increased self-concept, self-efficacy, and competency; decreased alienation
- Reduced violent delinquency
- Less depression
- Increased moral reasoning
- More positive attitudes toward adults; better development of mature relationships; increased social competence outside school; increased empathy
- Increased problem-solving skills
- Increased community involvement as an adult; increased political participation and interest; increased positive attitudes toward community involvement; positive civic attitudes; belief that one can make a difference in community; leadership positions in community organizations
- Increased personal and social responsibility; increased perceived duty to help others; increased effi-

cacy in helping others; increased altruism; increased concern for others' welfare; increased awareness of social problems

These research findings speak volumes with regard to the power of volunteering to positively impact youth's lives. However, a word of caution is necessary: Volunteering may bring negative consequences unless it is carefully monitored. For example, community service may be an intrusion in the life of the receiver of services, it may be more of a relief for the teenage helper than for the helped, or it may convince the person who is receiving help of the inadequacy of their coping abilities and foster their tendency to depend on others. Thus, care must be taken when engaging in community service to be sensitive to the real needs of those being assisted.

Civic Responsibility and
Age Segregation
Social changes that have occurred over the past century have led to a movement toward an age-segregated society, in which young and old have become disconnected and feel isolated from each other. When young people have little more than themselves to believe in—and therefore no hope or optimism—community cohesion is greatly weakened. Engagement in community service empowers teens to achieve a civic ethic, to realize that when they contribute to the community both they and the community benefit. Service draws teens out of themselves and provides them hope and optimism because it allows them to believe in something greater than themselves. By participating in service, young people shoulder some responsibility for others and for their communities. Therefore, participating in service in a community, whether that community is a classroom or a youth group (such as 4-H, Boy Scouts, or Girl Scouts), provides not only young people but people of all ages a chance to be productive citizens.

The movement to an age-segregated society means too many children raising each other with little stabilizing input from adults. Communities can or should offer intergenerational opportunities to learn from and share with each other through community service, opportunities that are important to the creation of nonmarket values. Furthermore, community service allows individuals to carve out a niche in life where the common, nonmarket values such as fellowship, solidarity, and social equality can flourish. Service within a supportive community allows young people to experience belonging, rather than being lost in a bureaucracy.

Community service bridges the gap between generations. It is a gateway for mutually beneficial and satisfying intergenerational interactions that tear down cross-generational alienation. When teens are involved in service, the community's perception of them changes from seeing them as the cause of problems to seeing them as a source of solutions. In addition, service gives young people the chance to be around the stabilizing influence of adults outside of home and school.

As America enters the twenty-first century, our role as parents and adults is to develop an ethic of service and lifelong learning within our youth so that they will be positive contributing members of society. This statement is reinforced by Urie Bronfenbrenner: "No society can long sustain itself unless its members have learned the sensitivities, motivations, and skills involved in assisting and caring for other human beings" (53).

Daniel F. Perkins
Lynne M. Borden

See also Moral Development; Social Development; Youth Outlook

References and further reading
Bass, Mary. 1997 *Citizenship and Young People's Role in Public Life.* Washington, DC: National Civic League.

Benard, Bonnie. 1991. *Fostering Resiliency in Kids: Protective Factors in the Family, School, and Community.* Portland, OR: Western Regional Center for Drug-Free Schools and Communities Far West Laboratory.

Benson, Peter L. 1997. *All Kids Are Our Kids.* San Francisco: Jossey-Bass.

Bronfenbrenner, Urie. 1979. *The Ecology of Human Development: Experiments by Nature and Design.* New York: Cambridge University Press.

Conrad, Diane, and Dan Hedin. 1989. *High School Community Service: A Review of Research and Programs.* Washington, DC: National Center on Effective Secondary Schools.

———. 1991. "School-Based Community Service: What We Know from Research and Theory." *Phi Delta Kappan* 72: 743–749.

Eckersley, Robert. 1993. "The West's Deepening Cultural Crisis." *The Futurist* 27, no. 6: 8–12.

Howe, Howard. 1986. "Can Schools Teach Values?" Remarks at Lehigh University Commencement. Bethelehem, PA (May).

Independent Sector. 1996. *Volunteering and Giving among American Teenagers 12 to 17 Years of Age.* Washington, DC: Independent Sector.

Johnson, Lloyd, Jerald Bachman, and Patrick Omalley. 1996. *Monitoring the Future: Questionnaire Responses from the Nation's High School Seniors.* Ann Arbor: Institute for Social Research, University of Michigan.

Lerner, Richard M. 1995. *America's Youth in Crisis: Challenges and Options for Programs and Policies.* Thousand Oaks, CA: Sage.

Perkins, Daniel F., and Joyce Miller. 1994. "Why Volunteerism and Service-Learning? Providing Rationale and Research." *Democracy & Education* 9: 11–16.

Scales, Peter, and Nancy Leffert. 1999. *Developmental Assets: A Synthesis of Scientific Research on Adolescent Development.* Minneapolis, MN: Search Institute.

Schine, Joan. 1989. *Young Adolescents and Community Service.* Working Paper for the Carnegie Council on Adolescent Development. Washington, DC.

Sundeen, Richard, and Sally Raskoff. 1995. "Teenage Volunteers and Their Values." *Nonprofit and Voluntary Sector Quarterly* 240: 337–357.

Toole, James, and Pamela Toole. 1992. *Key Definitions: Commonly Used Terms in the Youth Service Field.* Minneapolis, MN: National Youth Leadership Council.

W

Welfare

Welfare is a term typically used to refer to monthly income, and other support services given to families with children. Most welfare recipients are female-headed families with an average of two children. Families on welfare receive a monthly cash allotment, as well as certain services, which may include food stamps, Medicaid (government-funded health insurance), child care, clothing allotments, and housing services. Cash benefit levels and additional services vary state by state. Some of these services are funded with welfare money, and some are paid for through other funds.

History of Welfare

Early welfare programs in the United States came out of the Progressive Reform Movement, and were called "Mothers' Pensions" or "Widows Pensions." These "pensions" were funded and run at the state level, and were meant to provide a survival-level income to widows and their children. The goal of these programs was to enable women to stay at home to raise their children. In practice, this assistance was generally available only to Caucasian women. In addition, unmarried women and women who had divorced or had been deserted by their husbands did not qualify for these benefits.

In 1935, as part of the Social Security Act, Mothers' Pensions were replaced with a new federal-level program called Aid to Dependent Children (ADC). This program was a government response to socialist, labor, feminist, and social work movements of the time. Benefits still went to families where the father had died, but were expanded to include families where the father had deserted the family or was incapacitated and unable to work. The majority of the welfare recipients in the 1930s were Caucasian, but the 1940s and 1950s witnessed an increase in minority welfare recipients as more African American families began to reside in northern states (which were more likely to extend benefits to them).

During the 1960s, there was a brief period in which welfare rights activism helped many more families to access benefits, and ADC was changed to Aid to Families with Dependent Children (AFDC). Efforts were made to enroll more families, increase benefit amounts, and destigmatize welfare. Several Supreme Court decisions during this time period affirmed welfare benefits as an entitlement. From the late 1960s to the present, however, people opposed to more welfare expenditures succeeded in reducing welfare grants, increasing work requirements, and emphasizing marriage as a preferred alternative to public benefits. In the 1990s, with the passage of the Personal Responsibility and Work Opportunity Reconciliation Act (PRWORA), the number of families receiving benefits has decreased dramatically.

Welfare Reform: The Personal Responsibility and Work Opportunity Reconciliation Act

Welfare in the United States has a long history, but the system that is currently in place was passed by Congress in 1996. In August of that year, President Bill Clinton signed the Personal Responsibility and Work Opportunity Reconciliation Act. This welfare reform bill ended the federal entitlement of individuals to cash assistance under Aid to Families with Dependent Children, giving states complete flexibility to determine eligibility for and level of benefits. The assistance given to families is now called Temporary Assistance to Needy Families (TANF) and is intended to provide time-limited cash aid to needy families with or expecting children, and to provide parents with job preparation and support services. PRWORA requires work in exchange for public assistance.

The U.S. Department of Health and Human Services identifies the following four goals for TANF: (1) Aid needy families so that children may be cared for in their homes or those of relatives; (2) end dependence of needy parents upon government benefits by promoting job preparation, work, and marriage; (3) prevent and reduce out-of-wedlock pregnancies and establish goals for preventing and reducing their incidence; and (4) encourage formation and maintenance of two-parent families.

As the stated goals demonstrate, PRWORA contains statements reflecting strong moral values about family structure and reproduction. In particular, it implies that only married (presumably heterosexual) couples should bear children, that children should be raised in two-parent, mother-father homes, and that abortion rates should be reduced. PRWORA also stems from a belief that government welfare programs have contributed to an increase in poor, female-headed families, and that this phenomenon is the cause of many social problems.

The federal government hopes that PRWORA will achieve the goals listed above, but it is uncertain whether it will be successful. In many ways this is a very new type of welfare policy with which the government is experimenting.

AFDC was set up to provide services for everyone who qualified, and PRWORA replaced AFDC and other public assistance programs with a single block grant program, which allots states a capped sum of money to use for welfare. States now have more control over the provision of welfare to their residents, provided that they adhere to several new federal requirements. First of all, TANF benefits are only intended for families who are expecting children, or have children under the age of 18, and individuals may receive TANF for *no more than five years in total.*

There are also strict work requirements that must be met by families on TANF. Single parents with children who are over the age of five must participate in work activities for at least 30 hours per week. Single parents with children who are five years old and under must participate in work activities for at least 20 hours per week. (The federal law permits states, if they choose, to exempt single-parent families from these work requirements if they have a child under the age of one.) Two-parent families must participate in work activities for a total of at least 35 hours per week. If the two-parent family is receiving federally funded childcare, and neither adult is disabled in any way, the shared work requirement is 55 hours per week.

The new welfare laws prohibit a number of people from receiving TANF benefits. First, TANF benefits are not provided for illegal immigrant families. For legal immigrant families, TANF benefits are withheld for the first five years of their residency in the United States. After that, it is at the state's discretion whether or not to provide public assistance. Second, TANF benefits are not provided for anyone convicted of a drug-related felony after August 1996. Third, TANF benefits are not provided for any person who fails to comply with state child support requirements. Finally, TANF benefits may be reduced or denied to any mother who fails to provide the state with information about the father of her child. If she does not cooperate in establishing paternity, she will lose at least 25 percent of her benefits.

For teenage parents under the age of 18 to receive TANF benefits, they must live with their parents, or in another adult-supervised living arrangement. Adolescents without a high school diploma or equivalent must also attend school.

Welfare provision varies widely from state to state. Some states have welfare rules that are stricter than the federal requirements listed above, and some states have received permission to be more lenient about some of the rules.

Welfare and Teenagers

Although teenagers constitute a small percentage of the total women receiving benefits, adult women who began child-bearing as teenagers comprise almost half of the welfare caseload. Decision makers with strong moral preferences for two-parent families interpreted these numbers as a call for federal efforts to reduce out-of-wedlock pregnancies, especially for teenagers. Consequently, teenagers, specifically unwed teenagers, have a special role in the new welfare law. PRWORA includes some strict requirements for teenage mothers who are receiving assistance.

In order to receive TANF benefits, unwed teenage mothers under the age of 18 must live with their parents, or another adult relative, or in an adult-supervised living arrangement. Unwed teenage mothers under the age of 18 who have not attained a high school diploma or equivalent must attend school in order to receive assistance.

In most states, the school rules simply require teenagers to attend school. However, some states have more specific rules about teenagers and school attendance. In some states, teenagers must maintain a minimum grade-point average (GPA); in some states, education and training other than GED programs can be counted; and a very small number of states provide monetary bonuses for teens who complete a grade of school, have good attendance, graduate from high school, receive a GED, or maintain a high GPA. In most states, there are no formal criteria for permitting alternative education.

Despite the special challenges that face a poor teenager balancing child rearing, work, and school, they receive very little support under the new welfare laws. In most cases, teens do not receive any special priority for childcare, transportation, specialized case management, or other services. In over half the states, no additional state funds have been provided to assist teens in meeting the school/training requirements.

PRWORA also has numerous provisions aimed specifically at reducing teenage fertility. States have the flexibility to design any kind of adolescent pregnancy prevention program they want using TANF funds. However, the majority of federal funds targeting teenage fertility tend to emphasize abstinence rather than family planning programs that educate teenagers about and/or distribute birth control.

The federal program has developed some cash incentives to encourage states to reduce their out-of-wedlock births. These incentive programs are based on improvements that states show in reducing teenage pregnancy. However, many states are not collecting the data they may need to evaluate the success of their programs for teenage parents. For example, many states are not collecting data on numbers of teenagers living in each type of housing arrangement (with parents, guardians, adult relatives, other supervised settings, independently) or the numbers of teens who are noncompliant with this supervised living rule and are therefore being refused benefits.

Jessica Goldberg
Jennifer Douglas
Shireen Boulos

See also Poverty; Teenage Parenting: Childbearing; Teenage Parenting: Consequences; Work in Adolescence

References and further reading
Committee on Ways and Means, U.S. House of Representatives. 1998. *1998 Green Book*. Washington DC: U.S. House of Representatives.

Levin-Epstein, J. 1996. *Teen Parent Provisions in the Personal Responsibility and Work Opportunity Reconciliation Act of 1996.* Washington, DC: Center for Law and Social Policy.

Nathan, R. P., P. Gentry, and C. Lawrence. 1999. "Is There a Link between Welfare Reform and Teen Pregnancy?" *Rockefeller Reports*. Albany, NY: Nelson A. Rockefeller Institute of Government.

Wood, R. G., and J. Burghardt. 1997. *Implementing Welfare Requirements for Teenage Parents: Lessons from Experience in Four States.* Washington DC: Mathematica Policy Research, for the Office of the Assistant Secretary for Planning and Evaluation, U.S. Department of Health and Human Services.

White and American: A Matter of Privilege?

"White privilege"—trendy catchphrase or accurate depiction of modern-day American society? In thinking about this question, consider the following scenarios.

- Michelle, age eighteen, goes shopping at Wal-Mart—does she wonder if the security will keep a close eye on her as she walks around?
- Todd, age twenty, feels like taking his parents' new Jeep Cherokee for a drive—does he worry that the police will pull him over, whether or not they have good reason?

These scenarios have something to do with how people perceive each other. And one of the first things people often perceive is skin color. But if a person is white, issues of skin color may not be particularly salient, if thought about at all. Which means if a person hasn't considered what it would be like to be perceived by others based on this very visible human trait, perhaps the person simply never had to do so.

Being white and living in the United States translates into automatic membership in the racial majority. Not only does that make it much easier for a white person to blend into society as a whole, it also translates into tremendous power. Consider the following: Who is in the White House? Who controls most big businesses? Which Hollywood stars make the most money? In this country, on multiple levels, white people are firmly in charge.

The notion of white privilege helps further explain this reality. Simply put, being white in the United States affords certain advantages other racial groups may not have—like the freedom to walk into a store without being instantly scrutinized by security guards. But perhaps the biggest privilege is that in this country, white people, no matter how young or old, don't necessarily *have* to think about being white—a privilege that may be taken for granted, even when it comes at others' expense.

The more disheartening sides of white privilege are evidenced in many ways. For instance, African American adolescents (and males in particular) may be less confident than white students in their academic abilities and potential for school success, especially if African American students perceive that their own culture isn't being given the same focused attention as white students' cultural issues. Conversely, the more positive teacher and parent support African American students feel they are receiving, the more likely they may be to consider broader academic possibilities for themselves.

In direct contrast to these examples of the flip side of white privilege, consider the twenty-nine-year-old white physician who experienced all the benefits of being white right from the start. This person came from a wealthy family, was constantly praised by teachers throughout high school, and was never harassed by the police for his occasional rowdy behavior. Does he ever think about how being white influenced his relatively trouble-free existence thus far? Not really, he says—he merely assumed life would come easy, and it has.

Sometimes white privilege is this glaringly obvious, while at other times, its effects are subtler and less pronounced. But where does this sense of privilege come from? Historically speaking, white people have been in control from the moment they set foot on American soil. Early white settlers, often escaping from their own forms of persecution, perhaps believed they deserved to be here, regardless of who they may have displaced in the process. Sadly, with that sentiment comes the fact that white people haven't always considered the well-being of their nonwhite neighbors over time (slavery and the treatment of Native Americans being two of the more blatant examples).

And while U.S. society has certainly become more multicultural in recent years, the fact that white people's traditional power base may be in danger of slipping is a source of discomfort to some people. As proof, consider the growing number of "white power" hate groups and their increasing influence among various demographic groups, particularly adolescents and young adults whose value systems are still developing and changing. Yet even those white people who have no use for such extremism may, if they're truly honest with themselves, feel less than enthusiastic about this country's increasingly multicultural flavor. After all, when one's own privileges get called into question, one may start to feel uneasy, no matter how open-minded one purports to be. Social psychology literature refers to this phenomenon in terms of identification with one's own in-group in contrast to an undesirable out-group—in other words, an "us" versus "them" mentality.

At present, the issue of white privilege is even more important because by the middle of the year 2000, whites will no longer be in the racial majority—meaning the privileges they have always taken for granted may become less secure. So how can whites better prepare for this future reality—particularly concerning their relationships with nonwhites?

First comes awareness—realizing that if one is white and American, one has at least *some* degree of power and privilege due to skin color alone. And by being white, one automatically shares in the societal benefits of all white people historically—again, simply by virtue of racial group membership.

Along with awareness comes acknowledgement that in a country claiming to support equal opportunity for all, no citizen should have an advantage just because of skin color. Next comes action—the willingness to branch out beyond the safety of one's white contexts to connect with other cultures. The means by which people make this happen are certainly many and varied, but on a basic level could include attending a nonwhite cultural festival, interviewing a nonwhite teacher or professor, or talking to someone about what it's like to be nonwhite in the United States. Such approaches are especially suitable for adolescents in terms of giving them meaningful, concrete exposure to nonwhite cultural backgrounds. Indeed,

numerous studies over time have proven that meaningful interracial contact makes a significant difference in the attitudes one has toward people from other races—so the more positive experiences with nonwhite racial groups one seeks out, the better.

Of course, such a complex issue defies simplistic solutions. Understanding white privilege and working to diminish its downside is no easy task, considering that white privilege has been entrenched in American society for hundreds of years. But only through conscious awareness that such privilege does exist—and a determined effort not to let this awareness bypass one's ability (or willingness) to act—will the situation finally start to shift. Perhaps then people may begin appreciating skin color for the diversity it truly represents.

Jill C. Stoltzfus

See also Ethnic Identity; Racial Discrimination

References and further reading
Allen, Theodore. 1994. *The Invention of the White Race, Volume One: Racial Oppression and Social Control.* London: Verso.
Allport, Gordon W. 1954. *The Nature of Prejudice.* New York: Addison-Wesley.
Blanchard, F. A., C. S. Crandall, J. C. Brigham, and L. Vaughn. 1994. "Condemning and Condoning Racism: A Social Context Approach to Interracial Settings." *Journal of Applied Psychology* 79: 993–997.
Delgado, Richard, and Jean Stefancic, eds. 1996. *Critical White Studies: Looking behind the Mirror.* Philadelphia: Temple University Press.
Devine, Patricia G., and Andrew J. Elliot. 1995. "Are Racial Stereotypes *Really* Fading? The Princeton Trilogy Revisited." *Personality and Social Psychology Bulletin* 21: 1139–1150.
Devine, Patricia G., and Kristen A. Vasquez. 1998. "The Rocky Road to Positive Intergroup Relations." Pp.

234–262 in *Confronting Racism: The Problem and the Responses*. Edited by Jennifer L. Eberhardt and Susan T. Fiske. Thousand Oaks, CA: Sage.

Eberhardt, Jennifer L., and Susan T. Fiske, eds. 1998. *Confronting Racism: The Problem and the Responses*. Thousand Oaks, CA: Sage.

Feagin, Joe R., and Hernan Vera. 1995. *White Racism*. New York: Routledge.

Kaplan, Elaine B. 1999. "'It's Going Good: Inner-City Black and Latino Adolescents' Perceptions about Achieving an Education." *Urban Education* 34: 181–213.

Sanders, Mavis G. 1998. "The Effects of School, Family and Community Support on the Academic Achievement of African American Adolescents." *Urban Education* 33: 385–409.

Why Is There an Adolescence?

Adolescence as we know and experience it did not always exist. While the biological changes of the growth spurt years have always occurred and signaled the onset of the transition into adulthood, the nature and length of the transition has been undergoing continual change. Three broad social forces—the change from a rural/agricultural to urban/industrial society, mandatory schooling, and child labor laws—all acted to segregate children and adolescents from adults and helped shape the nature of adolescence. Similar social forces, such as the increase in the number of two-working-parent and single-parent families, the extension of schooling into and beyond the high school years, and the increasing delay in entering the workforce, have acted to lengthen the adolescent years. Improvements in nutrition and healthcare have resulted in the growth spurt occurring earlier, thereby extending the onset of adolescence to earlier ages. As a result of these changes we have lengthened the adolescent years by extending them upward in the age range and by their beginning sooner.

When we were largely an agricultural nation children were expected to contribute to the family's welfare by working on the farm. The home was the workplace; children, adolescents, and adults all worked together. With the spread of the industrial revolution and the attendant urbanization of the nation, home no longer was the workplace for increasing numbers of families. Large numbers of children "left" the workforce as their families moved to cities.

Mandatory education plunged most youth into schools. This established a formal separation of youth from adults and helped to formalize the role of youth as one distinct from that of adulthood. It also acted to increase contact with age-mates and reduce contact with adults. As age grading increased, this segregation became more refined, and younger, middle-aged, and older children were segregated from each other. Today, the school is the setting for the adolescent "society."

Child labor laws were instituted in part to keep children out of sweatshops, mines, and factories to improve their health and well-being. It also further segregated adolescents from adults and emphasized the idea that childhood and adolescence were uniquely different from adulthood.

The formalized separation of childhood from adulthood continues today. The percentage of adolescents living in two-working-parent and single-working-parent families has increased dramatically over the past twenty-five years. Children in these families have reduced contact with adults after school and during vacation times. Similarly, the number of adolescents seeking postsecondary training has been increasing. For these late adolescents the entrance into the full-time workforce also is delayed.

Each society creates its own version of adolescence. Adolescence in the United States reflects the desire and need for a well-educated citizenry as well as other social factors that act to create it. As our society continues to change so will the nature of adolescence and the adolescent experience.

Jerome B. Dusek

See also Identity; Puberty: Hormone Changes; Puberty: Physical Changes; Puberty: Psychological and Social Changes; Rites of Passage; Transition to Young Adulthood; Transitions of Adolescence

References and further reading
Bornstein, Marcus H., and Michael E. Lamb. 1999. *Developmental Psychology: An Advanced Textbook.* Mahwah, NJ: Erlbaum.
Crockett, Lisa J., and Rainer K. Silbereisen. 2000. *Negotiating Adolescence in Times of Social Change.* New York: Cambridge University Press.
Dusek, Jerome B. 1996. *Adolescent Development and Behavior.* Upper Saddle River, NJ: Prentice-Hall.

Work in Adolescence

Working is an integral part of American teenagers' lives. Many people think of adolescence as a time to have fun and enjoy a moratorium from adult responsibilities. It is also a time to prepare for future employment by doing well in school. However, most teenagers' daily schedules involve the simultaneous pursuit of both school and work. Eighty percent or more of contemporary adolescents are employed at least some time during their high school years. By the twelfth grade, close to three-quarters are employed during the school year. More than half of employed young people (fifteen- to seventeen-year-olds) work in the retail sector (in restaurants, fast-food outlets, grocery stores, department stores, gas stations, and the like); more than a fourth are in the service sector (entertainment and recreation, in private households, health, education, and so on) (Committee on the Health and Safety Implications of Child Labor, 1998). In addition to paid employment, today's youth are involved in other kinds of work. Most teenagers help their families by doing chores in their homes; many do volunteer or community service work. The widespread combination of schooling and working in adolescents' lives has spurred a lively controversy, as well as a growing body of systematic research about the developmental impacts of working, with both research and controversy especially focused on paid work activity.

It is widely believed that employment is good for youth, contributing to character development and positive work values. In fact, a series of highly prominent reports and commissions have proclaimed the benefits of youth employment and recommended that there be closer connections between schools and workplaces. More recently, many communities have developed "School-to-Work" initiatives, facilitated by the School-to-Work Opportunities Act of 1994. American parents generally approve of their teenage children's employment, as they believe that working fosters responsibility, independence, good work habits, and time management skills. In fact, when they look back on the jobs that they themselves held as adolescents, parents are nearly unanimous in their opinion that employment was a beneficial experience in their own lives.

The majority of contemporary adolescents are employed at least some time during their high school years. (Shirley Zeiberg)

The expectation that paid work will be beneficial for adolescents is reasonable, given that most young people, as they look forward to adulthood, anticipate that they will be employed and that working will be a significant part of their lives. Teenage boys and girls are now very similar in this regard. Paid work is the vehicle through which the "markers" of adulthood are acquired—residential and financial independence from the family of origin, the ability to nurture and support one's own children, and the capacity to acquire all the accoutrements of the desired "adult" lifestyle. Since employment is an integral feature of the future adult "possible self," successfully holding a paid job would likely signify to the adolescent, as well as to parents and others whose opinions matter, progress in moving toward an independent and highly valued adult status.

Aside from such symbolic significance, paid employment also conveys quite tangible benefits that are likely to foster subsequent success in the labor market, despite the relatively low levels of skill that most jobs for young people entail. For example, by performing part-time work in adolescence, the youth learns about how to acquire a job and how to behave at an interview. The young worker learns about the daily routines and how to comport oneself in the workplace, learning, for example, the importance of coming to work on time; the nature of appropriate clothing and demeanor; and how to relate to supervisors, coworkers, and clients. All of this will contribute to what is sometimes called "work readiness," the capacity to obtain, and to maintain, paid work. The young person may also learn specific skills that transfer to other jobs—for example, how to operate a cash register or a computer keyboard—and have opportunities to apply knowledge that is learned in school.

In addition to such elements of human capital, the employed youth also has the potential to gain social capital. Supervisors in early jobs can provide advice and act as references for future employers. Furthermore, since knowledge of job availability often occurs through informal networks, the youth may learn of better employment opportunities through coworkers or former coworkers. Indeed, building a network of occupational associates may be of great benefit in future job searches. In view of the salient symbolic meanings and practical consequences of work, it is no wonder that most adolescents in America want to work. Given this motivation and the continuing availability of suitable part-time jobs, employment among teenagers while school is in session, for at least some time during the high school career, has become almost universal.

There is, in fact, substantial evidence that employment in adolescence contributes to early adult occupational and income attainments. That is, youth who work during high school more easily acquire jobs after high school; they have less unemployment and higher income. Such gains have been found to persist nearly a dozen years after high school.

If all of these benefits accrue from paid work in adolescence, one might wonder what the controversy about teenage employment is all about. There is, however, reason to be cautious about adolescent work. In 1986, the publication of Ellen Greenberger and Laurence Steinberg's book, *When Teenagers Work*, alerted the scientific community, as well as the public at large, to the potential dangers of working in adolescence. In fact, their study of students in four California high schools showed that those who worked more hours had lower grades, were more likely to use alcohol and drugs, and were more likely to get in trouble at school. These findings generated considerable skepticism in the educational community about the benefits of working.

Instead of viewing work as enabling youth to implement positive "possible selves" as they move toward adulthood, Greenberger and Steinberg raised the specter of precocious development, echoing what has become an enduring concern among psychologists since the turn of the century. That is, the independence conferred by a job may encourage a premature adultlike identity and claim to adult status. Employed youths may begin to think of themselves as adults, coming to resent childlike roles that involve subordination to adult authorities such as teachers and school administrators. As their jobs make them less available to spend time with their families, the quality of the relationships teenagers have with their parents could deteriorate. Parents, seeing their children take on adultlike employment, may be less motivated (and less able) to closely monitor the behaviors of their employed teenagers.

Consequently, according to this argument, adolescents become prone to problem behavior in school and increasingly take on adultlike leisure-time activities, such as smoking, alcohol use, and other recreational drugs. Instead of investing their time and energy in school, building their human capital through educational achievement, employed youth could have less time to do their homework and become less interested and engaged in the educational enterprise more generally. There is concern that youth will prematurely withdraw from educational endeavors in favor of full-time work, early marriage, and parenthood.

This "dark side" of adolescent employment has been confirmed, at least in part, by several surveys that address youth activities and lifestyles. In fact, the more frequent alcohol use among teenagers who work longer hours is one of the most robust findings in this area of research. Hours of work have also been empirically linked to teenage smoking, the use of illegal drugs, minor delinquency, and other behavioral problems.

The assertion that investment in paid work will detract from students' grades, however, receives less consistent support, with some studies reporting that long work hours are associated with lower student grades, while others indicate no significant relationships between hours of work and grade-point average. Similarly, it has not been demonstrated that work hours decrease the amount of time spent doing homework. However, a large investment in work during high school predicts fewer years of postsecondary attainment. Still, there is evidence that teenagers who learn to balance school and working during high

school, by working almost continuously but limiting their hours of work to twenty or fewer hours per week, achieve more postsecondary schooling during the following years then their peers. Finally, there is no solid evidence that employed youth have poorer quality relationships with their parents than their nonworking counterparts.

In summary, both the "work is good" and the "work is bad" schools of thought receive some empirical support. Following employment during high school, youth move more easily into the adult workforce, achieving more stable employment, higher earnings, and other positive vocational outcomes. On the other hand, those teenagers who work more hours exhibit more frequent problem behaviors. But in some arenas, researchers report null findings—unable to demonstrate that hours worked either promotes or detracts from school performance or family relationships.

How can these diverse and seemingly contradictory findings be reconciled? In some ways, the advocates of both perspectives may be correct. That is, work experience does confer benefits with respect to the accumulation of human (and social) capital, which pay off in the early work career. As parents note, teenagers who work may actually become more responsible, more independent, and better time managers. But as they learn the ways of the workplace, take on adultlike responsibilities, and often work alongside older youth and adults, many employed youth do prematurely assume what most would consider undesirable components of adult lifestyle. Some chafe at adult authority and may act out in school. Thus, as youth take on a role that so clearly signifies adult status, they assume adultlike behaviors and capacities, some of which are highly approved and others frowned upon, at least when engaged in by minors.

The context in which youth are employed must be taken into account, however, in assessing the developmental consequences of work. That is, working in adolescence has different meanings and outcomes, depending on features of the broader social environment in which it occurs. For example, Shanahan et al. (1996) have shown that in rural and urban communities, teenagers' earnings are used in different ways, and have divergent implications for parent-child relationships. Comparing youth in St. Paul, Minnesota, with their counterparts in rural Iowa counties, they find that rural youth are more apt to use their earnings in ways that contribute to their families—by giving money to their parents or by spending their earnings on items, such as school expenses, that would otherwise be purchased by their parents. The urban youth were more apt to use earnings for entertainment and other more individualistic pursuits, enhancing their leisure time. Not surprisingly, as earnings increased, relationships between rural parents and their teenage children became more positive; earnings had no consequences for the quality of parent-child relations in the urban setting.

Likewise, employment during high school must be considered in the context of the other activities adolescents are engaged in. Shanahan and Flaherty's analysis of adolescent time use (in press) shows that most employed youth are involved in a wide variety of pursuits, including extracurricular activities in school, time with peers, and chores at home. The majority of youth who work at paid jobs spend about as much time at these activities, doing homework, and

engaging in volunteer work as their non-employed counterparts.

In fact, in their analysis the two most prevalent time use clusters among students in the eleventh grade had only one distinguishing characteristic: In the first, the youth were employed about seventeen hours per week; in the other, the teenagers were not employed. How can youth who work so many hours be so similar to their nonworking counterparts with respect to their investment in extracurricular life at school, homework, chores, and activities with their friends? The answer to this question is that employment, and any other single pursuit, is not a zero-sum game. There are many ways that young people can spend their time, and highly discretionary, less valuable activities may be the ones that are sacrificed when time becomes scarce. Schoenhals et al. (1998) report evidence that when youth work more hours, they spend less time watching television.

Though most discussion in the scientific and policy arenas has focused on adolescent hours of work (an element of youth employment readily alterable via parental restriction or even by child labor law), it should be recognized that youth who work perform different kinds of jobs and have varying work conditions. That is, young people may be employed in schools, hospitals, department stores, and landscaping businesses, as well as in restaurants and a host of other places. In each locale, there will be different job tasks, interactions with different kinds of people, and the use of varying tools and instruments. Some will have supervisors who take a strong interest in their work; others will work without supervision.

What may be most important from the perspective of the developing teen is whether the work environment provides experiences that help them to develop capacities that enhance their movement into adulthood. For example, having advancement opportunities and feeling that one is being paid well, and thus is valuable to the employer, builds a sense of efficacy in the workplace. Having a job that allows the acquisition of useful skills promotes positive occupational values. Alternatively, job pressures resulting from too much work, or other noxious work conditions, will generate feelings of distress and heighten depressive moods. Thus, to understand the impact of youth employment, it is important to consider the quality of the work experience as well as the time investment in working.

What can parents do to help to assure that working will be a beneficial experience for their teenagers? First, it is important for parents to monitor their teenagers' work so as to be sure that employment is not squeezing out other desirable activities or leading to excessive fatigue. As noted earlier, Shanahan and Flaherty's analysis showed that most adolescents are able to combine work with other pursuits. Working excessive hours, however, could jeopardize other developmentally beneficial activities.

Furthermore, parents should recognize the opportunities that employment presents for "teachable moments"—encouraging youth to attend to the prospect of future adult work, to consider the kinds of experiences in the workplace that they like (or dislike), to think about what tasks they are good at. Talking with young people about their work could help them become aware of the credentials needed to obtain the kind of adult work they are hoping to acquire. Contemporary American adolescents tend to give relatively little thought to such matters, in comparison to their counterparts in previous historical eras or in other Western societies. With stronger engagement in vocational issues, teenagers may become able to make better choices about what courses to take, in high school as well as subsequently, about what college or other postsecondary institution to attend, and about the kinds of experiences they should acquire (including work, internships, and other activities) that would facilitate more effective vocational exploration or enable them to realize their goals.

Jeylan T. Mortimer

See also Apprenticeships; Asian American Adolescents: Issues Influencing Identity; Employment: Positive and Negative Consequences; Mentoring and Youth Development; Vocational Development

References and further reading
Aronson, Pamela J., Jeylan T. Mortimer, Carol Zierman, and Michael Hacker. 1996. "Generational Differences in Early Work Experiences and Evaluations." Pp. 25–62 in *Adolescents, Work and Family: An Intergenerational Developmental Analysis.* Edited by Jeylan T. Mortimer and Michael D. Finch. Thousand Oaks, CA: Sage Publications.
Bachman, Jerald G., and John Shulenberg. 1993. "How Part-Time Work Intensity Relates to Drug Use, Problem Behavior, Time Use, and Satisfaction among High School Seniors: Are These Consequences or Merely Correlates?" *Developmental Psychology* 29: 220–235.
Carr, Rhoda V., James D. Wright, and Charles J. Brody. 1996. "Effects of High School Work Experience a Decade Later: Evidence from the National Longitudinal Survey." *Sociology of Education* 69: 66–81.
Committee on the Health and Safety Implications of Child Labor. 1998. *Protecting Youth at Work: Health, Safety and Development of Working Children and Adolescents in the United States.* Washington, DC: National Academy Press.

Greenberger, Ellen, and Laurence D. Steinberg. 1986. *When Teenagers Work: The Psychological and Social Costs of Adolescent Employment.* New York: Basic Books.

Mortimer, Jeylan T., and Monica Kirkpatrick Johnson. 1998. "New Perspectives on Adolescent Work and the Transition to Adulthood." Pp. 425–496 in *New Perspectives on Adolescent Risk Behavior.* Edited by Richard Jessor. New York: Cambridge University Press.

Mortimer, Jeylan T., and Helga Kruger. 2000. "Transition from School to Work in the United States and Germany: Formal Pathways Matter." In *Handbook of the Sociology of Education.* Edited by Maureen Hallinan. New York: Plenum Press.

Mortimer, Jeylan T., Michael D. Finch, Seongryeol Ryu, and Michael J. Shanahan. 1996. "The Effects of Work Intensity on Adolescent Mental Health, Achievement, and Behavioral Adjustment: New Evidence from a Prospective Study." *Child Development* 67: 1243–1261.

Mortimer, Jeylan T., Ellen Efron Pimentel, Seongryeol Ryu, Katherine Nash, and Chaimun Lee. 1996. "Part-Time Work and Occupational Value Formation in Adolescence." *Social Forces* 74 (June): 1405–1418.

Schneider, Barbara, and David Stevenson. 1998. *The Ambitious Generation: America's Teenagers, Motivated but Directionless.* New Haven: Yale University Press.

Schoenhals, Mark, Marta Tienda, and Barbara Schneider. 1998. "The Educational and Personal Consequences of Adolescent Employment." *Social Forces* 77 (December): 723–762.

Shanahan, Michael J., and Brian Flaherty. In press. "Dynamic Patterns of Time Use Strategies in Adolescence." *Child Development.*

Shanahan, Michael J., Glen H. Elder Jr., Margaret Burchinal, and Rand D. Conger. 1996. "Adolescent Earnings and Relationships with Parents: The Work-Family Nexus in Urban and Rural Ecologies." Pp. 97–128 in *Adolescents, Work and Family: An Intergenerational Developmental Analysis.* Edited by Jeylan T. Mortimer and Michael D. Finch. Thousand Oaks, CA: Sage Publications.

Steinberg, Laurence D., and Elizabeth Cauffman. 1995. "The Impact of Employment on Adolescent Development." *Annals of Child Development* 11: 131–166.

Y

Youth Culture

Youth distinguish themselves in many ways: dress, hairstyle, makeup, and jewelry; music and use of other media such as film and the Internet; language, recreation, even food and beverage choices. These distinguishing characteristics of youth qualify as culture according to the definitions offered by anthropology and cultural psychology.

Culture has been defined as the symbolic and behavioral inheritance received from the past that provides a community framework for what is valued. Whether symbolic and behavioral culture should be distinguished is controversial (Shweder et al., 1998). Culture is learned, socially shared, affects all aspects of the individual's life, and allows for individual variation (Roberts, 1993). The view that culture is learned and is all-encompassing has a long history in the field dating back to Margaret Mead and her teacher Franz Boas (Boas, 1911; Mead, 1961).

Establishing effective communication with youth requires understanding the cultural context of their lives (Harper and Harper, 1999). Contemporary teens grow up in a world saturated with mass media, advertising, and communications technologies. Teens watch television more than twenty hours per week and listen to music a similar amount of time. Advertising permeates their lives, and magazines are as important as television and radio; estimates from the Labor Department are that teens spent about $141 billion in 1998 on CDs, sneakers, clothes, and other products advertised to them. Estimates are that this figure rose to $160 billion in 1999 (Brown and Witherspoon, 2000). They also influence a sizable portion of the purchases made within the family, from computers to fruit snacks (Terry, 1998). Thus, teens are a big market for business.

A large part of teen culture includes top hits in TV, music, and movies. Paul Willis refers to the "common youth culture" of images, styles, and ideas that teens attend to in the media (1990). As C. Terry puts it, "Being cool is both a unifying factor and an unending quest" for teens aged twelve to eighteen years (1998). Media products become a core component of teen culture and hence a critical ingredient of peer conversations and social interactions. They constitute "cultural capital."

Adolescent researchers have described a pyramid of teen media use—the media diet of today's teen. At the broad base of the pyramid are those choices based wholly on the teen culture (including hit television shows and top ten songs and music videos). As one progresses toward the point, individual choices based on

Establishing effective communication with youth requires understanding their culture, which are the things in their world that are meaningful to them. (Shirley Zeiberg)

taste, age, personality, and demographics become important (Brown and Witherspoon, 2000; Brown, 1999).

Teen work is another aspect of culture. Teens work at a number of jobs, including fast-food restaurants, music shops, and other organizations connected to their culture. There is a sizable amount of research on teen work (Stern and Nakata, 1989), but little of it has explored its interaction with culture.

Hip-hop is one particularly prevalent form of current youth culture. The origins of hip-hop lie in the black and Hispanic communities of the inner city in

the 1970s; there are those that argue that its true source lies in ancient African traditions (Harper and Harper, 1999). Four traditions can be noted: break dancing, rap music, graffiti, and fashion.

Break dancing, a form of movement that is characterized as full of verve, originated as a competitive endeavor. It is highly athletic and acrobatic.

Rap music involves deejaying in which the person playing the music exercises his or her selection and sometimes comments on the music. The selection and order thus become critical aspects of the presentation. Scratching involves scratching the record to make a particular noise that becomes integral to the music. Hence, these two devices lead to a reformulation that enhances the rhythmic pattern of the music.

Graffiti art predated hip-hop in New York City. Graffiti art is, of course, art—designs or pictures, names, and other symbols drawn on subway cars, billboards, sides of buildings, and so forth, frequently with spray paint. The now deceased artist Keith Haring raised this art to the level at which it became appreciated by the art world.

Hip-hop fashion involves baggy or loose clothing, sportswear, hooded sweatshirts, skull and baseball caps, and faded denim. Today, major designers such as Tommy Hilfiger have entered the arena. Hip-hop is big business today and permeates youth culture, particularly among minority youth, the fastest growing segment of the youth population (Harper and Harper, 1999). Nonetheless, teens' interaction with hip-hop is poorly understood by academic researchers. What is its appeal? What is its impact on values and behaviors as youth make the transition to adulthood?

Sean "Puff Daddy" Combs is an influential mainstream trendsetter in today's youth culture. He has dominated the rap music industry and influenced the interests of youth worldwide. Puff Daddy thus becomes an important role model, particularly for minority youth. What message does he send through his lyrics and music videos? Sports are another purveyor of youth culture. Youth participate in sports and more importantly are spectators of professional sports, wear sports clothes and logos, read sports magazines, and idolize sports figures. They are responsible for inventions such as "extreme sports" that have spread to other segments of the population. *USA Today* has launched a focus on high school sports to attract teen readers. Perhaps one reason that figures like Puff Daddy and arenas like sports are so important to youth is that entertainment and sports represent two avenues for success for poor, minority youth. Again, research is needed.

Youth culture has not received much in the way of serious consideration by academic scholars of youth development. Social cognitive learning theory (Bandura, 1996) is one proposed mechanism by which culture operates through the media to impact youth. Youth attend to models such as Puff Daddy or Michael Jordan and emulate their behaviors, particularly in their choice of advertised products such as sneakers and beverages. Certainly marketers recognize that a model such as Michael Jordan is important to the marketing of their product. The business world has, in fact, appreciated the size and power of the youth market, and has shaped its marketing to youth on a solid basis of research, but that research is typically not available to the public. It is, in fact, proprietary, although it can be available for a price.

There are a number of interesting empirical questions needing research. For example, to what extent does the market create culture, to what extent does it mimic it? There are numerous examples of advertising that intentionally pit the youth market against adults regarding interests and preferences; products range from clothes to chewing gum and cereal. Do these ads mimic youth culture or create it through their product development, based on what they know from market research to be youth interests? A second example is the diffusion of youth culture to the wider society.

How does an innovation such as the style of baggy male pants hanging off the hips become so widely dispersed? This is a style that originated in inner-city poor neighborhoods because prisoners are not allowed to have belts and hence frequently find their pants in this position. Yet almost all teen boys now adopt this style, including white, middle-class suburban boys who are academically oriented. Methods such as ethnography may be particularly helpful in research in these areas, and in fact the private sector has relied on ethnography, focus groups, and other such methods.

Culture is a prevalent and powerful presence in the lives of youth. We cannot understand today's teenagers without attending to, studying, and understanding their culture. Academic research has much to learn from the business world about directing research effort at youth culture. Strategies need to be explored for increasing the interaction between the two communities.

Lonnie R. Sherrod

See also Appearance, Cultural Factors in; College; Computers; Dating; Ethnocentrism; Freedom; Media; Peer Groups; Rebellion; Sports and Adolescents; Television; Television, Effects of; Youth Outlook

References and Further Reading
Bandura, A. 1996. *Social Foundations of Thought and Action: A Social Cognitive Theory.* NJ: Prentice-Hall.
Boas, Franz. 1911. *The Mind of Primitive Man.* New York: Free Press.
Brown, J. D. 1999. "Adolescents and the Media." *Newsletter of the Society for Research on Adolescence.* Spring 1999, 1–2, 10.
Brown, J. D., and E. M. Witherspoon. 2000 (In press). "The Mass Media and Adolescents' Health in the United States." In *Media, Sex, Violence, and Drugs in the Global Village.* Edited by Y. R. Kamalipour. Boulder, CO: Rowman and Littlefield.
Harper, P. T., and B. M. Harper. 1999. *Hip-Hop's Influence within Youth Popular Culture.* Silver Springs, MD: McFarland.
Mead, M. 1961. *Coming of Age in Samoa: A Psychological Study of Primitive Youth for Western Civilization.* US: William Morrow.
Roberts, D. 1993. "Adolescents and the Mass Media." Pp. 171–186 in *Adolescence in the 1990's.* Edited by R. Takanishi. New York: Teachers College Press.
Shweder, R., J. Goodnow, G. Hatano, R. LeVine, H. Markus, and P. Miller. 1998. "The Cultural Psychology of Development: One Mind, Many Mentalities." Pp. 865–938 in *Handbook of Child Psychology.* Vol. 1, *Theoretical Models of Human Development.* Edited by W. Damon and R. Lerner. New York: Wiley.
Stern, D., and Y. Nakata. 1989. "Characteristics of High School Students' Paid Jobs, and Employment Experience after Graduation." In *Adolescence and Work: Influences of Social Structure, Labor Markets, and Culture.* Edited by D. Stern and D. Eichorn. Hillsdale, NJ: Erlbaum.
Terry, C. 1998. "Today's Target, Tomorrow's Readers." *Newspaper Youth Readership,* September.
Willis, P. 1990. *Common Culture.* Boulder, CO: Westview Press.

Youth Gangs

Introduction

Youth gangs have been a part of American culture since the Bowery Boys began hanging out on street corners after the American Revolution. Since that time, a consensus on the definition of a gang has not been reached. Although many gangs today are populated by young people from neighborhoods that are characterized by high unemployment rates and high educational dropout levels, as well as a general feeling of hopelessness, not

Present-day gangs are more diverse and complex than gangs of earlier times. In general, gang members behave in ways that set them apart from mainstream culture. (Daniel Laine/Corbis)

all gangs share an impoverished background. Today, youth gangs are springing up in affluent suburbs and in rural areas.

Early definitions of the term *gang* did not focus on criminal activity, but rather on delinquent behavior. Today, since no consensus on the definition has been reached, consequently every organization that comes in contact with youth gangs has created an operational definition that suits its own needs. Understandably, law enforcement's definition focuses on activities that are breaking the laws, yet not all jurisdictions use the same definition. The only consensus reached is that gangs vary by activity and membership.

Research in the last decade has provided varying definitions and characteristics of gangs and their members. According to Carl Taylor's research on Detroit, Michigan, gangs, it is possible to classify gangs into three categories: scavenger, territorial, and corporate. Scavenger gangs lack a purpose other than their impulsive behavior and need to belong. They are loose knit and have no particular goals, no purpose, and no substantial camaraderie. For the most part they are immoral but not criminal. When scavenger gangs become serious about organizing and set goals, they move into the territorial stage. A territorial gang claims territory as being the gang's, and their objective is to protect their turf from outsiders. The final category is the well-organized corporate gang, whose focus is on material gain and whose gang activities revolve around illegal means of making money.

The diversity of gangs is also growing with the rise of rural and affluent suburban gangs. Although gangs may vary in demographics (i.e., race, ethnicity, income, sex, age, and so on), some researchers have concluded that their similarities include lack of positive role models, low self-esteem, fear for physical safety, peer influence, and lack of family stability.

Historical Perspective
The earliest record of gangs in the United States may have been as early as the eighteenth century, at the end of the American Revolution, 1783. Some of these gangs were known as the Bowery Boys, the Smith Vly Gang, the Broadway Boys, and the Long Bridge Boys. These were noncriminal gangs who spent their time hanging out on street corners and having fistfights with rival gangs.

During the early years after the Civil War ended, immigration increased for industrial centers like New York, Chicago, and Detroit. The Irish, Polish, Jewish, and Italian immigrants who came were impoverished, and they formed gangs based on ethnicity. Due to the increase in population of the urban areas and depression in the economy, the gap between the rich and poor grew wider. According to Frederick Thrasher, there were 1,313 gangs in Chicago in the 1920s. Many, but not all, of these gangs were ethnic gangs. The increase of immigrants to urban areas continued throughout this century. In particular, in the early 1940s, large numbers of Puerto Ricans entered New York City. This fact, along with a growing African American population from the South, contributed to the large minority populations in northern cities. While the Eastern European ethnic groups were establishing their communi-ties, Puerto Ricans and African Americans became a strong presence.

Racial conflict at this time was clear in the big northern cities such as Detroit, where one of the worst race riots in American history took place in 1943. Groups of white youth gang members roamed the city attacking black citizens. Around the same time in Los Angeles, the Zoot Suit Riots of 1943 were under way. In these riots, white residents and visiting soldiers harassed and beat up young Chicano men who dressed in the popular zoot suit style of clothing.

The Watts riots of 1965 had the same results for African American youths as the Zoot Suit Riots of 1943 had for Mexican American youth. The outcome was that due to the media's negative portrayal of them, these youths began to see themselves differently. They chose to see themselves as defiant rather than defeated and to redefine exclusion as exclusivity. The media began their exaggerated view of a gangster from this era and can be blamed for the present-day stereotype. This stereotype includes the belief that a gang member is a Latino or African American illiterate youth who comes from a female-headed household in an impoverished urban area. At the same time suburban gangsters are not seen as a threat because they have been portrayed as literate, misunderstood youth who come from intact families in affluent communities.

Historically and currently, gangs in fact span the spectrum from whites to blacks, from rich to poor, from literate to illiterate, from nonviolent to violent, from noncriminal to criminal, from rural to urban, from tight-knit organizations to loosely knit groups. Whether or not a consensus is ever found on a definition, a realistic portrayal of the youth gang member is impossible without a respect for all people.

Influence of Media

The debate about what constitutes a gang has been underscored by the portrayal of gangs and gangsters in the media. Entertainment has become a big business as an industry that promotes and sells gangsters, action heroes, and violence. The media have been developing a bio-sketch of a gang member since the Zoot Suit Riots of 1943 and using it to keep fear of diversity in the minds of all who are willing to be taken in.

For the past five decades the entertainment industry has had ever-increasing interaction with our youth. The practice of society during this time has been to blame the popular culture (i.e., music, style of dress, media, cinema, and so on) for all the ills it encounters. In the 1950s, popular music was blamed for lowering the morals of our children. In the 1960s, communism was said to be idealized by popular music, and in the 1970s the drug use of young people was also blamed on popular culture. In the 1980s, this same culture was blamed for causing teen suicide and encouraging gang violence. The 1990s blamed popular culture for all the school violence. Whether or not we can put the blame on popular culture isn't fully known; what is suggested is that pop culture has had a hand in desensitizing our youth toward violence and delinquency.

The American cinema has had a long history of gangster movies. From *West Side Story* to the more hard-core portrayal of criminal street gangsters today, the cinema has literally been a training ground for gang wanna-bes. Classic movies such as *The Godfather* give an excellent example of Frederick Thrasher's evolution of

street gangs rising from neighborhood play groups and evolving into successful criminal street gangs. From the portrayal of rebelling youth *(Rebel without a Cause, Blackboard Jungle, Wild Ones),* to the portrayal of star-crossed love *(West Side Story),* to the portrayal of the hard-core reality of street gangsters *(Menace II Society, 187, Heat, Boys in the Hood),* the youth of America did not have to look far for gangster role models.

Society, especially the media, have been ready to assign responsibility for brutal acts exclusively to so-called vicious gangs. But the reality is that gang members are of all kinds, with only about 10 percent of gangs being composed of hard-core, violent constituents. Researchers have found that most gang members are peripherally involved in violence, with only a small percentage of gang members actually being responsible for the violence.

Gang Myths

In order to properly gauge the gang influence in a community, one must first address and dispel popular myths about gangs. Although there are many myths in existence today, the following are a select few that tend to come up often.

Myth 1: All street gangs are turf oriented.
Reality: There are gangs that claim ownership to a particular territory, but this is not the exclusive type of gang. Others include scavenger and corporate gangs.

Myth 2: Females are not allowed to join gangs.
Reality: Females are joining gangs in record numbers. One study of female gangs showed females in

autonomous gangs involved in organized criminal activities.

Myth 3: There are no gangs in my neighborhood.
Reality: Today, no neighborhood, regardless of economic status, is immune to gang membership. Gangs can be found in rural areas and suburban areas, as well as urban areas.

Myth 4: Gang members wear baggy clothes and athletic team baseball caps.
Reality: Baggy clothing has become the "cool" style of dress and not a uniform that only gang members wear.

Myth 5: All gangs have a single leader and a tight structure.
Reality: Some gangs are loosely knit organizations, virtually having no leadership.

Myth 6: Gangs are a law enforcement problem.
Reality: Gangs are a problem for every member of society, including parents, teachers, and clergy, as well as police.

Myth 7: I know a gang member when I see one.
Reality: This statement opens the door to racism. Using traditional ideas of gang membership would mean that only Latino and African American youths would be targeted. It is important to remember that youth gang members are diverse in color, style of dress, activities they engage in, and economic backgrounds.

Conclusion

Historically, youth gangs began as a group of young people hanging out on street corners. The majority of these early gang members were bonded by their ethnicity. Ethnicity is the common denominator the media and society focus on when discussing gangs. Our nation's gang problem continues to grow, emphasizing the need to stop the cycle of new members. In order to better address the needs of youth today, we need to be aware of the fact that gangs are no longer an urban issue. Currently we are seeing a rapid growth of suburban and rural gangs. The majority of these are not ethnic gangs. Society needs to change the way it uses the term *gang*, taking into account the fact that gangs are diverse and range from noncriminal to criminal and from loosely knit to highly structured; members come from diverse ethnic backgrounds; they experience different reasons for joining; and they pursue different activities. Youth gangs should be defined by the behavior that is associated with gangs and not by ethnic makeup.

Carl S. Taylor
Wilma Novalés Wibert

See also Aggression; Delinquency, Mental Health, and Substance Abuse Problems; Ethnic Identity; Identity; Juvenile Crime; Juvenile Justice System; Peer Groups; Peer Pressure; Peer Status; Rites of Passage; Violence

References and further reading
Cromwell, Paul, D. Taylor, and W. Palacios. 1992. "Youth Gangs: A 1990's Perspective." *Juvenile & Family Court Journal* 43, no. 3: 25–31.
Curry, G. David, and Irving A. Spergel. 1992. "Gang Involvement and Delinquency among Hispanic and African-American Adolescent Males." *Journal of Research in Crime and Delinquency* 29: 273–291.

Evans, William P., Carla Fitzgerald, Daniel Weigel, and Sara Chvilicek. 1999. "Are Rural Gang Members Similar to Their Urban Peers? Implications for Rural Communities." *Youth & Society* 30, no. 3: 267–282.

Fagan, Jeffre E. 1989. "The Social Organization of Drug Use and Drug Dealing among Urban Gangs." *Criminology* 27: 633–669.

Goldstein, Arnold P., and Ronald Huff. 1993. *The Gang Intervention Handbook*. Champaign, IL: Research Press.

Goldstein, Arnold P., and Fernand I. Soriano. 1994. "Juvenile Gangs." In *Reason to Hope: A Psychosocial Perspective on Violence and Youth*. Edited by Leonard D. Eron, Jacqueline H. Gentry, and P. Schlegel. Washington DC: American Psychological Association.

Huff, C. Ronald. 1990. *Gangs in America*. Newbury Park, CA: Sage.

Monti, D. J. 1993. "Origins and Problems of Gang Research in the United States." In *Gangs*. Edited by S. Cummings and D. J. Monti. Albany: State University of New York Press.

Moore, J. W. 1978. *Homeboys: Gangs, Drugs and Prison in the Barrios of Los Angeles*. Philadelphia: Temple University Press.

Osman, Karen. 1992. *Gangs*. San Diego: Lucent Books.

Sante, Luc. 1991. *Low Life: Lures and Snares of Old New York*. New York: Vintage Books.

Shaw, C. R., and H. D. McKay. 1942. *Juvenile Delinquency and Urban Areas*. Chicago: University of Chicago Press.

Shelden, Randell G., Sharon K. Tracy, and William B. Brown. 1997. *Youth Gangs in American Society*. Wadsworth Publishing.

Spergel, Irving A., and David G. Curry. 1993. "The National Youth Gang Survey: A Research and Development Process." In *The Gang Intervention Handbook*. Edited by Arnold P. Goldstein and C. Ronald Huff. Champaign, IL: Research Press.

Taylor, Carl S. 1990. *Dangerous Society*. East Lansing: Michigan State University Press.

———. 1993. *Girls, Gangs, Women and Drugs*. East Lansing: Michigan State University Press.

Thrasher, Frederick M. 1927. *The Gang*. Chicago: University of Chicago Press.

Youth Outlook

Americans have become increasingly concerned about what they perceive as the degenerating moral values and behavior of young people. Supported by a nostalgia for the past and a litany of statistics on youth violence and teenage suicide, this view shapes the way Americans understand adolescence. Their willingness to believe in the moral degeneration of youth was shown last year when police arrested two boys under ten years old in Chicago for the murder of an eleven-year-old girl. Americans were initially shocked, but quickly adjusted to the idea. Even after the children were exonerated, the media focused on the complicity of the police, not our eagerness to believe that two young boys might commit such a crime. Their willingness to believe may stem from a trend in the way that adolescents are thought about and portrayed in the media. Writers, journalists, and many researchers focus on the cynicism, despair, and demoralization of contemporary youth, characterizing them as hopeless, aimless, materialistic, hedonistic, even nihilistic. National attention is paid to adolescents who indeed may be some or all of these things.

But is this true of most adolescents? Looking for an answer to this question, we went into the heartland of America to find out what adolescents, ones whose voices are not typically heard in the media, had to say about themselves and the world they live in. Our study describes what these adolescents say when they reach for their deepest insights into the laws that govern their lives.

We studied essays written by teenagers for the Templeton Foundation's Laws of Life Essay Contest. Sir John Templeton began the Laws of Life Essay Contest to encourage young people to reflect on and articulate the moral principles and ideals

Many youth maintain a positive outlook on themselves and their world.
(Wartenberg/Picture Press/Corbis)

that govern their lives. The contest provides students with the opportunity to forge or clarify their personal moral understandings. It asks teens to reflect on their intuitions about the way the world works and encourages them to do their best, to test the limits of their wisdom, and to critically reflect on and support their positions. The essays suggest trends in the content of adolescents' moral understandings, provide a picture of the spiritual, emotional, and intellectual assets they draw upon when faced with complex personal dilemmas, and suggest some age and gender differences on these issues. From what students omit in their

essays, the study also reveals what adolescents may need to learn in order to cope with the challenges of modern living and citizenship.

A General Description of the Adolescents Who Participated

We examined 476 essays from five schools. The schools were located in two areas of the country. The majority of the essays (259) came from two public middle schools located in a rural section of the Bible Belt. Most of the students from these schools come from families of middle and lower socioeconomic status. Fifty-two essays were written by students from a private Catholic K–8 school located in an urban area. This school serves an "at-risk" population of primarily African Americans. Of the total essays, 311 came from these three middle schools. The two high schools in the sample were both private religious schools. One was a long established parochial school in an urban area, from which 136 essays came. The school is located in a distressed neighborhood and draws from a diverse population. Another high school in the sample provided 29 essays from eleventh and twelfth graders. Located in an upper-middle-class suburb, this school has a reputation for providing a Christ-centered education. Females wrote 262 of the essays; 214 were from males. The authors of the essays were all between the ages of twelve and seventeen.

TABLE 1

	Type	Ages	Males	Females	Totals
Schools 1 & 2	Rural/ Public	12, 13, 14	111	148	259
School 3	Urban/ Relig	12, 13	26	26	52
School 4	Urban/ Relig	14, 15, 16, 17	62	74	136
School 5	Suburban/ Relig	16, 17	15	14	29

What the Essays Revealed

Six basic themes emerged from the essays: Responsibility to Self, Responsibility to Others, Positive Emotional Orientations to Life and Other People, Spirituality/Religion, Skepticism, and Outliers. Outliers are essays that lay outside the first five themes. (Note that many essays express more than one theme or law of life.)

Responsibility to Self. First, 42 percent of the students expressed the wisdom of feeling or showing deferential regard for one's self. The theme of Responsibility to Self included a range of student concerns. The majority of the essays discussed the need to persevere and work hard. One student wrote: "Hard work in my dictionary is the force put into something to make one's life better. That is what my dad has raised me up by, and that is what I'm going to do" (twelve-year-old male). Many essays reflected the importance of being self-confident, of exercising good judgment, of using self-control for one's own good, and of accepting suffering. The theme also included the idea that, as a general rule, one ought to strive to improve one's self. An offshoot of this line of thought was the mention of the wisdom of establishing goals and pursuing education. One young woman wrote, "I felt like I was going around in circles and was never moving on. Right then and there I realized that I had no goals. . . . In order for me to go to law school, I had to finish high school, and in order for me to get into high school, I had to take the test. . . . As Georgia Douglas Johnson would say, "Your world is as big as you make it" (thirteen-year-old female).

A group of essays within this theme articulated the importance of retaining one's integrity and individuality, even treating it as an obligation: "People tell me every day that I'm weird. If they want to think that, it is fine with me. . . . Like I said earlier, it doesn't bother me" (twelve-year-old female). The theme also included concerns with honesty, patience, and humility. The contents of one essay was the following moral story:

> There once was a little boy who wanted a new bike for his birthday. Unfortunately, his mother and father didn't have the money to get him a new bike. Every day while coming home from school he stopped by the bikeshop. He looked and looked for hours until he couldn't take it any more. So he decided to steal it from a young man with wealthy parents. He thought to himself "they won't mind." One day before his birthday his father received a promotion that he hadn't expected. So he decided to surprise him with the new bike he wanted. They [sic] next morning when the boy was up, he came downstairs to see the brand new bike. All of a sudden he did not feel too good. He started to wish he had the patience to wait. (Thirteen-year-old male)

Responsibility to Others. The second significant theme students articulated was the importance of feeling or showing deferential regard to others. Thirty-two percent of the teenagers discussed this. The significant difference between Responsibility to Others and Responsibility to Self is that actions taken under the rubric of the former are intended to benefit others, not self. For example, concern for honesty in this theme aims at creating civil harmony and interpersonal trust, not personal gain:

Honor is a part of honesty but honesty is more than that. It is partially trust. If somebody lies to you, it breaks that trust. Honesty is a strange thing sometimes. A little kid could have more honesty than a politician. Honesty, like honor, is needed in order to have a happy and good civilization. (Thirteen-year-old male)

Realizing why one has a responsibility to others is the fundamental element in one's development of a responsibility toward others. Although I do not claim to have fully attained a complete grasp of integrity, I have attempted to practice maintaining it. It is, in a certain perspective, a definition of who we are, and what we give to others. (Fourteen-year-old male)

Responsibility to Others was also dominated by concern for respect:

I feel respect is a crucial value that my children must have to be virtuous individuals. With this virtue they will treat others fairly. They will also consider their feelings. If they are respectful they will listen to and adhere to my advice and be obedient. My children also won't prejudge people. They will treat everyone equally and hold everyone in their same regard until they get to know them and their personality. (Fourteen-year-old male)

Respect is a quality which I feel is needed in a special sort of dual relationship. This type of relationship consists of having the respect of others, and at the same time giving them the respect which they are due. . . . [I]f a person gains the respect of another, then they will most likely also gain their trust and open-mindedness. . . . [I]f a person always respects others, then they will learn to look at the good inside of others and they will gain that person's respect in return. (Fifteen-year-old male)

Responsibility to others also included paying attention to the Golden Rule, keeping an open mind, and maintaining harmony by exercising self-control. Concern with loyalty and trustworthiness were also included.

Positive Emotional Orientations to Life and Other People. The most popular theme, by far, was Positive Emotional Outlook to Life and Other People; 67 percent of the essays articulated laws related to this theme. This theme was quite broad and differs from the previous in that it focuses on the emotional connection between the essay writers and others in the world. By far, the law of love was the most popular:

Love, an essence at the core of all humans, can be the only true happiness. (Sixteen-year-old male)

Love is the key to living. . . . When I think of love, I think of God, Jesus, family and friends. I believe that there would be a lot less violence if everyone had love in his or her heart. . . . I say that love is the greatest law of life. (Thirteen-year-old female)

Calls to live life fully and enjoyably, to be grateful for what you have, and to be particularly grateful for your family and friends were also present:

I learned a very important lesson from Christina's death. . . . I learned that you have to cherish each moment for what it is and enjoy life while you have the chance to live it. (Seventeen-year-old female)

Please remember to respect your brother or sister no matter what the age. Be thankful that you were blessed with them. I SURE AM! (Thirteen-year-old female)

Gratefulness teaches a person to be thankful for everything, and to be more particular about what you need and don't need in your life. Most importantly, gratefulness of your own possessions, and capabilities helps create a more giving heart that desires to reach out to others that are truly in need. (Sixteen-year-old female)

The importance of forgiveness, generosity, trust, kindness, compassion, and the general attitude of hopefulness also indicated the positive emotional orientation of the students.

Spirituality/Religion. Eighteen percent of the students expressed secure belief in the truth and value of God. Many of the essays discussed the importance of loving God and expressed strong faith and a hopeful optimistic relationship with God:

Then, one day, he came over on his week leave, and told us that he was going to war in thirty days. He didn't seem nervous or scared of it. He was very brave. . . . It is a very tragic thing for us and his family, but mostly for him. . . . I know in my heart that if me and Donny are brave, always pray, and trust in God, everything will eventually turn out okay. Even if Donny gets hurt or killed, God will deliver us, tell us what to do, and give

us the strength to do it. (Twelve-year-old female)

Our God, who knows and sees all, certainly does not miss those who choose enduring faithfulness. . . . At Christ's judgment, God promises to reward those who have been faithful to his calling. (Seventeen-year-old female)

Others spoke of the importance of fearing God:

I picked [Jesus] to be my savior because I do not want to go to the lake of fire when I die. I also love him. (Thirteen-year-old male)

Skepticism. A remarkably small number of students (.02 percent) articulated skeptical laws of life. Out of 476 essays, only 11 were skeptical, and 7 of these came from a single senior class. They focused on such issues as the unfairness of life:

For some reason it finally sunk in. Life can deal a good hand or it can deal a bad hand. My mother was dealt a bad hand and she lost the game. [She was diagnosed with a chronic disease.] (Seventeen-year-old male)

Not everyone gets a fair chance to accomplish his or her goals no matter how hard he or she tries at it. (Seventeen-year-old male)

These essays also articulated the necessity of depending only upon yourself in the world:

Throughout my life I have learned many lessons, but there is one that I will never forget. The lesson is that people sometimes take advantage of others' good nature. People do this because their needs come first, no matter what the circumstances. . . . People are for themselves in this world. All you have is yourself. Everyone will look to get over on you to meet their needs no matter how it effects another. To this day, I am still angry about what happened. (Seventeen-year-old male)

Although many of the essays were purely skeptical, a postive note can be heard in some.

Dad was right, life wasn't fair. He thought about all the unfair things that had happened to him, and all the unfair things that had happened to others. Joey knew he had a bad day, but he also realized that while it could have been a lot better, it also could have been a lot worse. (Sixteen-year-old male)

Outliers. The final theme consisted of oddball and street-smart laws of life. Only .05 percent of the essays were outliers. They included the following:

> Wear a seatbelt.
> Don't drink and drive.
> Keep Humor in Your Life.
> Exercise Freedom of Speech.
> Reality is Mysterious.
> Play sports.
> Learn sign language.
> Own a dog.
> Have a hero in the Worldwide
>   Wrestling Federation.

The distribution of theme by frequency and gender is shown in Figure 1. Clearly, teenagers most frequently revealed the importance of a Positive Emotional Outlook on Life and Others. This was followed by Respect for Self and then Respect for Others. Spirituality and Religion also was important to many adolescents. Suprisingly, there were very few Skeptical and Outlying essays.

As shown in Figure 1, some of these themes were distributed differently across gender. On the whole, females were more positive than males; nearly twice as many females (201) expressed Positive Emotional laws of life as did males (119). It is also worth noting that all eleven Skeptical essays were written by males. Again, seven of them were from a single high school class. Eighty percent of the Outliers were also written by males.

The essays were also analyzed by age. The trends worth noting in the analysis by age and gender include the relative stability of Positive Emotional Orientations to Life over time (see Figure 2). Interestingly, as a sense of Responsibility to Self increases from ages twelve to seventeen, a sense of Responsibility to Others declines (see Figure 3).

What the Essays Say about Youth Outlook

On the whole, the essays coalesce into an unusual portrait of adolescent thinking on moral laws of life. Instead of painting a cynical, materialistic, and demoralized picture of youth, the essays reflect persons with strong and positive veins of moral wisdom from which to draw. What the media and many researchers find most compelling about adolescents may be what is most unusual: adolescents who are "at risk" or already involved in the penal system, or who exemplify the traits of what has come to be known as Generation X. Indeed, the essays suggest

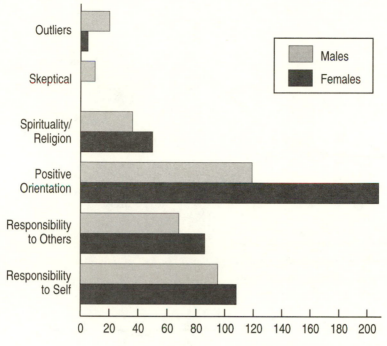

Figure 1: Frequency by Theme and Gender

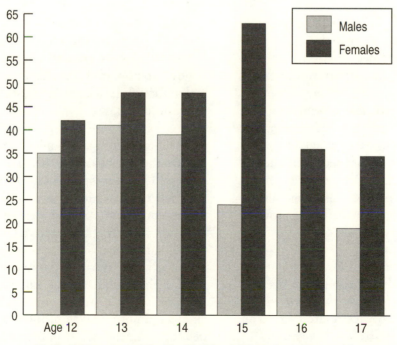

Figure 2: Frequency of Positive Emotional Orientation by Age and Gender

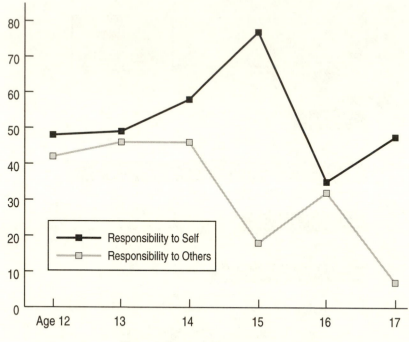

Figure 3: Sense of Responsibility over Time

that skepticism is low to the point of being negligible among males and nonexistent among females. Positivity dramatically outweighs negativity in the essays we examined.

In addition to the absence of the expected cynicism and demoralization, the essays demonstrated a lack of materialism as well. Students spoke eloquently of being grateful, but not for their material possessions. The following clearly represents the sentiments of the group in general:

So often I see myself buying something new, going out to eat, or even watching my favorite TV show without realizing how fortunate I am to be able to do these things. Many of us take for granted the things we have

and can do in our daily lives . . . the school we go to, the sports we play or the abilities we possess. . . . It is unbelievable how much we have yet we don't think twice about it. (Sixteen-year-old female)

The teens expressed thanks for personal health and the health of their family and friends. They also spoke of how fortunate they felt to have friends and to be receiving an education. As a whole, the sample was not from highly privileged families. Some subportions were privileged economically, but most of the writers came from either moderate or disadvantaged families. The positivity expressed in the essays did not come from the fulfillment of material desires but out of a sense of appreciation of what they had.

Most of the laws of life came out of teenagers' personal experience and from moral exemplars. Many laws of life were articulated as responses to things that had happened to students, what we commonly think of as unfortunate or traumatic life events. Students were assimilating deaths, disappointments, and conflicts, and coping with dilemmas of trust and integrity. The positive spin they placed on these experiences is notable in that it is usually considered a special sign of wisdom. The essay writers seemed to find joy in unexpected places and inspiration in small moments. One young woman found unexpected happiness in taking care of her disabled sister. Another young man rediscovered his faith in God in a small moment with his girlfriend. It also seems that students were highly attuned to the behavior of moral exemplars. One young woman tells us about her cousin who died: "The laws of my life, which are to live to the fullest, to appreciate your family, and to accept the hardships in your life, were modeled through my cousin Chris. Live" (fifteen-year-old female).

Not surprisingly, the essays reflected an increasing sense of Responsibility to Self for adolescents over time. Adolescence is commonly understood as a time of identity formation and focus. However, it is surprising, even alarming, that at the same time Responsibility to Self increases, Responsibility to Others diminishes (see Figure 3). This second point highlights a major difference from what both Jean Piaget and Eric Erickson found in their studies on developing adolescents conducted earlier this century. A hallmark of adolescence for Piaget and Erickson was that along with an increasing cognitive ability to generalize arose a growing concern with and sense of responsibility

to society at large. This hallmark was clearly lacking in this study.

It may also be cause for concern that the thinking in the essays on moral issues was, on the whole, consistently confined to small and local communities. In general, students' circle of concern extended to self, family, friends, and congregation. Only a few essays expressed concern about or exhibited positive connections to worlds outside their own small circle. The shape of adolescents' sense of positivity toward life becomes apparent in conjunction with students' general lack of concern for communities outside their own, their focus on their own experience, and their diminishing sense of responsibility toward others. Given the fact of cultural pluralism in the United States and increasing trends of globalization, these conditions have the potential to become problematic. It may be cause for concern that students' positive moral attitude extends only toward a narrow segment of the population and does not include a sense of responsibility even toward members of that group.

The trends in the essays, however, may have been influenced by the nature of the sample and the study; the data were constrained by both. First, essays were drawn from only two locales; thus, the sample cannot be considered representative of adolescents across the nation. Nor was the sample random; all the schools chose to be involved in the contest. Although the majority of the essays came from public middle schools, it is important to note that three out of the five schools were religious. All of the data from fifteen- to seventeen-year-olds came from students enrolled in Christian or Catholic high schools. Due to a misunderstanding, one of the high schools sent only the top twenty-nine finalists from the contest. In addition to the post hoc analysis, no predetermined scale was used to assess or evaluate the essays. The sample was not random, and so analysis across socioeconomic status could not be done. Nor could an analysis of the difference between urban and rural students be done. Even the analysis of age was confounded by the fact that the data from all fifteen- to seventeen-year-olds came from students in religious schools. And, although the Templeton Foundation provided teachers with a contest guidebook, there was no controlling for the instructions teachers provided their students. The instructions allow teachers and schools tremendous latitude in framing the purposes and requirements of participation in the contest. For example, some of the essays were geared to fulfill a particular assignment for a class. One teacher used the contest as a vehicle to teach her students how to write a five-paragraph essay. Another teacher required students to write about their biblical laws of life.

The fact that the essays were written for a competitive event may also have influenced the young people's thinking on what they presented as their laws of life. Some of the essays were graded by teachers as well as adjudicated and rewarded through the contest. The fact that the essays were part of a contest and may have been graded by a teacher both helps and hinders us as researchers. Although this may have biased the students' responses in that they might, on some level, have written to please the judges and teacher, it may also have been the catalyst for deep critical thinking. The competition and critique may have provided incentive to go beyond what

they might otherwise have written. It is clear in any case that the contest invites young people to dig deeper into their moral and social philosophies. In some schools, this seemed to have happened; batches of essays were deeply thoughtful and provocative, even profound. In others, depth of reflection was not present, particularly when the essays were used as a vehicle toward some other curricular end, like the learning of the five-paragraph essay. It seems less likely that these students were clarifying or forging their moral positions than fulfilling an assignment. The question of whether the essays are a clear reflection of students' moral laws of life remains.

Final Implications

The student essays that we examined revealed a number of noteworthy characteristics. Most importantly, the vast majority of students expressed a more positive view of life than is commonly recognized in popular or media portrayals of today's teens. Moreover, most of the essays showed a great deal of compassion, spirituality, and personal and social responsibility. All of these characteristics suggest a cohort of youngsters that has a strong moral sense.

But it is a moral sense that seems to be confined to the boundaries of students' immediate interpersonal relationships—their friends and family in particular. The contents of the essays reflected little concern about the larger society beyond home, school, or neighborhood. Concepts such as civic duty and patriotism were all but absent. Nor was there much mention of social causes, political leaders, or news events.

If the essays we examined are representative of contemporary society's adolescent population, this is a dramatic and unsettling change from prior cohorts. All of the classic developmental theories—Piaget, Erikson, Sullivan, Hall—mark adolescence as an age when young people work out their larger societal beliefs and concerns, a process that includes intense reflection about ideological belief systems. This process is a necessary precursor to citizenship. If it is not taking place today, one wonders how the institutions of a free and democratic society will be maintained in the future. Of course, it could be that the process is simply delayed in today's world. But it may also be that the cynicism associated with public life has caused teenagers to turn inward, at the expense of their civic growth.

Susan Verducci
William Damon

See also Ethnocentrism; Identity; Moral Development; Peer Groups; Political Development; Social Development; Youth Culture

BIBLIOGRAPHY

Abma, J., A. Chandra, W. Mosher, L. Peterson, and L. Piccinino, 1997. "Fertility, Family Planning, and Women's Health: New Data from the 1995 National Survey of Family Growth, National Center for Health Statistics." *Vital Health Statistics* 23, no.19.

Abramovitch, Rona, Jonathon L. Freedman, and Patricia Pliner. 1991. "Children and Money: Getting an Allowance, Credit Versus Cash, and Knowledge of Pricing." *Journal of Economic Psychology* 12: 27–45.

Acuña, Rodolfo. 1988. *Occupied America: A History of Chicanos*, 3rd ed. New York: HarperCollins.

———. 1996. *Anything but Mexican: Chicanos in Contemporary Los Angelos.* London: Verso.

Adams, Gerald. R. 1991. "Physical Attractiveness and Adolescent Development." Pp. 785–789 in *Encyclopedia of Adolescence.* Edited by Richard M. Lerner, Anne C. Petersen, and Jeanne Brooks-Gunn. New York: Garland.

Adams, G. R., and G. Munro. 1979. "Portrait of North American Runaways: A Critical Review." *Journal of Youth and Adolescence* 8: 359–371.

Adams, G. R., T. Gulotta, and M. A. Clancy. 1985. "Homeless Adolescents: A Descriptive Study of Similarities and Differences between Runaways and Throwaways." *Adolescence* 20: 715–724.

Adams, Gerald R., and Sheila K. Marshall. 1996. "A Developmental Social Psychology of Identity: Understanding the Person-in-Context." *Journal of Adolescence* 19: 429–442.

Adelman, Clifford. 1999. *Answers in the Tool Box: Academic Intensity, Attendance Patterns, and Bachelor's Degree Attainment.* Washington, DC: U.S. Department of Education, Office of Educational Research and Improvement.

Ahmed, Paul I., and Nancy Ahmed., eds. 1985. *Coping with Juvenile Diabetes.* Springfield: Thomas.

Ainsworth, Mary. 1982. "Attachment: Retrospect and Prospect." Pp. 3–30 in *The Place of Attachment in Human Behavior.* Edited by C. M. Parkes and J. Stevenson-Hinde. New York: Basic Books.

Ainsworth, Mary. 1989. "Attachments beyond Infancy." *American Psychologist* 44: 709–716.

Alan Guttmacher Institute, http://www.agi-usa.org

Alan Guttmacher Institute. 1994. *Sex and America's Teenagers.* New York: Alan Guttmacher Institute.

Alan Guttmacher Institute. 1994. *Sex and America's Teenagers.* Washington, DC: Author.

Alexander, Karl L., and Aaron Pallas. 1983. "Private Schools and Public Policy: New Evidence on Cognitive Achievement in Public and Private Schools." *Sociology of Education* 56, no. 4: 170–182.

Allen, Marylee, Karen Bonner, and Linda Greenan. 1988. "Federal Legislative Support for Independent Living." Pp. 19–32 in *Independent-Living Services for at-Risk Adolescents.* Edited by Edmund Mech. Washington DC: CWLA.

Allen, Theodore. 1994. *The Invention of the White Race, Volume One: Racial Oppression and Social Control.* London: Verso.

Allen, Vernon L., and David A. Wilder. 1979. "Social Support in Absentia: The Effect of an Absentee Partner on Conformity." *Human Relations* 32: 103–111.

Allgood-Merten, Betty P., Lewinsohn, Peter, and Hyman Hops. 1990. "Sex Differences in Adolescent Depression." *Journal of Abnormal Psychology* 99, no. 1: 55–63.

Allison, Paul D., and Frank F. Furstenberg, Jr. 1989. "Marital Dissolution Affects Children: Variations by Age and Sex." *Developmental Psychology* 25: 540–549.

Allport, Gordon W. 1950. *The Individual and His Religion: A Psychological Interpretation.* New York: Macmillan.

———. 1954. *The Nature of Prejudice.* New York: Addison-Wesley.

Almeida, David M., and Nancy L. Galambos. 1991. "Examining Father Iinvolvement and the Quality of Father-Adolescent Relations." *Journal of Research on Adolescence* 1, no. 2: 155–172.

———. 1993. "Continuity and Change in Father-Adolescent Relations." Pp. 27–40 in *Father-Adolescent Relationships.* Edited by Shmuel Shulman and W.

Andrew Collins. San Francisco: Jossey-Bass.

Almeida, David M., and Daniel A. McDonald. 1998. "Weekly Rhythms of Parents' Work Stress, Home Stress, and Parent Adolescent Tension." Pp. 53–67 in *Temporal Rhythms in Adolescence: Clocks, Calendars, and the Coordination of Daily Life.* Edited by Ann C. Crouter and Reed Larson. San Francisco: Jossey-Bass.

Almeida, David M., Elaine Wethington, and Daniel A. McDonald. In press. *Daily Variation in Paternal Engagement and Negative Mood: Implications for Emotionally Supportive and Conflictual Interactions.*

Alterman, Alan, and Ralph E. Tarter. 1983. "The Transmission of Psychological Vulnerability: Implications for Alcoholism Etiology." *Journal of Nervous and Mental Disorders* 171, no. 3: 147–154.

Alves, Julio. 1993. "Transgressions and Transformations: Initiation Rites among Urban Portuguese Boys." *American Anthropologist* 95, no. 4: 894–928.

Amabile, Teresa M. 1983. *The Social Psychology of Creativity.* New York: Springer-Verlag.

Amato, Paul R. 1993. "Children's Adjustment to Divorce: Theories, Hypotheses, and Empirical Support." *Journal of Marriage and the Family* 55: 23–38.

Amato, Paul R., and Bruce Keith. 1991. "Parental Divorce and the Well-being of Children: A Meta-Analysis." *Psychological Bulletin* 100: 26–46.

American Academy of Pediatrics. 1999. "Adolescent Pregnancy—Current Trends and Issues: 1998." *Pediatrics* 103, no. 2: 516–520.

American Association of University Women. 1992. *How Schools Shortchange*

Girls: The AAUW Report. Washington, DC: American Association of University Women Educational Foundation.

American Council on Education. Web site: http://www.acenet.edu/ (select GED link).

American Psychiatric Association 1994. *Diagnostic and Statistical Manual of Mental Disorders, Fourth Edition. (DSM-IV).* Washington, DC: American Psychiatric Association.

American Psychological Association. 1992. "Ethical Principles of Psychologists and Code of Conduct." *American Psychologist* 47: 1597–1611.

American Psychological Association Commission on Violence and Youth. 1993. *Violence and Youth: Psychology's Response.* Washington, DC: Public Interest Directorate.

American Social Health Association and Centers for Disease Control and Prevention hot line information website: http://www.ashastd.org

American Social Health Association, http://www.iwannaknow.org

Ammerman, Robert T., Vincent R. Kane, Gregory T. Slomka, Donald H. Reigel, Michael D. Franzen, and Kenneth D. Gadow. 1998. "Psychiatric Symptomatology and Family Functioning in Children and Adolescents with Spina Bifida." *Journal of Clinical Psychology in Medical Settings* 5: 449–465.

Anastasi, Anne. 1988. *Psychological Testing,* 6th ed. New York: Macmillan.

Anaya, Rodolfo A., Francisco Lomeli, eds. 1989. *Atzlan.* Albuquerque, NM: El Norte Publications.

Anderman, Eric M., and Martin Maehr. 1994. "Motivation and Schooling in the Middle Grades." *Review of Educational Research* 64: 287–309.

Anderson, Barbara J., and James C. Coyne. 1993. "Family Context and Compliance Behavior in Chronically Ill Children." Pp. 77–89 in *Developmental Aspects of Health Compliance Behavior.* Edited by Norman A. Krasnegor. Hillsdale, NJ: Erlbaum.

Anderson, Betsy, and Janet Vohs. 1992. "Another Look at Section 504." *Coalition Quarterly* 10, no. 1: 1–4.

Anderson, Elijah. 1999. *Code of the Street: Decency, Violence, and the Moral Life of the Inner City.* New York: Norton.

Anderson, E. R., E. M. Hetherington, and W. G. Clinempeel. 1989. "Transformations in Family Relations at Puberty: Effects of Family Context." *Journal of Early Adolescence* 9, no. 3: 310–334.

Anderson, Ronald E. 2000. "Youth and Information Technology." Unpublished manuscript, University of Minnesota.

Anthony, E. James, and Bertram J. Cohler, eds. 1987. *The Invulnerable Child.* New York: Guilford Press.

Anzaldúa, Gloria. 1987. *Borderlands: La Frontera, the New Mestiza.* San Francisco: Aunt Lute Books.

Appleton, P. L., P. E. Minchom, N. C. Ellis, C. E. Elliott, V. Boll, and P. Jones. 1994. "The Self-Concept of Young People with Spina Bifida: A Population-Based Study." *Developmental Medicine and Child Neurology* 36: 198–215.

Aquilino, William S. 1997. "From Adolescence to Young Adult: A Prospective Study of Parent-Child Relations during the Transition to Adulthood." *Journal of Marriage and Family* 59: 670–686.

Arbetter, Sandra. 1995. "Am I Normal? Those Teen Years." *Current Health* 2, no. 21: 6–7.

Arllen, Nancy L., Robert A. Gable, and Jo M. Hendrickson. 1994. "Toward an Understanding of the Origins of Aggression." *Preventing School Failure* 38, no. 3: 18–23.

Arnett, Jeffrey J. 1995. "Adolescents' Uses of Media for Self-Socialization." *Journal of Youth and Adolescence* 24: 519–533.

———. 1999. "Adolescent Storm and Stress, Reconsidered." *American Psychologist* 54: 317–326.

Aronson, Pamela J., Jeylan T. Mortimer, Carol Zierman, and Michael Hacker. 1996. "Generational Differences in Early Work Experiences and Evaluations." Pp. 25–62 in *Adolescents, Work and Family: An Intergenerational Developmental Analysis.* Edited by Jeylan T. Mortimer and Michael D. Finch. Thousand Oaks, CA: Sage.

Ary, D. V., T. E. Duncan, A. Biglan, C. W. Metzler, J. W. Noell, and K. Smolkowski. 1999. "Development of Adolescent Problem Behavior." *Journal of Abnormal Child Psychology* 27: 141–150.

Asher, Steven R., Shelly Hymel, and Peter D. Renshaw. 1984. "Loneliness in Children." *Child Development* 55: 1456–1464.

Association of Reproductive Health Professionals, http://www.arhp.org.

Attie, Ilana, and Jeanne Brooks-Gunn. 1989. "Development of Eating Problems in Adolescent Girls: A Longitudinal Study." *Developmental Psychology* 25: 70–79.

Babb, Linda. 1999. *Ethics in American Adoption.* Westport: Bergin and Garvey.

Bachman, Jerald G., and John Schulenberg. 1993. "How Part-Time Work Intensity Relates to Drug Use, Problem Behavior, Time Use, and Satisfaction among High School Seniors: Are These Consequences, or Merely Correlates?" *Developmental Psychology* 29, no. 2: 220–236.

Bachrach, C. A., C. C. Clogg, and D. R. Entwisle, eds. 1993. "Pathways to Childbearing and Childbirth Outcomes of Adolescent and Older Mothers." [Special issue]. *Journal of Research on Adolescence* 3 no.4.

Baddley, Alan D. 1986. *Working Memory.* Oxford, UK: Clarendon Press.

Bahr, S. J., R. D. Hawks, and G. Wang. 1993. "Family and Religious Influences on Adolescent Substance Abuse." *Youth and Society* 24: 443–465.

Bakker, A. B., B. P. Buunk, and A. S. R. Manstead. 1997. "The Moderating Role of Self-Efficacy Beliefs in the Relationship between Anticipated Feelings of Regret and Condom Use." *Journal of Applied Social Psychology* 17, no. 2: 2001–2014.

Baltes, Paul B., and Orville G. Brim Jr., eds. 1979. *Life-Span Development and Behavior,* Vol. 2. New York: Academic Press.

Baly, Iris. 1989. "Career and Vocational Development of Black Youth." Pp. 249–265 in *Black Adolescents.* Edited by Reginald Jones. Berkeley: Cobb and Henry Publishers.

Bancroft, John, and June Machover Reinisch, eds. 1990. *Adolescence and Puberty.* New York: Oxford University Press.

Bandura, Albert. 1986. *Social Foundations of Thought and Action: A Social Cognitive Theory.* Englewood Cliffs, NJ: Prentice-Hall.

Bandura, A. 1996. *Social Foundations of Thought and Action: A Social Cognitive Theory.* New Jersey: Prentice-Hall.

Barber, Brian. 1994. "Cultural, Family, and Personal Contexts of Parent-Adolescent Conflict." *Journal of Marriage and the Family* 56: 375–386.

———. 1996. "Parental Psychological Control: Revisiting a Neglected Construct." *Child Development* 67: 3296–3319.

Barber, Brian K., and Joseph A. Olsen. 1997. "Socialization in Context: Connection, Regulation, and Autonomy in the Family, School, and Neighborhood, and with Peers." *Journal of Adolescent Research* 12: 287–315.

Barber, Nigel. 1998. *Parenting: Roles, Styles and Outcomes.* Huntington, N.Y.: Nova Science Publishers.

Bardy, Margitta. 1994. "The Manuscript of the 100-Year Project: Toward a Revision." Pp. 299–317 in *Social Theory, Practice and Politics.* Edited by Jan Qvortttup, Margitta Bardy and Hans Winterberger. Aldeshot, England: Avebury Press.

Barkley, Russell. 1998. *Attention-Deficit/Hyperactivity Disorder: A Handbook for Diagnosis and Treatment.* New York: Guilford Press.

Barkley, Russell, George DuPaul, and Mary McMurray. 1990. "A Comprehensive Evaluation of Attention Deficit Disorder with and without Hyperactivity." *Journal of Consulting and Clinical Psychology* 58: 775–789.

Baron, Jonathan, and Rex V. Brown, eds. 1991. *Teaching Decision Making to Adolescents.* Mahwah, NJ: Erlbaum.

Barth, Richard P. 1990. "On Their Own: The Experiences of Youth After Foster Care." *Child and Adolescent Social Work* 7, no. 5: 419–440.

Barton, John, Laurie Chassin, Clark C. Presson, and Steven J. Sherman. 1982. "Social Image Factors as Motivators of Smoking Initiation in Early and Middle Adolescents." *Child Development* 53: 1499–1511.

Bass, Ellen, and Kate Kaufman. 1996. *Free Your Mind: The Book for Gay, Lesbian, and Bisexual Youth—and Their Allies.* New York: HarperPerennial.

Bass, Mary. 1997 *Citizenship and Young People's Role in Public Life.* Washington, DC: National Civic League, Inc.

Batson, C. Daniel, Patricia Schoenrade, and W. Larry Ventis. 1993. *Religion and the Individual: A Social-Psychological Perspective.* New York: Oxford University Press.

Baughman, James L. 1997. *The Republic of Mass Culture: Journalism, Filmmaking, and Broadcasting.* Baltimore: Johns Hopkins University Press.

Baumeister, Roy F. 1986. *Identity: Cultural Change and the Struggle for Self.* New York: Oxford Press.

Baumrind, Diana. 1971. "Current Patterns of Parental Authority." *Developmental Psychology Monographs* 4: 1–103.

———. 1973. "The Development of Instrumental Competence through Socialization." Pp. 3–46 in *Minnesota Symposia on Adolescent Psychology,* vol. 7. Edited by Anne D. Pick. Minneapolis: University of Minnesota Press.

———. 1975. *Early Socialization and the Discipline Controversy.* Morristown, NJ: General Learning Press.

———. 1989. "Rearing Competent Children." Pp. 349–378 in *Child Development Today and Tomorrow.* Edited by William Damon. San Francisco: Jossey-Bass.

———. 1991. "The Influence of Parenting Style on Adolescent Competence and Substance Use." *Journal of Early Adolescence* 11, no. 1: 56–95.

———. 1991. "Parenting Styles and Adolescent Development." Pp. 746–758 in *Encyclopedia of Adolescence,* vol. 2. Edited by Richard M. Lerner, Anne C.

Peterson, and Jeanne Brooks-Gunn. New York: Garland.

Bebeau, Muriel, and Mary M. Brabeck. 1989. "Ethical Sensitivity and Moral Reasoning among Men and Women in the Professions." Pp. 144–163 in *Who Cares? Theory, Research and Educational Implications of the Ethic of Care.* Edited by Mary M. Brabeck. New York: Praeger.

Belenky, Mary F., Blythe M. Clinchy, Nancy Goldberger, and Jill M. Tarule. 1986. *Women's Ways of Knowing: The Development of Self, Voice and Mind.* New York: Basic Books.

Bell, Laurie. 1987. *Good Girls/Bad Girls: Feminists and Sex Trade Workers Talk Face to Face.* Toronto: The Women's Press.

Bell, Ruth, and other coauthors of *Our Bodies, Ourselves,* with members of the Teen Book Project. 1998. *Changing Bodies, Changing Lives,* 3rd ed. New York: Random House.

Belter, Ronald W., and Thomas Grisso. 1984. "Children's Recognition of Rights Violations in Counseling." *Professional Psychology and Practice* 15: 899–910.

Benard, Bonnie. 1991. *Fostering Resiliency in Kids: Protective Factors in the Family, School, and Community.* Portland, OR: Western Regional Center for Drug-Free Schools and Communities Far West Laboratory.

Benedict, Ruth. 1938. "Continuities and Discontinuities in Cultural Conditioning." *Psychiatry* 1: 161–167.

Bengtson, Vern L. 1985. "Diversity and Symbolism in Grandparental Roles." Pp. 11–26 in *Grandparenthood.* Edited by Vern L. Bengtson and Joan F. Robertson. Beverly Hills: Sage.

Benson, A. Jerry, and Joan M. Benson. 1993. "Peer Mediation: Conflict

Resolution in Schools." *Adolescence* 28, no. 109: 244–245.

Benson, Peter. 1997. *All Kids Are Our Kids: What Communities Must Do to Raise Caring and Responsible Children and Adolescents.* San Francisco: Jossey-Bass.

Benson, Peter L., Anu R. Sharma, and Eugene C. Roehlkepartain. 1994. *Growing Up Adopted: A Portrait of Adolescents and Their Families.* Minneapolis: Search Institute.

Benson, Peter L., Nancy Leffert, Peter C. Scales, and Dale A Blyth. 1998. "Beyond the 'Village' Rhetoric: Creating Healthy Communities for Children and Adolescents." *Applied Developmental Science* 2: 138–159.

Benson, Peter L., Peter C. Scales, Nancy Leffert, and Eugene C. Roehlkepartain. 1999. *A Fragile Foundation: The State of Developmental Assets among American Youth.* Minneapolis: Search Institute.

Berk, Laura E. 1997. *Child Development.* 4th ed. Boston: Allyn and Bacon.

———. 1999. *Infants, Children, and Adolescents,* 3rd ed. Needham Heights, MA: Allyn and Bacon.

Berk, Sheryl. 1999. *The Ultimate Prom Guide.* New York: HarperCollins Juvenile Books.

Berkow, Robert B., ed. 1997. *The Merck Manual of Medical Information: Home Edition.* Whitehouse Station, NJ: Merck Research Laboratories.

Berman, Alan L., and D. A. Jobes. 1991. *Adolescent Suicide: Assessment and Intervention.* Washington, DC: American Psychological Association.

Berndt, Thomas J. 1979. "Developmental Changes in Conformity to Peers and Parents." *Developmental Psychology* 15: 608–616.

———. 1996. "Transitions in Friendship and Friends' Influence." Pp. 57–84 in *Transitions through Adolescence: Interpersonal Domains and Context*. Edited by Julia A. Graber, Jeanne Brooks-Gunn, and Anne C. Petersen. Mahwah, NJ: Erlbaum.

Berndt, Thomas J., and Keuho Keefe. 1995. "Friends' Influence on Adolescents' Adjustment to School." *Child Development* 66: 1312–1329.

Bersoff, Donald N. 1983. "Children as Participants in Psychoeducational Assessment." Pp. 149–178 in *Children's Competence to Consent*. Edited by Gary B. Melton, Gerald P. Koocher, and Michael J. Saks. New York: Plenum Press.

Best, Karin M., Stuart T. Hauser, and Joseph P. Allen. 1997. "Predicting Young Adult Competencies: Adolescent Parent and Individual Influences." *Journal of Adolescent Research* 12, no. 1: 90–112.

Beyth-Marom, Ruth, and Baruch Fischhoff. 1997. "Adolescents' Decisions about Risks: A Cognitive Perspective." Pp. 110–135 in *Health Risks and Developmental Transitions during Adolescence*. Edited by John Schulenberg, Jennifer L. Maggs, and Klaus Hurrelmann. Cambridge: CambridgeUniversity Press.

Biddle, Stuart, and Nanette Mutrie. 1991. *Psychology of Physical Activity and Exercise*. London: Springer-Verlag.

Biederman, Joseph, Jerrold Rosenbaum, Jonathon Chaloff, and Jerome Kagan. 1995. "Behavioral Inhibition as a Risk Factor for Anxiety Disorders." Pp. 61–81 in *Anxiety Disorders in Children and Adolescents*. Edited by John March. New York: Guilford Press.

Bimstein, Enrique. 1991. "Periodontal Health in Children and Adolescents." *Pediatric Clinics of North America* 38 (October): 1183–1207.

Birch, Leann L., and Jennifer O. Fisher. 1998. "Development of Eating Behaviors Among Children and Adolescents." *Pediatrics* 101 (suppl.): 539–549.

Bireley, Marlene, and Judy Genshaft, eds. 1997. *Understanding the Gifted Adolescent: Educational, Developmental, and Multicultural Issues*. New York: Teachers College Press.

Bjarnson, Thoroddur. 1998. "Parents, Religion, and Perceived Social Coherence: A Durkheimian Framework of Adolescent Anomie." *Journal for the Scientific Study of Religion* 37, no. 4: 742–754.

Black, M. M., and Howard Dubowitz. 1999. "Child Neglect: Research Recommendations and Future Directions." Pp. 261–277 in *Neglected Children*. Edited by Howard Dubowitz. Thousand Oaks, CA: Sage.

Blanchard, F. A., C.S. Crandall, J.C. Brigham, and L. Vaughn. 1994. "Condemning and Condoning Racism: A Social Context Approach to Interracial Settings." *Journal of Applied Psychology* 79: 993–997.

Blank, Rolf, and Doreen Langesen. 1999. *State Indicators of Science and Mathematics Education: State by State Trends and New Indicators from the 1997–98 School Year*. Washington, DC: Council of Chief State School Officers.

Block, Jack. 1971. *Lives through Time*. Berkeley: Bancroft Books.

Bloom, Benjamin S., ed. 1985. *Developing Talent in Young People*. New York: Ballantine.

Blos, Peter. 1979. *The Adolescent Passage*. New York: International Universities Press.

Blos, Peter. 1979. *The Adolescent Passage: Developmental Issues*. New York: International Universities Press.

Blum, Robert W. 1992. "Chronic Illness and Disability in Adolescence." *Journal of Adolescent Health* 13, no. 5: 364–368.

Blyth, Dale, Roberta G. Simmons, and David F. Zakin. 1985. "Satisfaction with Body Image for Early Adolescent Females: The Impact of Pubertal Timing in Different School Environments." *Journal of Youth and Adolescence* 14: 207–225.

Boas, Franz. 1911. *The Mind of Primitive Man*. New York: Free Press.

Boesel, David, Nabeel Alsalam, and Thomas Smith. 1998. *Research Synthesis: Educational and Labor Market Performance of GED Recipients*. Washington, DC: U.S. Department of Education.

Booth, A., and J. F. Dunn, eds. 1996. *Family-School Links: How Do They Affect Educational Outcomes?* New Jersey: Erlbaum.

Borhek, Mary V. 1993. *Coming Out to Parents: A Two-Way Survival Guide for Lesbians and Gay Men and Their Parents*. 2nd ed. Cleveland: Pilgrim.

Bornstein, Marcus H., and Michael E. Lamb. 1999. *Developmental Psychology: An Advanced Textbook*. Mahwah, NJ: Erlbaum.

Boston Women's Health Collective. 1998. *Our Bodies, Ourselves for the New Century*. New York: Simon and Schuster.

Boteach, Stanley. 1999. *Kosher Sex*. New York: Doubleday.

Boucher, C. A. B., and J. M. Schapiro. 1999. "Drug-Resistance Genotyping in HIV-1 Therapy: The VIRADAPT Randomised Controlled Trial." *The Lancet* 353: 2195–2199.

Bourgeois, Paulette, and Martin Wolfish. 1994. *Changes in You and Me: A Book about Puberty, Mostly for Girls*. Kansas City: Andrews and McMeel.

———. 1994. *Changes in You and Me: A Book about Puberty, Mostly for Boys*. Kansas City: Andrews and McMeel.

Bourgignon, J., and T. M. Plant, eds. 2000. *The Onset of Puberty in Perspective. Proceedings of the 5th International Conference on the Control of the Onset of Puberty*. Amsterdam: Elsevier.

Bowen, William G., and Derek Bok. 1998. *The Shape of the River: Long-Term Consequences for Considering Race in College Admissions*. Princeton, NJ: Princeton University Press.

Boyd, Gale M., Jan Howard, and Robert A. Zucker, eds. 1995. *Alcohol Problems among Adolescents: Current Directions in Prevention Research*. Hillsdale, NJ: Erlbaum.

Boyer, Ernest. 1990. *Scholarship Reconsidered: Priorities of the Professoriate*. Princeton, NJ: Carnegie Foundation.

Brabeck, Mary. 1983. "Moral Judgment: Theory and Research on Differences between Males and Females." *Developmental Review* 3: 274–291.

———. 1984. "Longitudinal Studies of Intellectual Development during Adulthood: Theoretical and Research Models." *Journal of Research and Development in Education* 17, no. 3: 12–27.

———. 1996. "The Moral Self, Values, and Circles of Belonging." Pp. 145–165 in *Women's Ethnicities: Journeys through Psychology*. Edited by K. Wyche and F. Crosby. Boulder, CO: Westview Press.

Brabeck, Mary, and Ann G. Larned. 1996. "What We Do Not Know about Women's Ways of Knowing." Pp. 261–269 in *Psychology of Women: Ongoing Debates*, 2nd ed. Edited by Mary R. Walsh. New Haven, CT: Yale University Press.

Brandtstädter, Jochen, and Richard M. Lerner. 1999. "Introduction: Development, Action, and Intentionality." Pp. ix–xx in *Action and Self-Development: Theory and Research Through the Life Span*. Edited by Jochen Brandtstädter and Richard M. Lerner. Thousand Oaks, CA: Sage.

Brassard, Marla R., David, B. Hardy, and Stuart N. Hart. 1993. "The Psychological Maltreatment Rating Scales." *Child Abuse and Neglect* 17, no. 1: 715–729.

Brega, Angela G., and Lerita M. Coleman. 1999. "Effects of Religiosity and Racial Socialization on Subjective Stigmatization in African-American Adolescents." *Journal of Adolescence* 22: 223–242.

Bremer, Jennifer, and Paula K. Rauch. 1998. "Children and Computers: Risks and Benefits." *Journal of the American Academy of Child and Adolescent Psychiatry* 37: 559–560.

Briere, John N., and Diana M. Elliott. 1994. "Immediate and Long-Term Impacts of Child Sexual Abuse." *The Future of Children* 4, no. 2: 54–69.

Brindis, Claire D., and Philip R. Lee. 1991. "Adolescents' Conceptualization of Illness." Pp. 534–540 in *Encyclopedia of Adolescence*. Edited by Richard M. Lerner, Anne C. Petersen, and Jeanne Brooks-Gunn. New York: Garland.

Brinthaupt, Thomas, and Richard Lipka, eds. 1992. *The Self: Definitional and Methodological Issues*. Albany: State University of New York Press.

Brody, Gene H., and Zolinda Stoneman. 1996. "Sibling Relationships." Pp. 189–212 in *Sibling Relationships: Their Causes and Consequences*. Edited by Gene H. Brody. Norwood, NJ: Ablex Publishing.

Brody, Gene H., Douglas Flor, and Nicole M. Gibson. 1999. "Linking Maternal Efficacy Beliefs, Developmental Goals, Parenting Practices, and Child Competence in Rural Single-Parent African-American Families." *Child Development* 70: 1197–1208.

Brody, Gene H., ed. 1996. *Sibling Relationships: Their Causes and Consequences*. Norwood, NJ: Ablex Publishing.

Brodzinsky, David M., and Marshall D. Schechter, eds. 1990. *The Psychology of Adoption*. New York: Oxford University Press.

Brodzinsky, David M., Daniel W. Smith, and Anne B. Brodzinsky. 1998. *Children's Adjustment to Adoption: Developmental and Clinical Issues*. Thousand Oaks, CA: Sage.

Bronfenbrenner, Urie, Peter McClelland, Elaine Wethington, Phyllis Moen, and Stephen J. Ceci. 1996. *State of Americans*. New York: Free Press.

Bronfenbrenner, Urie. 1979. *The Ecology of Human Development: Experiments by Nature and Design*. New York: Cambridge University Press.

———. 1980. "Ecology of Childhood." *School Psychology Review* 9, no.4: 294–297.

———. 1989. "Ecological Systems Theory." Pp. 187–248 in *Annals of Child Developmen*. Edited by Ross Vasta. Greenwich, CT: JAI Press.

———. 1991. "What Do Families Do?" *Family Affairs* 4: 1–2.

Brook, Judith S., Ann. S. Gordon, Adam Brook, and David W Brook. 1989. "The Consequences of Marijuana Use on Intrapersonal and Interpersonal Functioning in Black and White Adolescents." *Genetic, Social, and General Psychology Monographs* 15: 351–369

Brook, Judith S., Elinor B. Balka, Thomas Abernathy, and Beatrix A. Hamburg. 1994. "Sequence of Sexual Behavior and Its Relationship to Other Problem Behaviors in African American and Puerto Rican Adolescents." *Journal of Genetic Psychology* 155: 107–114.

Brooks-Gunn, Jeanne. 1988. "Antecedents and Consequences of Variations in Girls' Maturational Timing." *Journal of Adolescent Health Care* 9: 365–373.

———. 1991. "How Stressful Is the Transition to Adolescence for Girls?" Pp. 131–149 in *Adolescent Stress: Causes and Consequences.* Edited by M. E. Colten and S. Gore. New York: Aldine de Gruyter.

Brooks-Gunn, Jeanne, and E. O. Reiter. 1990. "The Role of Pubertal Process." Pp. 16–53 in *At the Threshold: The Developing Adolescent.* Edited by S. Shirley Feldman and Glen R. Elliott. Cambridge, MA: Harvard University Press.

Brooks-Gunn, Jeanne, and Frank F. Furstenberg. 1989. "Adolescent Sexual Behavior." *American Psychologist* 44: 249–257.

Brooks-Gunn, Jeanne, and Roberta L. Paikoff. 1993. "'Sex Is a Gamble, Kissing Is a Game': Adolescent Sexuality and Health Promotion." In *Promoting the Health of Adolescents: New Directions for the Twenty-First Century.* Edited by Susan G. Millstein, Anne C. Petersen, and Elena O. Nightingale. New York: Oxford University Press.

Brooks-Gunn, Jeanne, Guang Guo, and Francis F. Furstenberg. 1993. "Who Drops Out of and Continues beyond High School? A 20-Year Follow-Up of Black Urban Youth." *Journal of Research on Adolescence* 3, no. 3: 271–294.

Brovermann, I. K., S. R. Vogel, D. M. Broverman, F. E. Clarkson, and P. S.

Rosenkrantz. 1994. "Sex-Role Stereotypes: A Current Appraisal." Pp. 191–210 in *Caring Voices and Women's Moral Frames: Gilligan's View.* Edited by B. Puka. New York: Garland.

Brown, Bradford B. 1989. "The Role of Peer Groups in Adolescents' Adjustment to Secondary School." Pp. 188–215 in *Peer Relationships in Child Development.* Edited by Thomas J. Berndt and Gary W. Ladd. New York: Wiley.

Brown, B. Bradford, Donnie Rae Classen, and Sue Ann Eicher. 1986. "Perceptions of Peer Pressure, Peer Conformity Dispositions, and Self-Reported Behavior among Adolescents." *Developmental Psychology* 22: 521–530.

Brown, Bradford B., Margaret S. Mory, and David Kinney. 1994. "Casting Adolescent Crowds in a Relational Perspective: Caricature, Channel, and Context." Pp. 123–167 in *Personal Relationships during Adolescence.* Edited by Raymond Montemayor, Gerald R. Adams, and Thomas P. Gullotta. Newbury Park, CA: Sage.

Brown, Duane. 1998. *Dropping Out or Hanging In: What You Should Know before Dropping Out of School.* NTC Publishing Group.

Brown, J. D. 1999. "Adolescents and the Media." *Newsletter of the Society for Research on Adolescence.* Spring, 1999, 1–2, 10.

Brown, J. D., and E. M. Witherspoon. 2000 (In press). "The Mass Media and Adolescents' Health in the United States." In *Media, Sex, Violence, and Drugs in the Global Village.* Edited by Y. R. Kamalipour. Boulder, CO: Rowman and Littlefield Publishers.

Brown, Jonathon W. 1998. *The Self.* Boston: McGraw-Hill.

Brown, Larry K., Ralph J. DiClemente, and Nancy I. Beausoleil. 1992. "Comparison of Human Immunodeficiency Virus Related Knowledge, Attitudes, Intentions, and Behaviors Among Sexually Active and Abstinent Young Adolescents." *Journal of Adolescent Health* 13: 140–145.

Brown, Roy I. 1996. "Partnership and Marriage in Down Syndrome." *Down Syndrome: Research and Practice* 4: 96–99.

Brownell, R. D. 1991. "Dieting and the Search for the Perfect Body: Where Physiology and Culture Collide." *Behavioral Therapy* 22: 1–12.

Brumberg, Jacobs. 1997. *The Body Project: An Intimate History of American Girls.* New York: Random House.

Bruun, Erik, and Robin Getzen, eds. 1996. *The Book of American Values and Virtues: Our Tradition of Freedom, Liberty, and Tolerance.* New York: Black Dog & Leventhal Publishers, Inc.

Buchanan, Christy. M. 2000. "The Impact of Divorce on Adjustment during Adolescence." Pp. 179–216 in *Resilience across Contexts: Family, Work, Culture, and Community.* Edited by Ronald D. Taylor and Margaret C. Wang. Mahwah, NJ: Erlbaum.

Buchanan, Christy M., and Grayson N. Holmbeck. 1998. "Measuring Beliefs about Adolescence Personality and Behavior." *Journal of Youth and Adolescence* 27: 607–627.

Buchanan, Christy M., Eleanor E. Maccoby, and Sanford M. Dornbusch. 1996. *Adolescents after Divorce.* Cambridge, MA: Harvard University Press.

Buis, Joyce, and Dennis Thompson. 1989. "Imaginary Audience and Personal Fable: A Brief Review" *Adolescence* 24, no. 96: 774–781.

Bukowski, William M., Andrew F. Newcomb, and Willard M. Hartup. 1996. *The Company They Keep: Friendship in Childhood and Adolescence.* New York: Cambridge University Press.

Burnett, Bruce B. 1993. "The Psychological Abuse of Latency Age Children: A Survey." *Child Abuse and Neglect* 17, no. 1: 441–454.

Burns, Barbara, Carl A. Taube, and John E. Taube. 1990. *Use of Mental Health Sector Services by Adolescents: 1975, 1980, 1986.* Paper prepared under contract for the Carnegie Council on Adolescent Development and the Carnegie Corporation of New York, for the Office of Technology Assessment, U.S. Congress, Washington, DC. Springfield, VA: National Technical Information Service (NTIS No. PB 91–154 344/AS).

Burns, R. B. 1979. *The Self Concept in Theory, Measurement, Development and Behavior.* New York: Longman.

Burton, Linda M. 1995. "Intergenerational Patterns of Providing Are Found in African-American Families with Teenage Childbearers: Emergent Patterns in an Ethnographic Study." Pp. 79–96 in *Adult Intergenerational Relations: Effects of Societal Change.* Edited by Vern L. Bengtson, K. W. Schaie, and L. M. Burton. New York: Springer.

Buss, Arnold H., and Robert Plomin. 1975. *A Temperament Theory of Personality Development.* New York: Wiley.

Bynner, John. 1992. "Experiencing Vocational Preparation in England and Germany." *Education and Training* 34, no. 4: 1–8.

Byrnes, James P. 1998. *The Nature and Development of Decision Making: A Self-Regulation Model*. Mahwah, NJ: Erlbaum.

Cadogan, Donald A. 1999. "Drug Use Harm." *American Psychologist* 54: 841–842.

Cain, Kathleen, and Carol Dweck. 1989. "The Development of Children's Conceptions of Intelligence: A Theoretical Framework." Pp. 47–82 in *Advances in the Psychology of Human Intelligence*, Vol. 5. Edited by R. J. Sternberg. Hillsdale, NJ: Erlbaum.

Caldwell, C. H., and T. C. Antonucci. 1997. "Childbearing during Adolescence: Mental Health Risks and Opportunities." Pp. 220–245 in *Health Risks and Developmental Transitions during Adolescence*. Edited by J. Schulenberg, J. L. Maggs, and K. Hurrelmann. New York: Cambridge University Press.

California Senate Office Research. 1997. *Issue Brief: California Strategies to Address Teenage Pregnancy*. Sacramento, CA: Senate Printing Office.

Callan, Victor J., and Debra Jackson. 1986. "Children of Alcoholic Fathers and Recovered Alcoholic Fathers: Personal and Family Functioning." *Journal of Studies on Alcohol* 47, no. 2: 180–182.

Camerena, Phame. 1991. "Conformity in Adolescence." In *Encyclopedia of Adolescence*. Edited by Richard Lerner, Anne Petersen, and Jeanne Brooks-Gunn. New York: Garland.

Camerena, Phame M., Mark Stemmler, and Anne C. Petersen. 1994. "The Gender-Differential Significance of Work and Family: An Exploration of Adolescent Experience and Expectation." Pp. 201–221 in *Adolescence in Context*. Edited by R. Silbereisen and E. Todt. New York: Springer.

Campbell, J. R., and Kristen E. Voelkl et al. 1997. *Trends in Academic Progress*. Washington, DC: U.S. Government Printing Office.

Capaldi, D. M., L. Crosby, and M. Stoolmiller. 1996. "Predicting the Timing of First Sexual Intercourse for At-Risk Adolesent Males." *Child Development* 67: 344–359.

Capelli, M., Patrick J. McGrath, C. E. Heick, N. E. MacDonald, William Feldman, and P. Rowe, P. 1989. "Chronic Disease and Its Impact: The Adolescent's Perspective." *Journal of Adolescent Health Care* 10, no. 4: 283–288.

Carducci, Bernado, and Philip Zimbardo. 1995. "Are You Shy?" *Psychology Today* 28: 34–40.

Carelli, Anne O. 1988. *Sex Equity in Education*. Springfield, MA: Charles C. Thomas.

Carlson Maya, and Felton Earls. 1997. "Psychological and Neuroendocrinological Sequelae of Early Social Deprivation in Institutionalized Children in Romania." *Annals of the New York Academy of Science* 807: 419–428.

Carlson, Neil R.1998. *Physiology of Behavior*. Boston: Allyn and Bacon.

Carnegie Corporation of New York. 1995. *Great Transitions: Preparing Adolescents for a New Century*. New York: Carnegie Corporation of New York.

Carnegie Council on Adolescent Development. 1992. *A Matter of Time: Risk and Opportunity in the Nonschool Hours*. New York: Carnegie Corporation.

———. 1995. *Great Transitions: Preparing Adolescents for a New Century*. New York: Carnegie Corporation.

Carr, Janet. 1995. *Down Syndrome: Children Growing Up*. London: Cambridge University Press.

Carr, Rhoda V., James D. Wright, and Charles J. Brody. 1996. "Effects of High School Work Experience a Decade Later: Evidence from the National Longitudinal Survey." *Sociology of Education* 69 (January): 66–81.

Case, Robbie. 1985. *Intellectual Development: Birth to Adulthood.* New York: Academic Press.

———. 1992. *The Mind's Staircase: Exploring the Conceptual Underpinnings of Children's Thought and Knowledge.* Hillsdale, NJ: Erlbaum.

Caspi, Avshalom. 1998. "Personality Development across the Life Course." Pp. 311–388 in *Handbook of Child Psychology.* Edited by W. Damon and N. Eisenberg. New York: Wiley.

Caspi, Avshalom, Glen Elder, and Ellen Herbener. 1990. "Childhood Personality and the Prediction of Life-course Patterns." In *Straight and Devious Pathways from Childhood to Adulthood.* Edited by Lee N. Robins and Michael Rutter. Cambridge: Cambridge University Press.

Cassidy, Jude, and Steven R. Asher. 1992. "Loneliness and Peer Relations in Young Children." *Child Development* 63: 350–365.

Castlebury, Susan, and John Arnold. 1988. "Early Adolescent Perceptions of Informal Groups in a Middle School." *Journal of Early Adolescence* 8, no. 1: 97–107.

Cates, Willard, Jr. 1999. "Estimates of the Incidence and Prevalence of Sexually Transmitted Diseases in the United States." *American Social Health Association Panel: Sexually Transmitted Disease* (Suppl.): S2–S7.

Centers for Disease Control, http://www.cdc.gov

Centers for Disease Control (CDC). 1991. "Homicide among Young Black Males: United States, 1978–1987." *Journal of the American Medical Association* 265: 183–184.

———. 1991. "Children at Risk from Ozone Air Pollution in the United States." *Morbidity and Mortality Weekly Report* 44: 309–312.

———. 1996. *Exposure to Second-Hand Smoke Widespread.* Center For Disease Control (April).

———. 1997. "State-Specific Pregnancy Rates Among Adolescents-United States, 1990–1996." *MMWR* 46: 837–842.

———. 1998. *HIV/AIDS Surveillance Report.10 (No. 2).* Atlanta, GA.

———. 1998. "Youth Risk Behavior Surveillance—United States, 1997." *CDC Surveillance Summaries Morbidity and Mortality Weekly Report 4,* no. SS-3. Atlanta, GA.

———. 1999. *Suicide Deaths and Rates Per 100,000.* Available at: http://www.cdc.gov/ncipc/data/us9794/suic.htm

———. 2000. HIV/AIDS Surveillance in Adolescents. L265 Slide Series through 1999. Atlanta, GA.

———. 1999. *HIV/AIDS Surveillance Report.11 (No. 1).* Atlanta, GA.

———. 2000. *CDC Update: A Glance at the HIV Epidemic.* Atlanta, GA.

———. 2000. "Profile of the Nation's Health." In *CDC Factbook 2000/2001.* Washington, DC: Department of Health and Human Services.

———. 2000. *The Programs That Work (PTW) Project.* Atlanta, Georgia.

———. 2000. *Sexually Transmitted Disease Surveillance, 1999.* Atlanta, GA. CDC's Web site for this report and other information: http://www.cdc.gov/nchstp/dstd/dstdp.html. Diagnostic slides in color are at http://www.cdc.gov/nchstp/dstd/

Stats_Trends/1999Surveillance/99Slides. htm

Center on Juvenile Justice and Criminal Justice. 2000. Web site: www.cjcj.org.

Center for Law and Social Policy. 1999. *Emancipated Teen Parents and the TANF Living Arrangement Rules.* Washington, DC.

Centerwall, Brandon S. 1989. "Exposure to Television as a Risk Factor for Violence." *American Journal of Epidemiology* 129, no. 4: 643–652.

Chalfie, D. 1994. *Going It Alone: A Closer Look at Grandparents Parenting Grandchildren.* Washington, DC: American Association of Retired People Women's Initiative.

Chamberlain, Patricia, and John Reid. 1998. "Comparison of Two Community Alternatives to Incarceration for Chronic Juvenile Offenders." *Journal of Consulting and Clinical Psychology* 66, no. 4: 624–633.

———.1991. "Using a Specialized Foster Care Community Treatment Model for Children and Adolescents Leaving the State Mental Hospital." *Journal of Community Psychology* 19, no. 3: 266–276.

Champion, Dean J. 1992. *The Juvenile Justice System: Delinquency, Processing, and the Law.* New York: Macmillan.

Chao, Ruth K. 1994. "Beyond Parental Control and Authoritarian Parenting Style: Understanding Chinese Parenting through the Cultural Notion of Training." *Child Development* 65: 1111–1119.

———. 1996. "Chinese and European American Mothers' Beliefs about the Role of Parenting in Children's School Success." *Journal of Cross Cultural Psychology* 27, no. 4: 403–423.

Chassin, Laurie, Clark C. Presson, Steve J. Sherman, Daniel Montello, and John McGrew. 1986. "Changes in Peer and Parent Influence during Adolescence: Longitudinal versus Cross-Sectional Perspectives on Smoking Initiation." *Developmental Psychology* 22: 327–334.

Chassin, Laurie, Clark C. Presson, Steven J. Sherman, Eric Corty, and Richard Olshavsky. 1984. "Predicting the Onset of Cigarette Smoking in Adolescents: A Longitudinal Study." *Journal of Applied Social Psychology* 14: 224–243.

Chassin, Laurie, Clark C. Presson, Steven J. Sherman, and Debra Edwards. 1990. "The Natural History of Cigarette Smoking: Predicting Young Adult Smoking Outcomes from Adolescent Smoking Patterns." *Health Psychology* 9: 701–716.

Chassin, Laurie, Patrick J. Curran, Andrea M. Hussong, and Craig R. Colder. 1996. "The Relation of Parent Alcoholism to Adolescent Substance Use: A Longitudinal Follow-Up Study." *Journal of Abnormal Psychology* 105, no. 1: 70–80.

Chen, Chaunsheng, and Harold W. Stevenson. 1995. "Motivation and Mathematics Achievement: A Comparative Study of Asian American, Caucasian American, and East Asian High School Students." *Child Development* 66: 1215–1234.

Chen, Chuansheng, and Stevenson, Harold W. 1995. "Motivation and Mathematics Achievement: A Comparative Study of Asian American, Caucasian American, and East Asian High School Students." *Child Development* 66: 1215–1234.

Chen, Zeng-Yin, and Sanford M. Dornbusch. 1998. "Relating Aspects of Adolescent Emotional Autonomy to Academic Achievement and Deviant Behavior." *Journal of Adolescent Research* 13: 293–319.

Cherlin, Andrew, and Frank Furstenberg. 1986. *The New American Grandparent: A Place in the Family, a Life Apart.* New York: Basic Books.

Chesney-Lind, Meda, and Randall G. Shelden. 1998. *Girls, Delinquency, and Juvenile Justice.* 2nd ed. Belmont: West/Wadsworth.

Children's Defense Fund. 1996. *The State of America's Children.* Washington, DC: Children's Defense Fund.

Chipman, Susan F., Lorielei R. Brush, and Donna M. Wilson. 1985. *Women and Mathematics: Balancing the Equation.* Hillsdale, NJ: Erlbaum.

Christenson, Peter G., and Donald F. Roberts. 1998. *It's Not Only Rock and Roll: Popular Music in the Lives of Adolescents.* Cresskill, NJ: Hampton Press.

Chuansheng, Chen, Ellen Greenberger, Julia Lester, Qi Dong, and Miaw-Schue Guo. 1998. "A Cross-Cultural Study of Family and Peer Correlates of Adolescent Misconduct." *Developmental Psychology* 34, no. 4: 770–781.

Cicchetti, Dante, and Fred A. Rogosch. 1999. "Psychopathology as Risk for Adolescent Substance Use Disorders: A Developmental Psychopathology Perspective." *Journal of Clinical Child Psychology* 28, no. 3: 355–365.

Cicchetti, Dante, and Marjorie Beeghly, eds. 1990. *Children with Down Syndrome: A Developmental Perspective.* New York: Cambridge University Press.

———. 1990. *The Self in Transition: Infancy to Adulthood.* Chicago: University of Chicago Press.

Cicirelli, Victor G. 1995. *Sibling Relationships across the Lifespan.* New York: Plenum Press.

Citro, Connie, and Robert Michael. 1995. *Measuring Poverty: A New Approach.* Washington, DC: National Academy Press.

Clark, Nancy. 1996. *Nancy Clark's Sports Nutrition Guidebook.* Champaign, IL: Human Kinetics Publishers.

Clayman, Charles B., ed. 1994. *The American Medical Association Family Medical Guide,* 3rd ed. New York: Random House.

Clegg, Averil, and Anne Woollett. 1983. *Twins: From Conception to Five Years.* New York: Van Nostrand Reinhold.

Cobb, Nancy J. 1998. *Adolescence: Continuity, Change and Diversity.* Mountain View, CA: Mayfield Publishing.

Cocking, Rodney R., and Patricia M. Greenfield. 1994. "Diversity and Development of Asian Americans: Research Gaps in Minority Child Development." *Journal of Applied Psychology* 15: 301–303.

Cohen, Deborah A., and Janet C. Rice. 1995. "A Parent-Targeted Intervention for Adolescent Substance Use Prevention: Lessons Learned." *Evaluation Review* 19: 159–180.

Cohn, Lawrence, Susan Macfarlane, Claudia Yanez, and Walter Imai. 1995. "Risk-Perception: Differences between Adolescents and Adults." *Health Psychology* 14, no. 3: 217–222.

Colangelo, Nicholas, Susan Assouline, and DeAnn Ambroson, eds. 1992. *Talent Development: Proceedings from the 1991 Henry B. and Jocelyn Wallace National Research Symposium on Talent Development.* Unionville, NY: Trillium Press.

Colby, Anne, Lawrence Kohlberg, John Gibbs, and Marcus Liebermann. 1983. "A Longitudinal Study of Moral Judgment." *Monographs of the Society for Research in Child Development* 48 (issues 1–2, Serial No. 200).

Cole, Letha B., and Mary Winkler. 1994. *The Good Body: Asceticism in Contemporary Culture*. New Haven: Yale University Press.

Coleman, John. 1978. "Current Contradictions in Adolescent Theory." *Journal of Youth and Adolescence* 7: 1–11.

Coleman, John, and D. Roker, eds. 1998. *Teenage Sexuality: Health, Risk and Education*. Canada: Harwood Academic Publishers.

Coleman, John, and Leo B. Hendry. 1999. *The Nature of Adolescence*, 3rd ed. New York: Routledge.

Coleman, John, and T. Hoffer. 1987. *Public and Private High Schools: The Impact of Communities*. New York: Wiley.

Coles, R. 1997. *The Youngest Parents*. New York: Norton.

College Board Online. 2000. http://www.collegeboard.com

Collins, W. Andrew. 1990. "Parent-Child Relationships in the Transition to Adolescence: Continuity and Change in Interaction, Affect, and Cognition." Pp. 85–106 in *Advances in Adolescent Development: From Childhood to Adolescence: A Transitional Period?* Vol. 2. Edited by R. Montemayor, G. Adams, and T. Gullotta. Beverly Hills, CA: Sage.

Collins, W. Andrew, and Daniel J. Repinski. 1994. "Relationships during Adolescence: Continuity and Change in Interpersonal Perspective." Pp. 7–36 in *Personal Relationships during Adolescence*. Edited by Raymond Montemayor, Gerald R. Adams, and Thomas P. Gullotta. Thousand Oaks, CA: Sage.

Committee on the Health and Safety Implications of Child Labor. 1998. *Protecting Youth at Work: Health, Safety and Development of Working Children and Adolescents in the United States*. Washington, DC: National Academy Press.

Committee on Ways and Means, United States House of Representatives. 1998. *1998 Green Book*. Washington D.C.: United States House of Representatives.

Compas, Bruce E., B. R. Hinden, and C. A. Gerhardt. 1995. "Adolescent Development: Pathways and Processes of Risk and Resilience." *Annual Review of Psychology* 46: 265–293.

Conger, Rand D., Glen H. Elder, Jr., F. O. Lorenz, K. J. Conger, R. L. Simmons, L. B. Whitbeck, J. Huck, and J. N. Melby. 1990. "Linking Economic Hardship and Marital Quality and Instability." *Journal of Marriage and the Family* 52: 643–656.

Conrad, Diane, and Dan Hedin. 1989. *High School Community Service: A Review of Research and Programs*. Washington, DC: National Center on Effective Secondary Schools.

———. 1991. "School-Based Community Service: What We Know from Research and Theory." *Phi Delta Kappan* 72: 743–749.

Constanzo, Philip, Shari Miller-Johnson, and Heidi Wence. 1995. "Social Development." Pp. 82–108 in *Anxiety Disorders in Children and Adolescents*. Edited by John March. New York: Guilford Press.

Cornell, S., and D. Hartmann 1998. *Ethnicity and Race*. Thousand Oaks, CA: Pine Forge Press.

Cosby, William H., Jr. 1986. *Bill Cosby: Fatherhood*. Garden City, NY: Doubleday & Company.

Coughlin, Eileen V., ed. 1997. *Successful Drug and Alcohol Prevention Programs*. San Francisco: Jossey-Bass.

Courtney, Mark E., and Irving Pillavin. 1998. *Youth Transitions to Adulthood:*

Outcomes 12–18 Months after Leaving Out-of-Home Care. Madison, WI: University of Wisconsin.

Covey, Sean. 1998. *The 7 Habits of Highly Effective Teens: The Ultimate Success Guide.* New York: Simon and Schuster.

Crick, Nicki R. 1996. "The Role of Overt Aggression, Relational Aggression, and Prosocial Behavior in the Prediction of Children's Future Social Adjustment." *Child Development* 67: 2317–2327.

Crick, Nicki R., and Jennifer K. Grotpeter.1995. "Relational Aggression, Gender, and Social-Psychological Adjustment." *Child Development* 66: 710–722.

Crockett, Lisa J., and Anne C. Crouter. 1995. "Pathways through Adolescent Individual Development in Relation to Social Contexts." Mahwah, NJ: Erlbaum.

Crockett, Lisa J. and Rainer K. Silbereisen. 2000. *Negotiating Adolescence in Times of Social Change.* New York: Cambridge University Press.

Cromwell, Paul, D. Taylor, and W. Palacios. 1992. "Youth Gangs: A 1990's Perspective." *Juvenile & Family Court Journal* 43, no. 3: 25–31

Crouter, Ann C., and Mary C. Maguire. 1998. "Seasonal and Weekly Rhythms: Windows into Variability in Family Socialization Experiences in Early Adolescence." *New Directions for Child and Adolescent Development* 82: 69–82.

Crouter, Ann C., and Susan M. McHale. 1993. "Temporal Rhythms in Family Life: Seasonal Variation in the Relation between Parental Work and Family Processes." *Developmental Psychology* 29: 198–205.

Crouter, Ann C., H. Helms-Erikson, K. Updegraff, and Susan M. McHale. 1999. "Conditions Underlying Parents' Knowledge about Children's Daily Lives in Middle Childhood: Between- and Within-Family Comparisons." *Child Development* 70: 246–259.

Csikszentmihalyi, Mihaly. 1975. *Beyond Boredom and Anxiety.* San Francisco: Jossey-Bass.

———. 1990. *Flow: The Psychology of Optimal Experience.* New York: Harper and Row.

———. 1997. *Finding Flow: The Psychology of Engagement with Everyday Life.* New York: Basic Books.

Csikszentmihalyi, Mihaly, and Reed Larson. 1984. *Being Adolescent.* New York: Basic Books.

Csikszentmihalyi, Mihaly, Kevin Rathunde, and Samuel Whalen. 1997. *Talented Teenagers: The Roots of Success and Failure.* New York: Cambridge University Press.

Cummins, Jim. 1986. "Empowering Minority Students: A Framework for Intervention." *Harvard Educational Review* 56, no. 1: 18–36.

Cummings, E. Mark, and Patrick Davies. 1994. *Children and Marital Conflict: The Impact of Family Dispute and Resolution.* New York: Guilford Press.

Cunningham, Michael. 1999. "African American Adolescent Males' Perceptions of Their Community Resources and Constraints: A Longitudinal Analysis." *Journal of Community Psychology* 5: 569–588.

Curcio, Joan L., and Patricia F. First. 1993. *Violence in the Schools: How to Proactively Prevent and Defuse It.* Newbury Park, CA: Corwin Press.

Curry, G. David, and Irving A. Spergel. 1992. "Gang Involvement and Delinquency among Hispanic and African-American Adolescent Males." *Journal of Research in Crime and Delinquency* 29: 273–291.

D'Emilio, John D., and Estelle B. Freedman. 1997. *Intimate Matters: A History of Sexuality in America*. Chicago, IL.: University of Chicago Press.

Dacey, John S., and Alex J. Packer. 1992. *The Nurturing Parent*. New York: Fireside.

Damon, William. 1983. *Social and Personality Development: Infancy through Adolescence*. New York, NY: Norton.

———. 1997. *The Youth Charter: How Communities Can Work Together to Raise Standards for All Our Children*. New York: Free Press.

Damon, William, and Daniel Hart. 1988. *Self Understanding in Childhood and Adolescence*. Cambridge: Cambridge University Press.

Daniel, William A., Jr. 1991. "Training in Adolescent Health Care." Pp. 450–453 in *Encyclopedia of Adolescence*. Edited by Richard M. Lerner, Anne C. Petersen, and Jeanne Brooks-Gunn. New York: Garland.

Darling, Nancy, and Laurence Steinberg. 1993. "Parenting Style as Context: An Integrative Model." *Psychological Bulletin* 113, no. 3: 487–496.

Darling, Nancy, Patricio E. Cumsille, and Bonnie Dowdy. 1998. "Parenting Style, Legitimacy of Parental Authority, and Adolescents' Willingness to Share Information with Their Parents: Why Do Adolescents Lie?" Paper presented at the June 1998 meeting of the International Society for the Study of Personal Relationships, Saratoga, NY.

Davidson, Ann Locke. 1996. *Making and Molding Identity in Schools: Student Narratives on Race, Gender, and Academic Engagement*. New York: State University of New York Press.

Davies, E., and A. Furham. 1986. "Body Satisfaction in Adolescent Girls." *British Journal of Medical Psychology* 59: 279–287.

Davies, Patrick T., and Michael Windle. 2000. "Middle Adolescents' Dating Pathways and Psychosocial Adjustment." *Merrill-Palmer Quarterly* 46: 90–118.

Davis, Fred. 1992. *Fashion, Culture and Identity*. Chicago: University of Chicago Press.

DeBiase, Christina. 1991. *Dental Health Education: Theory and Practice*. Philadelphia: Lea and Febiger.

Decker, Jeffrey L. 1994. "The State of Rap: Time and Place in Hip Hop Nationalism." Pp. 99–12 in *MicrophoneFiends: Youth Music and Youth Culture*. Edited by A. Ross and Tricia Rose. New York: Routledge.

Delgado, D. 1994. "The Annie E. Casey Foundation's Plain Talk Initiative." *PSAY Network* 2: 1–12.

Delgado, Richard, and Jean Stefancic, eds. 1996. *Critical White Studies: Looking Behind the Mirror*. Philadelphia: Temple University Press.

Demo, D. H., S. A. Small, and R. C. Savin-Williams. 1987. "Family Relations and the Self-Esteem of Adolescents and Their Parents." *Journal of Marriage and the Family* 49: 705–715.

Demo, David, and Alan C. Acock. 1993. "Family Diversity and the Division of Domestic Labor." *Family Relations* 42: 323–331.

Demos, David. 1986. *Past, Present, and Personal*. New York: Oxford University Press.

Demos, John. 1986. *Past, Present, and Personal*. New York: Oxford University Press.

DePanfilis, Diane. 1999. "Intervening with Families When Children Are Neglected." Pp. 211–236 in *Neglected*

Children. Edited by Howard Dubowitz. Thousand Oaks, CA: Sage.

Department of Health and Human Services. 1991. "Protection of Human Subjects." *Code of Federal Regulations*. Title 45 Public Welfare, Part 46. Washington, DC: DHHS.

Department of Health and Human Services: Substance Abuse and Mental Health Services Administration. 2000. *1999 National Household Survey on Drug Abuse*. Rockville:, MD.

Derryberry, Douglas, and Mary K. Rothbart. 1985. "Emotion, Attention, and Temperament." Pp. 132–166 in *Emotion, Cognition, and Behavior*. Edited by Carroll E. Izard, Jerome Kagan, and Robert Zajonc. New York: Cambridge University Press.

Deshler, Donald, E. S. Ellis, and B. K. Lenz. 1996. *Teaching Adolescents with Learning Disabilities: Strategies and Methods*. 2nd ed. Denver, CO: Love.

DeVesa, S. S., W. J. Blot, B. J. Sonte, B. A. Miller, R. E. Tarove, and J. F. Fraumeni, Jr. 1995. "Recent Cancer Trends in the United States." *Journal of the National Cancer Institute* 87: 175–182.

Devine, Patricia G., and Andrew J. Elliot. 1995. "Are Racial Stereotypes *Really* Fading? The Princeton Trilogy Revisited." *Personality and Social Psychology Bulletin 21:* 1139–1150.

Devine, Patricia G., and Kristen A. Vasquez. 1998. "The Rocky Road to Positive Intergroup Relations." Pp. 234–262 in *Confronting Racism: The Problem and the Responses*. Edited by Jennifer L. Eberhardt and Susan T. Fiske. Thousand Oaks, CA: Sage.

Diamond, Lisa M. 2000. "Passionate Friendships among Adolescent Sexual-Minority Women." *Journal of Research on Adolescence* 10: 191–209.

DiClemente, Ralph J., William Hansen, and Lynn Ponton, eds. 1996. *Handbook of Adolescent Health Risk Behavior*. New York: Plenum Publishing.

Dictionary of Postsecondary Institutions, Vol. 2. 1997. Washington, DC: U.S. Department of Education.

Dietz, William H. 1998. "Health Consequences of Obesity in Youth: Childhood Predictors of Adult Disease." *Pediatrics* 101 (suppl.): 518–525.

Dietz, William H., and S. L. Gortmaker. 1985. "Do We Fatten Our Children at the Television Set? Obesity and Television Viewing in Children and Adolescents." *Pediatrics* 75: 807–812.

DiGirolamo, A. M., A. L. Quittner, V. Ackerman, and J. Stevens. 1997. "Identification and Assessment of Ongoing Stressors in Adolescents with a Chronic Illness: An Application of the Behavior-Analytic Model." *Journal of Clinical Child Psychology* 26, no. 1: 53–66.

Donelson, Elaine. 1999. "Psychology of Religion and Adolescents in the United States: Past to Present." *Journal of Adolescence* 22: 187–204.

Dorn, Lorah D., Stacie F. Hitt, and Deborah Rotenstein. 1999. "Psychological and Cognitive Differences in Children with Premature vs. on-Time Adrenarche." *Archives of Pediatrics and Adolescent Medicine* 153: 137–145.

Dorn, Sherman. 1996. *Creating the Dropout: An Institutional and Social History of School Failure*. Westport, CT: Praeger.

Dornbusch, Sanford M., Kristan L. Glasgow, and I-Chun Lin. 1996. "The Social Structure of Schooling." Pp. 401–429 in *Annual Review of Psychology*, Vol. 47. Palo Alto, CA: Annual Reviews.

Dote, Martha. 1999. "Emotionally and Behaviorally Disturbed Children in the Child Welfare System: Points of Preventative Intervention." *Children and Youth Services Review* 21, no. 1: 7–29

Drewnowski, Adam, Candace L. Kurth, and Dean D. Krahn. 1995. "Effects of Body Image on Dieting, Exercise, and Anabolic Steroid Use in Adolescent Males." *International Journal of Eating Disorders* 17: 381–386.

Dryfoos, Joy G. 1990. *Adolescents at Risk: Prevalence and Prevention.* New York: Oxford University Press.

———. 1994. *Full Service Schools: A Revolution in Health and Social Services for Children, Youth, and Families.* San Francisco: Jossey-Bass.

———. 1995. "Full Service Schools: Revolution or Fad?" *Journal of Research on Adolescence* 5, no. 2: 147–172.

———.1998. *Safe Passage: Making It through Adolescence in a Risky Society.* New York: Oxford University Press.

Dubovsky, Steven L. 1997. *Mind-Body Deceptions: The Psychosomatics of Everyday Life.* New York: Norton.

Duggan, Hayden A. 1978. *A Second Chance: Empathy in Adolescent Development.* Lexington, MA: Lexington Books.

Dukette, Rita. 1984. "Values in Present-day Adoption." *Child Welfare* 63, no. 3: 233–243.

Duncan, Greg J., and Willard L. Rodgers. 1988. "Longitudinal Aspects of Childhood Poverty." *Journal of Marriage and the Family* 50 (November): 1007–1021.

Dunham, Richard M., Jeannie S Kidwell, and Stephen M. Wilson. 1986. "Rites of Passage at Adolescence: A Ritual Process Paradigm." *Journal of Adolescent Research* 1, no. 2: 139–154.

Dunn, Judy, and Robert Plomin. 1990. *Separate Lives: Why Siblings Are So Different.* New York: Basic Books.

Dunn, Judy, and Shirley McGuire. 1992. "Sibling and Peer Relationships in Childhood." *Journal of Child Psychology and Psychiatry* 33, no. 1: 67–105.

DuPaul, George, Russell Barkley, and Daniel Connor. 1998. "Stimulants." Pp. 510–551 in *Attention-Deficit/ Hyperactivity Disorder: A Handbook for Diagnosis and Treatment.* New York: Guilford Press.

Durant, J., P. Clevenbergh, P. Halfon, P. Delguidice, S. Porsin, P. Simonet, N. Montagne,

Durham, M. G. 1998. "Dilemmas of Desire: Representations of Sexuality in Two Teen Magazines." *Youth and Society* 29: 369–389.

Durlack, Joseph A. 1998. "Common Risk and Protective Factors in Successful Prevention Programs." *American Journal of Orthopsychiatry* 68: 512–520.

Dusek, Jerome B. 1996. *Adolescent Development and Behavior.* Upper Saddle River, NJ: Prentice-Hall.

Dweck, Carol S. 1999. *Self-Theories: Their Role in Motivation, Personality, and Development.* Philadelphia: Psychology Press/Taylor and Francis.

Earls, Felton, and Maya Carlson. 1999. "Children at the Margins of Society: Research and Practice." *Homeless and Working Youth around the World: Exploring Developmental Issues.* Edited by Marcela Raffaelli and Reed Larson. San Francisco, CA, Jossey-Bass.

East, P. L. 1996. "Do Adolescent Pregnancy and Childbearing Affect Younger Siblings?" *Family Planning Perspectives* 28: 148–153.

East, P. L. and Felice, M. E. 1996. *Adolescent Pregnancy and Parenting: Findings from a Racially Diverse Sample.* Mahwah, NJ: Erlbaum.

Eberhardt, Jennifer L., and Susan T. Fiske, eds. 1998. *Confronting Racism: The Problem and the Response.* Thousand Oaks, CA: Sage.

Eccles, Jacquelynne S. 1991 "Academic Achievement." In *Encyclopedia of Adolescence.* Edited by Richard M. Lerner, Anne C. Petersen, and Jeanne Brooks-Gunn. New York: Garland.

Eccles, Jacqueline, Carol Midgley, and Terry Adler. 1984. "Grade-Related Changes in the School Environment." Pp. 283–331 in *Advances in Motivation and Achievement.* Edited by M. L. Maehr. Greenwich, CT: JAI.

Eccles, Jacquelynne S., Diane Early, Kari Frasier, Elaine Belansky, and Karen McCarthy. 1997. "The Relation of Connection, Regulation, and Support for Autonomy to Adolescents' Functioning." *Journal of Adolescent Research* 12: 263–286.

Eccles, Jacquelynne S., Sarah Lord, and Christy Miller Buchanan. 1996. "School Transitions in Early Adolescence: What Are We Doing to Our Young People?" Pp. 251–284 in *Transitions through Adolescence: Interpersonal Domains and Context.* Edited by Julie A. Graber and Jeanne Brooks-Gunn. Mahwah, NJ: Erlbaum.

Eccles, Jacquelynne, Carol Midgley, Allan Wigfield, and Christy M. Buchanan. 1993. "Development during Adolescence: The Impact of Stage Environment Fit on Young Adolescents' Experiences in Schools and in Families." *American Psychologist* 48, no. 2: 90–101.

Eckenrode, John, Molly Laird, and John Doris. 1993. "School Performance and Disciplinary Problems among Abused and Neglected Children." *Developmental Psychology* 29, no. 1: 53–62.

Eckersley, Robert. 1993. "The West's Deepening Cultural Crisis." *The Futurist* 27, no. 6: 8–12.

Egeland, Byron. 1993. "A History of Abuse Is a Major Risk Factor for Abusing the Next Generation." Pp. 197–208 in *Current Controversies on Family Violence.* Richard J. Gelles and Donileen R. Loseke–. Newbury Park, California: Sage.

Eisenberg, Nancy, ed. 1989. *Empathy and Related Emotional Responses.* San Francisco: Jossey-Bass.

Elder, Glen H. Jr. 1974. *Children of the Great Depression: Social Change in Life Experience.* Chicago: University of Chicago Press.

Elder, Glen H. Jr., John Modell, and Ross D. Parke, eds. 1993. *Children in Time and Place: Developmental and Historical Insights.* New York: Cambridge University Press.

Elder, Glen H. Jr., Rand D. Conger, E. Michael Foster, and Monika Ardelt. 1992. "Families under Economic Pressure." *Journal of Family Issues* 13: 5–37.

Elkind, David. 1967. "Egocentrism in Adolescence." *Child Development* 38: 1025–1034.

———. 1971. "The Development of Religious Understanding in Children and Adolescents." Pp. 655–685 in *Research on Religious Development.* Edited by M. P. Strommen.

———. 1978. "Understanding the Adolescent." *Adolescence* 13, no. 49: 127–134.

———. 1982. *The Hurried Child.* New York: Addison-Wesley.

———. 1985. "Egocentrism Redux." *Developmental Review* 5: 218–226.

————. 1998. *All Grown Up and No Place to Go*, rev. ed. Cambridge, MA: Perseus.

Elkind, David., and Richard. Bowen. 1979. "Imaginary Audience Behavior in Children and adolescents." *Developmental Psychology* 15: 38–44.

Elliott, Delbert S., David Huizinga, and Suzanne S. Ageton. 1985. *Explaining Delinquency and Drug Use.* Beverly Hills, CA: Sage.

Emery, Robert E. 1999. *Marriage, Divorce, and Children's Adjustment*, 2nd ed. Newbury Park, CA: Sage.

Endo, K., and T. Hashimoto. 1998. "The Effect of Sex-Role Identity on Self-Actualization in Adolescence." *Japanese Journal of Educational Psychology* 46: 86–94.

Eng, T. R., and W. T. Butler, eds. 1997. *The Hidden Epidemic: Confronting Sexually Transmitted Diseases.* Washington, DC: National Academy Press: Institute of Medicine.

English, Diana. 1998. "The Extent and Consequences of Child Maltreatment." The *Future of Children* 8, no. 1: 39–51.

Ennew, Judith, Kusum Gopal, Janet Heeran, and Heather Montgomery. 1996. *Children and Prostitution: How Can We Measure and Monitor the Commercial Sexual Exploitation of Children?* New York: UNICEF.

Enright, Robert D., et al. 1979. "Adolescent Egocentrism in Early and Late Adolescence." *Adolescence* 14: 687–695.

Ensminger, Margaret E., Rebecca P. Lamkin, and Nora Jacobson. 1996. "School Leaving: A Longitudinal Perspective Including Neighborhood Effects." *Child Development* 67: 2400–2416.

Epps, Roselyn P., Marc W. Manley, and Thomas J. Glynn. 1995. "Tobacco Use among Adolescents: Strategies for Prevention." *Substance Abuse* 42 (April): 389–401.

Epstein, Joyce L. 1989. "The Selection of Friends: Changes across the Grades and in Different School Environments." Pp. 158–187 in *Peer Relationships in Child Development.* Edited by Thomas J. Berndt and Gary W. Ladd. New York: Wiley.

Epstein, Joyce, and Nancy Karweit. 1983. *Friends in School.* New York: Academic Press.

Epstein, Joyce L., and S. Lee. 1995. "National Patterns of School and Family Connections in the Middle Grades." Pp 108–154 in *The Family-School Connection: Theory, Research, and Practice.* Edited by B. A. Ryan, G. R. Adams, T. P. Gullotta, R. P. Weissberg, and R. L. Hampton. Thousand Oaks, CA: Sage.

Epstein, Joyce L., and Susan L. Dauber. 1995. "Effects on Students of an Interdisciplinary Program Linking Social Studies, Arts, and Family Volunteers in the Middle Grades." *Journal of Early Adolescence* 15, no. 1: 114–144.

Erickson, David. 1992. "Knowledge of Disability in Adolescents with Spina Bifida." *Canadian Journal of Rehabilitation* 5: 171–175.

Erickson, David, and Laurel Erickson. 1992. "Knowledge of Sexuality in Adolescents with Spina Bifida." *Canadian Journal of Human Sexuality* 14: 195–199.

Erickson, Joseph A. 1992. "Adolescent Religious Development and Commitment: A Structural Equation Model of the Role of the Family, Peer Group, and Educational Influences." *Journal for the Scientific Study of Religion* 31, no. 2: 131–152.

Erikson, Erik H. 1950. *Childhood and Society*, 1st ed. New York: Norton.

———. 1968. *Identity: Youth and Crisis.* New York: Norton.

———. 1985. *Childhood and Society*, 35th anniversary ed. New York: Norton.

———. 1993. *Childhood and Society.* New York: Norton.

Ernst, John M., and John T. Cacioppo. 1999. "Lonely Hearts: A Psychological Perspective on Loneliness." *Applied and Preventive Psychology* 8: 1–22.

Esman, Aaron H. 1990. *Adolescence and Culture.* New York: Columbia University Press.

Essed, P. 1991. *Understanding Everyday Racism: An Interdisciplinary Theory.* Newbury Park: Sage.

Evans, Ellis D., J. Rutberg, C. Sather, and C. Turner. 1991. "Content Analysis of Contemporary Teen Magazines for Adolescent Females." *Youth and Society* 23: 99–120.

Evans, Ellis D., and Delores Craig. 1991. "Teacher and Student Perceptions of Academic Cheating in Middle and Senior High Schools." *Journal of Educational Research* 84, no. 1: 41–52.

Evans, William P., Carla Fitzgerald, Daniel Weigel, and Sara Chvilicek. 1999. "Are Rural Gang Members Similar to Their Urban Peers? Implications for Rural Communities." *Youth & Society* 30, no. 3: 267–282.

Eysenck, Michael. 1990. "Anxiety and Cognitive Functioning." Pp. 419–435 in *Handbook of Anxiety*, Vol. 2, *The Neurobiology of Anxiety.* Edited by Graham D. Burrows, Martin Roth, and Russell Noyes. New York: Elsevier Science Publishers.

Fagan, Jeffre E. 1989. "The Social Organization of Drug Use and Drug Dealing among Urban Gangs." *Criminology* 27: 633–669.

Fairchild, Betty, and Nancy Hayward. 1989. *Now That You Know: What Every Parent Should Know about Homosexuality*, updated ed. San Diego: Harcourt Brace Jovanovich.

Fallon, April, and Paul Rozin. 1985. Sex Differences in Perceptions of Desirable Body Shape. *Journal of Abnormal Psychology* 94: 102–105.

Farris, C. 1976. "Indian Children: The Struggle for Survival." *Social Work* 21: 386–389.

Fauci, Anthony S. 1999. "The AIDS Epidemic. Considerations for the 21st Century." *The NewEngland Journal of Medicine* 341, no. 14: 1046–1050.

Faulkenberry, Ray, M. Vincent, A. James, and W. Johnson. 1987. "Coital Behaviors, Attitudes, and Knowledge of Students Who Experience Early Coitus." *Adolescence* 22: 321–332.

Favazza, Armando R. 1996. *Bodies under Siege: Self-Mutilation and Body Modification in Culture and Pyschiatry*, 2nd ed. Baltimore: Johns Hopkins University Press.

———. 1989. "Why Patients Mutilate Themselves." *Hospital and Community Psychiatry* 40, no. 2: 137–145.

Favazza, Armando R., and Karen Conterio. 1988. "The Plight of Chronic Self-Mutilators." *Community Mental Health Journal* 24, no. 1: 22–30.

Feagin, Joe R., and Hernan Vera. 1995. *White Racism.* New York: Routledge.

Featherstone, Helen. 1980. *A Difference in the Family.* New York: Basic Books.

Federal Bureau of Investigation. 1997. *Crime in the United States: 1996.* Washington, DC: Government Printing Office.

Federal Glass Ceiling Commission. 1995. *Good for Business: Making Full Use of the Nation's Human Capital. The Environmental Scan.* Washington DC: U.S. Government Printing Office.

Feinberg, Leslie. 1993. *Stone Butch Blues.* Ithaca, NY: Firebrand.

Feldman, Shirley S., and Glen R. Elliot. 1990. *At the Threshold: The Developing Adolescent.* Cambridge, MA: Harvard University Press.

Feldman, Shirley S., Rebecca N. Turner, and Katy Araujo. 1999. "Interpersonal Context as an Influence on Sexual Timetables of Youths: Gender and Ethnic Effects." *Journal of Research on Adolescence* 9, no. 1: 25–52.

Fetterman, David M., Shakeh J. Kaftarian, and Abraham Wandersman, eds. 1996. *Empowerment Evaluation: Knowledge and Tools for Self-Assessment and Accountability.* Thousand Oaks, CA: Sage.

Fielding, Elizabeth N. 1999. *Learning Differences in the Classroom.* Delaware: International Reading Association.

Fine, Michelle. 1986. "Why Urban Adolescents Drop into and out of Public High School." *Teachers College Record* 87: 393–409.

———. 1991. *Framing Dropouts: Notes on the Politics of an Urban High School,* Albany, NY: State University of New York Press.

Finkelhor, David. 1994. "Current Information on the Scope and Nature of Child Sexual Abuse." *The Future of Children* 4, no. 2: 31–53.

Finkelhor, David, Gerald Hotaling, I. A. Lewis, and Christine Smith. 1990. "Sexual Abuse in a National Survey of Adult Men and Women: Prevalence, Characteristics, and Risk Factors." *Child Abuse and Neglect* 14: 19–28.

Finn, Jeremy. 1993. *School Engagement and Students at Risk.* Washington, DC: National Center for Education Statistics, U.S. Department of Education.

Fischer, Paul, Meyer Schwartz, John Richards, Adam Goldstein, and Tina Rojas. 1991. "Brand Logo Recognition by Children Aged 3–6 Years: Mickey Mouse and Joe the Camel." *Journal of the American Medical Association* 266: 3145–3148.

Fisher, Celia B. 1993. "Integrating Science and Ethics in Research with High Risk Children and Youth." *Social Policy Report. Society for Research in Child Development* 7, no. 4: 1–27.

Fisher, Celia B., Kimberly Hoagwood, and Peter Jensen. 1996. "Casebook on Ethics: Issues in Research with Children and Adolescents with Mental Disorders." Pp. 135–238 in *Ethical Issues in Research with Children and Adolescents with Mental Disorders.* Edited by Kimberly Hoagwood, Peter Jensen, and Celia B. Fisher. Mahwah, NJ: Lawrence.

Fisher, Celia B., Michi Hatashita-Wong, and Lori Isman Greene. 1999. "Ethical and Legal Issues in Clinical Child Psychology." Pp. 470–486 in *Developmental Issues in the Clinical Treatment of Children and Adolescents.* Edited by Wendy K. Silverman and Thomas H. Ollendick. Boston: Allyn and Bacon.

Fisher, Celia B., S. A. Wallace, and R. E. Fenton. 2000. "Discrimination Distress during Adolescence." *Journal of Youth and Adolescence* 29: 679–695.

Fisher, David E. 1996. *Tube: The Invention of Television.* Washington, DC: Counterpoint.

Flanagan, Constance A., and Corrina Jenkins Tucker. 1999. "Adolescents' Explanations for Political Issues: Concordance with their Views of Self and

Society." *Developmental Psychology* 35, no. 5: 1198–1209.

Flanagan, Constance A., and Leslie S. Gallay. 1995. "Reframing the Meaning of 'Political' in Research with Adolescents." *Perspectives on Political Science* 24: 34–41.

Flanagan, Constance A., Jennifer Bowes, Britta Jonsson, Beno Csapo, and Elena Sheblanova. 1998. "Ties That Bind: Correlates of Adolescents' Civic Commitments in Seven Countries." In *Political Development: Youth Growing up in a Global Community. Journal of Social Issues* 54, no. 3: 457–475.

Flannery, Daniel J., David C. Rowe, and Bill L. Gulley. 1993. "Impact of Pubertal Status, Timing, and Age on Adolescent Sexual Experience and Delinquency." *Journal of Adolescent Research* 8: 21–40.

Folman, Rosalind D. 1994. "Risk and Protective Factors among Children and Youth in Foster Care." Paper presented at the 24th annual conference of the National Foster Parent Association, Grand Rapids, MI.

———. 1995. "Resiliency and Vulnerability among Abused and Neglected Children in Foster Care." Doctoral dissertation, University of Michigan. Abstract in *Dissertation Abstract International* 56(08-B), p. 4601.

———. 1996. "Foster Care Experiences: How They Impact the Transition to Adulthood." Pathways to Adulthood National Conference, San Diego, CA.

Folman, Rosalind D., and John Hagen. 1996. "Foster Children Entering Adolescence: Factors of Risk and Resilience." Poster presented at the biennial meeting of the Society for Research on Adolescence, Boston.

Ford, Kathleen, and Anne Norris. 1993. "Urban Hispanic Adolescents and Young Adults: Relationship of Acculturation to Sexual Behavior." *Journal of Sex Research* 30: 316–323.

Fordham, Signithia, and John U. Ogbu. 1986. "Black Students' School Success: Coping with the Burden of 'Acting White.'" *Urban Review* 18, no. 3: 176–206.

Forehand, R., K. S. Miller, R. Dutra, and M. W. Chance. 1997. "Role of Parenting in Adolescent Deviant Behavior: Replication across and within Two Ethnic Groups." *Journal of Consulting and Clinical Psychology* 65: 1036–1041.

Fowler, James W. 1981. *Stages of Faith: The Psychology of Human Development and the Quest for Meaning.* San Francisco: Harper and Row.

Fowler, Mary. 1992. *Attention Deficit Disorders: An In-Depth Look from an Educational Perspective. C.H.A.D.D. Educators Manual.* Fairfax, VA: CASET Associates, Ltd.

Fox, Kenneth R., ed. 1997. *The Physical Self: From Motivation to Well-Being.* Champaign, IL: Human Kinetics.

Freedman, Benjamin. 1975. "A Moral Theory of Informed Consent." *Hastings Center Report* 5, no 4: 32–39.

Freedman, Jonathan L. 1984. "Effects of Television Violence on Aggressiveness." *Psychological Bulletin* 96: 227–246.

Freiberg, K. L. 1998. *Annual Editions: Human Development.* Guilford, CT: Dushkin/McGraw-Hill.

Freud, Anna. 1958. "Adolescence." *Psychoanalytic Study of the Child* 13: 255–278.

Freud, Anna. 1958. "Adolescence." *Psychoanalytical Studies of Children* 13: 231–258.

Freud, Sigmund. 1925. *Some Psychical Consequences of the Anatomical Distinction between the Sexes. (The*

Standard Edition of the Complete Psychological Works of Sigmund Freud, vol. 19.) Translated and edited by James Strachey. London: The Hogarth Press, 1961.

Frey, William H. 1985. *Crying: The Mystery of Tears.* New York: Harper Row.

Fricke, Aaron. 1981. *Reflections of a Rock Lobster: A Story about Growing Up Gay.* Boston: Alyson.

Friedman, S. B., M. M. Fisher, S. K. Schoenberg, and E. M. Alderman. 1998. *Comprehensive Adolescent Health Care.* St. Louis: Mosby.

Frisch, Rose E. 1983. "Fatness, Puberty, and Fertility: The Effects of Nutrition and Physical Training on Menarche and Ovulation." Pp. 29–50 in *Girls at Puberty: Biological and Psychosocial Perspectives.* Edited by Jeanne Brooks-Gunn and Anne C. Petersen. New York: Plenum Press.

Frome, Pamela M., and Jacquelynne S. Eccles. 1998. "Parents' Influence on Children's Achievement-Related Perceptions." *Journal of Personality and Social Psychology* 74: 435–452.

Fulgini, Andrew J., and Harold W. Stevenson.1995. "Time Use and Mathematics Achievement among American, Chinese, and Japanese High School Students." *Child Development* 66: 830–842.

Fuligni, Andrew J., and Jacquelynne S. Eccles. 1993. "Perceived Parent/Child Relationships and Early Adolescents' Orientation toward Peers." *Developmental Psychology* 29: 622–632.

Funk, Jeanne B. 1993. "Reevaluating the Impact of VideoGames." *Clinical Pediatrics* 32: 86–90.

Funk, Jeanne B., Geysa Flores, Debra D. Buchman, and Julie N. Germann. 1999. "Rating Electronic Video Games: Violence Is in the Eye of the Beholder." *Youth and Society* 30: 283–312.

Furman, Wyndol. 1989. "The Development of Children's Social Networks." Pp. 151–172 in *Children's Social Networks and Social Supports.* Edited by Deborah Belle. New York: Wiley.

Furnham, Adrian, and Paul Thomas. 1984. "Adults' Perception of the Economic Socialization of Children." *Journal of Adolescence* 7: 217–231.

Furstenberg, F. F., and A. J. Cherlin. 1991. *Divided Families: What Happens to Children When Parents Part.* Cambridge, MA: Harvard University Press.

Furstenberg, F. F., J. Brooks-Gunn, and S. P. Morgan. 1987. *Adolescent Mothers in Later Life.* New York: Cambridge University Press.

Gable, Robert A., Lyndal M. Bullock, and Dana L. Harader. 1995. "Schools in Transition: The Challenge of Students with Aggressive and Violent Behavior." *Preventing School Failure* 39: 29–34.

Garcia, Alma M., ed. 1997. *Chicana Feminist Thought: The Basic Historical Writings.* New York: Rutledge.

Garcia, Eugene E. 1991. *The Education of Linguistically and Culturally Diverse Students: Effective Instructional Practices* (Educational Practice Report 1). Washington, DC: National Center for Research on Cultural Diversity and Second Language Learning.

Gager, Constance T., Teresa M. Cooney, and Kathleen Thiede Call. 1999. "The Effects of Family Characteristics and Time Use on Teenagers' Household Labor." *Journal of Marriage and the Family* 61: 982–994.

Galambos, Nancy L., and David M. Almeida. 1992. "Does Parent-Adolescent Conflict Increase in Early Adolescence?" *Journal of Marriage and the Family* 54: 737–747.

Galanter, M. 1996. "Cults and Charismatic Group Psychology." Pp. 269–296 in *Religion and the Clinical Practice of Psychology*). Edited by E. P. Shafranske. Washington, DC: American Psychological Association.

Galbraith, John Kenneth.1958. *The Affluent Society*. Boston: Houghton Mifflin.

Gallup, Gordon, Jr. 1987. *The Gallup Poll: Public Opinion 1986*. Washington, DC: Scholarly Resources.

Gardner, Chadwick N. 1994/1995. "Don't Come Crying to Daddy! Emancipation of Minors: When Is a Parent 'Free at Last' from the Obligation of Child Support?" *University of Louisville Journal of Family Law* 33: 927–948.

Gardner, Howard. 1983. *Frames of Mind: The Theory of Multiple Intelligences*. New York: Basic Books.

———. 1993. *Creating Minds*. New York: Basic Books.

———. 1993. *Frames of Mind: The Theory of Multiple Intelligences*. 10th anniversary ed. New York: Basic Books.

Garrison, Carol Z., et al. 1997. "Incidence of Major Depressive Disorder and Dysthymia in Young Adolescents." *Journal of the Academy of Child and Adolescent Psychiatry* 36: 458–465.

Gaudin, J. M. 1999. "Child Neglect: Short-Term and Long-Term Outcomes." Pp. 89–108 in *Neglected Children*. Edited by Howard Dubowitz. Thousand Oaks, CA: Sage.

Gaylin, Willard, and Ruth Macklin. 1982. *Who Speaks for the Child: The Problems of Proxy Consent*. New York: Plenum Press.

Geary, David C. 1998. *Male, Female: The Evolution of Human Sex Differences*. Washington, DC: American Psychological Association.

Geiser, Robert L. 1973. *The Illusion of Caring: Children in Foster Care*. Boston: Beacon Press.

Gelles, R. J. 1999. "Policy Issues in Child Neglect." Pp. 278–298 in *Neglected Children*. Edited by Howard Dubowitz. Thousand Oaks, CA: Sage.

Gemelli, Ralph. 1996. *Normal Child and Adolescent Development*. Washington, DC: American Psychiatric Press.

Gennep, Arnold Van. 1960. *The Rites of Passage*. Translated by Monika B. Vizedom and Gabrielle L. Caffee. Chicago: University of Chicago Press. (Original work published in 1908.)

Gerber, Sterling, and Brenda Terry-Day. 1999. "Does Peer Mediation Really Work?" *Professional School Counseling* 2, no. 3: 169–171.

Gerzon, Robert. 1998. *Finding Security in the Age of Anxiety*. New York: Bantam Books.

Gesell, Arnold, et al. 1956. *Youth: The Years from Ten to Sixteen*. New York: Harper.

Gilbert, Daniel, Susan Fiske, and Gardner Lindzey, eds. 1998. *The Handbook of Social Psychology*. New York: McGraw-Hill.

Gibbs, John, and Marcus Liebermann. 1983. "A Longitudinal Study of Moral Judgment." *Monographs of the Society for Research in Child Development* 48: 1–124.

Gilligan, Carol. 1977. "In a Different Voice: Women's Conceptions of Self and of Morality." *Harvard Educational Review* 47: 481–517.

———. 1982. *In a Different Voice: Psychological Theory and Women's Development*. Cambridge, MA: Harvard University Press.

Gittler, Josephine, M. Quigley-Rick, and Michael J. Saks. 1990. *Adolescent Health Care Decision-Making: The Law and Public Policy*. Washington, DC: Carnegie Council on Adolescent Development.

Gjerde, Per F. 1986. "The Interpersonal Structure of Family Interaction Settings: Parent-Adolescent Relations in Dyads and Triads." *Developmental Psychology* 22, no. 3: 297–304.

Gjerde, Per F., and Jack Block. 1991. "Preadolescent Antecedents of Depressive Symptomatology at Age 18: A Prospective Study." *Journal of Youth and Adolescence* 20: 217–231.

Gluck, George M., and Warren M. Morganstein. 1998. *Jong's Community Dental Health*. St. Louis: Mosby.

Gochman, David, and Jean-Francois Saucier. 1982. "Perceived Vulnerability in Children and Adolescents." *Health Education Quarterly* 9, nos. 2 and 3: 46–58, 142–154.

Goldscheider, Francis K., and Linda J. Waite. 1991. *New Families, No Families: The Transformation of the American Home*. Berkeley: University of California Press.

Goldsmith, H. Hill, Arnold Buss, Robert Plomin, Mary Rothbart, Alexander Thomas, Stella Chess, Robert Hind, and Robert McCall. 1987. "Roundtable: What Is Temperament? Four Approaches." *Child Development* 58: 505–529.

Goldstein, Arnold P., and Fernand I. Soriano. 1994. "Juvenile Gangs." In *Reason to Hope: A Psychosocial Perspective on Violence and Youth*. Edited by Leonard D. Eron, Jacqueline H. Gentry, and P. Schlegel. Washington DC: American Psychological Association.

Goldstein, Arnold P., and Ronald Huff. 1993. *The Gang Intervention Handbook*. Champaign: Research Press.

Gonzalez, Nancy A., Ana Mari Cauce, Ruth J. Friedman, and Craig A. Mason. 1996. "Family, Peer, and Neighborhood Influences on Academic Achievement among African-American Adolescents: One Year Prospective Effect." *American Journal of Community Psychology* 24, no. 3: 365–387.

Goodnough, Gary E., and Vivian Ripley. 1997. "Structured Groups for High School Seniors Making the Transition to College and to Military Service." *The School Counselor* 44 (January): 230–234.

Goodnow, Jacqueline J. 1988. "Children's Household Work: Its Nature and Functions." *Psychological Bulletin* 103: 5–26.

Goodnow, Jacqueline J., and S. Delaney. 1989. "Children's Household Work: Task Differences, Styles of Assignment, and Links to Family Relationships. *Journal of Applied Developmental Psychology* 10: 209–226.

Goodwin, Donald W., Fini Schulsinger, L. Hermansen, Samuel B. Guze, and George Winokur 1973. "Alcohol Problems in Adoptees Raised Apart from Alcoholic Biological Parents." *Archives of General Psychiatry* 28: 238–243.

Goosens, F. X., et al. 1992. "The Many Faces of Egocentrism: Two European Replications." *Journal of Adolescent Research* 7: 43–58.

Gore, Susan A., and R. H. Aseltine. 1995. "Protective Processes in Adolescence: Matching Stressors with Social Resources." *American Journal of Community Psychology* 23: 301–327.

Gore, Susan, Robert H. Aseltine, and Mary Ellen Colten. 1993. "Gender, Social-Relational Involvement, and Depression." *Journal of Research on Adolescence* 3, no. 2: 101–125.

Gorsuch, Richard L. 1988. "Psychology of Religion." *Annual Review of Psychology* 39: 201–221.

Gortmaker, Steven L., Charles A. Salter, D. K. Walker, and William R. Dietz. 1990. "The Impact of Television Viewing on Mental Aptitude and Achievement: A Longitudinal Study." *Public Opinion Quarterly* 54: 594–604.

Gortmaker, Steven L., Jerome Kagan, Avshalom Caspi, and Phil A. Silva. 1997. "Daylength during Pregnancy and Shyness in Children: Results from Northern and Southern Hemispheres." *Developmental Psychobiology* 31: 107–114.

Gottfried, Adele E. 1985. "Academic Intrinsic Motivation in Elementary and Junior High School. *Journal of Educational Psychology* 77: 631–645.

———. 1986. *Children's Academic Intrinsic Motivation Inventory.* Odessa, FL: Psychological Assessment Resources.

———. 1991. "Maternal Employment in the Family Setting: Developmental and Environmental Issues." Pp.63–84 in *Employed Mothers and their Children.* Edited by J. V. Lerner and N. L. Galambos. New York: Garland.

Gottfried, Adele E., and Allen W. Gottfried. 1996. "A Longitudinal Study of Academic Intrinsic Motivation in Intellectually Gifted Children: Childhood through Early Adolescence." *Gifted Child Quarterly* 40: 179–183.

Gottfried, Adele E., James S. Fleming, and Allen W. Gottfried 1994. "Role of Parental Motivational Practices in Children's Academic Intrinsic Motivation and Achievement." *Journal of Educational Psychology* 86: 104–113.

———. 1998. "Role of Cognitively Stimulating Home Environment in Children's Academic Intrinsic Motivation: A Longitudinal Study." *Child Development* 69: 1448–1460.

———. 2001. "Continuity of Academic Intrinsic Motivation from Childhood through Late Adolescence: A Longitudinal Study." *Journal of Educational Psychology.*

Gould, Madelyn S., et al. 1998. "Psychopathology Associated with Suicidal Ideation and Attempts among Children and Adolescents." *Journal of the American Academy of Child and Adolescent Psychiatry* 37: 915–923.

Gould, Madelyn S., Prudence Fisher, Michael Parides, Michael Flory, and David Shaffer. 1996. "Psychosocial Risk Factors of Child and Adolescent Completed Suicide." *Archives of General Psychiatry* 53: 1155–1162.

Graber, Julia A., Anne C. Petersen, and Jeanne Brooks-Gunn, eds. 1996. "Pubertal Processes: Methods, Measures, and Models." Pp. 23–53 in *Transitions through Adolescence: Interpersonal Domains and Context.* Mahwah, NJ: Erlbaum.

Graber, Julia A., Jeanne Brooks-Gunn, Roberta L. Paikoff, and Michelle P. Warren. 1994. "Prediction of Eating Problems: An Eight-Year Study of Adolescent Girls." *Developmental Psychology* 30: 823–834.

Graber, Julia A., Peter M. Lewinsohn, John R. Seeley, and Jeanne Brooks-Gunn. 1997. "Is Psychopathology Associated with the Timing of Pubertal Development?" *Journal of the American Academy of Child and Adolescent Psychiatry* 36: 1768–1776.

Graham, Sandra, and Jaana Juvonen. 1998. "A Social Cognitive Perspective on Peer Aggression and Victimization." *Annals of Child Development* 13: 21–66.

———. 1998. "Self-Blame and Peer Victimization in Middle School: An

Attributional Bias." *Developmental Psychology* 34: 587–598.

Graham, Sandra, April Z. Taylor, and Cynthia Hudley. 1998. Exploring Achievement Values among Ethnic Minority Early Adolescents." *Journal of Educational Psychology* 90, no. 4: 606–620.

Grand Rapids Youth Groups. 2000. Nishnabek Youth Leadership Council and People of Our Time. Personal communication (January 25).

Granqvist, Pehr. 1998. "Religiousness and Perceived Childhood Attachment: On the Question of Compensation or Correspondence." *Journal for the Scientific Study of Religion* 37, no. 2: 350–367.

Gray, Marjory R., and Laurence Steinberg. 1999. "Unpacking Authoritative Parenting: Reassessing a Multidimensional Construct." *Journal of Marriage and the Family* 61: 574–587.

Gray, William M., and Lynne M. Hudson. 1984. "Formal Operations and the Imaginary Audience." *Developmental Psychology* 20: 619–627.

Green, Patricia, Bernard L. Dugoni, and Steven Ingels. 1995. *Trends among High School Seniors, 1972–1992.* Washington, DC: U.S. Department of Education.

Greenberg, Bradley S., Jane D. Brown, and Nancy Buerkel-Rothfuss. 1993. *Media, Sex, and the Adolescent.* Cresskill, NJ: Hampton Press.

Greenberger, Ellen, and Laurence D. Steinberg. 1986. *When Teenagers Work: The Psychological and Social Costs of Adolescent Employment.* New York: Basic Books.

Greene, Maxine. 1995. *Releasing the Imagination.* San Francisco: Jossey-Bass.

Griesler, Pamela C., Denise B. Kandel and Mark Davies. 1998. "Maternal Smoking during Pregnancy and Smoking by Adolescent Daughters." *Journal of Research on Adolescence* 8: 159–185.

Griffen, J. E., and S. R. Ojeda. 1996. *Textbook of Endocrine Physiology.* New York: Oxford University Press.

Griffin, Carolyn W., Marian J. Wirth, and Arthur G. Wirth. 1986. *Beyond Acceptance: Parents of Lesbians and Gays Talk about Their Experiences.* Englewood Cliffs, NJ: Prentice-Hall.

Grisso, Thomas, and Linda Vierling. 1978. "Minors' Consent to Treatment: A Developmental Perspective." *Professional Psychology* 9: 412–427.

Grossman, Jean B., and Jean E. Rhodes. In press. "The Test of Time: Predictors and Effects of Duration in Youth Mentoring Relationships." *American Journal of Community Psychology.*

Grotevant, Harold D. 1998. "Adolescent Development in Family Contexts." Pp. 1097–1150 in *Handbook of Child Psychology,* Vol. 3, *Social, Emotional, and Personality Development,* 5th ed. Edited by W. Damon and N. Eisenberg. New York: Wiley.

———. 1997. "Family Processes, Identity Development, and Behavioral Outcomes for Adopted Adolescents." *Journal of Adolescent Research* 12, no. 1: 139–161.

Grotevant, Harold D., Ruth G. McRoy, Carol L. Elde, and Deborah L. Fravel. 1994. "Adoptive Family System Dynamics: Variations by Level of Openness in the Adoption." *Family Process* 33: 125–146.

Grubb, Norton, and John Tuma. 1991. "Who Gets Student Aid?: Variation in Access to Aid." *Review of Higher Education* 14, no. 3: 359–382.

Grumbach, Melvin M., and Dennis M. Styne. 1998. "Puberty: Ontogeny, Neuroendocrinology, Physiology, and Disorders." Pp. 1509–1625 in *Williams*

Textbook of Endocrinology. Edited by Jean D. Wilson, Daniel W. Foster, and Henry M. Kronenberg. Philadelphia: W. B. Saunders Publishing.

Grusec, Joan E., Jacqueline J. Goodnow, and Lorenzo Cohen. 1996. "Household Work and the Development of Concern for Others." *Developmental Psychology* 32: 999–1007.

Grych, J. H., and F. D. Fincham. 1999. "Children of Single Parents and Divorce." Pp. 321–341 in *Developmental Issues in the Clinical Treatment of Children.* Edited by W. K. Silverman and T. H. Ollendick. Boston: Allyn and Bacon.

Guerney, Louise, and Joyce. Arthur. 1984. *Adolescent Social Relationships.* In *Experiencing Adolescents: A Sourcebook for Parents, Teachers, and Teens.* Edited by Richard M. Lerner and N. Galambos. New York: Teachers College Press.

Gullota, Thomas P., Gerald R. Adams, and Carol A. Markstrom. 2000. *The Adolescent Experience.* 4th ed. San Diego: Academic Press.

Gullota, Thomas P., Gerald R. Adams, and Richard Montemayor, eds. 1995. *Substance Misuse in Adolescence.* Thousand Oaks: Sage.

"Hackers Are Necessary." Retrieved from the World Wide Web on 5/17/99: http://www.cnn.com/TECH/specials/hackers/qandas/

"Hacking Is a Felony." Retrieved from the World Wide Web on 5/17/99: http://www.cnn.com/TECH/specials/hackers/qandas/.

Hagan, John, and Bill McCarthy. 1997. *Mean Streets: Youth Crime and Homelessness.* New York: Cambridge University Press.

Hagen, John, Jennifer T. Myers, and Jennifer S. Allswede. 1992. "The Psychological Impact of Children's Chronic Illness." Pp. 27–47 in David

Featherman, Richard Lerner, and Marion Perlmutter, eds., *Lifespan Development and Behavior,* Vol. 11. Hillsdale, NJ: Erlbaum.

Hagestad, G. O. 1985. "Continuity and Connectedness." Pp. 31–48 in *Grandparenthood.* Edited by Vern L. Bengtson and Joan F. Robertson. Beverly Hills: Sage.

Haignere, Clara S., Rachel Gold, and Heather J. McDanel, 1999. "Adolescent Abstinence and Condom Use: Are We Sure We Are Really Teaching What Is Safe?" *Health Education and Behavior* 26: 43–54.

Halfon, Neal, Ana Mendonca, and Gale Berkowitz. 1995. "Health Status of Children in Foster Care." *Archives of Pediatric and Adolescent Medicine* 149: 386–392.

Hall, G. Stanley. 1904. *Adolescence: Its Psychology and Its Relations to Physiology, Anthropology, Sociology, Sex, Crime, Religion, and Education,* Vols. 1 and 2. New York: Appleton.

Hallowell, Edward M. 1997. *Worry: Hope and Help for a Common Condition.* New York: Ballantine Books.

Halpern-Felsher, Bonnie L., Susan G. Millstein, Jonathan M. Ellen, Nancy E. Adler, Jeanne Tschann, and Michael C. Biehl. In press. "The Role of Behavioral Experience in Judging Risks." *Health Psychology.*

Hamilton, Stephen F. 1990. *Apprenticeship for Adulthood: Preparing Youth for the Future.* New York: Free Press.

Hamilton, Stephen F., and Wolfgang Lempert. 1996. "The Impact of Apprenticeship on Youth: A Prospective Analysis." *Journal of Research on Adolescence* 6, no. 4: 427–455.

Hammer, Torild. 1996. "Consequences of Unemployment in the Transition from

Youth to Adulthood in Life Course Perspective." *Youth & Society* 27, no. 4: 450–468.

Hammill, Donald. D., J. E. Leigh, G. McNutt, and S. C. Larsen. 1981. "A New Definition of Learning Disabilities." *Learning Disability Quarterly* 4: 336–342.

Hanson, C. L., J. R. Rodrique, S. W. Henggeler, M. A. Harris, R. C. Klesges, and D. L. Carle. 1990. "The Perceived Self-Competence of Adolescents with Insulin-Dependent Diabetes Mellitus: Deficit or Strength?" *Journal of Pediatric Psychology* 15, no. 5: 605–618.

Hareven, Tamara K., and Maris A. Vinovskis, eds. 1978. *Family and Population in Nineteenth-Century America.* Princeton, NJ: Princeton University Press.

Harper, P. T., and B. M. Harper. 1999. *Hip-Hop's Influence within Youth Popular Culture.* Silver Springs, MD: McFarland and Associates.

Hart, Daniel. 1988. "The Adolescent Self-Concept in Social Context." Pp. 71–90 in *Self, Ego, and Identity.* Edited by Daniel Lapsley and F. Clark Power. New York: Springer-Verlag.

Hart, Jordana. 1998. "Young and on the Run after Fleeing Home, They Often Find a World of Rape, Prostitution and Drugs." *The Boston Globe,* February 2, A1.

Harter, Susan. 1996. "Teacher and Classmate Influences on Scholastic Motivation, Self-Esteem, and Level of Voice in Adolescents." Pp. 11–42 in *Social Motivation: Understanding Children's School Adjustment.* Edited by Jaana Juvonen and Kathryn Wentzel. New York: Cambridge University Press.

———. 1999. *The Construction of the Self: A Developmental Perspective.* New York: Guilford Press.

Hartman, Virginia F. 1995. "Teaching and Learning Style Preferences: Transition through Technology." *VCCA Journal* 9, no. 2: 18–20.

Hartup, Willard. 1993a. "Adolescents and Their Friends." *New Directions for Child Development* 60: 3–22.

———. 1993b. "The Company They Keep: Friendships and Their Developmental Significance." *Child Development* 67: 1–13.

Hatcher, Robert A., James Trussell, Felicia Stewart, Willard Cates, Jr., Gary K. Stewart, Felicia Guest, and Deborah Kowal. 1998. *Contraceptive Technology.* 17th revised ed. New York: Ardent Media.

Haugaard, Jeffrey J., Amy Schustack, and Karen Dorman. 1998. "Searching for Birth Parents by Adult Adoptees." *Adoption Quarterly* 1, no. 3: 77–83.

Havinghurst, Robert J. 1972. *Developmental Tasks and Education.* New York: David McKay.

Hawkins, J. David, ed. 1996. *Delinquency and Crime: Current Theories.* New York: Cambridge University Press.

Hawkins, J. David, Richard F. Catalano, and Janet Y. Miller. 1992. "Risk and Protective Factors for Alcohol and Other Drug Problems in Adolescence and Young Adulthood: Implications for Substance Abuse Prevention." *Psychological Bulletin* 112: 64–105.

Hayes, Cheryl D. 1987. *Risking the Future: Adolescent Sexuality, Pregnancy, and Childbearing.* Washington, DC: National Academy Press.

Hayward, Christopher, Joel D. Killen, Darrell M. Wilson, Lawrence D. Hammer, Iris F. Litt, Helena C. Kraemer, Farish Haydel, Ann Varaday, and C. Barr Taylor. 1997. "Psychiatric Risk Associated with Early Puberty in Adolescent Girls." *Journal of the American Academy of*

Child and Adolescent Psychiatry 36: 255–262.

Head, John. 1997. *Working with Adolescents: Constructing Identity.* Washington, DC: The Falmer Press.

Healy, Jane M. 1994. *Your Child's Growing Mind: A Practical Guide to Brain Development and Learning from Birth to Adolescence.* New York: Doubleday.

Helms, Janet E. 1992. "Why Is There No Study of Cultural Equivalence in Standardized Cognitive Ability Tests?" *American Psychologist* 49 no. 7: 1038–1101.

Hendee, William R., ed. 1991. *The Health of Adolescents.* San Francisco: Jossey-Bass.

Henderson, Lynne, and Philip Zimbardo. 1998. "Shyness." Pp. 497–509 in *Encyclopedia of Mental Health*, Vol. 3. Edited by Howard S. Friedman. San Diego: Academic Press.

Hendren, Robert L. 1990. "Stress in Adolescence." Pp. 247–265 in *Childhood Stress.* Edited by L. E. Arnold. New York: Wiley.

Henggeler, Scott W., Sonja K. Schoenwald, Charles M. Borduin, Melisa D. Rowland, and Phillippe B. Cunningham. 1998. *Multisystemic Treatment of Antisocial Behavior in Children and Adolescents.* New York,: Guilford Press.

Henry, James. 1997. "System Intervention Trauma to Child Sexual Abuse Victims Following Disclosure." *Journal of Interpersonal Violence* 12: 499–512.

Herbert, Martin.1987. *Conduct Disorders of Childhood and Adolescence: A Social Learning Perspective.* New York: Wiley.

Herdt, Gilbert, ed. 1989. *Gay and Lesbian Youth.* New York: Harrington Park Press.

Herman, Judith. 1992. *Trauma and Recovery: The Aftermath of Violence—from Domestic Abuse to Political Terror.* New York: Basic Books.

Herman-Giddens, Marcia E, Eric J. Slora, Richard C. Wasserman, Carlos J. Bourdony, Manju V. Bhapkar, Gary G. Koch, and Cynthia Hasemeier. 1997. "Secondary Sexual Characteristics and Menses in Young Girls Seen in Office Practice: A Study from the Pediatric Research in Office Settings Network." *Pediatrics* 99: 505–512.

Hernandez, Donald J. 1993. *America's Children: Resources From Family, Government, and the Economy.* New York: Russell Sage Foundation.

———. 1996a. "Population Change and the Family Environment of Children." Pp. 231–342 in *Trends in the Well-Being of Children and Youth: 1996.* Washington, DC: U.S. Department of Health and Human Services.

———. 1996b. "Child Development and Social Demography of Childhood." *Child Development* 68, no. 1: 149–169.

———. 1997. "Poverty Trends" Pp. 18–34 in *Consequences of Growing Up Poor.* Edited by Greg J. Duncan and Jeanne Brooks-Gunn. New York: Russell Sage Foundation.

———. 2000. Calculated by author from U.S. Census Bureau's *Current Population Survey*, March 2000.

Heron, Ann, ed. 1994. *Two Teenagers in Twenty: Writings by Gay and Lesbian Youth.* Boston: Alyson.

Hetherington, E. Mavis. 1989. "Coping with Family Transitions: Winners, Losers, and Survivors." *Child Development* 60: 1–14.

Hetherington, E. Mavis, and W. G. Clingempeel. 1992. "Coping with Marital Transitions." *Monographs of the Society* for *Research in Child Development* 57 (2–3, Serial No. 227).

Hetherington, E. Mavis, David L. Featherman, and Karen A. Camara. 1981. *Intellectual Functioning and Achievement of Children in One-Parent Households.* Washington DC: National Institute of Education.

Hetherington, E. Mavis, David Reiss, and Robert Plomin. 1994. *Separate Social Worlds of Siblings: The Impact of Nonshared Environment on Development.* Hillsdale, NJ: Erlbaum.

Hetherington, E. Mavis, Richard M. Lerner, and Marion Perlmutter, eds. 1988. *Child Development in Life-Span Perspective.* Hillsdale, NJ: Erlbaum.

Hicks, M. John, and Catherine M. Flaitz. 1993. "Epidemiology of Dental Caries in the Pediatric and Adolescent Population: A Review of Past and Current Trends." *Journal of Clinical Pediatric Dentistry* 18 (Fall): 43–49.

Hieshima, Joyce A., and Barbara Schneider. 1994. "Intergenerational Effects on the Cultural and Cognitive Socialization of Third and Fourth Generations of Japanese Americans." *Journal of Applied Developmental Psychology* 15: 319–327.

Hill, Craig, Judith Blakemore, and Patrick Drumm. 1997. *Mutual and Unrequited Love in Adolescence and Young Adulthood,* Vol. 4, *Personal Relationships.* New York: Cambridge University Press.

Hill, James O., and John C. Peters. 1998. "Environmental Contributions to the Obesity Epidemic." *Science* 280: 1371–1374.

Hill, John P., and Grayson Holmbeck. 1986. "Attachment and Autonomy during Adolescence." *Annals of Child Development* 3: 145–189.

"A History of Hacking." Retrieved from the World Wide Web on 8/17/99: http://www.sptimes.com/Hackers/history.hacking.html

Hobbs, Frank, and Laura Lippman. 1990. "Children's Well-Being: An International Comparison." U.S. Bureau of the Census, International Population reports, Series P-95, No. 80. Washington, DC: U.S. Government Printing Office.

Hodapp, Robert M. 1996. "Down Syndrome: Developmental, Psychiatric, and Management Issues." *Child and Adolescent Psychiatric Clinics of North America* 5: 881–894.

Hofer, Myron. 1995. "An Evolutionary Perspective on Anxiety." Pp. 17–38 in *Anxiety as Symptom and Signal.* Edited by Steven Roose and Robert Glick. Hillsdale, NJ: Analytic Press.

Hoffman, Martin L. 1983. "Empathy, Guilt, and Social Cognition." Pp. 1–52 in *The Relationship between Social and Cognitive Development.* Edited by Willis F. Overton. Hillsdale, NJ: Erlbaum.

Hogan, K., and M. Pressley, eds. 1997. *Scaffolding Student Learning: Instructional Approaches and Issues.* Cambridge, MA: Brookline.

Holder, Angela R. 1981. "Can Teenagers Participate in Research without Parental Consent?" *Irb: Review of Human Subjects Research* 3: 5–7.

Holland, John L. 1994. *Self-Directed Search: Assessment Booklet.* Odessa, FL: Psychological Assessment Resources.

———. 1997. *Making Vocational Choices: A Theory of Vocational Personalities and Work Environments,* 3rd ed. Odessa, FL: Psychological Assessment Resources.

Hollifield, John H. 1995. "Parent Involvement in Middle Schools." *Principal* 74, no. 3: 14–16.

Holmbeck, Grayson N. 1994. "Adolescence." Pp. 17–28 in *Encyclopedia of Human Behavior*, Vol. 1. Edited by V.S. Ramachandran. San Diego: Academic Press.

———. 1996. "A Model of Family Relational Transformations during the Transition to Adolescence: Parent-Adolescent Conflict and Adaptation." In *Transitions Through Adolescence: Interpersonal Domains and Context.* Edited by J. Graber, J. Brooks-Gunn, and A. Peterson. Mahwah, NJ: Erlbaum.

Holmbeck, Grayson N., and John P. Hill. 1988. "Storm and Stress Beliefs about Adolescence: Prevalence, Self-Reported Antecedents, and Effects of an Undergraduate Course." *Journal of Youth and Adolescence* 17: 285–305.

Holmbeck, Grayson, Roberta Paikoff, and Jeanne Brooks-Gunn. 1995. "Parenting Adolescents." In *Handbook of Parenting*, Vol. 1. Edited by Marcus Bornstein. Mahwah, NJ: Erlbaum.

Holmbeck, Grayson, and Wendy Shapera. 1999. "Research Methods with Adolescents." In *Handbook of Research Methods in Clinical Psychology.* Edited by P. Kendall, J. Butcher, and G. Holmbeck. New York: Wiley.

Holmes, K. K., et al. 1999. *Sexually Transmitted Diseases, 3rd* ed. New York: McGraw-Hill.

Hood, Ralph W. Jr., Bernard Spilka, Bruce Hunsberger, and Richard Gorsuch. 1996. *The Psychology of Religion: An Empirical Approach.* New York: Guilford Press.

Hoover, J., R. Oliver, and R. Hazler. 1992. "Bullying: Perceptions of Adolescent Victims in Midwestern USA." *School Psychology International* 13: 5–.

Horowitz, Allan V., and Helen R. White. 1998. "The Relationship of Cohabitation and Mental Health: A Study of Young Adult Cohort." *Journal of Marriage and the Family* 60: 505–514.

Hovell, Melbourne F.,et al. 1994. "A Behavioral-Ecological Model of Adolescent Sexual Development: A Template for AIDS Prevention." *Journal of Sex Research* 31: 267–281.

Howard, M., and McCabe, J. 1990. "Helping Teenagers Postpone Sexual Involvement." *Family Planning Perspectives* 22: 21–26.

Howe, Howard. 1986. "Can Schools Teach Values?" Remarks at Lehigh University Commencement, May. Bethelehem, PA.

Hoyenga, Katharine B. 1993. *Gender-Related Differences: Origins and Outcomes.* Boston: Allyn and Bacon.

Hoyert, Donna L., Kenneth D. Kochanek, and Sherry L. Murphy. 1999. "Deaths: Final Data for 1997." *National Vital Statistics Reports* 47, no 19. Hyattsville, MD: National Center for Health Statistics.

Hsu, L. K. George. 1990. *Eating Disorders.* New York: Guilford Press.

Huff, C. Ronald. 1990. *Gangs in America.* Newbury Park, CA: Sage.

Hughes, C. A., and S. K. Suritsky. 1993. "Notetaking Skills and Strategies for Students with Learning Disabilities." *Preventing School Failure* 38, no. 1: 7–11.

Hughes, M. E., Furstenberg, F. F., and Teitler, J. O. 1995. "The Impact of an Increase in Family Planning Services on the Teenage Population of Philadelphia." *Family Planning Perspectives* 27: 60–65.

Humes, Edward. 1997. *No Matter How Loud I Shout: A Year in the Life of Juvenile Court.* New York: Simon and Schuster.

Hundleby, Marion, Joan Shireman, and John Triseliotis. 1997. *Adoption: Theory, Policy, and Practice.* London: Cassell.

Hunter, E. 1998. Adolescent Attraction to Cults. *Adolescence* 33: 709–714.

Hurrelmann, Klaus, and Stephen F. Hamilton, eds. 1996. *Social Problems and Social Contexts in Adolescence: Perspectives across Boundaries.* New York: Aldine de Gruyter.

Huston, A. C., and J. C. Wright. 1998. "Mass Media and Child Development." In *Handbook of Child Psychology,* Vol. 3, *Child Psychology in Practice.* Edited by I. E. Sigel and K. Renninger. New York: Wiley.

Hutchins, Loraine, and Lani Kaahumana, eds. 1991. *Bi Any Other Name: Bisexual People Speak Out.* Boston: Alyson.

Hutson, S., and M. Liddiard. 1994. *Youth Homelessness: The Construction of a Social Issue.* London: Macmillan.

Hyde, Janet S. and Marcia Linn. 1988. "Gender Differences in Verbal Ability: A Meta-Analysis." *Psychological Bulletin* 104: 53–69.

Hyde, Janet S., Elizabeth Fennema, and Susan J. Lamon. 1990. "Gender Differences in Mathematics Performance: A Meta-Analysis." *Psychological Bulletin* 107: 139–155.

Inciardi, James A., Ruth Horowitz, and Anne E. Pottieger. 1993. *Street Kids, Street Drugs, Street Crime.* Belmont: Wadsworth Publishing.

Independent Sector. 1996. *Volunteering and Giving Among American Teenagers 12 to 17 Years of Age.* Washington, DC: Independent Sector.

InfoStreet, Inc. 1999. *InstantWeb: Online Computing Dictionary.* http://www.instantweb.com/~foldoc/contents.html

Ingersoll, G. M., D. P. Orr, A. J. Herrold, and M. P. Golden. 1986. "Cognitive Maturity and Self-Management among Adolescents with Insulin-Dependent Diabetes Mellitus." *Journal of Pediatrics* 10, no. 4: 620–623.

Inhelder, Barbel, and Jean Piaget. 1958. *The Growth of Logical Thinking from Childhood Through Adolescence.* New York: Basic Books.

International Dyslexia Association Web site at http://www.interdys.org. 1–800–222–3123

International Food Information Council Foundation (IFIC) http://ificinfo.health.org/insight/teentrnd.htm

Irvine, Janice M. 1994. *Sexuality Education across Cultures.* San Francisco: Jossey-Bass.

Israelashvili, Moshe. 1997. "School Adjustment, School Membership and Adolescents' Future Expectations." *Journal of Adolescence* 20: 525–535.

Jacklin, Carol Nagy. 1992. *The Psychology of Gender.* New York: New York University Press.

Jacobs, Fran. 1988. "The Five-Tiered Approach to Evaluation: Context and Implementation." Pp. 37–68 in *Evaluating Family Programs.* Edited by H. B. Weiss and F. Jacobs. Hawthorne, NY: Aldine.

Jacobson, K. C., and L. J. Crockett. 2000. "Parental Monitoring and Adolescent Adjustment: An Ecological Perspective." *Journal of Research on Adolescence* 10: 65–97.

Jacobs-Quadrel, Marilyn, Baruch Fischhoff, and Wendy Davis. 1993. "Adolescent (In)vulnerability." *American Psychologist* 48, no. 2: 102–116.

Jesson, Jill. 1993. "Understanding Adolescent Female Prostitution: A Literature Review." *British Journal of Social Work* 23, no. 5: 517–530.

Jessor, Richard, and Shirley L. Jessor. 1977. *Problem Behavior and Psychosocial Development.* New York: Academic Press.

Johnson, David W., and Roger T. Johnson. 1996. "Conflict Resolution and Peer Mediation Programs in Elementary and Secondary Schools: A Review of the Research." *Review of Educational Research* 66, no. 4: 459–506.

Johnson, Lloyd D., Patrick M. O'Malley, and Jerald G. Bachman. 1999. *National Survey Results from the Monitoring the Future Study: 1975–1998.* Washington, DC: U.S. Government Printing Office.

Johnson, Norine G., Michael C. Roberts, and Judith Worell, eds. 1999. *Beyond Appearance: A New Look at Adolescent Girls.* Washington, DC.: American Psychological Association.

Johnson, Penny, Carol I. Yoken, and Ron Voss. 1995. "Foster Care Placement: The Child's Perspective." *Child Welfare* 74, no. 5: 959–974.

Johnston, Lloyd D., Jerald Bachman, and Patrick M. O'Malley. 1996. *Monitoring The Future: Questionnaire Responses from the Nation's High School Seniors.* Ann Arbor: Institute for Social Research, University of Michigan.

———. 1999. *National Survey Results on Drug Use from the Monitoring the Future Study, 1975–1998.* U.S. Department of Health and Human Services, National Institute on Drug Abuse, NIH Publication No. 99–4661. Washington, DC: U.S. Government Printing Office.

———. 1999. *The Monitoring of the Future Study.* Washington, DC: U.S. Department of Health and Human Services.

———. 2000. *Monitoring the Future: National Survey Results on Drug Use, 1975–1999,* Vol. 1: Secondary Students." (NIH Publication No. 00–4802) Washington, DC: National Institute on Drug Abuse.

———. 2000. *Monitoring the Future: National Results on Adolescent Drug Use: Overview of Key Findings, 1999* (NIH Publication No. 00–4690). Rockville, MD: National Institute on Drug Abuse.

Joint Committee on Testing Practices. 1988. *Code of Fair Testing Practices in Education.* Washington, D.C.: Joint Committee on Testing Practices.

Jones, Doug. 1996. *Physical Attractiveness and the Theory of Sexual Selection.* Ann Arbor: University of Michigan.

Jones, LeAlan, Lloyd Newman, and David Isay. 1997. *Our America.* New York: Simon and Schuster.

Joy, Elizabeth, et al. 1997. "Team Management of the Female Athlete Triad. Part I: Optimal Treatment and Prevention Tactics." *The Physician and Sportsmedicine* 25: 94.

———. 1997. "Team Management of the Female Athlete Triad. Part II: What to Look For, What to Ask." *The Physician and Sportsmedicine* 25: 55.

Juang, Linda P., Jacqueline V. Lerner, John McKinney, and Alex von Eye. 1999. "The Goodness of Fit of Autonomy Expectations between Asian-American Late Adolescents and Their Parents." *International Journal of Behavioral Development* 23, no. 4: 1023–1048.

Juel-Nielsen, Niels. 1980. *Individual and Environment: Monozygotic Twins Reared Apart.* New York: International Universities Press.

Juvonen, Jaana. 1996. "Self-Presentation Tactics Promoting Teacher and Peer Approval: The Function of Excuses and Other Clever Explanations." Pp. 43–65 in *Social Motivation: Understanding Children's School Adjustment.* Edited by Jaana Juvonen and Kathryn Wentzel. New York: Cambridge University Press.

Juvonen, Jaana, and Sandra Graham, eds. 2000. *Peer Harassment in School: The Plight of the Vulnerable and Victimized.* New York: Guilford Press.

Kagan, Jerome, J. Reznick, and Nancy Snidman. 1987. "The Physiology and Psychology of Behavioral Inhibition in Children." *Child Development* 58: 1459–1473.

Kaiser Family Foundation. 2000. "The State of the HIV/AIDS Epidemic in America." *Capitol Hill Briefing Series on HIV/AIDS*, April: 1–8.

Kaiser, Susan. 1997. *The Social Psychology of Clothing: Symbolic Appearances in Context*, 2nd ed., rev. New York: Fairchild.

Kamphaus, Randy W. 1993. *Clinical Assessment of Children's Intelligence.* Boston: Allyn and Bacon.

Kandel, Denise B. 1978. "Homophily, Selection, and Socialization in Adolescent Friendships." *American Journal of Sociology* 84: 427–436.

Kaplan, Elaine B. 1999. "'It's Going Good: Inner-City Black and Latino Adolescents' Perceptions about Achieving an Education. " *Urban Education 34:* 181–213.

Kaplan, Harold I., Benjamin J. Sadock, and Jack A. Grebb. 1994. *Kaplan and Sadock's Synopsis of Psychiatry: Behavioral Sciences, Clinical Psychiatry.* 7th ed. Baltimore: Williams & Wilkins.

Kaplowitz, Paul B., Sharon E. Oberfield, and the Drug and Therapeutics and Executive Committee of the Lawson Wilkins Pediatric Endocrine Society. "Reexamination of the Age Limit for Defining When Puberty Is Precocious in Girls in the United States: Implications for Evaluation and Treatment." *Pediatrics* 104: 936–941.

Kardiner, Abram, and Lionel Ovessey. 1951. *The Mark of Oppression.* Cleveland: World Publishing Company.

Karniol, Rachel, Rivi Gabay, Yael Ochion, and Yeal Harari. 1998. "Is Gender or Gender-Role Orientation a Better Predictor of Empathy in Adolescence?" *Sex Roles* 39: 45–59.

Kastner, Laura, and Jennifer Wyatt. 1997. *The Seven Year Stretch.* New York: Houghton Mifflin.

Katchadourian, Herant. 1977. *The Biology of Adolescence.* San Francisco: Freeman.

———. 1991. "Sexuality." In *At the Threshold: The Developing Adolescent.* Edited by Shirley S. Feldman and Glen R. Elliott. Cambridge, MA: Harvard University Press.

Kaufman, Alan S. 1990. *Assessing Adolescent and Adult Intelligence.* Boston: Allyn and Bacon.

Kaufman, Sandra Z. 1999. *Retarded Isn't Stupid, Mom!* Baltimore, MD: Paul H. Brookes.

Kavlock, R. J., and G. T. Ankley. 1996. "A Perspective on the Risk Assessment Process for Endocrine-Disruptive Effects on Wildlife and Human Health." *Risk Analysis* 16: 731–739.

Kawamoto, Walter T., and Tamara C. Cheshire. 1999. "Contemporary Issues in the Urban American Indian Family." Pp. 94–104 in *Family Ethnicity: Strength in Diversity*, 2nd ed. Edited by Harriette P. McAdoo. Thousand Oaks, CA: Sage.

Kaysen, Susanna. 1993. *Girl Interrupted.* New York: Vintage Books.

Kazdin, Alan. 1987. *Conduct Disorders in Childhood and Adolescence* Vol. 9, *Developmental Clinical Psychology and Psychiatry.* London: Sage.

Keel, Pamela K., Jayne A. Fulkerson, and Gloria R. Leon. 1997. "Disordered Eating

Precursors in Pre- and Early Adolescent Girls and Boys." *Journal of Youth and Adolescence* 26: 203–216.

Kegan, Robert. 1982. *The Evolving Self: Problem and Process in Human Development.* Cambridge, MA: Harvard University Press.

Keidel, K. C. 1970. "Maternal Employment and Ninth Grade Achievement in Bismarck, North Dakota. *Family Coordinator* 19: 95–97.

Keidel, K. C. 1970. "Maternal Employment and Ninth Grade Achievement in Bismarck, North Dakota. *Family Coordinator* 19: 95–97.

Keith-Spiegel, Patricia. 1983. "Children and Consent to Participate in Research." Pp. 179–211 in *Children's Competence to Consent.* Edited by Gary B. Melton, Gerald P. Koocher, and Michael J. Saks. New York: Plenum Press.

Kelder, Steven H., Cheryl L. Perry, Knut-Inge Klepp, and Leslie L. Lytle. 1994. "Longitudinal Tracking of Adolescent Smoking, Physical Activity, and Food Choice Behaviors." *American Journal of Public Health,* 84, no. 7: 1121–1126.

Kellam, Susan. 1999a. "New School, New Problems: Foster Children Struggle in U.S. Schools." Web site: http://connectforkids.org.

———. 1999b. "Voices of Foster Care: People Who Make a Difference." Web site: http:www.connectforkids.org.

Kelly, Alison. 1987. *Science for Girls?* Philadelphia: Open University Press.

Kendall, Philip. 2000. *Childhood Disorders.* United Kingdom: Psychology Press.

Kendall-Tackett, Kathleen A., Linda M. Williams, and David Finkelhor. 1993. "Impact of Sexual Abuse on Children: A Review and Synthesis of Recent Empirical Studies." *Psychological Bulletin* 113: 164–180.

Kennedy, Suzanne E., Sherri D. Garcia Martin, John M. Kelley, Brian Walton, Claudia K. Vlcek, Ruth S. Hassanein, and Grace E. Holmes. 1998. "Identification of Medical and Nonmedical Needs of Adolescents and Young Adults with Spina Bifida and Their Families: A Preliminary Study." *Children's Health Care* 27: 47–61.

Kent, Angela, Waller, Glenn. 1998. "The Impact of Childhood Emotional Abuse: An Extension of The Child Abuse and Trauma Scale." *Child Abuse and Neglect* 22, no. 5: 393–399.

Kett, Joseph F. 1977. *Rites of Passage: Adolescence in America, 1790 to the Present.* New York: Basic Books.

Kihlstrom, John F., and Stanley B. Klein. 1997. "Self-Knowledge and Self-Awareness." Pp. 5–17 in *The Self across Psychology: Self-Recognition, Self-Awareness, and the Self Concept.* Edited by Joan Gay Snodgrass and Robert L. Thommpson. New York: New York Academy of Sciences.

Kim, Uichol, and Maria B. J. Chun. 1994. "Educational "Success" of Asian Americans: An Indigenous Perspective." *Journal of Applied Developmental Psychology* 15: 329–343.

Kindermann, Thomas A., Tanya McCollam, and Ellsworth Gibson. 1996. "Peer Networks and Students' Classroom Engagement during Childhood and Adolescence." Pp. 279–312 in *Social Motivation: Understanding Children's School Adjustment.* Edited by Jaana Juvonen and Kathryn R. Wentzel. New York: Cambridge University Press.

Kingsley, Jason, and Mitchell Levitz. 1994. *Count Us In: Growing Up with Down Syndrome.* San Diego: Harcourt Brace.

Kirby, Douglas. 1997. *No Easy Answers: Research Findings on Programs to Reduce Teen Pregnancy.* Washington, DC: The National Campaign to Prevent Teen Pregnancy.

———. 1999. "Reducing Adolescent Pregnancy: Approaches That Work." *Contemporary Pediatrics* 16: 83–94.

Kist, Jay. 1997. "Dealing with Depression." *Current Health* 23, no. 5: 25–28.

Kivett, Vira. 1991. "The Grandparent-Grandchild Connection." *Journal of Marriage and Family Review* 19: 26–34.

Kivnick, Helen Q. 1993. "Everyday Mental Health: A Guide to Assessing Life Strengths." Pp. 19–36 in *Mental Health and Aging: Progress and Prospects.* Edited by M. A. Smyer. New York: Springer.

Kivnick, Helen Q., and Heather Sinclair. 1996. "Grandparenthood." Pp. 611–624 in *Encyclopedia of Gerontology.* Edited by J. E. Birren. New York: Academic Press.

Klaw, Elena L., and Jean E. Rhodes. 1995. "Mentor Relationships and the Career Development of Pregnant and Parenting African-American Teenagers." *Psychology of Women Quarterly* 19: 551–562.

Klein, Karla, Rex Forehand, Lisa Armistead, and Patricia Long. 1997. "Delinquency during the Transition to Early Adulthood: Family and Parenting Predictors from Early Adolescence." *Adolescence* 32: 203–219.

Klerman, Lorraine V. 1991. "Barriers to Health Services for Adolescents." Pp. 470–474 in *Encyclopedia of Adolescence.* Edited by Richard M. Lerner, Anne C. Petersen, and Jeanne Brooks-Gunn. New York: Garland.

Koch, Patricia. 1991. "Sex Education." In *Encyclopedia of Adolescence.* Edited by Richard Lerner, Anne Petersen, and Jeanne Brooks-Gunn. New York: Garland.

Kohlberg, Lawrence. 1969. "Stage and Sequence: The Cognitive Developmental Approach to Socialization." Pp. 347–480 in *Handbook of Socialization Theory.* Edited by D. A. Goslin.

———. 1981. *The Philosophy of Moral Development: Moral Stages and the Idea of Justice.* San Francisco: Harper and Row.

Kohnstamm, Gedolph A., John E Bates, and Mary K. Rothbart, eds. 1995. *Temperament in Childhood.* UK: Wiley.

Kolaric, G. C., and Nancy L. Galambos. 1995. "Face-to-Face Interactions in Unacquainted Female-Male Adolescent Dyads: How Do Girls and Boys Behave?" *Journal of Early Adolescence* 15, no. 3: 363–382.

Kolb, David A. 1984. *Experiential Learning: Experiences as the Source of Learning and Development.* Englewood Cliffs, NJ: Prentice-Hall, Inc.

Kolvin, I., and C. Kaplan. 1988. "Anxiety in Childhood." Pp. 259–275 in *Handbook of Anxiety,* Vol. 1, *Biological, Clinical and Cultural Perspectives.* Edited by Martin Roth, Russell Noyes Jr., and Graham Burrows. New York: Elsevier Science Publishers.

Koocher, Gerald P., and Patricia C. Keith-Spiegel. 1990. *Children, Ethics, and the Law.* Lincoln: University of Nebraska Press.

Koss, Mary P., Lisa A. Goodman, Angela Browne, Louise F. Fitzgerald, Gwendolyn Puryear Keita, and Nancy Felipe Russo. 1994. *No Safe Haven: Male Violence against Women at Home, at Work, and in the Community.* Washington, D.C.: American Psychological Society.

Kovacs, Maria. 1997. "Depressive Disorder in Childhood: An Impressionistic Landscape." *Journal of Child Psychology and Psychiatry* 38: 287–298.

Kovar, Mary Grace. 1991. "Health of Adolescents in the United States: An Overview." Pp. 454–458 in *Encyclopedia of Adolescence*. Edited by Richard M. Lerner, Anne C. Petersen, and Jeanne Brooks-Gunn. New York: Garland

Kowalski, Kathiann M. 1998. "Peer Mediation Success Stories: In Nearly 10,000 Schools Nationwide, Peer Mediation Helps Teens Solve Problems Without Violence." *Current Health* 25, no. 2: 13–15.

Kracke, Baerbel. 1997. "Parental Behaviors and Adolescents' Career Exploration." *The Career Development Quarterly* 45(4): 341–350.

Kramer-Koehler, Pamela, Nancy M. Tooney, and Devendra P. Beke. 1995. "The Use of Learning Style Innovations to Improve Retention." In ASEE/ISEE *Frontiers in Education '95: Proceedings*. Purdue University. http://fie.engrng.pitt.edu/fie95/4a2/4a22/4a22htm

Krauss, Marty W., Marsha M. Seltzer, Rachel Gordon, and Donna H. Friedman. 1996. "Binding Ties: The Roles of Adult Siblings of Persons with Mental Retardation." *Mental Retardation* 34, no. 2: 83–93.

Krisberg, B., and James F. Austin. 1993. *Reinventing Juvenile Justice*. Newbury Park, CA: Sage.

Kuhn, Deanna, and Michael Weinstock. In press. "What Is Epistemological Thinking and Why Does It Matter?" In *Epistemology: The Psychology of Beliefs about Knowledge and Knowing*. Edited by Barbara Hofer and Paul Pintrich. Mahwah, NJ: Erlbaum.

Kuhn, Deanna, Victoria Shaw, and Mark Felton. 1997. "Effects of Dyadic Interaction on Argumentive Reasoning." *Cognition and Instruction* 15: 287–315.

Kulish, Nancy. 1998. *First Loves and Prime Adventures: Adolescent Expressions in Adult Analyses*, Vol. 72, *Psychoanalytic Quarterly*. New York: Psychoanalytic Quarterly Press.

Kumin, L. 1994. *Communication Skills in Children with Down Syndrome*. Rockville, MD: Woodbine House.

Lamb, M. E. 1997. *The Role of the Father in Child Development*, 3rd ed. New York: Wiley.

Lampel, Anita K. 1996. "Children's Alignment with Parents in Highly Conflicted Custody Cases." *Family and Conciliation Courts Review* 34: 229–239.

Lamphear, Vivian S. 1985. "The Impact of Maltreatment on Children's Psychosocial Adjustment: A Review of the Research." *Child Abuse and Neglect* 9, no. 2: 251–263.

Lampkin, B. C. 1993. "Introduction and Executive Summary." *Cancer* 71: 3199–3201.

Landrigan, P. J. 1992. "Commentary: Environmental Disease—A Preventable Epidemic." *American Journal of Public Health* 82: 941–943.

Langhout, Regina E., Lori N. Osborne, Jean B. Grossman, and Jean E. Rhodes. 2000. *An Exploratory Study of Volunteer Mentoring: Toward a Typology of Relationships*. Unpublished manuscript.

Lapsley, Daniel, Matt Milstead, Stephen Quintana, Daniel Flannery, and Raymond Buss. 1986. "Adolescent Egocentrism and Formal Operations: Tests of a Theoretical Assumption." *Developmental Psychology* 22, no. 6: 800–807.

Larner, Mary B., Lorraine Zippiroli, and Richard E. Behrman. 1999. "When School Is Out: Analysis and Recommendations." *The Future of Children* 9: 4–20.

Larson, Reed. 1995. "Secrets in the Bedroom: Adolescents' Private Use of Media." *Journal of Youth and Adolescence* 24: 535–550.

Larson, Reed W., and David M. Almeida. 1999. "Emotional Transmission in the Daily Lives of Families: A New Paradigm for Studying Family Process." *Journal of Marriage and the Family* 61: 5–20.

Larson, Reed W., and Maryse H. Richards. 1994. *Divergent Realities: The Emotional Lives of Mothers, Fathers, and Adolescents.* New York: Basic Books.

Larson, Reed, Gerald L. Clore, and Gretchen A. Wood. 1999. "The Emotions of Romantic Relationships: Do They Wreak Havoc on Adolescents?" Pp. 19–49 in *Contemporary Perspectives in Adolescent Romantic Relationships.* Edited by Wyndol Furman, B. Bradford Brown, and Candice Feiring. New York: Cambridge University Press.

Larson, Reed W., Maryse H. Richards, Giovanni Moneta, Grayson Holmbeck, and Elena Duckett. 1996. "Changes in Adolescents' Daily Interactions with Their Families from Ages 10 to 18: Disengagement and Transformation." *Developmental Psychology.* 32, no. 4: 744–754.

Laskaris, George. 2000. *Color Atlas of Oral Diseases in Children and Adolescents.* Stuttgart: Thieme.

Lasser, Carol. 1987. *Educating Men and Women Together: Coeducation in a Changing World.* Urbana: University of Illinois Press.

Laumann, Edward O., John Gagnon, Robert T. Michael, and Stuart Michaels. 1994. *The Social Organization of Sexuality: Sexual Practices in the United States.* Chicago: University of Chicago Press.

Laursen, Brett. 1993. "Conflict Management among Close Peers." *New Directions for Child Development* 60: 39–54.

Laursen, Brett, Katherine C. Coy, and W. Andy Collins. 1998. "Reconsidering Changes in Parent-Child Conflict across Adolescence: A Meta-Analysis." *Child Development* 69: 817–832.

Laws of the Fifty States, District of Columbia and Puerto Rico Governing the Emancipation of Minors. 2000. Cornell University: Legal Information Institute. Retrieved on January 14, 2000, from the World Wide Web at http://www.law.cornell.edu.

Lazarus, Richard S., and Susan Folkman. 1991. *Stress, Appraisal, and Coping,* 3rd ed. New York: Springer-Verlag.

Learning Disabilities Association of America (LDA): 1–888–300–6710 (www.ldanatl.org)

Learning Disabilities Online (www.ldonline.com)

Lee, John A. N. 1999. *The Machine That Changed the World.* http://ei.cs.vt.edu/~history/TMTCTW.html

Lee, S. J. 1994. "Behind the Model Minority Stereotype: Voices of High and Low Achieving Asian American Students." *Anthropology and Education Quarterly* 25, no. 4: 413–429.

Lee, Valerie E., and Anthony S. Bryk. 1986. "Effects of Single-Sex Secondary Schools on Student Achievement and Attitudes." *Journal of Educational Psychology* 78, no. 5: 331–339.

Lee, Valerie, Robert Croninger, Eleanor Linn, and Xianglei Chen. 1996. "The Culture of Sexual Harassment in Secondary Schools." *American Educational Research Journal* 33: 383–417.

Leffert, Nancy, Peter L. Benson, Peter C. Scales, Anu R. Sharma, Dy R. Drake, and Dale A. Blyth. 1998. "Developmental Assets: Measurement and Prediction of Risk Behaviors among Adolescents." *Applied Developmental Science* 2: 209–230.

Lehman, Darrin R., and Richard E. Nisbett. 1990. "A Longitudinal Study of the Effects of Undergraduate Training on Reasoning." *Developmental Psychology* 26: 952–960.

Lemberg, Raymond, and Leigh Cohn, eds. 1999. *Eating Disorders: A Reference Sourcebook.* Arizona: Oryx Press.

Lennon, Sharron J., Nancy A. Rudd, Bridgette Sloan, and Jae Sook Kim. 1999. "Attitudes toward Gender Roles, Self-Esteem, and Body Image: Application of a Model. *Clothing and Textile Research Journal* 17, no. 4: 191–202.

Lepper, Mark R., Sheena Sethi, Dialdin Dania, and Michael Drake. 1997. "Intrinsic and Extrinsic Motivation: A Developmental Perspective." Pp. 23–50 in *Developmental Psychopathology: Perspectives on Adjustment, Risk, and Disorder.* Edited by Suniya S. Luthar, Jacob A. Burack, Dante Cicchetti, and John Weisz. New York: Cambridge University Press.

Lerner, Janet. 1997. *Learning Disabilities: Theories, Diagnosis, and Teaching Strategies.* 7th ed. Boston: Houghton Mifflin.

Lerner, Richard M. 1985. "Adolescent Maturational Changes and Psychosocial Development: A Dynamic Interactional Perspective." *Journal of Youth and Adolescence* 14: 355–372.

———. 1986. *Concepts and Theories of Human Development,* 2nd ed. New York: Random House.

———. 1994. "Schools and Adolescents." *Visions 2010: Families and Adolescents* 2, no. 1: 14–15, 42–43. Minneapolis, MN: National Council on Family Relations.

———. 1995. *America's Youth in Crisis: Challenges and Options for Programs and Policies.* Thousand Oaks, CA: Sage.

———. 1998. "Adolescent Development: Challenges and Opportunities for Research, Programs, and Policies." *Annual Reviews of Psychology* 49: 413–446.

———. In press. *Adolescence: Development, Diversity, Context, and Application.* Upper Saddle River, NJ: Prentice-Hall.

Lerner, Richard M., A. C. Petersen, and Jeanne Brooks-Gunn, eds. 1991. *Encyclopedia of Adolescence.* New York: Garland.

Lerner, Richard M., and Galambos, Nancy. 1998. "Adolescent Development: Challenges and Opportunities for Research, Programs, and Policies." Pp. 413–446 in *Annual Review of Psychology,* Vol. 49. Edited by J. T. Spence. Palo Alto, CA: Annual Reviews, Inc.

Lerner, Richard M., and Nancy L. Galambos, eds. 1984. *Experiencing Adolescents: A Sourcebook for Parents, Teachers, and Teens.* New York: Garland.

Lerner, Richard M., Celia B. Fisher, and Richard A. Weinberg. 2000. "Toward a Science for and of the People: Promoting Civil Society through the Application of Developmental Science." *Child Development* 71: 11–20.

Lester, Marilyn. 1984. "Self: Sociological Portraits." Pp. 19–68 in *The Existential Self in Society.* Edited by Joseph A. Kotarba and Andrea Fontana. Chicago: The University of Chicago Press.

Levenkron, Steven. 1998. *Cutting: Understanding and Overcoming Self-Mutilation.* New York: Norton.

Levin, Jerome D. 1992. *Theories of the Self.* Washington, DC: Hemisphere Publishing.

Levine, Mel. 1994. *Educational Care: A System for Understanding and Helping Children with Learning Problems at Home and in School.* Cambridge, MA: Educators Publishing Service.

Levine, R., and D. Campbell. 1992. *Ethnocentrism: Theories of Conflict, Ethnic Attitudes and Group Behavior.* New York: Wiley.

Levin-Epstein, J. 1996. *Teen Parent Provisions in the Personal Responsibility and Work Opportunity Reconciliation Act of 1996.* Washington, D.C.: Center for Law and Social Policy.

Levinson, Daniel J. 1978. *The Seasons of a Man's Life.* New York: Knopf.

———. 1996. *The Seasons of a Woman's Life.* New York: Random House.

Levy, Barrie, ed. 1991. *Dating Violence: Young Women in Danger.* Seattle: Seal Press.

Lewinsohn, Peter M., Paul Rohde, and John R. Seeley. 1996. "Adolescent Suicidal Ideation and Attempts: Prevalence, Risk Factors, and Clinical Implications." *Clinical Psychology: Science and Practice* 3: 25–46.

Lewinsohn, Peter M., Robert E. Roberts, John R. Seeley, Paul Rohde, Ian H. Gotlib, and Hyman Hops. 1994. "Adolescent Psychopathology. II. Psychosocial Risk Factors for Depression." *Journal of Abnormal Psychology* 103: 302–315.

Lewis, C. C. 1981. "How Adolescents Approach Decisions: Changes over Grades Seven to Twelve and Policy Implications." *Child Development* 52: 538–544.

Lewis, Michael, and Jeannette M. Haviland, eds. 1993. *The Handbook of Emotions.* New York: Guilford Press.

Lewis, Michael, and Suzanne M. Miller, eds. 1990. *Handbook of Developmental Psychopathology.* New York: Plenum Press.

Lewis, Theodore, James Stone III, Wayne Shipley, and Svjetlana Madzar. 1998. "The Transition from School to Work: An Examination of the Literature." *Youth and Society* 29, no. 3: 259–292.

Lickona, Thomas. 1994. "The Neglected Heart." *American Educator,* Summer, 34–39.

Liker, J. K., and Glen H. Elder, Jr. 1983. "Economic Hardship and Marital Relations in the 1930s." *American Sociological Review* 48: 343–359.

Lindsay, Paul. 1998. "Conflict Resolution and Peer Mediation in Public Schools: What Works?" *Mediation Quarterly* 16, no. 1: 85–99.

Loeber, Rolf, and Dale Hay. 1997. "Key Issues in the Development of Aggression and Violence from Childhood to Early Adulthood." *Annual Review of Psychology* 48: 371–410.

Loeber, Rolf, and David P. Farrington, eds. 1998. *Serious and Violent Juvenile Offenders: Risk Factors and Successful Interventions.* Thousand Oaks: Sage.

Loeber, Rolf, and Magda Stouthamer-Loeber. 1998. "Development of Juvenile Aggression and Violence: Some Common Misconceptions and Controversies." *American Psychologist* 53: 242–259.

Loevinger, Jane. 1976. *Ego Development.* San-Francisco: Jossey-Bass.

Loftus, Elizabeth F. 1980. *Memory, Surprising and New Insights into How We Remember and Why We Forget.* Reading, MA: Addison-Wesley Publishers.

Lopez, David. 1978. "Chicano Language Loyalty in an Urban Setting." *Sociology and Social Research* 62, no. 2: 267–278.

Lord, Jan, Nicole Varzos, Bruce Behrman, John Wicks, and Dagmar Wicks. 1990. "Implications of Mainstream Classrooms for Adolescents with Spina Bifida." *Developmental Medicine and Child Neurology* 32: 20–29.

Lott, Juanita Tamayo. 1998. *Asian Americans: From Racial Categories to Multiple Identities.* Walnut Creek, CA: Alta Mira Press.

Lovett, Maureen. 1992. "Developmental Dyslexia." Pp. 163–185 in *Handbook of Neuropsychology,* Vol. 7. Edited by Sydney J. Segalowitz. Amsterdam: Elsevier Science Publishing.

Lovinger, Sophie L., Lisa Miller, and Robert J. Lovinger. 1999. "Some Clinical Applications of Religious Development in Adolescence." *Journal of Adolescence* 22: 269–277.

Lucas, Samuel R. 1999. *Tracking Inequality: Stratification and Mobility in American High Schools.* New York: Teachers College Press.

Luster, Tom, and Stephen A. Small. 1997. "Sexual Abuse History and Number of Sex Partners among Female Adolescents." *Family Planning Perspectives* 29: 204–211.

———. 1997. "Sexual Abuse History and Problems in Adolescence: Exploring the Effects of Moderating Variables." *Journal of Marriage and the Family* 59: 131–142.

Lykken, David T. 1997. "Factory of Crime." *Psychological Inquiry* 8: 261–270.

Lyman, Howard B. 1986. *Test Scores and What They Mean,* 4th ed. Englewood Cliffs, NJ: Prentice-Hall.

Maccoby, Eleanor, and Carol Jacklin. 1974. *The Psychology of Sex Differences.* Stanford, CA: Stanford University Press.

Maccoby, Eleanor, and John Martin. 1983. "Socialization in the Context of the Family: Parent-Child Interaction." Pp. 1–102 in *Handbook of Child Psychology,* Vol. 4. Edited by E. M. Hetherington. New York: Wiley.

Maccoby, Eleanor E., and John A. Martin. 1983. "Socialization in the Context of the Family: Parent-Adolescent Interactions." Pp. 1–101 in *Handbook of Adolescent Psychology,* vol. 4. Edited by Paul H. Mussen. New York: Wiley.

Maccoby, Eleanor M., and Robert H. Mnookin. 1992. *Dividing the Child: Social and Legal Dilemmas of Custody.* Cambridge, MA: Harvard University Press.

MacCoun, R. 1998. "Toward a Psychology of Harm Reduction." *American Psychologist* 53: 1199–1208.

MacDonald, Kevin. 1991. "Rites of Passage." Pp. 944–945 in *Encyclopedia of Adolescence.* Vol 2. Edited by Richard M. Lerner, Anne C. Petersen, and Jeanne Brooks-Gunn. New York: Garland.

MacGillivray, Maureen, and Jeannette Wilson. 1997. "Clothing and Appearance in Early, Middle and Late Adolescents." *Clothing and Textile Research Journal,* 15: 43–49.

Mann, L., R. Harmoni, and C. Power. 1989. "Adolescent Decision-Making: The Development of Competence." *Journal of Adolescence* 12: 265–278.

Mannheim, Karl. 1952. "The problem of generations." Pp. 276–322 in *Essays on the Sociology of Knowledge.* London: Routledge and Kegan Paul. (Original work published 1928).

Manning, Wendy D. 1990. "Parenting Employed Teenagers." *Youth and Society* 22: 184–200.

Marano, Hara Estroff. 1998. *Why Doesn't Anybody Like Me?* New York: William Morrow Company.

Marcia, James E. 1967. "Development and Validation of Ego-Identity Status." *Journal of Personality and Social Psychology* 3: 551–558.

Markstrom, Carol A. 1999. "Religious Involvement and Adolescent Psychosocial Development." *Journal of Adolescence* 22: 205–221.

Markus, Hazel, and Paula Nurius. 1986. "Possible Selves." *American Psychologist* 41: 954–969.

Marsh, Herbert W. 1991. "Employment during High School: Character Building or a Subversion of Academic Goals?" *Sociology of Education* 64: 172–189.

Martin, Carole A., and James E. Johnson. 1992. "Children's Self-Perceptions and Mothers' Beliefs about Development and Competencies." In *Parental Belief Systems: The Psychological Consequences for Children.* Edited by Irving E. Sigel, Ann V. McGillicuddy-DeLisi, and Jacqueline J. Goodnow. Hillsdale, NJ: Erlbaum.

Martinez, Elizabeth. 1998. *De Colores Means All of Us: Latina Views for a Multi-Colored Century.* Cambridge, MA: South End Press.

Martz, Geoff, and Laurice Pearson (contributor). 1999. *Cracking the GED, 2000.* New York: Random House (published annually).

Mastropieri, Margo. 1991. *Teaching Students Ways to Remember: Strategies for Learning Menmonically.* Cambridge, MA: Brookline.

McAnarney, Elizabeth R. 1985. "Social Maturation: A Challenge for Handicapped and Chronically Ill Adolescents." *Journal of Adolescent Health Care* 6, no. 2: 90–101.

McCarney, Stephen B., ed. 1994. *Attention Deficit Disorders Intervention Manual.* Columbia, MS: Hawthorne Educational Services, Inc.

McCormick, John F. 1995. "'But, Nobody Told Me about . . . ': A Program for Enhancing Decision Making by College-Bound Students." *The School Counselor* 42 (January): 246–248.

McDermott, Virginia A. 1987. "Life Planning Services: Helping Older Placed Children with Their Identity." *Child and Adolescent Social Work* 4: 97–115.

McGuire, Shirley, Beth Manke, Afsoon Eftekhari, and Judy Dunn. 2000. "Children's Perceptions of Sibling Conflict during Middle Childhood: Issues and Sibling (Dis)similarity." *Social Development* 9: 173–190.

McHugh, Mary. 1999. *Special Siblings: Growing Up with Someone with a Disability.* New York: Hyperion.

McKeachie, James, Sandra Lindsay, Sandy Hobbs, and M. Lavalette. 1996. "Adolescents' Perceptions of the Role of Part-Time Work." *Adolescence* 31, no. 121: 193–204.

McLaughlin, Rose D., and Steven M. Rose. 1989. "Student Cheating in High School: A Case of Moral Reasoning vs. 'Fuzzy Logic.'" *The High School Journal* 72, no. 3: 97–104.

McWhirter, J. Jeffries, Benedict T. McWhirter, Anna M. McWhirter, and Ellen Hawley McWhirter. 1993. *At-Risk Youth: A Comprehensive Response.* Pacific Grove, CA: Brooks-Cole.

Mead, Margaret. 1928. *Coming of Age in Samoa: A Psychological Study of Primitive Youth for Western Civilization.* New York: Morrow.

————. 1961. *Coming of Age in Samoa: A Psychological Study of Primitive Youth for Western Civilization.* US: William Morrow.

Meadows, A. T., and Hovvie, W. L. 1986. "The Medical Consequences of Cure." *Cancer*, 58: 524–528.

Measor, Lynda, with Coralie Tiffin. 2000. *Young People's Views on Sex Education: Education, Attitudes, and Behavior.* London and New York: Routledge/Falmer.

Mekos, Debra, E. M. Hetherington, and D. Reiss. 1996. "Sibling Differences in Problem Behavior and Parental Treatment in Nondivorced and Remarried Families." *Child Development* 67: 2148–2165.

Mercer, Cecil. 1997. *Students with Learning Disabilities.* Columbus, OH: Merrill.

Mercugliana, Marianne. 1999. "What Is Attention-Deficit/Hyperactivity Disorder?" *Pediatric Clinics of North America* 46, no. 5: 831–843.

Merino, Barbara. 1991. "Promoting School Success for Chicanos: The View from Inside the Bilingual Classroom." Pp. 119–148 in *Chicano School Failure and Success: Research and Policy Agendas for the 1990s,* edited by Richard Valencia. New York: Falmer Press.

Mickelson, Roslyn Arlin. 1990. "The Attitude-Achievement Paradox among Black Adolescents." *Sociology of Education* 63: 44–61.

Microsoft Corporation. 1999. *Microsoft Corporation Interactive Software and Computer History Museum.* http://www.microsoft.com/mscorp/museum/home.asp.

Midgely, Carol, Revathy Arunkumar, and Timothy C. Urdan. 1996. "'If I Don't Do Well There's a Reason': Predictors of Adolescents' Use of Academic Self-Handicapping Strategies." *Journal of Educational Psychology* 88, no. 3: 423–434.

Mihalic, Sharon W., and Delbert Elliot. 1997. "Short- and Long-Term Consequences of Doing Work." *Youth and Society* 28, no. 4: 464–498.

Miller, B. A., L.A.G. Ries, F. R. Hankey, F. L. Kosary, A. Harras, S. S. Devesa, and B. K. Edwards, eds. 1993. "SEER Cancer Statistics Review: 1973–1990." NIH Publication Number 93–2789. Bethesda, MD: National Cancer Institute.

Miller, Brent C., and Kristin A. Moore. 1990. "Adolescent Sexual Behavior, Pregnancy, and Parenting: Research through the 1980s." *Journal of Marriage and the Family* 52: 1025–1044.

Miller, Joan. 1994. "Cultural Diversity in the Morality of Caring: Individually Oriented Versus Duty-Based Interpersonal Moral Codes." *Cross-Cultural Research* 28: 3–39.

Miller, Kim A., Rex Forehand, and Beth A. Kotchick. 1999. "Adolescent Sexual Behavior in Two Ethnic Minority Samples: The Role of Family Variables." *Journal of Marriage and the Family* 61, no. 1: 85–98.

Miller, R. B., and Vern L. Bengtson. 1991. "Grandparent-Grandchild Relations." Pp. 414–418 in *Encyclopedia of Adolescence.* New York: Garland.

Miller-Jones, Dalton. 1989. "Culture and Testing." *American Psychologist* 44, no. 2: 360–366.

Millstein, Susan G. 1993. "Perceptual, Attributional, and Affective Processes in Perceptions of Vulnerability throughout the Life Span." Pp. 55–65 in *Adolescent Risk Taking.* Edited by Nancy Bell and Robert Bell. Newbury Park, CA: Sage.

Milne, Ann M. 1996. Family Structure and the Achievement of Children." Pp. 32–65 in *Education and the American Family: A Research Synthesis.* Edited by

W. J. Weston. New York: New York University Press.

Minkler, M., and K. M. Roe. 1993. *Grandmothers as Caregivers*. Newbury Park, CA: Sage.

Mirsky, Allan. 1996. "Disorders of Attention: A Neuropsychological Perspective." Pp. 71–96 in *Attention, Memory, and Executive Function*. Edited by G. Reed Lyon and Norman Krasnegor. Baltimore: Paul H. Brookes.

Modell, J. 1985. *A Social History of American Adolescents, 1945–1985*. Pittsburgh, PA: Carnegie Mellon University.

Moe, Barbara. 1998. *Adoption: A Reference Handbook*. Santa Barbara: ABC-CLIO.

Moffitt, Terrie E. 1993. "'Adolescent-Limited' and 'Life-Course-Persistent' Antisocial Behavior: A Developmental Taxonomy." *Psychological Review* 100: 674–701.

Montemayor, Raymond, Gerald R. Adams, and Thomas P. Gullotta, eds. 1994. *Personal Relationships during Adolescence*. Thousand Oaks, CA: Sage.

Monti, D. J. 1993. "Origins and Problems of Gang Research in the United States." In *Gangs*. Edited by S. Cummings and D. J. Monti. Albany: State University of New York Press.

Moody, William J. 1990. *Artistic Intelligences: Implications for Education*. New York: Teachers College Press.

Moore and Snyder. 1994. *"Facts at a Glance."* Annual newsletter on teen pregnancy. Washington, DC: Child Trends.

Moore, J. W. 1978. *Homeboys: Gangs, Drugs and Prison in the Barrios of Los Angeles*. Philadelphia, PA: Temple University Press.

Moore, K. A., B. W. Sugland, C. Blumenthal, D. Glei, and N. Snyder. 1995.

Adolescent Pregnancy Prevention Programs: Interventions and Evaluations. Washington, DC: Child Trends, Inc.

Moraga, Cherrie, and Gloria Anzaldua, eds. 1981. *This Bridge Called Me Back: Writings by Radical Women of Color*. New York: Kitchen Table: Women of Color Press.

Mortimer, Jeylan T., and Helga Kruger. 2000. "Transition from School to Work in the United States and Germany: Formal Pathways Matter." In *Handbook of the Sociology of Education*. Edited by Maureen Hallinan. New York: Plenum Publishers.

Mortimer, Jeylan T., and Marcia K. Johnson. 1997. "Adolescent Part-Time Work and Post-Secondary Transition Pathways: A Longitudinal Study of Youth in St. Paul, Minnesota." Paper presented at the New Passages, Toronto, Canada.

———. 1998. "New Perspectives on Adolescent Work and the Transition to Adulthood." Pp. 425–496 in *New Perspectives on Adolescent Risk Behavior*. Edited by Richard Jessor. New York: Cambridge University Press.

Mortimer, Jeylan T., Ellen Efron Pimentel, Seongryeol Ryu, Katherine Nash, and Chaimun Lee. 1996. "Part-Time Work and Occupational Value Formation in Adolescence." *Social Forces* 74 (June): 1405–1418.

Mortimer, Jeylan T., Katherine Dennehy, Chaimun Lee, and Michael D. Finch. 1994. "Economic Socialization in the American Family: The Prevalence, Distribution, and Consequences of Allowance Arrangements." *Family Relations* 43: 23–29.

Mortimer, Jeylan T., Michael D. Finch, Seongryeol Ryu, and Michael J. Shanahan. 1996. "The Effects of Work Intensity on Adolescent Mental Health, Achievement, and Behavioral Adjustment: New

Evidence from a Prospective Study." *Child Development* 67: 1243–1261.

Mortimer, Jeylan, Michael Shanahan, and Seongryeol Ryu. 1994. "The Effects of Adolescent Employment on School-Related Orientations and Behavior." Pp. 304–326 in *Adolescence in Context*. Edited by R. Silbereisen and R. Todt. New York: Springer.

Moshman, David. 1993. "Adolescent Reasoning and Adolescent Rights." *Human Development* 36: 27–40.

Mounts, Nina S., and Laurence Steinberg. 1995. "An Ecological Analysis of Peer Influence on Adolescent Grade Point Average and Drug Use." *Developmental Psychology* 31: 915–922.

Munoz, Kathryn A., Susan M. Krebs-Smith, Rachel Ballard-Barbash and Linda E. Cleveland. 1997. "Food Intakes of U.S. Children and Adolescents Compared with Recommendations." *Pediatrics* 100, no. 3: 323–329.

Munro, Thomas, and Herbert Read. 1960. *The Creative Arts in American Education*. Cambridge, MA: Harvard University Press.

Murphy, Debra A., Mary Jane Rotheram-Borus, and Helen M. Reid. 1998. "Adolescent Gender Differences in HIV-Related Sexual Risk Acts, Social-Cognitive Factors and Behavioral Skills." *Journal of Adolescence* 21, no. 2: 197–208.

Murphy, Kevin, and Finnis Welch. 1989. "Wage Premiums for College Graduates: Recent Growth and Possible Explanations." *Educational Researcher* 18, no. 4: 17–26.

Myers, Jennifer, and John Hagen, 1993. "The Impact of Chronic Illness on the Late Adolescent/Early Adult Transition: Focus—Insulin-Dependent Diabetes Mellitus." (Presentation.) *Family Relationships and Psychosocial Development in Physically Impaired and Chronically Ill Adolescents*, G. Holmbeck, chair. Symposium conducted at the biennial meeting of the Society for Research in Child Development (SRCD), New Orleans.

Myers-Briggs, Isabel. 1989. *Manual: A Guide to the Development and Use of the Myers-Briggs Type Indicator: From Theory to Practice*. Austin, TX: Pro-Ed.

Myrtek, M., C. Scharff, G. Brugner, and W. Muller. 1996. "Physiological, Behavioral and Psychological Effects Associated with Television Viewing in Schoolboys: An Exploratory Study." *Journal of Early Adolescence* 16, no. 3: 301–323.

Namnoum, A., B. Koehler, and S. E. Carpenter. 1994. "Abnormal Uterine Bleeding in the Adolescent." *Adolescent Medicine: State of the Art Reviews* 5: 157–170.

Nathan, R. P., Gentry, P., & Lawrence, C. 1999. "Is There a Link between Welfare Reform and Teen Pregnancy?" *Rockefeller Reports*. Albany, NY: The Nelson A. Rockefeller Institute of Government.

National Academy of Sciences. 1985. *Injury in America*. Washington, DC: National Academy Press.

National Adolescent Health Survey. 1989. *A Report on the Health of America's Youth*. Oakland, CA: Third Party.

National Center for Education Statistics (NCES). 1996. *Projections of Education Statistics to 2006*. Washington, DC: U.S. Department of Education.

———. 1997. *Postsecondary Persistence and Attainment*. Washington, DC: U.S. Department of Education, Office of Educational Research and Improvement.

———. 1997. *Public and Private Schools: How Do They Differ?* Washington, DC:

U.S. Department of Education Office of Educational Research and Improvement.

———. 1998. *Digest of Education Statistics.* Washington, DC: U.S. Department of Education.

———. 1999. *The Condition of Education 1999.* Washington, DC: U.S. Department of Education.

National Center for Juvenile Justice. 2000. Web site: www.ncjj.org.

National Center for Learning Disabilities: 1–800–575–7373 (www.ncld.org)

National Center of Education Statistics. 1997. *Digest of Education Statistics, 1997.* Washington, DC: National Center of Education Statistics.

National Clearinghouse on Child Abuse and Neglect Information. 1999. "Child Fatalities Fact Sheet." (pp 1–3). Washington, DC: United States Government Printing Office.

National Council on Alcoholism and Drug Dependence (NCADD).1999. *Youth, Alcohol and Other Drugs: An Overview.* http://www.ncadd.org.

National Crime Center and Crime Victims Research and Treatment Center. 1992. *Rape in America: A Report to the Nation.* Arlington: VA.

National Household Survey on Drug Abuse. 1998. News Release.

National Information Center for Children and Youth with Disabilities: 1–800–695–0285 (www.nichcy.org)

National Institute for Children and Youth with Disabilities (NICHCY). 1999. *Fact Sheet No. 7 (FS7).* Available by mail: P.O. Box 1492 Washington, DC 20013 or by phone, 1–800–695–0285.

National Institute for Occupational Safety and Health (NIOSH). 1991. *Current*

Intelligence Bulletin 54: Environmental Tobacco Smoke in the Workplace.

National Mentoring Working Group. 1991. *Elements of Effective Practice.* Washington, DC: United Way of America and One to One/The National Mentoring Partnership.

National Middle School Association. 1995. *This We Believe: Developmentally Responsive Middle-Level Schools.* Columbus, OH: National Middle School Association.

National Opinion Research Corporation. 1976. *National Statistical Survey on Runaway Youth.* Princeton, New Jersey: NORC.

National Research Council (NRC). 1993. *Pesticides in the Diets of Infants and Children.* Washington, DC: National Academy Press.

Needleman, H. L., A. Schell, and D. Bellinger. 1990. "The Long-Term Effects of Exposure to Low Doses of Lead in Childhood: 11-Year Follow-Up Report." *New England Journal of Medicine* 322: 83–88.

Needleman, H. L., and C. A. Gatsonis. 1990. "Low-Level Lead Exposure and the IQ of Children: A Meta-Analysis of Modern Studies." *Journal of American Medical Association* 263: 673–678.

Neisser, U., et al. 1996. "Intelligence: Knowns and Unknowns." *American Psychologist* 51, no. 2: 77–101.

Nemours Foundation. Kids Health www.kidshealth.org/teen/index.html

Neumark-Szainer, Dianne, and Jillian K. Moe. 2000. "Weight-Related Concerns and Disorders among Adolescents." Pp. 288–317 in *Nutrition throughout the Life Cycle.* Edited by Bonnie S. Worthington-Roberts and Sue Rodwell Williams. Boston: McGraw-Hill.

Newcombe, Nora, and Judith S. Dubas. 1992. "A Longitudinal Study of Predictors of Spatial Ability in Adolescent Females." *Child Development* 63: 37–46.

———. 1998. "Guidelines for Treatment of Sexually Transmitted Diseases." *Morbidity and Mortality Weekly Report* 47, no. RR-1: 1–116.

Nolen-Hoeksema, Susan, and Joan S. Girgus. 1995. "Explanatory Style and Achievement, Depression, and Gender Differences in Childhood and Early Adolescence." Pp. 57–70 in *Explanatory Style*. Edited by G. M. Buchanan and M. E. P. Seligman. Hillsdale, NJ: Erlbaum.

Norlander, T., A. Erixon, and T. Archer. 2000. "Psychological Androgyny and Creativity: Dynamics of Gender-Role and Personality Trait." *Social Behavior and Personality* 28: 423–435.

Nottelmann, Editha D., Elizabeth J. Susman, Gale E. Inoff-Germain, Gordon B. Cutler Jr., D. Lynne Loriaux, and George P. Chrousos. 1987. "Developmental Processes in American Early Adolescents: Relationships between Adolescent Adjustment Problems and Chronological Age, Pubertal Stage, and Puberty-Related Serum Hormone Levels." *Journal of Pediatrics* 110: 473–480.

Nummenmaa, Anna R., and Tapio Nummenmaa. 1997. "Intergenerational Roots of Finnish Women's Sex-Atypical Careers." *International Journal of BehavioralDevelopment* 21, no. 1: 1–14.

Nycum, Benjie. 2000. *The XY Survival Guide: Everything You Need to Know about Being Young and Gay*. San Francisco: XY Publishing.

O'Malley, Patrick M., and Lloyd D. Johnston. 1999. "Drinking and Driving among U.S. High School Seniors, 1984–1997." *American Journal of Public Health* 89: 678–684.

O'Malley, Patrick M., Lloyd D. Johnston, and Jerald G. Bachman. 1998. "Alcohol Use among Adolescents." *Alcohol Health and Research World* 22: 85–93.

Oakes, Jeannie. 1985. *Keeping Track: How Schools Structure Inequality*. New Haven, CT: Yale University Press.

Office of Juvenile Justice and Delinquency Prevention. 1996. (March). *Combating Violence and Delinquency: The National Juvenile Justice Action Plan*. Washington, DC: U.S. Department of Justice, Office of Juvenile Justice and Delinquency Prevention.

Office of National Drug Control Policy. 1997. "The National Drug Control Strategy." http://www.ncjrs.org/htm/chapter2.htm

Ogbu, John U. 1981. Origins of Human Competence: A Cultural-Ecological Perspective. *Child Development* 52: 413–429.

———. 1990. "Minority Education in Comparative Perspective." *Journal of Negro Education* 59: 45–57.

Olivier, Carolyn, Bill Cosby, Rosemary Bowler. 1996. *Learning to Learn*. New York: Fireside.

Olson, David, and Janet Astington. 1993. "Thinking about Thinking: Learning How to Take Statements and Hold Beliefs." *Educational Psychologist* 28: 7–23.

Oltmanns, Thomas F., and Robert E. Emery. 1998. *Abnormal Psychology*. 2nd ed. Upper Saddle River, NJ: Prentice-Hall.

Olweus, Dan. 1991. "Bully/Victim Problems among School Children: Basic Facts and Effects of a School-Based Intervention Program." Pp. 411–454 in *The Development and Treatment of Childhood Aggression*. Edited by Debra Pepler and Kenneth Rubin. Hillsdale, NJ: Erlbaum.

———. 1993. *Bullying at School. What We Know and What We Can Do.* Cambridge, MA: Blackwell.

Olweus, Dan, Ake Mattsson, Daisy Schalling, and Hans Low. 1988. "Circulating Testosterone Levels and Aggression in Adolescent Males: A Causal Analysis." *Psychosomatic Medicine* 50: 261–272.

Oppenheimer, Valerie Kincade. 1970. *The Female Labor Force in the United States.* Population Monograph Series, no. 5. Institute of International Studies. Berkeley: University of California Press.

———.1982. *Work and the Family.* New York: Academic Press.

Orenstein, Peggy. 1994. *Schoolgirls: Young Women, Self-Esteem, and the Confidence Gap.* New York: Anchor Books.

Orr, D. P., S. C. Weller, B. Satterwhite, and Ivan B. Pless. 1984. "Psychosocial Implications of Chronic Illness in Adolescence." *Journal of Pediatrics* 104, no. 1: 152–157.

Osherson, Daniel N., and Ellen M. Markman. 1975. "Language and the Ability to Evaluate Contradictions and Tautologies." *Cognition* 2: 213–226.

Osman, Karen. 1992. *Gangs.* San Diego: Lucent Books.

Otis, Carol L., Barbara Drinkwater, Mimi Johnson, Anne Loucks, and Jack Wilmore. 1997. "American College of Sports Medicine Position Stand on The Female Athlete Triad." *Medicine and Science in Sports and Exercise* 29: i–ix.

Ozorak, Elizabeth Weiss. 1989. "Social and Cognitive Influences on the Development of Religious Beliefs and Commitment in Adolescence." *Journal for the Scientific Study of Religion* 24, no. 4: 448–463.

Page, Angela and Kenneth R. Fox. 1997. "Adolescent Weight Management and the Physical Self." Pp. 229–256 in *The Physical Self: From Motivation to Well-Being.* Edited by Kenneth R. Fox. Champaign, IL: Human Kinetics

Paikoff, Roberta L., and Jeanne Brooks-Gunn. 1991. "Do Parent-Child Relationships Change during Puberty?" *Psychological Bulletin* 110: 47–66.

Paikoff, Roberta L., Sheila H. Parfenoff, Stephanie A. Williams, and Anthony McCormick. 1997. "Parenting, Parent-Child Relationships, and Sexual Possibility Situations among Urban African American Preadolescents: Preliminary Findings and Implications for HIV Prevention." *Journal of Family Psychology* 11, no. 1: 11–22.

Paikoff, Roberta, and Jeanne Brooks-Gunn. 1991. "Do Parent-Child Relationships Change during Puberty? *Psychological Bulletin* 110: 47–66.

Pandina, Robert, and Robert Hendren. 1999. "Other Drugs of Abuse: Inhalants, Designer Drugs, and Steroids." Pp. 171–184 in *Addictions: A Comprehensive Guidebook.* Edited by Barbara S. McCrady and Elizabeth E. Epstein. New York: Oxford University Press.

Parfenoff, Sheila H., and Roberta L. Paikoff. 1997. "Developmental and Biological Perspectives on Minority Adolescent Health." Pp. 5–27 in *Health-Promoting and Health-Compromising Behaviors among Minority Adolescents.* Edited by Dawn K. Wilson, James R. Rodrigue, and Wendell C. Taylor. Washington, DC: American Psychological Association.

Pargament, Kenneth I., Bruce W. Smith, Harold G. Koenig, and Lisa Perez. 1998. "Patterns of Positive and Negative Religious Coping with Major Life Stressors." *Journal for the Scientific Study of Religion* 37, no. 4: 710–724.

Parikh, Bindu. 1980. "The Development of Moral Judgment and Its Relation to Family Environmental Factors in Indian and American Families." *Child Development* 51: 1030–1039.

Park, Eun-ja. 1994. "Educational Needs and Parenting Concerns of Korean American parents." *Psychological Reports* 75: 559–562.

Parker, Jeffrey G., and Steven R. Asher. 1993. "Friendship and Friendship Quality in Middle Childhood: Links with Peer Group Acceptance and Feelings of Loneliness and Social Dissatisfaction." *Developmental Psychology* 29: 611–621.

Parker, Sheila, Mimi Nichter, Mark Nichter, Nancy Vuckovic, Colette Sims, and Cheryl Ritenbaugh. 1995. "Body Image and Weight Concerns among African American and White Adolescent Females: Differences That Make a Difference." *Human Organization* 54: 103–114.

Parrott, Andy C. 1999. "Does Cigarette Smoking Cause Stress?" *American Psychologist* 54: 817–820.

Partnership for a Drug-Free America. 1999. News Release. http://www. drugfreeamerica.org.

Paterson, Charlotte J., Janis B. Kupersmidt, and Nancy A. Vaden. 1990. "Income Level, Gender, Ethnicity, and Household Composition as Predictors of Children's School-Based Competence." *Child Development* 61: 485–494.

Patterson, Gerald R. 1982. *Coercive Family Processes.* Eugene, OR: Castalia.

———. 1986. "Performance Models for Antisocial Boys." *American Psychologist* 41: 432–444.

Patterson, Gerald R., and M. Stouthamer-Loeber. 1984. "The Correlation of Family Management Practices and Delinquency." *Child Development* 55: 1299–1307.

Patterson, Gerald R., J. Reid, and Thomas Dishion. 1992. *Antisocial Boys.* Eugene, OR: Castalia.

Patterson, Lewis E., and Elizabeth Reynold Welfel. 2000. *The Counseling Process.* 5th ed. Belmont, CA: Wadsworth.

Patzer, Gordon. 1985. *The Physical Attractiveness Phenomenon.* New York: Plenum Press.

Paulson, S. E. 1994. Relations of Parenting Style and Parental Involvement with Ninth-Grade Students' Achievement. *Journal of Early Adolescence* 14: 250–267.

Paxton, Robert. 1997. "'Someone with Like a Life Wrote It': The Effects of a Visible Author on High School History Students." *Journal of Educational Psychology* 89: 235–250.

Pearl, Peggy S. 1996. "Psychological Abuse." Recognition of Child Abuse for the Mandated Reporter. (pp. 120–146) St. Louis, Missouri: G.W. Medical Publishing Inc.

Peñalosa, Fernando. 1980. *Chicano Sociolinguistics.* Rowley, MA: Newbury House Publishers.

Peplau, Letitia A., and Daniel Perlman. 1982. *Loneliness: A Sourcebook of Current Theory, Research, and Therapy.* New York: Wiley.

Pergamit, Michael R. 1995. "Assessing School to Work Transitions in the United States. Discussion Paper" (NLS 96–32). Washington, DC: U.S. Bureau of Labor Statistics.

Perkins, Daniel F., and Joyce Miller. 1994. "Why Volunteerism and Service-Learning? Providing Rationale and Research." *Democracy & Education* 9: 11–16

Perreault, Stephanie, and Richard Y. Bourhis. 1999. "Ethnocentrism, Social Identification, and Discrimination."

Personality and Social Psychology Bulletin 25: 92–103.

Peters, Elizabeth H., and Natalie C. Mullis. 1997. "The Role of Family Income and Sources of Income in Adolescent Achievement." Pp. 340–381 in *Consequences of Growing Up Poor.* Edited by Greg J. Duncan and Jeanne Brooks-Gunn. New York: Sage.

Petersen, Anne. 1985. "Pubertal Development as a Cause of Disturbance: Myths, Realities, and Unanswered Questions." *Genetic, Social, and General Psychology Monographs* 111: 205–232.

———. 1988. "Adolescent Development." Pp. 583–607 in *Annual Review of Psychology*, Vol. 39. Edited by R. M. Rosenzweig. Palo Alto, CA: Annual Reviews, Inc.

Peterson, Anne C., Nancy Leffert, and Barbara Graham. 1995. "Adolescent Development and the Emergence of Sexuality." *Suicide and Life-Threatening Behaviors* 25: 4–17.

Peterson, S., and Brindis, C. 1995. *Adolescent Pregnancy Prevention: Effective Strategies.* San Francisco, CA: National Adolescent Health Information Center.

Peterson-Lewis, Sonja. 1991. "A Feminist Analysis of theDefenses of Obscene Rap Lyrics." *Black Sacred Music: A Journal of Theomusicology* 5: 68–80.

Petrie, Keith J., and John A. Weinman, eds. 1997. *Perceptions of Health and Illness.* Amsterdam: Hardwood Academic Publishers.

Phelan, P., A. L. Davidson, and H. T. Cao. 1991. "Students' Multiple Worlds: Negotiating the Boundaries of Family, Peer, and School Cultures." *Anthropology and Education Quarterly* 22: 224–250.

Phillip, Kay, Andrea Estepa, and Al Desetta, eds. 1998. *Things Get Hectic: Teens Write about the Violence That Surrounds Them.* New York: Touchstone.

Phinney, Jean S., and V. Chavira. 1995. "Parental Ethnic Socialization and Adolescent Coping with Problems Related to Ethnicity." *Journal of Research on Adolescence* 5: 31–53.

Phinney, Jean S., and Alipuria, Linda L. 1990. "Ethnic Identity in College Students from Four Ethnic Groups." *Journal of Adolescence* 13: 171–183.

Piaget, Jean. 1932. *The Moral Judgment of the Child.* Harmondsworth: Penguin Books. (Reprinted in 1965.)

———. 1936. *The Origins of Intelligence in Children.* New York: International Universities Press. (Reprinted in 1952.)

———. 1950. *The Psychology of Intelligence.* London: Routledge and Kegan Paul.

Piaget, Jean and Barbel Inhelder. 1969. *The Psychology of the Child.* New York: Basic Books.

Pierce, John, and Elizabeth Gilpin. 1995. "A Historical Analysis of Tobacco Marketing and the Uptake of Smoking by Youth in the United States: 1890–1977." *Health Psychology* 14: 500–508.

Pierce-Baker, Charlotte. 1998. *Surviving the Silence: Black Women's Stories of Rape.* New York: Norton.

Pipher, Mary. 1994. *Reviving Ophelia: Saving the Selves of Adolescent Girls.* New York: Ballantine Books.

Pirog-Good, Maureen, and Jan E. Stets, eds. 1989. *Violence in Dating Relationships: Emerging Social Issues.* New York: Praeger Publishers.

Pitts, Marian, and Keith Phillips. 1998. 2nd ed. *The Psychology of Health. An Introduction.* London: Routledge.

Planned Parenthood, http://www.plannedparenthood.org, http://www.teenwire.com

Pleck, Joseph H. 1997. "Parental Involvement: Levels, Sources, and Consequences." Pp. 66–103 in *The Role of the Father in Child Development*. Edited by Michael E. Lamb. New York: Wiley.

Pojman, Louis P., and Francis J. Beckwith, comps. 1998. *The Abortion Controversy*. Belmont, CA: Wadsworth.

Polhemus, Ted. 1994. *Streetstyle: From Sidewalk to Catwalk*. New York: Thames and Hudson.

Pong, Suet-Ling. 1997. "Family Structure, School Context, and Eighth-Grade Math and Reading Achievement." *Journal of Marriage and the Family* 59: 734–746.

Poppema, Suzanne P., with Mike Henderson. 1996. *Why I Am an Abortion Doctor*. Amherst, NY: Prometheus Books.

Powers, Mick J. 1999. "Sadness and Its Disorders." Pp. 497–519 in *Handbook of Cognition and Emotion*. Edited by Tim Dalgleish and Mick J. Power. Chichester, England: Wiley.

Prochaska, Janice M., and James O. Prochaska. 1985. "Children's Views of the Causes and 'Cures' of Sibling Rivalry." *Child Welfare* 114: 427–433.

Prout, H. Thompson, and Douglas T. Brown. 1998. Counseling and Psychotherapy with Children and Adolescents, 3rd ed. New York: Wiley.

Pueschel, Sigfried M., and Maria Sustrova. 1997. *Adolescents with Down Syndrome: Toward a More Fulfilling Life*. Baltimore: Paul H. Brookes Publishing Co.

Pugh, Mary Jo V., and Daniel Hart. 1999. "Identity Development and Peer Group Participation." Pp. 55–70 in *New Directions for Child and Adolescent Development: The Role of Peer Groups in Adolescent Social Identity: Exploring the Importance of Stability and Change*, no. 84. Edited by Jeffrey A. McLellan and Mary Jo V. Pugh. San Francisco: Jossey-Bass.

Quinn, Jane. 1995. "Positive Effects of Participation in Youth Organizations." Pp 274–303 in *Psychosocial Disturbances in Young People: Challenges for Prevention*. Edited by M. Rutter. New York: Cambridge University Press.

Raffaelli, Marcela. 1992. "Sibling Conflict in Early Adolescence." *Journal of Marriage and the Family* 54: 652–663.

———. 1997. "Young Adolescent's Conflicts with Siblings and Friends." *Journal of Youth and Adolescence* 26: 539–557.

Rahn, Wendy M., and John E. Transue. 1998. "Social Trust and Value Change: The Decline of Social Capital in American Youth, 1976–1995." *Political Psychology* 19: 545–565.

Rainwater, Lee. 1974. *What Money Buys: Inequality and the Social Meanings of Income*. New York: Basic Books.

Rapoport, Judith. 1989. *The Boy Who Couldn't Stop Washing*. New York: Plume.

Rathunde, Kevin. 1996. "Family Context and Talented Adolescents' Optimal Experience in School-Related Activities." *Journal of Research on Adolescence* 6, no. 4: 605–628.

Rau, Jean-Marie B. 1997. *The Ability of Minors to Define and Recognize Their Rights in Research*. Dissertation #97–30, 105. Fordham University, NY.

Ray, Oakley, and Charles Ksir. 1996. *Drugs, Society and Human Nature*, 7th ed. St. Louis: Mosby Year Book, Inc.

Raychaba, Brian. 1988. *To Be on Our Own with No Direction from Home*. Ottawa: National Youth in Care Network.

Reid, William J., and Timothy Donovan. 1990. "Treating Sibling Violence." *Family Therapy* 152: 49–59.

Reinisch, June Machover, Leonard A. Rosenblum, and Stephanie A. Sanders, eds. 1987. *Masculinity/Femininity: Basic Perspectives.* New York: Oxford University Press.

Rendón, Laura I. 1996. "Life on the Border." About Campus (November–December): 14–20.

Renshaw, Peter D., and Peter J. Brown. 1993. "Loneliness in Middle Childhood: Concurrent and Longitudinal Predictors." *Child Development* 64: 1271–1284.

Reschly, David. 1981. "Psychological Testing in Educational Classification and Placement." *American Psychologist* 36 no. 10: 1094–1102.

Resnick, J. Steven, Jerome Kagan, Nancy Snidman, Michelle Gersten, Katherine Baak, and Allison Rosenberg. 1986. "Inhibited and Uninhibited Children: A Follow-Up Study." *Child Development* 57, no. 3: 660–680.

Rest, James. 1979. *Development in Judging Moral Issues.* Minneapolis: University of Minnesota Press.

Reynolds, Arthur J., and Judy A. Temple. 1998. "Extended Early Childhood Intervention and School Achievements: Age Thirteen Findings from the Chicago Longitudinal Study." *Child Development* 69: 231–246.

Reynolds, William M., and Hugh F. Johnston, eds. 1994. *Handbook of Depression in Children and Adolescents.* New York: Plenum.

Rhodes, Jean E., and Anita A. Davis. 1996. "Supportive Ties between Nonparent Adults and Urban Adolescent Girls." Pp. 213–225 in *Urban Girls: Resisting Stereotypes, Creating Identities.* Edited by Bonnie J. R. Leadbeater, and Niobe Way. New York: New York University Press.

Rhodes, Jean E., Jean B. Grossman, and Nancy L. Resch. In press. "Agents of Change: Pathways through Which Mentoring Relationships Influence Adolescents' Academic Adjustment." *Child Development.*

Rhodes, Jean E., Josefina M. Contreras, and Sarah C. Mangelsdorf. 1994. "Natural Mentor Relationships among Latina Adolescent Mothers: Psychological Adjustment, Moderating Processes, and the Role of Early Parental Acceptance." *American Journal of Community Psychology* 22: 211–227.

Rhodes, Jean E., Lori Ebert, and Karla Fischer. 1992. "Natural Mentors: An Overlooked Resource in the Social Networks of Young, African-American Mothers." *American Journal of Community Psychology* 20: 445–461.

Rhodes, Jean E., Wendy L. Haight, and Ernestine C. Briggs. 1999. The Influence of Mentoring on the Peer Relationships of Foster Youth in Relative and Non-Relative Care. *Journal of Research on Adolescence* 9: 185–201.

Ricciuti, Henry R. 1999. "Single Parent-hood and School Readiness in White, Black, and Hispanic 6- and 7-Year-Olds." *Journal of Family Psychology* 13: 450–465.

Ridley, C. 1995. *Overcoming Unintentional Racism in Counseling and Therapy.* Thousand Oaks: Sage.

Rierdan, Jill, and Elissa Koff. 1997. "Weight, Weight-Related Aspects of Body Image, and Depression in Early Adolescent Girls." *Adolescence* 32, no. 127: 615–625.

Rigby, Ken. 1996. *Bullying in Schools and What to Do about It.* Melbourne: Australian Council for Educational Research.

Riordan, Cornelius. 1990. *Girls and Boys in School: Together or Separate?* New York: Teachers College Press.

Rizzini, Irene, Irma Rizzini, Monica Munoz-Vargas, and Lidia Galeano. 1994. "Brazil: A New Concept of Childhood." Pp. 55–99 in *Urban Children in Distress: Global Predicaments and Innovative Strategies*. Edited by Cristina Szanton Blanc. Langhorne, PA: Gordon and Breach Science Publishers.

Roberts, D. 1993. "Adolescents and the Mass Media." Pp. 171–186 in *Adolescence in the 1990's*. Edited by R. Takanishi–. New York: Teachers College Press.

Roberts, Donald F., Ulla G. Foehr, Victoria J. Rideout, and Mollyann Brodie. 1999. *Kids and Media @ the New Millennium*. Menlo Park, CA: Henry J. Kaiser Foundation.

Roberts, R.E.L., L. N. Richards, and Vern L. Bengtson. 1991. "Intergenerational Solidarity in Families: Untangling the Ties That Bind." Pp. 11–46 in *Marriage and Family Review*, Vol. 16, *Families: Intergenerational and Generational Connections*. Edited by S. K. Pfeifer and M. B. Sussman. Binghamton, NY: Haworth.

Robins, Lee. 1966. *Deviant Children Grown Up*. Baltimore: Williams and Wilkins.

Robinson, Thomas N., Joel D. Killen, Iris F. Litt, Lawrence D. Hammer, Darrell M. Wilson, K. Farish Haydel, Chris Hayward, and C. Barr Taylor. 1996. "Ethnicity and Body Dissatisfaction: Are Hispanic and Asian Girls at Increased Risk for Eating Disorders?" *Journal of Adolescent Health* 19: 384–393.

Rodriguez, Luis J. 1993. *Always Running: La Vida Loca: Gang Days in L.A.* New York: Touchstone.

Rogers, Audrey Smith, Lawrence D'Angelo, and Donna Futterman. 1994.

"Guidelines for Adolescent Participation in Research: Current Realities and Possible Resolutions." *Irb: Review of Human Subjects Research* 16: 1–6.

Rolf, Jon E., Ann S. Masten, Dante Cicchetti, Keith H. Nuechterlein, and Sheldon Weintraub, eds. 1990. *Risk and Protective Factors in the Development of Psychopathology*. Cambridge, UK: Cambridge University Press.

Romer, Daniel, Maureen Black, Izabel Ricardon, Susan Feigelman, Linda Kaljee, Jennifer Galbraith, Rodney Nesbit, Robert C. Hornik, and Bonita Stanton. 1994. "Social Influences on the Sexual Behavior of Youth at Risk for HIV Exposure." *American Journal of Public Health* 84: 977–985.

Romo, Harriett D., and Toni Falbo. 1996. *Latino High School Graduation: Defying the Odds*. Austin: University of Texas Press.

Roscoe, Bruce, Lauri E. Cavanaugh, and Donna R. Kennedy. 1988. "Dating Infidelity: Behaviors, Reasons, and Consequences." *Adolescence* 23: 35–43.

Rosenberg, Elinor B. 1992. *The Adoption Life Cycle*. New York: The Free Press.

Rosenheim, M. K., and M. F. Testa, eds. 1992. *Early Parenthood and Coming of Age in the 1990s*. New Brunswick, NJ: Rutgers University Press.

Roth, Jodie, Jeanne Brooks-Gunn, Lawrence Murray, and William Foster. 1998. "Promoting Healthy Adolescents: Synthesis of Youth Development Program Evaluations." *Journal of Research on Adolescence* 8: 423–459.

Rotheram-Borus, Mary J. 1990. "Adolescents' Reference-Group Choices, Self-Esteem, and Adjustment." *Journal of Personality and Social Psychology* 59: 1075–1081.

———. 1993. "Biculturalism among Adolescents." Pp. 81–102 in *Ethnic Identity: Formation and Transmission among Hispanics and Other Minorities.* Edited by M. E. Bernal and G. P. Knight. Albany: State University of New York Press.

Rowland, Julia H. 1998. "Developmental Stage and Adaptation: Child and Adolescent Model." Pp. 519–543 in *Handbook of Psychooncology: Psychological Care of the Patient with Cancer.* Edited by Jimmie C. Holland and Julia H. Rowland. New York: Oxford University Press.

Rubenstein, Ruth P. 1995. *Dress Codes: Meanings and Messages in American Culture.* Boulder, CO: Westview Press.

Rubin, Kenneth A. 1998. "Peer Interaction, Relationships, and Groups." Pp. 619–700 in *Handbook of Child Psychology*, Vol. 3, *Social, Emotional, and Personality Development*, 5th ed. Edited by W. Damon and N. Eisenberg. New York, Wiley.

Rudolph, Frederick. 1990. *The American College and University: A History.* Athens/London: University of Georgia Press.

Ruggles, Patricia. 1990. *Drawing the Line: Alternative Poverty Measures and Their Implications for Public Policy.* Washington, DC: The Urban Institute Press.

Rutter, Michael. 1991. "Age Changes in Depressive Disorders: Some Developmental Considerations." Pp. 273–300 in *The Development of Emotion Regulation and Dysregulation.* Edited by Judy Garber and Kenneth Dodge. Cambridge: Cambridge University Press.

Rutter, Michael, Henri Giller, and Ann Hagell, eds. 1998. *Antisocial Behavior by Young People.* New York: Cambridge University Press.

Ruusuvaara, Leena. (997. "Adolescent Sexuality: An Educational and Counseling Challenge. Pp. 411–413 in *Adolescent Gynecology and Endocrinology: Basic and Clinical Aspects.* Edited by G. Creatsas, G. Mastorakos, and G. Chrousos. New York: Annals of the New York Academy of Science, Vol. 816.

Ryan, B. A., and G. R. Adams. 1995. "The Family-School Relationships Model." Pp. 3–28 in *The Family-School Connection: Theory, Research, and Practice.* Edited by B. A. Ryan and associates. Thousand Oaks, CA: Sage.

———. 1999. "How Do Families Affect Children's Success in School?" *Education Quarterly Review* 6: 30–43 (Available in English and French).

Ryan, Caitlin, and Donna Futterman. 1998. *Lesbian and Gay Youth: Care and Counseling.* Philadelphia: Hanley and Belfus.

Ryan, R., and R. Kuczkowski. 1994. "The Imaginary Audience, Self-Consciousness, and Public Individuation in Adolescence." *Journal of Personality* 62: 219–238.

Ryan, Richard M., and John H. Lynch. 1989. "Emotional Autonomy versus Detachment: Revisiting the Vicissitudes of Adolescence and Young Adulthood." *Child Development* 60: 340–356.

Rycek, K. E., S. L. Stuhr, J. McDermott, J. Benker, and M. D. Swartz. 1998. "Adolescent Egocentrism and Cognitive Functioning during Late Adolescence." *Adolescence* 33: 746–750.

Saarni, Carolyn. 1999. *The Development of Emotional Competence.* New York: Guilford Press.

Sachdev, Paul, ed. 1985. *Perspectives on Abortion.* Metuchen, NJ: Scarecrow Press.

Sadker, Myra P., David M. Sadker, and Susan Klein. 1991. "The Issue of Gender in Elementary and Secondary Education." *Review of Research in Education* 17: 269–334.

Salmivalli, Christina. 1999. "Participant Role Approach to School Bullying: Implications for Intervention." *Journal of Adolescence* 22: 453–459.

Salmivalli, Christina, Karl M. Lagerspetz, Kaj Björkqvist, Karin Österman, and Anna Kaukiainen. 1996. "Bullying as a Group Process: Participant Roles and Their Relations to Social Status within the Group." *Aggressive Behavior* 22: 1–15.

Salzman, S. A. 1987. "Meta-Analysis of Studies Investigating the Effects of Father Absence on Children's Cognitive Performance." Paper presented at the annual meeting of the American Educational Research Association, Washington, DC (April).

Sanders, Christopher, Tiffany Field, Miguel Diego, and Michele Kaplan. 2000. "Moderate Involvement in Sports Is Related to Lower Depression Levels among Adolescents." *Adolescence* 35: 793–797.

Sanders, Mavis G. 1998. "The Effects of School, Family and Community Support on the Academic Achievement of African American Adolescents." *Urban Education* 33: 385–409.

Sanfilippo, J. S., and Hertwick, S. P. 1998. "Physiology of Menstruation and Menstrual Disorders." Pp. 990–1017 in *Comprehensive Adolescent Health Care.* Edited by S. B. Friedman, M. Fisher, S. K.Schoenberg, E. M. Adlerman, and E. Mosby. New York: Random House.

Sante, Luc. 1991. *Low Life: Lures and Snares of Old New York.* New York, NY: Vintage Books.

Santrock, John W. 1992. *Life-Span Development.* 4th ed. Dubuque, IA: W. C. Brown Publishers.

———. 1996. *Adolescence: An Introduction,* 6th ed. Dubuque, IA: Brown & Benchmark Publishers.

———. 1998. *Adolescence.* Boston: McGraw-Hill.

Satter, Ellyn. 1987. *How to Get Your Kid to Eat . . . But Not Too Much: From Birth to Adolescence.* Palo Alto: Bull Publishing.

Sattler, Jerome M. 1992. *Assessment of Children,* 3rd ed. San Diego: Jerome M. Sattler.

Savin-Williams, Ritch C. 2001. *"Mom, Dad. I'm Gay." How Families Negotiate Coming Out.* Washington, DC: American Psychological Association Press.

———. 1998. *". . .And Then I Became Gay": Young Men's Stories.* New York: Routledge.

Savin-Williams, Ritch C., and Kenneth M. Cohen. 1996. *The Lives of Lesbians, Gays, and Bisexuals: Children to Adults.* Forth Worth, TX: Harcourt Brace College Publishing.

Savin-Williams, Ritch C., and Thomas J. Berndt. 1990. "Friendships and Peer Relations during Adolescence." Pp. 277–307 in *At the Threshold: The Developing Adolescent.* Edited by Shirley S. Feldman and Glen R. Elliott. Cambridge, MA: Harvard University Press.

Sayer, Aline G., Stuart T. Hauser, Alan M. Jacobson, John B. Willett, and Charlotte F. Cole. 1995. "Developmental Influences on Adolescent Health." Pp. 22–51 in *Adolescent Health Problems: Behavioral Perspectives Advances in Pediatric Psychology.* Edited by J. L. Wallander and L. J. Siegel. New York: Guilford Press.

Scales, Peter C. 1991. *A Portrait of Young Adolescents in the 1990s: Implications for Promoting Health Growth and*

Development. Minneapolis: Search Institute/Center for Early Adolescence.

Scales, Peter C., and Nancy Leffert. 1999. *Developmental Assets: A Synthesis of the Scientific Research on Adolescent Development.* Minneapolis: Search Institute.

Scales, Peter C., Peter L. Benson, and Nancy Leffert. 2000. "Contribution of Developmental Assets to the Prediction of Thriving among Adolescents." *Applied Developmental Science* 4: 27–46.

Schab, Fred, 1991. "Schooling without Learning: Thirty Years of Cheating in High School." *Adolescence* 26, no. 104: 839–847.

Schecter, Sandra, Diane Sharken-Taboada, and Robert Bayley. 1996. "Bilingual by Choice: Latino Parents' Rationales and Strategies fo Raising Children with Two Languages." *The Bilingual Research Journal* 20, no. 2: 261–281.

Scheibe, Karl E. 1995. *Self Studies.* Westport, CT: Praeger.

Schine, Joan. 1989. *Young Adolescents and Community Service.* Working Paper for the Carnegie Council on Adolescent Development. Washington, DC.

Schissel, Bernard, and Kari Fedec. 1999. "The Selling of Innocence: The Gestalt of Danger in the Loves of Youth Prostitutes." *Canadian Journal of Criminology* 41, no. 1: 33–56.

Schmidt, Louis A., and Jay Schulkin, eds. 1999. *Extreme Fear, Shyness, and Social Phobia: Origins, Biological Mechanisms, and Clinical Outcomes.* New York: Oxford University Press.

Schmittroth, L., ed. 1994. *Statistical Record of Children.* Detroit: Gale Research.

Schneider, Barbara, and David Stevenson. 1998. *The Ambitious Generation: America's Teenagers, Motivated but*

Directionless. New Haven: Yale University Press.

Schneider, Barbara, Fengbin Chang, Christopher Swanson, and David Stevenson. 1999. "Social Exchange and Interests: Parents' Investments in Educational Opportunities." Paper presented at the annual meeting of the American Sociological Association, Chicago (August).

Schoenhals, Mark, Marta Tienda, and Barbara Schneider. 1998. "The Educational and Personal Consequences of Adolescent Employment." *Social Forces* 77 (December): 723–762.

Schorr, Lee B. 1988. *Within Our Reach: Breaking the Cycle of Disadvantage.* New York: Doubleday.

Schulenberg, J., J. L. Maggs, K. Steinman, and R. A. Zucker (in press). "Development Matters: Taking the Long View on Substance Abuse Etiology and Intervention during Adolescence. In P. M. Monti, S. M. Colby, and T. A. O'Leary, eds., *Adolescents, Alcohol, and Substance Abuse: Reaching Teens through Brief Intervention.* New York: Guilford Press.

Schulenberg, John, Fred W. Vondracek, and Ann Crouter. 1984. "The Influence of the Family on Vocational Development." *Journal of Marriage and the Family* 46: 129–143.

Schwartz, Irma M., ed. 1992. *Juvenile Justice and Public Policy.* New York: Macmillan.

Schwartz, J. 1994. "Societal Benefits of Reducing Lead Exposure." *Environmental Resources* 66: 105–124.

Scott, Elizabeth R., N. Dickon Reppucci, and Jennifer Woolard. 1995. "Evaluating Adolescent Decision Making in Legal Contexts." *Law and Human Behavior* 19, no. 3: 221–244.

Scott-Jones, D. 1993. "Adolescent Childbearing: Whose Problem? What Can We Do?" *Phi Delta Kappan*, 75, 1–12.

Sebald, Hans. 1985. "Adolescents' Shifting Orientation toward Parents and Peers: A Curvilinear Trend over Recent Decades." *Journal of Marriage and the Family* 48: 5–13.

Secretary's Commission on Achieving Necessary Skills. 1991. *What Work Requires of Schools: A SCANS Report for America 2000.* Washington, DC: U.S. Department of Labor.

Secada, Walter, et al. 1998. *No More Excuses: Final Report of the Hispanic Dropout Project.* Washington, DC: Hispanic Dropout Project.

Sedlak, Andrea J., and Diane D. Broadhurst. 1996. *The Third National Incidence Study of Child Abuse and Neglect.* Washington, DC: National Clearinghouse on Child Abuse and Neglect Information.

Seiffge-Krenke, Inge. 1995. *Stress, Coping, and Adaptation.* New York: Cambridge University Press.

———. 1995. *Stress, Coping, and Relationships in Adolescence.* Mahwah, NJ: Erlbaum.

———. 1998. *Adolescents' Health: A Developmental Perspective.* Mahwah, NJ: Erlbaum.

———. 1998. "Chronic Disease and Perceived Developmental Progression in Adolescence." *Developmental Psychology* 34, no. 5: 1073–1084.

———. 2001. *Diabetic Adolescents and Their Families: Stress, Coping, and Adaptation.* New York, NY: Cambridge University Press.

Shackelford, Todd K., and David M. Buss. 1997. "Cues to Infidelity." *Personality and Social Psychology Bulletin* 23: 1034–1045.

Shafer, William G., Maynard K. Hine, and Barnet M. Levy. 1983. *Oral Pathology.* Philadelphia: W. B. Saunders.

Shaffer, David, and Leslie Craft. 1999. "Methods of Adolescent Suicide Prevention." *Journal of Clinical Psychiatry* 60: 70–74.

Shanahan, Michael J., and Brian Flaherty. In press. "Dynamic Patterns of Time Use Strategies in Adolescence." *Child Development.*

Shanahan, Michael J., Glen H. Elder, Jr., Margaret Burchinal, and Rand D. Conger. 1996. "Adolescent Earnings and Relationships with Parents: The Work-Family Nexus in Urban and Rural Ecologies." Pp. 97–128 in *Adolescents, Work and Family: An Intergenerational Developmental Analysis.* Edited by Jeylan T. Mortimer, and Michael D. Finch. Thousand Oaks, CA: Sage.

Shanahan, Michael J., Glenn H. Elder, Jr., Margaret Burchinal, and Rand D. Conger. 1996. "Adolescent Paid Labor and Relationships with Parents: Early Work-Family Linkages." *Child Development* 67: 2183–2200.

Shapiro, Daniel, and Margaret Goertz. 1998. "Connecting Work and School: Findings from the 1997 National Employer Survey." Paper presented at the annual meeting of the American Educational Research Association, San Diego (April).

Sharf, Richard S. 1997. *Applying Career Development Theory to Counseling.* 2nd ed. Pacific Grove, CA: Brooks/Cole.

Sharp, Charles William, Fred Beauvais, and Richard Spence, eds. 1992. *National Institute on Drug Abuse Research Monograph Series*, No. 129. *Inhalant Abuse: A Volatile Research Agenda.* Rockville: National Institute on Drug Abuse.

Sharp, Paul M., and Barry W. Hancock, eds. 1998. *Juvenile Delinquency: Historical, Theoretical, and Societal Reactions to Youth.* 2nd ed. Upper Saddle River: Prentice-Hall.

Shaw, C. R., and H. D. McKay. 1942. *Juvenile Delinquency & Urban Areas.* Chicago: University of Chicago Press.

Shaywitz, Sally. 1998. "Dyslexia." *New England Journal of Medicine* 338, no 5: 307–312.

Shelden, Randell G., Sharon K. Tracy, and William B. Brown. 1997. *Youth Gangs in American Society.* Wadsworth Publishing.

Sheppart, Viveca J., Eileen S. Nelson, and Virginia Andreoli-Mathie. 1995. "Dating Relationships and Infidelity: Attitudes and Behaviors. *Journal of Sex and Marital Therapy* 21: 202–212.

Sher, Ken J. 1991. *Children of Alcoholics: A Critical Appraisal of Theory and Research.* Chicago: University of Chicago Press.

Sherrod, Lonnie R., Robert J. Haggerty, and David L. Featherman. 1993. "Late Adolescence and the Transition to Adulthood." *Journal of Research on Adolescence* 3: 217–226.

Shoho, Alan R. 1994. "A Historical Comparison of Parental Involvement of Three Generations of Japanese Americans (Isseis, Niseis, Sanseis) in the Education of Their Children." *Journal of Applied Developmental Psychology* 15: 305–311.

Shulman, Shmuel, and W. Andrew Collins, eds. 1997. *Romantic Relationships in Adolescence: Developmental Perspectives.* San Francisco: Jossey-Bass.

Shweder, Richard A., Jacqueline Goodnow, Giyoo Hatano, Robert A. LeVine, Hazel Markus, and Peggy Miller. 1998. "The Cultural Psychology of Development: One Mind, Many Mentalities." Chap. 15 in *Handbook of Child Psychology,* Vol. 1,

Theoretical Models of Human Development. Edited by W. Damon and R. Lerner. New York: Wiley.

Shweder, Richard, M. Mahapatra, and Joan Miller. 1987. "Culture and Moral Development in India and the United States." Pp. 1–90 in *The Emergence of Morality in Young Children.* Edited by Jerome Kagan and Sharon Lamb. Chicago: University of Chicago Press.

Sickmund, Melissa, Howard Snyder, and Eileen Poe-Yamagata. 1997. *Juvenile Offenders and Victims: 1997 Update on Violence.* Washington, DC: U.S. Department of Justice, Office of Juvenile Justice and Delinquency Prevention.

Silbereisen, Rainer K., Fred W. Vondracek, and Lucianne A. Berg. 1997. "Differential Timing of Initial Vocational Choice: The Influence of Early Childhood Family Relocation and Parental Support Behaviors in Two Cultures." *Journal of Vocational Behavior* 50: 41–59.

Silver, Larry, B. 1991. *The Misunderstood Child: A Guide for Parents of Children with Learning Disabilities.* 2nd ed. New York: McGraw-Hill.

———. 1998. *The Misunderstood Child: Understanding and Copingwith Your Child's Learning Disabilities,* 3rd ed. New York: McGraw-Hill.

Silverman, Wendy K., and Thomas M. Ollendick, eds. 1999. *Developmental Issues in the Clinical Treatment of Children.* Boston: Allyn and Bacon.

Simmons, Roberta, and Dale Blyth. 1987. *Moving into Adolescence: The Impact of Pubertal Change and School Context.* New York: Aldine.

Simon, Gary. 1999. *How I Overcame Shyness: 100 Celebrities Share Their Secrets.* New York: Simon and Schuster.

Simon, Leonore M. J. 1998. "Does Criminal Offender Treatment Work?"

Applied and Preventative Psychology 7, no. 3: 137–159.

Simons, Ronald. L., Kuei-Hsiu Lin, Leslie C. Gordon, Rand D. Conger, and Frederick O. Lorenz. 1999. "Explaining the Higher Incidence of Adjustment Problems among Children of Divorce Compared with Those in Two-Parent Families." *Journal of Marriage and the Family* 61: 1020–1033.

Simpson, Sharon M., Barbara G. Licht, Richard K. Wagner, and Sandra R. Stader. 1996. "Organization of Children's Academic Ability-Related Self-Perceptions." *Journal of Educational Psychology* 88: 387–396.

Singer, M. T. 1995. *Cults in Our Midst.* San Francisco: Jossey-Bass.

Singh, S., and J. E. Darroch. 2000. "Adolescent Pregnancy and Childbearing: Levels and Trends in Developed Countries." *Family Planning Perspectives* 32: 14–23.

Sipowicz, Hugh, and Marty Zanghi. 1998. "Maine Youth Are Speaking Up and Reaching Out!" *Common Ground* (December).

Skinner, Ellen, James Welborn, and James Connell. 1990. "What It Takes to Do Well in School and Whether I've Got It: A Process Model of Perceived Self-Control and Children's Engagement and Achievement in School." *Journal of Educational Psychology* 82, no. 1: 22–32.

Slee, Phillip T. 1993. "Bullying: A Preliminary Investigation of Its Nature and the Effects of Social Cognition." *Early Child Development and Care* 87: 47–57.

Sloane, L. 1991. "With Allowances, Every Parent Differs." *New York Times* November 2: 12.

Smeeding, Timothy M., and Barbara Boyle Torrey. 1993. "Poor Children in Rich Countries," *Science* 242: 873–877.

———. 1995. "Revisiting Poor Children in Rich Countries," unpublished manuscript.

Smetana, Judith G. 1995. "Parenting Styles and Conceptions of Parental Authority during Adolescence." *Child Development* 66: 299–316.

Smetana, Judith, and Bruce Bitz. 1996. "Adolescents' Conceptions of Teachers' Authority and Their Relations to Rule Violations in School." *Child Development* 67: 1153–1172.

Smith Adam. 1776. *Wealth of Nations* (London: Everyman's Library, cited in "Alternative Measures of Poverty," A Staff Study Prepared for the Joint Economic Committee (of the U.S. Congress), October 18, 1989, p. 10.

Smith, Anthony, ed. 1998. *Television: An International History.* Oxford; New York: Oxford University Press.

Smith, Corinne, Lisa Strick. 1999. *Learning Disabilities A to Z.* New York: Simon and Schuster.

Smith, Peter K., Yohji Morita, Josine Junger-Tas, Dan Olweus, Richard F. Catalano, and Phillip Slee. 1999. *The Nature of School Bullying: A Cross-National Perspective.* London, UK: Routledge.

Smith, Sally, L. 1995. *No Easy Answers: The Learning Disabled Child at Home and at School.* New York: Bantum Books.

———. 1993. *Succeeding against the Odds: How the Learning Disabled Can Realize Their Promise.* California: J. P. Tarcher.

Smucker, Mervin R., Edward W. Craighead, Linda Wilcoxen, and Barbara J. Green. 1986. "Normative and Reliability Data for the Children's Depression Inventory." *Journal of Abnormal Child Psychology* 14, no a: 25–39.

Snarey, John. 1985. "Cross-Cultural Universality of Social-Moral Development: A Critical Review of Kohlbergian Research." *Psychological Bulletin* 97: 202–232.

———. 1993. *How Fathers Care for the Next Generation.* Cambridge, MA: Harvard University Press.

Snyder, Howard N., and Melissa Sickmund. 1999. *Juvenile Offenders and Victims: 1999 National Report.* Washington, DC: Juvenile Justice Clearinghouse, Office of Juvenile Justice and Delinquency Prevention. Web site: www.ncjj.org.

Society for Research in Child Development. 1993. "Ethical Standards for Research with Children." Pp. 337–339 in *Directory of Members.* Ann Arbor, MI: SRCD.

Sontag, M. Suzanne, Mihaela Peteu, and Jongnam Lee. 1997. "Clothing in the Self-System of Adolescents: Relationships among Values, Proximity of Clothing to Self, Clothing Interest, Anticipated Outcomes and Perceived Quality of Life." Research Report 556. East Lansing: Michigan Agricultural Experiment Station.

Soriano, Marcel, Fernando L. Soriano, and Evelia Jimenez. 1994. "School Violence among Culturally Diverse Populations: Sociocultural and Institutional Considerations." *School Psychology Review* 2: 216–235.

Spear, Bonnie A. 2000. "Adolescent Nutrition: General." Pp. 262–287 in *Nutrition throughout the Life Cycle.* Edited by Bonnie S. Worthington-Roberts and Sue Rodwell Williams. Boston: McGraw-Hill.

Spencer, Herbert. 1873. "Psychology of the Sexes." *Popular Science Monthly* 4: 31–32.

Spencer, Margaret. 1990. "Identity, Minority Development of." Pp. 111–130 in *Encyclopedia of Adolescence.* Edited by Richard M. Lerner, Anne C. Petersen and Jeanne Brooks-Gunn New York: Garland.

———. 1995. "Old Issues and New Theorizing about African American Youth: A Phenomenological Variant of Ecological Systems Theory." Pp. 37–70 in *Black Youth: Perspectives on their Status in the United States.* Edited by Ronald L. Taylor. Westport, CT: Praeger.

———. 1999. "Social and Cultural Influences on School Adjustment: The Application of an Identity Focused Cultural Ecological Perspective." *Educational Psychologist* 34: 43–57.

Spencer, Margaret B., David Dupree, Dena P. Swanson, and Michael Cunningham. 1996. "Parental Monitoring and Adolescents' Sense of Responsibility for Their Own Learning: An Examination of Sex Differences." *Journal of Negro Education* 65: 30–43.

Spencer, Margaret Beale, and Carol Markstrom-Adams. 1990. "Identity Processes among Racial and Ethnic Minorities in America." *Child Development* 61: 290–310.

Spencer, Margaret Beale, David Dupree, and Tracy Hartmann. 1997. "A Phenomenological Variant of Ecological Systems Theory (PVEST): A Self-Organization Perspective in Context." *Development and Psychopathology* 9: 817–833.

Spencer, Margaret Beale, Vinay Harpalani, and Tabitha Del' Angelo. In press. "Structural Racism and Community Health: A Theory-Driven Model for Identity Intervention."

Spencer, Thomas, Joseph Biederman, and Timothy Wilens. 1998. Pharmacotherapy of ADHD with Antidepressants." Pp. 552–563 in *Attention-Deficit/Hyperactivity Disorder: A Handbook for Diagnosis and Treatment.* Edited by Russell Barkley. New York: Guilford Press.

Spergel, Irving A., and David G. Curry. 1993. "The National Youth Gang Survey: A Research and Development Process." In *The Gang Intervention Handbook.* Edited by Arnold P. Goldstein and C. Ronald Huff. Champaign, IL: Research Press.

Spivek, Howard, Alice J. Hausman, and Deborah Prothrow-Stith. 1989. "Practitioners' Forum: Public Health and the Primary Prevention of Adolescent Violence: The Violence Prevention Project." *Violence and Victims* 4: 203–212.

Spurlock, Jeanne, and Donna M. Norris. 1991. "The Impact of Culture and Race on the Development of African Americans in the United States." *American Psychiatric Press Review of Psychiatry* 10: 594–607.

Sroufe, Alan, Robert Cooper, and Ganic DeHart, eds. 1996. *Child Development: Its Nature and Course.* New York: McGraw-Hill.

Steele, C. M. 1997. "A Threat in the Air: How Stereotypes Shape Intellectual Identity and Performance." *American Psychologist* 52: 613–629.

Steele, Claude M., and Robert A. Josephs. 1990. "Alcohol Myopia: Its Prized and Dangerous Effects." *American Psychologist* 45: 921–933.

Steele, Jeanne R., and Jane D. Brown. 1995. "Adolescent Room Culture: Studying Media in the Context of Everyday Life." *Journal of Youth and Adolescence* 24: 551–576.

Stein, Nan. 1996. *Bullyproof.* Wellesley, MA: Wellesley Center for Research on Women.

Steinberg, L. 1988. "Reciprocal Relation between Parent-Child Distance and Pubertal Maturation. *Developmental Psychology* 24: 122–128.Steinberg, Laurence. 1989. "Communities of Families and Education." In *Education and the American Family: A Research Synthesis.* Edited by W. J. Weston. New York: New York University Press.

Steinberg, Laurence. 1990. "Autonomy, Conflict, and Harmony in the Family Relationship." In *At the Threshold: The Developing Adolescent.* Edited by S. Feldman and G. Elliott. Cambridge, MA: Harvard University Press.

———. 1996. *Adolescence.* 4th ed. Boston: McGraw-Hill.

———. 1999. *Adolescence.* Boston: McGraw-Hill.

———. 1999. "Families." Pp.118–149 in *Adolescence,* 5th ed. Boston: McGraw-Hill.

———. 1999. *Adolescence,* 5th ed. New York: McGraw-Hill.

Steinberg, Laurence D., and Elizabeth Cauffman. 1995. "The Impact of Employment on Adolescent Development." *Annals of Child Development* 11: 131–166.

———. 1996. "Maturity of Judgment in Adolescence: Psychosocial Factors in Adolescent Decision Making." *Law and Human Behavior* 20, no. 3: 249–272.

Steinberg, Laurence, and Ann Levine. 1990. *You and Your Adolescent: A Parent's Guide for Ages 10 to 20.* New York: Harper Perennial.

Steinberg, Laurence, and Sanford Dornbusch. 1991. "Negative Correlates of Part-Time Employment during Adolescence: Replication and Elaboration." *Developmental Psychology* 27: 304–313.

Steinberg, Laurence, and Susan Silverberg. 1986. "The Vicissitudes of Autonomy in Early Adolescence." *Child Development* 57: 841–851.

Steinberg, Laurence, and Wendy Steinberg. 1994. *Crossing Paths: How Your Child's Adolescence Can Be an*

Opportunity for Your Own Personal Growth. New York: Simon and Schuster.

Steinberg, Laurence, Nina Mounts, Susie Lamborn, and Sanford M. Dornbusch. 1991. "Authoritative Parenting and Adolescent Adjustment across Varied Ecological Niches." *Journal of Research on Adolescence* 1, no. 1: 19–36.

Steinberg, Laurence, Susie D. Lamborn, Nancy Darling, Nina S. Mount, and Sanford M. Dornbusch. 1994. "Over-Time Changes in Adjustment and Competence among Adolescents from Authoritative, Authoritarian, Indulgent, and Neglectful Families." *Child Development* 65: 754–770.

Steiner-Adair, Catherine. 1986. "The Body Politic: Normal Adolescent Development and the Development of Eating Disorders." *Journal of the American Academy of Psychoanalysis* 14: 95–114.

Stern, D., and Y. Nakata. 1989. "Characteristics of High School Students' Paid Jobs, and Employment Experience after Graduation." In *Adolescence and Work: Influences of Social Structure, Labor Markets, and Culture*. Edited by D. Stern and D. Eichorn. Hillsdale, NJ: Erlbaum.

Sternberg, Robert. 1985. *Beyond IQ—The Triarchic Theory*. New York: Cambridge University Press.

Sternberg, Robert, ed. 1992. *Intellectual Development*. Cambridge, New York: Cambridge University Press.

Sternberg, Robert, and Janet Davidson. 1987. *Conceptions of Giftedness*. New York: Cambridge University Press.

Stevenson, D. L., and D. P. Baker. 1987. The Family-School Relation and the Child's School Performance. *Child Development* 58: 1348–1357.

Stevenson, David, Julie Kochanek, and Barbara Schneider. 1998. "Making the Transition from High School: Recent Trends and Policies." Pp. 207–226 in *The Adolescent Years: Social Influences and Educational Challenges*, National Society for the Study of Education Yearbook. Edited by Kathryn Borman and Barbara Schneider. Chicago: University of Chicago Press.

Stevenson, Harold C. 1997. "Missed, Dissed, and Pissed": Making Meaning of Neighborhood Risk, Fear and Anger Management in Urban Black Youth. *Cultural Diversity and Mental Health* 3, no. 1: 37–52.

Stevenson, Howard C. 1997. "Managing Anger: Protective, Proactive, or Adaptive Racial Socialization Identity Profiles and African American Manhood Development." Pp. 35–62 in *Manhood Development in Urban African-American Communities*. Edited by R. J. Watts and R. Jagers. New York: Hawthorne Press.

Stevens-Simons, C., and E. R. McAnarney. 1996. "Adolescent Pregnancy." In *Handbook of Adolescent Health Risk Behavior*. Edited by R. J. DiClimente, W. B. Hansen, and L. E. Ponton. New York: Plenum Press.

Stevens-Simons, C., and M. White. 1991. "Adolescent Pregnancy." *Pediatric Annals* 20: 322–331.

Stinson, M. S., K. Whitmire, and T. N. Kluwin. 1996. "Self-Perceptions of Social Relationships in Hearing-Impaired Adolescents." *Journal of Educational Psychology* 88, no. 1: 132–143.

Stipek, Deborah J., and Douglas Mac Iver. 1989. "Developmental Change in Children's Assessment of Intellectual Competence." *Child Development* 60: 521–538.

Stodolsky, Susan, Scott Salk, and Barbara Glaessner. 1991. "Student Views about Learning Math and Social Studies."

American Educational Research Journal 28: 89–116.

Stomfay-Stitz, Aline M. 1994. "Conflict Resolution and Peer Mediation: Pathways to Safer Schools." *Childhood Education* 70, no. 5: 279–282.

Stone, Gregory P. 1962. "Appearance and the Self." Pp. 86–116 in *Human Behavior and the Social Processes: An Interactionist Approach.* Edited by Arnold M. Rose. New York: Houghton Mifflin.

Stone, James R., Jeylan T. Mortimer. 1998. "The Effects of Adolescent Employment on Vocational Development: Public and Educational Policy Implications." *Journal of Vocational Behavior* 53: 184–214.

Stoolmiller, M. 1994. "Antisocial Behavior, Delinquent Peer Association and Unsupervised Wandering for Boys: Growth and Change from Childhood to Early Adolescence." *Multivariate Behavioral Research* 29: 263–288.

Story, Mary, Simone A. French, Michael D. Resnick, and Robert W. Blum. 1995. "Ethnic/Racial and Socioeconomic Differences in Dieting Behaviors and Body Image Perceptions in Adolescents." *International Journal of Eating Disorders* 18: 173–179.

Strasburger, Victor C. 1995. *Adolescents and the Media: Medical and Psychological Impact.* Thousand Oaks, CA: Sage.

Straus, Murray A., and Glenda K. Kantor. 1994. "Corporal Punishment of Adolescents by Parents: A Risk Factor in the Epidemiology of Depression, Suicide, Alcohol Abuse, Child Abuse, and Wife Beating." *Adolescence* 29, no. 115: 543–560.

Strauss, David Levi. 1992. "A Threnody for Street Kids: The Youngest Homeless." *The Nation* 254 (June 1): 752–755.

Strayer, Janet, and William Roberts. 1997. "Facial and Verbal Measure of Children's

Emotions and Empathy." *International Journal of Behavioral Development* 20: 627–649.

Streib, Heinz. 1999. "Off-Road Religion? A Narrative Approach to Fundamentalist and Occult Orientations of Adolescents." *Journal of Adolescence* 22: 255–267.

Strong, Marilee. 1998. *A Bright Red Scream: Self-Mutilation and the Language of Pain.* New York: Viking.

Substance Abuse and Mental Health Services Administration (SAMSHA). 1998. "Prevention Works." News Release. http://www.samhsa.gov.

Sullivan, Mercer L. 1993. "Culture and Class as Determinants of Out-of-Wedlock Childbearing and Poverty during Late Adolescence. *Journal of Research on Adolescence* 3, no. 3: 295–316.

Sundeen, Richard, and Sally Raskoff. 1995. "Teenage Volunteers and Their Values." *Nonprofit and Voluntary Sector Quarterly* 240: 337–357

Super, Donald E. 1964. "A Developmental Approach to Vocational Guidance: Recent Theory and Results." *Vocational Guidance Quarterly* 13: 1–10.

———. 1990. "A Life-Span Life-Space Approach to Career Development." Pp. 197–261 in *Career Choice and Development,* 2nd ed. Edited by D. Brown and L. Brooks. San Franscisco, CA: Jossey-Bass.

Suris, J. C., N. Parera, and C. Puig. 1996. "Chronic Illness and Emotional Distress in Adolescence." *Journal of Adolescent Health* 19, no. 2: 153–156.

Susman, Elizabeth, Gale Inoff-Germain, Editha Nottleman, D. Lynn Loriaux, Gordon Cutler, and George Chrousos. 1987. "Hormones, Emotional Dispositions, and Aggressive Attributes in Young Adolescents." *Child Development* 58: 1114–1134.

Suyemoto, Karen L., and Marian L. McDonald. 1995. "Self-Cutting in Female Adolescents" *Psychotherapy* 32, no. 1: 162–171.

Swanson, Dena P., Margaret B. Spencer, and Anne Petersen. 1998. "Identity Formation in Adolescence." Pp. 18–41 in *The Adolescent Years: Social Influences and Educational Challenges.* Edited by Kathy Borman and B. Schneider. Chicago: University of Chicago Press.

Swanson, Dena Phillips, and Margaret Beale Spencer. 1995. "Developmental and Contextual Considerations for Research on African American Adolescents." In *Children of Color: Research, Health and Public Policy Issues.* Edited by Hiram E. Fitzgerald, Barry M. Lester, and Barry S. Zuckerman. New York: Garland.

Takanishi, Ruby, ed. 1993. *Adolescence in the 1990s.* New York: Teachers College Press.

Tanenbaum, Andrew S. 1998. *Structured Computer Organization.* Englewood Cliffs: Prentice-Hall.

Taylor, Carl S. 1990. *Dangerous Society.* East Lansing, MI: Michigan State University Press.

———. 1993. *Girls, Gangs, Women and Drugs.* East Lansing, MI: Michigan State University Press.

Taylor, Ronald. 1996. "Kinship Support, Family Management, and Adolescent Adjustment and Competence in African-American Families." *Developmental Psychology* 32: 687–695.

Taylor, Ronald D., Robin Casten, Susanne M. Flickinger, Debra Roberts, and Cecil D. Fulmore. 1994. "Explaining the School Performance of African-American Adolescents." *Journal of Research on Adolescence* 4: 21–44.

Terry, C. 1998. "Today's Target, Tomorrow's Readers." *Newspaper Youth Readership*, September.

Thomas, Alexander, and Stella Chess. 1977. *Temperament and Development.* New York: Brunner/Mazel.

Thompson, Ross A. 1990. "Vulnerability in Research: A Developmental Perspective on Research Risk." *Child Development* 61: 1–16.

———. 1992. "Developmental Changes in Research Risks and Benefits. A Changing Calculus of Consensus." Pp. 31–64 in *Social Research on Children and Adolescents.* Edited by Barbara Stanley and Joan E. Sieber. Newbury Park, CA: Sage.

Thornton, M. C., L. M. Chatters, R. J. Taylor, and W. R. Allen. 1990. "Sociodemographic and Environmental Correlates of Racial Socialization by African American Parents." *Child Development* 61: 401–409.

Thrasher, Frederick M. 1927. *The Gang.* Chicago, IL: University of Chicago Press.

Thullen, Manfred, et al. 1997. *Cooperating with a University in the United States.* Washington, DC: NAFSA.

Tieger, Todd. 1980. "On the Biological Bases of Sex Differences in Aggression." *Child Development* 51: 943–963.

Tolan, Patrick H., and Bertram J. Cohler, eds. 1993. *Handbook of Clinical Research and Practice with Adolescents.* New York: Wiley.

Toole, James, and Pamela Toole. 1992. *Key Definitions: Commonly Used Terms in the Youth Service Field.* Minneapolis, MN: National Youth Leadership Council.

Treas, Judith, and Ramon Torrecilha. 1995. "The Older Population." Pp. 47–92 in *State of the Union: America in the*

1990s, Vol. 2, *Social Trends.* Edited by Reynolds Farley. New York: Russell Sage Foundation.

Trickett, Penelope K., and Frank W. Putnam. 1998. "Developmental Consequences of Child Sexual Abuse." Pp. 39–56 in *Violence against Children in the Family and the Community.* Edited by Penelope K. Trickett and Cynthia J. Schellenbach. Washington, DC: American Psychological Association.

Troiana, Richard P., and Katherine M. Flegal. 1998. "Overweight Children and Adolescents: Description, Epidemiology, and Demographics." *Pediatrics* 101 (suppl.): 497–504.

Troll, L. E. 1983. "Grandparents: The Family Watchdogs." Pp. 63–74 in *Family Relationships in Later Life.* Edited by T. Brubaker. Beverly Hills, CA: Sage.

———. 1985. "The Contingencies of Grandparenting." Pp. 135–149 in *Grandparenthood.* Edited by Vern L. Bengtson and J. F. Robertston. Beverly Hills, CA: Sage.

Trow, Martin. 1989. "American Higher Education: Past, Present, and Future." *Studies in Higher Education* 14: 5–22.

Tucker, Corinna J., Kimberly A. Updegraff, Susan M. McHale, and Ann C. Crouter. 1998. "Older Siblings as Socializers of Younger Siblings' Empathy." *Journal of Early Adolescence* [special issue: *Prosocial and Moral Development in Early Adolescence,* Pt. 2] 19: 176–198.

Turner, John C., and Rina S. Onorato. 1999. "Social Identity, Personality, and the Self-Concept: A Self-Categorization Perspective." Pp. 11–46 in *The Psychology of the Social Self.* Edited by Tom R. Tyler, Roderick M. Kramer, and Oliver P. John. Mahwah, NJ: Lawrence Elbaum Associates.

Turner, Rebecca A., Charles E. Irwin, Jeanne M. Tschann, and Susan G. Millstein. 1993. "Autonomy, Relatedness, and the Initiation of Health Risk Behaviors in Early Adolescence." *Health Psychology* 12, no. 3 (May): 200–208.

U. S. Census Bureau. 1999. *Current Population Survey,* Racial Statistics Branch, Population Division.

———. 1992a. *Workers with Low Earnings: 1964 to 1990.* Current Population Reports, Series P-60, no. 178. Washington, DC: U.S. Government Printing Office.

———. 1992b. *Measuring the Effects of Benefits and Taxes on Income and Poverty: 1979 to 1991.* Current Population Reports, Series P-60, no. 183. Washington, DC: US. Government Printing Office.

———. 1998. "Poverty and the United States: 1997." Current Populations reports, Series p–60, No. 178. Washington, DC: U.S. Government Printing Office.

U.S. Congress. 1989. "Alternative Measures of Poverty." A Staff Study Prepared for the Joint Economic Committee, October 18.

U.S. Congress, Office of Technology Assessment. 1991. *Adolescent Health,* Vol. 1, *Summary and Policy Options,* OTA-H-468 (pp. 105–107). Washington, DC: U.S. Government Printing Office.

U.S. Department of Education, National Center for Education Statistics. 1989. "Dropout Rates in the United States: 1988." ED 313–947. Washington, DC: U.S. Department of Education.

———. 1994–1995. *Teacher Follow-Up Survey, 1994–1995.* Washington, DC: National Center for Education Statistics.

———. 1998. *National Assessment of Educational Progress, Trends Almanac: Writing, 1984 to 1996.* Washington, DC.

———. 2000. "Dropout Rates in the United States: 1998." NCES 2000–022. Washington, DC: U.S. Department of Education.

———. 2001. "Dropout Rates in the United States: 1999." NCES 2001–022. Washington, DC: U.S. Department of Education.

U.S. Department of Health and Human Services (USDHHS), Administration on Children, Youth, and Families. 1997. *Child Maltreatment 1997: Reports from the States to the National Child Abuse and Neglect Data System.* Washington, DC: U.S. Government Printing Office.

———. 1999. Child Maltreatment 1997: Reports from the States to the National Child Abuse and Neglect Data System. Washington, DC: Government Printing Office.

U.S. Department of Health and Human Services. 1990. *Healthy People 2000: National Health Promotion and Disease Prevention Objectives.* Washington, DC: U.S. Government Printing Office.

U.S. Department of Health and Human Services. *The Health Consequences of Smoking: Nicotine Addiction. A report of the Surgeon General.* Public Health Service, Centers for Disease Control, Center for Health Promotion and Education, Office on Smoking and Health, DHHS Publication No. (CDC) 88–8046. Washington, DC: U.S. Government Printing Office.

———. 1996. *Trends in the Well Being of America's Children and Youth; 1996.* Washington DC.: U.S. Department of Health and Human Services.

———. 1997. *Ninth Special Report to the U.S. Congress on Alcohol and Health.* Washington, DC: U.S. Government Printing Office.

———. 1999. *The AFCARS Report.* Web site: http://www.acf.dhhs.gov.

U.S. Department of Justice. 1992. *Child Rape Victims.* Washington: DC.

U.S. Department of Justice. 1997. *The Sourcebook of Criminal Justice Statistics, 1997.* Washington, DC: Bureau of Justice Statistics.

U.S. Environmental Protection Agency. 1994. *Indoor Air Pollution: An Introduction for Health Professionals,* GPO Number 1994–523–217/81322. Compiled by the U.S. Environmental Protection Agency, the American Lung Association, the Consumer Product Safety Commission, and the American Medical Association.

———. 1997a. *Criteria Pollutants (Greenbook): National Ambient Air Quality Standards.* U.S. Environmental Protection Agency, Office of Air and Radiation.

———. 1997b. *Special Report on Endrocrine Disruption: An Effects Assessment and Analysis,* Publication Number EPA 630-R-96–012. U.S. Environmental Protection Agency, Office of Research and Development.

U.S. Government Printing Office. 1993. *Injury Control.* Morbidity and mortality weekly reports. Reprints #733–260/80519

U.S. Public Health Service. 1964. *Smoking and Health: Report of the Advisory Committee to the Surgeon General of the Public Health Service.* U.S. Department of Health, Education, and Welfare, Public Health Service, Center for Disease Control, PHS Publication No. 1103. Washington, DC: U.S. Government Printing Office.

U.S. Sentencing Commission. 1995. *Special Report to the Congress: Cocaine and Federal Sentencing Policy.* Washington, DC: Author.

Uba, Laura. 1994. *Asian Americans: Personality Pattern, Identity, and Mental Health.* New York: Guilford Press.

Udry, J. Richard. 1988. "Biological Predispositions and Social Control in Adolescent Sexual Behavior." *American Sociological Review* 53: 709–722.

Udry, J. Richard, Luther M. Talbert, and Naomi M. Morris. 1986. "Biosocial Foundations for Adolescent Female Sexuality." *Demography* 23: 217–227.

UNAIDS. 1999. *AIDS Epidemic Update: December 1999.* Switzerland: UNAIDS.

UNICEF. 1995. *State of the World's Children.* New York: Oxford University Press.

University of Michigan. 1999. (December 18). "Drug Use among American Young People Begins to Turn Downward." *News and Information Services Press Release.*

Urberg, Kathryn A., Serdar M. Degirmencioglu, Jerry M. Tolson, and Kathy Halliday-Scher. 1995. "The Structure of Adolescent Peer Networks." *Developmental Psychology* 31: 540–547.

Urberg, Kathryn, Rochelle Robbins. 1984. "Perceived Vulnerability in Adolescents to the Health Consequences of Cigarette Smoking." *Preventive Medicine* 13: 367–376.

Urquiza, Anthony J., and Cynthia Winn. 1999. "Treatment for Abused and Neglected Children: Infancy to Age 18." National Clearinghouse on Child Abuse and Neglect Information. (pp 1–16) Washington, DC: United States Government Printing Office.

Valenzuela, Angela. 1999. *Subtractive Schooling: U.S.-Mexican Youth and the Politics of Caring.* New York: State University of New York Press.

Van Bueren, Geraldine. 1995. *The International Law on the Rights of the Child.* Dordrecht, Germany: Martinus Nijhoff Publishers.

Vandell, Deborah L., and Mark D. Bailey. 1992. "Conflicts between Siblings." Pp. 242–269 in *Conflict in Child and Adolescent Development (Cambridge Studies in Social and Emotional Development).* Edited by Carolyn U. Shantz and William H. Hartup. New York: Cambridge University Press.

Varni, James W., Ronald L. Blount, and Daniel L. L. Quiggins. 1998. "Oncological Disorders." Pp. 313–346 in *Handbook of Pediatric Psychology and Psychiatry,* Vol. 11: *Disease, Injury, and Illness.* Boston: Allyn and Bacon.

Verba, Sidney, Kay Lehman Schlozman, and Henry E. Brady. 1995. *Voice and Equality: Civic Voluntarism in American Politics.* Cambridge: Harvard University Press.

Velasquez, Roberto J., Leticia M. Arellano, and Amado M. Padilla. 1999. "Celebrating the Future of Chicano Psychology: Lessons from the Recent National Conference." Hispanic Journal of Behavioral Sciences 21, no. 1: 3–13.

Verlinden, Stephanie, Hersen, Michael, and Jay Thomas. 2000. "Risk Factors in School Shootings." *Clinical Psychology Review* 20: 3–56.

Veysey, Lawrence. 1965. *The Emergence of the American University.* Chicago: University of Chicago Press.

Viira, Roomet, and Lennert Raudsepp. 2000. "Achievement Goal Orientation, Beliefs about Sports Success and Sport Emotions as Related to Moderate and Vigorous Physical Activity of Adolescents." *Psychology and Health* 15: 625–633.

Vittinghoff, Eric, Susan Scheer, Paul O'Malley, Grant Colfax, Scott D. Holmberg, andSusan P. Buchbinder. 1999. "Combination Antiretroviral Therapy and Recent Declines in AIDS Incidence and Mortality." *Journal of Infectious Diseases* 179: 717–720.

Vondracek, Fred W., Richard M. Lerner, and John E. Schulenberg. 1986. *Career Development: A Life-Span Developmental Approach.* Hillsdale, NJ: Erlbaum.

Walker, Lawrence, and John Taylor. 1991. "Family Interactions and the Development of Moral Reasoning." *Child Development* 62: 264–283.

Walsh, Barent W., and Paul M. Rosen. 1988. *Self-Mutilation: Theory, Research, and Practice.* New York: Guilford Press.

Walsh, Timothy B., and Michael J. Devlin. 1998. "Eating Disorders: Progress and Problems." *Science* 280: 1387–1390.

Wang, Po-Ching. 1996. *Gardner's Multiple Intelligences.* Penn State Educational Systems Design Home Page: Penn State University. http://www.ed.psu.edu/

Ward, L. Monique. 1995. "Talking about Sex: Common Themes about Sexuality in the Prime-Time Television Programs Children and Adolescents View Most." *Journal of Youth and Adolescence* 24: 595–616.

Warren, Michelle. 1983. "Physical and Biological Aspects of Puberty." Pp. 3–28 in *Girls at Puberty: Biological and Psychosocial Perspectives.* Edited by Jeanne Brooks-Gunn and Anne C. Petersen. New York: Plenum Press.

Waters, Tony. 1999. *Crime and Immigrant Youth.* Thousand Oaks: Sage.

Watts, Roderick J., and Jaleel. K. Abdul-Adil. 1997. "Promoting Critical Consciousness in Young, African-American Men." Pp. 63–86 in *Manhood Development in Urban African-American Communities.* Edited by R. J. Watts and R. Jagers. New York: Hawthorne Press.

Webster's New Riverside University Dictionary. 1988. Boston: Houghton Mifflin.

Wegar, Katarina. 1997. *Adoption, Identity, and Kinship.* New Haven: Yale University Press.

Weinberg, Richard A. 1989. "Intelligence and IQ: Landmark Issues and Great Debates." *American Psychologist* 44 no. 2: 98–104.

Weinert, Franz and Marion Perlmutter, eds. 1988. *Memory Development: Universal Changes and Individual Differences.* Hillsdale, NJ: Erlbaum.

Weisberg, D. Kelly. 1985. *Children of the Night: A Study of Adolescent Prostitution.* Lexington, MA: Lexington Books.

Weithorn, Lois A. 1983. "Children's Capacities to Decide about Participation in Research." *Irb: Review of Human Subjects Research* 5: 1–5.

Weithorn, Lois A., and Susan B. Campbell. 1982. "The Competency of Children and Adolescents to Make Informed Treatment Decisions." *Child Development* 53: 1589–1598.

Wellman, Henry M. 1990. *The Child's Theory of Mind.* Cambridge, MA: MIT. Press.

Wentzel, Kathryn R. 1997. "Student Motivation in Middle School: The Role of Perceived Pedagogical Caring." *Journal of Educational Psychology* 89, no. 3: 411–419.

———. 1998. "Social Support and Adjustment in Middle School: The Role of Parents, Teachers, and Peers." *Journal of Educational Psychology* 90: 202–209.

———. 1999. "Social-Motivational Processes and Interpersonal Relationships: Implications for Understanding Students' Academic Success." *Journal of Educational Psychology* 91: 76–97.

———. 2000. *Middle School Teachers' Educational Goals and Perceptions of*

Their Students. Unpublished manuscript, University of Maryland, College Park.

Werner, Emily E. 1986. "Resilient Offspring of Alcoholics: A Longitudinal Study from Birth to Age 18." *Journal of Studies on Alcohol* 47, no. 1: 34–40.

Werner, Emmy E., and Ruth S. Smith. 1982. *Vulnerable but Invincible: A Study of Resilient Children.* New York: McGraw-Hill.

West, Linda L., ed. 1991. *Effective Strategies for Dropout Prevention of At-Risk Youth.* Gaithersburg, MA: Aspen.

Westat, Inc. 1991. *A National Evalutaion of Title IV-E Foster Care Independent Living Programs for Youth.* Washington, DC: HHS.

White, Lynn K., and David B. Brinkerhoff. 1981. "Children's Work in the Family: Its Significance and Meaning." *Journal of Marriage and the Family* 43: 789–798.

Whitehead, James R., and Charles B. Corbin. 1997. "Self-Esteem in Children and Youth: The Role of Sport and Physical Education." Pp. 175–203 in *The Physical Self: From Motivation to Well-Being.* Edited by Kenneth R. Fox. Champaign, IL: Human Kinetics.

Who's Who among American High School Students. 1993. "24th Annual Survey of High Achievers." Lake Forest, IL: Educational Communications.

Widom, Cathy S. 1989. "Does Violence Beget Violence? A Critical Examination of the Literature." *Psychological Bulletin* 106, no. 1: 3–28.

Wiehe, Vernon, and Anne Richards. 1995. *Intimate Betrayal: Understanding and Responding to the Trauma of Acquaintance Rape.* Thousand Oaks: Sage.

Wigfield, Allen, Jacquelynne Eccles, Douglas Mac Iver, David Reuman, and Carol Midgley. 1991. "Transitions at Early Adolescence: Changes in Children's Domain-Specific Self-Perceptions and General Self-Esteem across the Transition to Junior High School." *Developmental Psychology* 27: 552–565.

Wigfield, Carol, and Jacquelynne Eccles. 1994. "Children's Competence Beliefs, Achievement Values, and General Self-Esteem: Change across Elementary School and Middle School." *Journal of Early Adolescence* 14, no. 2: 107–138.

Wilcox, Brian, and Hans Neimark. 1991. "The Rights of the Child: Progress towards Human Dignity. *American Psychologist* 46: 49–55.

Williams, T. B., ed. 1986. *The Impact of Television: A Natural Experiment in Three Communities.* New York: Academic Press.

Williams-Morris, Ruth S. 1996. "Racism and Children's Health: Issues in Development." *Ethnicity and Disease* 6: 69–82.

Willis, P. 1990. *Common Culture.* Boulder, CO: Westview Press.

Wills, Karen E., Grayson N. Holmbeck, Katherine Dillon, and David G. McLone. 1990. "Intelligence and Achievement in Children with Myelomeningocele." *Journal of Pediatric Psychology* 15: 161–176.

Wilson, William Julius. 1987. *The Truly Disadvantaged: The Inner City, The Underclass, and Public Policy.* Chicago: University of Chicago Press.

Winchel, Ronald M., and Michael Stanley. 1991. "Self-Injurious Behavior: A Review of the Behavior and Biology of Self-Mutilation." *American Journal of Psychiatry* 148, no. 3: 306–317.

Windle, Michael. 1994. "A Study of Friendship Characteristics and Problem

Behaviors among Middle Adolescents." *Child Development* 65: 1764–1777.

———. 1999. *Alcohol Use among Adolescents.* Thousand Oaks, CA: Sage.

Windle, Michael, and John S. Searles. 1990. *Children of Alcoholics: Critical Perspectives.* New York: Guilford Press.

Winger, G., Hofmann, F. G., and Woods, J. F. 1992. *A Handbook on Drug and Alcohol Abuse: The Biomedical Aspects.* New York: Oxford University Press.

Wolf, Maryanne, and Patricia G. Bowers. 1999. "The Double-Deficit Hypothesis for the Developmental Dyslexias." *Journal of Educational Psychology* 91, no. 3: 1–24.

Wolf, Naomi. 1991. *The Beauty Myth: How Images of Beauty Are Used Against Women.* New York: Doubleday.

Wolman, Clara, and Deborah E. Basco. 1994. "Factors Influencing Self-Esteem and Self-Consciousness in Adolescents with Spina Bifida." *Society of Adolescent Medicine* 15: 543–548.

Wong, Bonnie. Y. L., ed. 1991. *Learning about Learning Disabilities.* San Diego: Academic Press.

Wood, Peter B., and W. Charles Clay. 1996. "Perceived Structural Barriers and Academic Performance among American Indian High School Students." *Youth and Society* 28, no. 1: 40–61.

Wood, R. G. & Burghardt, J. 1997. *Implementing Welfare Requirements for Teenage Parents: Lessons from Experience in Four States.* Washington DC: Mathematica Policy Research Inc., for the Office of the Assistant Secretary for Planning and Evaluation, United States Department of Health and Human Services.

Woodcock, Richard, and M. Bonner Johnson. 1989. *Woodcock-Johnson Tests of Achievement-Revised.* Boston: Houghton-Mifflin.

Wright, John, Aletha Huston, Alice Reitz, and Suwatchara Piemyat. 1994. "Young Children's Perceptions of Television Reality: Determinants and Developmental Differences. *Developmental Psychology* 30: 229–239.

Wulff, David M. 1991. *Psychology of Religion: Classic and Contemporary Views.* New York: Wiley.

Yee, Albert H. 1992. "Asians as Stereotypes and Students: Misperceptions That Persist." *Educational Psychology Review* 4, no. 1: 95–132.

Young, R. L., et al. 1983. "Runaways: A Review of Negative Consequences." *Family Relations* 32: 275- 289.

Youniss, James. 1980. *Parents and Peers in Social Development: A Sullivan-Piaget Perspective.* Chicago: University of Chicago Press.

Youniss, James, and Jacqueline Smollar. 1985. *Adolescent Relations with Mothers, Fathers, and Friends.* Chicago: University of Chicago Press.

Youniss, James, Jeffrey A. McLellan, and Miranda Yates. 1997. "What We Know about Engendering Civic Identity." *American Behavioral Scientist* 40: 620–631.

———. 1999. "Religion, Community Service, and Identity in American Youth." *Journal of Adolescence* 22: 243–253.

Youniss, Richard P. 1958. *Conformity to Group Judgments in Its Relation to the Structure of the Stimulus Situation and Certain Personality Characteristics.* Washington, DC: Catholic University of America Press.

Zabin, L., and S. Hayward. 1993. *Adolescent Sexual Behavior and Childbearing.* Newbury Park, CA: Sage.

Zabin, L. S., M. B. Hirsch, E. A. Smith, R. Street, and J. Hardy. 1986. "Evaluation of a Pregnancy Prevention Program for Urban Teenagers." *Family Planning Perspectives* 14: 15–21.

Zahm, S. H., and S. S. Devesa. 1995. "Childhood Cancer: Overview of Incidence Trends and Environmental Carcinogens." *Environmental Health Perspectives* 103 (Supplement 6): 177–184.

Zeagans, Susan, and Leonard Zeagans. 1979. "Bar Mitzvah: A Rite for a Transitional Age." *The Psychoanalytic Review* 66, no. 1: 117–132.

Zelizer, Viviana A. 1985. *Pricing the Priceless Child: The Changing Social Value of Children*. New York: Basic Books.

Zill, Nicholas, Christine W. Nord, and Laura S. Loomis. 1995. *Adolescent Time Use: Risky Behavior and Outcomes: An Analysis of National Data*. Washington, DC: U.S. Department of Health and Human Services.

Zill, Norman. 1996. "Family Change and Student Achievement: What We Have Learned, What It Means for Schools." Pp. 139–174 in *Family-School Links: How Do They Affect Educational Outcomes?* Edited by Alan Booth and Judith F. Dunn. Mahwah, NJ: Erlbaum.

Zimbardo, Philip, and Shirley Radl. 1981/1999. *The Shy Child: A Parent's Guide to Preventing and Overcoming Shyness from Infancy to Adulthood*, 2nd ed. Cambridge, MA: Malor Books.

Zinnbauer, Brian J., and Kenneth I. Pargament. 1998. "Spiritual Conversion: A Study of Religious Change among College Students." *Journal for the Scientific Study of Religion* 37, no. 1: 161–180.

Zuckerman, Marvin. 1991. *Psychobiology of Personality*. Cambridge: Cambridge University Press.

INDEX

Note: Page numbers in **boldface** indicate an encyclopedia entry devoted to that topic.